I0867411

This study, following on from the author's acclaimed book *I Will Not Surrender a Hair of a Horse's Tail*, commences with Victorio's return to New Mexico in January 1880. The US army's January to February campaign illustrates the operational decoy strategy employed by Victorio to protect his own logistic support whilst simultaneously undermining that of his opponents. The Hembrillo Canyon operation in April 1880 saw the largest battle of the Victorio Campaign. By the end of May 1880, Victorio's warriors had rendered the Ninth Cavalry unfit for field service. This was achieved through the Apache strategy of directly and indirectly targeting the US army's horses and mules. Yet the Apaches also suffer their first major defeat of the campaign at the end of May. After regrouping up and engaging in widespread raiding in northern Mexico, Victorio engaged the Tenth Cavalry in Western Texas during July-August 1880. Failing to break through that regiment's defences he retreated back into Mexico. This allowed the US army in New Mexico to rest and recover. By September 1880, the US army had negotiated a cross border operation of questionable legality. Known as the Buell Expedition, the aim was to coordinate with Mexican state troops to destroy the Apaches. This volume will end with Mexican state troops, led by Colonel Joaquin Terrazas', inflicting a major defeat upon the Apaches at Tres Castillos. It will be argued that the setbacks in Western Texas and at Tres Castillos demonstrate the employment of strategies and tactics by the Apaches which came very close to succeeding.

Dr Robert N. Watt is a lecturer in the Department of Political Science and International Studies (POLSIS) at the University of Birmingham, UK. His main area of research is into the Apache Wars of 1860-1886, with particular reference to the Victorio Campaign of 1879-1881. He has published articles on Victorio, the Apaches and the US Army in *Small Wars & Insurgencies*, *The New Mexico Historical Review*, *War in History*, *Southwestern Historical Quarterly* and *The Journal of Military History*. He was awarded a 2017 Moncado Prize for his article '"An Exodus to Nowhere"?: Victorio's Tres Castillos Campaign' in *The Journal of Military History* by The Society for Military History. He has also published two books with Osprey on The Apache Warrior and Apache Tactics. He has made numerous archive and field trips to the USA and has visited most of the areas where the Victorio Campaign took place – including Tres Castillos in Northern Mexico, where Victorio was killed in October 1880. Dr Watt has taught a module on American Indian Wars for the History Department, the University of Birmingham. He has also published an article on the Red Army in the Second World War and has lectured on Soviet Deep Battle/ Operations for a module in the same department. In 2018 Helion published the first part of his trilogy on the Victorio Campaign, *'I will not Surrender the Hair of a Horse's Tail': The Victorio Campaign 1879.* The final instalment *'With My Face to My Foes' Nana's War 1880–1881* was published in 2019.

'HORSES WORN TO MERE SHADOWS'

The Victorio Campaign 1880

Robert N. Watt

Helion & Company Limited

Helion & Company Limited
Unit 8 Amherst Business Centre
Budbrooke Road
Warwick
CV34 5WE
England
Tel. 01926 499619
Email: info@helion.co.uk
Website: www.helion.co.uk
Twitter: @helionbooks
blog.helion.co.uk/

Published by Helion & Company 2019. Reprinted in paperback 2022
Designed and typeset by Mach 3 Solutions Ltd (www.mach3solutions.co.uk)
Cover designed by Paul Hewitt, Battlefield Design (www.battlefield-design.co.uk)

ISBN 978-1-915113-03-0

British Library Cataloguing-in-Publication Data.
A catalogue record for this book is available from the British Library.

For details of other military history titles published by Helion & Company Limited contact the above address, or visit our website: http://www.helion.co.uk.

We always welcome receiving book proposals from prospective authors.

Contents

Appendices
Due to the volume of appendices attached to this volume it has been decided to make the extensive documentary annex available as a free download. Please follow the link to access the file: http://www.helion.co.uk/hwms-annex.pdf

List of Plates

These monochrome photos were originally in colour. If you wish to have colour copies of these photos email me at r.n.watt@bham.ac.uk. Please note that any further use of these photos is strictly forbidden unless given the express permission of the author.

List of Contemporary Photographs

List of Maps

A master map for the Victorio Campaign is included in Volume One.

In colour section

Key to maps

Map 1.1

1.	2 January	Prospectors attacked in the Florida Mountains.
2.	4 January	Major Morrow ordered into the field from Fort Bayard. Apache scouts are sent to the Florida Mountains, while at least two companies are sent to Fort Cummings.
3.	6 January	A large party of Apache warriors, accompanied by some women and children and 200 horses, encounters Chapman's wagon train at Mule Springs.
4.	6 or 7 January	Telegraph wire between Fort Cummings and La Mesilla is severed. Repair crew find the break near the Goodsight Mountains and report a large trail heading north. The location suggests that the Apaches encountered at Mule Springs are the culprits. There is no effort to conceal either the break in the telegraph line or the trail.
5.	8 January	Reports received of 40-50 Apaches seen in the vicinity of McEvers' Ranch.
6.	9 January	Morrow sets out in pursuit of Victorio from Fort Cummings, picking up his trail as it moves north from the telegraph line towards McEvers' Ranch, having ordered the rest of his command to march to Fort Cummings and follow his trail.
7.	7 January	Colonel Cisneros, one of General Trevino's officers, sends word that his scouts are moving from the Mexican border in the general direction of La Mesilla.
	10–13 January	Mexican Traders discover a large Apache trail going from the vicinity of the Florida Mountains towards Magdalena Canyon, presumably Magdalena Gap, in the southern reaches of the Sierra Uvas.

Map 2.1

Key to Map One

1.	6 or 7 January	Telegraph wire between Fort Cummings and La Mesilla is severed. Repair crew find the break near the Goodsight Mountains and report a large trail heading north.
2.	8 January	Reports received of 40-50 Apaches seen in the vicinity of McEvers' Ranch.
3.	9 January	Morrow sets out in pursuit of Victorio from Fort Cummings, picking up Victorio's trail as it moves north from the telegraph line towards McEvers', Ranch, having ordered the rest of his command to march to Fort Cummings and follow his trail.
4.	12 January	Morrow, having gathered his scattered detachments together, engages Victorio on the Rio Percha between Hillsboro and Kingston. The Apaches hold their positions for several hours before the deployment of a mountain howitzer breaks the deadlock. The Apaches fade away to the north.
5.	13 January	One of Morrow's cavalry companies has a brief skirmish with some Apaches.

6.	16 January	Victorio with at least 60 warriors holds a conference with Andrew Kelley at Canada Alamosa. The conference is terminated two hours later by the arrival of Morrow's battalion.
7.	16 January	Morrow pursues the Apaches to the southern reaches of the San Mateo Mountains. That evening he holds a parley with Victorio somewhere along Nogal Canyon.
	17 January	Morrow's troops engage Victorio's warriors in the same area. Once again, the Apaches hold their positions until the mountain howitzer is brought into action. They move north deeper into the San Mateo Mountains.
8.	17 January	Morrow leads his battalion to Ojo Caliente to replenish his supplies.
9.	17–22 January	Andrew Kelley is sent into the San Mateo Mountains and returns to report that Victorio has moved to the northern end of the San Mateo Mts.
10.	22 to 26 January	Victorio leads Morrow's battalion on a gruelling march through the San Mateo Mountains. Inconclusive skirmishing continues as Victorio keeps one jump ahead of the US troops.
11.	23 January	Andrew Kelley goes back into the San Mateo Mts. in an effort to contact Victorio and persuade him to enter into peace negotiations.
12.	27 January	Morrow's battalion arrives at Canada Alamosa having failed to catch Victorio.
13.	27 to 29 January	Kelley appears to have successfully contacted Victorio and a second parley between Victorio and Morrow is arranged. It is unclear whether this conference took place.
14.	30 January	Morrow with dwindling supplies sets out with his command for Fort Bayard.
15.	30 January	Capt. Rucker, attached to a supply train out of Fort Bayard commanded by Capt. Carroll, is detached to pursue Apaches into the Caballo Mts. Joined by a number of civilian volunteers they are ambushed (probably in or near Mescal Canyon) and driven back across the Rio Grande.
16.	1 to 2 February	The news of Rucker's defeat reaches Morrow who swings his command around, crosses the Rio Grande and picks up a trail moving through Aleman and on into the San Andres Mts.
17.	3 February	Morrow and Victorio's men engage in a prolonged running battle (probably in or near Hospital Canyon) on the eastern side of the San Andres Mts.
18.	4 February	Morrow arrives at Tulerosa.
19.	4 February	Detachments led by Capt's Carroll & Hooker make for San Augustin Pass in an attempt to prevent Victorio making for Mexico.
20.	6 February	Morrow tracks some Apaches to Malpais Springs where the Apaches rendezvoused after scattering out of the San Andres Mts. on 3 February. Once again the Apaches scattered and Morrow suspects that the Apaches have fresh horses hidden on the Mescalero reservation to the east but fails to discover more than a few small trails.
21.	10 February	Morrow's battalion returns to Tulerosa having lost contact with Victorio. His command is completely exhausted after a month's pursuit of the Apaches.

22.	11 to 20 February	On hearing rumours of Apache raiders in the Caballo Mts. Morrow's battalion marches west to scout this range. Finding little sign of Apaches he moves his forces first to Las Palomas to rest and refit. By 20 February he had returned to Ojo Caliente.

Map 4.2

A – The road crosses the main arroyo.
B – The road ascends a steep incline, rising between 50 and 60 feet.
C – The road levels out for approximately 200-300 yards.
D – Finally, the road rises by approximately another 20 feet to complete its ascent from the arroyo.

As the second of the two wagons entered C, the Apaches had their quarry in a perfect trap. The Apaches were *probably* stationed on the small hillocks at points E, F and G, and along the low ridge H, which was no more than 20 feet high. Alternatively, rather than being positioned along Point H, some Apaches may have been posted in the small depression marked J. Whichever of these it was, they could have remained hidden until they opened fire at point blank range. It is believed that the rear wagon attempted to flee between E and H, but was quickly cut off and the occupants slain.

Map 5.1

Note: The three broad blue arrows labelled A, B and C indicate Hatch's plan before the operation. The narrower blue arrows numbered 1–12 outline how the First and Second Battalions, New Mexico Troops, executed the Hembrillo Canyon Operation.

Key to Map 5.1

The Intended Plan:

A	Major Morrow with the First Battalion, NM Troops, to start from their base at Las Palomas and move east to strike the Apaches based in the San Andres Mountains.
B	The Second Battalion, NM Troops, commanded by Captain Carroll, to move from Fort Stanton to Tulerosa to cover the east side of the San Andres Mountains and support the First Battalion when the latter engage the Apaches.
C	Captain Hooker with the Third Battalion, NM Troops, to proceed from Annaya Springs to Malpais Springs on the Tulerosa Road. Colonel Hatch in three different communications instructs Hooker that his battalion should cover the east, north and west of the San Andres Mountains.

The Hembrillo Canyon Operation

Captain Carroll's Second Battalion, NM Troops

Date		Event
1.	4 April	Carroll marches with his battalion from Tulerosa to Malpais Springs.
2.	5 April	Carroll sends Lieutenant Conline's company ahead of the battalion towards the San Andres Mountains. After a march of about 37 miles Conline discovers a trail leading into Hembrillo Canyon. He follows the trail a short distance into the canyon before he is attacked by Apaches and retreats at nightfall, rejoining the rest of the battalion at around 11:00 p.m.

	Date	Event
3.	6 April	Carroll splits his command in two. He leads two companies up Sulphur Canyon and enters the Hembrillo Basin from the north, thereby avoiding using the Hembrillo Canyon route from the west, as attempted by Lieutenant Conline. Late in the afternoon, Carroll is ambushed and trapped by the Apaches.
4.	6 April	Carroll sends Lieutenant Cusack, with the other two companies, to scout south along the San Andres Mountains.
5.	7 April	Lieutenant Cusack, with the other two companies, arrives, following Carroll's trail, having been recalled by courier. They arrive at the same time as the Apache scouts from the First Battalion, NM Troops, arrive from the west. The former having mistakenly been fired upon by the latter, the two sets of reinforcements join forces to relieve Carroll's command.

Major Morrow's First Battalion, NM Troops

Date		Event
6.	29 March	Morrow, with 98 men and 63 Apache scouts, leaves Fort Bayard to rendezvous with the rest of his battalion at Las Palomas. The latter is made up of a composite company of Sixth Cavalrymen led by Captain McLellan and Apache scouts led by Lieutenant Gatewood.
7.	27 March	Captain McLellan leaves Camp Ojo Caliente for Las Palomas.
8.	1–3 April	The First Battalion NM Troops congregates at Las Palomas.
9.	4–5 April	The First Battalion, plagued by logistical difficulties, finds its departure for Aleman Wells delayed. Major Morrow leaves for Aleman on 4 April. Captain McLellan leaves for Aleman on 5 April.
10.	6 April	On arrival at Aleman Wells, the troops are again delayed by the slow rate at which their stock can be watered. Colonel Hatch, having gone ahead of the First Battalion to Aleman on 4 April, orders McLellan's Sixth Cavalry detachment and the Apache scouts to draw water first and proceed from Aleman across the Jornada and into the San Andres Mountains. They set off near midnight on 6 April.
11.	7 April	McLellan's force, having crossed to the eastern rim of the San Andres Mountains by dawn, hears the gunfire from the battle between Carroll and the Apaches and moves to their relief. (See Note 5.)
12.	7 April	The rest of the First Battalion takes on water and between 4:00 p.m. and 5:00 p.m. arrives in Hembrillo Canyon.

Map 5.2

1. Vidette posted to the left and rear of Conline's position.
2. Videttes stationed on the southern slope of Hembrillo Canyon.
3. Videttes deployed on the northern slope of Hembrillo Canyon.
4. Conline's skirmish line.
5. Conline's horse herd.
6. 30-50 Apaches approach Conline's command by moving rapidly down Hembrillo Canyon.
7. The videttes in advance of Conline's position skirmish with the Apaches as they withdraw. Presumably, the vidette(s) posted above and to the rear of Conline's position return to the skirmish line.

8. An Apache, identified as Victorio, is seen to be directing the opening moves of his men from approximately this point.
9. A few Apaches occupy these positions to engage Conline's company.
10. Some of the Apaches, using dead ground, occupy positions in front of the Ninth Cavalrymen.
11. A number of Apaches use an arroyo running up the southern side of Hembrillo Canyon to work their way to firing positions above and to the left of Conline's skirmish line.

Map 5.3

Conline's company (1) engage the Apaches to their front (2) and left and above (3), in a general fire-fight at an approximate distance of 200 yards. The Apaches then launch an attack (4) on the right of Conline's position by working their way through the rough terrain at that point. This possibly distracts the Ninth Cavalrymen from the Apaches working their way around Conline's right flank (5) using the depression created by a dry arroyo. These Apaches successfully work their way around to the rear (6) and they open fire on Conline's horses, some using the arroyo for cover (7), whilst at least one Apache climbs up the north side of the Canyon (8) and another moves out of the arroyo (9) to take a position directly behind Conline's first skirmish line. It would appear that some men from the first skirmish line and some of the men guarding the horses form a second skirmish line (10) to counter this flank attack. Fading light would appear to prevent the Apaches from pressing home their advantage, and they withdraw up Hembrillo Canyon.

Maps 5.4–5.7 are derived from Laumbach's book on the recent archaeological survey of the Hembrillo battlefield.

Map 5.4

Carroll was spotted by Apache lookouts, giving Victorio time to set up a trap for him between two converging ridges, each lined with Apache warriors. Once Carroll marched into the trap, the Apache warriors opened fire. Instead of retreating, Carroll's men stormed what is now known as Carroll's Ridge. Other Apache warriors occupied positions between Carroll's command and Rock House Spring.

Map 5.5

Carroll creates a defensive position along the lower end of Carroll's Ridge. The Apaches occupy positions higher up Carroll's Ridge. They occupy Victorio Ridge, to the south; and those on Apache Ridge shift position southwards to bring Carroll's position under fire. A number of Apache warriors occupy the area around Rock House Spring and the small stream running past and below Carroll's position. These warriors successfully prevent Carroll's troopers from gaining more than a few canteens of water. Finally, other Apaches infiltrated in towards Carroll's position during the night. As first light arrives, the Ninth Cavalrymen come under increasing attack. At one point, the Apaches press so close to them that they have to resort to their revolvers to hold their line.

Map 5.6

McLellan's command arrives from the north-west and Cusack links up with Carroll from the north. The hostile Apaches abandon their position around Carroll's Ridge and Rock House Spring to form a defence line along Victorio Ridge. It is probable that the Apache Camp scatters initially to the south and south-east, before the Mescaleros flee to the east and the Warm Springs/Chiricahuas turn and move to the west.

Map 5.7

While McLellan and Cusack launch their cavalrymen in a frontal assault on Victorio Ridge, the Apache scouts launch a flanking attack. By 9:00 a.m. Rock House Spring is taken. The Apaches detach men from their line to hold back the scouts, but once the US cavalrymen are in position to overrun Victorio Ridge, the Apaches fall back. Some mount horses and escape down Hembrillo Canyon. Others continue a rearguard action, falling back towards Victorio Peak. Upper Hembrillo Spring is secured in the mid-afternoon as the last Apache warriors retreat from Victorio Peak. Having covered their dependents' retreat, the Apache warriors break contact and withdraw from Hembrillo Canyon.

Map 7.1

1. The US army reports of this campaign are not detailed enough to pinpoint the movements of the various detachments with any certainty; but an effort has been made to pinpoint as many of the locations as possible to map Victorio's raiding and the attempts made to pursue him.
2. We know that Morrow left Ojo Caliente on 4 May and Hooker, with his battalion, left on 5 May. The clearest hint as to the direction taken by the Ninth Cavalry's pursuit is given by Captain Parker of K Company (Hooker's battalion), who stated that he had followed a trail from Chase's Ranch on the Rio Cuchillo Negro across the Black Range, the Mogollons, into the Negrieta Mountains (possibly the San Francisco Mountains), on to Old Fort Tularosa, and back to Ojo Caliente, by 23 May.
3. The sheepherders killed by Victorio appear to have been struck on the northern slopes of the Mogollon Mountains, Squares E5 and E6.
4. The mining camps attacked by Victorio in late April would appear to be concentrated in Square E5.
5. The scout by Captain Madden's Sixth Cavalry and civilian volunteers from Silver City meandered through Squares E, D and C4–5.
6. Captain Kramer was camped on Ash Creek, but the actual location of Rocky Canyon is unclear. It may be somewhere in Square E1, but is probably further west, just off the map. Tupper appears to have pursued Washington's raiders through Squares E1, E2, D3, D4, D5 and C5.
7. The Apache scouts led by H.K. Parker appear to have started their scout, either from the San Francisco River or somewhere between that point and the Datil Mountains, on 17 May. They reached Ojo Caliente on 21 May. On 23 May they located Victorio's camp to the south of Ojo Caliente, two to three miles east of Hermosa. At dawn on 24 May, they attacked the camp.

Map 10.1

[1] Lt Finley leaves his emplacement to confront **[2]** Apaches seen approaching from the south-east. His detachment is fired upon from the flank and rear by Apaches **[3]** who have infiltrated through the thick terrain. Finley's detachment **[4]** moves back to **[5]** and engages the Apaches in a prolonged firefight. Finley's detachment is in the process of clearing a rocky outcrop **[6]** of Apache defenders when he is fired upon by reinforcements arriving from Eagle Springs **[7]** and is forced to retreat **[8]** back to his emplacement. Grierson's small detachment gives surprise covering fire **[9]** to repulse the pursuing Apaches **[10]** who withdraw to a small ridge to the south **[11]**.

The reinforcements from Eagle Springs assault **[12]** this ridge and drive the Apaches off **[13]**. Skirmishing continues in the thick brush until additional reinforcements from Fort Quitman arrive **[14]** and that Apaches elect to withdraw **[15]**.

Map 11.1

	Date	Event
1.	Mid July	Mexican state and federal troops unsuccessfully attempt to trap Victorio in the Sierra el Fierro.
2.	21 July	Colonel Valle's forces clash with Victorio at Ojo del Pino in the Sierra de Los Pinos. The Apaches withdraw south towards the Sierro el Fierro.
3.	22 July	Colonel Grierson arrives at Vieja Pass.
4.	23 July	Colonel Grierson travels to Eagle Springs via Van Horn's Wells.
5.	25 July	Colonel Valle once again fights Victorio in the Sierra de Los Pinos.
6.	27 July	Colonel Grierson travels to Old Fort Quitnam.
7.	28 July	Colonel Grierson meets with Colonel Valle at Old Fort Quitnam.
8.	29 July	Travelling back to Eagle Springs, Colonel Grierson encounters an Apache scout at Tinaja de las Palmas. Reports arriving from scouts out of Old Fort Quitnam and Eagle Springs give news of a large party of Apaches moving towards Grierson from the Rio Grande.
	30 July	Skirmish between Victorio and Grierson at Tinaja de las Palmas.
9.	30 July	Colonel Grierson moves his forces back to Eagle Springs.
10.	1 August	Colonel Grierson sends out scout detachments to scout to the south of Eagle Springs. One detachment sent to Alamo Springs.
11.	3 August	The detachment at Alamo Springs engages a large party of Apaches in a running battle moving north-east towards Van Horn Mountains.
12.	1 August	Captain Lebo, scouting the Sierra Diablo, captures a camp full of supplies. He pursues the Apaches north out of these mountains.
13.	3–4 August	News of the clash between the detachment at Alamo Springs and Apaches convinces Colonel Grierson to move his troops to Van Horn Wells and beyond.
14.	4 August	A detachment of Tenth Cavalry is ambushed in the Guadalupe Mountains, probably by the same Apaches who were attacked by Captain Lebo.
15.	5–6 August	Very early on 5 August, Colonel Grierson realises that the Apaches have outmanoeuvred him. He gathers his command and by the early hours of 6 August has marched his forces northwards to Rattlesnake Springs.
16.	6 August	Inconclusive battle with Victorio at Rattlesnake Springs.
17.	7 August	Colonel Grierson sends detachments to picket Apache and Sulphur Springs to the north. (Note: the locations of these water holes are approximate.)
18.	8 August	Colonel Grierson is joined by a company from the Eighth Cavalry, with Lipan Apache scouts, at Rattlesnake Springs. They are sent to scout to the south and later return to confirm that Victorio has retreated from Rattlesnake Springs. He has withdrawn into the Sierra Diablo. Texas Rangers also join Grierson at Rattlesnake Springs.
19.	9 August	Sierra Diablo scouted by Pueblo and Lipan Indian scouts and the infantry accompanying Grierson's battalion.

	Date	Event
20.	10 August	Colonel Grierson sends troops under Captain Nolan to Fresno Springs to scout the southern end of Sierro Diablo.
21.	10 August	Grierson travels to Sulphur Springs and orders troops under Captain Carpenter to move west, then scout south, along the west side of the Sierra Diablo.
22.	11 August	Victorio's trail is finally discovered by Captain Carpenter. It goes west towards Fort Bliss, then turns south towards the Rio Grande. Carpenter estimates that he is a day and a half behind the Apaches. By the end of the day, he has to break off the pursuit, as his horses are exhausted. He sends word to Captain Nolan, who joins him at Eagle Springs at around midnight.
23.	12 August	Nolan picks up the trail two miles from Tinaja de las Palmas and follows it south to the Rio Grande where it turns east and makes for Ojo Caliente.
24.	13 August	Nolan confirms that the Apaches have crossed back into Mexico.

Map 11.2

	Date	Event
1.	29–30 July	Victorio splits his force into two groups. He takes the first group, made up exclusively of warriors, across the Rio Grande in an attempt to decoy Grierson's troops away from Eagle Springs. By attacking Grierson at Tinaja de las Palmas, he attracts the attention of forces stationed at Eagle Springs and Old Fort Quitman.
2.	29–31 July	If Victorio and his group of warriors are successful in drawing the forces at Eagle Springs westwards, this should give the second group, made up of Victorio's dependents and plunder, escorted by a few warriors, the opportunity to pass northwards towards New Mexico, by passing between the Eagle and Van Horn Mountains. This group is camping somewhere between Sierra el Alambre and Sierra los Pilares. **Failure No. 1.** Victorio fails to move Grierson west, as the latter is already aware, through information received from both Mexican army scouts and his own scouts, that there is a large group of Apaches just across the border between the Sierra el Alambre and Sierra los Pilares.
3.	30 July	Grierson quickly moves his forces back to Eagle Springs. This point is relatively high on the northern slope of the Eagle Mountains and affords a good view of the area between the Eagle and Van Horn Mountains, and north to the Carrizo Mountains. From Eagle Springs, Grierson sends small scouting patrols southwards to monitor movements of Apaches camped at 2.
4.	2–4 August	Grierson, based on knowledge of the location of a second group of Apaches, decides that the next likely spot for a border incursion is to the east of Eagle Springs, and moves some of his troops to Van Horn Wells and beyond. Later, news of an attack on the patrol sent to Alamo Springs convinces the Colonel to move the rest of his force to Van Horn Wells and beyond, in an effort to head off the Apaches.
5.	4 August	The telegraph line between Old Fort Quitman and Eagle Springs is cut. Once again, this appears to be an attempt to draw Grierson westwards to allow the second group of Apaches an unimpeded passage north to New Mexico.

	Date	Event
		Failure No. 2. The scouting party which encountered the second group of Apaches near Alamo Springs manages to alert Grierson. By the time the telegraph line is cut, Grierson is already aware of the approximate location of the second group and has moved east in an attempt to intercept them.
6.	3–5 August	Apaches hold off the scouting party and move to north and east, towards Van Horn Mountains. Once they have escaped from the patrol, they change their line of march to the northwest and make for Fresno Springs. Here they probably rendezvous with Victorio's party of warriors. **Failure No. 3.** Grierson's scout patrols and stagecoach employees warn the Colonel that he has probably been outmanoeuvred in sufficient time for him to redeploy his forces and move north.
7.	5–6 August	Grierson manages to get his forces to Rattlesnake Springs in advance of Victorio, forcing Apaches to retreat back to the south. Despite losing track of Victorio between 7 and 11 August, this manoeuvre wins the campaign for Grierson, as Victorio is forced to return to Mexico with his plunder.

Map 14.2

	Date	Event
1.	6 September	A stagecoach is ambushed, and the occupants killed, 16 miles east of Fort Cummings. The wreckage is discovered by a detachment of Sixteenth Infantrymen escorting a railroad survey team. Their commander, Captain Hale, sends a courier to Fort Cummings, who arrives there at 10:00 p.m.
2.	6–7 September	At midnight, Captain Parker, with A Company, Fourth Cavalry, and 10 Apache scouts, proceeds from Fort Cummings to the site of the ambush. He is ordered to pursue the Apaches from that point.
3.	6–7 September	At 12:00 midnight, Major Noyes departs Fort Cummings with H Company, Fourth Cavalry and 10 Apache Scouts for the Florida Mountains, in an attempt to intercept the Apache raiders should they make for that point. He is also ordered to contact Lieutenants Maney and Goodwin, currently scouting in this area with their Apache scouts, and put them in pursuit of the Apaches. He arrives at the Little Floridas at dawn and works his way down the Floridas, but finds insufficient water and returns to the Little Floridas.
4.	7 September	Parker's detachment reaches the site of the ambush. At 8:00 a.m., he pursues the trail southwards, probably along the eastern side of the Goodsight Mountains, until, at approximately 11:00 a.m. he is ambushed at the southern end of these mountains. He loses three men killed and three wounded. Parker sends a courier to Captain Hale requesting that he telegraph for reinforcements from Fort Cummings. Unable to shift the Apaches from their positions on the ridge, Parker pulls back about eight miles to regroup.
5.	7 September	This request is received at about 1:30 p.m. and Lieutenant Colonel Dudley mounts a large battalion of Ninth Cavalry and sets out at about 2:15 p.m. Colonel Buell also puts some Fifteenth Infantrymen in wagons and sets off with them on the road at 2:45 p.m.

	Date	Event
6.	7 September	Captain Hale marches to the aid of Parker and arrives just before the Ninth Cavalry arrive from Fort Cummings.
7.	7 September	On the approach of reinforcements, the Apaches scatter and re-congregate at a nearby camp in a canyon running down out of the Goodsight Mountains.
8.	7 September	Lieutenant Colonel Dudley takes command and pursues the Apaches to a point two miles beyond their camp, before darkness makes it impossible to follow the trail.
9.	7 September	Seeing that they are still being pursued, the Apaches poison the water at their camp using horse entrails and then retreat into Mexico. They are earlier spotted by Dudley, from the southern escarpment of the Goodsight Mountains, 15 miles distant, making for Mexico.
10.	7–8 September	Major Noyes finds no sign of Apaches in or around the Florida Mountains. He is met by a courier from Buell and ordered to march to the Goodsight Mountains. By dawn on 8 September he is approximately 10 miles from the Goodsights.
11.	8 September	Buell and Dudley return to Cummings via Hale's railroad surveying camp. They are joined by Major Noyes who, on reaching the Goodsight Mountains, had spotted their dust and followed them. Buell and Dudley had both concluded that to pursue the Apaches further would be futile, given their lack of supplies sufficient for a prolonged pursuit. It would also have involved a premature entry into the Republic of Mexico.

Map 15.1

Colonel Terrazas	Having gathered his state troops from the townships to the south, he would advance north towards Guzman and Santa Maria Lakes and attack Victorio from the south.
Colonel Buell	Would advance south from Fort Cummings to Palomas Lake. His forces would then spread out and advance south towards the lakes and attack Victorio from the north.
Colonel Carr	Would advance east from Fort Bowie and blockade the passes to the east of Guzman and Santa Maria Lakes, to prevent Victorio's escape to the west.

To the east, Chihuahuan state troops raised from the settlements along the Rio Grande and the Carrizal area would form a cordon to prevent Victorio escaping to the east. A small group of Texas Rangers were to join this force, as were a small scouting detachment of Tenth Cavalrymen under civilian scout Charles Berger. The Tenth Cavalry's blockade of the waterholes on the US side of the Rio Grande would be maintained to prevent Victorio getting away, should he break through this cordon.

Map 15.2

Part 1: Terrazas' Campaign (Green Arrows)

1.	25–26 August	Joaquin Terrazas leaves Chihuahua City and progresses through northern Chihuahua gathering recruits. He links up with Juan Mata Ortiz at Corralitos. The latter has already sent scouts to Guzman and Santa Maria Lakes.
2.	27 September	The combined forces of Terrazas and Mata Ortiz move to the Vado de Santa Maria, where they are joined by Mata Ortiz's scouts. The latter report that the Apaches appear to have left the lakes, moving east.
3.	28 September	Terrazas moves on to Ojo Caliente, Mexico, while scouting parties are sent to the north.
4.	29 September	Terrazas arrives at the Laguna de Patos to rendezvous with state troops raised from the Rio Brazos region. He also sends scouts out to check the Candelaria Mountains. Other troops raised in his earlier recruitment drive catch up with him at this point.
5.	17 September to 3 October	A small group of Texas Rangers under Baylor, and a larger group of Chihuahua State troops raised from along the Rio Grande, take up a position at Aranda's Ranch, somewhere to the east of the Candelaria Mountains. Signal fires are seen to the east, and a trail is discovered to the south of the Sierra la Rancheria on 19 September. The troops are sent to picket these mountains until being sent to join Terrazas at Laguna de Patos, arriving on 3 October. A large trail of Apaches going east from the Candelarias is discovered going in the direction of the Sierra el Pino on 23 September.
6.	28 September	Charles Berger and six Tenth Cavalrymen arrive at the Tinajas de Cantarrecio. They move to join Terrazas, in the vicinity of the Candelaria Mountains, probably at San Jose.
7.	1 October	Terrazas marches to the Sierra la Alcaparra.
8.	1 October	Mata Ortiz marches a detachment towards the Tinajas de Cantarrecio to meet a supply train from El Paso del Norte.
9.	2–3 October	Terrazas searches the vicinity of the Sierra Alcaparra.
10.	4 October	En route to the north-east and a rendezvous in the Sierra Borracho with Juan Mata Ortiz, Terrazas finds the traces of a large Apache camp at Lagunita (possibly present-day Laguna las Flores). Assuming that Victorio might be making for the Sierra Borracho, and thereby threatening his supply train, Terrazas marches straight to the rendezvous point with Mata Ortiz.
11.	5 October	Terrazas and Mata Ortiz reunite somewhere in the Sierra Borracho. Scouts are sent on towards the Sierra de Los Pinos.
	7 October	Terrazas' command is re-supplied from El Paso del Norte.
12.	8–9 October	Terrazas' command marches down to the Sierra de Los Pinos. Confident he is between Victorio and the Rio Grande, he requests Buell, via Lieutenants Maney and Schaeffer, to withdraw to the USA. Scouts have reached Terrazas from the Laguna el Cuervo (I), stating that Apaches have passed by but are now moving south. Terrazas also reduces his command to 260 effectives, sending 90 men home.

13.	9–10 October	Terrazas marches to the Laguna el Cuervo (I), only to find that the tracks left are those of a small party of Apaches.
14.	11–12 October	Terrazas moves south to the Ojo del Carrizo. He doles out the remaining supplies to his troops.
15. & 16.	12–13 October	While Terrazas scouts onto the plains west of Ojo Del Carrizo, Mata Ortiz sets off southwards with a detachment, to scout the Sierra Tosesihua.
17.	13 October	Terrazas' scouts find signs out on the plain that a large body of Apaches has passed, apparently going towards Tres Castillos, a few days previously. Terrazas sends a courier to Mata Ortiz ordering him to rejoin the command. That night, a scouting party is despatched towards Tres Castillos, but returns to report plenty of tracks but no Apaches.
18.	14 October	Terrazas leads a small scouting party to Tres Castillos. From this point, he sees dust clouds to the south, and he returns to pick up his command. At dusk, the Chihuahua state troops attack Victorio at Tres Castillos...

Part 2: Buell's Campaign (Blue Arrows)

A.	23–24 September	Buell's forces, stationed at Fort Cummings and Knight's Ranch, rendezvous at Palomas Lake. The forces from Fort Cummings depart that point between 19 and 21 September.
	24 September	Lieutenant S. Mills' company of Apache scouts from Carr's command joins Buell at Palomas Lake.
B.	23–24 September	During the night, Maney's Apache scout company moves from the West Potrillo Mountains into Chihuahua.
C.	23 September	Under cover of darkness, Captain Beyer, based in the East Potrillo Mountains, crosses the border into Mexico.
D.	25 September	Buell's forces march to Laguna de Guzman, where he is joined by Lieutenant Maney's Apache scouts and presumably Captain Beyer's detachment.
E.	26–27 September	Buell moves his forces from Laguna de Santa Maria on 26 September and waits there for a day to see if Carr's forces make their appearance.
F.	28–29 September	Buell sends out Captain Beyer's company of Ninth Cavalry to scout the Candelaria Mountains. Buell follows and hides his command behind (probably) the Sierra los Muertos.
G.	28 September to 2 October	Buell sends his supply train up the Santa Maria River across to Ojo Caliente, Mexico, El Carrizal, the Laguna de Patos and on to El Lucero.
H.	29–30 September	Buell's command reaches the Candelaria Mountains and scouts this range, only to find their quarry four days departed.
I.	1 October	Buell arrives at El Lucero.
J.	4 October	Buell reaches the Tinajas de Cantarrecio.
K.	5–9 October	Buell's command marches to San Ignacio (5 October), then along the Rio Grande to 18 miles south-east of Fort Quitman (6–9 October).
L.	9–10 October	Buell receives Terrazas' request that he return to the USA.
M	8–10 October	Lieutenants Maney and Schaeffer, with a mixed detachment of Apache scouts and Ninth Cavalrymen, meet Terrazas' forces in the Sierra de Los Pinos.

Map 16.1

Part 1: Terrazas' Campaign (Green Arrows)

11.	5 October	Terrazas and Mata Ortiz reunite somewhere in the Sierra Borracho. Scouts are sent on towards the Sierra de Los Pinos.
	7 October	Terrazas' command is re-supplied from El Paso del Norte.
12.	8–9 October	Terrazas' command marches down to the Sierra de Los Pinos. Confident he is between Victorio and the Rio Grande, he requests Buell, via Lieutenants Maney and Schaeffer, to withdraw to the USA. Scouts have reached Terrazas from the Laguna el Cuervo (I), stating that Apaches have passed by but are now moving south. Terrazas also reduces his command to 260 effectives, sending 90 men home.
13.	9–10 October	Terrazas marches to the Laguna el Cuervo (I), only to find that the tracks left are those of a small party of Apaches.
14.	11–12 October	Terrazas moves south to the Ojo del Carrizo. He doles out the remaining supplies to his troops.
15. & 16.	12–13 October	While Terrazas scouts onto the plains west of Ojo Del Carrizo, Mata Ortiz sets off southwards with a detachment, to scout the Sierra Tosesihua.
17.	13 October	Terrazas' scouts find signs out on the plain that a large body of Apaches has passed, apparently going towards Tres Castillos, a few days previously. Terrazas sends a courier to Mata Ortiz ordering him to rejoin the command. That night, a scouting party is despatched towards Tres Castillos, but returns to report plenty of tracks but no Apaches.
18.	14 October	Terrazas leads a small scouting party to Tres Castillos. From this point, he sees dust clouds to the south, and he returns to pick up his command. At dusk, the Chihuahua state troops attack Victorio at Tres Castillos…

Part 2: Buell's Campaign (Blue Arrows)

K.	5–9 October	Buell's command marches to San Ignacio (5 October), then along the Rio Grande to 18 miles south-east of Fort Quitman (6–9 October).
L.	9–10 October	Buell receives Terrazas' request that he return to the USA.
M	8–10 October	Lieutenants Maney and Schaeffer, with a mixed detachment of Apache scouts and Ninth Cavalrymen, meet Terrazas' forces in the Sierra de Los Pinos.

List of Figures

List of Tables

Preface & Acknowledgements

In the first volume to this trilogy concerning the Victorio Campaign, *'I Will Not Surrender the Hair of the Horse's Tail'*, I wrote quite a long Preface/Acknowledgements and the comments made there are as germane to this volume and need not be repeated.

However, research is an on-going process and I would like to thank the following people for their assistance in gaining access to several sites in New Mexico and Texas in June. Glen Sample Ely suggested that I contact the Hudspeth Co. Appraisal District. C.R. "Kit" Bramblett and his wife Jerry for helping to gain access to the battle site at Tinaja de Las Palmas (see Chapter 10). I would also like to thank Gary and Gracie Zent for granting permission to visit and Prudella McMillan for contacting them on our behalf. Finally, Karl and Toni Laumbach for arranging the trip out to Texas and for their support in general.

Karl, Toni and Deni Seymour deserve my deep appreciation for their general support and advice this year. In addition, we also had great fun presenting a panel on how archaeology can inform history and vice versa at the 2018 Society for Military History conference in Louisville, Kentucky. Thanks also go to Willy Dobak and Lance Blyth for making the panel work so well.

I would also like to thank Forestry Service District Archaeologist, Chris Adams and District Ranger, Michael N. Hutchins for their advice and acknowledgement concerning the Palomas River battle of May 1880. (See Chapter 8)

The usual suspects also deserve a mention: Dan Aranda, Eric, Kathy and Ruby Fuller, Emilio Tapia and Juan Rojelio were, as ever, generous hosts. Bill and Jill Cavaliere were, again, as usual, outstanding hosts. Thanks to Bill, I finally got some good photos of a Northern Cardinal, a Mexican Cardinal, Acorn Woodpecker and got within touching distance of a Javelina, all in the space of fifteen minutes at Portal, Arizona. Also got very close to a pair of Barn Owls, a pair of Screech Owls and their three chicks and a plethora of other wild life at his ranch. I think the incident involving me, an eight-foot wood baton, a large tree and a Bull Snake is probably best forgotten.

The people of Portal braved some of the heaviest rain I've seen in the southwest to hear me talk about the Victorio Campaign in an event organised by the Cochise County Historical Society. I have to commend Bill Cavaliere for organising this event and keeping his eyeballs on both the audience and the speaker in particular. I also had the great pleasure and honour of finally meeting Henrietta Stockel, another icon in the pantheon of great Apache historians.

As ever, thanks goes to my wife Catherine for her constant encouragement and support. Our cat, Kira, also, very occasionally, shows her support. She also occasionally reminds me that cats are just as careful and cautious as the Chiricahua Apaches, and just as lethal.

However, I have to end with the very sad news that Ed Sweeney passed away on 6 September, 2018. Ed played a key early role in facilitating my contact with people in the Southwest, particularly Dan Aranda. This initiated the field-study side of my research which proved to be an essential component of this work. He was always very supportive, even to the extent of telling me what he'd said as a referee to some of my articles, even though they were supposed to be anonymous. This would never fail to encourage me to endeavour to persevere with this project.

My abiding memory of Ed would be during September 2009, when he, Dan Aranda, Emilio Tapia and I ended up camping on the continental divide at the northern end of the Black Range. We talked Apaches and all sorts of things into the early hours of the morning around a campfire.

I then spent most of the rest of the night in a camp-bed looking at the stars, planes, satellites, shooting stars and seeing the flashes on the eastern horizon from a distant, inaudible electric storm. A city-dweller such as myself rarely gets the opportunity to talk with the experts and experience the Southwest at the same time.

Ed leaves an outstanding legacy as an authority on Chiricahua Apache history. He will also be greatly missed as a good friend.

Author's Notes

A couple of issues came up as a result of some feedback on the first volume of this trilogy.

The Apache warrior on the front cover of Volume One is not Victorio. He is an Apache warrior named Frijole. There were a couple of comments which reached my ears that I was either being disingenuous or ignorant by passing this photograph off as Victorio. This surprised me as I had quite deliberately chosen this image for the front cover. I wanted to have a front cover image which did two things: first, give a flavour of the terrain and two, show an image of one of the lesser-known participants. Frijole was in Nana's following so almost certainly fought throughout the Victorio Campaign. The more obvious approach was to have used the alleged Victorio photograph for Volume One, Edward Hatch for Volume Two and Nana for the final book of this trilogy. I have used a quote attributed to Victorio and Nana for the titles of Volumes One and Three. I have used a phrase used in a letter sent by Colonel Hatch for this Volume in his correspondence for the title of Volume Two. The correspondence would have worked well.

However, separate research by Radbourne, and more recently Aranda, in my opinion, conclusively established that the two photographs said to be Victorio are not of the Apache leader.[1] I thought, if anything, it would have been dishonest to use a photograph which I was convinced was not Victorio. As an alternative I decided to eschew the use of leading actor images and opt to utilise photographs of lesser-known participants.

The young officer on the front cover of this volume is Walter Finley, Ninth Cavalry. It is one of the few contemporary photographs of one of the junior participants in the Victorio Campaign. Most US army officer photographs either pre-date the conflict significantly often being images taken during the American Civil War or post-date the campaign by some years. When looking for photographs of even US army participants in the Victorio War images of veteran First Lieutenants and Captains photographs often date back to the Civil War. The images of junior officers in that same period are often post-1900. Nevertheless, there are some photographs of officers such as Lieutenants Gatewood and Mills dressed for rough service in Apacheria. However, it was the discovery of a contemporary photograph of Finley which reached the front cover. First, his beard cannot disguise the fact that he still looks young enough to be in High School and not facing Victorio's warriors in a night battle in October 1879. Second, his private correspondence proved to be the key which allowed Karl Laumbach to challenge the accepted version of what happened at Hembrillo Canyon in April 1880. It was this information which prompted me to look very carefully at US army accounts of this operation in order to further challenge accounts of this battle. Finally, despite his youth, Finley's private correspondence shows a very mature analysis of the reasons for Victorio's resistance.

I intend to use an image of Sergeant Brent Woods as part of the cover image for Volume Three.

The use of footnotes also generated quite a discussion, particularly on Facebook, in response to a number of people objecting to the use of footnotes.

My position on this is unequivocal: I loathe endnotes. I am an academic. If another author piques my interest by unearthing new information or advancing an alternative explanation of events, I do

1 See short discussion of this issue in Chapter 16.

not want to be constantly moving back and forth between endnotes and the narrative. This impedes the flow of the narrative. If I can quickly glance down I can see the source and carry on with the reading virtually uninterrupted.

For those who don't like footnotes, I fail to see how the presence of footnotes causes any problem: simply ignore them and carry on reading.

1

Victorio's Decoy Strategy, January 1880

Victorio and his following, broadly prompted by the same reasons as Juh, moved back towards south-western New Mexico in late December 1879-early January 1880. Governor Terrazas contacted General Pope, informing him that General Trevino was to move against Victorio on 28 December. A few days later, Terrazas asked US forces to help prevent the Apaches reaching the United States, predicting the critical area would be the Florida Mountains.[1] The Apaches were believed to be based around the Laguna de Guzman and Santa Maria suggesting that any northward movement to avoid Trevino would be centred on the Florida Mountains. Major Morrow, at Fort Bayard, was instructed to take to the field to cooperate with Trevino's forces.[2] By 6 January, the Mexican authorities thought the Apaches were definitely making for the Florida Mountains.[3]

In response to Terrazas' information that Victorio was moving towards the Florida Mountains, General Pope immediately ordered Major Morrow into the field and, if necessary, to use the Ninth Cavalry Companies based at Forts Bliss and Stanton to help hunt down any Apaches who crossed into the United States. When Morrow did not immediately leave Fort Bayard, General Pope repeated his instruction to move immediately into the field. Pope added that Morrow could call upon all the troops in southern New Mexico and should act decisively to 'end this trouble as soon as possible'.[4] General Pope reminded Major Morrow that the latter was in command of field operations, and that his authority was not to be hindered by post commanders.[5] At the same time, Morrow was told that the Department of Arizona had been informed of Trevino's operation, and

1 Luis Terrazas to Acting Assistant Adjutant General (Hereafter referred to as 'AAAG') 2 Jan., 1880, NA, RG393, Part 3, Entry 439, pp.472-473; See also Pope to Whipple. AAG Headquarters (Hereafter referred to as 'HQ'), Military Division of the Missouri, 9 Jan., 1880, 'Victorio Campaign, Feb. 1879-Nov. 1880' in "Special Files" Created by the Military Division of the Missouri. Records of U.S. Army Continental Commands, 1821-1920, (Hereafter referred to as the 'Victorio Files') NA, RG393, M1495, Roll 14; As above in Papers relating to military operations against Chief Victorio's band of Mescalero Apache in southern New Mexico, 1879-81 in Letters Rec'd by the Adjutant General's Office, 1871-80, (Hereafter referred to as the 'Victorio Papers'), NA, M666, Roll 526.

2 Loud to CO Fort Bayard, 2 Jan., 1880, Telegrams Sent DoNM (Hereafter referred to as 'DoNM'), Vol.3, Jan. – Nov. 1880 NA, RG393, Part 3, Entry 431, pp.5-6.

3 Loud to CO Fort Bayard, 2 Jan., 1880, Telegrams Sent DoNM, Vol.3, Jan. – Nov. 1880 NA, RG393, Part 3, Entry 431, pp.5-6; Pope to Carr, 7 Jan., 1880, NA, RG393, Part 1, Entry 236; Thrapp, 1974, p.260.

4 Loud to Morrow, 4 Jan., 1880 reporting instructions from Gen. Pope rec'd at Santa Fé (Hereafter referred to as 'SF'), 3 Jan., 1880, Telegrams Sent DoNM, Vol.3, Jan. – Nov. 1880 NA, RG393, Part 3, Entry 431, p.10.

5 Loud to Morrow 4 Jan., 1880, repeating instructions from Platt Assistant Adjutant General (Hereafter referred to as 'AAG'), Department of the Missouri (Hereafter referred to as 'DoM')and General Pope rec'd at SF, 3 Jan., 1880, Telegrams Sent DoNM, Vol.3, Jan. – Nov. 1880 NA, RG393, Part 3, Entry 431, pp.9-10.

had been asked to cooperate with the major in his operations against the Apaches.[6] In a further missive, General Pope also ordered Morrow to use some of his force from Bayard and Stanton to 'suppress promptly' the raiding activities of the Mescalero Apaches. Pope also ordered that every available infantryman and cavalryman should take the field.[7] Pope seems to have been unaware of the exact geography of the region, and he does seem, despite his own protestations to the contrary,[8] to have been prone to demanding immediate responses from his field commanders when they should probably have been left to organise their own operations.[9] Pope even went so far as to demand that couriers be sent after Morrow to deliver further instructions (a repeat of instructions already issued) and obtain a written acknowledgement of these from the Major.[10]

In the meantime, and interfering superiors notwithstanding, Major Morrow alerted three guard posts at McEvers', Mason's and Knight's Ranches, occupied by small sections of Ninth Cavalrymen detached from Fort Bayard.[11] If the Apaches were making for the Floridas, and beyond, these pickets would be the most likely to detect any such movement. Morrow also:

> sent Maney with his Indians to the [F]lorida Mts to hunt up Indian trails Beyer to [C]ow [S] prings with his own & M company. Purington [D]awson and Humphreys to Cummings. I leave here at daylight tomorrow. Am provided with Thirty days rations and will cooperate with Mexican Troops. Will not want the Stanton or Bliss Companies.[12]

Despite the Major's statement that he would not need them, District Headquarters ordered that the troops at Fort Bliss be placed on standby to be ready to join Morrow's command if called upon.[13] It was more realistic to use the Fort Bayard and Fort Bliss troops to counter the threat from below the border, while the Fort Stanton garrison would counter the Mescalero Raiders, the latter being judged by Morrow as not presenting a serious threat.[14]

The first indication that the Apaches had crossed the border came from the Florida Mountains, as predicted by the Mexican authorities, on 2 January 1880. A group of prospectors was attacked in the Florida Mountains. (See document file no. 25.[15]) One of these prospectors, John Adair, later reported that he had been part of a 10-man party drawn from Pinos Altos, Georgetown and the Lower Mimbres. They had worked their way down the western side of the Florida Mountains and had been

6 Loud AAAG to Major Morrow, 4 Jan., 1880, Telegrams Sent DoNM, Vol.3, Jan. – Nov. 1880 NA, RG393, Part 3, Entry 431, p.12 see also p.18; Pope to Whipple. AAG HQ Military Division of the Missouri, (Hereafter referred to as the 'MDoM'), 9 Jan., 1880, 'Victorio Files', NA, RG393, M1495, Roll 14.

7 Loud to CO Fort Bayard, 4 Jan., 1880, Telegrams Sent DoNM, Vol.3, Jan. – Nov. 1880 NA, RG393, Part 3, Entry 431, pp.10-11.

8 'He [Morrow] can judge better than I what force it is necessary to use on or near the Pecos and what force to help General Trevino with.' (Loud (repeating Gen. Pope's instructions rec'd at SF) to Morrow, 5 Jan., 1880, Telegrams Sent DoNM, Vol.3, Jan. – Nov. 1880 NA, RG393, Part 3, Entry 431, p.19).

9 See for example Loud to Major Morrow, 4 Jan., 1880, Telegrams Sent DoNM, Vol.3, Jan. – Nov. 1880 NA, RG393, Part 3, Entry 431, pp.12-13.

10 Hatch to Co Fort Bayard, 5 Jan., 1880, Telegrams Sent DoNM, Vol.3, Jan. – Nov. 1880 NA, RG393, Part 3, Entry 431, p.20.

11 Billington, 1991, p.93.

12 Morrow Bayard to Loud AAAG SF, 4 Jan., 1880, NA, RG393, Part 3, Entry 439, p.474; Loud to AAG Fort Leavenworth, 14 Jan.1880, Telegrams Sent DoNM, Vol.3, Jan. – Nov. 1880 NA, RG393, Part 3, Entry 431, p.14.

13 Loud AAAG to CO Fort Bliss, 4 Jan., 1880, Telegrams Sent DoNM, Vol.3, Jan. – Nov. 1880 NA, RG393, Part 3, Entry 431, p.13.

14 Morrow, 5 Jan., 1880, Telegrams Sent DoNM, Vol.3, Jan. – Nov. 1880 NA, RG393, Part 3, Entry 431, pp.20-21; see also Hatch to CO Fort Stanton, 5 Jan., 1880, Telegrams Sent DoNM, Vol.3, Jan. – Nov. 1880 NA, RG393, Part 3, Entry 431, p.22.

15 Documentary annex available as a free download at <http://www.helion.co.uk/hwms-annex.pdf>.

Plates 1.1 and 1.2 Two shots of the remains of Slocum's or Mason's Ranch, one of the sites where Major Morrow chose to station guard detachments to detect the return of Victorio to New Mexico. The ranch seems to be a mix of stone and adobe build, and is being steadily eroded as the years pass. The upper photo also shows the obvious threat of erosion of the walls through flood damage. (Photos: Author)

camped at some natural water tanks at the south-eastern end of the Floridas. On the morning of 2 January, they had cleaned their guns and had fired off some shots 'in order to more thoroughly clean them'.[16] Up till that point, they had seen no sign of the presence of Apaches and obviously felt that such a noisy process would not be dangerous. Four of the men remained in camp while six men left the camp to prospect, two including Adair, on their own, and four others in a small group. At about 9:00 a.m. Adair heard heavy firing from the direction of their camp. He and the other men hastily returned to the camp and found it under attack by Apache warriors. The prospectors took cover behind some rocks but could catch glimpses of Apaches working their way around their flanks. They pulled back for some distance to avoid being trapped, but doing this left their horses and mules out of range of their guns, and the Apaches promptly ran their stock off and disappeared.[17]

Of the four men left in the camp, three had been hit, probably in the first volley: Edward Fulton was killed and F.C. Bell and J.J. Baxter wounded. The prospectors lost all of their stock, apart from some burros that had remained in the range of their rifles. The survivors made their way to Fort Cummings.[18] Adair thought that they had killed two of the 28 to 30 Apaches who had attacked them.[19] However, Adair himself noted the heavy firing, and that the Apaches, rather than holding their positions, had made it obvious to their opponents that they were shifting positions. This suggests that the Apaches were employing the tactic of combining heavy gunfire with rapid movement through rough terrain, to give the impression of greater numbers than were actually present. If there had been approximately 30 Apaches, there would have been more than enough warriors present to pick off the whole party while it was scattered around the camp. It is also clear that the obvious effort by the Apaches to outflank the miners had been carried out with the intention of forcing the prospectors to retreat beyond rifle range of their stock.

Morrow received news of this attack on 4 January,[20] and the following day set out in pursuit of Victorio for the second time in less than five months. The Department of Arizona also received the news of Victorio's return to New Mexico via the Commanding Officer for the Department of the Missouri on or around 6 January 1880.[21] Lieutenant Blocksom's company of Apache scouts was sent to join Morrow, and that of Lieutenant Gatewood was ordered out to patrol the country between the Gila and San Francisco Rivers.[22] Lieutenant Howard's Apache scout company was also ordered to prepare itself for field service.[23] In fact, as noted in the last chapter of the previous book, Gatewood's A Company, Indian scouts, was already in the field scouting that very country.[24]

---

16 John Adair's Account of an Attack upon Prospectors in the Florida Mountains on the 2 Jan., 1880 in the 'Correspondence' Section of the *Grant County Herald* 17 Jan., 1880.

17 John Adair's Account of an Attack upon Prospectors in the Florida Mountains on the 2 Jan., 1880 in the 'Correspondence' Section of the *Grant County Herald,* 17 Jan., 1880.

18 Lt Allen to Loud SF, 3 Jan., 1880, NA, RG393, Part 3, Entry 439, pp.470-471; Gibson Operator Grant to Carr Fort Thomas, 3 Jan., 1880, NA, RG393, Part 1, Entry 236; John Adair's Account of an Attack upon Prospectors in the Florida Mountains on 2 Jan., 1880 in the 'Correspondence' Section of the *Grant County Herald,* 17 Jan., 1880; Thrapp, 1974, p.260.

19 John Adair's Account of an Attack upon Prospectors in the Florida Mountains on 2 Jan., 1880 in the 'Correspondence' Section of the *Grant County Herald,* 17 Jan., 1880.

20 Loud AAAG to Commanding Officer (Hereafter referred to as 'CO'), Fort Bayard 4 Jan., 1880, Telegrams Sent DoNM, Vol.3, Jan. – Nov. 1880 NA, RG393, Part 3, Entry 431, p.11.

21 Willcox to AAG, Presidio, San Francisco, 6 Jan., 1880, NA, RG393, Part 1, Entry 169, Vol. 10, pp.6-7

22 Martin to AAG, DoNM, 6 Jan., 1880, NA, RG393, Part 1, Entry 169, Vol. 10, p.5; Loud to CO Fort Bayard, 8 Jan., 1880, Telegrams Sent DoNM, Vol.3, Jan. – Nov. 1880 NA, RG393, Part 3, Entry 431, p.25 & 27.

23 Kerr AAAG, Howard, (Through CO Camp Huachuca), 6 Jan., 1880, Troops in SE Arizona, Dept. of Arizona, (Hereafter referred to as DoAz), NA, RG393, Part 1, Entry 232, Vol.5, 13 Dec., 1879-7 May, 1880, Letter No.11, pp.24-25.

24 HQ, Troops in the field in South Eastern Arizona, Fort Apache, Special Orders No.12, 31 Dec., 1879, Special Orders Oct. 1879-Jan. 1881, DoAz, Vol. 1, NA, RG393, Part 1, Entry 239, pp.9-10.

James P. Martin, Assistant Adjutant General to General Willcox, also informed Colonel Carr, Sixth Cavalry, that a major campaign could not be mounted in New Mexico by troops from the Department of Arizona due to the poor condition of troops and transportation. However, Martin thought that a smaller scale scouting and support operation could be mounted to aid the joint operation of General Trevino and Major Morrow. Thus, it was judged that the international line from the juncture of Arizona and New Mexico territories to the Florida Mountains could be patrolled,[25] and on 6 January, Blocksom's Apache scouts were sent to cover the 100 or so miles between the Arizona line and the Florida Mountains.[26] Three days later, Major D. Perry, Sixth Cavalry, was sent out to follow Blocksom to the Floridas. Perry was instructed to cooperate with Major Morrow but not to go beyond the Mimbres River unless sure that such a move would achieve positive results against the Apaches.[27] This detachment of four officers and 73 cavalrymen, with 24 Apache scouts, patrolled the country between Fort Bowie and Fort Bayard, arriving at the latter post on 13 January, and departed for Fort Bowie on 18 January.[28] These orders were issued too late to block Victorio's move into New Mexico but they did allow Morrow to concentrate more immediately available troops from New Mexico on the pursuit of the Apaches.

Major Perry's instructions also reflected the uncertainty of the moment:

> I do not think you can do better than to wait near Fort Bayard till Morrow is heard from or there is some different news of where the Indians are – Department Commander expects you to return as soon as the emergency is over.[29]

In approving Carr's decision to send Perry into New Mexico, General Willcox did so with the proviso that Perry must cooperate with Morrow and return to Arizona as soon as the campaign was over.[30] Willcox was clearly worried that Juh and his following might leave to join Victorio. Lieutenant Haskell was informed of Trevino's operation and instructed to be very vigilant towards Juh and his warriors.[31] There was also the problem of different military commands trying to retain control of their own forces. For instance, in contrast to Willcox's instructions to Perry, Carr made it clear that Blocksom's Apache scouts were not intended to join with Morrow. He ordered that the Apache scouts should operate independently to prevent the Apaches moving west of the Florida

25 Martin to Carr, 6 Jan., 1880, NA, RG393, Part 1, Entry 169, Vol. 10, pp.3-4; Kerr to Carr, 6 Jan., 1880, Troops in SE Arizona, DoAz, NA, RG393, Part 1, Entry 232, Vol.5, 13 Dec., 1879-7 May, 1880, Letter No.8,pp.21-22.

26 Carr to Blocksom (through CO Fort Bowie), 6 Jan., 1880, Troops in SE Arizona, DoAz, NA, RG393, Part 1, Entry 232, Vol.5, 13 Dec., 1879-7 May, 1880, Letter No.6, p.20; Carr to Blocksom (through CO Fort Bowie), 6 Jan., 1880, Troops in SE Arizona, DoAz, NA, RG393, Part 1, Entry 232, Vol.5, 13 Dec., 1879-7 May, 1880, Letter No.10, pp.23-24.

27 Carr to Perry, 8 Jan., 1880, Troops in SE Arizona, DoAz, NA, RG393, Part 1, Entry 232, Vol.5, 13 Dec., 1879-7 May, 1880, Letter No.33, pp.45-46; Carr to AAAG SF, 9 Jan., 1880, NA, RG393, Part 3, Entry 439, pp.488-490; See also Report of Col. EA Carr 29 Aug., 1880; Kerr AAAG to Morrow, Fort Bayard, Troops in SE Arizona, DoAz, NA, RG393, Part 1, Entry 232, Vol.5, 13 Dec., 1879-7 May, 1880, Letter No.12, pp.25-26.

28 Medical History, Fort Bayard NM May 1879, NA, RG94, Entry 257, Vol. 896, p.21; See also Comdg Bowie to Adjutant General (Hereafter referred to as 'AG'), 8 Jan., 1880, NA, RG393, Part 1, Entry 236; Carr, 10 Jan., 1880, Telegrams Sent DoNM, Vol.3, Jan. – Nov. 1880 NA, RG393, Part 3, Entry 431, p.33; See also 'Town and County', the *Grant County Herald*, 17 Jan., 1880; Bi-Monthly Company Muster Rolls for Company C, 6th Cavalry, Jan./Feb. 1880 in NA, RG94.

29 Comdg Fort Bowie to Major Perry, 13 Jan., 1880, NA, RG393, Part 1, Entry 236.

30 Martin to Carr, 19 Jan., 1880, NA, RG393, Part 1, Entry 169, Vol. 10, p.15.

31 Martin to Haskell, 6 Jan., 1880, NA, RG393, Part 1, Entry 169, Vol. 10, p.5.

Mountains.[32] These specific instructions were probably provoked by instructions from Colonel Hatch that troops from Arizona should report to Morrow.[33]

US Army Blues: Déjà Vu in the Black Range and San Mateo Mountains, January 1880[34]

The post surgeon at Fort Bayard noted that, '8 Officers and 174 men of the Ninth Cavalry and 24 Indian Scouts left the post for the field to operate against Victorio's hostile band of Apache Indians January 5th.'[35] The attack on the prospectors in the Florida Mountains clearly confirmed that Apaches were now inside the USA. The first indication that Victorio had *also* evaded the Morrow's border blockade came on 6 or 7 January, with the cutting of the telegraph line east from Fort Cummings. The repairman found the break near the Goodsight Mountains. He also found an 'Indian trail crossing road at that point. 150 feet wire taken.'[36] The *Arizona Citizen* of 17 January 1880 reported that several hundred yards of wire were taken then 'dropped a hundred yards or so to the north of the road.'[37] Fort Cummings was also alerted to the sighting of 55 Apaches preparing to attack McEvers' Ranch early on 8 January.[38] The ranches to the north, including McEvers, Fountains and Mossner Ranches, were subsequently reported to have been attacked, with 30 cattle slaughtered and another 60 driven off.[39] A courier was despatched to find Major Morrow and the news was passed on to Fort Bayard. Lieutenant Martin B. Hughes was ordered to proceed from Fort Bayard to McEvers' Ranch *poste haste* with a detachment of 38 cavalrymen. Each man was issued 100 rounds and rationed till 31 January.[40] Lieutenant Taylor, commanding the small detachment of Ninth Cavalrymen at McEvers' Ranch, was ordered to remain there and scout the surrounding county thoroughly to ascertain the truth of this report.[41]

The departure of Lieutenant Hughes left no mounted troops stationed at Fort Bayard.[42] For once, the courier reached Morrow in record time. The Major immediately countermanded the order to send Lieutenant Hughes to McEvers' Ranch. Instead, Hughes was to march to Fort Cummings, where further orders from Morrow awaited him.[43] Morrow had stationed himself at

32 Carr 10 Jan., 1880, Telegrams Sent DoNM, Vol.3, Jan. – Nov. 1880 NA, RG393, Part 3, Entry 431, p.33.
33 Loud to Col. Carr, 5 Jan., 1880, Telegrams Sent DoNM, Vol.3, Jan. – Nov. 1880 NA, RG393, Part 3, Entry 431, p.24.
34 See Map 2.1 for a summary of Morrow's campaign against Victorio during January-February 1880.
35 Medical History, Fort Bayard NM May 1879, NA, RG94, Entry 257 Vol. 896, p.21.
36 Lt Allen Silver City to Loud SF, 8 Jan., 1880, NA, RG393, Part 3, Entry 439, p.481; Carr to AG DoAz, 8 Jan., 1880, Troops in SE Arizona, DoAz, NA, RG393, Part 1, Entry 232, Vol.5, 13 Dec., 1879-7 May, 1880, Letter No.20. pp.29-30.
37 *Arizona Citizen*, 17 January, 1880 in Library of Congress 'Chronicling America' website <http://chroniclingamerica.loc.gov/> (accessed 10/09/2018).
38 Loud to Carr, 8 Jan., 1880, Telegrams Sent DoNM, Vol.3, Jan. – Nov. 1880 NA, RG393, Part 3, Entry 431, p.24.
39 *Thirty-Four*, 15 Jan., 1880; Loud to CO Fort Bayard, 8 Jan., 1880, Telegrams Sent DoNM, Vol.3, Jan. – Nov. 1880 NA, RG393, Part 3, Entry 431, p.25; Carr to AG DoAz, 8 Jan., 1880, Troops in SE Arizona, DoAz, NA, RG393, Part 1, Entry 232, Vol.5, 13 Dec., 1879-7 May, 1880, Letter No.20. pp.29-30.
40 Humphreys Bayard to AAAG DoNM, 8 Jan., 1880, NA, RG393, Part 3, Entry 439, pp.476-480; Medical History, Fort Bayard NM May 1879, NA, RG94, Entry 257 Vol. 896, p.21; Hatch to Carr, 8 Jan., 1880, NA, RG393, Part 1, Entry 236.
41 Loud to CO Fort Bayard, 8 Jan., 1880, Telegrams Sent DoNM, Vol.3, Jan. – Nov. 1880 NA, RG393, Part 3, Entry 431, p.25 & p.26.
42 Humphreys Bayard to AAAG DoNM, 8 Jan., 1880, NA, RG393, Part 3, Entry 439, pp.484-485.
43 Humphrey Bayard to AAAG SF, 8 Jan., 1880, NA, RG393, Part 3, Entry 439, pp.482-485; Loud to AAG Fort Leavenworth, 9 Jan., 1880, Telegrams Sent DoNM, Vol.3, Jan. – Nov. 1880 NA, RG393, Part 3, Entry 431, pp.27-28.

Fort Cummings, after leaving Fort Bayard, and had sent out a couple of detachments to scout the surrounding country. The Major had also scouted the Florida Mountains. On receipt of the news that the telegraph line to the north had been cut, he moved very swiftly. By 8 January, he had sent out orders to his scattered detachments ordering them to move to Fort Cummings to either join him or follow up his trail:[44]

> I expect Dawson to overtake me tomorrow night. Beyer with his command has gone astray his orders were to report to me in the Florida Mts which he failed to do & I fear he is on a wild goose chase. I think however I have force enough to get away with Victorio.[45]

Morrow left Fort Cummings with Captain Purington, Lieutenants Humphrey and Maney, and 46 men, moving to the north towards McEvers' Ranch, on the morning of 9 January 1880.[46] The major felt that he had sufficient force to deal with Victorio and that the Apaches would be caught within two days.[47] It would appear that Lieutenant Hughes's detachment joined Morrow on 9 January, at Macho Springs, that Lieutenants Dawson and Hugo left Fort Cummings with their detachment on the same morning, and that Beyer left Cummings to join Morrow early on 10 January.[48] L Company, Ninth Cavalry, had also left Fort Bliss on 8 January to join Morrow's battalion.[49]

Morrow, having reached his old supply camp at McEvers' Ranch, picked up a large trail leading into the Black Range.[50] Humphreys, at Fort Bayard, reported that the Apache trail led north into the Black Range, and private letters from Lieutenants Day and French informed him that they were expecting to engage the Apaches on 11 January.[51]

Even as Morrow was trying to coordinate his forces, further information concerning the numbers and movement of Apaches arrived at Fort Bayard. On 12 January, a 'commissary train arrived yesterday, man in charge reports having seen sixty-six Indians near Black ?Sakes? about 12 miles east of Macho going north about Wed Jan 7th.'[52]

War: Skirmish on the Rio Percha …

On 12 January 1880, Morrow caught up with Victorio on the Rio Percha, by which time it was clear that all his scattered detachments had re-joined his command (see Table 1.1).[53]

---

44 Loud to AAG Fort Leavenworth Ks., 9 Jan., 1880, Telegrams Sent DoNM, Vol.3, Jan. – Nov. 1880 NA, RG393, Part 3, Entry 431, p.27.

45 Loud to AAG Fort Leavenworth, 10 Jan., 1880, Telegrams Sent DoNM, Vol.3, Jan. – Nov. 1880 NA, RG393, Part 3, Entry 431, pp.34-35; Morrow McEvers Ranch to Loud AAAG, 9 Jan., 1880, NA, RG393, Part 3, Entry 439, pp.494-495; Pope to AAG HQ MDoM, 11 Jan., 1880, 'Victorio Files', NA, RG393, M1495, Roll 14; 'Indian Affairs' *Army & Navy Journal,* Vol.17, 17 Jan., 1880, p.465.

46 Humphreys Bayard to AAAG SF 13 Jan., 1880, NA, RG393, Part 3, Entry 439, p.508.

47 Allen Bayard to Lt Stedman SF, 9 Jan., 1880, NA, RG393, Part 3, Entry 439, p.499.

48 Humphreys Bayard to AAAG SF, 13 Jan., 1880, NA, RG393, Part 3, Entry 439, pp.508-509.

49 Returns for Dec. 1879 & Jan., 1880 in Returns From U.S. Military Posts 1800-1916, Fort Bliss, Texas, Jan. 1872-Dec. 1885, NA, M617, Roll 117.

50 Morrow McEvers Ranch to Loud AAAG SF, 9 Jan., 1880, NA, RG393, Part 3, Entry 439, p.494; Morrow to Loud, 9 Jan., 1880 in 'Victorio Papers', NA, M666, Roll 526; Loud to AAG Fort Leavenworth, 10 Jan., 1880, Telegrams Sent DoNM, Vol.3, Jan. – Nov. 1880 NA, RG393, Part 3, Entry 431, pp.34-35; Thrapp, 1974, p.261.

51 Humphreys Bayard to AAAG SF, 13 Jan., 1880, NA, RG393, Part 3, Entry 439, p.510.

52 Humphreys, Bayard to AAAG SF, 13 Jan., 1880, NA, RG393, Part 3, Entry 439, p.509.

53 Bayard to CO, DoNM, 15 Jan., 1880, NA, RG393, Part 3, Entry 439, pp.514-515; *Thirty-Four Extra,* 15 Jan., 1880.

Table 1.1 Roster of Major Morrow's Battalion, 5 January 1880.[54] (See Document File No. 26.)

Officer	Company	Number of Soldiers/Scouts
Major Morrow with Lieutenants Day and Finley		
Captain Dawson and Lieutenant Hugo	B Company, 9th Cavalry	20 soldiers
Captain Beyer and Lieutenant Humphreys	C Company, 9th Cavalry	36 soldiers
No officer	F Company, 9th Cavalry	25 soldiers
Captain Purington	H Company, 9th Cavalry	15 soldiers
Lieutenant French	M Company, 9th Cavalry	30 soldiers
Lieutenant Maney, 15th Infantry	A Company Indian scouts	24 Apache Scouts
	D Company 9th Cavalry	13 soldiers
Lieutenant Hughes (with a detachment drawn from the Fort Bayard garrison including a Hotchkiss mountain howitzer)	B Company, 9th Cavalry	10 soldiers
	F Company, 9th Cavalry	2 soldiers
	H Company, 9th Cavalry	2 soldiers
	D Company, 9th Cavalry	24 soldiers
	Doctors	2
	Guides	2
	Teamsters	3

The Chihenne Apaches used the rough country to hold off their foes from early afternoon till the light failed. Morrow noted that Victorio 'made a strong stand & evidently thought he could check us but he finally gave it up & went off on the jump.'[55] Morrow claimed several Apache warriors killed and wounded, with a Sergeant Gross killed and one scout[56] wounded in return.[57] There are some discrepancies in the number of casualties sustained, but this can probably be put down to delays in filling out returns for the Ninth Cavalry rather than an attempt to play down the fatalities sustained.[58]

---

54 Humphreys to AAAG SF, 10 Jan., 1880, NA, RG393, Part 3, Entry 439, pp.491-493; See also CO Fort Bayard, 10 Jan., 1880, Telegrams Sent DoNM, Vol.3, Jan. – Nov. 1880 NA, RG393, Part 3, Entry 431, p.34; Humphreys Bayard to AAAG SF, 9 Jan., 1880, NA, RG393, Part 3, Entry 439, pp.486-487; See also Telegrams Sent DoNM, Vol.3, Jan. – Nov. 1880 NA, RG393, Part 3, Entry 431, p.32

55 Platt quoting both Morrow's Report & Hatch's endorsement to AAG HQ MDoM, 14 Jan., 1880, 'Victorio Files', NA, RG393, M1495, Roll 14; Whipple to Sherman, 14 Jan., 1880 in 'Victorio Papers', NA, M666, Roll 526.

56 Medical History, Fort Bayard NM May 1879, NA, RG94, Entry 257 Vol. 896, p.21 Notes that the scout sustained a flesh wound in the thigh.

57 Morrow to Loud AAAG, 13 Jan., 1880 Telegrams Sent DoNM, Vol.3, Jan. – Nov. 1880 NA, RG393, Part 3, Entry 431, p.47; Whipple to Sherman, 14 Jan., 1880, NA, RG393, Part 1, Entry 2539, Press Copies of Letters and Endorsements Sent, MDoM, Vol. 13, p.41; Morrow to Loud AAAG SF, 13 Jan., 1880, NA, RG393, Part 3, Entry 439, pp.512-513; Bi-Monthly Company Muster Rolls for Company F, 9th Cavalry, Jan./Feb.1880 in NA, RG94; Report of The Surgeon General in Annual Reports of the War Department 1880, (Hereafter referred to as 'AR-WD'), NA, M997, Roll 35, 1880 Vol. I, p.520; Platt quoting both Morrow's Report & Hatch's endorsement to AAG HQ MDoM, 14 Jan., 1880, 'Victorio Files', NA, RG393, M1495, Roll 14; Medical History, Fort Bayard NM May 1879, NA, RG94, Entry 257 Vol. 896, p.21; *Thirty-Four*, 14 Jan., 1880; *Thirty-Four Extra*, 15 Jan., 1880; 'Town and County', the *Grant County Herald*, 17 Jan., 1880; See also Thrapp, 1974, p.261; Record of Engagements, p.93; web article The Ninth Regiment of Cavalry by Lt G. Hutcheson; Wellman, 1957, p.164; Webb, 1976, p.87.

58 The Regimental Return for Jan. lists both Gross and Pvt. D.H. Jones as being killed in action. (Record of Events Jan., 1880 in Returns From Regular Army Cavalry Regiments 1833-1916, 9th Cavalry

During the fight, Lieutenant Day:

> commanded Troop "C" 9th Cavey in two charges, both successful. The first a charge by Company. Then crossing the valley, was fourth man up in the charge by battalion. After an hour's fighting Lt (now Capt Hughes) Lieuts Day and Maney (15th Infty) collected about 40 men, moved off by the flank and made a charge on the flank, which was repulsed. Lieut Day and about 8 men reaching within 50 feet of the breast high natural wall of rock which crowned the crest of the gulch. Lieut Day alone sustained the entire fire of the hostile line at this point while climbing to a position which commanded the hostiles on the flank, Capt Hughes with five men holding a similar position in front, to liberate Lt Maney and the soldiers in the bottom and sides of the gulch.[59]

It was even reported, in the *Grant County Herald* of 21 February 1880, that one of the two Apaches claimed to have been killed was shot by Major Morrow himself.[60] The fighting ended at about 5:00 p.m., when the troops were able to bring their mountain howitzer into action, at which point the Apaches withdrew, though it was noted that until that point the Apaches had shown no inclination to flee from Morrow's command.[61] The fighting could be heard in the Animas River area and sheep herders straggled into Hillsboro reporting hearing heavy firing, including cannon fire, all afternoon.[62] One sheepherder claimed to have been detained by the Apaches, who confiscated his gun, almost certainly a breech-loading rifle of some description, but compensated with some clothes. Among these items of clothing was a shawl which was recognised as belonging to a victim of the September 1879 Jaralosa massacre.[63] The man also erroneously claimed that Victorio and Loco were dead, and that the Apaches were led by Nana.[64]

Morrow spoke 'in highest terms of hotchkiss gun'[65] during the engagement. The Apaches were no strangers to artillery. They certainly first came up against artillery at Apache Pass in 1862, when attempting to contest the passage of General Carleton's California Volunteer column during the American Civil War.[66] The *Grant County Herald* claimed that six Apaches had been killed by howitzer fire.[67] Morrow also estimated that Victorio had between 50 and 60 warriors.[68] (See document file no. 27.)

Regimental Returns 1873-1880, NA, M744, Roll 88) Two enlisted men were recorded as having been killed and one wounded (Chronological List, p.48; see also O'Neal, p.177; Haley, 1981, p.324).

Private Issac Jones of F Company, Ninth Cavalry, died from wounds received after the Hembrillo Canyon battle of 6 and 7 Apr., 1880. and it seems too close a coincidence that F Company should lose two men with the same surname within three months of each other.

59 Personal File Matthias W. Day, NA, RG94, Entry 297, Box 1; See also Kenner, 1999, p.197.
60 S.M. Ashenfelter, 'Maj. Morrow's Campaign', the *Grant County Herald*, 21 Feb., 1880.
61 *Thirty-Four Extra*, 15 Jan., 1880.
62 Ibid.
63 This occurred on 10 or 11, Sept., 1879. See Watt 'I Will Not Surrender the Hair of a Horse's Tail: The Victorio Campaign 1879, Chapter 6.
64 *Thirty-Four Extra*, 15 Jan., 1880.
65 Bayard to CO DoNM, 15 Jan., 1880, NA, RG393, Part 3, Entry 439, pp.514-515.
66 See Sweeney, 1998, pp.430-437 & 1991, pp.198-202 for a detailed account.
67 'Town and County', the *Grant County Herald*, 17 Jan., 1880.
68 Bayard to CO DoNM 15 Jan., 1880, NA, RG393, Part 3, Entry 439, pp.514-515.

... and Peace: Parley at Canada Alamosa

Morrow hoped to catch Victorio the next day near either the Animas River or the Cuchillo Negro River, but once again the Apaches out-paced him.[69] There was a brief skirmish between one of Morrow's companies (H Company, Ninth Cavalry) and the Apaches on 13 January, but, so far, no further details have emerged.[70] Hatch certainly hoped for another confrontation as he was confident that the Apaches would not be able to cope with another severely punishing onslaught.[71] Just what led both Morrow and Hatch to conclude that they had inflicted dire chastisement on their opponents can only be a matter of speculation. Hatch also contacted the Department of Arizona to alert those in command to the possibility that Victorio might try to evade Morrow by passing down the Gila Valley.[72] Captain Hooker, at Ojo Caliente, was again warned that Morrow was in pursuit of Victorio, and that a sharp lookout for the Apaches should be maintained by patrols from that post.[73]

On 16 January, Victorio contacted Andrew Kelley,[74] known and trusted by the Warm Springs Apaches. As noted earlier, Kelley had played a leading role in persuading Victorio to surrender at Ojo Caliente in February 1879.[75] Kelley was certainly based at Canada Alamosa in April-May 1880, as he corresponded with *Thirty-Four* from that location with reference to illegal trade with the Apaches.[76] This conference probably occurred in the vicinity of Canada Alamosa, as it was reported in *Thirty-Four* that the citizens there had had a conference with Victorio and 60 warriors. As far as these people could tell, there were no warriors missing from Victorio's following, and the Apaches showed little concern about being pursued by US troops. Victorio reiterated his desire for a reservation at Ojo Caliente.

Two hours later, Morrow arrived with his troops, and the Apaches quietly dispersed into the surrounding hills.[77] Kelley stated that Victorio had been accompanied by approximately 60 warriors with good mounts and well provided with modern arms and ammunition. He also added that Victorio did not want to negotiate with the US army over a possible return to Ojo Caliente.[78] Such distrust of the army may have dated back to the attempt to arrest him at Ojo Caliente in April 1879. Captain Hooker's post return (see document file no. 31) confirms that, on 15 January 1880,

---

69 Morrow to Loud AAAG SF, 13 Jan., 1880, NA, RG393, Part 3, Entry 439, p.513; Whipple to Sherman, 14 Jan., 1880, in Press Copies of Letters and Endorsements Sent, MDoM, NA, RG393, Part 1, Entry 2539, Vol. 13, p.41; Bayard to CO, DoNM, 15 Jan., 1880, NA, RG393, Part 3, Entry 439, p.515.

70 Record of Events Jan., 1880 in Returns From Regular Army Cavalry Regiments 1833-1916, 9th Cavalry Regimental Returns 1873-1880, NA, M744, Roll 88 & Bi-Monthly Company Muster Rolls for Company H, 9th Cavalry, Jan./Feb. 1880 in NA, RG94.

Both sources clearly state that Company H engaged hostile Apaches on 12, 13 and 17 Jan. with no casualties sustained in these encounters. It was reported that one sheepherder had been killed on 13 Jan., while his two companions were able to make their escape. (*Thirty-Four Extra*, 15 Jan., 1880).

71 Platt quoting both Morrow's Report & Hatch's endorsement to AAG HQ MDoM, 14 Jan., 1880, 'Victorio Files', NA, RG393, M1495, Roll 14.

72 Platt quoting both Morrow's Report & Hatch's endorsement to AAG HQ MDoM, 14 Jan., 1880, 'Victorio Files', NA, RG393, M1495, Roll 14; See also Whipple to Sherman, 14 Jan., 1880 in 'Victorio Papers', NA, M666, Roll 526.

73 Hatch to Hooker, 13 Jan., 1880, Telegrams Sent DoNM, Vol.3, Jan. – Nov. 1880 NA, RG393, Part 3, Entry 431, p.44; Telegrams Sent DoNM, Vol.3, Jan. – Nov. 1880 NA, RG393, Part 3, Entry 431, p.48.

74 Andrew Kelly is mentioned as a beef contractor supplying 'fresh beef on the hoof.' (2 Mar., 1880, Telegrams Sent DoNM, Vol.3, Jan. – Nov. 1880 NA, RG393, Part 3, Entry 431, p.175).

75 Thrapp, 1988, p.764.

76 Report from Andrew Kelley concerning illegal trade with Apaches at Canada Alamosa as reported in *Thirty-Four*, 5 May, 1880.

77 *Thirty-Four*, 28 Jan., 1880.

78 Thrapp, 1974, p261-262; Laumbach p.121.

Plate 1.3 The San Mateo Mountains seen from the road from Canada Alamosa to Nogal Canyon. The modern road winds its way up into the mountains, up to a high saddle out of sight behind the closer of the two ridges on the left and middle of the photo. The road then drops rapidly down into Nogal Canyon. This is the sort of terrain Victorio would use to exhaust his pursuers. (Photo: Author)

Plate 1.4 Opposite view looking down the same valley as shown in plate 1.3. The other side of the prominent rocky outcrop just above the pine trees can be seen in Plate 1.3. This shows the terrain Victorio led Morrow's battalion after the former's parlay with Andrew Kelley in Canada Alamosa on 16 January, 1880. This image, taken in conjunction with the previous photograph, also illustrates the difficulty in judging distances in Apacheria. The vegetation shown in Plate 1.3 can easily be mistaken for small trees and bushes when, in fact, they turn out to be fully grown pinewoods. (Author's Photo)

he had taken his company to Canada Alamosa as rumours had been received that Victorio wanted to parley. He makes no mention of any meeting with Victorio and notes that he met with a detachment from D Company, who were under orders from Morrow to join the Captain at Ojo Caliente. They returned to Ojo Caliente that same evening.[79]

This may have been the first of two conferences held by Victorio on 15-16 January, the second apparently being held about dusk with Major Morrow 'just below the highest peak of the San Mateos.'[80] Lieutenant Day's personal file states that 'before this engagement [San Mateo Mountains 17 January 1880] Lt. Day accompanied Col. Morrow to conference with hostiles.'[81] This time Victorio took no chances and, while the Apaches displayed a flag of truce, Victorio remained on top of the cliff. He reiterated his desire to be settled at Ojo Caliente with his family and other previous requests. Morrow, unfortunately, could only inform him that if the Apaches surrendered and gave up their arms and horses they would be treated as prisoners of war. The Major, quite honestly, revealed that he could not guarantee any conditions.[82] While Victorio would have appreciated Morrow's integrity, his suspicions of potential foul play, should he elect to surrender, could only have been reinforced by such candour. With the onset of night, it was agreed that the parley would be resumed in the morning.[83]

Victorio's Decoy Strategy

In the meantime, Mexican forces had also tracked Victorio to the border. General Trevino had contacted the United States authorities on 10 January 1880, to inform them that the Apaches had moved from the Florida Mountains towards La Mesilla.[84] As this was clearly US territory, General Trevino also informed them that his punitive expedition was over. There appears to be no record of any clashes between the Apaches and this large force of mixed Mexican federal and state troops.[85] Governor Wallace contacted Alexander Ramsey, the Secretary of War, on 10 January, reporting that Mexican troops had now reached the border and asking if they could be invited to continue their pursuit into the United States. Ramsey wholeheartedly approved, with the proviso that if the Mexican troops captured any Apaches, they should be turned over to US troops.[86] This condition was received with great opprobrium by both the territorial press[87] and the Governor of Chihuahua.[88] (See document file no. 29.4.) As far as the *Grant County Herald* was concerned: 'If any of these red devils are captured they ought to be turned over to the tender mercies of the troops from over the line. The Mexican government understands how to deal with this question.'[89] Colonel Hatch wrote to the Governor of Chihuahua on 12 January, through the CO Fort Bliss, informing him of this

79 Record of Events Jan., 1880 in Returns From U.S. Military Posts 1800-1916, Ojo Caliente, N.M. May 1879-Mar. 1882, NA, M617, Roll 877.
80 S.M. Ashenfelter, 'Maj. Morrow's Campaign', the *Grant County Herald*, 21 Feb., 1880.
81 Personal File Matthias W. Day, NA, RG94, Entry 297, Box 1.
82 S.M. Ashenfelter, 'Maj. Morrow's Campaign', the *Grant County Herald*, 21 Feb., 1880.
83 Ibid.
84 Thrapp, 1974, p.260.
85 Stout, p.121; Thrapp, 1974, p.260.
86 Wallace to Ramsey, 10 Jan., 1880 & Ramsey to Wallace, 14 Jan., 1880, , 'Victorio Files', NA, RG393, M1495, Roll 14; AGO (Hereafter referred to as 'AGO') to Commanding General DoM, 20 Jan., 1880 in 'Victorio Papers', NA, M666, Roll 526; 'Indian Affairs' *Army & Navy Journal*, Vol.17, 17 Jan., 1880, p.465.
87 Ashenfelter Editorial, the *Grant County Herald*, 17 Jan., 1880.
88 Terrazas to Gen Edward Hatch Comd DoNM, 17 Jan., 1880 NA, RG393, Part 3, Entry 439, pp.429-430.
89 Ashenfelter Editorial, the *Grant County Herald*, 17 Jan., 1880.

development and inviting Mexican troops to cross the border and cooperate with US troops.[90] Forts Bliss and Bayard acknowledged receipt of this information from District Headquarters on the same day, and the latter sent couriers to inform Major Morrow and all other detachments in the field of this development.[91] (See document file no. 29.) However, it would appear that no Mexican troops crossed the border. Mexican traders travelling with Colonel Cisneros until he reached the border later reported that the Mexican troops were not inclined to cross the line.[92].

A column of both federal and state troops, led by Colonel Cisneros, followed the Apaches to the border before disbanding on 10 January 1880, with the local Mexican troops returning to their homes and the 187 *federales* marching to El Paso.[93] Colonel Cisneros sent word on 7 January, from 'Stoney Ford on the Guzman River', that according to his scouts:

> the Indians to the number of a hundred and more including their families have taken the road towards Mesilla in the direction ???? having with them a considerable amount of plunder & having committed great depredations.[94]

The message was delivered to the telegraph office at Mesilla by a Mexican courier travelling directly from Cisneros's command. Thus, it did not reach Santa Fé until 9 January, by which time Morrow was already pursuing the Apaches north of McEvers' Ranch. Cisneros's dispatch is interesting in that plunder and families are mentioned, whereas, so far, events would indicate that Morrow was in pursuit of a group of between 50 and 60 warriors alone. What is far more interesting is that this intelligence, if combined with other reports, can be used to argue that Victorio was in the process of deploying a very clever decoy strategy. This was aimed at protecting his own logistics while targeting that of his enemies. (See Map 1.1.)

First, a party of 30 Mexican traders was attacked in or near the Florida Mountains. These men had all of their animals stolen, though they later recovered them.[95] *Thirty-Four*, from information received from the Mexican merchant in charge of the train, reported that two Apaches had stolen the Mexicans' horses. The traders had managed to catch up with the pair and recover their stock before the latter managed to join a larger party of Apaches.[96] This attack must have occurred between 10 and 12 January, as the merchants had left Colonel Cisneros's command on the 9 January, and arrived at Las Cruces, New Mexico, on 12 January.[97] The Mexican merchant stated that the

90 Hatch to Terrazas, 12 Jan., 1880 in Telegrams Sent DoNM, Vol.3, Jan. – Nov. 1880 NA, RG393, Part 3, Entry 431, pp.38-39.

91 Osborne, CO Fort Bliss to AAAG DoNM, 12 Jan., 1880, NA, RG393, Part 3, Entry 439, p.500; Humphreys, CO Fort Bayard to AAAG SF 12 Jan., 1880, NA, RG393, Part 3, Entry 439, p502-505; Loud to Morrow, 12 Jan., 1880 in Telegrams Sent DoNM, Vol.3, Jan. – Nov. 1880 NA, RG393, Part 3, Entry 431, pp.41-42; Loud to CO Fort Bayard, 12 Jan., 1880 in Telegrams Sent DoNM, Vol.3, Jan. – Nov. 1880 NA, RG393, Part 3, Entry 431, p.42.

92 *Thirty-Four*, 14 Jan., 1880.

93 Humphreys Bayard to AAAG SF, 13 Jan., 1880, NA, RG393, Part 3, Entry 439, pp.506-507; Hatch to AAG Fort Leavenworth, 13 Jan., 1880, Telegrams Sent DoNM, Vol.3, Jan. – Nov. 1880 NA, RG393, Part 3, Entry 431, p.45; Platt to AAG HQ MDoM, 14 Jan., 1880, 'Victorio Files', NA, RG393, M1495, Roll 14; *Thirty-Four*, 14 Jan., 1880.

94 Cisneros to Col. In Chief SF rec'd, 9 Jan., 1880, NA, RG393, Part 3, Entry 439, pp.496-498; see also Loud (citing Letter from Cisneros from Stony Ford on the Guzman River, 7 Jan., 1880) to CO Fort Bayard to forward to Major Morrow, 9 Jan., 1880, Telegrams Sent DoNM, Vol.3, Jan. – Nov. 1880 NA, RG393, Part 3, Entry 431, p.28-29.

95 Humphreys Bayard to AAAG SF, 13 Jan., 1880, NA, RG393, Part 3, Entry 439, p.506.

96 *Thirty-Four*, 14 Jan., 1880.

97 'Dispatch just received from Bayard repeating dispatch received from S.H. Newman, and which has been sent to CO Bliss and Col. Carr states a party of 30 Mexican merchants arrived at Las Cruces last night [12 Jan., 1880] They were attacked in Florida Mountains and their animals stolen but recovered. They

trail of the Apaches was 300 yards wide, indicating that the party had about 500 horses and mules. The trail was making for Magdalena Canyon (presumably Magdalena Gap).[98] The important point is that a very large group of horses and mules was reported to be on the move from the Florida Mountains towards the Sierra Uvas *after* Morrow's detachments had left the area to pursue the Apaches who had cut the telegraph line between Fort Cummings and La Mesilla.

Secondly, the *Grant County Herald* of 17 January 1880 reported that a wagon train loaded with supplies for Fort Bayard had encountered a large group of Apaches on 6 January, at Mule Springs, between Cooke's Range and the Black Range Mountains.[99] This consisted of approximately 90 warriors with women, children and 200 horses laden with 'plunder'. The freighters prepared for a fight but three Apaches approached the train and asked to trade for flour and 150 pounds was handed over. The Apaches were noted as departing the springs in a northerly direction.[100] (See document file no. 28.) Apaches from this party could easily have cut the line between Fort Cummings and La Mesilla. These two points indicate that there were at least two groups of Apaches moving into New Mexico in early January.

Third, there may have been another group of Warm Springs Apaches moving from Mexico into the USA. On 7 January 1880, Apaches attacked a merchant convoy in Chihuahua, killing nine men, and taking 80 mules and $10,000 worth of goods.[101] While there may have been two groups of Apaches already in the USA, there may also have been a relatively strong rear-guard party lingering in northern Mexico. These warriors would have been tasked with monitoring and even delaying the Mexican armed forces sent against the Apaches. However, if they were not being closely pursued, they might well have taken advantage of any target or opportunity which presented itself.

Finally, a report from Agent Russell, at the Mescalero reservation, stated that on 17 January, Lieutenant G.W. Smith, travelling between Tulerosa and Fort Stanton, had crossed an Indian trail of between 70 to 80 Apaches who were travelling towards the Agency from the south. It was assumed by Lieutenant Smith that these were Apaches belonging to Victorio's band; and though Russell discounted this possibility, he also noted that two of Victorio's men had recently been seen within approximately four miles of the Agency.[102] Agent Russell was sufficiently alarmed by such reports to request that troops be sent to protect the Agency.[103] Lieutenant-Colonel Swain, previously unimpressed with Russell as an ineffective agent, did comment that, 'knowing he [Russell] is a man not easily frightened. I fear he has good cause for alarm and that the matter is more serious than I can well attend to under the circumstances.'[104]

When studying the actions of the Apaches, it is important to remember that they rarely undertook any action without reason. The problem facing Victorio was how to get, if possible, all of the

were with Mexican Troops from eighth till tenth. The Mexican auxiliary troops forces were disbanded and the regulars under Colonel Cisneros started for El Paso, they numbered one hundred and eighty.' (Hatch to AAG Fort Leavenworth, 13 Jan., 1880, Telegrams Sent DoNM, Vol.3, Jan. – Nov. 1880 NA, RG393, Part 3, Entry 431, p.45; Platt to AAG HQ MDoM, 14 Jan., 1880, 'Victorio Files', NA, RG393, M1495, Roll 14; *Thirty-Four*, 14 Jan., 1880).

98 *Thirty-Four*, 14 Jan., 1880.

99 As the *Grant County Herald* is published every Saturday, this meeting occurred on 6 Jan., 1880 based on the point that the paper being published on the Saturday most of it would have been written before Saturday. If this is so, the phrase 'Tuesday of last week', suggests this date rather than 13 Jan., 1880.

100 'Town and Country' Section of the *Grant County Herald*, 17 Jan., 1880.

101 *Thirty-Four*, 14 Jan., 1880.

102 Russell to Commissioner of Indian Affairs, (Hereafter referred to as 'CoIA'), 22 Jan., 1880 in 'Victorio Papers', NA, M666, Roll 527.

103 Russell to Col. Swain, CO Fort Stanton, 17 Jan., 1880 in 'Victorio Papers', NA, M666, Roll 527.

104 Swain to AAAG, DoNM, 18 Jan., 1880 in Letters Received, DoM 1868-98, RG 393, Entry A1-1 2601, Box 87.

plunder taken in Mexico to places where he could sell it without being blocked by the US army. Victorio also had to consider the threat presented by General Trevino's offensive. So, with an advance party of mainly warriors, he crossed the border into New Mexico. At least some of these warriors were involved in attracting the attention of the US army by attacking the prospectors in the Florida Mountains; but the main aim was to get through to Mule Springs. As noted by the freighters who encountered the Apaches at Mule Springs, there were also some women and a large number of pack horses. Therefore, the pack horses and the women, with some of the warriors, may have been held back, for example, in the Tres Hermanas Mountains, until the Apache scouts had moved from Fort Bayard to investigate the Florida Mountains. This group could then have crossed behind the scouts and the cavalry Morrow took from Bayard to Cummings and reconvened at Mule Springs. The pack horses spotted at Mule Springs may have been carrying such plunder as could be traded at Canada Alamosa and Las Palomas. The group could then have been split up, with some warriors and the women and pack horses moving north to trade their plunder, while Victorio, with 60 warriors, diverted attention by cutting the telegraph line and leaving an obvious trail to the north. This occurred on 6 or 7 January; but Morrow did not catch up with the diversionary group until 12 January, which would have left plenty of time for the group with the pack horses to move far ahead of the pursuit.

Still to be accounted for is the large herd of horses and mules whose trail was spotted by the Mexican traders moving from the Florida Mountains towards the Sierra Uvas. This group's ultimate destination may have been the Mescalero reservation, travelling via the Sierra Uvas, across the Rio Grande, and through the San Andres Mountains. The large number of horses, mules and possibly some cattle in the herd does not necessarily mean that it was accompanied by a large number of Apache warriors. This group was probably driven by a small number of warriors, travelling with the remainder of the Apaches – the old, the women and the children. If so, detection of this herd would entail its abandonment and the loss of fresh supplies of rifles and ammunition. It was imperative that the US army did not detect this group. Thus, the cutting of the telegraph wire makes very good sense: why else attract the attention of the US army when the Apaches had successfully passed through Morrow's picket lines undetected? This action was meant to give the second group the best chance of getting through to the Mescalero reservation.

There were two other problems facing the Apaches. First, how could they coordinate the movements of the two groups? How could the first group let the second group know when it was safe to move? They could have used mounted couriers, but they may well have used a simple set of signal fires. As the first group moved into the USA, single warriors, the older and the most reliable, could have been left in the Florida Mountains, Cooke's Range and in the southern reaches of the Black Range above Mule Springs. Once Victorio knew that he had a large number of Ninth Cavalry and Apache scouts on his trail, all he needed to do was to signal the lookouts in the Black Range. So before starting this operation, Victorio could have simply arranged for a set of signals to be transmitted down to, for example, the Tres Hermanas. If two fires were lit on the Black Range and seen on Cooke's Range, this signal would be passed on to the Florida Mountains and then on to the Tres Hermanas. The leader of the second group would then know that it was safe to make the attempt to get their plunder over to the Mescalero reservation. If the effort to decoy the US army away from the area failed, then only one fire would be lit, and this would let the second group know that they would have to improvise. The Apaches must have managed to get far enough ahead of the Mexican armed forces to allow them the time to linger for some days in the region of Palomas Lake and the Tres Hermanas. Colonel Cisneros reached the Guzman River (probably the Corralitos River) on 7 January, and did not arrive at the US border until two days later. The wiping out of a merchant convoy in Chihuahua suggests that a relatively strong rear-guard was left

Plate 1.5 Entrance to the Goodsight Mountains campsite. What looks to be an innocuous canyon from the plain winds its way back and forth up into the mountains and develops into a deep canyon with steep sides and natural rock breastworks. (Photo: Author)

Plate 1.6 Another view down the canyon from deeper within the ravine. Again, one can see the natural rock breastworks that the Apaches could use to hold off an assault while the rest of the group and their dependents could make good their escape. Both this and the photo above were taken from near Point F on Map 1.2. (Photo: Author)

Plate 1.7 View looking down into the area (Point C on Map 1.2) where the canyon opens into a natural corral where stolen stock could be penned with a good supply of water at certain times of the year. (Photo: Author)

Plate 1.8 The Goodsight Mountain campsite seen from upper Point B on Map 1.2. The point where the photograph was taken is only about 200 yards from Point C on the map, yet the presence of this Apache cantonment could hardly be guessed, which helped to prevent accidental discovery while the Apaches were not using the site. (Photo: Author)

Plate 1.9 Shot taken from the 'crow's nest' at Point E.2 on Map 1.2. Again, though this was taken at a much higher elevation than the previous photograph, the presence of a quite deep canyon does not make itself obvious to the casual observer, who might thus be surprised to stumble upon the site. (Photo: Author)

in Chihuahua to give the group waiting in the Tres Hermanas sufficient warning of approaching Mexican troops.

The second problem was how to keep such the waiting group's herd watered and fit for sale. Thus the apparent delay in an area where water was available (Palomas Lake and the Tres Hermanas) could only benefit their stock. However, they also had to get their stock from that point to the Mescalero reservation. The trail seen by the Mexican traders going towards Magdalena Pass may have turned northwards, going up the eastern side of the Goodsight Mountains to a good campsite which was not discovered by the Army until December 1881. (See Map 1.2.) The herd could then have been driven through the Sierra Uvas, across the Rio Grande, and across the Jornada del Muerto to the San Andres Mountains in successive stages with, they would have hoped, the minimum of loss.

Any horses or mules which did not keep up could be abandoned or eaten. The reports of 80 Apaches making for the Mescalero reservation may have referred to part of this herd driven by a few Apaches. With the herd safely stationed in the San Andres Mountains, the Apaches could have afforded to break it into smaller groups and drive these across to the Mescalero reservation to trade them for fresh munitions.

In the meantime, Major Morrow was engaged in an exhausting pursuit of 60 well-armed and well-mounted Apaches far to the north, along the eastern side of the Black Range and into the San Mateo Mountains. Thus, while he preserved his own logistic support, Victorio targeted that of his enemies by leading them on a gruelling pursuit across southern New Mexico.

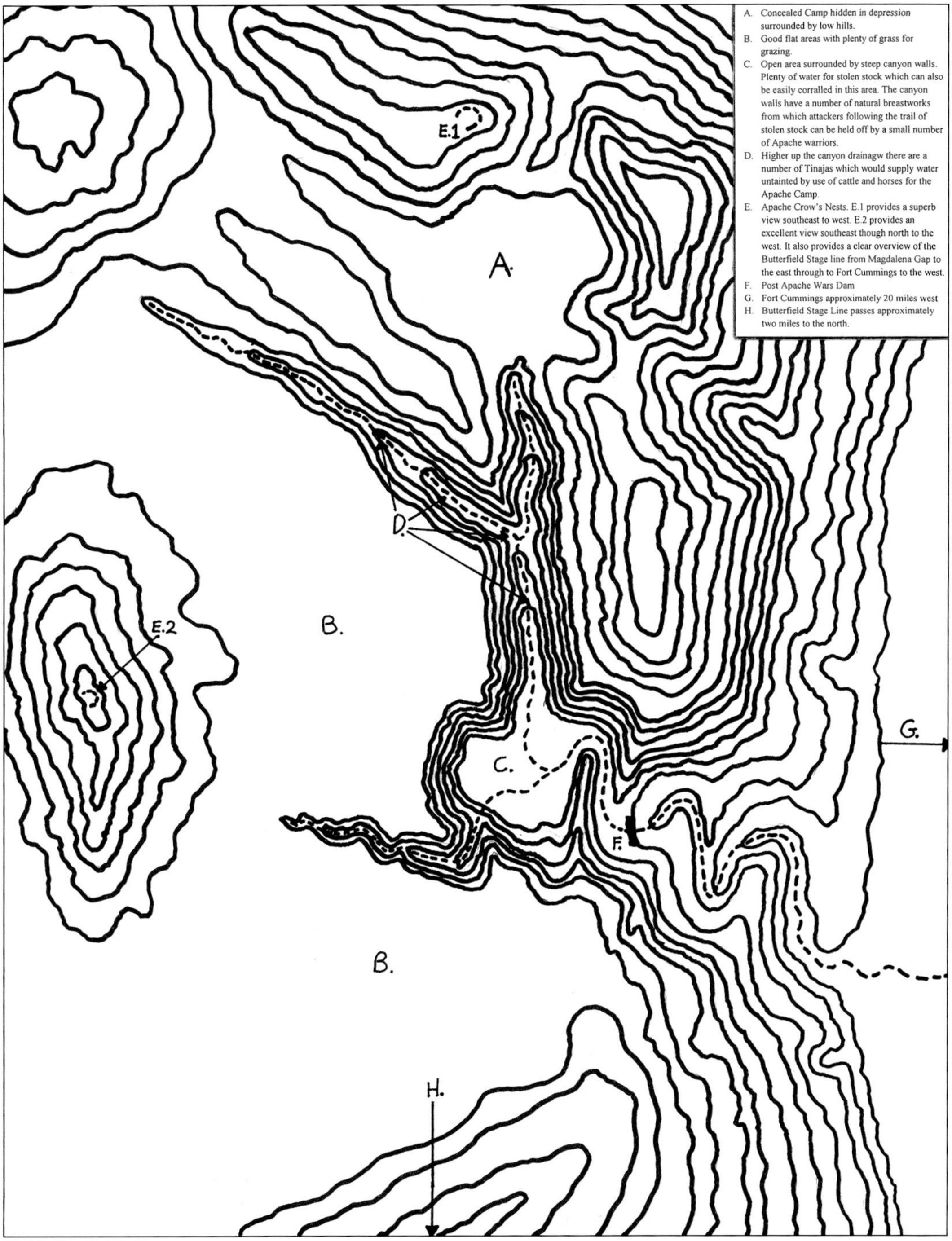

Map 1.2 Goodsight Mountains Apache Camp Site. (Author)

Victorio also benefitted from the activities of other Apaches not allied to him. He was blamed for the earlier attacks reported to the east of Fort Stanton in the vicinity of Roswell and the Black and Delaware Rivers.[105] A further alarm was raised when it was reported that Mescaleros and Mexicans were fighting near the Mescalero reservation. This turned out to have been the result of a drunken binge which resulted in the death by drowning of one Mescalero Apache. The Mescaleros retaliated by burning a hay train of seven wagons.[106]

Hatch also informed Colonel Grierson that reports had been received on 15 January that a wagon train had been attacked at Crow Springs, 75 miles from El Paso. The train was abandoned and the drivers and others accompanying the wagons arrived in El Paso and requested an escort to return with them to recover what property they could. Hatch stated that the culprits were from Indian Territory; but the location would suggest that the raiders were far more likely to have been Mescalero Apaches. As all his troops were in the field at that point, Hatch requested that Grierson supply this escort. He also stated that the site of the attack was in the District of the Pecos, in order to further shift the responsibility for providing this escort to Grierson.[107] If Hatch could attribute blame, legitimately or not, to raiders from outside the District of New Mexico, he could divert demands for protection away from his already stretched military resources.

Nevertheless some reports could not be ignored. A Tenth Cavalry detachment patrolling along the Delaware River reported that, a week earlier, two Mescaleros had passed through driving stolen stock in the direction of the Mescalero reservation.[108] In response to the activities of these Mescalero raiders, Hatch ordered the transfer of an infantry company from Fort Bliss to the Mescalero Indian agency.[109] Hatch also ordered D Company, Ninth Cavalry, to move from Fort Union to Santa Fé.[110] While these Apaches were almost certainly not allied with Victorio, the Chihenne leader still benefitted from such activities, as this forced Hatch to divert troops which otherwise could have been assigned to Major Morrow.

105 Press Copies of Letters and Endorsements Sent, MDoM, NA, RG393, Part 1, Entry 2539, Vol. 13, p.14 & p.17.
106 Lt. G.W. Smith, 10 Jan., 1880, Telegrams Sent DoNM, Vol.3, Jan. – Nov. 1880 NA, RG393, Part 3, Entry 431, pp.33-34.
107 Hatch to CO District of the Pecos (Hereafter referred to as 'DoP'), 17 Jan., 1880 in Register of Telegrams Rec'd 11 Oct., 1879-8 Oct., 1880, HQ Records DoP 1878-1881, NA, RG393, M1381, Roll 2, p.69, Letter No.27.
108 Grierson Ft Concho to COSF, 18 Jan., 1880, NA, RG393, Part 3, Entry 439, pp.522-523.
109 Hatch, 21 Jan., 1880, Telegrams Sent DoNM, Vol.3, Jan. – Nov. 1880 NA, RG393, Part 3, Entry 431, p.67
110 Ibid, p.69.

2

Morrow's Campaign, January–February 1880

A squadron of cavalry riding slow
Crosses the plains in search of the foe,
Which rides ever ahead.
The red man's trail may be plain to the eye,
And the hunters may chase as the crow doth fly-
They will ever be led,
For the red man rides with lightning speed.
No rest for rider, no rest for steed-
'Til the hidden lair is won.
The soldier in chase may tire or fall,
Worn by the race, or struck by the ball,
Leaving his work undone
Anonymous.[1]

Renewed Hostilities: Skirmishing in the San Mateo Mountains

We left Major Morrow's pursuit of Victorio after the Major's conference with the Apache leader on the evening of 16 January 1880. The following day hostilities were renewed, once it was clear that the Apaches had no intention of renewing negotiations.[2] Morrow had found time to send orders to Hooker, at Ojo Caliente, to cover the western and southern sides of the San Mateo Mountains while Morrow was covering the northern and eastern sides. Hooker made no contact with any Apaches and returned to Ojo Caliente on 20 January 1880.[3] If we look at Map 2.1, we can see that Morrow would have had time to send a courier to Ojo Caliente asking Hooker to move his troops directly west, then south, along the San Mateo Mountains, while he himself moved north-west from Canada Alamosa, crossing a high ridge below Vicks Peak,[4] before dropping down into Nogal Canyon. Morrow probably turned east and north before encountering and parlaying with Victorio on the evening of 16 January 1880

1 Powers, p.92.
2 S.M. Ashenfelter, 'Maj. Morrow's Campaign', the *Grant County Herald*, 21 Feb., 1880.
3 Returns From U.S. Military Posts 1800-1916 Ojo Caliente, N.M. May 1879-Mar. 1882, M 617 Roll 877.
4 The author has travelled this route twice and according to the USGS 1:250, 000 Map 'Tularosa' the road passes immediately below this peak. One suspects that 'Vicks' is a shortening of 'Victorio'.

On 17 January, Morrow's battalion had a 'brisk'[5] skirmish, with the Apaches, who were in possession of a strong position and an abundance of ammunition.[6] Second Lieutenant French was killed and two Apache scouts[7] were wounded. Morrow had no idea how many casualties, if any, were inflicted on the Apaches.[8] This skirmish occurred in the upper reaches of Nogal Canyon.[9] The canyon meanders out of the San Mateos to the east, and its upper reaches are dominated by pine-topped cliffs. It is not clear whether the skirmish took place at the site of the previous day's conference, or if the Apaches had shifted to an even more defensible site nearby.

Major Morrow had appointed Lieutenant Day as his adjutant in the field, and during this fight, this veteran of the Las Animas of September 1879 physically transmitted Morrow's orders to each company as they attempted to close with the Apaches. This suggests that the terrain was too rough for Morrow to be able to keep all of his battalion under his direct command. It also suggests that the Apaches were able to use the terrain to move round the flanks of their enemies and disrupt Morrow's efforts to coordinate his forces. Day was then attached to Captain Purington's company and, with the aid of some troopers, who boosted him up the canyon face with their carbines, reached a point where he gained a good view of the Apache positions. At this point, the Apaches managed to attain a position where they could open fire on the horses of Purington's company and Lieutenant Day scrambled back down the mountainside and led the horses to safety.

Lieutenant Day then contacted the officer in charge of the mountain howitzer and gave him the information necessary to bring the Apache positions under fire.[10] Once the Lieutenant had indicated a site for the howitzer, it must have been manhandled up to its firing position, though it is unlikely that the Apaches would have ignored this development. It was no accident that the one Ninth Cavalryman[11] who was killed during the fight on the Rio Perchas on 12 January was directing the fire of the howitzer. As soon as the Apaches spotted the howitzer, the effort to move it into position must have come under constant fire. Once the howitzer was brought into action, the Apaches killed the few horses that were with them, scaled the precipices behind their own cliff-top positions, and disappeared. Their main supply of horses, it was supposed, were secreted elsewhere, deeper in the mountains. [12] However, Morrow could make no pursuit without abandoning his horses and mules, and he withdrew to Ojo Caliente to replenish his food and ammunition stocks.[13]

---

5 Thrapp, 1974, p.262.

6 *Thirty-Four*, 28 Jan., 1880.

7 A wounded Indian scout was brought into Fort Bayard on 25 Jan., 1880. ('By Telegraph', the *Grant County Herald*, 31 Jan., 1880); See also *Thirty-Four*, 28 Jan., 1880; Report of The Surgeon General in AR-WD 1880, NA, M997, Roll 35, 1880 Vol. I, p.520.

8 Morrow, Canada Alamosa, 18 Jan., 1880 in 'Victorio Papers', NA, M666, Roll 526; Hatch (reporting telegram dated 18 Jan., 1880) to AAG Fort Leavenworth, 20 Jan., 1880, Telegrams Sent DoNM, Vol.3, Jan.–Nov. 1880 NA, RG393, Part 3, Entry 431, pp.61-62; NA, RG393, Part 1, Entry 2539, Press Copies of Letters and Endorsements Sent, MDoM, Vol. 13, pp.45-46; Morrow HQ Troops in the Field Camp near Canada Alamosa to Loud AAAG, 18 Jan., 1880, NA, RG393, Part 3, Entry 439, pp.525-526; See also Humphreys Bayard to AAAG SF, 20 Jan., 1880, NA, RG393, Part 3, Entry 439, p.527; Carr to AG DoAz, 19 Jan., 1880, Troops in SE Arizona, DoAz, NA, RG393, Part 1, Entry 232, Vol.5, 13 Dec., 1879–7 May, 1880, pp.52-53; Medical History, Fort Bayard NM, May 1879, NA, RG94, Entry 257 Vol. 896, p.21; 'Town and County', the *Grant County Herald*, 24 Jan., 1880; Thrapp, 1974, p.262; Thrapp, 1967, p.192; Stout, p.121; Record of Engagements, p.93; Wellman, 1957, p.164; Haley, 1981, p.324; Webb, 1976, pp.87-88.

9 Letter from Van Smith to *Thirty-Four*, 7 May, 1880.

10 Personal File Matthias W. Day, NA, RG94, Entry 297, Box 1.

11 See Appendix 2.1.

12 S.M. Ashenfelter, 'Maj. Morrow's Campaign', the *Grant County Herald*, 21 Feb., 1880.

13 Morrow to Loud AAAG HQ Troops in the field Camp near Canada Alamosa, 18 Jan., 1880, NA, RG393, Part 3, Entry 439, p.526; Morrow Canada Alamosa, 18 Jan., 1880 in 'Victorio Papers', NA, M666, Roll 526; S.M. Ashenfelter, 'Maj. Morrow's Campaign', the *Grant County Herald*, 21 Feb., 1880; See also Thrapp, 1974, p.262.

Lieutenant French, variously described as 'promising',[14] a 'valuable scout',[15] and 'intrepid',[16] was officially reported to have been killed in action, shot through the head[17] 'while gallantly commanding Company "M," Ninth Cavalry'.[18] Nothing was further from the truth. Lieutenant Finley thought that Lieutenant French, who had been in the army for some time but had no combat experience, had become disoriented and lost contact with the rest of the troops and had failed to return to camp that evening. Finley stated that, half an hour after the search party returned to camp, three gunshots were heard, but that it was too dark for the search party to discover anything, and French's body was not discovered until the following morning.[19] (See document file no. 27.2.) Surgeon MacPherson, though not present himself, also reported that Lieutenant French was missing for 12 hours before his body was found.[20] This was a clear example of 'wiping the slate clean', as less than a month before his demise, French was cited in the *Army & Navy Journal* as facing court martial proceedings.[21] A general court martial verdict against Lieutenant French in 1879 was to 'be dissolved and that officer will be released from arrest and returned to duty.' This order was dated 19 January, 1880, two days after Lieutenant French was killed.[22] The fact that three shots were heard almost certainly rules out suicide, and the unfortunate man had probably been picked off by the Apaches. Immediately prior to his departure in pursuit of Victorio, on 3 January 1880, Major Morrow had put in a personal request to General Pope that French be released from arraignment of a charge of being drunk on duty. Morrow described French as 'an efficient and valuable officer and I need his services in the field. I will hold myself responsible for his future sobriety.'[23] However, Morrow also made it quite clear that he did not wish that this request be placed on the post records. This might simply mean that Morrow did not wish a charitable act of support to become a matter of public knowledge. Another implication is that Morrow may have needed every available officer, no matter how troubled, for his pursuit of the Apaches. Morrow's unofficial support would not have interfered with a future court-martial, should French have survived the expedition, but would have given the unfortunate Lieutenant the chance to redeem himself.

On 20 January, 1880, 10,000 rations were under escort of one NCO and Seven privates to be delivered to Ojo Caliente. (Telegrams Sent DoNM, Vol.3, Jan. – Nov. 1880 NA, RG393, Part 3, Entry 431, p.64) This information was reiterated on 24 January, but Hatch added that replacement horses and mules were on their way to Morrow's command. In addition, 30,000 rounds of ammunition had been ordered from the Fort Union arsenal. (Loud to Morrow, 24 Jan., 1880, Telegrams Sent DoNM, Vol.3, Jan. – Nov. 1880 NA, RG393, Part 3, Entry 431, p.72).

14 *Army & Navy Journal,* Vol.17, 24 Jan., 1880, p.484.

15 *Army & Navy Journal,* Vol.17, 31 Jan., 1880, p.509.

16 Ibid.

17 'The ball penetrated the mastoid portion of the temporal bone on the right side, passed through right temple and brain, and emerged one inch from the median line through the right supra orbital process of frontal bone, 6 inches from the wound of entrance. Wound of exit 1 ½ inches in diameter. Cranium fractured through the whole of right Parietal and temporal bones. Right ear cut through the middle of right cartilage. Fracture of nasal bones. Ecchymosis in left side of head. Face very much swollen. A deep incised wound was found on right buttock, extending from the anterior superior process of the flinm to 1½ inches from the tuberosity of the lochium, 4 inches deep, 5 inches long, extending upwards 2 inches from spinal column.' (Personal File James Hansell French, NA, RG94, Entry 297, Box 448; See also Nolan, 1994, p.38).

18 Personal File James Hansell French, NA, RG94, Entry 297, Box 44; Bi-Monthly Company Muster Rolls for Company M, 9th Cavalry, Jan./Feb. 1880 in NA, RG94; 'Indian Affairs' *Army & Navy Journal,* Vol.17, 24 Jan., 1880, p.491 & *Army & Navy Journal,* Vol.17, 14 Feb., 1880, p.552.

19 Letter dated Ojo Caliente, 20 Jan., 1880 in The Walter Lowry Finley Collection.

20 Letter 15 Mar., 1880 in MacPherson Letters 1 Jan. 1879 to 3 Sept., 1880, University of Virginia at Charlottesville.

21 *Army & Navy Journal,* Vol.17, 20 Dec., 1879, p.380.

22 Telegrams Sent DoNM, Vol.3, Jan. – Nov. 1880, NA, RG393, Part 3, Entry 431, p.58.

23 Morrow to Pope, 3 Jan., 1880 in Letters Received, DoM 1868-98, RG 393, Entry A1-1 2601, Box 87.

Plate 2.1. The San Mateo Mountains photographed from their southern end. This shows the rocky scrubland which is one of the features of the southern reaches of these mountains. (Photo: Author)

Plate 2.2. Pinewoods in Rosedale Canyon, the San Mateo Mountains. It was through varied terrain such as that shown in these two photographs that Victorio led Morrow's battalion in late January 1880. (Photo: Author)

One major obstacle to progress in the campaign against Victorio was the time taken to transmit news of it, as it unfolded, to District Headquarters and beyond. Morrow's command dropped in and out of communication twice with District Headquarters (7-8 January and 12-15 January) prompting periodic appeals for information as to his whereabouts.[24] In response to these difficulties in communication, Hatch ordered Hooker to 'establish and maintain a suitable courier line between telegraph office at Ft. Craig and Ojo Caliente.'[25] Of course, this was fine only for as long as the Apaches obligingly operated in the general vicinity of Ojo Caliente. This situation made it very difficult for District Headquarters to coordinate other troops, outside of Morrow's immediate control, in sufficient time to lend meaningful support to the Major's campaign against Victorio.

Morrow was also sent authorisation to 'follow Victorio on to any reservation', though the problems of actually delivering such a message become apparent: 'This dispatch will be forwarded from here [Fort Bayard] to McEvers' Ranch to be forwarded from there as chance opportunity may present.'[26] General Pope made it quite clear that he wanted Victorio and his followers 'crushed as early as possible. No exertion must be spared to do so.'[27] Pope urged that any Apaches captured should not be turned over to the reservation authorities but held at an army post and put to work. Any prisoners against whom there was strong evidence should be placed in irons and put on trial.

On 21 January, Lieutenant Emmett arrived at Fort Bayard not only accompanied by a detachment of 12 Navajo scouts,[28] but also carrying a message from Mariano, a Navajo chief. The latter offered to select 100 Navajo warriors and to lead them against the Apaches, provided that the US army armed and provisioned them. Mariano expected no pay but requested that they be allowed to 'retain such plunder as may be captured from Apaches.' Mariano also offered to guarantee that the property of US citizens would be protected. This proposal was prompted by the killing of the two Navajo scouts in Las Animas Canyon during September 1879.[29] Hatch certainly welcomed the offer to the extent that he instructed the CO Fort Wingate to send these volunteers, under command of Lieutenant W.W. Tyler, Ninth Cavalry, to join the troops in the field operating against Victorio. They would be armed on passing through Ojo Caliente, Fort Craig or at some other point along the Rio Grande.[30] Pope recommended that Hatch be allowed to take up this offer of assistance,[31] but ultimately, the offer of approximately 100 Navajo warriors fell through, due to the poor winter condition of their mounts.[32] The 100 Navajo warriors would also have violated the instructions, laid down by Congress, which put a strict limit of 25,000 on the number of men to be employed

24 See Telegrams Sent DoNM, Vol.3, Jan. – Nov. 1880 NA, RG393, Part 3, Entry 431, p.23, p.43 & p.51.
25 Hatch to Hooker, 20 Jan., 1880, Telegrams Sent DoNM, Vol.3, Jan. – Nov. 1880 NA, RG393, Part 3, Entry 431, p.63.
26 Humphreys Bayard to AAAG SF, 19 Jan., 1880, NA, RG393, Part 3, Entry 439, p.524; See also Hatch to Morrow, 19 Jan., 1880, Telegrams Sent DoNM, Vol.3, Jan. – Nov. 1880 NA, RG393, Part 3, Entry 431, p.p.60.
27 HQ DoNM to Morrow, 15 Jan., 1880, Telegrams Sent DoNM, Vol.3, Jan. – Nov. 1880 NA, RG393, Part 3, Entry 431, p.50.
28 Medical History, Fort Bayard NM, May 1879, NA, RG94, Entry 257 Vol. 896, p.21.
29 Both scouts are named in the telegram but only one name 'Baraja' is legible. Humphreys Bayard to AAAG SF, 19 Jan., 1880, NA, RG393, Part 3, Entry 439, pp.519-521; see also Hatch to DoM, 19 Jan., 1880, Telegrams Sent DoNM, Vol.3, Jan. – Nov. 1880 NA, RG393, Part 3, Entry 431, p.60.
30 Loud to Capt. Bennett, CO Fort Wingate, 27 Jan., 1880 in Letters Sent by the 9th Military Department, the Department of New Mexico, and the DoNM 1849-1890, (Hereafter referred to as '9MD/DNM/DoNM', NA, RG393, M1072, Roll 6, Jan., 1880-Aug. 1881, Letter No.43, pp.30-31.
31 Pope to AG Washington DC, 20 Jan., 1880, 'Victorio Files', NA, RG393, M1495, Roll 14; See also Pope to AG, Wash. D.C., 20 Jan., 1880 in 'Victorio Papers', NA, M666, Roll 526.
32 Hatch to AAG Fort Leavenworth, 9 Feb., 1880, Telegrams Sent DoNM, Vol.3, Jan. – Nov. 1880 NA, RG393, Part 3, Entry 431, p.113) some doubt as to the legality of such an endeavour (Ramsey, Secretary of War, 26 Jan., 1880? in 'Victorio Papers', NA, M666, Roll 526.

by the US army.[33] In the meantime, Emmett and his Navajo scouts were instructed to join Major Morrow's command which was believed to be at Ojo Caliente.[34]

Logistics Failure turns the Tide …

Major Morrow departed Ojo Caliente early on 22 January 1880, with the addition of E Company, Ninth Cavalry, under the command of Captain Hooker. Morrow had not found sufficient supplies at Ojo Caliente and had had had to requisition what stores were available from Fort Cummings, with the result that his men were on half rations.[35] On 7 January 1880, a large and surprisingly variable list of supplies was earmarked for delivery to Ojo Caliente from Fort Craig's stores, though there is no indication as to whether this was intended for Ojo Caliente's garrison or was being sent in anticipation of a campaign against Victorio. (See Appendix 2.2.) A large requisition of 10,000 rations[36] had been ordered for sending to Ojo Caliente by District Headquarters on 20 January, [37] but the required rations clearly had not reached Ojo Caliente by the time Morrow departed. It also emerged that the telegraph line was not necessarily to be relied on, as some messages transmitted by army personnel had miscarried and not reached their intended recipients, further hampering military operations.[38]

A picket of 20 dismounted Ninth Cavalrymen was left to guard Ojo Caliente under the command of Lieutenant Hughes. He had 'part rations for nine days' and only broken-down horses, which crippled his ability to maintain the courier service to Fort Craig demanded by General Pope. Hughes also noted that Captain Beyer had reported sick and was making his way back to Fort Bayard.[39] In the meantime, Hatch assured Lieutenant Hughes that supplies were being hurried on to Ojo Caliente and reiterated the importance of maintaining the courier line to Fort Craig.[40] Victorio's technique of exhausting his enemy was beginning to have an effect on both men and horses. It was also playing havoc with the US army's logistics and hence its ability to keep troops in the field. Overall, Morrow's command was in poor shape and the Major was clearly finding the strategy and tactics deployed by the Apaches as deeply frustrating. (See document file no. 30.) Despite his conviction that he had inflicted severe punishment on Victorio, and his claim to have recaptured over 100 horses, some laden with loot, he found that he could not bring Victorio to a decisive battle. He noted that Victorio, when they thought they had him at bay in the late afternoon, tended to turn and fight till nightfall before slipping away. These engagements were usually preceded by long pursuits over the most difficult terrain and as a result he predicted that his command would 'soon be *hors de combat*.'[41] As such, Morrow was not optimistic as to the chances of bringing the

33 Charles Devens, Attorney General to Alexander Ramsey, Secretary of War, 29 Jan., 1880 in 'Victorio Papers', NA, M666, Roll 526.

34 Loud AAAG to CO Fort Bayard, 25 Jan., 1880, Telegrams Sent DoNM, Vol.3, Jan. – Nov. 1880 NA, RG393, Part 3, Entry 431, p.73.

35 Hughes Ojo Caliente to AAAG SF, 22 Jan., 1880, NA, RG393, Part 3, Entry 439, pp.528-529; Morrow to Hatch SF, 23 Jan., 1880, NA, RG393, Part 3, Entry 439, pp.532-538.

36 My colleague, Willy Dobak informs me that a 'ration' was the amount considered necessary for sustaining a soldier in the field for one day. Email communication 17 Aug., 2013.

37 Loud to Chief Commissary of Subsistence, DoNM, SF, 20 Jan., 1880 in Letters Sent by '9MD/DNM/DoNM', NA, RG393, M1072, Roll 6, Jan., 1880-Aug. 1881, Letter No.24, p.17.

38 Loud to Joseph M. Gough, Manager Western Union Telegraph Company, SF, 12 Feb., 1880 in Letters Sent by '9MD/DNM/DoNM', NA, RG393, M1072, Roll 6, Jan., 1880-Aug. 1881, Letter No.71, p.51.

39 Hughes Ojo Caliente to AAAG SF, 22 Jan., 1880, NA, RG393, Part 3, Entry 439, pp.529-530.

40 Loud to Lt. Hughes, CO Ojo Caliente, 25 Jan., 1880, Telegrams Sent DoNM, Vol.3, Jan. – Nov. 1880 NA, RG393, Part 3, Entry 431, p.75.

41 Morrow to Hatch SF, 23 Jan., 1880, NA, RG393, Part 3, Entry 439, pp.532-538.

pursuit of Victorio to a speedy conclusion and recommended that 150 Apache scouts be employed to prosecute the war.[42] It is clear that Major Morrow appreciated the impact this campaign was having on his troops. Morrow did not comprehend that, when he engaged in such long pursuits, punctuated by ineffective skirmishes, he and his men were merely doing what Victorio wanted. Each gun battle tempted the US troops into believing that their pursuit was wearing down the Apaches when all that was accomplished was their own exhaustion.

Therefore, it should come as no surprise to find that Morrow tried to arrange another meeting to discuss terms with Victorio. On 21 January, he telegraphed Hatch with the following query: 'Should Victorio surrender what terms am I authorised to offer he insists upon keeping this reservation as a *sine qua non* can I promise it to him?'[43] This elicited an unequivocal response from Hatch: 'Should Victorio surrender inform him he will remain on the Ojo Caliente Reservation, which has been so decided by the War Department.'[44] Morrow appears to have used Andrew Kelley as a scout or emissary, though it is not clear from the archives exactly when Kelley was recruited. Kelley had returned from scouting in the San Mateo Mountains on 22 January, to inform Morrow that Victorio had moved to the north-western end of this range.[45] Kelley was reported due to leave on 23 January, in an attempt to make further contact with Victorio, with a view to negotiating a peace agreement.[46]

Nevertheless, while exploring the peace option, Morrow maintained his pursuit of the Apaches after leaving Ojo Caliente on 22 January 1880. The Apaches led Morrow's battalion through the San Mateo Mountains for several days.[47] Hooker recorded this pursuit as marked by constant indirect harassment, with the Apaches declining to engage in battle and instead leading the soldiers over the roughest terrain they could find. The Apaches finally evaded the pursuit by fleeing out of the southern end of the mountains.[48] The apparently large numbers of Apaches present in these indecisive skirmishes led Hatch to believe that most of the independent Apaches living in Mexico had joined Victorio.[49] The District Commander failed to realise that Victorio's followers were past masters at using the terrain, and at producing a high rate fire from breech-loading and repeating rifles, so as to give the impressions of greater numbers than were actually present. Hatch concluded, probably correctly, that the employment of the maximum number of Apache and Navajo scouts was the only solution to their problem. The lack of grass and sheer inhospitable nature of the San Mateo Mountains was wreaking havoc on the Ninth Cavalry's stocks of horses and mules.[50]

However, peace negotiations were still being pursued. By 27 January, Lieutenant Hughes reported that Morrow's command had left the San Mateos and returned to Ojo Caliente, leaving on the same day 'for Canada for talk with Victorio.'[51] Lieutenant Hughes also stated that Victorio

42 Ibid.

43 Morrow Ojo Caliente via Cummings to Loud AAAG, 24 Jan., 1880, NA, RG393, Part 3, Entry 439, p.531.

44 Loud to Major Morrow, 24 Jan., 1880, Telegrams Sent DoNM, Vol.3, Jan. – Nov. 1880 NA, RG393, Part 3, Entry 431, p.72.

45 Hughes Ojo Caliente to AAAG SF, 22 Jan., 1880, NA, RG393, Part 3, Entry 439, pp.528-529

46 Ibid.

47 It would appear that Morrow may have returned, or at least sent a detachment from his command , to Ojo Caliente for further supplies on 25 January, 1880. (Hatch to AAG Fort Leavenworth, 25 Jan., 1880, Telegrams Sent DoNM, Vol.3, Jan. – Nov. 1880 NA, RG393, Part 3, Entry 431, p.77).

48 Record of Events Jan., 1880 in Returns From US Military Posts 1800-1916, Ojo Caliente, N.M. May 1879-Mar. 1882, NA, M617 Roll 877.

49 Hatch to AAG Fort Leavenworth, 25 Jan., 1880, Telegrams Sent DoNM, Vol.3, Jan. – Nov. 1880 NA, RG393, Part 3, Entry 431, p.77.

50 Ibid.

51 Hughes to AAAG, 30 Jan., 1880?, NA, RG393, Part 3, Entry 439, p.432; S.M. Ashenfelter, 'Maj. Morrow's Campaign', the *Grant County Herald*, 21 Feb., 1880.

'told Kelley he would not make peace until his families were brought here.'[52] One John Sullivan presented a bill for $45 'for nine days service with horse as bearer of messages between Major Morrow and Victorio @ $5.00 per day.'[53] The involvement of Kelley and Sullivan[54] would appear to lend strength to the argument that the citizens of Canada Alamosa acted as intermediaries between Victorio and Morrow for this second meeting;[55] but, so far, there is no evidence that the two men actually met during this time.[56]

This attempt to parley fell through, and by 30 January, the Apaches were last reported to have left Canada Alamosa 'followed by Hooker'.[57] It is not clear whether these negotiations took place with no result, or that fear of treachery, ever present in the minds of the Apaches, meant that no direct meeting took place. According to a letter sent to Jack Crawford 'the Poet Scout' by Andrew Kelley[58] Victorio did, in fact, meet with Captain Hooker but only after Kelley agreed to remain as a voluntary hostage in the hills with his warriors:

> Old Victorio came into the Cuchillo range and wanted a talk and as I was always trusted by the Indians he sent in for me and I went out in the afternoon and saw him and the commanding officer was anxious to see Vic and promised me a safe pass for him to come in and have a peace talk. Vic would not trust the C.O. until I passed my word that he would be all right. Then Vic said that if I stayed with his warriors as a hostage until his return he would go to the Fort, which he did and after a long talk there the Comd'g Officer wanted to arrest him and put him in irons and put him in the Guard House. Lieut Emmett reminded the C.O. that if he done so my life would be taken, he replied he did not give a d—m as Vic's arrest was worth a number of lives like mine, even tho I had a family depending upon me Emmett replied you are my comd'g officer but I will not allow you to have dishonor cast on a U.S. office by doing this, and I with my scouts will see you do not do so, and if necessary I will assume command and put you in arrest, and the C.O. came to his senses and let Vic go back.[59]

If Kelley's story is true then it shows the lengths some US army officers were prepared to go to catch Victorio, and both Victorio, and particularly Kelley, were lucky that Lieutenant Emmett refused to accept such a dishonourable solution. Moreover, if Victorio, all too conscious of the fate of his predecessor, Mangas Coloradas, had been aware that Hooker had tried to arrest him, it would only have reinforced his view that a fight to the finish was his only option. The only problem with this account is that Emmett, having brought 12 Navajo scouts to Fort Bayard, on 21 January, could not have been anywhere near the area when Hooker investigated claims that Victorio was near Canada Alamosa seeking peace talks on 15 January. (See previous chapter.) If Emmett was present at the attempted talks between 27 and 30 January, as we shall see below, he only left Fort Bayard on the

52 Hughes to AAAG, 30 Jan., 1880?, NA, RG393, Part 3, Entry 439, p.434.
53 Loud (querying the legitimacy of such a claim) to Hatch, Fort Craig, 22 Feb., 1880, Telegrams Sent DoNM, Vol.3, Jan. – Nov. 1880 NA, RG393, Part 3, Entry 431, p.152.
54 We last met John Sullivan when he tried to warn Captain Hooker that a large group of Apaches were near Ojo Caliente just before Victorio attacked E Company's horse-herd on 4 Sept., 1879.
55 S.M. Ashenfelter, 'Maj. Morrow's Campaign', the *Grant County Herald*, 21 Feb., 1880.
56 There is a strong local tradition that Morrow and Victorio met in late January in the Caballo Mountains and that Mexicans from Canada Alamosa and Las Palomas were involved in its arrangement (conversation with Emilio Tapia, September 2006) but so far I have not found any record which confirms this information.
57 Hughes to AAAG, 30 Jan., 1880?, NA, RG393, Part 3, Entry 439, p.432.
58 'Captain' Jack Crawford was recruited as a scout during the summer of 1880 and was based at both Fort Craig and Ojo Caliente during the latter part of 1880 and into 1881 so would have had ample opportunity to meet Kelley.
59 Kelley letter, 4 May, 1905 to Crawford, cited in Laumbach, p.122.

26 January and it is not clear whether he or his scouts had linked up with Captain Hooker by 30 January.

The only reasonably detailed contemporary summary of the meeting between Morrow's emissaries emerged in a private letter from Colonel Hatch to General Pope dated 24 February 1880. A clearly sceptical Hatch had written personally to Pope as the story was 'not reliable enough to be forwarded officially'. Hatch also dismissed Kelley as a 'primitive Squaw man'. The gist of the story is that on 23 January, Victorio and Nana (Hatch mentions both by name), showed a flag of truce on a mountain near to Ojo Caliente. Kelley and Sullivan answered the call, and Victorio suggested a parley in the San Mateo Mountains to:

> hear upon what terms they could come in. Major Morrow then sent Kelley out or said to him you can see him and inform him he can surrender at any time by coming in and giving up his arms and horses, the impression I think was Victorio did not meditate surrender but wished to gain time. Morrow thought by sending Kelley he could place the Indian camp so thoroughly he might be able to surround it.[60]

The willingness of both sides to be quite duplicitous is very interesting and has a distinct parallel with Hooker's alleged treacherous design. However, Hatch outlines the talk between Kelley and the Apaches: 'Victorio was inclined to surrender Nana remarked the country was as large as it was and that he had spent the most of last summer in preparing for a struggle with the troops.' The latter point fits well with what we know about Nana's activities on the Mescalero reservation from late 1878 to August 1879. The most intriguing point to Hatch was that Kelley stated that three quarters of the Apache warriors were unknown to him: 'he [Kelley] having issued rations for ten years or more to these Indians must have known all their faces.'[61] Unfortunately Hatch did not elaborate on this point. Hatch also noted that Nana apparently claimed to have visited the Indian Territory to speak to both the Kiowas and the Comanches and had gained the support of their young warriors. Nana also claimed to have done the same with 'all the Indians in Old Mexico.'[62] Hatch regarded this bit of information as thoroughly unreliable being a combination of 'the usual Indian boasting and retailed second hand by a Frontiers man.'[63] On one level Hatch is probably correct to dismiss this as a fiction but perhaps misses the point that the Apaches might have been trying to cause the army more disruption by attempting to make them stretch their already limited resources further in response to such a threat.

What is clear is that the parlous state of US army logistical support probably encouraged Morrow in his attempt to open a dialogue with Victorio, no matter the duplicitous intent. It also suggests that Victorio and Nana were aware of at least some of the problems facing the US army and were more than happy to see if they could cause further problems by giving the impression of a wider Indian insurrection.

Captain Carroll, based at Fort Bayard, attempted to relieve the logistical problems, notifying District Headquarters that he could provide 3,000 rations by 'contract train' which he would start towards Morrow on 25 January. Carroll also stated that he would also leave that post 'with available men on Monday [26 January 1880].'[64] In response, Hatch instructed Carroll to carry 5,000, or, if

60 Hatch to Pope, 24 Feb., 1880 in Letters Received, DoM 1868-98, RG 393, Entry A1-1 2601, Box 88.
61 Ibid.
62 Ibid.
63 Ibid.
64 Carroll Bayard to AAAG DoNM SF, 24 Jan., 1880, NA, RG393, Part 3, Entry 439, p.531. See perpetual Calendar RR1250-1251, Cambridge Encyclopaedia, 2nd Edition, Editor David Crystal.

possible, as much as 10,000 rounds of carbine ammunition to Morrow.[65] The troops leaving Fort Bayard consisted of four officers and 55 Ninth Cavalrymen. They were joined by the 12 recently arrived Navajo scouts, presumably under the command Lieutenant Emmett.[66] At the same time, Lieutenant C.W. Taylor, then in Albuquerque, was also instructed by District Headquarters to find and bring forward a train of four wagons recently departed from Santa Fé. These wagons were carrying rations destined for Ojo Caliente and the troops at Ojo Caliente were reported to have run out of rations.[67] A few days later, Hatch asked Lieutenant Taylor, now at Fort Craig to find out whether, and at what price, corn could be purchased in the vicinity of Fort Craig.[68]

The Apaches regain the Initiative

After the breakdown of these peace talks Morrow appears to have temporarily lost contact with Victorio; and District Headquarters once again lost contact with Morrow. On 30 January, Lieutenant Hughes had to report that the current location of Hooker and Morrow was not known.[69] He also passed on a rumour of 'one Indian wounded & held prisoner by Mexicans at Canada.'[70]

Morrow may have assumed that Victorio was now heading back to Mexico, as he informed District Headquarters that his command would be going directly to Fort Bayard.[71] By the end of January, the earlier optimism concerning the imminent defeat of Victorio seems to have dissipated. On receipt of the news that Morrow intended to return to Fort Bayard, Hatch immediately ordered him to maintain pressure on the Apaches, and to remain in the field for as long as it took to achieve a result. He also promised Morrow that essential supplies would soon arrive at Ojo Caliente.[72] A note of desperation entered Hatch's efforts to rouse support for defeating the Apaches:

> any person desiring to join Major Morrow in his operations against those Indians will be permitted to do so and rations furnished them, if necessary they will be armed also.[73]

Major Morrow was also informed that he could recruit 'any persons, white, black or Indian who may desire to join you,' and that the 'fight with Victorio's Apaches must be continued as long as one

---

65 Hatch to Carroll, 25 Jan., 1880, Telegrams Sent DoNM, Vol.3, Jan. – Nov. 1880 NA, RG393, Part 3, Entry 431, p.79.

66 Medical History, Fort Bayard NM May 1879, NA, RG94, Entry 257 Vol. 896, p.21; Loud to Capt. Carroll, CO Fort Bayard, 25 Jan., 1880, Telegrams Sent DoNM, Vol.3, Jan. – Nov. 1880 NA, RG393, Part 3, Entry 431, p.74.
According to the *Grant County Herald*, Captains Carroll and Rucker, Lt's Smith and Goodwin with 70 men from B, C, D, H & M, Ninth Cavalry plus Navajo scouts with 11 wagons and one mountain howitzer, commanded by Lt. Goodwin, Left to join Morrow on Jan. 26, 1880. ('By Telegraph', the *Grant County Herald*, 31 Jan., 1880).

67 Loud to Lt Taylor, Albuquerque, 25 Jan., 1880, Telegrams Sent DoNM, Vol.3, Jan. – Nov. 1880 NA, RG393, Part 3, Entry 431, pp.73-74.

68 Hatch to Lt Taylor, Fort Craig, 28 Jan., 1880, Telegrams Sent DoNM, Vol.3, Jan. – Nov. 1880 NA, RG393, Part 3, Entry 431, p.87.

69 Hughes to AAAG, 30 Jan., 1880?, NA, RG393, Part 3, Entry 439, p.432 & 433.

70 Ibid, p.433.

71 Hughes to AAAG, 30 Jan., 1880?, NA, RG393, Part 3, Entry 439, p.432.

72 Loud to Morrow, 1 Feb., 1880, Telegrams Sent DoNM, Vol.3, Jan. – Nov. 1880 NA, RG393, Part 3, Entry 431, pp.93-94.

73 Hatch to Operator at Mesilla N.M., 29 Jan., 1880, Telegrams Sent DoNM, Vol.3, Jan. – Nov. 1880 NA, RG393, Part 3, Entry 431, p.88.

is left with arms in his hands.'[74] Yet, by 7 February 1880, Hatch reported that there had been no uptake of this offer by the citizens of New Mexico.[75]

There were two or three report of clashes between the Apaches and various Ninth Cavalry detachments towards the end of January; but these, when we consider them, mainly indicate the difficulties of transmitting accurate reports from different detachments in the field through to District Headquarters. From Ojo Caliente Lieutenant Taylor reported that:

> couriers just in from Lt Hughes report that last night they were joined at Canada Alamosa by three couriers from Maj Morrow, with dispatches for Capt Hooker asking for cooperation in surrounding the Indians near Palomas. Capt Carroll had a fight at this point on the 29th & reported two or three men wounded one Indian [hostile or scout not clear] killed can't determine knowledge possessed by couriers how many men Carroll had but think a detachment of his company & one company under Hugo. Maj Morrow was at Palomas yesterday enroute for Bayard the Indians attacked a supply train for Ojo Caliente which Carroll was taking in which began the fight.[76]

It was reported that 'Carroll and Rucker had fight and Indians well punished.'[77] Hatch repeated this information not necessarily realising that Taylor's version might have been garbled as a result of being second hand. Hatch thought that Carroll had taken the opportunity to block Victorio's attempt to reach Mexico, allowing Hooker to attack from the west and Morrow to advance from the north, thus driving Victorio across the Rio Grande into the Caballo Mountains.[78] There also exists an intriguing telegram from Lt. Hughes at Ojo Caliente, possibly dated 30 January 1880, which mentions an attack in which a wagon train, with an escort of 30 men, was driven back to Canada Alamosa on 25 January.[79] This report prompted Hatch to warn Governor Terrazas that the Apaches might be going south towards the Florida Mountains and back to Mexico, and to suggest that Mexican military units should guard the passes in those mountains.[80] Earlier, we saw that inaccurate reports from civilians could cause problems; but in this case, it would appear that the reports relied on were garbled army versions of one fight between a Ninth Cavalry detachment and the Apaches in the Caballo Mountains.

---

74 Loud to Major Morrow, 28 Jan., 1880, Telegrams Sent DoNM, Vol.3, Jan. – Nov. 1880 NA, RG393, Part 3, Entry 431, p.84.

75 Hatch to AAG Fort Leavenworth, 7 Feb., 1880, Telegrams Sent DoNM, Vol.3, Jan. – Nov. 1880 NA, RG393, Part 3, Entry 431, p.109.

76 Taylor to AAAG SF, 31 Jan., 1880, NA, RG393, Part 3, Entry 439, pp.435-437.

77 Loud to CO Fort Bayard, 2 Feb., 1880, Telegrams Sent DoNM, Vol.3, Jan. – Nov. 1880 NA, RG393, Part 3, Entry 431, p.98.

78 Hatch to AAG, Fort Leavenworth 2 Feb., 1880, NA, RG393, Part 1, Entry 2546, pp.383-385; Hatch to CO Fort Bliss, 2 Feb., 1880, Telegrams Sent DoNM, Vol.3, Jan. – Nov. 1880 NA, RG393, Part 3, Entry 431, pp.98-99; Hatch to AAG, Fort Leavenworth, 2 Feb., 1880 in 'Victorio Papers', NA, M666, Roll 526; Hatch to AAG, DoM, Fort Leavenworth, 14 Feb., 1880 in Letters Sent by '9MD/DNM/DoNM', NA, RG393, M1072, Roll 6, Jan., 1880-Aug. 1881, Letter No.82, pp58-65.

79 Hughes to AAAG SF, 30 Jan., 1880? NA, RG393, Part 3, Entry 439, p.433. According to Thrapp, Rucker and Carroll attacked Victorio on the Animas River west of Las Palomas, losing one man killed, two wounded plus several horses shot. They then pursued the Apaches to the Rio Grande. (Thrapp, 1974, p.262; Worcester, p.225) On 30 January, Stout states that Captain Rucker with M Company and Captain Hooker with E Company attacked Victorio four miles north of Las Palomas as they were crossing the river, probably the Rio Grande. One Navajo Scout was slain and two troopers injured and a few horses killed. (Stout, pp.122-123) These two versions have enough similarities to be potentially garbled accounts of the same engagement.

80 Hatch to Governor Luis Terrazas, 1 Feb., 1880, Telegrams Sent DoNM, Vol.3, Jan. – Nov. 1880 NA, RG393, Part 3, Entry 431, p.95.

Plate 2.3. Looking north along the main spine of the Caballo Mountains. The main part of the mountains would be impassable to large groups of cavalry or driven herds, which suggests that the Rucker fight took place in the passable sections at either the northern or the southern end of the range. Nevertheless, the tops of these mountains provide an excellent overview of the surrounding terrain, making them an ideal point for a possible peace talk between Victorio and Morrow, as it would be very difficult to trap the Apaches in such terrain. (Photo: Author)

Plate 2.4 Mescal Canyon at the northern end of the Caballo Mountains. About a mile up from the Rio Grande, the Canyon opens out into a natural amphitheatre. The photograph is taken from the centre of this location and shows the type of cover the Apache Warriors could easily have deployed for concealment, and then protection once they opened fire. However, it may also illustrate why Rucker sustained relatively few casualties during the ambush: the cover is too far away to allow the Apaches to pick off many horses, let alone men. (Photo: Author)

The bi-monthly company return for M Company, Ninth Cavalry, makes no mention of an attack on a wagon train. Nor does Captain Hooker's quite detailed report on his company's activities during January 1880. (See document file no. 31.) The bi-monthly return for M Company *does*, however, make reference to a battle between Captain Rucker's company and the Apaches in the Caballo Mountains on 30 January 1880.[81] Lieutenant Finley also noted that the only skirmish he was aware of during this period was the defeat of a small detachment of 15 men in the Caballo Mountains on that day.[82]

What appears to have happened is that, while moving his wagon train up towards Palomas, Carroll came across signs of a party of Apaches and detailed Captain Rucker to pursue them across the Rio Grande. The fact that Rucker was attached to Carroll's command may have given rise to a 'Chinese whisper' that Carroll's train had been attacked. On entering the foothills towards the northern end of the Caballo Mountains, probably a mile or so up Mescal Canyon,[83] Captain Rucker, commanding a detachment of men from B and M Companies, Ninth Cavalry, walked into a classic Apache ambush. Rucker had been joined by some Mexican volunteers; and at least some of Lieutenant Emmett's Navajo scouts were also present. Proceeding up the canyon, they came upon a herd guarded by three or four older women who, apparently surprised by the soldiers' appearance, appeared to panic and try to drive the stock away. Rucker's detachment charged and when they were about to overrun their quarry, Apache marksmen opened fire from all directions.[84]

The historian Joseph A. Stout Jr places this skirmish four miles to the north of Palomas,[85] which puts it in or near Mescal Canyon. What is striking about this canyon is that it is quite wide, with relatively low walls, and at first glance it does not look particularly dangerous. About one and a half miles in, it widens out briefly into a natural bowl before it again narrows and enters the northern reaches of the Caballo Mountains. This natural bowl in Mescal Canyon was the perfect place for the decoy herd to be placed, the relatively low canyon walls providing excellent cover for the Apaches. Once Rucker's command was well within this natural amphitheatre, the Apaches stationed above and around them would have opened fire, catching their enemies in a withering crossfire. One Navajo scout was killed,[86] Sergeant Albert Stout was shot through the left shoulder, and Privates Bolt and Shaw were also wounded.[87] Many of the detachment panicked and fled. Captain Rucker, with a second unidentified officer and approximately a dozen men, formed a rear-guard and skirmished their way back down the canyon.[88] The Apaches, most likely on foot, kept

81 Record of Events Jan., 1880 in Returns From US Military Posts 1800-1916, Ojo Caliente, N.M. May 1879-Mar. 1882, NA, M617, Roll 877.

82 Letter dated Tulerosa, 11 Feb., 1880 in The Walter Lowry Finley Collection. The Chronological List relates a skirmish in the Caballo Mountains on 30 January. It names Captain L.H. Rucker as officer-in-charge and states that three enlisted men were wounded. Chronological List, p.48 Lt G. Hutcheson reports that Capt. Rucker with Companies B and M clashed with the Apaches in the Caballo Mountains. Three troopers were wounded. See web article The Ninth Regiment of Cavalry by Lt G. Hutcheson.

83 I visited the area with Dan Aranda and Emilio Tapia in September 2006 (Apache Canyon) and June 2007 (Mescal Canyon). Emilio was certain that the ambush could not have happened in the main part of the high Caballo Mountains and thought that it would either be in Apache Canyon at the southern end of the Caballo or in Mescal Canyon to the northern end of the Caballo Mountains. Having seen the western face of the main range of the Caballo Mountains I am inclined to agree with him. The western side of these mountains present a formidable series of high precipices and while not presenting a problem to unencumbered Apaches on foot; it would not have been possible to drive a herd of horses and cattle through such terrain.

84 S.M. Ashenfelter, 'Maj. Morrow's Campaign', the *Grant County Herald*, 21 Feb., 1880.

85 Stout, pp.122-123.

86 S.M. Ashenfelter, 'Maj. Morrow's Campaign', the *Grant County Herald*, 21 Feb., 1880.

87 Bi-Monthly Company Muster Rolls for Company M, 9th Cavalry, Jan./Feb. 1880 in NA, RG94.

88 S.M. Ashenfelter, 'Maj. Morrow's Campaign', the *Grant County Herald*, 21 Feb., 1880.

pace with Rucker's dismounted rearguard, constantly pushing its flanks from above, until the latter reached more open ground at the river.

While Rucker's encounter with the Apaches ended in defeat, it did suggest that the latter had moved east of the Rio Grande in the general direction of the San Andres Mountains and on in the direction of the Mescalero reservation. On or around 1 or 2 February, 1880, Morrow's command crossed the Rio Grande, passing through the Caballo Mountains, and followed a trail north-east[89] through Aleman Well,[90] across the desolate Jornada del Muerto (Dead Man's Journey) and into the San Andres Mountains.[91] Morrow caught up with Victorio again on 3 February 1880, on the eastern face of the San Andres Mountains.[92] He had elements of five Ninth Cavalry companies and Indian scouts. In a canyon on the eastern side of the San Andres Mountains, they were opposed by Victorio's warriors, who fell back from position to position, as the Ninth Cavalrymen and Apache scouts advanced.[93] The site of this skirmish may have been Hospital Canyon, to the south of the Hembrillo Basin in the San Andres Mountains.[94]

Captain Louis Rucker.
On 30 January, 1880, he led a small detachment of Ninth Cavalrymen and civilian volunteers into an ambush in the Caballo Mountains and driven back across the Rio Grande. (National Archives)

Years later, Major Morrow, in a letter to Captain Carrol l, stated that the latter had commanded the assault upon:

> the right of Victorio's line which at the time occupied two high ridges to our left front. You succeeded in capturing the ridges and turning the Indian's right, in doing which, you had several men wounded.[95]

Lieutenant Finley also noted that:

89 This would suggest that Morrow passed through the southern pass in the Caballo Mountains. (See Note 16 – Map One).
90 The name of this waterhole apparently commemorates a family of German immigrants wiped out by Apaches sometime before 1860. (Carmony, p.126) Local tradition tells a very different and far older origin to this tale dating back to the 1600s.
91 *Thirty-Four*, 4 Feb., 1880.
92 'Major Morrow's Campaign' *Army & Navy Journal*, Vol.17, 7 Feb., 1880, p.530.
93 Stout, p.124; Thrapp, 1967, p.192; Thrapp, 1974, pp.262-263; Haley, 1981, p.325.
94 Laumbach, p.55 & p.122; The Bi-monthly Return for B Company, Ninth Cavalry stated that they had 'had an engagement with Indians in the Membres Canon San Andres Mountains' (Bi-Monthly Company Muster Rolls for Company B, 9th Cavalry, Jan./Feb. 1880 in NA, RG94).
95 Letter from Morrow to Carroll, 14 Apr., 1890 in Personal File Henry Carroll, NA, RG94, Entry 297, Box 476.

> The hostiles occupied the strongest position they have had yet while our force has been much weakened by sending in our dismounted men to Bayard. We fought from 9:39 A.M. until after dark and drove them from two positions but they held the third and strongest. We went into camp and in the morning found them waiting for us in the same place. This time we did not attempt to charge up the hill but went around some eight miles in sight of their position all the time and came up on more favorable ground in their rear. When they saw what we were after they decamped.[96]

The Army again claimed to have killed several warriors, yet found no bodies. They lost one Apache scout killed and four Ninth Cavalrymen wounded.[97] The wounded men were Sergeant Brent Woods and Private Stephen H. Garnett, of B Company, and Privates James Johnson and Stanley Osborne, both of F Company.[98] Osborne had been shot through the thigh and was still out of action in June 1880.[99] (For accounts of the skirmishes between 30 January and 3 February 1880, see document file no, 32.)

Morrow reported that the Apaches had been 'routed' and that he expected to catch up with them in the Organ or Sacramento Mountains. He also reported that if a detachment led by Captains Carroll and Hooker managed to get across the San Augustin Pass quickly enough, Victorio would not be able to seek refuge in Mexico.[100] Hatch took the precaution of warning both the commanding officer, Fort Bliss, and the Mexican authorities that Victorio might be making for Chihuahua.[101] Morrow estimated that Victorio would then try to return to either his San Mateo or his Black Range mountain strongholds.[102] As usual, the Apaches did not act as predicted. Instead of riding for Mexico, they turned east, then north, and scattered into numerous small parties. Morrow reached Tulerosa on the edge of the Mescalero reservation on the day after the battle, and his battalion was described as short of rations, with their clothing in tatters.[103] By 6 February, Morrow was at Malpais Springs, where the Apaches had rendezvoused after the battle in the San

96 Lt Finley, Letter 11 Feb., 1880 cited in Laumbach, p.100.

97 Hatch to AAG Fort Leavenworth, 5 Feb., 1880 in 'Victorio Papers', NA, M666, Roll 526; Pope to AAG, MDoM, 6 Feb., 1880, NA, RG393, Part 1, Entry 2546, p.315; Hatch to AAG, Fort Leavenworth, 5 Feb., 1880, Telegrams Sent DoNM, Vol.3, Jan. – Nov. 1880 NA, RG393, Part 3, Entry 431, p.104; 'By Telegram', the *Grant County Herald*, 7 Feb., 1880; Report of The Surgeon General in AR-WD 1880, NA, M997, Roll 35, 1880 Vol. I, p.520; See also Webb, 1976, p.88.

98 Special Order No 17, par 2, 5 Feb., 1880, NA, RG393, Part 3, Entry 450; Loud to CO Fort Bayard, 5 Feb., 1880, Telegrams Sent DoNM, Vol.3, Jan. – Nov. 1880 NA, RG393, Part 3, Entry 431, p.107; Bi-Monthly Company Muster Rolls for Company's B & F, 9th Cavalry, Jan./Feb. 1880 in NA, RG94.

These wounded men were sent to Aleman on 4 February, 1880 (Loud to CO Fort Bayard, 5 Feb., 1880, Telegrams Sent DoNM, Vol.3, Jan. – Nov. 1880 NA, RG393, Part 3, Entry 431, p.105) where they were fed by a Mrs Martin until they could be sent back to Fort Bayard by stagecoach. (Loud to Mrs Martin, Aleman, 5 Feb., 1880,Telegrams Sent DoNM, Vol.3, Jan. – Nov. 1880 NA, RG393, Part 3, Entry 431, pp.104-105; *Army & Navy Journal*, Vol.17, 21 Feb., 1880, p.576).

99 Bi-Monthly Company Muster Rolls for Company F, 9th Cavalry, May/Jun. 1880 in NA, RG94.

100 Pope to AAG, MDoM, 6 Feb., 1880, NA, RG393, Part 1, Entry 2546, p.315; Hatch to AAG Fort Leavenworth, 5 Feb., 1880, Telegrams Sent DoNM, Vol.3, Jan. – Nov. 1880 NA, RG393, Part 3, Entry 431, p.104.

101 Hatch to CO Fort Bliss, 3 or 4 Feb., 1880, Telegrams Sent DoNM, Vol.3, Jan. – Nov. 1880 NA, RG393, Part 3, Entry 431, pp.101-102.

102 Pope to AAG, MDoM, 6 Feb., 1880, NA, RG393, Part 1, Entry 2546, p.315; Hatch to AAG Fort Leavenworth, 5 Feb., 1880, Telegrams Sent DoNM, Vol.3, Jan. – Nov. 1880 NA, RG393, Part 3, Entry 431, p.104.

103 'Correspondence Mesilla NM, 12 Feb., 1880' *Grant County Herald*, 21 Feb., 1880.

Plate 2.5 The Jornada del Muerto (Dead Man's Journey) from the top of the Caballo Mountains, looking towards the San Andres Mountains on the horizon. It was across this dry, arid terrain that Victorio led Morrow's battalion at the beginning of February 1880. (Photo: Author)

Plate 2.6 Hembrillo Canyon in the San Andres Mountains. On this lower terrain, the Apaches could make a stand on a ridge until, either flanked by Morrow's troops or fired on by the mountain howitzer, they retreated to the next ridge and repeated the process. If pressed too closely, they could simply retreat deeper into the mountains and draw their enemies into a further, horse-killing, pursuit; or they could scatter and reconvene at a pre-arranged rendezvous. (Photo: Author)

Andres Mountains.[104] Troops at Fort Stanton were sent to Dog Canyon but did not intercept any Apaches, who may or may not have gone that way. Hatch suspected that the Apaches had fresh horses concealed on the Mescalero reservation and would scatter. His only consolation was that the Apaches had been so closely pursued as to prevent them from attacking the local populace.[105] This fails to account for two important points. First, the main purpose of Victorio's confrontation with the US army, in January and early February 1880, was to run the Ninth Cavalry's pursuit into the ground while keeping the whereabouts of his dependents and plunder (taken in Mexico) secret. Second, for the very same reason, it made no sense for the Apaches to raid any settlements in New Mexico at this time. Many of the Apache warriors were concentrating on keeping the US army's attention securely focused upon their activities, while the remaining Apaches made sure that their plunder was transported to points where it could be traded for guns and ammunition. Raiding in New Mexico was simply not yet on Victorio's agenda. That state of affairs would soon change. Hatch claimed that the Apaches were almost dismounted, with hardly enough animals to transport their wounded, due to Morrow's persistent pursuit. Yet, the simple truth was that the Ninth Cavalry pursuit had finally exhausted itself, with little evidence that the Apaches had been in any way discomfited.

Morrow's forces had finally lost contact with the Apaches by 10 February,[106] when both his detachments returned to Tulerosa having found only small trails[107]. As late as 18 February, District Headquarters in Santa Fé had to send a report to Hatch (then making his way to Fort Craig) stating that, up to that date, neither they, nor Fort Bayard, had received any information as to the

---

104 Hatch to AAG, Fort Leavenworth, 14 Feb., 1880, NA, RG393, Part 1, Entry 2546, p.653; Hatch to AAG Fort Leavenworth, 14 Feb., 1880, Telegrams Sent DoNM, Vol.3, Jan. – Nov. 1880 NA, RG393, Part 3, Entry 431, pp.125-126.

105 Hatch to AAG, Fort Leavenworth, 14 Feb., 1880, NA, RG393, Part 1, Entry 2546, pp.653-654; Hatch to AAG Fort Leavenworth, 14 Feb., 1880, Telegrams Sent DoNM, Vol.3, Jan. – Nov. 1880 NA, RG393, Part 3, Entry 431, pp.125-126.

106 Thrapp and others argue that Morrow withdrew after the 3 February fight in the San Andres Mountains and. Captain Rucker's unit was left to continue the pursuit of Victorio. (Stout, p.124; Thrapp, 1967, p.192; Thrapp, 1974, pp.262-263; Haley, 1981, p.325) Thrapp, in 'Victorio and the Mimbres Apaches', states that Rucker pursued for six days in the San Andres Mountains. In 'Conquest of Apacheria', he maintains that it was for two days, when they walked right into a prepared ambush in a 'narrow and rough canyon', 'Several men and horses fell' and the command seems to have panicked. (Thrapp, 1974, p.263, 1967, pp.192-193) The Apaches sensed a victory and charged. The company was routed and was pursued across 'the river'. (Thrapp, 1974, p263; Thrapp, 1967 p.193) Rucker's command is reported as losing its rations, bedding and other supplies in the rout. (Thrapp, 1974, p.263; Thrapp, 1967, p.193; Haley, 1981, p.325) In fact, the earlier comment by Lt. Finley suggests that this ambush is a more detailed account of the clash between Apaches and Cavalrymen under Rucker on 30 January, in the Caballo Mountains! Nevertheless, this skirmish was quite widely reported in newspapers across the US If one goes on to the Library of Congress 'Chronicling America' website <http://chroniclingamerica.loc.gov/> (accessed 10/09/2018) and searches for 'Fort' and 'Bayard' between 1879-1881 there were no less than five newspaper reports of this battle all of which placed it in the San Andres Mts and/or on 9 February, 1880 with interesting variations on the spelling of 'Rucker'. See *Daily Globe*, 16 February; *Salt Lake Herald*, 17 February; *Memphis Daily Appeal*, 17 February; *Shenandoah Herald*, 18 February and *Little Falls Transcript*, 20 February, 1880.

There is another issue, which is a recurring theme of this campaign; the playing down or failure to report embarrassing defeats. Thrapp himself notes that this engagement is not acknowledged in official sources, being reported in a despatch to the Arizona Star. (Thrapp, 1967, pp.192-193; Thrapp, 1974, p.263 & note 47 p.368) Is this a case of media exaggeration or fantasy or another case of the suppression of an 'unfortunate incident' for the US army?

107 'Maj. Morrow's Campaign', the *Grant County Herald*, 21 Feb., 1880; *Thirty-Four*, 18 Feb., 1880.

current whereabouts of Morrow's command.[108] Rumours of Apaches operating from the Caballo Mountains, and raiding in the vicinity of El Colorado, were waiting for Morrow when he arrived at Tulerosa. The following day, the battalion returned through the San Andres Mountains and across the Jornada del Muerto to scour the Caballo Mountains. Morrow's command found traces of small groups of Apaches but nothing worth pursuing; so, he returned to Palomas to rest and refit after a hard campaign.[109] And hard it had been: 'His men were ragged, many of them barefooted and nearly one half without horses. All were hungry and jaded.'[110] (See document file no. 33.) It was also reported that all of the officers in Morrow's battalion had been affected by exposure.[111] Hatch later reported that the horses in Morrow's command were 'worn to mere shadows.[112]

There was some indication that small bands of Apaches had returned to the Black Range and rumours were rife that Victorio was by then regrouping in strength in those mountains.[113] Morrow's command found Lieutenant Dimmick at Palomas with a large stock of much needed stores and the Major was informed that further 'rations, forage, pack mules and ammunition' were on their way to Fort Craig and could be sent where the Major required.[114] Boots were still in short supply and Lieutenant Dimmick was instructed to give a clearer requisition so that these needs could be met as soon as practicable.[115] By 20 February, Morrow was back at Ojo Caliente but was in no position to take any offensive action against any Apaches that might have been in the vicinity, as his horses were in very poor condition.[116]

The Ninth Cavalry's regimental return shows an overall increase in unserviceable horses. It also records that the Ninth Cavalry lost 70 horses during January and February 1880. The effect of campaigning against the Apaches can also be clearly demonstrated by examining the Ninth Cavalry's bi-monthly company returns for the period January to February 1880. If we compare the ratio of available men to serviceable horses with that for November to December 1879 (see Table 2.1) we can see that the failure to provide sufficient mounts for the available troopers continued. If we also highlight the Ninth Cavalry companies serving with Morrow (bold type) in January-February 1880, apart from C Company, whose results were not entered on the original form, those companies experienced significant and in some cases quite drastic reductions in their pool of serviceable horses. Only L Company recorded a relatively small drop in the number of serviceable horses. Those companies not involved in this mini-campaign appear to have generally benefited from their non-participation (where recorded), either increasing the number of serviceable horses

---

108 Loud to Hatch (to be picked up on latter's arrival at Fort Craig), 18 Feb., 1880, Telegrams Sent DoNM, Vol.3, Jan. – Nov. 1880 NA, RG393, Part 3, Entry 431, p.132.

109 Morrow to AAG SF, 16 Feb., 1880 (relayed to SF from Aleman on the 17 Feb., 1880, Telegrams Sent DoNM, Vol.3, Jan. – Nov. 1880 NA, RG393, Part 3, Entry 431, p.133; Hatch, 18 Feb., 1880, DoNM General and Special Field Orders, Letters and Telegrams, (Hereafter referred to as 'DoNM/GSFO/L&T', NA, RG393, Part 3, Entry 475, Vol. 5, p.402; See also 'Maj. Morrow's Campaign', the *Grant County Herald*, 21 Feb., 1880.

110 'Maj. Morrow's Campaign', the *Grant County Herald*, 21 Feb., 1880; *Thirty-Four*, 18 Feb., 1880.

111 *Thirty-Four*, 18 Feb., 1880.

112 Hatch to AAG, Dept of the Missouri, Fort Leavenworth, Kansas, 25 February, 1880, in District of New Mexico General and Special Field Orders, Letters and Telegrams, RG 393, Part 3, Entry 475, Vol.5

113 'Town and County', the *Grant County Herald*, 21 Feb., 1880.

114 Loud to Morrow, Palomas, 18 Feb., 1880, Telegrams Sent DoNM, Vol.3, Jan. – Nov. 1880 NA, RG393, Part 3, Entry 431, pp.134-135; Loud to Hatch, enroute to Fort Craig, 18 Feb., 1880, Telegrams Sent DoNM, Vol.3, Jan. – Nov. 1880 NA, RG393, Part 3, Entry 431, pp.133-134.

115 Loud to Dimmick, Palomas, 17 Feb., 1880, Telegrams Sent DoNM, Vol.3, Jan. – Nov. 1880 NA, RG393, Part 3, Entry 431, p.135.

116 Hatch, Ft. Craig, to AAAG SF, 20 Feb., 1880, 'DoNM/GSFO/L&T', NA, RG393, Part 3, Entry 475, Vol. 5, p.408; Return for Feb. 1880 in Returns From US Military Posts 1800-1916, Ojo Caliente, New Mexico, May 1879-Mar. 1882, NA, M617, Roll 877.

or at least being able to provide enough horses for the available men. The other critical point to note is that *before* these companies engaged in the January–February campaign, apart from E Company, they were *already* short of sufficient serviceable horses to mount the available men.

This did not stop Hatch from claiming all four engagements in the January–February campaign (12, 17, 30 January and 3 February) as great successes against the Apaches. He consistently stated that the latter had had great punishment inflicted upon them in each skirmish;[117] but this is simply not true. Had Victorio sustained four clear defeats of the magnitude suggested by Morrow and Hatch, then his reputation would have suffered, and he would have lost many of his associates. Such failure would find little forgiveness in Apache society. It is quite clear that while both Hatch and Morrow understood facets of Apache warfare, they failed to see that they had been completely outmanoeuvred by Victorio. Thus, the latter's standing as a successful leader was reinforced amongst the Warm Springs Apaches; among some members of other Apache groups it had probably gained new heights.

Table 2.1 Available Men to Serviceable Horses, Ninth Cavalry, November–December 1879 and January–February 1880.[118]

Company	Available Men Nov–Dec 1879	Serviceable Horses Nov–Dec 1879	Available Men Jan–Feb 1880	Serviceable Horses Jan – Feb 1880
A	57	31	55	No entry
B	55	32	55	17
C	53	33	59	No entry
D	55	53	60	40
E	48	51	37	25
F	56	47	47	34
G	55	35	54	35
H	57	36	56	17
I	48	No entry	49	57
K	47	47	61	63
L	54	39	57	34
M	57	44	52	12

Unfortunately for Colonel Hatch, *Thirty-Four* had a different view on the failure to defeat Victorio:

> Major Morrow has for some months enjoyed an unusual opportunity of making a reputation and winning promotion. With 300 white soldiers, Victorio's band could by this time have been annihilated. Morrow has done as well as possible under the circumstances and is unfortunate in not having at his command the material with which to win the fame of a Crook.[119]

117 Hatch to General Willcox, 5 Feb., 1880, Telegrams Sent DoNM, Vol.3, Jan. – Nov. 1880 NA, RG393, Part 3, Entry 431, pp.105-106; Hatch to AAG, Fort Leavenworth, 2 Feb., 1880, NA, RG393, Part 1, Entry 2546, pp.383-385; Hatch to CO Fort Bliss, 2 Feb., 1880, Telegrams Sent DoNM, Vol.3, Jan. – Nov. 1880 NA, RG393, Part 3, Entry 431, pp.98-99; Hatch to AAG, Fort Leavenworth, 2 Feb., 1880 in 'Victorio Papers', NA, M666, Roll 526.

118 Derived Bi-Monthly Company Muster Rolls for Nov./Dec. 1879 & Jan./Feb. 1880, 9th Cavalry in NA, RG94

119 *Thirty-Four*, 11 Feb., 1880.

This largely unwarranted poor opinion of the Ninth Cavalry (Crook did not win fame in Apacheria by employing white troops, but Apache scouts), combined with Hatch's over-optimistic evaluation of the most recent campaign, would soon create a quite savage territorial press campaign against Hatch.

In the meantime, the District Commander was faced with the difficult task of bringing the current Apache war to a successful conclusion. General Pope had a clear idea of what should be done, strongly recommending that preparations be made to occupy the Mescalero reservation for the purpose of disarming and dismounting the Apaches.[120]

> Everybody knows, beyond the probability of dispute, that the Indians on this Reservation (like all the Apaches) are a miserable, brutal race, cruel, deceitful, and wholly irreclaimable. Although for years they have been fed by the Government and "civilized" by their Agent, they are in no respect different from what they were when the process began.
>
> There is no game in that country upon which they can subsist and they therefore have no use for arms and horses except to depredate. They should, if kept there, be sufficiently fed to obviate the necessity of hunting game. The safety of the whole New Mexico and Texas Frontiers along the Pecos demands vigorous and conclusive action with the Indians. They can do nothing with Arms & horses except rob and murder; and surely it is the merest common sense to take away from them what they can use for no purpose except a harmful one.[121]

Surprisingly, given the apparent antipathy between the US army and the Office of Indian Affairs, Carl Schurz, Secretary of the Interior, broadly concurred with Pope's opinion that the Mescaleros should be disarmed and dismounted as soon as possible.[122] In September 1879, the Acting Commissioner of Indian Affairs described the Mescaleros as 'uncivilised and turbulent' and that their Agent had clear orders to recover stolen stock and punish the perpetrators. He suggested that the army be called upon to station a detachment close enough to the reservation to easily render aid when called.[123] In February 1880, the Secretary of Interior requested that 'troops be stationed at Mescalero Agency to protect government property.'[124] Pope noted that the Commanding Officer for the District of New Mexico had ordered troops from Fort Bliss for that very purpose on 21 January 1880 and a telegram dated 14 February, confirmed their arrival.[125]

120 Pope to Whipple, AAG, HQ, MDoM, 9 Jan., 1880, 'Victorio Files', NA, RG393, M1495, Roll 14.
121 Pope to Whipple, AAG, HQ, MDoM, 9 Jan., 1880, 'Victorio Files', NA, RG393, M1495, Roll 14; As above in 'Victorio Papers', NA, M666, Roll 526.
122 Schurz, Secretary of the Interior to The Secretary of War, 11 Feb., 1880, 'Victorio Files', NA, RG393, M1495, Roll 14; Schurz to Secretary of the Interior to The Secretary of War, 11 Feb., 1880 in 'Victorio Papers', NA, M666, Roll 526.
123 Acting CoIA to the Secretary of the Interior, 23 Sept., 1879 in Letters Received by HQ DoNM Sept. 1865-Aug. 1890, NA, RG393, M1088, Roll 39, Oct.-Dec. 1879.
124 Pope to AAG, 23 Feb., 1880, NA, RG393, Part 1, Entry 2546, p.335.
125 Pope to AAG, 23 Feb., 1880, NA, RG393, Part 1, Entry 2546, p.335.

3

Colonel Hatch Reviews the Situation, February–March 1880

As it became clear that Victorio had returned to the United States, Colonel Hatch made the decision to take direct control of the campaign on or around 10 January, 1880.[1] Hatch had been widely criticised in the territorial press for not taking an interest in events in New Mexico. However, one only has to see the volume of field orders, letters and telegrams generated by the Ute Crisis in the autumn of 1879 to realise that this criticism is unfair.[2] Hatch had also been instructed to join a commission charged with determining the guilt, or otherwise, of the Utes in their recent conflict with the United States.[3] He could not deal with two conflicts at once; and it was quite plain that higher command in the US army considered the Ute conflict as the first priority for action.

Despite these constraints Hatch did not lose sight of the conflict with the Apaches, and immediately tried to free up the maximum number of Ninth Cavalry companies to deal with the Chihenne Apaches. He also contacted his superiors to ask that those troops that had been detached from Fort Stanton to help keep the peace in Lincoln County, be sent back to Fort Stanton and made available for field service against the Apaches. His reasoning was that, as the territorial governor had been authorised to raise, and arm, a militia of 1,000 men, there was no need for the Ninth Cavalry to assist the civil authorities.[4] This request was duly granted on 28 February.[5]

Hatch arrived at Fort Craig by 19 February 1880,[6] bringing with him two additional Ninth Cavalry companies from Fort Union and the Ute country (I and K Companies, Ninth Cavalry).[7] These two companies, with new recruits and horses, were sent to join Captain Hooker at Ojo Caliente; and the reinforcements were accompanied by a further 16 recruits and additional horses assigned to E Company. A new pack mule train assigned to Hooker's expanded force was also en route to Ojo Caliente, and Hatch assured Hooker that much-needed supplies would be sent, and

---

1 Pope's Annual Report Year ending 22 Sept., 1880, NA, RG393, Part 1, Entry 2546, p.612; Report of General John Pope, 22 Sept., 1880 in AR-WD, NA, M997, Roll 35, 1880 Vol. I-II, p.86; See also Stout, p.124; Thrapp, 1967, p.193; Thrapp, 1974, p.263; Utley, 1973, p.361; Worcester, p.226; Lockwood, p.230; Haley, 1981, p.325.

2 See 'DoNM/GSFO/L&T', NA, RG393, Part 3, Entry 475, Vol.4.

3 Whipple AAG to Hatch, 29 Oct., 1879 in Letters Received by HQ DoNM Sept. 1865-Aug. 1890, NA, RG393, M1088, Roll 39, Oct.-Dec. 1879.

4 Hatch to AAG, DoM, Fort Leavenworth, 3 Feb., 1880 in Letters Sent by '9MD/DNM/DoNM', NA, RG393, M1072, Roll 6, Jan. 1880-Aug. 1881, Letter No.58, pp39-40.

5 Loud to CO Fort Stanton, 28 Feb., 1880 in Letters Sent by '9MD/DNM/DoNM', NA, RG393, M1072, Roll 6, Jan. 1880-Aug. 1881, Letter No.108, pp.84-85.

6 Loud to Cunningham, Fort Craig 18 Feb., 1880, Telegrams Sent DoNM, Vol.3, Jan. – Nov., 1880 NA, RG393, Part 3, Entry 431, p.131; Hatch to AAG Fort Leavenworth, 14 Feb., 1880, Telegrams Sent DoNM, Vol.3, Jan.-Nov. 1880, NA, RG393, Part 3, Entry 431, p.125; See also 'Maj. Morrow's Campaign', the *Grant County Herald*, 21 Feb., 1880.

7 Hatch to CO Fort Union, 5 Feb., 1880, Telegrams Sent DoNM, Vol.3, Jan.-Nov. 1880, NA, RG393, Part 3, Entry 431, p.107; Hatch to AAG Fort Leavenworth, 7 Feb., 1880, Telegrams Sent DoNM, Vol.3, Jan.-Nov. 1880, NA, RG393, Part 3, Entry 431, p.109.

that he would be provided with a Hotchkiss Gun 'if it can be obtained'.[8] Replacement horses were also sent to A and H Companies, Ninth Cavalry[9] However, this was just the beginning, as Colonel Hatch was preparing a comprehensive redeployment and reorganization of the Ninth Cavalry, in order to focus the entire Regiment on the pursuit and defeat of Victorio.[10]

Hatch met, and saw for himself the state of, Morrow's command after it arrived at Ojo Caliente on 22 February 1880.[11] On the strength of this meeting, Hatch notified Headquarters of his first overall impression of the Victorio War. While Victorio was the leader credited with directing this war, in Hatch's opinion, Nana was the most talented leader, and had a far larger following than Victorio.

Finally, Hatch reported that the Apaches had chosen to make their stands in the most impossible terrain, with highly detrimental effects on both soldiers and mounts.[12] He also acknowledged that the campaign would take some months, as the Apaches were 'fighting very well and seem determined to hold out'.[13] Therefore, Hatch, with Morrow's support, repeated his request of 25 January 1880 to employ as many Indian scouts as possible.[14] In his opinion, at least 100 'Arizona foot Indians' were necessary if the Apaches were to be defeated. If Apache scouts could not be officially employed, Hatch suggested that they should be hired as 'guides trailers or packers, at fifteen dollars per month will not amount to the actual loss in horses, judging from the horses left by Morrow when he crossed the Rio Grande'.[15]

Hatch's arrival at Ojo Caliente quickly revealed the difficulty of coordinating and supervising the campaign against Victorio. On 27 February 1880, Captain Loud, at Santa Fé, informed the Assistant Adjutant General, Department of the Missouri, that information from the latter destined for Hatch had been forwarded to Ojo Caliente by letter. Loud had arranged, by telegraph, for the letter to be deposited with the postmaster at Paraje, from where a courier detached from Fort Craig would carry it to Ojo Caliente.[16]

8 Hatch to Hooker, Ojo Caliente, 9 Feb., 1880, Telegrams Sent DoNM, Vol.3, Jan.-Nov. 1880, NA, RG393, Part 3, Entry 431, pp.112-113.

9 Loud to Stedman, RQM 9th Cavalry, SF, 8 Feb., 1880 in Letters Sent by '9MD/DNM/DoNM', NA, RG393, M1072, Roll 6, Jan. 1880-Aug. 1881, Letter No.63 p.45; See also *Army & Navy Journal,* Vol.17, 21 Feb., 1880, p.576.

10 Hatch to AAG, Fort Leavenworth, 14 Feb., 1880, NA, RG393, Part 1, Entry 2546, pp.654-655; Hatch to AAG Fort Leavenworth, 14 Feb., 1880, Telegrams Sent DoNM, Vol.3, Jan.-Nov. 1880, NA, RG393, Part 3, Entry 431, pp.125-126; Special Field Orders No. 6, 1 Feb., 1880, 'DoNM/GSFO/L&T', NA, RG393, Part 3, Entry 475, Vol. 7, pp.139-140; Medical History, Fort Bayard NM May 1879, NA, RG94, Entry 257 Vol. 896, p.23.

11 Return for Feb., 1880 in Returns From U.S. Military Posts 1800-1916, Ojo Caliente, New Mexico, May 1879-Mar. 1882, NA, M617, Roll 877.

12 Hatch to AAG, DoM, Ft. Leavenworth, Kansas, 23 Feb., 1880, 'DoNM/GSFO/L&T', NA, RG393, Part 3, Entry 475, Vol. 5; See also similar comments made Hatch to AAG Fort Leavenworth, 25 Jan., 1880, Telegrams Sent DoNM, Vol.3, Jan.-Nov. 1880, NA, RG393, Part 3, Entry 431, p.77; Hatch to AAG DoM, 16 Mar., 1880, 'Victorio Files', NA, RG393, M1495, Roll 14.

13 Hatch to Pope, 4 Mar., 1880 in Letters Received, DoM 1868-98, RG 393, Entry A1-1 2601, Box 88.

14 Hatch to AAG, DoM, Ft. Leavenworth, Kansas, 23 Feb., 1880, 'DoNM/GSFO/L&T', NA, RG393, Part 3, Entry 475, Vol. 5; See also similar comments made Hatch to AAG Fort Leavenworth, 25 Jan., 1880, Telegrams Sent DoNM, Vol.3, Jan.-Nov. 1880, NA, RG393, Part 3, Entry 431, p.77; Hatch to AAG DoM, 16 Mar., 1880, 'Victorio Files', NA, RG393, M1495, Roll 14.

15 Hatch to AAG Fort Leavenworth, 20 Feb., 1880, Telegrams Sent DoNM, Vol.3, Jan.-Nov. 1880, NA, RG393, Part 3, Entry 431, p.151; Hatch to AAG, DoM, Ft. Leavenworth, Kansas, 23 Feb., 1880, 'DoNM/GSFO/L&T', NA, RG393, Part 3, Entry 475, Vol. 5; Hatch, Ojo Caliente to AAG Fort Leavenworth, 22 Feb., 1880, Telegrams Sent DoNM, Vol.3, Jan.-Nov. 1880, NA, RG393, Part 3, Entry 431, p.154; See also similar comments made Hatch to AAG Fort Leavenworth, 25 Jan., 1880, Telegrams Sent DoNM, Vol.3, Jan.-Nov. 1880, NA, RG393, Part 3, Entry 431, p.77.

16 Loud to AAG, DoM, in Letters Received, DoM 1868-98, RG 393, Entry A1-1 2601, Box 88.

There was a bloodless 'confrontation' between Mescalero Apaches under Nautzilla and A Company, Ninth Cavalry, under Lieutenant John Conline, in the Sacramento Mountains on 13 February 1880.[17] Conline was not willing to provoke a conflict, since he thought these Mescaleros might have been camped within the bounds of the reservation; although he later reported that he had seen what he suspected was the Terrazas brand on some of the horses at the camp. Two citizens named Eubank and Roberts were with Conline's patrol, and Eubank identified a Mescalero whom he claimed to have wounded in the Ashby skirmish.[18] He also spotted two colts belonging to Ashby amongst the horse herd. Roberts claimed to have seen a Mescalero riding one of his own horses. He also claimed to have scouted down a canyon nearby and found several small groups of horses hidden there.[19] (See document file no. 34.)

Such reports only underlined the perceived need to clamp down on illicit trade networks on the Mescalero reservation. But as we have seen from General Pope's earlier comments, the wheels of that particular project were already in motion. Ever since reports had started to surface of an illicit trade in goods looted by Victorio and other Apache raiders taking place on the Mescalero Reservation, the idea of disarming and dismounting the Mescalero Apaches had gathered momentum. As early as 22 October 1879, General Sheridan stated:

> It has been pretty well established that most of the raids made by our Indians have their origin on the Fort Stanton Indian Reservation. I have repeatedly called the attention of the authorities to this fact and to the impossibility of stopping them unless the reservation is placed directly under the control of the military, when I am satisfied we would be able to put an end to them.[20]

As we saw earlier, General Pope, commander of the Department of the Missouri, had also recommended disarming and dismounting the Mescaleros on 9 January 1880.[21] In response to Pope's recommendation, Carl Schurz, Secretary of the Interior contacted the Secretary of War:

> I am in receipt of a letter of reply from the Indian Office concurring in the views of General Pope that, in the case of the capture of any of the hostile Indians they "not only be disarmed and dismounted but confined as prisoners in the guard house of some post where they will be made to work and those against whom sufficient testimony of hostile acts especially murders is found will be ironed and held for trial."

So far as the recommendation concerning the Mescalero Apaches was concerned, further concurrence is expressed as follows:

> The Mescalero Indians as indicated by General Pope have no use for their arms and horses except to depredate as there is but little game in that vicinity and the best and most economical

17 See Lt. Conline's Report cited in Loud to Hatch, Fort Craig, 15 Feb., 1880, Telegrams Sent DoNM, Vol.3, Jan.-Nov. 1880, NA, RG393, Part 3, Entry 431, pp.138-139; Webb, 1976, p.88; Captain Steelhammer's Report cited in Loud to Hatch, Fort Craig, 18 Feb., 1880, Telegrams Sent DoNM, Vol.3, Jan.-Nov. 1880, NA, RG393, Part 3, Entry 431, pp.140-141.

18 See Watt, 'I Will Not Surrender the Hair of a Horse's Tail: The Victorio Campaign' Chapter 13, p.310.

19 Captain Steelhammer's Report cited in Loud to Hatch, Fort Craig, 18 Feb., 1880, Telegrams Sent DoNM, Vol.3, Jan.-Nov. 1880, NA, RG393, Part 3, Entry 431, pp.140-141; Lt. Conline's Report cited in Loud to Hatch, Fort Craig, 15 Feb., 1880, Telegrams Sent DoNM, Vol.3, Jan.-Nov. 1880, NA, RG393, Part 3, Entry 431, pp.138-139.

20 Sheridan to Townsend, AG Army 22 Oct., 1879, NA, RG393, Part 1, Entry 2538, p.214.

21 Thrapp, 1974, pp.261-262 & Note 34 p.367.

> policy is to compel the Indians to remain upon their reservation and furnish them with sufficient supplies to obviate the necessity of their hunting for game.
>
> This Department concurs in the recommendation of the Indian Office based upon those of General Pope in regard to the disposal of Victoria's and other bands and also in regard to disarming dismounting and guarding the Mescalero Indians and I have respectfully to request that the necessary orders may be issued at the proper time to carry the same into effect.
>
> I have also to request that when those Indians have been disarmed and dismounted and the question of the disposal of their ponies is considered a sufficient number of the largest and best of the ponies be reserved to be used by them for agricultural purposes.[22]

Thus it would appear that both the Secretary of the Interior and his Commissioner of Indian Affairs clearly supported General Pope's recommendation as to the treatment of Apache prisoners of war and, most importantly, that the Mescalero Apaches be disarmed, dismounted and confined. As we shall see, the devil would be in the army's detailed implementation of these instructions, and in the fact that local employees of the OIA do not appear to have been informed of their superior's support for General Pope's recommendations.

Captain Steelhammer, recently returned to Fort Stanton from his investigation of Captain Hooker, held a council with the Mescalero Apache leaders on 19 February. (See document file no. 35.) On being informed that it was believed that a large number of Mescalero Apaches were raiding, these leaders promised to bring in all of their followers to be inspected on 21 February. By 26 February, Steelhammer had seen only 53 warriors, and he stated that he believed there were 29 more men on the reservation who had not reported to him, but were not engaged in hostile activity. However, according to the reservation rolls, this left 75 warriors still at large. Steelhammer considered it likely that these men were hiding out on the reservation, raiding either independently of, or in direct alliance with, Victorio.[23] This information must have reinforced the belief that a significant number of Mescalero Apaches were hostile to the United States, even if not directly allied to Victorio.

Hatch, fearing the Apaches would move west to contact their relatives still living in San Carlos, alerted troops in eastern Arizona, including Gatewood's Apache scouts.[24] In response to a request from Hatch, on 9 February, Colonel Carr furnished a detachment of Sixth Cavalrymen for service in New Mexico to reinforce the already stretched Ninth Cavalry. This unit consisted of 37 men from L Company under the command of Lieutenant T.A. Touey.[25] They were first stationed at Fort Cummings, arriving there on 25 February,[26] but by 10 March they had moved to Hillsboro. Here,

---

22 Schurz to the Secretary of War, 11 Feb., 1880, in Letters Received, DoM 1868-98, RG 393, Entry A1-1 2601, Box 88.

23 Loud to General Hatch, Fort Bayard, 3 Mar., 1880, Telegrams Sent DoNM, Vol.3, Jan.-Nov. 1880, NA, RG393, Part 3, Entry 431, pp.183-186.

24 Hatch to Gen. Willcox, 5 Feb., 1880, Telegrams Sent DoNM, Vol.3, Jan.-Nov. 1880, NA, RG393, Part 3, Entry 431, p.105; Thrapp, 1974, p.264.

25 Carr to Hatch, 9 Feb., 1880, Troops in SE Arizona, DoAz, NA, RG393, Part 1, Entry 232, Vol.5, 13 Dec., 1879 – 7 May, 1880, p.63; HQ, Troops in the field in SE Arizona, Fort Apache, Special Orders No.4, 9 Feb., 1880, Special Orders Oct. 1879-Jan. 1881, DoAz, Vol. 1, NA, RG393, Part 1, Entry 239, pp.14-15; Report of Col E.A. Carr, 29 Aug., 1880; see also Carr to Hatch, NA, RG393, Part 3, Entry 439, p.70; NA, RG94, Entry 257 Vol. 896, Medical History, Fort Bayard NM May 1879, p.23; Willcox to Hatch, 8 Feb., 1880, NA, RG393, Part 1, Entry 169, Vol. 10, p.57; Record of Events Feb., 1880 in Returns From Regular Army Cavalry Regiments 1833-1916, 6th Cavalry Regimental Returns 1875 to 1880, NA, M744, Roll 63; Bi-Monthly Company Muster Rolls for Company L, 6th Cavalry, Jan./Feb., 1880 in NA, RG94.

26 Bi-Monthly Company Muster Rolls for Company L, 6th Cavalry, Jan./Feb., 1880 in NA, RG94; See also Medical History, Fort Bayard NM May 1879, NA, RG94, Entry 257 Vol. 896, p.23; 'By Telegraph', the *Grant County Herald*, 28 Feb., 1880 which estimated that they had arrived on the 22 or 23 Feb., 1880.

they were joined by their company commander, Captain C.B. McLellan, who brought a further composite detachment of 29 men from F, G, L and M Companies, Sixth Cavalry, and a company of Apache scouts under Lieutenant Stephen Mills.[27] Prior to his detachment to assist the troops in New Mexico, Touey described the scouts as being in perfect physical condition and well equipped with a mule train.[28] Lieutenant Blocksom was also placed on notice that he might be required to move into New Mexico.[29] General Willcox even offered Hatch the use of a tripod-mounted Gatling gun, packed on mules, which had recently been ordered for use in the Department of Arizona.[30] Carr used this offer to highlight the shortage of mules and forage in the Department of Arizona: if the Gatling was required, it should be collected by troops from New Mexico, who had far greater stocks of both mules and forage.[31] General Pope also requested 'another Hotchkiss Mountain Gun, with three hundred rounds ammunition'.[32]

The First, Second and Third Battalions, New Mexico Troops

Setting up a field headquarters at Ojo Caliente,[33] Hatch reorganised his troops into three battalions – the First, Second and Third – of New Mexico Troops.[34] While these orders were finalised in late February, it was clear Hatch had decided to reorganise his troops into three battalions by the end of January 1880.[35] (See document file no. 36.) This was not as straightforward as it might appear, and on 9 March 1880, Hatch admitted to General Pope that in refitting his three battalions 'nearly every detail requires my personal attention … I am now busy on pack saddles and hope to improve them, so badly are they constructed.'[36] While these battalions were in the process of being organised and refitted, Hatch concentrated 'all of the dismounted men into the field in one column in the Black Range'.[37] This detachment consisted of all those dismounted men based at Fort Bayard. It was to be based at McEvers' Ranch and was expected to scout in the field with Captain Beyer's

27 Carr to CO Fort Bowie & AG DoAz, 25 Feb., 1880, Troops in SE Arizona, DoAz, NA, RG393, Part 1, Entry 232, Vol.5, 13 Dec., 1879-7 May, 1880,Letter No.'s 76 & 77, pp.74-75; Carr to CO Camp Huachuca, 25 Feb., 1880, Troops in SE Arizona, DoAz, NA, RG393, Part 1, Entry 232, Vol.5, 13 Dec., 1879-7 May, 1880,Letter No.79, p.76; Report of Capt. C.B. McLellan, 16 May, 1880; McLellan to Post Adjutant, Fort Bowie, 16 May, 1880 in 'Victorio Papers', NA, M666, Roll 527; 'Town and County', the *Grant County Herald*, 13 Mar., 1880.

28 Touey to Loud AAAG, NA, RG393, Part 3, Entry 439, p.71; Loud to Hatch, Fort Craig, 16 Feb., 1880, Telegrams Sent DoNM, Vol.3, Jan.-Nov. 1880, NA, RG393, Part 3, Entry 431, p.130.

29 Carr to CO Fort Bowie & AG DoAz, 25 Feb., 1880, Troops in SE Arizona, DoAz, NA, RG393, Part 1, Entry 232, Vol.5, 13 Dec., 1879-7 May, 1880,Letter No.'s 76 & 77, pp.74-75.

30 Willcox to Hatch, 6 Mar., 1880, NA, RG393, Part 1, Entry 169, Vol. 10, p.102.

31 Carr to AG DoAz, 3 Mar., 1880, Troops in SE Arizona, DoAz, NA, RG393, Part 1, Entry 232, Vol.5, 13 Dec., 1879-7 May, 1880, Letter No.85, p.80.

32 Pope to AAG, MDoM, 12 Feb., 1880, NA, RG393, Part 1, Entry 2546, p.316.

33 'DoNM/GSFO/L&T', NA, RG393, Part.3, Entry 475, Vol. 5, pp.4-6.

34 General Field Orders No. 1, 23 Feb., 1880, 'DoNM/GSFO/L&T', NA, RG393, Part 3, Entry 475, Vol. 5, p.390; See also the *Grant County Herald*, 14 Feb., 1880; Thrapp, 1974, p.265; Thrapp, 1967, p.194; Stout, p.129; Leckie, 1967, p.215; Billington, 1991, pp.93-94; Laumbach, pp.135-137.

35 *Army & Navy Journal*, Vol.17, 31 Jan., 1880, p.508.

36 Hatch to Pope, 9 Mar., 1880 in Letters Received, DoM 1868-98, RG 393, Entry A1-1 2601, Box 88.

37 Hatch, Ojo Caliente to AAG Fort Leavenworth, 22 Feb., 1880, Telegrams Sent DoNM, Vol.3, Jan.-Nov. 1880, NA, RG393, Part 3, Entry 431, p.154; Hatch, Ojo Caliente, to AAAG SF, 22 Feb., 1880, 'DoNM/GSFO/L&T', NA, RG393, Part 3, Entry 475, Vol. 5, pp.412-413.

Lt. Mills and Gatewood. This photo gives a clear image of the field dress of officers in charge of Apache scout companies. This is in clear contrast with many of the dress uniform photos of officers shown elsewhere in this volume. (Carlisle Barracks)

company of cavalry, who were already stationed there.[38] For this purpose, Hatch requested enough horses to furnish these dismounted troopers with fresh mounts.[39]

The First Battalion, commanded by Major Morrow, headquartered at Fort Bayard,[40] was made up from five companies of the Ninth Cavalry. Lieutenant Humphries and 10 men of the Fifteenth Infantry provided the crews for a Hotchkiss mountain howitzer. McLellan's composite company from the Sixth Cavalry, including two companies of Apache scouts under Lieutenants Gatewood and Mills, were ultimately assigned to this battalion.[41] Hatch specifically requested the services of Lieutenant Gatewood to assist in the forthcoming campaign and, once clear information of

38 Hatch to Morrow 23? Feb., 1880 in 'DoNM/GSFO/L&T', NA, RG393, Part 3, Entry 475, Vol. 5; see also a slightly garbled version of the above development in *Thirty-Four*, 10 Mar., 1880.
39 Hatch to AAG Fort Leavenworth, 23 Feb., 1880, Telegrams Sent DoNM, Vol.3, Jan.-Nov. 1880, NA, RG393, Part 3, Entry 431, p.156.
40 Station of Troops by Companies – Troops in the Field, Mar. 1880, NA, RG393, Part 1, Entry 183
41 General Field Orders No.1, 23 Feb., 1880, 'DoNM/GSFO/L&T', NA, RG393, Part 3, Entry 475, Vol. 5, p.390.

Victorio's movements finally surfaced,[42] Gatewood's company was ordered to New Mexico on 5 March 1880.[43]

Lieutenant Maney commanded a third Apache scout company, which had been raised specifically for operations against Victorio in New Mexico. However, their term of enlistment expired at the end of March. The problem was that the current members of Maney's scout company seemed reluctant to sign on for another three months' service. Hatch also noted that the 25 scouts currently with Morrow had also had enough after their gruelling pursuit of Victorio.[44] Willcox approved the raising of an Apache scout company specifically for service in New Mexico, as 'Morrow has taken all the fight out of those in New Mexico'.[45]. However, it should be remembered that this particular Apache scout company would have served six months by the end of March 1880, and had already participated in two hard campaigns against Victorio. To replace this company, Lieutenant Maney was sent to San Carlos to recruit Apache scouts. Once recruited, his company was to report to Major Morrow at Fort Bayard, where his scouts would be 'armed and equipped for the field'.[46] The bureaucracy inherent in this procedure is made all too clear by the fact that Hatch had to be very precise when discharging serving Apache scouts:

> The term of enlistment of the twenty-four (24) Apache Scouts now at this Post expires on the 31st of March. They will be discharged on the 20th of March to enable Lieutenant Maney to enlist Scouts at San Carlos on the same date.[47]

However, it would appear that Hatch recruited a second company of Apache scouts. Special Field Order No. 7 (2 March, 1880) clearly ordered 'HK Parker Chief of Scouts' to 'proceed to San Carlos for the purpose of obtaining thirty seven (37) Apache Scouts to be enlisted pursuant to authority from the General of the Army'.[48] One hundred Springfield rifles and 10,000 rounds of ammunition were ordered from the Fort Union Arsenal for the purpose of arming Indian scouts.[49] At the same time, Hatch asked for authority to disband the Navajo scouts and recruit Apache scouts in

---

42 Martin to Carr, 9 Feb., 1880, NA, RG393, Part 1, Entry 169, Vol. 10, p.58.

43 Carr to Gatewood, 5 Mar., 1880, Troops in SE Arizona, DoAz, NA, RG393, Part 1, Entry 232, Vol.5, 13 Dec., 1879-7 May, 1880, p.82; 'DoNM/GSFO/L&T', NA, RG393, Part 3, Entry 475, Vol. 5, p.40; Martin to Carr, 5 Mar., 1880, NA, RG393, Part 1, Entry 169, Vol. 10, p.98; Hatch, Fort Bayard, to Willcox, 4 Mar., 1880, 'DoNM/GSFO/L&T', NA, RG393, Part 3, Entry 475, Vol. 5, p.433; The order to move only arrived late on 4 March, 1880 and Surgeon MacPherson noted that the detachment would set out for Fort Bayard on the following day. (See Letter 4 Mar., 1880 in MacPherson Letters 1 Jan., 1879 to 3 Sept., 1880, University of Virginia at Charlottesville).

44 Hatch, Ojo Caliente, to Willcox, Prescott Arizona, 23 Feb., 1880, 'DoNM/GSFO/L&T', NA, RG393, Part 3, Entry 475, Vol. 5, p.416.

45 Willcox to Chaffee, 25 Feb., 1880, NA, RG393, Part 1, Entry 169, Vol. 10, p.79; See also Whipple to Commanding General, Dept of Texas (Hereafter referred to as 'DoTx'), , NA, RG393, Part 1, Entry 2539, Press Copies of Letters and Endorsements Sent, MDoM, Vol. 13, p.78; See also McDowell to Colonel Whipple, AAG Chicago, 27 Feb., 1880, NA, RG393, Part 1, Entry 2546, p.341.

46 Special Field Order No. 9, 14 Mar., 1880, NA, RG393, Part.3, Entry 450; 'DoNM/GSFO/L&T', NA, RG393, Part 3, Entry 475, Vol. 5, p.64; Special Field Orders No. 9, 'DoNM/GSFO/L&T', NA, RG393, Part 3, Entry 475, Vol. 5, p.307 'Town and County', the *Grant County Herald*, 20 Mar., 1880.

47 Special Field Orders No. 12, Paragraph 1, 18 Mar., 1880, NA, RG393, Part.3, Entry 450; See also 'DoNM/GSFO/L&T', NA, RG393, Part 3, Entry 475, Vol. 5, p.310.

48 Special Field Orders No. 7, 'DoNM/GSFO/L&T', NA, RG393, Part 3, Entry 475, Vol. 5, p.305; See also 'DoNM/GSFO/L&T', NA, RG393, Part.3, Entry 475, Vol.5, p.36.

49 Loud to Capt. Shoemaker, Fort Union Arsenal, N.M., 24 Feb., 1880 in Letters Sent by '9MD/DNM/DoNM', NA, RG393, M1072, Roll 6, Jan. 1880-Aug. 1881, Letter No.95, p.75.

their stead.[50] Lieutenant Emmett disbanded his company of 12 Navajo scouts at Ojo Caliente on 2 March 1880.[51] Hatch stated that, some having been killed in action, the Navajo scouts 'were of no value, were so completely cowed they wouldn't leave the column to search for trails'.[52] It was no coincidence that the Navajo scouts were disbanded on the same day that Parker was ordered to San Carlos. Whether Hatch had the authority to replace 12 Navajo scouts with 37 Apache scouts will be discussed later.

The Second Battalion, under the command of Captain Carroll, consisted of four companies (A, D, F and G) of the Ninth Cavalry. The battalion was headquartered at Fort Stanton, and the order for its formation was given on 22 February 1880.[53] Acting Assistant Surgeon Handy was ordered to accompany it in the field.

The Third Battalion, led by Captain Hooker, was formed from E, I and K Companies, Ninth Cavalry, and H Company, Fifteenth Infantry. It was originally authorised to have a Navajo scout company, under Lieutenant Emmett, before this was disbanded in favour of hiring Apache scouts in their stead. The battalion was stationed at Ojo Caliente, and Hooker was also instructed to 'maintain a suitable "Courier-Line," between the telegraph office at Fort Craig and Ojo Caliente'.[54] A Hotchkiss Gun had also been ordered for this battalion, but it had still not arrived by 10 March.[55] The Hotchkiss Gun, with a full supply of ammunition, finally arrived at Santa Fé on 23 March, and was estimated to arrive at Fort Craig by 1 April.[56] A flurry of telegrams, dated 2 April 1880, from Headquarters, District of New Mexico, concerning the whereabouts of the Hotchkiss gun strongly suggests that the mountain howitzer had failed to appear in time for the Third Battalion's participation in the Hembrillo Canyon Operation.[57] (See Chapter 5.)

The formation of the Third Battalion, in particular, illustrates one of the key problems concerning the US army's competence in dealing with Apaches: they did not have adequate numbers of troops to cover the whole District of New Mexico. Therefore, troops had to be shifted from one 'hotspot' to another. Hooker's battalion took almost a month to constitute, its component parts having to move from a number of points in northern New Mexico and southern Colorado to Ojo Caliente.[58] This task took time, and even when accomplished still left Colonel Hatch with insufficient troops to

50 Hatch, 23 Feb., 1880, 'DoNM/GSFO/L&T', NA, RG393, Part 3, Entry 475, Vol. 5, p.415; Special Field Orders No. 7, 'DoNM/GSFO/L&T', NA, RG393, Part 3, Entry 475, Vol. 5, p.305; Hatch to AAG Fort Leavenworth, 23 Feb., 1880, Telegrams Sent DoNM, Vol.3, Jan.-Nov. 1880, NA, RG393, Part 3, Entry 431, p.156.

51 NA, RG393 Part 3, Entry 475 Vol. 5. p.34 & p.35.

52 Hatch to Pope, 4 Mar., 1880 in Letters Received, DoM 1868-98, RG 393, Entry A1-1 2601, Box 88.

53 Special Field Order No. 5, Paragraphs 1-10, NA, RG393, Part.3, Entry 450; Hatch, Ojo Caliente, to AAAG SF, 22 Feb., 1880, 'DoNM/GSFO/L&T', NA, RG393, Part 3, Entry 475, Vol. 5, pp.412-413; General Field Orders No.1, 23 Feb., 1880, 'DoNM/GSFO/L&T', NA, RG393, Part 3, Entry 475, Vol. 5, p.390; Station of Troops by Companies – Troops in the Field, Mar. 1880, NA, RG393, Part 1, Entry 183; Special Field Order No.5, 22 Feb., 1880, 'DoNM/GSFO/L&T', NA, RG393, Part 3, Entry 475, Vol. 5, pp.300-302.

54 NA, RG393, Part 3, Entry 450, p. Special Order 9 par 8, 19 Jan., 1880; Station of Troops by Companies – Troops in the Field, Mar. 1880, NA, RG393, Part 1, Entry 183; General Field Orders No.1, 23 Feb., 1880, 'DoNM/GSFO/L&T', NA, RG393, Part 3, Entry 475, Vol. 5, p.390.

55 Telegrams Sent DoNM, Vol.3, Jan.-Nov. 1880, NA, RG393, Part 3, Entry 431, p.215.

56 Loud to Hooker, Fort Craig, 23 Mar., 1880, Telegrams Sent DoNM, Vol.3, Jan.-Nov. 1880, NA, RG393, Part 3, Entry 431, p.240.

57 Loud to Hooker 2 Apr., 1880, Loud to Operator Fort Craig, 2 Apr., 1880, Telegrams Sent DoNM, Vol.3, Jan.-Nov. 1880, NA, RG393, Part 3, Entry 431, p.273; Loud to Hatch 3 Apr., 1880, Telegrams Sent DoNM, Vol.3, Jan.-Nov. 1880, NA, RG393, Part 3, Entry 431, p.276.

58 NA, RG393, Part 3, Entry 450, p. Special Order 9 par 2, 5, 6 & 8, Jan. 19 1880; Station of Troops by Companies – Troops in the Field, Mar. 1880, NA, RG393, Part 1, Entry 183; General Field Orders No.1, 23 Feb., 1880, 'DoNM/GSFO/L&T', NA, RG393, Part 3, Entry 475, Vol. 5, p.390.

counter the Apaches effectively. This was not the only challenge facing Colonel Hatch in February and March 1880.

'Friends' as Enemies 1: The Territorial Press takes the Offensive

While the territorial press had been critical of the US army's conduct of the campaign in 1879, they had also highlighted corruption in the reservation system, a lack of federal government interest, and illicit trade of arms and ammunition. During Morrow's six-week campaign in January and February 1880, the press confined themselves to reporting the campaign as it progressed. As Morrow's second campaign staggered to a close in mid-February, the papers took up the offensive. First, they reiterated the accusation that Canada Alamosa, Palomas and Ojo Caliente and their environs were bases for an illegal trade in arms, ammunition and alcohol. This trade was organised by unscrupulous Mexicans and Anglo-Americans, in exchange for plunder taken by the Apaches.[59] The people of Canada Alamosa and Ojo Caliente were also accused of harbouring some of Victorio's wounded warriors.[60]

Second, the press also reiterated another criticism by launching a stinging attack upon the African-American soldiers.

> The people of this part of the country are thoroughly convinced that the troops now in the field are entirely unfit to follow or fight Indians. Maj. Morrow is no doubt an efficient and energetic officer, but he is doubtless like a good many others, lacks faith and confidence in his troops.[61]

The *Grant County Herald* did take one crumb of comfort from this state of affairs, declaring, 'At least the attempt to use the African to chastise him [Victorio] has proved a decided failure.'[62]

This was but the opening salvo of a press attack on the US army that, while initially aimed at the rank and file of the Ninth Cavalry, would soon find its main target in the form of Colonel Edward Hatch. The attack was first provoked by Hatch's attempts to explain his long-term strategy to reach a successful conclusion of the Victorio War. Hatch argued that the Apaches in small raiding parties were too difficult to destroy until these groups had re-united.[63] In the meantime, Hatch explained, he was establishing a supply camp at Hillsboro, and had stationed small detachments at known waterholes, in preparation for the next offensive against Victorio.[64] Second, Hatch also played down the number of casualties inflicted by the Apaches on the citizens of New Mexico during the previous six months, and strongly implied that reports of higher casualties were fabricated.[65] He requested that the press and citizens moderate their criticisms as it 'disheartens' the troops.[66] Finally, he pointed out that citizens were not familiar with the difficulties of combating Apache guerrillas.[67] While Hatch was broadly correct in much of what he said, the argument that the level of warfare had been very much exaggerated was politically inept. His stupidity unleashed

59 *Thirty-Four*, 17 Mar., 1880; 'Ashenfelter Editorial', the *Grant County Herald*, 13 Mar., 1880.
60 'Ashenfelter Editorial', The Grant County Herald, 13 Mar., 1880.
61 'Correspondence', the *Grant County Herald*, 13 Mar., 1880; See 'In the Name of the Prophet!' and 'The Situation', the *Grant County Herald*, 27 Mar., 1880.
62 In the Name of the Prophet!', the *Grant County Herald*, 27 Mar., 1880.
63 'Town and County', the *Grant County Herald*, 13 Mar., 1880
64 Ibid.
65 Hatch to AAG, DoM, Fort Leavenworth, 14 Feb., 1880 in Letters Sent by '9MD/DNM/DoNM', NA, RG393, M1072, Roll 6, Jan. 1880-Aug. 1881, Letter No.82, pp58-65.
66 *Thirty-Four*, 17 Mar., 1880; 'Town and County', the *Grant County Herald*, 13 Mar., 1880
67 'Town and County', the *Grant County Herald*, 13 Mar., 1880.

a torrent of abuse which did not really abate until he and the Ninth Cavalry left New Mexico at the end of 1881:

> Not by word of mouth, General. Not by dogmatic expression of the opinion that not thirty men had been killed during this entire campaign. Not by forcing yourself into a Ute Commission with a view to newspaper notoriety. Not by misrepresenting the strength of Maj. Morrow's command. Not by the establishment of supply camps and other methods known to modern military science. Not by any of these is Victorio to be brought to terms. In fact, it were better for this frontier, to say nothing of your own reputation, if your time were devoted to sharp, energetic action against hostile Indians, rather than the ventilation of your own opinion at public places on every favourable opportunity.[68]

Thirty-Four rejoiced in the conversion of the *Grant County Herald* to its way of thinking and renewed its accusations that 'negro troops are worthless as Indian fighters and that Hatch should be investigated' and removed.[69] *Thirty-Four* would later take the dubious credit for being the first paper to start the anti-Hatch campaign, in late 1879.[70]

This situation cannot have been helped by the passing of joint resolutions by the New Mexico Council and the House of Representatives lauding Hatch's conduct of the Apache war, on 13 February 1880.[71] (See document file no. 43.1.) In response to this resolution *Thirty-Four* published a resolution condemning the conduct of the war against the Apaches. (See document file no. 43.2.) What is particularly interesting is that both Hatch himself, and his planned 'campaign', were dismissed as 'farcical' *before* he launched his first attempt to crush the Apaches in early April 1880.[72] At this point, the *Grant County Herald* was already demanding Hatch's court martial for gross misrepresentation of the facts and general incompetence in handling his command.[73]

The press attack on the US army from this point on in the campaign focused on the following themes. First, it dismissed Hatch's policy of concentrating his forces in March 1880 (see next chapter) thus, in their view, allowing the Apaches to raid unhindered. Second, Hatch and other officers were accused of underplaying the seriousness of the Apache war in Washington D.C. Third, the army, and in particular Hatch, was accused of exaggerating the success of his troops, to the extent of claiming victory when, in fact, his soldiers had been defeated by the Apaches. As we have seen, there was certainly truth in the accusation that Hatch, with no good reason, had trumpeted the success of the troops in January and February 1880. There may also be some basis for the charge that Hatch was not giving his superiors an accurate picture of events. For example, General Pope was to state, near the end of March 1880, that there had been no attacks on the citizens of New Mexico for a number of months.[74] In fact, during March, the Apaches had launched a series of raids in the Rio Grande valley. (See Chapter 4.) Over and above the writers' fury at Hatch's public statements, the reason for the vociferousness of these attacks was clear: Apache guerrillas were

68 'Hatch vs Breech Clouts [Veni Vidi Vici], the *Grant County Herald*, 20 Mar., 1880; See also 'In the Name of the Prophet!', the *Grant County Herald*, 27 Mar., 1880.
69 *Thirty-Four*, 24 Mar., 1880.
70 Ibid, 28 Apr., 1880.
71 *Army & Navy Journal*, Vol.17, 27 Mar., 1880, p.684; See also copy in Letters Received, DoM 1868-98, RG 393, Entry A1-1 2601, Box 88.
72 'Town and County', the *Grant County Herald*, 20 Mar., 1880.
73 Ibid, 27 Mar., 1880.
74 Pope to Col. W.D. Whipple, AAG, Chicago, 26 Mar., 1880, NA, RG393, Part 1, Entry 2546, pp.353-356.

paralysing the economic development of the region.[75] It must be noted that the press did accurately reflect the anger of local citizens at the army's lack of success against the Apaches.

The press were also, for the moment, somewhat ambivalent concerning the increased use of Apache scouts.

> Well if this war cannot be ended without them, let it be so. Upon general principles we dislike this policy. It teaches the Indian the use of arms. It increases his vanity and sense of his own importance. It makes him impudent and proud. It belittles the white man in his estimation. But anything to end this trouble – even a bad treaty is better than getting whipped.[76]

The solution offered by the press was to use local volunteers. These were argued to have been historically successful against the Utes, Navajos and Mescaleros. However, this call was based on the assumption that the Federal Government would not only to authorise the militia, but also to feed outfit and arm these volunteers.[77] First, this call for federal support seems to be somewhat at odds with the 'get up and go' independent attitude one might associate with settlers on the American frontier. For example, the *Grant County Herald* decried the apathy of the people in the territory, not because they failed to take up arms, but because they failed to write to the Government about Apache depredations and the poor performance of US troops.[78] Second, when New Mexican volunteer forces did attempt to tackle Apaches, they were notable in their lack of success. So far, two groups of armed citizens, (the Hillsboro men, on 11 September 1879 and Van Patten, on 13 October 1879) sustained heavy casualties when they were ambushed by Apaches.

However, the press undermined its own position by indulging in gross misrepresentations of the situation in southern New Mexico. This was compared unfavourably to the Modoc and Seminole wars. In the former, it was argued, Captain Jack (the Modoc leader) had had far more men than Victorio. How was it that the former was defeated in a month, but the latter still at large after almost a year?[79] We have already seen that a simple comparison of opposing numbers is not an accurate reflection on the reality of war with the Apaches. In comparison to the inaccessible Seminole Swamps, it was argued, 'Victorio has the plains and hills, which are as well known to his enemies as to him. His country is comparatively open.'[80] The truth of the matter was that the area of operations covered by the Victorio war was vast in comparison to that covered by the Modoc conflict. The statement that Apacheria was as well-known to their enemies as to the Apaches was contradicted by the very same press. The *Grant County Herald* warned that any citizen entering the Black Range and its environs pre-1880 was entering unknown territory and could expect to be attacked and killed by Apaches.[81] It was simply not true that the US army and citizens in New Mexico knew the territory as well as the Apaches.

As for the charge of incompetence levelled at Hatch, while the Colonel may not have conducted a perfect campaign, he had a clear notion of how to attempt to fight the Apaches with the limited resources at his disposal. Even while Morrow was in the field pursuing Victorio in January 1880, Hatch was thinking ahead to future operations against the enemy. He had a clear idea of the direction of future operations, and took the opportunity to form the Third Battalion from troops

75 'Resolution criticising the Conduct of the War' passed in La Mesilla on 29 Mar., 1880 and published in *Thirty-Four* on 31 Mar., 1880 (presented with general approval of the meeting by: A.J. Fountain, Jacinto Armijo, Rafael Ruelas, Euginio Moreno, Carlos Armijo and S.H. Newman).

76 'The Situation', the *Grant County Herald*, 27 Mar., 1880.

77 The *Grant County Herald*, 27 Mar., 1880.

78 Ibid, 3 Apr., 1880.

79 'Town and County', the *Grant County Herald*, 27 Mar., 1880.

80 Ibid.

81 'The Black Range', the *Grant County Herald*, 18 Dec., 1880.

not currently committed to the pursuit of Victorio. This was accomplished even as other troops, who would make up the First and Second Battalions, were still 'in the field' in hot pursuit of the Apaches. Hatch also made enquiries, in mid-January, as the possibility of raising additional Apache scout units. This does not suggest incompetence, but shows a commander who, even as some of his troops were still committed to field operations, was planning for future operations. It was also quite plain that the Colonel was well acquainted with the challenges which faced any officer charged with tackling Apache guerrillas. In a letter addressed to the Assistant Adjutant General, Department of the Missouri, Hatch comprehensively summarised these obstacles (see document file no, 37) and even went so far as to respond to the critical comparison with the Modoc War by concluding that:

> It is impossible to describe the exceeding roughness of such mountains as the Black range and the San Mateo. The well known Modoc Lava Beds are a lawn – compared with them.[82]

Hatch exaggerated the situation when he asserted that US army detachments were consistently outnumbered by the Apaches. In fact, within a month of taking over command he made a number of quite inaccurate observations in a private letter to General Pope. While he admitted that campaigning against Victorio had been hard field service, he claimed that in each engagement the Apaches had sustained more casualties than the army; that the Apaches had twice escaped certain destruction through the advent of 'dark nights';[83] and that the mountain howitzers had inflicted serious casualties on their foe. In the last case, Hatch stated that he had learned 'from a wounded Indian found in the chaparral after a fight, that one shell killed and wounded six Indians'.[84] He rightly pointed out that in January and February 1880 not a civilian had been killed; nor had travel or freight been disrupted.[85] Yet, as we have seen, Victorio's primary effort during this period was directed at disrupting the Ninth Cavalry's ability to operate successfully. As we shall see, in March 1880, Victorio turned his attention to targeting the local populace and a large number of US civilians were killed or wounded and there was severe disruption to travel and trade. Finally, Hatch blamed the 'Indian Bureau' for provoking the war on two counts. First for its 'floundering'[86] concerning where to settle the Warm Springs Apaches; and second, for 'lull[ing]' the army into a false sense of security by reporting that Victorio was content to stay on the Mescalero reservation.[87]

---

82 Hatch to AAG, DoM, Fort Leavenworth, Kansas, 25 Feb., 1880, in 'DoNM/GSFO/L&T', NA, RG393, Part 3, Entry 475, Vol. 5; same letter in Letters Received, DoM 1868-98, RG 393, Entry A1-1 2601, Box 88; See also slightly edited version in Personal File Albert, P. Morrow, NA, RG94, Entry 297, Boxes 71 & 72; Hatch to AAG DoM, 25 Feb., 1880, 'Victorio Files', NA, RG393, M1495, Roll 14; Hatch to AAG Dept. Mo., 25 Feb., 1880 in 'Victorio Papers', NA, M666, Roll 526; See also *Army & Navy Journal,* Vol.17, 20 Mar., 1880, p.664; Thrapp, 1974, pp.264-65.

It is worth noting that the *Grant County Herald*, Saturday, 27 September 1879 makes a similar comment. "From the latest information we can gather, Major Morrow, who has taken the field with all the available troops and scouts, is now at McEvers' ranch, near Hillsborough. His force is said to be about two hundred strong, and he only awaits certain movements of Apache scouts from Arizona to move forward against Victorio's position, which is said to be fully as strong as was that of the Modocs in the lava beds of the northwest." (Ashenfelter, 'The Fight on the Animas' *Grant County Herald*, Saturday 27 Sept. 1879).

83 Hatch to Pope, 13 Feb., 1880 in Letters Received, DoM 1868-98, RG 393, Entry A1-1 2601, Box 88.

84 Ibid. This is the only mention of a wounded Apache being taken prisoner by US troops in January or February 1880 and the author has come across no mention of this event in any other correspondence relating to this period.

85 Ibid.

86 Ibid.

87 Ibid.

While not completely untrue, his early communication with Pope shows either an inability to check the facts or a wilful distortion of the truth.

Yet, Hatch did give the reader a clear idea of the difficulties of trying to defeat Apache guerrillas, particularly the loss rate in army mounts in such an endeavour, and the economic chaos caused by the raiding Apaches. With these observations, Hatch very quickly gained the support of General Sherman, who clearly had his own ideas as to how to defeat the Apaches:

> I am directed by the General of the Army to say that he is well satisfied with the operations of the troops in Southern New Mexico, knows the difficult nature of the country and does not expect impossibilities.
>
> The General remarks that there is no necessity for great haste, only to prepare for the coming emigrant and subdue these Apaches in the course of time.[88]

One can only imagine how the New Mexico press would have reacted to such sentiments. If this was Sherman's prescription for success against the Apaches, it was even less proactive than the policy adopted by Colonel Hatch.

However, the territorial press were not the only source of problems for the US army in New Mexico.

'Friends' as Enemies 2: False Reporting of Apache Raids

In an undated telegram from Fort Bayard to Santa Fé, Morrow made the following comment:

> The report about Indians at point of rocks may be true but I do not believe it. Every day since my return I have received reports of Indians on the road about cummings[89] and masons[90] and in every instance the Indians have proven to be Mexicans or deer or troopers.[91]

The Ninth Cavalry had few enough resources to pursue actual Apache raiders, without having to expend these resources on investigating unsubstantiated rumours. Far to the east, along the Rio Grande between Texas and Coahuila, reports of raiding by Mescaleros allied to Victorio prompted the dispatch of four detachments of Eighth Cavalry troopers and one detachment of Twenty-Fourth Infantrymen to scour the borderland for traces of these raiders.[92] Each detachment reported no trace of Indians having gone into Mexico from the United States and concluded that reports of Indians on the United States side of the river were the product of vivid imagination.[93] One Lieutenant Phelps, Eighth Cavalry, noted:

88 Townsend, Adjutant General to Commanding General, DoM, 13 March 1880, same letter in Letters Received, DoM 1868-98, RG 393, Entry A1-1 2601, Box 88.

89 Fort Cummings.

90 Masons Ranch.

91 Morrow to Loud AAAG, either 10 Mar., 1880 or 10 Nov. or Dec., 1879 in NA, RG393, Part 3, Entry 439, p.9 (This entry in the archives is not stored in any particular order and this telegram is dated the 10 but no further indication of the date is given.) See also much later but similar comment from Hatch to Loud AAAG, 26 Aug., 1881 in NA, RG393, Part 3, Entry 439, p.129.

92 Ord to the AG, MDoM, 30 Mar., 1880, NA, RG393, Part 1, Entry 2546, pp.359-380.

93 Ord to the AG, MDoM, 30 Mar., 1880, NA, RG393, Part 1, Entry 2546, pp.359-380; Tabular Statement of Expeditions and Scouts against Indians, &c., made in the DoTx, During the Year ending September 30, 1880., NA, RG393, Part 1, Entry 2546, pp.629-630.

> on three different occasions, I met a Mexican, who on catching sight of us, instantly fled, and when overhauled and questioned, they stated, that seeing a mounted party they at once took us for Indians, and if not undeceived would have spread the alarm of Indians far and wide. This fear of Indians may possibly account for the numerous abound stories I heard of Indians.[94]

The key point was that amongst the many false rumours, there would be accurate reports. Two detachments of Eighth Cavalrymen did pursue a trail of eight Indians believed to be from the Mescalero reservation. Captain Morris and then Captain Randlett pursued these Indians from 9 to 15 March, until they lost the trail when it crossed into Mexico.[95]

Many officers felt that such rumours were often started quite deliberately in the hope that US army detachments would be stationed in the area. Not only would these detachments provide local protection, they would also prove to be lucrative additions to the local economy. The US army did not have the resources to protect every settlement from attack. Yet few people outside the army appreciated this fact. There were individuals within the local populace who, while clamouring for protection, were motivated either by fear or by hope of personal gain, which only compounded the difficulties faced by the US army in its attempts to combat the Apaches.

False reporting of Apache raiding was probably a further disincentive for the District of New Mexico, which already had poor relations with the papers, to share news with the local press. This in turn opened a new line of attack for the press. On 10 March 1880, *Thirty-Four* complained that it could not give more information relating to Apaches to local citizens as the military were refusing to share information:

> Have they [the citizens] no right to know when their lives are in danger? Have the troops been for the past six months so successful in protecting the people as to inspire perfect confidence in their all-protecting arms? No! But *theoretically*, the troops are for our protection; and resting secure in the *theory*, we must calmly fold our arms and be plundered. Such was the protection received by the party of a dozen who were massacred on the road near Mason's last October[96]. Such was the protection received by the victims of the Jarralosa massacre[97] about the same time. In the name of humanity we again call upon the military to "spread the news."[98]

This was unfair to the military. Censorship of military telegrams was relaxed in late March to allow the communication of Apache depredations to citizens, on condition that the papers did not publish details of troop deployments.[99] Moreover, District Headquarters was by now painfully aware that a significant proportion of intelligence received was either outdated or inaccurate, and to share such information would likely provide the territorial press with an additional rod with which to beat the military.

94 Ord to the AG, MDoM, 30 Mar., 1880, NA, RG393, Part 1, Entry 2546, p.365.

95 Tabular Statement of Expeditions and Scouts against Indians, &c., made in the DoTx, During the Year ending September 30, 1880., NA, RG393, Part 1, Entry 2546, pp.625-626.

96 This refers to the carreta convoy wiped out on the 13 Oct., 1879. (See Watt, 'I Will Not Surrender the Hair of a Horse's Tail: The Victorio Campaign 1879, p.247).

97 This attack occurred around about the 10/11 Sept. 1879. (See Watt, 'I Will Not Surrender the Hair of a Horse's Tail: The Victorio Campaign 1879', pp.187-188).

98 *Thirty-Four*, 10 Mar., 1880

99 Ibid, 31 Mar., 1880

'Friends' as Enemies 3: Illicit Trade Networks

As noted earlier, the New Mexico press accused certain Mexican settlements of trading with, and sheltering, Apaches; but this was not the only source of illicit supplies of guns, ammunition, food and intelligence which were reaching the Apaches. Hatch complained that:

> Every Mexican who has a sheep herd out of anxiety to procure his property is ready to afford them with ammunition and information. The country has cattle nearly every where if no game could be obtained there is abundance for them to subsist upon. [100]

What the Army failed to understand was that these shepherds were caught between the US army and the Apaches. It would have been a brave Mexican shepherd who relied on theoretical US army protection in refusing to trade when confronted by Apache warriors. This relationship, in some cases, may have amounted to a 'protection racket' where landowners would supply their employees with ammunition on the understanding that this be given to the local Apaches in return for their not attacking the flocks and their shepherds. The economics of cattle ranching were such that the ranchers, in the face of the Apaches, had a choice of either employing large numbers of cowboys or confining the cattle to specific areas. Either option would undermine their profit margins, whereas the loss of small numbers of steers to the Apaches may have been the least worse option for the ranching community. Again, one should not rule out the possibility that individual ranchers may have come to more explicit arrangements with the Chihenne Apaches to protect their economic interests. As Benjamin E. Davis, Postmaster, San Augustin, New Mexico noted:

> I have had to employ armed men to guard our sheep herds and employees at a monthly cost of $350. About six weeks ago one of my employees was killed and last week we had ten horses stolen from the ranch, and a set of troughs 300 feet long that we use for watering sheep was so badly damaged as to render them useless, all of which Damage was caused by Indians.[101]

This clearly sums up the cumulative economic effect of Apache guerrilla warfare: costs in terms of lost lives lost, property destroyed, and the need for added protection of property. Against the local population population's concern for their profit margin, the interests of the US army when campaigning against independent Apaches would have weighed little, at best rousing fleeting individual regret.

Asymmetric Warfare?

Hatch was not an incompetent commander, but he did not fully comprehend his opponents. While he correctly identified the fact that Victorio had been operating free of dependants in January and February 1880, he incorrectly assumed that all of these dependants were sheltering on reservations in New Mexico and Arizona.[102]

The fundamental problem facing the US army was a combination of failing to fully comprehend the methods of warfare used by the Apaches and not having nearly enough resources to cover the

100 Hatch to Pope, 4 March, 1880 in Letters Received, DoM 1868-98, RG 393, Entry A1-1 2601, Box 88.
101 Newspaper clipping of letter from Benjamin E. Davies in Letters Received, DoM 1868-98, RG 393, Entry A1-1 2601, Box 89.
102 Hatch to AAG, DoM, Fort Leavenworth, 14 Feb., 1880 in Letters Sent by '9MD/DNM/DoNM', NA, RG393, M1072, Roll 6, Jan. 1880-Aug. 1881, Letter No.82, pp58-65; Laumbach, 2001, p.122.

Plate 3.1. Cuchillo Negro, a village that, along with Canada Alamosa (Monticello) and Las Palomas, was widely believed to have amicable trading relations with the Chihenne Apaches up to 1880. (Photo: Author)

Plate 3.2. Remains of the original Las Palomas village near the banks of the Rio Grande. Unlike the settlements of Canada Alamosa and Cuchillo Negro, the current settlement of Las Palomas has moved slightly from its original location. (Photo: Author)

amount of territory involved. Many officers, including Hatch, appreciated that to give their troops any chance against Victorio, they required enough Apache scouts, as the most 'economical and expeditious manner'[103] by which a quick end to this Apache war could be achieved:

> Without these Indians as trailers the troops can do nothing and even with all the caution of the Indians, the first intimation of the hostiles position is usually a volley. I believe the hostiles must be hunted out of the mountain fastnesses, and the experience of General Crook in Arizona has shown this is the most effectual and economical to accomplish the end desired. This may look like delegating the work of the soldiers to the Indians, it is based upon experience and has sound reasons to recommend the course advised.[104]

Hatch was far more candid in a private letter to General Pope concerning the political economy of using Apache scouts:

> I am in favour of employing Indians to operate against Indians. The animosity between the tribes as fostered here [means there] can be no concert of action against us by all the tribes, and whether they kill the hostiles or we lose the auxiliary, it [is] merely hastening the end inevitable at cost to the Indian. There is great economy in the use of the foot Indian.[105]

Despite Hatch's requests, his superiors dilly-dallied over whether to allow him to recruit the additional Apache scouts he wanted, thus leaving him with too few scouts and troops to complete the very job his superiors wanted.

My Kingdom for a Horse ...

As February passed, the US army not only reorganised its structure but also had to refit its men. Special Order No. 18, of 8 February 1880, is mostly concerned with the effective delivery of recruits and replacement horses.[106] Indeed Hatch's somewhat 'grand' reorganisation of the Ninth Cavalry into three battalions looks to have been somewhat undermined if we compare the numbers of available men to serviceable horses. By the end of February 1880, the First, Second and Third Battalions would have been able to field 119, 157 and 145 mounts respectively to give a total of 421 Ninth Cavalrymen ready for mounted field service. By the end of March, these figures had increased to 141, 147 and 149, to give Hatch a total of 437 mounted troops. (See Tables 3.1 to 3.3.) Therefore, Hatch made an urgent request to General Pope for 100 horses 'to replace the horses in the Ninth Cavalry disabled by hard service during the past three months'.[107] In a personal letter to General Pope, Hatch added that:

103 Hatch to AAG, DoM, Fort Leavenworth, Kansas, 26 Feb., 1880, 'DoNM/GSFO/L&T', NA, RG393, Part 3, Entry 475, Vol. 5; same letter in Letters Received, DoM 1868-98, RG 393, Entry A1-1 2601, Box 88; See also 'DoNM/GSFO/L&T', NA, RG393, Part 3, Entry 475, Vol. 5, p.23.

104 Ibid.

105 Hatch to Pope, 4 Mar., 1880 in Letters Received, DoM 1868-98, RG 393, Entry A1-1 2601, Box 88.

106 Special Order No. 18 Feb. 8 1880, NA, RG393, Part 3, Entry 450.

107 Pope to Whipple, AAG, Chicago, 25 Feb., 1880, NA, RG393, Part 1, Entry 2546, p.342.

> the horses brought out by Dodge at great expense last winter are melting away like snow, [due to] the fearful mountain trails, scant grass with no water or very little need of grain when in the mountains combined with forced marches to which they readily succumb.[108]

However, these numbers have to be balanced by the fact that the monthly regimental returns reveal that, at the end of February, the Ninth Cavalry had 671 troops available for active service, whereas by the end of the following month, this figure had fallen slightly to 664 men. In other words, Colonel Hatch could only mount 62.7 percent of his available men at the end of February; but by the end of March he could deploy 65.8 percent of the Ninth Regiment as cavalrymen. Furthermore, these tables also reveal that Hatch's strategy of trying to 'rest' his forces met with mixed success. Both the First and Third Battalions managed slowly to reduce the number of unserviceable horses; but the Second Battalion actually had an increase in the number of its broken-down horses. What the tables suggest is that the rate of recovery for broken-down horses was very slow. Of the 114 unserviceable horses with the First and Third Battalions in February 1880, 99 were still unserviceable at the end of March.

On a more positive note all three battalions managed to reduce the number of horses lost during this period. However, for Hatch, expected to launch his operation against the Apaches by the beginning of April, it was obvious that he needed additional fresh horses, and more time to allow those horses broken down by field service to recover. He would be given neither. Plainly put, the Ninth Cavalry was expected to keep the federal peace in New Mexico on a shoestring. This may explain Hatch's exaggeration of the number of Apache warriors before press criticism became sustained. Originally, this over-estimation may have been a symptom of the scarce resources at his disposal. In other words, Hatch was caught in a bureaucratic cleft stick when reporting to federal authorities in Washington. On the one hand, he had to point out the lack of human, equine and material resources. On the other hand, how far could the deteriorating situation at the hands of a numerically inferior opponent be outlined without adverse publicity threatening, for example, officer's promotions or the reputation of their regiment?

Table 3.1 First Battalion, New Mexico Troops, Available Men to Serviceable Horses, February–March 1880.[109]

Company	Available Men	Serviceable Horses	Unserviceable	Lost Horses
First Battalion, New Mexico Troops, February 1880				
B	55	17	21	3
C	60	39	0	2
H	54	17	15	0
L	57	34	5	1
M	54	12	30	7
Totals	280	119	71	13
First Battalion, NM Troops, March 1880				
B	60	27	13	0
C	53	21	17	1
H	56	25	22	1

108 Hatch to Pope, 20 Feb., 1880 in Letters Received, DoM 1868-98, RG 393, Entry A1-1 2601, Box 88.

109 Derived from Returns From Regular Army Cavalry Regiments 1833-1916, 9th Cavalry 1873-1880, NA, M744, Roll 88

L	57	34	5	0
M	60	34	8	0
Totals	286	141	65	2

Table 3.2 Second Battalion New Mexico Troops, Available Men to Serviceable Horses, February–March 1880.[110]

Company	Available Men	Serviceable Horses	Unserviceable	Lost Horses
Second Battalion, New Mexico Troops, February 1880				
A	57	31	10	2
D	55	53	1	0
F	55	38	0	13
G	54	35	6	1
Totals	221	157	17	16
Second Battalion, NM Troops, March 1880				
A	49	42	9	0
D	45	25	23	6
F	45	33	5	0
G	58	47	4	0
Totals	197	147	41	6

Table 3.3 Third Battalion, New Mexico Troops, Available Men to Serviceable Horses, February–March 1880.[111]

Company	Available Men	Serviceable Horses	Unserviceable	Lost Horses
Third Battalion, New Mexico Troops, February 1880				
E	52	25	33	4
I	56	57	3	0
K	62	63	5	0
Totals	170	145	41	4
Third Battalion, NM Troops, March 1880				
Company				
E	53	29	27	2
I	66	57	3	0
K	62	63	4	0
Totals	181	149	34	2

Other areas requiring attention included the need to transport a qualified signal corpsman and a civilian telegraph operator to key points on the telegraph network.[112] A second Hotchkiss mountain

110 Derived from Returns From Regular Army Cavalry Regiments 1833-1916, 9th Cavalry 1873-1880, NA, M744, Roll 88

111 Derived from Returns From Regular Army Cavalry Regiments 1833-1916, 9th Cavalry 1873-1880, NA, M744, Roll 88

112 Special Order No. 18, 8 Feb., 1880, NA, RG393, Part 3, Entry 450, par 3.

gun was in the process of being sent to Hatch, though it seems to have become lost in transit as the Colonel telegraphed a request for its whereabouts to be confirmed or at least ascertained.[113]

Finally, several civilian guides were attached to Hatch's force. Laumbach mentions one Mexican guide serving with McLellan's company, and attached Apache scouts.[114] He also argues that Henry Parker (Chief of Scouts) and Van C. Smith may have been present. Both men were certainly with Apache scout companies during April and May 1880. Parker had been recruited as early as October 1879 and was based at Fort Bayard.[115] This would suggest that he was attached to Lieutenant Maney's scout company. Parker was also noted as leading Apache scouts into the Florida Mountains in December 1879, but finding no trace of Apaches.[116] Finally, Laumbach states that Carroll's battalion was accompanied by Jose Carillo,[117] interpreter at the Mescalero reservation, and a man variously named as Enbank, Eubank or Burbank.[118] Recent research confirms that he was called William Eubank.[119]

This re-organisation was arranged in tandem with that of units in both western Texas and Arizona. By 12 March 1880, Hatch had submitted the basic outline of a plan to disarm and dismount the Mescalero Apaches. He would use New Mexico troops, including those sent by the Department of Arizona, to drive the Apaches eastwards across the Rio Grande and on to the Mescalero reservation. At the same time troops from Texas would advance north-west towards the same reservation and sweep up any raiding parties in the process. (See document file no. 38) The two forces were set to rendezvous at the Mescalero agency on 12 April 1880. Hatch thought that because Victorio 'feels strong', the Apache leader might stand and fight. If so, Hatch was confident that he could inflict a defeat of such magnitude upon the Apaches that the subsequent operation to disarm and dismount the Mescaleros would be a formality.[120]

By this time Hatch believed that Victorio's following, which he thought now included the Warm Springs, Mescalero and Mexican Apaches, were based in the San Andres Mountains.[121] General Pope agreed the detail of the plan on or around 26 March[122] and it was further approved by General Sheridan on 30 March 1880.[123]

---

113 Platt AAG to AAAG DoNM SF, 11 Mar., 1880, NA, RG393, Part 3, Entry 439, p.81.

114 Laumbach notes that Morrow's battalion met a party of militia, led by Gregorio Miranda, from the village of El Colorado in the Caballo Mountains. He suggests that the guide may have been recruited from Miranda's party the rest returning home after confirming that the Apache were no longer an immediate threat to their livestock grazing in the Caballo mountains. (p.165).

115 *Thirty-Four*, 15 Oct., 1879.

116 Ibid, 17 Dec., 1879.

117 This is the same man who eventually calmed Victorio down when he or Kaytennae attacked Agent Godfroy in Aug. 1879.

118 Laumbach, pp.147-148. This must be the same man who accompanied Lt. Conline to Nautzilla's camp in early Feb., 1880.

119 William Eubank is sometimes referred to as 'Enbank' or 'Burbank' but is clearly named as such in First Lieutenant Clark, Dillard Hazelrig, Fifteenth Infantry, AAQM, Fort Stanton to AAG, DoM, 31 May, 1880 in Letters Received, Dept. of Missouri 1868-98, RG 393, Entry A1-1 2601, Box 91.

120 Loud to General Pope, Fort Leavenworth, 12 Mar., 1880, Telegrams Sent DoNM, Vol.3, Jan.-Nov. 1880, NA, RG393, Part 3, Entry 431, pp.219-220; See also Thrapp, 1974, p.265; Thrapp, 1967, pp.193-194; Stout, p126; Leckie, 1967, pp.216-218; Worcester, p.226; Haley, 1981, p.325.

121 Hatch, Ojo Caliente to AAG Fort Leavenworth, 22 Feb., 1880, Telegrams Sent DoNM, Vol.3, Jan.-Nov. 1880, NA, RG393, Part 3, Entry 431, p.154.

122 Pope to Col. W.D. Whipple, AAG, Chicago, 26 Mar., 1880, NA, RG393, Part 1, Entry 2546, pp.353-356.

123 Whipple to Pope, 30 Mar., 1880 in NA, RG393, Part 1, Entry 2539, Press Copies of Letters and Endorsements Sent, MDoM, Vol. 13, p.132.

Returning the Ojo Caliente Reservation to the Chihenne Apaches: The US Army Examines the Peace Option

It must be acknowledged that while Colonel Hatch and his superiors were planning for war, they also explored the possibility of a negotiated settlement with the Warm Springs Apaches.[124] Hatch may have misinterpreted some of the tactics being used by Victorio, but he fully understood the reasons for the Apache leader's hostility. He argued that the decision to remove the Warm Springs Apaches to San Carlos was central to the continuing hostilities. 'I am satisfied old Victorio and many of his Indians [would] rather die than go to San Carlos.'[125] Hatch recommended that Victorio be granted his wish and be returned to Ojo Caliente. This reversal of policy seems to have been accepted by the Department of the Interior, as instructions were sent to Acting Agent Lieutenant Chaffee at San Carlos to send the Warm Springs Apaches living there to Ojo Caliente, in the charge of a reliable employee and escorted by the San Carlos Indian Police.[126]

There was a further, less humanitarian[127] reason, for Hatch's recommendation. He thought Victorio enjoyed an additional advantage in that many of his dependents were still living on the San Carlos Reservation being fed by the United States. 'It is a great mistake for us not to have the women and children in our hands.'[128]Thus they were not a constraint on Victorio's actions. Both Hatch and Pope were convinced that this measure would persuade most of the independent Apaches, including Victorio, to surrender. The newly resettled Apaches might then be prevailed upon to help finish off any remaining renegades.[129] This was not the first time that this option had been considered. In March 1879, whilst Victorio had been staying at Ojo Caliente, Hatch had suggested recruiting some of the Warm Springs Apaches as scouts once the existing Navajo scouts had been discharged.[130] Hatch also thought that if the San Carlos Indian Police were used to escort the Warm Springs Apaches back to Ojo Caliente, these policemen could then be used in the short term to hunt down any remaining Apache renegades.[131] Hatch also tried to justify what was a fairly

124 Including General Sherman, who had a talent for camouflaging any sympathy for American Indians with the most genocidal of statements.

125 Hatch, Fort Craig NM, to AAAG SF, 20-22 Feb., 1880, (The date on this letter is unclear but was placed between letters dated the 20 and 22 of Feb., 1880) 'DoNM/GSFO/L&T', NA, RG393, Part 3, Entry 475, Vol. 5, p.411; See also Laumbach, pp.123-124.

126 Brookes, Acting Commissioner, Bureau of Indian Affairs, to Chaffee 8 Mar., 1880, Telegrams Sent DoNM, Vol.3, Jan.-Nov. 1880, NA, RG393, Part 3, Entry 431, pp.235-236; Schurz to the Secretary of War, 10 Mar., 1880, 'Victorio Files', NA, RG393, M1495, Roll 14; Feb., 1880 in Letters Received, DoM 1868-98, RG 393, Entry A1-1 2601, Box 88.

127 During the Ute Conflict in 1879, Hatch had advocated that a substantial amount of Navajos should be armed and sent against the Utes retaining the women and stock captured during such an operation. (Hatch to Pope, 2 Oct., 1879, Telegrams Sent DoNM, Vol.2, Jan.-Dec. 1879, NA, RG393, Part 3, Entry 431, p.266).

128 Hatch to Pope, 9 Mar., 1880 in Letters Received, DoM 1868-98, RG 393, Entry A1-1 2601, Box 88.

129 Hatch, Fort Craig NM, to AAAG SF, 20-22 Feb., 1880, 'DoNM/GSFO/L&T', NA, RG393, Part 3, Entry 475, Vol. 5, p.411; see also Hatch to AAG Fort Leavenworth 20 Feb., 1880, Telegrams Sent DoNM, Vol.3, Jan.-Nov. 1880, NA, RG393, Part 3, Entry 431, pp151-152; Hatch, Ojo Caliente, to AAAG SF, 22 Feb., 1880, 'DoNM/GSFO/L&T', NA, RG393, Part 3, Entry 475, Vol. 5, pp.412-413; Hatch, Ojo Caliente, to AAAG 26 Feb., 1880, 'DoNM/GSFO/L&T', NA, RG393, Part 3, Entry 475, Vol. 5, pp.420-421; Pope to AAG HQ MDoM, 21 Feb., 1880, 'Victorio Files', NA, RG393, M1495, Roll 14; Pope to Sherman, 24 Feb., 1880 & Hatch to AAG Fort Leavenworth 20 Feb., 1880 in 'Victorio Papers', NA, M666, Roll 526.

130 Hatch to AAG Fort Leavenworth, 25 Mar. 1879, Telegrams Sent DoNM, Vol.2, Jan.-Dec. 1879, NA, RG393, Part 3, Entry 431, p.72.

131 Hatch, Ojo Caliente to AAG Fort Leavenworth, 26 Feb., 1880, Telegrams Sent DoNM, Vol.3, Jan.-Nov. 1880, NA, RG393, Part 3, Entry 431, p.161; Hatch to AAG Dept. Mo., 25 Feb., 1880 in 'Victorio Papers', NA, M666, Roll 526.

blatant attempt to inflate the number of Apache scouts at his disposal[132] by arguing that as the San Carlos Police had already let the Warm Springs Apaches escape twice, 'It seems proper they should assist in their recapture.'[133] If this was actually true then this is surely a good argument for not employing them. To be fair, Hatch's concern was even if the Apaches were either persuaded peacefully to surrender, or beaten into submission, there would be small bands of holdouts. Such independent Apaches would continue to depredate among the miners and prospectors scattered over the country. Hatch was convinced that moving the San Carlos Warm Springs Apaches to Ojo Caliente would minimise the number of such renegades and at the same time maximise the number of potential scouts to combat these holdouts.[134]

It must also be noted that between March and October 1880, Colonel Hatch, depending upon how much pressure he was under, and perhaps depending on the audience addressed, veered back and forth from being clearly sympathetic to Victorio's case to advocating his complete destruction by any means. At one point, he suggested that Apaches tasked with meeting Victorio could be paid to bring in his head.[135] In the light of Hatch's initiative to return Ojo Caliente to the Chihennes, one should be wary of statements made, in the heat of the moment, by a sometimes very harassed District Commander.

By 30 March, Hatch, still hearing nothing of the proposed movement of the Warm Springs Apaches to Ojo Caliente, enquired as to their whereabouts.[136] His efforts were frustrated by what was, at first glance, a most surprising source. Lieutenant Chaffee had reported back to the Commissioner of Indian Affairs that the Warm Springs Apaches residing at San Carlos, including Victorio's wife, stated that they wished to remain at San Carlos.[137] On being informed of the Warm Springs Apaches refusal to leave San Carlos on 1 April 1880,[138] Hatch was at first dumbfounded, finding this reluctance to move 'singular'.[139] Initially, Hatch thought that this undermined Victorio's claim that he had only declared war because he had not been allowed to remain at Ojo Caliente with his people.[140] However, on reflecting more deeply on the matter Hatch concluded that:

132 As employees of the Department of the Interior, (Hereafter referred to as the 'DoI'),the San Carlos police might not count as being members of the US army and thereby avoid political problems concerning Congress-approved manpower limits upon their standing army.

133 Hatch, Ojo Caliente to AAG Fort Leavenworth, 26 Feb., 1880, Telegrams Sent DoNM, Vol.3, Jan.-Nov. 1880, NA, RG393, Part 3, Entry 431, p.161; Hatch to AAG Dept. Mo., 25 Feb., 1880 in 'Victorio Papers', NA, M666, Roll 526.

134 Hatch to AAG Fort Leavenworth, 11 Mar., 1880, Telegrams Sent DoNM, Vol.3, Jan.-Nov. 1880, NA, RG393, Part 3, Entry 431, pp.215-216; Pope to AAG HQMDoM, 12 Mar., 1880, 'Victorio Files', NA, RG393, M1495, Roll 14.

135 Hatch to Carr, Camp Thomas, 11 Jul., 1880, Telegrams Sent DoNM, Vol.3, Jan.-Nov. 1880, NA, RG393, Part 3, Entry 431, p.600.

136 Loud to AAG Fort Leavenworth, 30 Mar., 1880, Telegrams Sent DoNM, Vol.3, Jan.-Nov. 1880, NA, RG393, Part 3, Entry 431, p.263.

On 1 April, 1880, Hatch was informed that Sherman was vigorously pursuing this question. (Loud to Hatch, Aleman, 1 Apr., 1880, Telegrams Sent DoNM, Vol.3, Jan.-Nov. 1880, NA, RG393, Part 3, Entry 431, pp.269-270).

137 Chaffee to CoIA, 12 Mar., 1880 in 'Victorio Papers', NA, M666, Roll 526.

138 Chaffee, San Carlos to Hatch, Aleman, 1 Apr., 1880, Telegrams Sent DoNM, Vol.3, Jan.-Nov. 1880, NA, RG393, Part 3, Entry 431, p.275; See also CoIA to Secretary of the Interior, 7 Apr., 1880 in 'Victorio Papers', NA, M666, Roll 526.

139 Hatch, Fort Bayard to Capt. Chaffee, San Carlos, 13 Mar.,1880 in 'DoNM/GSFO/L&T', NA, RG393, Part 3, Entry 475, Vol. 5, p.466; Hatch to AAG Dept. Mo. 16 Mar., 1880 in 'Victorio Papers', NA, M666, Roll 526; Same letter in Letters Received, DoM 1868-98, RG 393, Entry A1-1 2601, Box 88.

140 Hatch to AAG DoM, 16 Mar., 1880, 'Victorio Files', NA, RG393, M1495, Roll 14.

> Of course these families object to be put into my hands knowing they would be held as hostages for the good behaviour of the Indians now out on the warpath it would be infinitely better if they were loose today with the hostiles instead of being taken care of and fed while the men are on the warpath.[141]

General Pope, unaware that the Warm Springs Apaches at San Carlos had refused to move, blamed the Department of the Interior and contacted General Sherman to register his frustration, arguing that it was clear that Victorio and his men would never accept San Carlos as a reservation. He added that until this fact was appreciated, there would be many more 'unnecessary'[142] fatalities amongst both Apaches and citizens, and the sooner that all the Warm Springs Apaches at San Carlos were sent back to Ojo Caliente, the better for all concerned. He concluded that it simply made no sense to feed and clothe the families in Arizona while many of their men were wreaking havoc in New Mexico.[143] The refusal of the Warm Springs Apaches to move from San Carlos probably gave the on-going feud being waged by the Indian Bureau and the Department of the Interior against the War Department enough oxygen to reignite the administrative conflict. The Office of Indian Affairs reverted to its short-sighted insistence on the continuation of the concentration policy and the harsh treatment for those who resisted. Such a policy was ultimately of dubious legality as the US Supreme Court, in 1901, backed the US Court of Claims in stating that damage caused by 'non-treaty' Indians should be regarded as 'a distinct political entity in a state of war'.[144] This recognition of political legitimacy was also (rightly) extended to Victorio's Warm Springs Apaches and their Mescalero allies.[145] In the meantime, such a policy ensured that the Victorio and like-minded Apaches would continue to resist to the bitter end.

However, despite the auxiliary intention to use Victorio's dependents to force a settlement, it is quite clear that a number of officers were well aware of the reasons for Victorio's continued resistance and were willing to promote an ultimately honourable settlement with the Warm Springs Apaches.[146] (See document file no. 39.) While the continued feuding over the direction of Indian

141 Loud to AAG Fort Leavenworth, 3 Apr., 1880,Telegrams Sent DoNM, Vol.3, Jan.-Nov. 1880, NA, RG393, Part 3, Entry 431, pp.275-276; Hatch to AAAG, NA, RG393, Part 3, Entry 439, pp.19-20, & Hatch to AAAG SF, NA, RG393, Part 3, Entry 439, pp.37-38; See also Hatch, Aleman 2 Apr., 1880, 'DoNM/GSFO/L&T', NA, RG393, Part 3, Entry 475, Vol. 5, p.369; Hatch first made this recommendation to the AAG Fort Leavenworth on the 20 Feb., 1880, Telegrams Sent DoNM, Vol.3, Jan.-Nov. 1880, NA, RG393, Part 3, Entry 431, pp151-152; Pope to Sheridan, 4 Apr., 1880, 'Victorio Files', NA, RG393, M1495, Roll 14; Pope to Sheridan, 4 Apr., 1880 in 'Victorio Papers', NA, M666, Roll 526.

142 Pope to Sheridan, 4 Apr., 1880, 'Victorio Files', NA, RG393, M1495, Roll 14; Pope to Sheridan, 4 Apr., 1880 in 'Victorio Papers', NA, M666, Roll 526.

143 Pope to Sherman, 25 Mar., 1880, 'Victorio Files', NA, RG393, M1495, Roll 14; Pope to Sherman, 25 Mar., 1880 in 'Victorio Papers', NA, M666, Roll 526; See also General Sherman's endorsement of Hatch and Pope's views in Sherman to Secretary of the Interior, 30 Mar., 1880 in 'Victorio Papers', NA, M666, Roll 526 & in Letters Received, DoM 1868-98, RG 393, Entry A1-1 2601, Box 88.

144 Skogen, 1996, p.148.

145 Ibid, p.147.

146 Hatch to AAG, DoM, Fort Leavenworth, 14 Feb., 1880 in Letters Sent by '9MD/DNM/DoNM', NA, RG393, M1072, Roll 6, Jan. 1880-Aug. 1881, Letter No.82, pp58-65.

Hatch was accused of trying to manufacture a stunning victory by "unconditionally" surrendering to Victorio while presenting this to the public as having brought peace to the region. ('Town and County', the *Grant County Herald* 20 Mar., 1880) The paper believed that if such a peace deal was struck, Victorio would be back on the warpath in six months. "However, it would be a fitting termination to Hatch's farcical campaign." ('Town and County', the *Grant County Herald* 20 Mar., 1880)

policy continued, General Pope could only ask Hatch to be patient and to treat any captured Apaches as prisoners-of-war,[147] a policy upheld by General Sherman.[148]

In general, both sides, needing some rest, recuperation and re-supply, seem to have laid low for the rest of February 1880. Lieutenant Conline, with A Company, Ninth Cavalry, again clashed with Apaches in the Sacramento Mountains on 28 February 1880. In a strategy that contrasted with that of his earlier encounter with the Mescaleros, Conline's command launched a two-pronged attack on a camp of Mescalero Apaches on a rocky hill in the 'south-east branch of Alamo Canon'.[149] A party under Lieutenant Clark managed to surround the horse herd, while Lieutenant Conline and the rest of his force launched an attack on the camp, which consisted of seven lodges with an estimated 17 occupants. Conline claimed to have captured and burned the camp and 'captured sixteen horses and five mules'.[150] No casualties were recorded for either side.[151] It was believed that the Mescaleros were led by 'Capitan Blanco'.[152]

By early March 1880, hints that a decision has been reached by the US army concerning the 'dismounting and disarming'[153] of the Mescaleros are contained in several telegrams 'the contents of which I cannot telegraph'[154] to Hatch from Department Headquarters. Hatch planned to 'kill two birds with one stone'. If given enough time to rest and refit his forces, he calculated that he might be able to disguise his operation to disarm and dismount the Mescaleros.[155] He would mount an operation that would appear to be aimed at Victorio, and which would be timed to 'conveniently' arrive at the Mescalero reservation by 'operational chance'. It was hoped that this 'happenstance' would not alert the Mescalero Apaches until it was too late.[156]

On 2 March 1880, reports were received that Apaches had been seen on the Mescalero reservation and that both Victorio and Nana were camped in the White Mountains.[157] Yet Hatch remained convinced that the Apaches were based in the San Andres Mountains. Accordingly, he

147 Platt AAG Fort Leavenworth to CO DoNM 24 Feb., 1880, NA, RG393, Part 3, Entry 439, p.79

148 Sherman to Pope 29 Feb., 1880, Telegrams Sent DoNM, Vol.3, Jan.-Nov. 1880, NA, RG393, Part 3, Entry 431, p.169.

149 Loud to Hatch, Fort Bayard, 10 Mar., 1880, Telegrams Sent DoNM, Vol.3, Jan.-Nov. 1880, NA, RG393, Part 3, Entry 431, pp.209-210 see also pp.210-211; 'Striking Indians', *Army & Navy Journal,* Vol.17, 13 Mar., 1880, p.643.

150 Personal File John Conline, NA, RG94, Entry 297, Box 279; Bi-Monthly Company Muster Rolls for Company A, 9th Cavalry, Jan./Feb., 1880 in NA, RG94; Loud to Hatch, Fort Bayard, 10 Mar., 1880, Telegrams Sent DoNM, Vol.3, Jan.-Nov. 1880, NA, RG393, Part 3, Entry 431, pp.209-210 see also pp.210-211; See also Record of Events Feb., 1880 in Returns From Regular Army Cavalry Regiments 1833-1916, 9th Cavalry Regimental Returns 1873-1880, NA, M744, Roll 88; Return for Mar. 1880 in Returns From U.S. Military Posts 1800-1916, Fort Stanton, New Mexico, Jan. 1878-Dec. 1887, NA, M617, Roll 1218 'By Telegraph', the *Grant County Herald*, 13 Mar., 1880; 'Striking Indians', *Army & Navy Journal,* Vol.17, 13 Mar., 1880, p.643.

151 Chronological List, p.49 See also Record of Events Feb., 1880 in Returns From Regular Army Cavalry Regiments 1833-1916, 9th Cavalry Regimental Returns 1873-1880, NA, M744, Roll 88.

152 Bi-Monthly Company Muster Rolls for Company A, 9th Cavalry, Jan./Feb., 1880 in NA, RG94.

153 Loud to Hatch, Ojo Caliente, 27 Feb., 1880, Telegrams Sent DoNM, Vol.3, Jan.-Nov. 1880, NA, RG393, Part 3, Entry 431, pp.162-163.

154 Loud to General Hatch, Fort Bayard, 1 Mar., 1880, Telegrams Sent, DoNM, Vol.3, Jan.-Nov. 1880, NA, RG393, Part 3, Entry 431, p.170.

155 Hatch To AAG Fort Leavenworth, 5 Mar., 1880, Telegrams Sent DoNM, Vol.3, Jan.-Nov. 1880, NA, RG393, Part 3, Entry 431, pp.189-190; Hatch, Fort Bayard, to AAAG SF, 5 Mar., 1880, 'DoNM/GSFO/L&T', NA, RG393, Part 3, Entry 475, Vol. 5, p.439.

156 Hatch To AAG Fort Leavenworth, 5 Mar., 1880, Telegrams Sent DoNM, Vol.3, Jan.-Nov. 1880, NA, RG393, Part 3, Entry 431, pp.189-190.

157 Hatch, Fort Bayard, 2 Mar., 1880, 'DoNM/GSFO/L&T', NA, RG393, Part 3, Entry 475, Vol. 5, p.428; Hatch to AAG Fort Leavenworth, 3 Mar., 1880, Telegrams Sent DoNM, Vol.3, Jan.-Nov. 1880, NA, RG393, Part 3, Entry 431, p.182.

ordered Captain Hooker's Third Battalion into the field, accompanied by Lieutenant Gatewood's detachment of Apache scouts.[158] These troops were to thoroughly scout the San Andres to confirm the Colonel's 'impression' that the Apaches were concentrated there. Hooker was to move from Ojo Caliente to Aleman (Martin's Wells), and from there he would follow Morrow's earlier trail into the San Andres. Hooker was to keep Hatch fully informed via the telegraph station at Aleman of his progress.[159]

Hatch gave very clear instructions that should Hooker encounter Apaches, and should the latter flee to the Mescalero reservation, he *was not* to pursue them, but rather he was to fall back on Aleman and await further instructions. 'It is not considered advisable to follow them on the Reservation until we are thoroughly prepared to strike a decisive blow.'[160] If the trails led away from the reservation, Hooker was to pursue them vigorously. He was also reminded to keep a close eye on the country on his flanks just in case Victorio attempted to move westwards towards the Black Range, or south into Mexico, rather than retreat to the Mescalero reservation.[161]

On 4 March 1880, Hatch also instructed the 'officer in charge', probably Captain Steelhammer, at the Mescalero agency, that should Victorio make contact, he was to be informed of the large force of US troops gearing up for an offensive against him:

> the object of this telegram is if possible to hold Victorio quiet and learn his position definitely until we are thoroughly prepared to crush these Indians out, and also not to alarm the Mescalleros by the movement of so large a number of troops.[162]

Hatch had already concluded that most of the Mescalero warriors had now sided with Victorio. He dismissed Agent Russell's estimate that only 35 Mescalero warriors were absent from the reservation.[163] As far as Hatch was concerned, he had what he regarded as reliable information that at least 100 Mescalero warriors were operating with Victorio.[164] His belief appears to have been confirmed by Captain Steelhammer a few days later when he noted that all but one small band of Mescalero Apaches had deserted the agency.[165] Hatch left it till 23 March before he wrote to Agent Russell at the Mescalero reservation and requested that the Mescaleros be gathered in with their stock no later than 12 April 1880. At that point he did not inform the Agent of his intention to disarm and dismount the Mescaleros. The preceding day, he had written to Fort Stanton instructing them

158 One suspects that, as Gatewood's scout company was not ordered to move to New Mexico until 5 Mar., 1880, it is unlikely that they were present. Hatch had personally requested Gatewood on 9 Feb., 1880, and perhaps had assumed that by this date Gatewood's company was serving in New Mexico.

159 Hatch, Fort Bayard, to CO, 3 Battalion NM Troops, Ojo Caliente, 5 Mar., 1880 in 'DoNM/GSFO/L&T', NA, RG393, Part 3, Entry 475, Vol. 5.

160 Ibid.

161 Hatch, Fort Bayard, to CO, 3 Battalion NM Troops, Ojo Caliente, 5 Mar., 1880 in 'DoNM/GSFO/L&T', NA, RG393, Part 3, Entry 475, Vol. 5.

162 Hatch, Fort Bayard, to Officer-in-Charge, Mescalero Agency, 4 Mar., 1880, 'DoNM/GSFO/L&T', NA, RG393, Part 3, Entry 475, Vol. 5, p.436.

163 Hatch to Loud, 18 Mar., 1880, Telegrams Sent DoNM, Vol.3, Jan.-Nov. 1880, NA, RG393, Part 3, Entry 431, p.230; See also Hatch to Pope, 4 Mar., 1880 in Letters Received, DoM 1868-98, RG 393, Entry A1-1 2601, Box 88.

164 Hatch to AAG Fort Leavenworth, 5 Mar., 1880, Telegrams Sent DoNM, Vol.3, Jan.-Nov. 1880, NA, RG393, Part 3, Entry 431, pp.189-190; Hatch, Fort Bayard, to AAAG SF, 5 Mar., 1880. 'DoNM/GSFO/L&T', NA, RG393, Part 3, Entry 475, Vol. 5, p.439.

165 Hatch, Fort Bayard, to AAAG SF, 11 Mar., 1880, 'DoNM/GSFO/L&T', NA, RG393, Part 3, Entry 475, Vol. 5, p.456; See also Hatch, Bayard to Gen. O.B. Willcox, Prescott, 18 Mar., 1880, NA, RG393, Part 1, Entry 235, p.38; Loud to AAG Fort Leavenworth, 12 Mar., 1880, Telegrams Sent DoNM, Vol.3, Jan.-Nov. 1880, NA, RG393, Part 3, Entry 431, p.217.

to send 20 days' rations and forage for the Tenth Cavalry, who were expected to arrive by that date.[166] Russell was not fooled and contacted the Commissioner of Indian Affairs. He stated that he thought that it was right that Hatch should ask the Mescaleros to come into the agency; but he warned that, if Hatch's intention was to disarm and dismount them, the Mescaleros would resist and probably retaliate by raiding neighbouring settlements. Russell added that, in his opinion, that while some Mescaleros were in sympathy with Victorio, they did not represent a majority of the tribe. He also concluded that, of this minority, only a few had actually joined Victorio.[167]

This appears to be a case of the right hand (the Department of the Interior) not letting the left hand (Russell, through the Commissioner of Indian Affairs) know about their support for the dismounting and disarming of the Mescalero Apaches mentioned earlier in this chapter.

In the meantime, the effort to refit the US forces ranged against the Apaches continued, with 100 horses being sent from Kansas City to Santa Fé on or around 7 March 1880. Additional rifles and ammunition were sent from the Fort Union Arsenal to Fort Bayard, though there were not enough wagons available at Santa Fé to supply this material as quickly as it was required.[168]

An important ruling on the 'hot pursuit' of Apaches into Mexico also arrived at Fort Bayard, and this removed an important operational option for Hatch. The directive from the Secretary of War stated that, as of 24 February 1880, the US army should 'consider the instructions of June 1st 1877, to General Ord which contemplates and provides that under certain circumstances he may pursue raiders across the border, as no longer in force'.[169] (See document file no. 40.)

This could not have come at a more inopportune moment. Within a fortnight of this directive, the Apaches renewed hostilities and plunged the troops in New Mexico into a prolonged campaign which would not end until the beginning of June.

166 Hatch to Russell, 23 Apr., 1880 & Hatch to CO Fort Stanton, 22 Mar., 1880 in Letters Sent Vol. 7, 25 Oct., 1880 – 24 Jun., 1881 in HQ Records of Fort Cummings, New Mexico, 1863-1873 & 1880-1884, NA, RG393, M1081, Roll 1. Note. I found these two telegrams at the beginning of vol. 7. See also Hatch to Russell, 23 Mar., 1880 NA, RG393 Part 3, Entry 475 p.91 & 94.

167 Russell to CoIA, 27 Mar., 1880 in Letters Received by HQ DoNM Sept. 1865-Aug. 1890, NA, RG393, M1088, Roll 40, Jan.-Jun. 1880; Russell to CoIA, 27 Mar., 1880 in 'Victorio Papers', NA, M666, Roll 526; R.E. Trowbridge to Secretary of the Interior, 6 Apr., 1880, in Letters Received, DoM 1868-98, RG 393, Entry A1-1 2601, Box 89; See also R.E. Trowbridge, Commissioner to The Secretary of the Interior, 5 May, 1880 with attached correspondence from Agent Russell in 'Victorio Papers', NA, M666, Roll 527.

168 Loud to Hatch, Fort Bayard, 5 Mar., 1880, Telegrams Sent DoNM, Vol.3, Jan.-Nov. 1880, NA, RG393, Part 3, Entry 431, p.192.

169 Alex Ramsey, Secretary of War to the General of the Army, 24 Feb., 1880 in Letters Received, DoM 1868-98, RG 393, Entry A1-1 2601, Box 88; See also Loud to General Hatch, Fort Bayard, 9 Mar., 1880, Telegrams Sent DoNM, Vol.3, Jan.-Nov. 1880, NA, RG393, Part 3, Entry 431, p.205.

4

Victorio Strikes the Rio Grande Valley, March 1880

If Hatch's message outlining the forces arrayed against the Apaches was ever delivered to Victorio via Captain Steelhammer, it did not have the desired effect. In March 1880, Victorio's warriors commenced raiding in the Rio Grande Valley (see Map 4.1), killing a number of people and stealing horses between Socorro and McEvers' Ranch. News of this arrived with a garbled report of the capture of 30 cases of Winchester rifles by the Apaches in Mexico.[1] If this rumour were true, for Hatch at least, it went some way to explaining the large amounts of modern weapons currently in the hands of the Apaches.[2] Hatch also noted that the Apaches were very well armed and had abundant supplies of ammunition. Here, he reiterated his long-held view that this equipment was gained from trade with a wide network of Mexicans, and he implied that this trade took place on both sides of the border. Trade in Mexico was not the only source of rifles and ammunition for the Apaches. Hatch ruefully commented that:

> It is unfortunate he should have captured 30 cases of Winchester rifles in Mexico. With abundance of ammunition I fear he will or has armed every Indian who will join him, he has shrewdly used the Mescalero Reservation for an asylum for his wounded, and it is to my impression he has cached large quantities of stolen property upon the reservation.[3]

One of the first parties of raiders attacked and killed a Mexican herder called Refugio Delgado, and ran off 15 head of cattle near Alamo Spring. A citizen called Wood and five other men followed the raiders' trail for 30 miles along the western side of the San Andres Mountains, until they were approximately opposite Aleman, where the trail joined a larger trail and turned into these mountains. Wood's party feared a trap and retired.[4]

Another party of raiders made their presence known near Hillsboro. A 'reliable' source informed Lieutenant Allen, signals officer in charge of telegraph lines in southern New Mexico, that a party of Apaches had crossed the Jornada del Muerto and the Rio Grande, ten miles south of Las Palomas, on the night of Monday 1 March, and that three men had been killed.[5] Further reports indicated that this party had moved towards Hillsboro, and that the three men had been killed on the 'main river road'.[6] Near Hillsboro, early on 2 March, a Mexican family was rescued from

1 Hatch, Fort Bayard, to AAAG, SF, 4 Mar., 1880, 'DoNM/GSFO/L&T', NA, RG393, Part 3, Entry 475, Vol. 5, pp.435-436.
2 Hatch To AAG Fort Leavenworth, 5 Mar., 1880, Telegrams Sent DoNM, Vol.3, Jan.-Nov. 1880, NA, RG393, Part 3, Entry 431, pp.189-190.
3 Hatch to Pope, 4 Mar., 1880 in Letters Received, DoM 1868-98, RG 393, Entry A1-1 2601, Box 88
4 *Thirty-Four*, 3 & 10 Mar., 1880.
5 Loud to Hatch, Fort Bayard 6 Mar., 1880, Telegrams Sent DoNM, Vol.3, Jan.–Nov. 1880, NA, RG393, Part 3, Entry 431, pp.195-196.
6 Loud to Hatch, Fort Bayard, 6 Mar., 1880, Telegrams Sent DoNM, Vol.3, Jan.–Nov. 1880, NA, RG393, Part 3, Entry 431, p.196.

the Apaches by three 'Wallace Rangers' (volunteer militia), though the Apaches made off with 10 mules in the direction of the Black Range.[7] By 6 March, Hatch was able to report that not only were the troops of the Sixth Cavalry on their tail, but that Captain Beyer, with 100 Ninth Cavalrymen[8] and Lieutenant Maney's Indian scouts, was also in the area. A further Apache scout company from Arizona had been instructed to advance to Hillsboro. As noted in the previous chapter, Captain Hooker's command was ordered to move into the San Andres Mountains. These particular Apache raiders inflicted no further casualties and faded away from view.[9]

Hatch's reliable acting assistant adjutant-general, Captain Loud at Santa Fé, also informed Hatch that no report of this raid had been sent to Department Headquarters, as Loud felt that it was Hatch's decision whether any such information was passed on.[10] These two attacks were only the first of a series of raids on the inhabitants of the Rio Grande valley.

Guadalupe Ascarate of Las Cruces reported sending two men and six mules to rendezvous with his pack train travelling from Las Vegas NM to Silver City. Both men and two mules were killed by Apaches near Las Palomas on or around 5 March.[11] The two men killed had been carrying two Winchester rifles, two Colt revolvers and 100 rounds of rifle and 60 rounds of pistol ammunition.[12]

Estanislao Montoya, 'personally known to almost every one of Victorio's band',[13] was raided by his former acquaintances. On 12 March 1880, at Nogal, approximately 40 miles north of San Jose, he lost 120 horses worth $3,000 to Apache raiders. The Apaches drove the horses off towards the Mescalero reservation, crossing the Rio Grande near San Jose.[14] On the same day, at Toussaint's[15] Ranch four mules and three horses were stolen.[16]

Two 'civilians' were slain near La Luz, approximately 10 miles to the south-east of the Tulerosa agency on the Mescalero reservation, sometime during March.[17] A citizen was reported killed at Blazer's Ranch on 15 March 1880.[18] Again during March, two wagons were ambushed between Hillsboro and Cummings, with three men killed. A woman and child survived and walked to Fort

7 *Thirty-Four*, 10 Mar., 1880.

8 What Hatch failed to point out to his AAAG, was that Captain Beyer was in charge of all the dismounted Ninth Cavalrymen from Fort Bayard backed up by 2 cavalry companies. (Hatch, Fort Bayard, to AAAG SF, 5 Mar., 1880, 'DoNM/GSFO/L&T', NA, RG393, Part 3, Entry 475, Vol. 5, p.439; See also Hatch to Morrow, 23? Feb., 1880 in 'DoNM/GSFO/L&T', NA, RG393, Part 3, Entry 475, Vol. 5).

9 Hatch to AAAG SF NM 6 Mar., 1880, NA, RG393, Part 3, Entry 439, pp.39-40.

10 Loud to Hatch, Fort Bayard, 9 Mar., 1880, Telegrams Sent DoNM, Vol.3, Jan.–Nov. 1880, NA, RG393, Part 3, Entry 431, p.208.

11 *Thirty-Four*, 10 Mar., 1880; 'Town and County', *The Grant County Herald*, 13 Mar., 1880.

12 *Thirty-Four*, 17 Mar., 1880.

13 Thrapp, 1988, p.1007.

14 E. Montoya to Wallace 23 Mar., 1880 in 'Victorio Papers', NA, M666, Roll 526; See also E. Montoya to Governor Wallace, 23 Mar., 1880 in Letters Received by HQ DoNM Sept. 1865-Aug. 1890, NA, RG393, M1088, Roll 40, Jan.-Jun. 1880; Luciano Chavez to Governor Lew Wallace, 27 Mar., 1880, Telegrams Sent DoNM, Vol.3, Jan.–Nov. 1880, NA, RG393, Part 3, Entry 431, p.257; Thrapp, 1974, p.267; Thrapp, 1988, pp.1006-1007. One Estanislado Montoya is reported as a San Antonio trader who was contracted to supply Fort McRae with corn in 1870. (Wilson, p.353).

15 See Lt Griffin's survey report concerning the area between Fort Stanton and Fort Bliss. The Jornada del Muerto covered in 'fine gamma grass' but worthless for grazing only four sources of water for 90 miles: Ojo del Muerto, Toussaint's Ranch, Martin's Well and the Stage station at Point of Rocks (p.2202) Notes little water in the Caballo Mts (p.2201) and that the San Andres even dryer than the Caballos (Report of Lt. E. Griffin, Corps of Engineers, submitted 26 Mar., 1879 in AR-WD, NA, M997, Roll 33, 1879 Vol. I-II, p.2202).

16 *Thirty-Four*, 17 Mar., 1880.

17 Chronological List, p.49; Webb, 1976, p.88; 'Hatch vs Breechclouts' [Veni Vidi Vici]', the *Grant County Herald*, 20 Mar., 1880; See also AAA Road Map, Arizona & New Mexico.

18 Webb, 1976, p.88.

Bayard, arriving on 25 March, to report the attack.[19] Captain Hooker reported parties of raiders leaving the San Mateo Mountains on 14 March, speculating that they were either going to the San Andres or the Mescalero reservation. The following day, in response to a report by Lieutenant Valois that Apaches were to the east of San Jose, Hooker, despite an outbreak of measles at Ojo Caliente,[20] stated his intent to pursue them, whether they continued going east or attempted to circle back to the San Mateo Mountains.[21]

On 17 March, Lieutenant Schaeffer, with a detachment of unknown size, trailed and then sighted a party of four Apaches, only to lose track of his quarry as darkness fell. Captain Beyer sent out a detachment of 10 men under Sergeant Boyne to take up the trail. Beyer later reported that this small party was moving south and estimated that they would probably be found lurking near McEvers' Ranch, or in the Goodsight Mountains.[22] Captain Steelhammer sent word from a 'reasonably reliable' source that Victorio, with a strong force of Apaches, was less than a day's march away from, and was making for, the Mescalero agency. Steelhammer dug in, requested reinforcements and awaited developments.[23]

On or around 20 March, a buckboard carrying mail was ambushed near Aleman, and the driver was reported slain and the mail scattered to the four winds.[24] The Apaches also struck the telegraph line running out of Fort Cummings, and troops had to be sent from that post to repair the line.[25] Two couriers from Fort Craig were sent down the line to find the break, and Hooker, on learning of the break, moved the Third Battalion down to Aleman.[26] Parties of Apaches were rumoured to be using the water near Aleman on a nightly basis, and mail drivers refused to operate their service unless escorted.[27] During the last week in March, it was reported that the stagecoaches running out of Las Cruces were also refusing to travel unless escorted.[28] By the beginning of April, mail runs were becoming more frequent across the Jornada, as enough troops were stationed at Round Mountain, Point of Rocks and Aleman to provide small detachments of three soldiers for each run.[29]

---

19 *Thirty-Four*, 31 Mar., 1880.

20 Hooker 13 Mar., 1880, reports that he has taken all necessary steps to avoid an epidemic, Telegrams Sent DoNM, Vol.3, Jan.–Nov. 1880, NA, RG393, Part 3, Entry 431, p.221.

21 Hooker to Hatch/Loud, NA, RG393, Part 3, Entry 439, p.36.

22 Beyer, to Morrow Fort Bayard, 18 Mar., 1880, Miscellaneous Records 1868-1889, NA, RG393, Part 3, Entry 453.

23 Loud to Gen. Hatch, Fort Bayard, 15 Mar., 1880, Telegrams Sent DoNM, Vol.3, Jan.–Nov. 1880, NA, RG393, Part 3, Entry 431, pp.225-226.

24 Loud to AAG Fort Leavenworth & to Hatch, Fort Bayard, both 23 Mar., 1880, Telegrams Sent DoNM, Vol.3, Jan.–Nov. 1880, NA, RG393, Part 3, Entry 431, pp.237-238; 'Town and County', the *Grant County Herald*, 27 Mar., 1880; See also Letter from Hatch dated 20 Mar., 1880 found between pages 29 & 30 in 'DoNM/GSFO/L&T', NA, RG393, Part 3, Entry 475, Vol. 5; 'Indian Affairs' *Army & Navy Journal*, Vol.17, 27 Mar., 1880, p.693.

25 Letter from Hatch dated 20 Mar., 1880 found between pages 29 & 30 in 'DoNM/GSFO/L&T', NA, RG393, Part 3, Entry 475, Vol. 5; See also Loud to AAG Fort Leavenworth & to Hatch, Fort Bayard, both 23 Mar., 1880, Telegrams Sent DoNM, Vol.3, Jan.–Nov. 1880, NA, RG393, Part 3, Entry 431, pp.237-238.

In a somewhat ambiguous statement Hatch stated that 'your last dispatch shows indications that Repairman is frightened he don't know where line is down.' If the lineman was afraid of encountering Apaches then one can hardly blame him. However, this could be read as indicating an earlier use of a trick noted from the later 'Geronimo' Campaigns where the line was cut and then spliced together with rawhide making it necessary for a minute examination of the line to spot the break. Being unaware of this tactic, the repairman may have checked the line and been unable to spot an obvious break.

26 Loud to AAG Fort Leavenworth & to Hatch, Fort Bayard, both 23 Mar., 1880, Telegrams Sent DoNM, Vol.3, Jan.–Nov. 1880, NA, RG393, Part 3, Entry 431, pp.237-238.

27 *Thirty-Four* 24 Feb., 1880.

28 Ibid, 31 Mar., 1880.

29 Ibid, 7 Apr., 1880.

Captain Beyer described how 10 Apaches raided Cienega Apache on 21 March, capturing 12 horses and mules. Lieutenant Gatewood, with his command, was in the vicinity and made towards the site of the attack. (See Appendix 1.) Lieutenant Wright and another man, being well in advance of the detachment, were confronted by the Apaches and chased several hundred yards before rejoining the command. Gatewood's detachment pursued the raiders for seven miles before they reached the Black Range. They were joined in the pursuit by Sergeant Boyne's detachment, who were returning from their unsuccessful pursuit of the Apaches spotted by Lieutenant Schaeffer on 17 March, and Captain Beyer, with 12 men. The Apaches were well mounted and scattered as they entered the mountains. Gatewood's detachment tried to continue the pursuit for another three miles, but gave up. Ten horses and mules were recovered[30]. (See document file no. 41.) That night, around midnight, a courier arrived at Gatewood's bivouac and reported that three men had been killed at a nearby ranch, and that the Apaches were still at the ranch. Lieutenant Cruse, Surgeon MacPherson, 18 Apache scouts and 15 troopers were immediately sent in pursuit, but failed to catch the Apaches.[31]

While the above raids were confirmed as occurring, Captain Beyer was also plagued by the usual rumour mill which rumbled into action whenever warfare with the Apaches flared up:

> Reported at Hillsboro that Indians ran off herd and Stage stock at Round Mountain on the Jornada on the eve of 14th inst – cannot trace the report to any reliable source – but I give it for what it is worth – Indians reported to have gone in direction of Mescalero Agency.[32]

Rynerson alerted the authorities that on 22 March, near Santa Barbara, the Apaches killed eight people, notably Don Santiago Gonzales, 'the father of a territorial senator', Green Worthly, 'an old and well known resident and a member of the old California Column', Juan Baca, 'two boys',[33] and three unknown 'Mexicans'.[34] It was later reported that only Worthly, Gonzales, Baca and a man named Victoriano Fajardo had been killed in this raid.[35] The same Apaches were believed to have slain eight sheepherders four miles north of McEvers' Ranch on Tierra Blanca Creek on the same day. Among the slain were John Christy, Jose Fuente, Jesus J. Jola and Jose Candelaria. Rynerson stated that this attack was 'only four miles from a camp of soldiers, and terribly heavy firing was

---

30 Beyer, Camp French to Morrow, Fort Bayard, 21 Mar., 1880, Miscellaneous Records 1868-1889, NA, RG393, Part 3, Entry 453; See also Letter 22 Mar., 1880 in MacPherson Letters 1 Jan., 1879 to 3 Sept., 1880, University of Virginia at Charlottesville.
Thrapp also reports a skirmish between Lt Wright's detachment and Apaches on 21 March, 1880 near to Hillsboro. (1988, p.1608).

31 Letter 22 Mar., 1880 in MacPherson Letters 1 Jan., 1879 to 3 Sept., 1880, University of Virginia at Charlottesville.

32 Beyer, Camp French to Morrow, Fort Bayard, 17 Mar., 1880, Miscellaneous Records 1868-1889, NA, RG393, Part 3, Entry 453; See also 'Indian Affairs' *Army & Navy Journal,* Vol.17, 27 Mar., 1880, p.693. The latter dates an attack, with the loss of twenty-five animals, on the Round Mountain stage station on 8 March, 1880.

33 Whether this refers to two cowhands or two children is unclear.

34 Rynerson to Governor Wallace, 25 Mar., 1880 in Letters Received by HQ DoNM Sept. 1865-Aug. 1890, NA, RG393, M1088, Roll 40, Jan.-Jun. 1880; Ritch, (citing Rynerson's letter of 25 Mar., 1880) Acting Governor, N.M. Territory to Schurz, Secretary of the Interior, 27 Mar., 1880 in 'Victorio Papers', NA, M666, Roll 526; See also Loud citing communication from Rynerson to Morrow via CO Fort Bayard, 24 Mar., 1880, Telegrams Sent DoNM, Vol.3, Jan.–Nov. 1880, NA, RG393, Part 3, Entry 431, p.246; the *Grant County Herald* of the 13 of Mar., 1880, reports four or five persons killed by Apaches near Santa Barbara. Later, the paper recorded that Santiago Gonzales, Juan Baca, Green Worthly and 'two boys' as killed north of Santa Barbara. ('By Telegraph', the *Grant County Herald*, 27 Mar., 1880; See also *Thirty-Four*, 24 Mar., 1880).

35 *Thirty-Four*, 31 Mar., 1880.

Plate 4.1. One of the old buildings still standing in Hillsboro, in 2006. Hillsboro was a focal point for Apache raiding in early March 1880. (Photo: Author)

Plate 4.2. A grave believed to be that of Green Worthly, one of many people killed by Apaches in the Rio Grande valley during March 1880. (Photo: Author)

heard from that direction.'[36] This may have been at Wheeler's Ranch,[37] which was said to have been attacked by over 20 Apaches with the loss of Jose Purrieta, Jose Candelaria and John Christie, on 22 March. Wheeler had reportedly killed an Apache when his, Christie's and Jojola's ranches were attacked.[38] From Camp French,[39] Captain Beyer dispatched Lieutenant Gatewood, newly arrived from his pursuit of the Apache raiding party, with his company of Apache scouts and Sixth Cavalrymen, to ascertain the truth of the report.[40]

Both the Rynerson and Estanislao Montoya claims were later investigated by Captain Edwin Pollack, Inspector General, District of New Mexico and both reports were found to be accurate apart from the fact that the three unknown Mexicans had in fact escaped. Pollack also noted that it would have been impracticable for the army to defend individual ranches or herds, even if they had had three times the number of troops present.[41]

A Ninth Cavalry courier was ambushed and killed near San Jose on 23 March 1880. Captain Hooker reported that:

> San Jose attacked by Indians this morning Two couriers killed between San Jose and Ojo Caliente Victorio reported in force near Canada Alamosa will concentrate my command there at once.[42]

In fact, one courier, Robert Kane of K Company, Ninth Cavalry, had been killed and his weapons and horse taken.[43] Two soldiers and three Mexicans sallied forth from San Jose to attack the Apaches and in the exchange of fire one of the Mexicans was killed,[44] but the Apaches were driven off.[45]

---

36 Rynerson to Governor Wallace, 25 Mar., 1880 in Letters Received by HQ DoNM Sept. 1865-Aug. 1890, NA, RG393, M1088, Roll 40, Jan.-Jun. 1880; Ritch, (citing Rynerson's letter of 25 Mar., 1880) Acting Governor, N.M. Territory to Schurz, Secretary of the Interior, 27 Mar., 1880 in 'Victorio Papers', NA, M666, Roll 526.

37 This was near McEvers Ranch. It was R.D. McEvers who sent a courier to Beyer informing him of the attack. (Beyer, Camp French to Morrow, Fort Bayard, 22 Mar., 1880, Miscellaneous Records 1868-1889, NA, RG393, Part 3, Entry 453) Wheeler's Ranch was said to be near the head of the Jarralosa. (*Thirty-Four*, 31 Mar., 1880).

38 *Thirty-Four*, 31 Mar., 1880.

39 The location of this camp is not clear. It was named after James Hansell French, after the officer killed by Apaches on 17 Jan., 1880. (See Chapter 2) It was initially called 'Camp James Hansell French, but this was quickly shortened to Camp French. Captain Beyer, his company and a large group of dismounted Ninth Cavalrymen were stationed there in March, 1880. This force was initially deployed at McEvers Ranche but appear to have been quickly moved to Camp French. My best guess that it was somewhere in the region between Hillsboro and Cuchillo Negro and Las Palomas.

40 Beyer, Camp French to Morrow, Fort Bayard, 22 Mar., 1880, Miscellaneous Records 1868-1889, NA, RG393, Part 3, Entry 472; See *Thirty-Four*, 24 Feb., 1880.

41 Pollack to AAAG, DoNM, 18 May, 1880 in Letters Received by HQ DoNM Sept. 1865-Aug. 1890, NA, RG393, M1088,p 393) Roll 40, Jan.-Jun. 1880; see same letter in Letters Received, DoM 1868-98, RG 393, Entry A1-1 2601, Box 89.

42 Hooker to Loud AAAG 22 Mar., 1880, NA, RG393, Part 3, Entry 439, p.26; See also Loud to Hatch, Fort Craig, 24 Mar., 1880, Telegrams Sent DoNM, Vol.3, Jan.–Nov. 1880, NA, RG393, Part 3, Entry 431, p.241.

43 Record of Events Mar. 1880 in Returns From Regular Army Cavalry Regiments 1833-1916, 9th Cavalry Regimental Returns 1873-1880, NA, M744, Roll 88; Return for Mar. 1880 in Returns From U.S. Military Posts 1800-1916, Ojo Caliente, New Mexico, May 1879-Mar. 1882, NA, M617, Roll 877.

44 According to the *Army & Navy Journal*, one soldier and one Mexican were killed in this skirmish.

45 Loud to AAG Fort Leavenworth, 30 Mar., 1880, Telegrams Sent DoNM, Vol.3, Jan.–Nov. 1880, NA, RG393, Part 3, Entry 431, p.264.

The following day, a representative of the Atchison, Topeka and Santa Fé Railroad requested protection from marauding Apaches for their engineers working near Paraje.[46] On 25 March, a telegram was sent from El Colorado asking for an escort for the mail service to Hillsboro as it had been 'driven back' close to where three men had been killed.[47]

More attacks were recorded on 25 March, with Reade and Woode's Ranch at San Nicholas (Spring?) raided, and 32 cattle killed and a further 100 driven off. At San Augustin, 10 horses were driven off towards Petia Blanca, presumably in or near the San Andres, as this is stated to be approximately three miles from Morrow's last contact with the Apaches in early February 1880. Finally, San Jose was attacked by 20 Apaches who killed three men.[48] Smith also reported that the previous day a small party of Apaches had passed from McEvers' Ranch to Hillsboro. This party attacked five herders but was driven off.[49]

On 26 March, two men were killed and a boy captured at Huning's Ranch, 15 miles to the west of Polvedra.[50] Three days later, Connelly's Ranch was also reported to have been attacked, 80 miles west of Las Lunas, with Connelly losing all of his horses and mules. These attacks were allegedly perpetrated by 40 well-armed and mounted Apaches. The raiders then moved on to Rito Quemado and ransacked a freight train and attacked other settlers and travellers. However, it was widely assumed at District Headquarters that these attacks were exaggerated if not fictitious.[51] Hatch was eventually directed to send an officer, Captain Pollack, to investigate the veracity of the claims.[52] When the Huning brothers were contacted by Pollack, it was found that, apart from the killing of two men, the rest of the information was hearsay. Connelly was also tracked down and stated that Victorio himself and five warriors had attacked his ranch and taken five horses and six mules, with a further six horses taken from the locality. The attack on Rito Quemado resulted in the taking of no more than four horses from the outskirts of the area. The locals opened fire and this was returned by approximately 25 Apaches. There was no indication of any casualties.[53]

Gatewood's scout company had been stationed in the vicinity of Las Palomas since 25 March 1880. Three days later, a small detachment of five scouts from the company, commanded by Lieutenant Cruse and accompanied by Surgeon MacPherson, buried two men who had been killed by Apaches several days earlier. These McPherson described as 'strangers from Missouri on their

46 WB Strong to Hatch 24 Mar., 1880, NA, RG393, Part 3, Entry 439, p.80; Strong to Hatch Telegrams Sent DoNM, Vol.3, Jan.–Nov. 1880, NA, RG393, Part 3, Entry 431, p.244.

47 Thomas B Lynch to The Dept Comdr, NA, RG393, Part 3, Entry 439, p.26; Loud to Morrow, Fort Bayard, 25 Mar., 1880, Telegrams Sent DoNM, Vol.3, Jan.–Nov. 1880, NA, RG393, Part 3, Entry 431, p.248.

48 *Thirty-Four*, 31 Mar., 1880.

49 Smith, Paymaster, Fort Cummings to Morrow, Fort Bayard, 25 Mar., 1880, Miscellaneous Records 1868-1889, NA, RG393, Part 3, Entry 453.

50 Luciano Chavez, Socorro to Lew Wallace, 27 Mar., 1880 in 'Victorio Papers', NA, M666, Roll 526; Luciano Chavez to Lew Wallace, 27 Mar., 1880 in Letters Received by HQ DoNM Sept. 1865-Aug. 1890, NA, RG393, M1088, Roll 40, Jan.-Jun. 1880; Pope to Col. W.D. Whipple, AAG, Chicago, 5 May, 1880, NA, RG393, Part 1, Entry 2546, pp.428-438.

51 Loud to Hatch, Aleman, 5 Apr., 1880, Telegrams Sent DoNM, Vol.3, Jan.–Nov. 1880, NA, RG393, Part 3, Entry 431, p.283; See also Loud to AAG Fort Leavenworth 4 May, 1880, Telegrams Sent DoNM, Vol.3, Jan.–Nov. 1880, NA, RG393, Part 3, Entry 431, p.374; Huning to Ritch, Acting Governor, 3 Apr., 1880 in 'Victorio Papers', NA, M666, Roll 526; See reports received of attacks on Huning and Connelly's property 27 and 29 Mar., 1880 in Letters Received by HQ DoNM Sept. 1865-Aug. 1890, NA, RG393, M1088, Roll 40, Jan.-Jun. 1880.

52 Loud to Hatch, Aleman, 27 Apr., 1880, Telegrams Sent DoNM, Vol.3, Jan.–Nov. 1880, NA, RG393, Part 3, Entry 431, pp339-340.

53 Pollack to AAAG, DoNM, 18 May, 1880 in Letters Received by HQ DoNM Sept. 1865-Aug. 1890, NA, RG393, M1088, Roll 40, Jan.-Jun. 1880.

Lt Thomas Cruse.
Though a damaged photograph it gives a reasonably clear image of Lt. Thomas Cruse, the tall thin officer sitting at the lower left of the picture. (Carlisle Barracks)

way to Silver City'.[54] It is more likely that they were two deserters from the Sixth Cavalry who were killed in very similar circumstances and at the same time. The two men were discovered by Lieutenant Cruse's detachment, and Surgeon MacPherson stated that they had:

> fought well considering they were armed only with pistols. We found their horses at least half a mile apart, but the men died together. One of them had eleven bullet holes in him and we trailed them half a mile by their blood.[55]

Hatch stated that two deserters from the Sixth Cavalry were killed after they had sold their weapons, and speculated that they might have been killed by Mexicans.[56] An anonymous letter dated Aleman, 5 April 1880, denouncing *Thirty-Four's* attacks on the troops also blamed Mexicans for killing the two deserters.[57] However. MacPherson described how the same Apaches had attacked a group of Mexicans on the same day, killing five of them and carrying off two children.[58]

---

54 Letter 2 Apr., 1880 in MacPherson Letters 1 Jan., 1879 to 3 Sept., 1880, University of Virginia at Charlottesville.
55 Ibid.
56 Hatch, Aleman to AAAG, SF, 4 Apr., 1880, 'DoNM/GSFO/L&T', NA, RG393, Part 3, Entry 475, Vol. 5, p.371.
57 *Thirty-Four*, 7 Apr., 1880.
58 Letter 2 Apr., 1880 in MacPherson Letters 1 Jan., 1879 to 3 Sept., 1880, University of Virginia at Charlottesville.

Lieutenant Cruse left a most vivid account of these two incidents[59]. In January 1880, he had been assigned to Lieutenant Gatewood's Apache scout company.[60] This detachment's supplies were carried by an accompanying mule train, which had a complement of mule packers and was guarded by a detachment of Sixth Cavalrymen. The company operated as follows: the Apache scouts would fan out and scour the countryside for Apaches, while the mule train and its defenders followed in the rear. Cruse makes it quite clear that he felt that these scout units were the most effective means of combating Apache raiders.[61] He also ascribes the Ninth Cavalry's travails in pursuing Victorio's warriors to their lack of such units.[62]

After leaving Hillsboro, the Apache scouts, under Gatewood and Cruse, linked up with one Captain Moore at Chase's Ranch, and the latter informed them of the destruction of a wagon train and its 20 emigrants by Nana's raiders.[63] Arriving at Las Palomas, Gatewood made contact with Captain McLellan, whose Sixth Cavalry detachment was camped at the small settlement of Cuchillo Negro.[64] McLellan asked Gatewood if he could verify a rumour that two Sixth Cavalrymen, George Allen and John Simmons,[65] who had deserted his command four days earlier, had been killed to the south of Las Palomas by the Apaches. Gatewood despatched Lieutenant Cruse with some Apache scouts to investigate.[66] Ten miles to the south of Las Palomas they encountered the remains of what Cruse referred to many years later as a large emigrant train.[67] (See document file no. 42.1.) They had been ambushed, just after they had climbed out of a deep arroyo (see Map 4.2), and had probably dropped their guard when the Apaches suddenly opened fire at virtually point blank range.

MacPherson also noted that efforts to combat Apaches raiding parties were hampered by false reports of their whereabouts. On 31 March, a Mexican sheepherder arrived at the camp and informed Lieutenant Cruse that he had seen four Apaches less than a mile away. Cruse, MacPherson and three Apaches scouts set out in pursuit, eventually cornering four Mexicans who had, in their turn, mistaken Cruse's party for Apaches. On their return to camp, Cruse and MacPherson, expressed their annoyance towards their source by confiscating two of his sheep, which proved a welcome addition to the officers' mess, on account of their having not had any meat rations for over a week.[68] On that basis, one wonders whether that particular shepherd would have considered his relations with the US army as much different from his relations with the Apaches.

Two Fifteenth Infantrymen on telegraph repair duty were posted missing, believed to have deserted. Private Norton was reported missing from La Mesilla, and Private Potter had been expected at El Paso. A description of the men and their equipment was circulated in the hope of

59 See Cruse, 1987, Chapter IV & V pp.46-73.

60 Cruse, 2001, p.262.

61 Cruse, 1987, p.54-55

62 Ibid, p.54

63 Ibid, 1987, p.67. No further details of Moore's unit are given by Cruse. It may be that the title was honorific dating back to service in the Civil War or earlier.

64 This appears to have been a small settlement founded in the 1850s near the mouth of the Cuchillo Negro River. (See Cuchillo Webpage Entry) However, Wilson states that the settlement was founded in 1871. (p.340) Gatewood seems to have contacted Capt. McLellan's detachment as it moved from Camp Ojo Caliente to Las Palomas.

65 Record of Events Mar. 1880 in Returns From Regular Army Cavalry Regiments 1833-1916, 6th Cavalry Regimental Returns 1875 to 1880, NA, M744, Roll 63; Laumbach, p.147.

66 Cruse, 1987, pp.67-68.

67 Ibid.

68 Letter 2 Apr., 1880 in MacPherson Letters 1 Jan., 1879 to 3 Sept., 1880, University of Virginia at Charlottesville.

their apprehension.[69] A third man, named Brickley, was posted as a deserter, having been reported seen in the company of these two men in La Mesilla on 30 March.[70] As we have seen, deserting was potentially a very dangerous activity; so it remains unclear whether these men had deserted, or been picked off by Apaches, or both.

Without naming the date, Hatch reports that, Mescalero Apaches killed one man in an attack near El Colorado.[71] Three men cutting hay near Ojo Caliente were also said to have been killed by Apaches.[72]

Further to the east, W.T. Shedd, of Shedd's Ranch, in the vicinity of San Augustine, reported a number of raids between the Organ Mountains and the Mescalero Reservation:

> Depredations committed in this vicinity, one man killed at the Cottonwoods Spring eight miles north from here at Mr Davis Sheep Camp, one horse taken and eight head of cattle at the same time. (David Woods with four men followed this trail north through San Andreas to the Embreo about sixty miles north from here) The miners at the Huera Mountains twenty [miles] east from here report Indians in that vicinity. Report of one man killed on the road between here and Tularosa [Tulerosa] three days since. The taking of five head of horse from here on the 23rd, also six head of horse from the adjoining Ranch on the same date. Trails of small bands passing to and from the Mescalero Reservation above and below this place are reported by nearly all parties coming in here. The herds of cattle owned by Woods and Read at San Nicholas are being rounded up and brought here for better protection. It is reported by parties that seem to be well informed that the Mescalero Indians are nearly all off the Reservation. Would it not be judicious to place a company of Cavalry here with a picket at San Nicholas to scout up and down the range and keep you informed of the movements any of the depredating bands in this vicinity. I feel more afraid of the Indians since they have broken up in small bands than when they were all together, when the military pursue them with some hope of success. I realize the difficulty of the military in subduing an enemy like the present one. I have been through the mile (as the saying is) in 69 and 70, when the San Augustine was the dread of the traveling public. If a company or picket is stationed here I will assist them every way I can in furnishing a guide whenever necessary to scout where they are unacquainted.[73]

Again while Shedd was clearly aware of the difficulties faced by the army, he was also a beneficiary of the army's logistics network, being one of the independent agents providing forage for army horses and mules. He would benefit financially from having such a company of cavalry stationed on his ranch if he exaggerated the extent of the raiding. Whether Shedd did so, or not, is unclear, but less than two weeks after he sent this letter, he was sacked as a forage agent for malpractice.[74] (See Chapter 5.)

69 Loud to CO Fort Bliss, 1 Apr., 1880, Telegrams Sent DoNM, Vol.3, Jan.–Nov. 1880, NA, RG393, Part 3, Entry 431, pp.271-272.

70 Loud to CO Fort Bayard, 3 Apr., 1880, Telegrams Sent DoNM, Vol.3, Jan.–Nov. 1880, NA, RG393, Part 3, Entry 431, p.278.

71 Hatch to AAAG SF, NA, RG393, Part 3, Entry 439, p.18; Hatch, Aleman, to AAG, SF, 4 Apr., 1880, 'DoNM/GSFO/L&T', NA, RG393, Part 3, Entry 475, Vol. 5, p.371.

72 'By Telegraph', the *Grant County Herald*, 27 Mar., 1880.

73 Shedd to Hatch, 25 Mar., 1880 in 'Victorio Papers', NA, M666, Roll 527.

74 Hatch to AAAG, DoNM, 6 Apr., 1880 in Letters Received by HQ DoNM Sept. 1865-Aug. 1890, NA, RG393, M1088, Roll 40, Jan.-Jun. 1880.

Plate 4.3. The burial site of the Mexicans killed by the Apaches to the south of Las Palomas. (Photo: Author)

Plate 4.4. One of the graves of the two Sixth Cavalry deserters killed by the same Apaches who killed the Mexicans, and were believed to have been led by Nana. (Photo: Author)

Long-Term Strategy vs Short-Term Response

The US army's response to this widespread raiding took the form of increased patrolling of the affected areas, and denial. Hatch believed that Victorio was still to the east and that having several detachments in the Rio Grande valley was more than enough to contain the Apaches.[75] He argued that many of these reports were exaggerations and that the whole country was in a panic over a few scattered raiding parties, clamouring for levels of protection the US army simply could not provide.[76]

Hatch's main concern was that his command should not be worn out in fruitless pursuit of real, but extremely mobile, Apache raiding parties; and he was adamant that his men and horses should not be wasted in pursuing figments of the local populace's imagination.[77] He was in the midst of planning a major operation, and he did not want his plans disrupted by the distractions posed by small bands of Apache raiders, no matter how distressing their activities might be for citizens. 'I don't wish anything to interfere with the general movement if it can be avoided.'[78]

By mid-March, Hatch's plans for an operation targeting the Mescalero reservation were advanced enough for him to inform Captain Steelhammer that troops under Grierson would be involved.[79] On 10 March, Hatch had requested the use of cavalry based in Texas.[80] In agreeing to his request, General Ord specified that while Texas troops were operating in New Mexico, he should be kept fully informed of their progress, and that they should have returned to Texas by 20 April 1880.[81]

Hatch also requested that troops from Arizona cover the area west of the Rio Grande, as his intended operation would result in many New Mexican troops being deployed to the east of that river.[82] In doing this, Carr was to ensure that such support did 'not unlock San Carlos' to Victorio.[83] Thus, Captain Daniel Madden with C Company, Sixth Cavalry, was sent into southern New Mexico to patrol the area between the Arizona line and the Rio Grande, while Hatch's troops were concentrating their efforts to the east.[84] Once arrived, they were tasked with patrolling the region encompassing Santa Barbara, Fort Cummings, McEvers' Ranch and Las Palomas.[85] (See Appendix 2.)

75 Hatch, San Jose, 26 Mar., 1880, 'DoNM/GSFO/L&T', NA, RG393, Part 3, Entry 475, Vol. 5, p.396; Hatch to AAAG SF, NA, RG393, Part 3, Entry 439, pp.27-29 This appears to be dated 26 March, 1880; It was noted in the Report of the Chief Signal Officer that the telegraph station at San Jose was used as an HQ by the District Commander that year. It was strategically situated as it lay three miles to the south and seven miles to the north of the two most popular trails across the Jornada used by Apache raiders. (Report of Chief Signal Operator in AR-WD, NA, M997, Roll 35, 1880 Vol. I-II, p.111).

76 Hatch to AAAG SF 26 Mar., 1880, NA, RG393, Part 3, Entry 439, p.28 & Hatch to AAAG SF 29 Mar., 1880, NA, RG393, Part 3, Entry 439, pp.33-34.

77 'DoNM/GSFO/L&T', NA, RG393, Part 3, Entry 475, Vol. 5, p.60.

78 Hatch, Palomas NM, 24 Mar., 1880, 'DoNM/GSFO/L&T', NA, RG393, Part 3, Entry 475, Vol. 5, p.400; See also Hatch, Fort Bayard to Willcox, Prescott, 18 Mar., 1880, NA, RG393, Part 1, Entry 235, pp.37-39.

79 Hatch, Fort Bayard, to Captain C. Steelhammer, 16 Mar., 1880, 'DoNM/GSFO/L&T', NA, RG393, Part 3, Entry 475, Vol. 5, pp.473-474.

80 Loud to AAG, Fort Leavenworth, 10 Jan., 1880, Telegrams Sent DoNM, Vol.3, Jan.–Nov. 1880, NA, RG393, Part 3, Entry 431, pp.208-209.

81 AAG Fort Leavenworth to AAAG, DoNM, 2 Apr., 1880 in Letters Received by HQ DoNM Sept. 1865-Aug. 1890, NA, RG393, M1088, Roll 40, Jan.-Jun. 1880; Loud to Hatch, Aleman, 5 Apr., 1880, Telegrams Sent DoNM, Vol.3, Jan.–Nov. 1880, NA, RG393, Part 3, Entry 431, p.282.

82 Martin to Carr, 25 Mar., 1880, NA, RG393, Part 1, Entry 169, Vol. 10, pp.124-125.

83 Martin to Carr, 27 Mar., 1880, NA, RG393, Part 1, Entry 169, Vol. 10, p.129.

84 Carr, Special Order No.6, 27 Mar., 1880, Special Orders Oct., 1879-Jan., 1881, DoAz, Vol. 1, NA, RG393, Part 1, Entry 239; Kerr AAAG Troops in SE Arizona, DoAz, NA, RG393, Part 1, Entry 232, Vol.5, 13 Dec., 1879-7 May, 1880, Letter No.103, p.97; Record of Events Apr. 1880 in Returns From Regular Army Cavalry Regiments 1833-1916, 6th Cavalry Regimental Returns 1875 to 1880, NA, M744, Roll 63.

85 Hatch, Aleman 5 Apr., 1880, 'DoNM/GSFO/L&T', NA, RG393, Part 3, Entry 475, Vol. 5, p.373; Report of Col E.A. Carr, 29 Aug., 1880.

Colonel Carr was willing to support Hatch and shared Hatch's view that Victorio should not be allowed to reach San Carlos. He was also worried that the recent arrival of Juh's followers at San Carlos might cause some problems. Some concern was expressed concerning apparent 'drunkenness and quarreling and dissatisfaction' amongst the recently arrived Chiricahuas on the San Carlos reservation, which might be the precursor to a breakout. Lieutenant Haskell thought that there was no danger of such a development, but Carr thought it was best to keep a close eye on the situation.[86] Lieutenant Blocksom was later ordered to move his detachment of Apache scouts and Sixth Cavalrymen to Camp Thomas. There he would be better placed to intercept any attempt by Victorio to reach San Carlos.[87] This was in response to rumours that Victorio was making for San Carlos;[88] but it would also place Blocksom in a good position to counter any move by the Chiricahua Apaches to leave San Carlos.

The widespread raiding in the Rio Grande Valley caused Hatch great concern that this might be the precursor of a general move west by Victorio. In fact, having safely established himself back in the US, and having successfully transported plunder taken in Mexico, principally to the Mescalero reservation, Victorio was now looking for fresh sources of loot to fund his war against the US and Mexico. The widespread raiding in the Rio Grande valley reflected a continued effort to gather material which could be traded for rifles and ammunition. So while Hatch may have been wrong to predict an imminent move to the west, he was correct in holding his main force in check until the intention of the enemy could be divined. For the moment, only small detachments of troops and Apache scouts were sent in pursuit of the raiders.

Unfortunately, as we have seen, such carefully thought-out inaction was not well-received by the New Mexican citizens or press. Indeed, when Estanislao Montoya sent word to Hooker that Apaches had stolen his horses, had crossed the Rio Grande, and were going towards the Mescalero reservation, Hooker allegedly responded that he could 'not arrange for their pursuit as he could neither divide his command nor move it.'[89] In fact, Hooker did send out a company from his battalion after the raiders,[90] but they were not quick enough to intercept them before they had moved into areas expressly forbidden to their pursuers. *We* know that Hooker was obeying orders to hold his command in readiness for future action; but this inaction led Montoya to assume that no protection was to be had from the US army. Montoya vented his frustration at Hooker's apparent refusal to break up his command to follow Apache raiders by contacting the Governor of New Mexico, expressing no confidence in the army. Instead he asked the Governor to provide arms and ammunition for, between 50 and 100 volunteers, who would endeavour to protect the citizens.[91]

Hatch allowed Hooker, who had become convinced that Victorio was in the San Mateo Mountains, to lead his men into those mountains. He felt that the imminent arrival of McLellan's company and Gatewood's Apache scouts could support Hooker's battalion if a large number of

86 Carr to AG DoAz, 25 Mar., 1880, Troops in SE Arizona, DoAz, NA, RG393, Part 1, Entry 232, Vol.5, 13 Dec., 1879-7 May, 1880, Letter No.100, pp.90-91.
87 Carr, Special Order No.7, 8 Apr., 1880, Special Orders Oct., 1879-Jan., 1881, DoAz, Vol. 1, NA, RG393, Part 1, Entry 239.
88 Carr to AG DoAz, 8 Apr., 1880, Troops in SE Arizona, DoAz, NA, RG393, Part 1, Entry 232, Vol.5, 13 Dec., 1879-7 May, 1880, Letter No.111, pp.101-102.
89 E. Montoya to Gov. Wallace, 23 Mar., 1880 in Letters Received by HQ DoNM Sept. 1865-Aug. 1890, NA, RG393, M1088, Roll 40, Jan.-Jun. 1880.
90 Hooker to Montoya, 17 Mar., 1880 in Letters Received by HQ DoNM Sept. 1865-Aug. 1890, NA, RG393, M1088, Roll 40, Jan.-Jun. 1880.
91 E Montoya to Wallace, 23 Mar., 1880 in 'Victorio Papers', NA, M666, Roll 526; E. Montoya to Gov. Wallace, 23 Mar., 1880 in Letters Received by HQ DoNM Sept. 1865-Aug. 1890, NA, RG393, M1088, Roll 40, Jan.-Jun. 1880.

Apaches were discovered.[92] For this reason, on 13 March, Captain McLellan's reinforced company of Sixth Cavalry was tasked with scouting the San Mateo Mountains.[93] McLellan established a base camp at Canada Alamosa and despatched his Apache scouts into the mountains. No recent signs of Apaches were found.[94] Yet, when Hooker then proposed to follow trails which led towards the San Andres Mountains, Hatch immediately forbade this manoeuvre and, on 17 March 1880, quickly re-deployed McLellan's detachment from Canada Alamosa to Ojo Caliente.[95] Hatch informed Hooker that the latter's intended move into the San Andres Mountains was premature and, 'as soon as we are prepared to move from the river, Carroll will move on the Indians from Stanton and by that time troops coming up from Texas will be in position.'[96] In forbidding this pursuit, Hatch implied that he wanted to wait for the arrival of Lieutenant Maney's additional company of Apache scouts, who were expected to arrive in the area around 28 March. Hatch needed accurate identification of Victorio's location, clearly arguing that US troops acting without Apache scouts would be unlikely to obtain this.[97] Hatch's sentiments about the nature of the terrain, and therefore the essential role of Apache scouts, was clearly underlined when he informed General Willcox that he was 'indebted' to him for the use of the Apache scouts.[98] Yet in response to some attacks, Hatch did send out troops to watch certain parts of the country, although without committing too many of the troops earmarked for his planned operation. On 16 March, he dispatched Lieutenant Gatewood from Fort Bayard to scout the region between Hillsboro, Chase's Ranch and Las Palomas.[99] We have already seen the vigorous scouting and similar pursuits undertaken by this officer's detachment. Around 20 March, Hatch also ordered Hooker to send one of his companies to Aleman, as the stage agent had reported that one of his drivers had been killed.[100] A patrol of one officer and 23 men of H Company, Ninth Cavalry, left Fort Bayard for field service on 19 March, returning on 27 March.[101] While no details of the route taken by this patrol have emerged, it would have had time to show itself to the settlements in the San Francisco valley and those along the Rio Mimbres, before returning to Bayard. On 23 March, Morrow was instructed to post a number of two-man dismounted escorts along the stage line between Fort Bayard and the Rio Grande.[102] Hatch also noted that the telegraph repairman based at Fort Cummings, a Fifteenth Infantryman, was unarmed, a situation he gave orders to rectify immediately.[103]

By 24 March, Lieutenant Gatewood's detachment of Apache scouts and Sixth Cavalrymen had been ordered to scout the Caballo Mountains.[104] Hatch noted that the detachment had been camped

92 Hatch, Fort Bayard , to Hooker, 12 Mar., 1880, 'DoNM/GSFO/L&T', NA, RG393, Part 3, Entry 475, Vol. 5, p.460; Hatch, Fort Bayard to Hooker, 16 Mar., 1880, 'DoNM/GSFO/L&T', NA, RG393, Part 3, Entry 475, Vol. 5, p.475.

93 'DoNM/GSFO/L&T', NA, RG393, Part 3, Entry 475, Vol. 5, p.60; McLellan to Post Adjutant, Fort Bowie, 16 May, 1880 in 'Victorio Papers', NA, M666, Roll 527.

94 Report of Capt. C.B. McLellan, 16 May, 1880.

95 Ibid.

96 'DoNM/GSFO/L&T', NA, RG393, Part 3, Entry 475, Vol. 5, pp.71-74.

97 'DoNM/GSFO/L&T', NA, RG393, Part 3, Entry 475, Vol. 5, pp.71-74; Hatch, Fort Cummings, to Hooker, Fort Craig, 22 Mar., 1880, 'DoNM/GSFO/L&T', NA, RG393, Part 3, Entry 475, Vol. 5, p.489.

98 Hatch, Bayard to Gen. O.B. Willcox, Prescott, 18 Mar., 1880, NA, RG393, Part 1, Entry 235, pp.38-39.

99 Special Field Order No.11, 16 Mar., 1880, Fort Bayard, 'DoNM/GSFO/L&T', NA, RG393, Part 3, Entry 475, Vol. 5, p.309.

100 'DoNM/GSFO/L&T', NA, RG393, Part 3, Entry 475, Vol. 5, p.86; See also Letter from Hatch dated 20 Mar., 1880 found between pages 29 & 30 in 'DoNM/GSFO/L&T', NA, RG393, Part 3, Entry 475, Vol. 5.

101 NA, RG 94, Entry 257 Vol. 896, Medical History, Fort Bayard NM May 1879, p.24.

102 Hatch, Fort Cummings, to Morrow, Fort Bayard, 23 Mar., 1880, Miscellaneous Records 1868-1889, NA, RG393, Part 3, Entry 453.

103 Ibid.

104 'DoNM/GSFO/L&T', NA, RG393, Part 3, Entry 475, Vol. 5, p.97 & 99.

'below Palomas to watch the pass they [the Apaches] will naturally take to get out. Gatewood will keep the trail ambushed with Indians during the day and use soldiers at night.'[105] This ambush was set up to catch the Apaches responsible for the killing of Captain Hooker's courier. The fact that Gatewood was now east of the Rio Grande suggests that he had either failed to find any trace of an attack on Wheeler's Ranch on 22 March, or had lost the trail of the raiders.

One NCO and nine enlisted men were sent from Fort Bliss to provide a guard on the mail line through the Jornada del Muerto. Four men, including the NCO, were stationed at Aleman, with the remainder split evenly between Point of Rocks and Round Mountain.[106] It had been decided that this detachment would be drawn from infantry or dismounted cavalrymen only.[107] In early April, Hatch instructed the Commanding Officer, Fort Bayard, to send some dismounted troopers to act as escorts for the stage line between Fort Cummings and Slocum's Ranch.[108] Captain Beyer was also instructed to maintain active patrols from his base at Hillsboro[109] as a show of force to deter the small parties of Apache raiders who had been active in the area.[110]

Most of this patrolling activity seems to have found plenty of trails left by the Apaches but produced little direct conflict.[111] Such tiny raiding parties proved almost impossible to counter, particularly when one also had to cope with the wild reporting of attacks, many of which proved to be false. On 24 March, Hatch had to again firmly remind Hooker not to use up his horses in futile pursuits of small bands of raiders into the Jornada del Muerto. Hatch argued that McLellan's company was of sufficient force to tackle these raiders.[112] He dismissed Hooker's report of Apaches in force as exaggerated, describing the Apaches responsible as a small scouting party of no more than a score of warriors.[113] He therefore ordered Hooker's battalion to protect the area around San Jose until 2 April, when the battalion was to move to Annaya Spring in preparation for 'active service in the field'.[114]

Yet even the reduced response deployed according to Hatch's orders had a negative effect on army logistics. By 26 March, Lieutenant Wright at Camp French was requesting the replacement of supplies recently issued to Gatewood's command.[115] The garrison of Fort Cummings ran dangerously low on ammunition, to the extent that they requested they be allowed to requisition munitions from a supply train destined for Fort Bayard.[116]

Lieutenant Cruse's narrative concerning the fate of the two Sixth Cavalry deserters raises two, related, issues of concern to the US army: first, low morale leading to increased desertion rates; and second, deserting soldiers as a potential source of weapons for the Apaches. As we have seen, the Apaches' main source of munitions was through illicit trade with some Mexican settlements in southern New Mexico. It should be noted that some Anglo-Americans living in these settlements were also more than happy to engage in such trade. This trade could be ascribed to the

105 Hatch, Palomas, NM, 24 Mar., 1880, 'DoNM/GSFO/L&T', NA, RG393, Part 3, Entry 475, Vol. 5, p.400.
106 This we believe to be the mountain now known as San Diego Peak.
107 Hatch to CO Fort Bliss, 31 Mar., 1880,Telegrams Sent DoNM, Vol.3, Jan.–Nov. 1880, NA, RG393, Part 3, Entry 431, p.277.
108 Hatch, Aleman, 1 Apr., 1880, 'DoNM/GSFO/L&T', NA, RG393, Part 3, Entry 475, Vol. 5, p.366.
109 Thus further suggesting that the location of Camp French was close to Hillsboro.
110 Hatch, Aleman to Captain Beyer Hillsboro, 2 Apr., 1880, 'DoNM/GSFO/L&T', NA, RG393, Part 3, Entry 475, Vol. 5, pp.366-367.
111 Hatch, Fort Cummings, to AAAG SF, 22 Mar., 1880, 'DoNM/GSFO/L&T', NA, RG393, Part 3, Entry 475, Vol. 5, p.484.
112 'DoNM/GSFO/L&T', NA, RG393, Part 3, Entry 475, Vol. 5, p.97.
113 Hatch, Palomas, NM, 24 Mar., 1880, 'DoNM/GSFO/L&T', NA, RG393, Part 3, Entry 475, Vol. 5, p.400.
114 'DoNM/GSFO/L&T', NA, RG393, Part 3, Entry 475, Vol. 5, pp.113-114.
115 Wright, Camp French to CO Fort Bayard, 26 Mar., 1880, Miscellaneous Records 1868-1889, NA, RG393, Part 3, Entry 453.
116 Smith, Paymaster, Fort Cummings to Morrow, Fort Bayard, 25 Mar., 1880, Miscellaneous Records 1868-1889, NA, RG393, Part 3, Entry 453.

Plate 4.5. The Caballo Mountains photographed from the south west. In an effort to intercept the Apaches who had killed Robert Kane, Hooker's courier, Apache scouts were sent to set up an ambush in these mountains. (Photo: Author)

Plate 4.6. Apache Canyon, probably the main pass through the Caballo Mountains, which was picketed by Gatewood's Apache scout company. (Photo: Author)

cordial relations Victorio's Warm Springs Apaches maintained with specific Mexican communities in southern New Mexico, Canada Alamosa being a prime example of a Mexican community which maintained trading contacts with Victorio's people. Las Palomas was another centre for the trading of illicit arms:

> One merchant in particular, a certain Juan Felano, did a booming business in cartridges and rifles when the military wasn't looking. Cartridges sold for a dollar a piece and a .45-55 carbine went for a hundred dollars. Mexican silver was the preferred item for exchange.[117]

The main source of guns and ammunition for Victorio was almost certainly through illicit trade networks on the Mescalero reservation. There appears to have been a brisk trade in stock stolen from both sides of the Mexican border on this reservation, and a lawlessness that revealed itself in the turmoil of the Lincoln County War and its aftermath during this same period.

However, Cruse's narrative shows that the two deserters, by selling their carbines and revolvers in Las Palomas had, in all probability, supplied these and at least 200 rounds of ammunition to the Apaches, the latter being the main customers for this trade. Thus the US army could find itself an unwitting commissariat for Victorio: witness the following telegram sent from Socorro NM by one Tilghman in 1880. 'There is a Negro soldier here now with horse & full equipment which he is trying to sell shall I have him arrested?'[118] A similar case occurred on 10 April 1880, in which Marshall Sherman from La Mesilla notified the army that another suspected deserter, a corporal from the Ninth Cavalry, had sold his carbine (number 40,952) at San Marical. The garrison of Fort Craig and the US Marshall were contacted and instructed to investigate this story and arrest the man and seize his horse and equipment if he turned out to be a deserter.[119] Later that month, from Albuquerque, Sherman reported that:

> Have in my possession govt carbine model eighteen seventy three no. eighteen thousand nine hundred twenty eight pawned here Apr fifteen by man in citizens clothing name P. Cady could this be one of the two deserters who sold govt horse mentioned in your dispatch I will hold gun till I hear from you.[120]

A sergeant and four men deserted from Captain Beyer's command at Camp French with horses and a full complement of arms and equipment on or around 17 April 1880. Fort Apache was alerted with a view to intercepting these men.[121] How many of these desertions resulted in arms sales to potentially hostile Apaches is difficult to determine. It was probably not a high figure in itself, but given the small number of Apaches involved in the Victorio War, the amount of government-issue weaponry that found its way into their hands may seem quite significant. It should be noted that the Ninth and Tenth Cavalry, on the whole, sustained far lower desertion rates in comparison to

117 Laumbach, p.161.

118 Tilghman to Loud AAAG SF, NA, RG393, Part 3, Entry 439, p.50.

119 Loud to Sherman, U.S. Marshall, Mesilla, 10 Apr., 1880; Loud to the NCO in Charge, Fort Craig, 10 Apr., 1880 and Loud to Mr Warden, Forage Agent, Fort Craig, 10 Apr., 1880, Telegrams Sent DoNM, Vol.3, Jan.–Nov. 1880, NA, RG393, Part 3, Entry 431, pp.297-298.

120 Sherman to Loud AAAG SF, NA, RG393, Part 3, Entry 439, pp.51-52; Loud to Lt Davenport AAAG in the field, Fort Craig & CO Fort Bayard, 29 Apr., 1880, Telegrams Sent DoNM, Vol.3, Jan.–Nov. 1880, NA, RG393, Part 3, Entry 431, p.346.

121 Loud to CO, Fort Apache, 17 Apr., 1880, Telegrams Sent DoNM, Vol.3, Jan.–Nov. 1880, NA, RG393, Part 3, Entry 431, pp310-311.) Towards the end of April, another supposed deserter was spotted passing Fort Craig. (Pease, Corpl, 15 Inf, to Operator Albuquerque, 30 Apr., 1880, Telegrams Sent DoNM, Vol.3, Jan.–Nov. 1880, NA, RG393, Part 3, Entry 431, p.350.

other US army formations stationed in the territories of New Mexico and Arizona. However, if we examine the Ninth Cavalry's desertion rates for 1879 to 1881, then the possibility that a dozen or so rifles, and ammunition for these, reached Victorio's followers is not outside the bounds of possibility. (See Figure 4.1.) If we examine the desertion rates for the Ninth and Sixth Cavalry Regiments and the Fifteenth Infantry Regiment for the years 1879 to 1881 (see Table 4.1), we see that even if only a fraction of these deserters sold their arms, or were picked off as they attempted to leave Apacheria, they could have provided a significant, if irregular, source of arms to the Apaches.

Considered today, Hatch's plan to conserve his forces for his main effort makes good sense. However, the increased activities of Apache raiders during March further undermined Hatch's already low standing with many citizens in southern New Mexico. Despite their small numbers, small parties of Apache warriors were paralysing economic activity over a vast area.

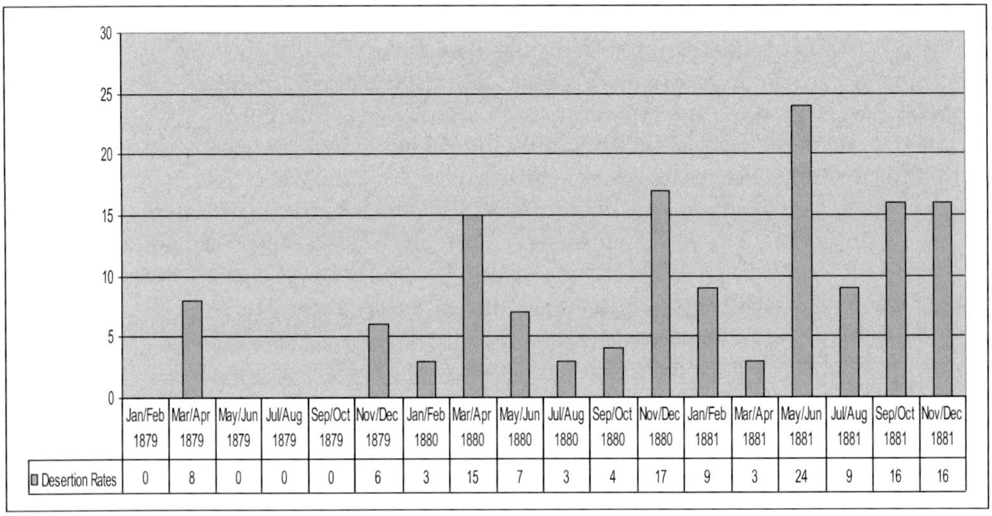

Figure 4.1 Ninth Cavalry, Desertion Rates, 1879–81.[122]

Table 4.1 Ninth and Sixth Cavalry and Fifteenth Infantry, Desertion Rates by Company, 1879–81.[123]

	A	B	C	D	E	F	G	H	I	K	L	M	Totals
1879													
Ninth	1	1	3	3	2	1	0	1	0	2	0	1	15
Sixth	2	5	21	9	9	11	6	9	10	4	6	9	101
Fifteenth	2	4	10	7	8	9	3	2	5	3	N/A	N/A	53
													169
1880													
Ninth	7	7	9	3	1	6	7	2	0	1	1	0	44
Sixth	6	13	11	8	5	10	10	7	8	6	9	8	101
Fifteenth	3	13	9	13	3	4	6	7	9	15	N/A	N/A	82
													227

122 Derived 9th Cavalry Bi-Monthly Company Muster Rolls 1879-1881: NA, RG94.

123 Derived from Returns From Regular Army Cavalry Regiments 1833-1916, 9th Cavalry 1873-1880 & 9th Cavalry 1881-1887, NA, M744, Roll 88 & 89: 6th Cavalry 1875-1880 & 6th Cavalry 1881-1887, NA, M744, Roll 63 & 64

	A	B	C	D	E	F	G	H	I	K	L	M	Totals
1881													
Ninth	5	2	10	5	14	12	10	3	6	4	3	7	81
Sixth	3	5	14	4	8	9	11	8	5	5	10	8	90
Fifteenth	13	3	4	4	7	12	17	8	8	5	N/A	N/A	81
													252

As time passed with no sign of the US army dealing with Victorio, the local media stirred up a storm of often unjustified and poisonous criticism:

> We are dreaming of a golden age – a future empire –and fifty dirty lousy Indians have us in a state of siege.[124]

This was but a fraction of the vitriol produced in the press.[125] (See document file no. 43.) For example, Hatch was accused of being paid to discourage immigration into the region.[126] He was also accused of effectively abandoning the territory and building supply camps, ignoring one of the most effective and, according to the newspapers, savage Apache leaders to have been let loose in New Mexico. (See document file no. 44.) This campaign of vilification was capped by the production of the 'Apache Chronicle' reproduced in the issue of *Thirty-Four* for 7 April 1880. This spoof journal claimed to be the official journal of 'General Victorio' and was supposedly a reply by the Apaches to the lies spread about their defeat by Colonel Hatch.[127] (See document file no. 45.) It was produced as a vehicle to accuse the US army in general, and Hatch in particular, of cowardice, incompetence, and lying to Washington concerning their inability to crush the Apaches. It also makes clear reference to Victorio's trading relations with Mexican settlements and individuals.

Not all of the newspapers were so hostile in their attitudes. The *Army & Navy Journal* reproduced a letter from a correspondent from Silver City to the *Philadelphia Times* in which both Morrow and his troops received high commendation. Indeed, the correspondent refers to the Ninth Cavalrymen as 'Buffalo Soldiers': a very rare contemporary usage of this term.[128] However, these positive reports were becoming the exception rather than the rule. More sober reflections tended to be drowned out by the clamour for more troops for a 'final solution'.

The press reports might have been exaggerated and poisonous, yet they pointed to a situation during March 1880 that the US army could not allow to continue. Something had to be done to defeat Victorio and his warriors. While unable to prevent the raiding in the Rio Grande valley, Hatch's command had been gearing up to strike at the Mescalero reservation, convinced that it provided Victorio's main source of arms, ammunition, supplies and recruits.

Moreover, as Hatch became increasingly convinced that Victorio was based in the San Andres Mountains, he began to formulate a plan for an offensive against the Apaches as a precursor to disarming the Mescalero Apaches. This involved a three-pronged attack that would culminate in a two-day engagement with Victorio in Hembrillo Canyon.

124 The *Grant County Herald*, 3 Apr., 1880; Ellis, p.276; Worcester, p.225 & Note 34 p357.
125 See Ellis, pp.276-277; See also Hart, p.44.
126 Ellis, p.277.
127 See also Ellis, pp.278-281 for a reproduction of the article.
128 'The Apache Campaign' *Army & Navy Journal*, Vol.17, 3 Apr., 1880, p.705.

5

The Battle of Hembrillo Canyon, April 1880

Toward the end of March, Colonel Hatch was ready to launch his offensive against the Warm Springs and Mescalero Apaches.

This operation was intended to unfold in two phases: an active operation in the field, centring on the San Andres Mountains; and once that manoeuvre was completed, a second phase disarming and dismounting the Mescalero Apaches by confronting them on their reservation. The first phase would involve the three battalions of New Mexico Troops, who would advance on the San Andres Mountains from different directions in an attempt to trap Victorio. The second phase would involve Hatch leading his three battalions across the White Sands and approaching the Mescalero reservation from the west. These troops would be joined in their endeavours by a Tenth Cavalry battalion, commanded by Colonel Grierson, which would approach the reservation from the south and east. All four battalions would converge on the reservation to dismount and disarm the Mescalero Apaches. As with many plans, even the best laid, this ambitious operation hit problems from the outset.

First, if we review the correspondence issued by the District of New Mexico prior to the first phase of the operation, this raises the suspicion that Hatch did not know the precise location of Victorio's camp in the San Andres Mountains. Indeed, it is clear that, for some time in March 1880, Hatch was unsure whether Victorio was based in the San Andres or the White Mountains. This suspicion is thoroughly reinforced by some of the orders issued, particularly those to Captain Hooker's Third Battalion of New Mexico Troops.

Second, the coordination of Hatch's three battalions broke down, a fact that is not highlighted in reports submitted after the event. This breakdown was inevitable, following a logistics failure which delayed the departure of the First Battalion. This battalion was directly under Hatch's control; but the delay was not transmitted to Captain Carroll, commanding the Second Battalion, and the latter battalion commenced field operations unaware that they were working to a timetable that was no longer valid.

The Quest for Victorio's Camp

On 23 February 1880, two of Victorio's men contacted Agent Russell and Captain Steelhammer, through Mescalero intermediaries, to discuss peace. The two Apaches did not want to speak to the US army and stated that Victorio was camped 60 miles away in the San Andres Mountains. They offered to talk directly to Russell and Steelhammer, if both men agreed to come out alone; but this was refused. The Apache emissaries then attempted to negotiate with Russell alone; but the agent did not wish to enter into any negotiations without authority from his superiors. These envoys remained in the vicinity for nearly two days then disappeared.[1] It is not clear from Steelhammer's report whether terms had been conveyed to the Warm Springs Apaches via the Mescalero Apaches; but he informed District Headquarters that he would have accepted Victorio's surrender under the following terms:

> the men to become prisoners of war to be fed as such by Military and to be deprived of all war material, ponies included, no promise of immunity for past offences but a return of tribe to Ojo Caliente to be recommended.[2]

In response to this approach, Hatch contacted Steelhammer and repeated his instructions (see previous chapter) that Steelhammer engage in negotiations, in order to hold Victorio in limbo until Hatch was ready to strike.

> Should Victorio come in he can surrender immediately. You can say to him I shall have his women and children at Ojo Caliente about the 1st of the month, and that I shall have soldiers and Indians enough to take him by the end of the month, it is only a question of time, when our preparations are completed. If he allows his people to kill women & children I will not protect his women & children from the people when at Ojo Caliente. You of course understand the object of talking with him, it is if possible to hold him quiet until we are ready. I shall be able on the last of the month to put one hundred Indian Scouts in the field and double the number of troops we have had out. Keep me posted in all Indian Affairs.[3]

Two prominent Mescalero chiefs, Ca-bal-le-so and San Juan, secured five-day passes from Russell on 3 and 8 March, 1880, respectively. Ostensibly Ca-bal-le-so had gone to contact Victorio and initiate peace negotiations, and San Juan had then gone to investigate Ca-bal-le-so's failure to re-appear after five days. On 16 March 1880, Russell acknowledged that 35 Apaches warriors had left to join Victorio.[4] However, Russell was convinced that only a small minority of Mescalero Apaches were inclined to join Victorio. He also reported the return of Ca-bal-le-so on the same day with a tentative peace proposal from Nana.[5] However, in his annual report for 1880, Russell states 'by the 1st of April, some two hundred to two hundred and fifty had left the reservation and gone to him [Victorio]; of this number fifty to sixty were men, and were of course of the worst Indians belonging to this agency.'[6]

Russell was not the only source that Hatch drew on to support his suspicions that Victorio was camped in the San Andres Mountains. We have already seen in the previous chapter that Hatch prevented Captain Hooker from leading his battalion, in pursuit of the Apaches, eastwards out of the San Mateo Mountains. By 18 March, Hatch was convinced that the Apaches were in the

---

1 Loud to General Hatch, Fort Bayard, 3 Mar., 1880, Telegrams Sent DoNM, Vol.3, Jan.-Nov. 1880 NA, RG393, Part 3, Entry 431, pp.183-186; See also 'By Telegraph', the *Grant County Herald*, 6 Mar., 1880; *Thirty-Four*, 3 Mar., 1880; Hatch, Fort Bayard, to Hooker, 'DoNM/GSFO/L&T', NA, RG393, Part 3, Entry 475, Vol. 5, p.460; Thrapp, 1974, p.266.

2 Loud to General Hatch, Fort Bayard, 3 Mar., 1880, Telegrams Sent DoNM, Vol.3, Jan.-Nov. 1880 NA, RG393, Part 3, Entry 431, pp.183-186.

3 Hatch to Captain Steelhammer, Mescalero Agency, 11 Mar., 1880, 'DoNM/GSFO/L&T', NA, RG393, Part 3, Entry 475, Vol. 5, p.458-459.

4 Loud to AAG Fort Leavenworth, 18 Mar., 1880, Telegrams Sent DoNM, Vol.3, Jan.-Nov. 1880 NA, RG393, Part 3, Entry 431, p.230; See also Thrapp, 1974, p.266; Laumbach, 2001, p.123.

5 Russell to CoIA, 27 Mar., 1880 in 'Victorio Papers', NA, M666, Roll 527; Thrapp, 1974, p.267.

6 Report of the CoIA. DoI, Office of Indian Affairs, (Hereafter referred to as the 'OIA'), Washington, 1 Nov., 1880, p.251.

San Andres Mountains.[7] However, by 21 March. 1880, he had drawn back from this conclusion, expressing only an 'impression'[8] that the Apaches were operating from the San Andres Mountains: 'I hope to get a fight out of him there.'[9] General Pope stated that scouts had located the Apaches in the San Andres Mountains on 26 March.[10] (See document file no. 46.) Whether the exact location of the camp was known, though, is unclear, for on 27 March, Hatch reported 'the main camp of the hostiles are now in the San Andres and White Mountains if fortunate to strike a blow there about the fourth of April matters will look better.'[11] By 31 March, Hatch stated that 'It is the impression the principal camp of the hostile Indians are in the San Andreas.'[12] Hatch clearly thought that it was important to defeat the Apaches in the field, as this would heavily incline them towards surrender.[13]

In fact, it turned out that Victorio was based in the Hembrillo Basin at the top of Hembrillo Canyon, on the eastern side of the San Andres, almost directly east from Aleman Well. Historian Karl Laumbach argues that Victorio's people had been camped there since the end of January.[14] A letter from Lieutenant Cruse stated that Apache scouts had only confirmed Victorio's location as being in the general vicinity of the Hembrillo Basin on 2 April 1880.[15] Yet Hatch's orders would suggest otherwise.

To elaborate on the argument that Hatch did not know the exact location of Victorio's base, we must first examine Hatch's plan to attack Victorio, and the details that were worked out in advance of the operation. The earliest version of this plan seems to have been formulated on 12 March 1880. At that point, the plan was that Hatch's forces should arrive at the Mescalero agency on 12 April 1880. However, Hatch also stated his intention to attack the Apaches during his move east from the Rio Grande towards the reservation 'for the moral effect it will have on the Mescaleros before going to Agency'.[16] (See document file no. 38.) However, Hatch only finalised the exact details on 5 April 1880, while at Aleman. (See Map 5.1.)

---

7 Hatch, Fort Bayard to AAAG SF, 18 Mar., 1880, 'DoNM/GSFO/L&T', NA, RG393, Part 3, Entry 475, Vol. 5, p.477. A few days prior to this Surgeon MacPherson vaguely noted that 'Victoria is on the other side of the journey of Death. (I have forgotten the Spanish name for it.)' (Letter 15 Mar., 1880 in MacPherson Letters 1 Jan., 1879 to 3 Sept., 1880, University of Virginia at Charlottesville).

8 Both letters were quite difficult to decipher.

9 Hatch, Fort Bayard, to AAAG SF, 12 Mar., 1880, 'DoNM/GSFO/L&T', NA, RG393, Part 3, Entry 475, Vol. 5, pp.461-462; 'DoNM/GSFO/L&T' NA, RG393, Part.3, Entry 475, Vol.5, pp.87-90.

10 Pope to Col. W.D. Whipple, AAG, Chicago, 26 Mar., 1880, NA, RG393, Part 1, Entry 2546, pp.353-356.

11 Hatch to AAAG SF 27 Mar., 1880, NA, RG393, Part 3, Entry 439, pp.30-31; See also Hatch to AAG, 27 Mar., 1880, 'DoNM/GSFO/L&T', NA, RG393, Part 3, Entry 475, Vol. 5, p.345; See also Loud to AAG, Fort Leavenworth, 29 Mar., 1880, Telegrams Sent DoNM, Vol.3, Jan.-Nov. 1880 NA, RG393, Part 3, Entry 431, p.258; Hatch to AAG, Fort Leavenworth, 27 Mar., 1880, 'Victorio Files', NA, RG393, M1495, Roll 14.

12 'DoNM/GSFO/L&T', NA, RG393, Part 3, Entry 475, Vol. 5, p.359.

13 Hatch, Fort Cummings, to AAAG SF, 22 Mar., 1880, 'DoNM/GSFO/L&T', NA, RG393, Part 3, Entry 475, Vol. 5, p.484; Loud to AAG Fort Leavenworth, 5 Apr., 1880, Telegrams Sent DoNM, Vol.3, Jan.-Nov. 1880 NA, RG393, Part 3, Entry 431, p.286.

14 Laumbach, 2001, p.122.

15 Laumbach, 2001, p.164; See also Cruse, 2001, p.263.

16 Hatch to AAAG SF 12 Mar., 1880, NA, RG393, Part 3, Entry 439, pp.41-44; See also Hatch, Fort Bayard, to AAAG SF, 12 Mar., 1880, 'DoNM/GSFO/L&T', NA, RG393, Part 3, Entry 475, Vol. 5, pp.461-462.

HEADQUARTERS DISTRICT OF NEW MEXICO
IN THE FIELD, ALEMAN, NEW MEXICO, April 5, 1880
SPECIAL FIELD ORDERS

NO. 18

1. The First Battalion New Mexico Troops will march in the following orders – Captain *McLellan* with his own Company ("L"), with detachments of 6th Cavalry and all Indian Scouts, will move to the San Andreas on the evening of the 6th instant as soon as it is dark enough to conceal the movement. He will report to the Battalion Commander for instructions.
2. All Companies of the 9th Cavalry present with the Battalion will move on the morning of the 7th instantly directly to the San Andreas, under direction of the Battalion Commander.
3. The Battalion will be rationed for ten days from the 5th instant. Owing to the condition of the pack animals, the command will move as light as possible, sending on train the supplies not required for the following ten days. The train will meet the command at Tulerosa on the 11th instant.
4. The Headquarters of the District Commander will be for the present with the First Battalion New Mexico Troops.
5. Under letter of instructions of April 4, 1880, from this office, the Third Battalion New Mexico Troops, under command of Captain *A.E. Hooker*, 9th Cavalry, will move on the 6th instant from Annaya Springs to Malpais Spring and cover west side of San Andreas Mountains.
6. Under letter of instructions of March 31, 1880, from this office, the Second Battalion New Mexico Troops, under command of Captain *Henry Carroll*, 9th Cavalry, will move on the 4th instant, up the east side of the San Andreas Mountains.

By command of Colonel HATCH
THOMAS C. DAVENPORT
First Lieutenant 9th Cavalry,
A.A.A. General in the field.[17]

The impression that the detail of this plan was not finalised until 5 April 1880 is reinforced by the fact that, by 4 April, Hooker's battalion was still not complete, Hatch having to order Captain Parker, with K Company, Ninth Cavalry, to move from Aleman, on 5 April, to join the Third Battalion.[18] The fact that the orders to proceed from Annaya Springs to Malpais Springs, issued to the Third Battalion of New Mexico troops, as noted above, were not changed from the orders issued on 4 April, shows that Hatch did not know the approximate, let alone the exact, location of Victorio's camp. Why else instruct this battalion to manoeuvre 25 miles from Hembrillo Canyon? Hatch's specific orders to Hooker also betray the fact that the Colonel did not know the location of Victorio's camp prior to launching his operation. It was only in hindsight that such knowledge was claimed. When Hatch wrote a summary of this operation on 5 August 1880, he claimed that:

17 Special Field Orders No.18, Aleman, New Mexico, 5 Apr., 1880 in 'Victorio Papers', M666. Roll 526; see also RG393, Part 3, Entry 450.
18 Special Field Order No.17 para.3, In the Field Aleman, N.M., 4 Apr., 1880, NA, RG393, Part.3, Entry 450.

> Hooker, 9th Cavalry, with one hundred men was sent by Anaya Springs to go through the pass of the northern point of the San Andreas and come down on the East side of those mountains[19]

Yet prior to the commencing of this operation, On 4 April, from Aleman,[20] Hatch issued orders to Hooker that he should march:

> from Annaya Springs to Malpais Spring on the road to Tularosa [Tulerosa]. At Malpais Springs (dispose?) of your force to cover the north side of the San Andreas Mountains. It is probable that you will find camp of hostile Indians in that vicinity.[21]

On the following day, in Special Field Orders, Number 18, Hatch instructed Hooker to 'cover west side of San Andreas Mountains.'[22] So, immediately prior to the operation, Hooker's Third battalion was given two different parts of the San Andres Mountains to cover, yet both sets of orders instructed Hooker to march from Annaya Springs to Malpais Springs. If Map 5.1 is examined, it would appear rather difficult for Hooker to cover either the north or west side of the San Andres Mountains from Malpais Spring. This suggests that Hatch was not at all familiar with the local geography. It was not until months after this operation that Hatch dropped the instruction to march to Malpais Spring, and changed his instructions to cover the east side of the San Andres Mountains. By that time he knew how the operation had unfolded, and he changed his instructions to give the impression that the location of Victorio's camp had been known before the operation.

It should also be noted that Hatch advised Hooker that he would 'probably' find an Indian camp on the north side of the San Andres Mountains. This shows that, up to the beginning of his offensive, Hatch was not remotely aware of an exact location of Victorio's camp. It also shows that Hatch was not averse to re-writing history. This was one of the key accusations already being levelled at him by some of the territorial press.

However, this was not the only problem with the coordination of the three battalions. It was also a fact that Hatch was unable to communicate delays in the proposed timetable for this operation to the Second Battalion of New Mexico troops, under the command of Captain Carroll.

Too Early or Too Late? Communication Breakdown between Colonel Hatch and his Second Battalion

On 20 March 1880, Captain Carroll was ordered to take the Second Battalion, New Mexico Troops, to Tulerosa as soon as it was ready for field service. He was to take 30 days' rations and use wagon transportation where possible, saving his pack mules for use in rough terrain.[23] (See document file no. 48.) These orders were relayed from Hatch to the telegraph operator at La Mesilla, and

19 Hatch to AAG, DoM, Fort Leavenworth, 5 Aug., 1880 in Letters Sent by '9MD/DNM/DoNM', NA, RG393, M1072, Roll 6, Jan. 1880-Aug. 1881, Letter No.407, pp.260-268; See also Report of Capt. C.B. McLellan, 16 May, 1880.

20 Hatch seems to have arrived there on 31 Mar. in advance of the 1 Battalion. (NA, RG393, Part.3, Entry 475, Vol.5, pp.113-114).

21 'DoNM/GSFO/L&T', NA, RG393, Part.3, Entry 475, Vol.5, pp.126-127.

22 Special Field Orders No.18, Aleman, New Mexico, 5 Apr., 1880 in 'Victorio Papers', NA, M666, Roll 526; See also 'DoNM/GSFO/L&T', NA, RG393, Part 3, Entry 475, Vol. 5, pp.320-321; NA, RG393, Part 3, Entry 450.

23 Letter found between pages 29 & 30 'DoNM/GSFO/L&T', NA, RG393, Part 3, Entry 475, Vol. 5.

thence to Carroll via courier, a procedure that would take about three days[24] These couriers had to cross territory known to present a high risk of encounters with Apaches. It should also be noted that the telegraph line was not necessarily in full working order, as the work required to bring the lines into full working order, as outlined by Lieutenant Allen on 2 December 1879, was not completed until 13 April 1880.[25] The quality of individual repairmen could also leave much to be desired: on 9 April 1880, one Private Michael McMahon was reported to have been drunk when on duty as a telegraph repairman.[26]

On 23 March 1880, Hatch informed District Headquarters that he hoped to commence his operation on 31 March.[27] On 2 April, he stated his intention to set out on the following day for the San Andres Mountains, where most of the Apaches were thought to be hiding.[28] Two days later (4 April 1880), Hatch informed Hooker that:

> Captain Carroll commanding 2nd Battalion is instructed to operate also [in the vicinity?] 1st Battalion with Indians ?????? move from this point on the 6th and will be on the San Andreas Mountains on the night of the 6th.[29]

However, an exhaustive search through the archives reveals no such instruction being sent to Captain Carroll, and once again Special Field Order Number 18 (written on 5 April 1880) strongly suggests that Carroll was not aware of these instructions. It states that Carroll was acting under 'letter of instruction' issued on 31 March 1880.[30] These instructions are worth quoting:

24 Loud, to Martin AAG Whipple Barracks, Arizona, 17 Apr., 1880, Telegrams Sent DoNM, Vol.3, Jan.-Nov. 1880 NA, RG393, Part 3, Entry 431, p.314. During mid-April, District HQ noted that telegraphic communications to Col. Hatch, who was then supervising the dismounting and disarming of the Mescalero Apaches (see next chapter), had to be sent to the operator at La Mesilla and then forwarded by courier to Tulerosa. (Loud to General Hatch, Tulerosa, 12 Apr., 1880, Telegrams Sent DoNM, Vol.3, Jan.-Nov. 1880 NA, RG393, Part 3, Entry 431, pp.303-303)

25 Lt. Allen to AAAG DoNM, 2 Dec., 1879 in Letters Received by HQ DoNM Sept. 1865-Aug. 1890, NA, RG393, M1088, Roll 39, Oct.-Dec. 1879; Allen, Signals Officer, New Mexico Division to AAAG, DoNM, 13 Apr., 1880 in Letters Received by HQ DoNM Sept. 1865-Aug. 1890, NA, RG393, M1088, Roll 40, Jan.-Jun. 1880. See also Watt, 'I Will Not Surrender the Hair of a Horse's Tail: The Victorio Campaign 1879', Chapter 13, p.303.

26 Allen, to AAAG, DoNM, 9 Apr., 1880 in Letters Received by HQ DoNM Sept. 1865-Aug. 1890, NA, RG393, M1088, Roll 40, Jan.-Jun. 1880.

27 Loud to AAG, Fort Leavenworth, 23 Mar., 1880, Telegrams Sent DoNM, Vol.3, Jan.-Nov. 1880 NA, RG393, Part 3, Entry 431, pp.237-238.

28 Loud to AAG Fort Leavenworth, 2 Apr., 1880, Telegrams Sent DoNM, Vol.3, Jan.-Nov. 1880 NA, RG393, Part 3, Entry 431, p.272.

29 Hatch to Hooker, 4 Apr., 1880, in 'DoNM/GSFO/L&T', NA, RG393, Part.3, Entry 475, Vol.5, pp.126-127.

30 Special Field Orders No.18, Aleman, New Mexico, 5 Apr., 1880 in 'Victorio Papers', M666. Roll 526; see also RG393, Part 3, Entry 450.

Hatch to Capt. Carroll, Ninth Cavalry Tulerosa, March 31, 1880.
(Operator Mesilla will forward by first mail[31])

It is the impression the principal camp of the hostile Indians are in the San Andreas, we shall move from here on the third, with Morrow's command, Sixth Cavalry and Indians. Hooker's Battalion in the mountains around Alamo Spring. You may be able to strike on the fourth. You should move upon the east side on the fourth to strike. Also if possible from San Andreas shall go to Reservation.
Hatch.[32]

Hatch to Captain H. Carroll, Ninth Cavalry, March 31, 1880.

... hope to strike them about the fourth or fifth [April] I have telegraphed you to come up on the east side of the mountains about the place of your last fight. [Hospital Canyon?] On the 4th Hooker will move through the pass above probably known as the Aleman [Alamo?] I shall take Morrows command, the Indians and Arizona troops directly to the camp. After that proceed to the Agency. You will not want to leave Tulerosa with more than five days forage.[33]

The above orders would strongly indicate that, if he was acting under letters of instruction, Carroll would be under the impression that Hatch intended to strike the Apaches no later than 5 April 1880. In Special Order 18, in which Hatch stated that some of his forces would move into the San Andres Mountains on the night of 6 April, with the rest moving in on the following day, he implied that Captain Carroll was aware of his latest orders. Yet it is clear that these do not match the instructions actually issued in letters to Carroll dated 31 March 1880. As we shall see later, the dramatic events involving Captain Carroll's battalion did not happen, as Hatch tried to suggest, because Captain Carroll engaged the Apaches in Hembrillo Canyon *too early*. They happened because Carroll thought he was *too late*. Indeed, by 26 June 1880, at least two New Mexican newspapers had published a garbled but recognisable version of events that echoes this interpretation.

Captain Carroll, the wounded officer who passed through Las Vegas last Saturday, owes his disablement and the killing of eight of his men to the carelessness and incompetency of General Hatch, who ordered him to be at a certain point on the 4th of May [April] when he would meet other troops. In order to reach the point in time, two night marches had to be made, and, upon reaching there, Captain Carroll and his soldiers met a hot reception from the Indians, who outnumbered them two to one. It was almost a miracle that the entire command were not murdered and scalped. It was afterwards learned that Gen. Hatch HAD MADE A MISTAKE, ordering Captain Carroll to be at the place designated two days before the rest of the troops. *Daily Optic*.[34]

31 Just how reliable this mail service was under the circumstances can be derived from the fact that Hatch had to detail small detachments of Infantry from Fort Bliss, with 30 days rations to protect the mail route across the Jornada on the very same date as these orders were issued. These were made up of one NCO and three privates based at Point of Rocks, Aleman and Round Mountain. (Hatch, Aleman, to CO, Fort Bliss TX, 31 Mar., 1880, 'DoNM/GSFO/L&T', NA, RG393, Part 3, Entry 475, Vol. 5, p.357).

32 'DoNM/GSFO/L&T', NA, RG393, Part 3, Entry 475, Vol. 5, p.359.

33 'DoNM/GSFO/L&T', NA, RG393, Part 3, Entry 475, Vol.5, p.117.

34 Cited in 'Town and County', the *Grant County Herald*, 26 Jun., 1880.

Problems with Logistics

While the *Grant County Herald* may be accurate in its report of the events that took place, the reason it gives for the delay in the timetable – that it was a mistake, the implication being that Hatch was an incompetent commander – was not accurate. Rather, the delay was the result of a number of unforeseen logistical difficulties. District Headquarters reported that:

> he [Hatch] is crippled in not having sufficient transportation now, that it is badly worn from its hard work during the winter, and the contractors have failed to deliver supplies in any reasonable time. Grain is very scarce.[35]

Prior to the operation, Captain Carroll himself reported that he was still trying to gather some 25 mounts for D and F Companies. He expected to lead 150 men out and would 'move in three days'.[36] Carroll also anticipated that he could expect high horse casualties 'if work proves severe'.[37]

Hatch was also experiencing significant difficulties in coordinating grain supplies for his horses in the two weeks prior to the Hembrillo Canyon operation,[38] writing that he was 'crucified not having efficient transportation' to move forage and other supplies, and that he had insufficient horses to mount all his troops.[39] It was reported, on 31 March, that Hatch had instructed the forage agents at San Augustin and South Fork (Mescalero reservation) to have on hand enough forage for 200 horses at the former and 10 days' worth of forage for 600 horses at the latter.[40] On 6 April, Hatch, from Aleman, issued instructions that Shedd, whose ranch was located on the eastern side of the San Augustin Pass, should have his appointment as forage agent terminated for 'improper practice'.[41] What this impropriety may have been is not specified. It should be noted that Shedd's Ranch was to the south and east of Aleman, on the eastern side of San Augustin Pass, so is almost certain that Shedd was the forage agent, referred to above, at San Augustin. Shedd may have been unable to supply forage as contracted; or he may have attempted to charge an exorbitant fee for his goods, knowing that he had a captive market; or he may have been guilty on both counts. Indeed, in the immediate aftermath of the Hembrillo Canyon operation, Hatch noted and condemned the extortionate price charged for grain in New Mexico since 1 January 1880. He even appears to have gone so far as to attempt to impose a set price for grain,[42] in response to the price of fodder being deliberately inflated by local civilians indulging in what might be called war-profiteering.[43]

It is worth noting that an application to become a forage agent submitted in April 1880 by George Williams of Williams' Ranch on the San Francisco River promised that, as agent, he would 'keep good Hay & Grain on hand at all times for any troops that may need it'.[44]

---

35 Loud to AAG Fort Leavenworth, 23 Mar., 1880, Telegrams Sent DoNM, Vol.3, Jan.-Nov. 1880 NA, RG393, Part 3, Entry 431, pp.239-240.
36 Carroll to Hatch 26 Mar., 1880 in 'Victorio Papers', NA, M666, Roll 527; Laumbach, 2001, p.164
37 Carroll to Hatch 26 Mar., 1880 in 'Victorio Papers', NA, M666, Roll 527.
38 'DoNM/GSFO/L&T', NA, RG393, Part 3, Entry 475 Vol. 5, pp.118-121 & p.136.
39 Hatch, Fort Cummings, 23 Mar., 1880, 'DoNM/GSFO/L&T', NA, RG393, Part 3, Entry 475, Vol. 5, p.496
40 *Thirty-Four*, 31 Mar., 1880.
41 Hatch to AAAG, DoNM, 6 Apr., 1880 in Letters Received by HQ DoNM Sept. 1865-Aug. 1890, NA, RG393, M1088, Roll 40, Jan.-Jun. 1880.
42 'DoNM/GSFO/L&T', NA, RG393, Part 3, Entry 475 Vol. 5, pp.138-139.
43 Hatch, Aleman to AAG, SF, 4 Apr., 1880, 'DoNM/GSFO/L&T', NA, RG393, Part 3, Entry 475, Vol. 5, p.372.
44 George Williams to Chief Quartermaster, DoNM, 17 Apr., 1880 in Letters Received by HQ DoNM Sept. 1865-Aug. 1890, NA, RG393, M1088, Roll 40, Jan.-Jun. 1880.

Hatch also experienced some difficulties getting the US army to furnish him with sufficient military supplies to fully equip his men prior to the Hembrillo Canyon battle. A letter from Headquarters, Division of the Missouri, authorising the purchase of 150 mules for service in New Mexico was issued on 29 March, one day after Hatch had originally intended to start his operation against the Apaches.[45] On 7 April 1880, the Chief Quartermaster, District of New Mexico, noting the authorisation to purchase these mules, contacted Hatch asking for instructions as to where the mules were to be sent once purchased.[46] Hatch also ordered 200 canteens to be shipped to Fort Stanton for urgent use by the Ninth Cavalry. If these were not available, Hatch authorised local purchase if that proved possible.[47] Two hundred canteens and straps were shipped from Fort Union to Santa Fé 'for immediate use of Troops in the field'.[48] These were to be shipped on the night of 6 April 1880.[49] On arrival at Santa Fé they were to be sent to Fort Stanton by wagon as soon as possible.[50] The canteens still had not arrived at Santa Fé by 9 April, prompting Loud, Acting Assistant Adjutant General, District of New Mexico, to contact the Fort Union Depot and remind them that this equipment was urgently needed for field service and that such delays were a serious matter.[51]

The canteens were a late requisition from Hatch (5 April 1880) and, as we shall see, this was probably prompted by problems with the water supply at Aleman. It is not certain when the additional mules were requested, but what is clear is that these mules were not delivered in time for Hatch's intended operation.

Hatch's proposed offensive was in trouble before it started, due to a combination of a lack of intelligence concerning the location of the Apaches, difficulties concerning the effective coordination of his three battalions, and logistic problems. These factors must be borne in mind when one studies the progress and outcome of the Hembrillo Canyon operation.

The Hembrillo Canyon Operation

The easiest starting point is to account for each battalion in reverse numerical order. Captain Hooker's Third Battalion marched via Round Mountain, Malpais Springs, Tulerosa and on to the Mescalero reservation.[52] Whatever instructions he had actually received, Hooker's command did not encounter any Apaches, underlining the fact that Hatch did not know the exact location of Victorio's camp. At first glance, Hooker's lack of Indian scouts may have contributed to this failure. His Navajo scouts supposedly deserted on 12 March 1880, with all their government–issue

45 Townsend, AG, to Commanding General, MDoM, Chicago, 29 Mar., 1880, NA, RG393, Part 1, Entry 2546, p.358.

46 Chief QM DoNM to AAAG, DoNM, 7 Apr., 1880 in Letters Received by HQ DoNM Sept. 1865-Aug. 1890, NA, RG393, M1088, Roll 40, Jan.-Jun. 1880.

47 Hatch, Aleman to AAG, DoNM, 5 Apr., 1880 in Letters Received by HQ DoNM Sept. 1865-Aug. 1890, NA, RG393, M1088, Roll 40, Jan.-Jun. 1880.

48 Loud to Capt. Shoemaker, Fort Union Arsenal, 6 Apr., 1880, Telegrams Sent DoNM, Vol.3, Jan.-Nov. 1880 NA, RG393, Part 3, Entry 431, p.288. Half were to be delivered to Lt Maney, in charge of Indian scouts, and the rest to the CO, Fort Stanton.

49 Loud to Depot Quartermaster, Fort Union, 5 Apr., 1880, Telegrams Sent DoNM, Vol.3, Jan.-Nov. 1880 NA, RG393, Part 3, Entry 431, p.288.

50 Loud to Hatch, Aleman, 6 Apr., 1880, Telegrams Sent DoNM, Vol.3, Jan.-Nov. 1880 NA, RG393, Part 3, Entry 431, p.289 & 290.

51 Loud to Capt Hunt, Depot Q.M., Fort Union, 9 Apr., 1880, Telegrams Sent DoNM, Vol.3, Jan.-Nov. 1880 NA, RG393, Part 3, Entry 431, p.196.

52 Bi-Monthly Company Muster Rolls for Company K, 9th Cavalry, Mar./Apr. 1880 in NA, RG94.

equipment, because they had become 'frightened'.[53] The reported desertion seems unlikely, however, given that there is evidence that the Navajo scouts were formally discharged at Fort Wingate on or around 22 March 1880.[54] Moreover, as noted in Chapter 3, instructions had been issued to discharge these scouts in order that additional Apache scouts could be recruited in their stead. Nevertheless Hatch and District Headquarters transmitted this story, though quite why they did so is not clear.[55] It certainly failed to convince the *Grant County Herald*. Such a charge was interpreted as an unjustified attempt to scapegoat the scouts and distract attention for other serious failings in the US army's conduct of the campaign.[56]

The experience of the Second Battalion of New Mexico Troops was very different to that of the Third. A number of sources state that Carroll's battalion was made up of approximately 100 troopers drawn from A, D, F and G Companies of the Ninth Cavalry.[57] Laumbach states that Carroll actually had 155 men with him when he left Fort Stanton.[58] If we examine the monthly regimental return for the end of March 1880, the Second Battalion of New Mexico Troops could provide mounts for 147 of its available men.

Table 5.1 Second Battalion, New Mexico Troops, Available Men to Serviceable Horses, March 1880.[59]

Second Battalion, New Mexico Troops, March 1880				
Company	**Available Men**	**Serviceable Horses**	**Unserviceable**	**Lost Horses**
A	49	42	9	0
D	45	25	23	6
F	45	33	5	0
G	58	47	4	0
Totals	197	147	41	6

This would certainly suggest that Laumbach's figure is the more accurate of the two, especially since Carroll's command was accompanied by water wagons, which could be escorted by a small number of dismounted men. These wagons were to keep pace with the Second Battalion by moving

53 Hatch, Fort Bayard, to AAAG SF, 12 Mar., 1880, 'DoNM/GSFO/L&T', NA, RG393, Part 3, Entry 475, Vol. 5, p.464; Loud to CO Fort Wingate, 13 Mar., 1880 in Letters Sent by '9MD/DNM/DoNM', NA, RG393, M1072, Roll 6, Jan. 1880-Aug. 1881, Letter No.146, p.108.

54 Bennett, CO Fort Wingate to AAAG, DoNM, 22 Mar., 1880 in Letters Received by HQ DoNM Sept. 1865-Aug. 1890, NA, RG393, M1088, Roll 40, Jan.-Jun. 1880.

55 See Hatch to AAG, DoM, Fort Leavenworth, 5 Aug., 1880 in Letters Sent by '9MD/DNM/DoNM', NA, RG393, M1072, Roll 6, Jan. 1880-Aug. 1881, Letter No.407, pp.260-268; 'Indian Affairs' *Army & Navy Journal,* Vol.17, 27 Mar., 1880, p.693.

56 'Victorio!', the *Grant County Herald*, 3 Apr., 1880.

57 Leckie, 1967, p.216; Thrapp, 1967, p.194; 1974, p.269; Billington, 1991, p.94; Utley, 1973, p.361; see also map in Thrapp, 1967, p.191. It should be noted that while this map shows Carroll moving down the west side of the San Andres Mountains, he actually marched down the eastern face of these mountains. Thrapp, in his later work on Victorio makes this clear. (Thrapp, 1974, p.268; see also note 4 p.369 of the same volume) Moreover, in the Public Affairs Office: White Sands Missile Range web page entitled 'Hembrillo Battlefield' it states that Carroll arrived in Hembrillo Canyon via Sulphur Canyon which is clearly marked on Thrapp's original map. Again this would indicate an approach from the eastern side of the San Andres Mountains.

58 Laumbach, 2001, p.170.

59 Derived from Returns From Regular Army Cavalry Regiments 1833-1916, 9th Cavalry 1873-1880, NA, M744, Roll 88

down the eastern edge of the San Andres Mountains. This is made clear in a letter from Lieutenant Finley written on 14 April 1880:

> The reason I was not in the last fight was that I had been appointed Asst. Quartermaster for the Battalion and had to stay with the train. I had two wagons loaded with water barrels and I camped out on the plain, three miles from the mountains in which the fight took place.[60] (See document file no. 50.1)

Lt. Walter Finley.
This is one of the few contemporary photographs of a participant in the Victorio campaign and, while smarter in appearance than Gatewood and Mills in Photograph 2 of this volume, this does give a good idea of the field service dress of a junior US Army officer. It was Finley's letter to his mother just after the Hembrillo Canyon which suggested to Karl Laumbach that the 'poisoned water' version of this battle should be challenged. (Fray Angelico Library)

The District of New Mexico included at least six[61] water wagons in its November 1880 listing of transportation allocated to specific posts.[62] They were essential equipment for this area of New Mexico, as it had suffered a period of drought since at least March 1879.[63] Even if there had been water available, a Table of Distances produced for the troops in New Mexico in 1878 stated that the waterholes were usually slightly alkaline, but could be much worse along the routes between Fort Stanton and Forts McRae and Craig (Route 21) and Fort Stanton and Fort Selden (Route 22). (See document file no. 50.2.) In other words, the water sources along these routes between the Sacramento Mountains and the San Andres Mountains were already known to contain water that was alkaline to varying degrees. Finally, Hatch notified Hooker, on 4 April, 'It is not probable there is any water between Annaya Springs & Malpais Spring at this ?????? if so it will be necessary to make

60 Letter dated Tularosa [Tulerosa] N.M., 18 Apr., 1880 in The Walter Lowry Finley Collection; Laumbach, 2001, p.174.

61 *Mea Culpa!* Of course I managed to miss out Fort Stanton's allocation by misaligning the photocopy. Something to avoid if one is based in Britain.

62 General Orders No.11. DoNM, 20 Nov., 1880 in General Orders, Circulars & Court Martial Orders 1870-1881, DoAz & DoNM NA, RG393, Part 1, Entry 183.

63 General Pope informed his superiors, in September, 1880, that an eighteen month drought had forced sheep herders to scatter their flocks across a wider area thus making them a tempting target as a source of subsistence for the Apaches. This information had officially come from a report submitted by Col. Hatch in May 1880. (Report of General John Pope, 22 Sept., 1880 in AR-WD, NA, M997, Roll 35, 1880 Vol. I-II, p.86; Hatch to AAG Dept. HQ, 26 May, 1880 in DoNM/GSFO/L&T, NA, RG393, Entry 475, Vol. 5, p.273). In fact Hatch had informed Pope of the drought on 4 March 1880: 'Never was there a season so bad as the present for operating last year was so dry the grass has nearly disappeared and it is almost impossible to subsist our animals.' (Hatch to Pope, in Letters Received, DoM 1868-98, RG 393, Entry A1-1 2601, Box 88)

a dry camp.'[64] The implication is that Hatch had also warned Hooker that he should make sure that his battalion was carrying enough water to complete the operation. As each battalion was operating in the same area, it would seem safe to assume that Carroll had been given the same instructions. Lieutenant Finley's letter confirms that Carroll's battalion was operating with water wagons.

However, before we cover the skirmishes and battles which took place between 5 and 7 April 1880, it is essential to note that modern battlefield archaeology has made a key contribution to our understanding of events in this chapter.[65] Due to its remote nature and the fact that it was on Department of Defense Land, this battlefield has been left virtually undisturbed. Using Cruse's memoirs, a team of archaeologists from Human Systems Research Inc. and New Mexico State University, led by Karl Laumbach, were able to discover and survey the site of the Hembrillo Canyon battle of 6–7 April 1880. They unearthed a wealth of artefacts, including temporary breastworks, spent bullets and cartridge cases. Using the same search techniques as used in surveying the Little Bighorn battle site, they set about mapping the exact locations of all the artefacts they could locate.[66] Once they had pinpointed the approximate location of the battle, they then thoroughly surveyed the site, producing a three-dimensional computer map of the area. Laumbach later carried out a comprehensive survey of Conline's skirmish of 5 April 1880, which occurred some distance down Hembrillo Canyon. As we shall see, these surveys reveal some very interesting details about both battles.

It was a detachment from Captain Carroll's battalion which made first contact with Victorio's warriors. On 5 April 1880, from Malpais Springs, Carroll sent 31 men of A Company under Lieutenant John Conline ahead of his command.[67] The reason Conline was sent ahead of Carroll's battalion is that Carroll thought he was running behind schedule. As far as he was aware, Hatch was intending to attack the Apaches no later than 5 April 1880; and his battalion was not yet in a position to support the First Battalion of New Mexico Troops.

The Battle of Hembrillo Canyon: Conline's Skirmish, 5 April 1880

After a march of 37 miles, at around 4:40 p.m., Conline discovered a trail of approximately 50 horses and 100 cattle entering Hembrillo Canyon on the eastern side of the San Andres Mountains. This trail was followed into the canyon until it narrowed; then Conline halted his company and sent a scouting party of six men further up the canyon. He also sent a courier back to Carroll. The advance party did not, at first, see any Apaches. Further back down the canyon, Conline, scanning the area with his binoculars, saw two Apaches moving down from the mountains into the canyon. Within seconds of this discovery, he spotted between 25 and 50 Apaches rapidly advancing down the canyon slightly to the right of these two warriors.[68]

---

64 'DoNM/GSFO/L&T', NA, RG393, Part 3, Entry 475 Vol. 5, pp.126-127.

65 See Laumbach, 'Hembrillo An Apache Battle field of the Victorio War: The Archaeology and History of the Hembrillo Battlefield' and 'Conline's Skirmish: An Episode of the Victorio War. Archaeological and Historical Documentation of an 1880s Skirmish Site on the White Sands Missile Range' Both are excellent additions to the Apache Wars literature. See also Wakeman & Laumbach, Chapter 22, pp.130-136; Wakeman & Laumbach webpage and the Bulletin of Las Cruces webpage.

66 Scott *et al*, 1989; Fox *et al*, 1993. Panzeri provides a very useful summary of their reconstruction of the Battle of the Little Big Horn in the Osprey Campaign Book of the same title.

67 Bi Monthly Return 'A' Company, 9th Cavalry Mar./Apr. 1880; Record of Events Apr. 1880 in Returns From Regular Army Cavalry Regiments 1833-1916, 9th Cavalry Regimental Returns 1873-1880, NA, M744, Roll 88.

68 Bi Monthly Return 'A' Company, 9th Cavalry Mar./Apr. 1880; Record of Events Apr. 1880 in Returns From Regular Army Cavalry Regiments 1833-1916, 9th Cavalry Regimental Returns 1873-1880, NA, M744, Roll 88; See also Correspondence from Newman (Editor of *Thirty-Four*) concerning Hembrillo Canyon and the Disarming of the Mescaleros published in *Thirty-Four* 21 Apr., 1880; The Chronological

Conline spotted his opponents at about 5:00 p.m., but the Apaches did not engage his detachment until about half an hour later, when they opened fire at 2–300 yards distance. Conline deployed his men in a skirmish line across the canyon and responded with several volleys, which forced the Apaches to take cover. A short and ferocious fire-fight was engaged in, which ended when the Apaches failed to turn both Conline's right and left flanks. During the fight, one of his guides, Jose Carillo, identified Victorio as the person directing the Apaches during the battle. The Apaches then kept up a harassing fire until about 7:30 p.m. when they withdrew. Conline withdrew his company 15 minutes later. He claimed to have sent four couriers to Captain Carroll.[69] (See document file no. 51.1.) Conline sustained two casualties, with Corporal Hawkins and citizen guide William Eubank both slightly wounded,[70] and two horses killed and one wounded.[71]

Lt. John Conline.
Though subject to periods of mental fatigue, Lt. John Conline wrote an unusually detailed account of the skirmish between his command and Victorio's warriors on 5 April, 1880 in Hembrillo Canyon. Despite this detail modern archaeology has shown his account to be incomplete. (National Archives)

It is interesting to note that one of the officers with Carroll's battalion later criticised Conline for unsaddling his horses and turning them loose before he was attacked.[72] Over 100 years later, the archaeological study of the site would reveal that Conline had given a less than complete account of this skirmish.[73] For example, the Lieutenant claimed that he secured his flanks on both sides of the Canyon; whereas it is clear that his skirmish line was deployed on the southern side of Hembrillo Canyon, and did not cover the entire canyon's width. There were also facts which he either did not appreciate or else chose not to reveal to his superiors. It is very clear that the good position from which he chose to fight was not ideal on three counts.

List, p.49; Stout p130; web article The Ninth Regiment of Cavalry by Lt G. Hutcheson; Wakeman & Laumbach p.130; Wakeman & Laumbach's web page.

69 Bi Monthly Return 'A' Company, 9th Cavalry Mar./Apr. 1880; Record of Events Apr. 1880 in Returns From Regular Army Cavalry Regiments 1833-1916, 9th Cavalry Regimental Returns 1873-1880, NA, M744, Roll 88; See also Correspondence from Newman (Editor of *Thirty-Four*) concerning Hembrillo Canyon and the Disarming of the Mescaleros published in *Thirty-Four* 21 Apr., 1880.

70 Eubank was certainly lightly wounded. On 31 May, 1880, William Eubank was paid $30.00 for the apprehension of Private Charles Wright who deserted from Company A, Ninth Cavalry while stationed at Fort Stanton. (1st Lieut Clark, Dillard Hazelrig, Fifteenth Infantry, AAQM Fort Stanton to AAG, DoM, 31 May, 1880 in Letters Received, Dept. of Missouri 1868-98, RG 393, Entry A1-1 2601, Box 91).

71 Bi Monthly Return 'A' Company, 9th Cavalry Mar./Apr. 1880; Record of Events Apr. 1880 in Returns From Regular Army Cavalry Regiments 1833-1916, 9th Cavalry Regimental Returns 1873-1880, NA, M744, Roll 88.

72 Personal File John Conline, NA, RG94, Entry 297, Box 279.

73 See Laumbach et al, 2005, pp.50-68 for an overview of what actually happened during this skirmish.

First, the Apaches were able to seize the higher ground overlooking his left flank. Second, the Apaches were able to use the dead ground to come within 60 yards (in one or two cases within 30 yards) of his skirmish line. Finally, the Apaches were able to utilise the arroyo to his right to move around that flank and threaten his rear. (See Plates 5.1 and 5.2.)

The archaeology shows that Conline played down the extent to which he had to bend his line to protect his horses from those Apaches attempting to turn Conline's right flank. His opponents managed to use the arroyo to open fire on his horses from behind his skirmish line. In this case, it appears that some Apaches were using arrows, possibly in an effort to wound some of the horses and provoke a stampede. One of these Apaches was firing Springfield rifle and carbine ammunition from the same gun. There were two metal arrowheads found in this area; one found within two metres of a spent Springfield Carbine cartridge case. This gives a clear impression of the close-range skirmishing during the fight. Walking over this site, one rapidly appreciates that Lieutenant Conline and his men had had a very narrow escape. They encountered the Apaches relatively late in the day; and these warriors were so convinced of the favourable odds, that they had launched an attack on the detachment. For Apaches to launch a direct attack on their opponents was very unusual. Yet they had judged the odds to perfection. By the time darkness fell, the beleaguered Ninth Cavalrymen were gradually being hemmed in by a successful turning of their right flank. To the front of A Company's skirmish line, Apache warriors were using the natural cover to full effect to work their way very close to the Ninth Cavalrymen, pinning them down. Finally, some warriors on Conline's left flank provided harassing fire from higher up the slopes of Hembrillo Canyon. It was a combination of the onset of darkness[74] and their refusal to panic that saved A Company from disaster. The Apaches must have decided that the steadfastness of Conline's men, and the onset of darkness, posed too much of a risk of casualties on their side, if they continued their attack as darkness fell. So, they withdrew; and Conline's detachment was able to withdraw and rejoin the Second Battalion.

Having returned to join the rest of the battalion, Lieutenant Conline was able to give his commanding officer his first clear idea of the location of the Apaches. Moreover, they had seen that the Apaches were more than willing to stand their ground. This factor must have been music to Captain Carroll's ears: that Victorio would stand and fight was exactly what Colonel Hatch had been hoping would happen. However, Carroll was also aware that Hatch had expressed his intention to arrive in the area no later than the morning of 5 April 1880. When Conline rejoined the battalion, it was approximately 11:00 p.m. on 5 April, and as far as Carroll was concerned, he was behind schedule – a schedule which, unknown to him, was now obsolete. Therefore, Carroll thought that he was in danger of ruining Hatch's operational timing. As Conline had been driven out of the lower reaches of Hembrillo Canyon, it was a reasonable assumption on Carroll's part that the Apaches' main camp was somewhere in the upper reaches of this canyon. Carroll was accompanied by guides, who could give advice as to how to outflank the Apaches who had stopped Conline's company. Intending to confront the Apaches in their camp, Carroll took command of D and F Companies and moved into Sulphur Canyon, roughly parallel to, and north of, Hembrillo Canyon, with the intention of entering Hembrillo Basin from the top of Sulphur Canyon. At the same time, Lieutenant Cusack was under instructions to move south, taking the remaining two companies from the battalion along the edge of the San Andres Mountains. It remains unclear whether this was to attract the attention of the Apaches, block the lower end of Hembrillo Canyon, or both.

74 Lt. C.W. Taylor stated that it was the onset of darkness which saved Company A from annihilation by the Apaches. (Personal File John Conline, NA, RG94, Entry 297, Box 279; See also Laumbach et al, 2005, p.54).

Plate 5.1. The extreme right of Conline's skirmish line was positioned just to the left of the road in the foreground. The Apaches attacked down Hembrillo Canyon towards where the camera is positioned. The broken line of darker foliage to the right of the road marks the dry arroyo down which some Apache warriors crept to get behind the Ninth Cavalrymen. (Photo: Author)

Plate 5.2. View up the arroyo used by the Apaches to turn Conline's right flank. (Photo: Author)

The Battle of Hembrillo Canyon.[75] Carroll's Siege, 6–7 April 1880

Conline's report of 30 to 50 warriors seriously underestimated the number of Apaches in the vicinity. With his Mescalero allies, Victorio may have commanded between 60 and 150 warriors when Carroll moved into Hembrillo Basin from the north. Laumbach argues that Victorio probably had reasonable warning of Carroll's approach. A lookout positioned high up on the north and west side of the Hembrillo Basin would have been able to see the Ninth Cavalrymen two miles away.[76] Nevertheless, Carroll, by not following Lieutenant Conline's route into Hembrillo Canyon, probably took Victorio by surprise; though the Apache warriors quickly occupied both Carroll's Ridge and Apache Ridge and set up a v-shaped trap.[77] (See Figure 5.3.) Laumbach, following the advice of fellow historian Ron Burkett, draws a very interesting distinction between 'trap' and 'ambush'. An ambush apparently has to have a 'close-range "killing ground"', whereas a trap 'is meant to contain the enemy'.[78] One must be very wary of applying US army concepts and terminology to the Apaches. However, on reflection this is a rather useful analogy, if used with a degree of qualification. Having been taken by surprise, the Apaches' first priority was to stop Carroll's detachment from breaking through to their camp. Laumbach argues that the Apaches also stationed warriors around Rock House Spring and along Victorio Ridge, as a second line of defence. Some Apache warriors quickly created some new, small breastworks facing northwards.[79] Hatch later observed that the Apache warriors 'had thrown up with much labor stone rifle pits where there were not natural defences'.[80] Again, the Apaches' immediate imperative was to prevent the Ninth Cavalrymen from breaking through to their camp should the first trap fail.

Carroll was therefore moving south through Hembrillo Basin, between Apache Ridge and Carroll's Ridge, when Victorio's warriors opened fire from both ridges. The archaeology reveals a wide range of weapons and equipment deployed by the Apaches during the battle.[81]

75 There seems to be some dispute in the various sources over the actual date of the battle. The earliest source seems to be provided by Capt. McLellan who clearly states that the battle was fought on the 6-7 of Apr., 1880. Until clear evidence to the contrary is provided I shall use these dates. (See for instance, Bi-Monthly Company Muster Rolls for Company L, 6th Cavalry, Mar./ Apr. 1880 in NA, RG94).

76 Laumbach, 2001, p.209. Having visited Hembrillo Canyon on the 22 September 2006 and seen the lie of the land I would agree with Karl on this matter. I did not reach the lookout position but Carroll's entry point from Sulphur Spring is clearly visible from lower ground and it would have taken the cavalrymen some time to march down into the Basin from this point. Incidentally, this entry point is quite high up on the northern side of Hembrillo Basin.

77 Laumbach, 2001, p.177 & p.209.

78 Laumbach email, 27/12/2002.

79 Laumbach, 2001, p.209.

80 Hatch to AAAG SF 10 Apr., 1880, NA, RG393, Part 3, Entry 439, p.67; See also Hatch, Tulerosa, to AAAG, SF, 10 Apr., 1880, 'DoNM/GSFO/L&T', NA, RG393, Part 3, Entry 475, Vol. 5, pp.387-388; Loud to AAG Fort Leavenworth, 12 Apr., 1880, Telegrams Sent DoNM, Vol.3, Jan.-Nov. 1880 NA, RG393, Part 3, Entry 431, p.301; Pope to AAG, MDoM13 Apr., 1880 in 'Victorio Papers', NA, M666, Roll 526.

81 Therefore, it should not be assumed that all of these weapons were deployed during the opening attack upon Carroll's command.

Table 5.2 Weapons Deployed by the Apaches in the Battle of Hembrillo Canyon.[82]

80	.45-55 Springfield Carbines
31	.50-70 1866 Springfield Rifles
15	.44-40 Winchester Repeating Rifles
8	.50-70 1868 Springfield Rifles
3	.50-70 Remington Rifles
3	.50 Sharps Rifles
3	.44 Henry/Winchester 1866 Repeating Rifles.
1	.44 extra-long Ballard Rifle
1	.44 extra-long Wesson Rifle
1	.45-70 Sharps Carbine

The large number of Springfield rifles somewhat undermines the stereotypical picture of the Apache warriors of the 1870s and 1880s being armed exclusively with Winchester and similar repeating rifles.[83]

Laumbach argues that Carroll had the choice of staying out in the open or retreating to a lower hill. Yet the Apaches on both ridges would have dominated both of these locations.[84] He was saved by launching a counterattack on the Apache positions on what is now known as Carroll's Ridge, which the archaeological survey suggests was held by far fewer Apache warriors than those stationed on Apache Ridge.[85] He was, as Conline had been the previous day, probably also saved by moving into Hembrillo Basin relatively late in the day.[86]

Nevertheless, Carroll and his men found themselves in deep trouble, even though they had managed to drive off the Apaches defending Carroll's Ridge and set up as good a defensive position as they could. This seems to have involved two skirmish lines, one facing north-east the other facing west. Laumbach estimates that approximately 21 men would have been required to control the horses and mules, leaving 50 men to fight the Apaches.[87] A rare account from the Mescalero Apache

Capt. Henry Carroll.
Commander of the Second Battalion, New Mexico Troops. On 6-7 April, 1880, he was trapped in Hembrillo Basin with half of his battalion and severely wounded, before being rescued by the remainder of his battalion and Apache scouts and Sixth Cavalrymen from the First Battalion, New Mexico Troops. (National Archives)

82 Wakeman & Laumbach, p.133; Laumbach, 2001, p.37 & p.209;

83 Note the K-H Butte survey, which also suggests that the popular image of Apache warriors armed to the teeth with Winchester repeating rifles may not be strictly accurate. (See Ludwig, L.L. & Stute, J.L., 1993, *The Battle at K-H Butte: Apache Outbreak – 1881: Arizona Territory* (Westernlore Press: Tucson Arizona).

84 Laumbach, 2001, p.177.

85 Laumbach, 2001, p.209

86 Ibid, p.179

87 Ibid, p.177 & pp.214 & 219

point of view is preserved in the Rare Manuscript Collections at Cornell University. A man named Old Paul was interviewed and remembered seeing Jose Carillo[88] among the soldiers after they had become pinned down on the ridge. The Mescaleros:

> called him [Carillo] by his Indian name there and said, "Today we're going to butcher you." He raised his rifle up and shot without sighting it he was so scared. They were all scared, those soldiers.[89]

The horses and mules were sheltered in a ravine at the southern end of Carroll's Ridge; but as darkness fell, this left them vulnerable to infiltrating Apaches.[90] Indeed, the cartridge analysis strongly suggests that the Apaches moved into this area as they closed in on Carroll's defences during the night.[91] (See Figure 5.4.) Though the Apaches were successful in killing or capturing approximately a quarter of the column's horses and mules, this suggests that the surviving stock was moved up onto Carroll's ridge under cover of darkness, for greater protection. With the troops probably last having filled their water bottles from the wagons that morning,[92] water became the critical issue. The archaeology also reveals that the Apaches knew the varying capabilities of the different models of breech-loading rifles, and deployed these weapons in an attempt to frustrate attempts by Carroll's men to reach water running down from Rock House Spring. Victorio concentrated most of those warriors armed with shorter-range but higher-rate-of-fire repeating rifles around the nearest source of water, while the ridgelines were occupied by warriors armed with longer-range single-shot breech-loading weapons.[93]

This is a plausible supposition, and one which can be extended. If groups of warriors operated together in battle, they may also have done so when acquiring weapons. Even if they were able to find an illicit arms dealer, they would not necessarily have been able to pick out a particular make of rifle. However, within the limited range of weapons and ammunition they had access to through raiding or trading, the Apaches were quite capable of modifying their tactics to take advantage of the best features offered by the various models of breech-loading rifles. Betzinez also noted that the older Apache warriors, no longer quite so active, preferred longer-range weapons; whereas the younger warriors tended to favour repeating rifles.[94] One can also see Apaches faced with Carroll's beleaguered men swapping arms and bullets among themselves to suit the immediate tasks allotted to them by their leaders.[95] These warriors managed to prevent the Ninth Cavalrymen from gaining all but a few canteens of water. Mescalero testimony suggests that while Carroll's men may have

---

88 Called 'Carrilla' in this document.

89 'Power from Black One Offered a Mexican' Box 39 #14/25/3238, Rare Manuscript Collections, Carl A. Kroch Library, Cornell University, Ithaca, New York, 14853-4302. Thanks go to Karl Laumbach for passing this information on to me.

90 Laumbach, 2001, pp.177-178.

91 Ibid, p.26 & pp.215-216.

92 Ibid, p.177.

93 Ibid, pp.211-213, p.219 & p.224.

94 Betzinez, 1959, p.77.

95 The closest example of such cooperation can be seen in a skirmish between two frontiersman and two Apaches in 1871: 'They fired three or four shots at me, one with a Henry rifle and the other with a six-shooter. I was jumping side-wise and trying to reload my rifle when Townsend sent a shot and broke the arm of the Indian who had the rifle. Then they both started to run, keeping as much as possible the brush between them and us. They had run only a few steps when they ran together, and the one with the six-shooter got the Henry rifle and gave the pistol to the one with the broken arm. All of this time I was trying to get a shot, but there was too much brush, and they were taking advantage of it.' (Genung, 2001, p.78).

been scared or confused at the beginning of the battle, they also remembered that as night closed in, Jose Carrillo made a successful attempt to reach water:

> He started towards the water. He kept on, bullets kicking the dust on all sides of him. He got to the water. He drank, filled canteens, and ran back. He would not make a second trip though they wanted him to do it.[96]

It is not clear from this account as to who 'they' refers to; it could mean that the trapped Ninth Cavalrymen wanted Carillo to make another dash to collect water. However, it could easily be read as the Mescalero Apaches wishing for a second opportunity to try to kill Carillo.

However, the Apache warriors managed to seriously wound Carroll and several of his men during these attempts to replenish their water supplies.[97]

This meant that the horses and mules were not watered that night and some of them were lost when they broke free to seek water. Two mules were discovered after the battle having drowned in a distant waterhole.[98] As Carroll established his position and attempted to reach the nearest water, the Apaches used the cover of darkness to change positions and close in around that position. They occupied the higher ground to the west, south and east of Carroll's Ridge.[99] At some point during the night, or perhaps around dawn, the northern skirmish line had to use their revolvers to drive off an Apache attempt to infiltrate their line.[100] According to Laumbach:

> darkness was indeed a factor in the night battle. The sun set of the evening of April 6, 1880, at 6:31 P.M. MST and twilight ended twenty-five minutes later. After that it was very dark. The moon did not rise until 4:25 A.M. on April 7. When it did rise, it was a waning crescent with only eight percent of the moon's visible surface illuminated. Sunrise followed a little more than one hour later, at 5:46 A.M.[101]

However, Apache warriors, always very reluctant to fight at night, may have refused to attack the cavalry on such a moonless night. No doubt, with their intimate knowledge of the terrain, Victorio and Nana and other experienced warriors had concocted a careful plan of attack to coincide with the dawn. At first light, Apache warriors started to close in, slipping down towards and around their foes through a network of arroyos and thickets of vegetation. This manoeuvre would have been undertaken by the younger, more active, warriors while the more mature warriors harassed the trapped Ninth Cavalrymen with long-range sniping from the higher ridges. This attack was focused upon 20 troopers holding a position facing to the north-east.[102]

> Early in the fight we have cartridges/weapons on Apache Ridge that are also found near to Carroll's position, suggesting that they were involved first from long range and then moved closer. The 3 Henry's are a case in point but several .45-55's appear to have joined that

96 'Power from Black One Offered a Mexican' Box 39 #14/25/3238, Rare Manuscript Collections, Carl A. Kroch Library, Cornell University, Ithaca, New York, 14853-4302.
97 Laumbach, 2001, p.179.
98 Ibid, p.179.
99 Ibid, pp.215 & 219.
100 Ibid, p.219
101 Ibid, p.179. Lumpkin states that there was a thumbnail moon from about 4.30 am onwards. (JJ Lumpkin, Albuquerque Journal, 23 Apr., 1999)
102 See Wakeman & Laumbach webpage.

> manoeuvre. So it is logical to posit a movement from Apache Ridge down the Area H especially as Hatch talks about the Apache closing in.[103]

Laumbach and fellow-archaeologist Wakeman point out that the Apaches attempted to outflank this position, forcing the Ninth Cavalrymen to use their revolvers to blaze away and discourage their tormentors. If we examine Wakeman and Laumbach's diagram[104] of the excavated line of spent cartridge cases, most of the Ninth Cavalrymen seem to have been moving from position to position along their skirmish line. Very few men remained at a single position on the line. One revolver (9) left spent cartridges at locations all along the line. This may represent an officer, or NCO, moving up and down the line directing the defence. The more localised movement of some of the spent cases may indicate troopers moving to cover comrades specifically threatened by the probing attacks of the Apache warriors. Laumbach also points out that such movement could also be due to 'rodents, visitors to the battlefield, wind, erosion and other natural processes'.[105]

Hatch stated that Carroll was wounded twice but that only one of these wounds was dangerous. He also noted seven enlisted men were seriously wounded.[106] In Carroll's case, the surgeon's report on his injuries states that, 'The course of the ball seriously endangered the axilliary artery, the brachial plexus, the head of the humerus and glenoid fossa, and, indeed it is difficult to understand how these parts escaped destruction.'[107] Two troopers, Privates Johnson and Lyle, were still out of action by the end of June. Lyle needed to have his left leg amputated,[108] and he was medically discharged from the army on 11 January 1881.[109] Another soldier, Trumpeter Guddy, was shot in both legs.[110] Three of Carroll's men subsequently died of their wounds: Issac James and William Sanders/Saunders died in April and July respectively,[111] and Private Morgan of D Company was also recorded as having died from wounds received at Hembrillo Canyon during April 1880.[112]

Immediately after the battle, Surgeon MacPherson estimated that three of Carroll's men were likely to die of their wounds.[113]

---

103 Laumbach Email, 27/12/2002.
104 Wakeman & Laumbach, p.134 see also Laumbach, 2001, p.221.
105 Laumbach email, 27/12/2002.
106 Hatch to AAAG SF 8 Apr., 1880, NA, RG393, Part 3, Entry 439, pp.16-17; Hatch, Tulerosa, to AAAG, SF, 10 Apr., 1880, 'DoNM/GSFO/L&T', NA, RG393, Part 3, Entry 475, Vol. 5, pp.387-388; Hatch to Sheridan 10 Apr., 1880, NA, RG393, Part 1, Entry 2539, Press Copies of Letters and Endorsements Sent, MDoM, Vol. 13, pp.155-156; Hatch to AAG, HQ, MDoM, Chicago, 13 Apr., 1880, NA, RG393, Part 1, Entry 2546, p.394; Pope's Annual Report Year ending 22 Sept., 1880, NA, RG393, Part 1, Entry 2546, p.612Loud to AAG Fort Leavenworth, 9 Apr., 1880, Telegrams Sent DoNM, Vol.3, Jan.-Nov. 1880 NA, RG393, Part 3, Entry 431, pp.294-295; Platt AAG Fort Leavenworth to Pope, 9 Apr., 1880, 'Victorio Files', NA, RG393, M1495, Roll 14; Sheridan to AG approximately quoting above report, 10 Apr., 1880 in 'Victorio Papers', NA, M666, Roll 526; See also Letter 10 Apr., 1880 in MacPherson Letters 1 Jan., 1879 to 3 Sept., 1880, University of Virginia at Charlottesville; Chronological List, p.49; Record of Engagements, p.94; Wellman, 1957, p.165.
107 Personal File Henry Carroll, NA, RG94, Entry 297, Box 476.
108 Bi-Monthly Company Muster Rolls for Company F, 9th Cavalry, May/Jun. 1880 in NA, RG94.
109 Bi-Monthly Company Muster Rolls for Company F, 9th Cavalry, Jan./Feb. 1881 in NA, RG94.
110 Bi-Monthly Company Muster Rolls for Company F, 9th Cavalry, May/Jun. 1880 in NA, RG94.
111 Record of Events Apr. & Jul. 1880 in Returns From Regular Army Cavalry Regiments 1833-1916, 9th Cavalry Regimental Returns 1873-1880, NA, M744, Roll 88; Bi-Monthly Company Muster Rolls for Company F, 9th Cavalry, Mar./Apr. & Jul./Aug. 1880 in NA, RG94; Laumbach, 2001, p.245 & 246.
112 Bi-Monthly Company Muster Rolls for Company D, 9th Cavalry, Mar./Apr. 1880 in NA, RG94.
113 Letter 10 Apr., 1880 in MacPherson Letters 1 Jan., 1879 to 3 Sept., 1880, University of Virginia at Charlottesville.

Plate 5.3. Photograph taken from the Apache position on Victorio Ridge. Carroll's command was trapped within the area marked by two faint curved lines forming a mirror image of each other in the middle of the photograph. The Apaches also occupied the two ridges to the left of this position, and the hill to the right of, and above, Carroll's position. Carroll's two companies had entered Hembrillo Basin somewhere along the left side of the horizon, giving Victorio time to react to the appearance of US troops from an unexpected direction. (Photo: Author)

Plate 5.4. Apache breastwork constructed on the ridge above Carroll's position. Victorio Peak can be seen to the left of the centre of the photograph, while part of Victorio Ridge can be seen on the right. (Photo: Author)

Plate 5.5. Victorio Ridge. It was from this position that the Apaches held off the reinforcements from both the First and Second Battalions of New Mexico Troops on 7 April. (Photo: Author)

Plate 5.6. A spent 45:70 cartridge case found below Carroll's position, so probably last handled by an Apache warrior working his way towards the Ninth Cavalrymen at dawn on 7 April 1880. (Photo: Author)

The Battle of Hembrillo Canyon: The Relief, 7 April 1880

We now return to the First Battalion of New Mexico Ttroops, under the immediate direction of Edward Hatch. The Battalion had started to come together as a unit towards the end of March. Major Morrow left Fort Bayard on 29 March 1880 with six officers, 86 Ninth Cavalrymen, six Fifteenth Infantrymen and 63 Apache scouts.[114] They rendezvoused with Captain McLellan, the composite Sixth Cavalry company and the Apache scouts under Lieutenant Gatewood, at Las Palomas. According to Captain McLellan, the rendezvous was scheduled for 1 April but Morrow did not arrive with the rest of his battalion until 3 April.[115] Captain McLellan remained at Las Palomas until 5 April, before being ordered to move on to Aleman. Morrow was ordered to move his element of the command to Aleman on 4 April.[116]

As the First Battalion congregated at Aleman, it was already clear that they would not be able to keep to the timetable that Captain Carroll was following. Unfortunately, the water pump at Aleman was broken, which further delayed their deployment into the San Andres Mountains. This meant that the horses and mules could only be watered at a fraction of the rate that might have been expected had the pump been working. The delay in Morrow's arrival at the rendezvous with McLellan at Las Palomas would also be explained by a delayed supply train. Newman, the editor of *Thirty-Four*, also noted that: 'It is now admitted that the troops from the west were a day behind, on account of the breaking down of a supply train and the well at Aleman getting out of order.'[117] (See document file no. 49.)

For these reasons, Hatch had to improvise the most efficient deployment of the troops at his disposal; and he had to deploy the Apache scouts first, and send them on to scout the San Andres Mountains. As the Apache scout companies were directly supported by detachments from the Sixth Cavalry, these had to be watered next. Late on 6 April, Hatch was able to send the Apache scouts and McLellan's command east from Aleman.[118] Morrow's Ninth Cavalry element of the battalion watered its horses and followed up as quickly as possible during the early hours and morning of 7 April.[119]

The Sixth Cavalry detachment, under Captain McLellan, with their accompanying Apache scouts, crested the San Andres Mountains above Hembrillo Canyon at daybreak. This was despite becoming lost after temporarily losing their guides during the night, and having to wait until the moon rose late in the night before they could reorient themselves.[120] Hearing heavy gunfire, McLellan gave orders that the supply train should be secured, and the balance of the troops and scouts, under Lieutenants Gatewood, Cruse and Maney, moved towards the sound of the guns.[121] McLellan also sent two couriers to inform Hatch's detachment.[122] Once again, Lieutenant Cruse left a graphic account of events. They found Carroll's beleaguered command and launched an attack, which drove the Apaches from their positions surrounding Carroll to a ridge to the south of Carroll's position, later called Victorio Ridge. (See Figure 5.5.) Cruse estimated that they appeared

114 NA, RG94, Entry 257 Vol. 896, Medical History, Fort Bayard NM May 1879, p.24; Hatch, San Jose, to Morrow, 29 Mar., 1880, 'DoNM/GSFO/L&T', NA, RG393, Part 3, Entry 475, Vol. 5, p.354.

115 Laumbach, 2001, p.161.

116 Morrow cited in Laumbach, 2001, p.161.

117 Correspondence from Newman (Editor of *Thirty-Four*) concerning Hembrillo Canyon and the Disarming of the Mescaleros published in *Thirty-Four* 21 Apr., 1880.

118 Report of Capt. C.B. McLellan, 16 May, 1880.

119 Hatch in Report to The Secretary of War for 1880, p.95; Leckie, 1967, p.216; Utley, 1973, p.361;Haley, 1981, p.326; Laumbach, 2001, p.167.

120 Laumbach, 2001, p.179 & p.181.

121 Report of Capt. C.B. McLellan, 16 May, 1880.

122 Cruse, 1987, pp.75-76.

to be confronted by at least 200 Apaches, which caused him some concern as Victorio had previously been estimated to lead about 75 warriors. The Apache scout companies were detailed to work their way around to the right to flank Victorio Ridge, while the Sixth Cavalry detachment launched a frontal attack on the Apache positions. (See Figure 5.6.) Cruse describes a leapfrog advance, where half the soldiers (those not assigned to horse-holding duty) would fire at the Apache positions while the other half moved forward under this covering fire. The latter would then halt and open fire while the former moved up, passing through to positions in advance of the firing line. These men would then open fire on the Apache positions. The process was repeated several times as they closed on Victorio Ridge. Cruse estimated that he had had to cover 600 yards to reach the crest of Victorio Ridge, and recalled that the Apaches opened a heavy fire on the advancing soldiers. Once the line got to within 150 yards of the top, they took cover and rested for some minutes. Cruse passed word along the line that, when he gave the command, all of the men were to charge the crest firing on the run. When they rose up and charged, they found that they received little return fire: the Apaches had mostly withdrawn and were now engaged in a furious gun battle with the Apache scouts.[123] (See document file no. 52.) On a more personal note, Cruse described his feelings during the Hembrillo Canyon battle:

> I didn't feel afraid when I first went in, but when several bullets had come uncomfortably close to me, I came to the conclusion that they were actually trying to shoot me, and that put a different light on the matter, and I didn't feel half so comfortable or confident. I am sure that I did not kill any Indians, because I did not see a single thing to shoot at; in fact, I saw nothing except a long ridge from which came white smoke and bullets.[124]

Captain McLellan reported that his force first engaged the Apaches at 7:30 a.m., and that the fight lasted until 3:30 p.m.[125] (See document file no. 53.)

What Cruse and McLellan failed to record was they were not the only US troops to arrive in the nick of time. Lieutenant Cusack, leading the rest of Carroll's Second Battalion, arrived at around the same time as McLellan's force and launched his own attack. Cusack's own account is frustratingly brief, merely noting that his company was engaged between 10:00 a.m. and 4:00 p.m. in driving the Apaches from 'the hill held by him [the Apaches]'.[126] Lieutenant Conline's original account remains almost as vague:

> On Apr 7, a little before 9 o'clock am [a.m.] joined Capt. Carroll near water in Membrillo Canon and about twenty minutes after, went into action, which closed at 5pm Apr 7, 80, after Victorio had been driven from the first water at 11 am, and the second at about 4pm, by the combined movements of Capt Carroll's and McFellan's commands.[127]

In the Ninth Cavalry regimental return, A Company was noted as being in skirmish lines from 8:00 a.m. to 5:00 p.m. on 7 April, and G Company was recorded as driving Apaches from positions in

123 Cruse, 1987, pp.74-76; see also Wakeman & Laumbach, p.136; Carter, USACMH, Webpage; Report of Capt. C.B. McLellan, 16 May, 1880.
124 Cruse, 2001, p.263.
125 Report of Capt. C.B. McLellan, 16 May, 1880. See also McLellan to Post Adjutant, Fort Bowie, 16 May, 1880 in 'Victorio Papers', NA, M666, Roll 527; See also Personal File Thomas Cruse, NA, RG94, Entry 297, Box 1428 where his file notes a 'severe fight lasting from 6.30 A.M. until 3 P.M.'.
126 Bi-Monthly Company Muster Rolls for Company G, 9th Cavalry, Mar./Apr. 1880 in NA, RG94.
127 Bi-Monthly Company Muster Rolls for Company A, 9th Cavalry, Mar./Apr. 1880 in NA, RG94.

Hembrillo Canyon.[128] D Company, led by Lieutenant Hughes, was noted as having fought continuously for nine hours each day on 6 and 7 April.[129] This additional information fits quite neatly with an account of the fight published in *Thirty-Four* on 14 April 1880.[130] (See document file no. 55.) Lieutenant Conline later stated (see document file no. 54) that Lieutenant Cusack's half of the battalion, recalled by courier, had marched at daylight on 7 April, and had joined Carroll under fire from the surrounding hills at around 8:30 a.m.[131] Some of the fire came from McLellan's Apache scouts who, unaware of the exact dispositions of Carroll's command, mistook the approaching cavalrymen for more Apaches.[132] Conline stated that the two companies of the Ninth Cavalry joined in the attack on Victorio Ridge. He also implied that some of the Second Battalion had provided covering fire for the Apache scouts as the latter had taken control of a second water hole (probably Upper Hembrillo Spring) at about 4:00 p.m.[133] Indeed, from the Apache perspective, James Kaywaykla notes that the deadlock between the US army and the Apaches was broken by the arrival of cavalry from the Tulerosa Basin. This clearly points to the arrival of the other two companies from Carroll's battalion.[134]

Skirmishing continued throughout the day as the Warm Springs and Mescalero Apaches faded back into the high ground to the south (see Map 5.7). Spent cartridges and bullets indicate that Victorio's warriors conducted a fighting withdrawal to a ridge to the south before finally breaking off the engagement. McLellan reported that Morrow reached him at 5:00 p.m. with Hatch following an hour later, both missing any chance to participate in the action.[135] When the action was broken off, the troops marching from Aleman had been without water, other than that which was in their canteens, for some hours. The troops under Carroll had been without water for almost two days.[136]

There is some debate[137] over the Apache casualties. McLellan and Cruse claimed three killed,[138] but the Apache scouts claimed to have killed approximately 20. Hatch stated that, while he knew of the claims of the Apache scouts, their reports had not been confirmed. As far as Hatch was concerned, he could only confirm that three Apache warriors had been killed.[139]. Hatch recognised

128 See Record of Events Apr. 1880 in Returns From Regular Army Cavalry Regiments 1833-1916, 9th Cavalry Regimental Returns 1873-1880, NA, M744, Roll 88.

129 Record of Events Apr. 1880 in Returns From Regular Army Cavalry Regiments 1833-1916, 9th Cavalry Regimental Returns 1873-1880, NA, M744, Roll 88.

130 *Thirty-Four*, 14 Apr., 1880.

131 Conline cited in Laumbach, 2001, p.182.

132 Laumbach, 2001, p.184 & p.224.

133 Conline cited in Laumbach, 2001, pp.189-190.

134 Ball, 1970, p.85.

135 Report of Capt. C.B. McLellan, 16 May, 1880; See also McLellan to Post Adjutant, Fort Bowie, 16 May, 1880 in 'Victorio Papers', NA, M666, Roll 527; Morrow cited in Laumbach p.191.

136 Hatch to AAG, 16 Apr., 1880, NA, RG393, Part 1, Entry 2546, p.412; Loud to AAG Fort Leavenworth, 18 Apr., 1880, Telegrams Sent DoNM, Vol.3, Jan.-Nov. 1880 NA, RG393, Part 3, Entry 431, p.318; Correspondence from Newman (Editor of *Thirty-Four*) concerning Hembrillo Canyon and the Disarming of the Mescaleros published in *Thirty-Four* 21 Apr., 1880.

137 See comments by Laumbach, 2001, p.246 It is certainly true that Department HQ sent a request concerning the numbers of Apaches killed and the number of horses killed or captured five days after the battle. (See Loud to Hatch, Aleman (to be forwarded from Mesilla by first opportunity), 12 Apr., 1880, Telegrams Sent DoNM, Vol.3, Jan.-Nov. 1880 NA, RG393, Part 3, Entry 431, p.) It should be noted that if the New Mexican Troops in the Field had had any indication of heavy casualties, this would have been among the first statistics transmitted.

138 Report of Capt. C.B. McLellan, 16 May, 1880. See also McLellan to Post Adjutant, Fort Bowie, 16 May, 1880 in 'Victorio Papers', NA, M666, Roll 527; Leckie, 1967, p.216. We might wish to remind ourselves of two of Thrapp's comments on the terms 'routed' and 'carried off their dead and wounded' when reading this report.

139 Hatch to AAG, 16 Apr., 1880, NA, RG393, Part 1, Entry 2546, p.412; See also Hatch to AAG, 16 Apr., 1880, 'DoNM/GSFO/L&T', NA, RG393, Part 3, Entry 475, Vol. 5, p.206; Thrapp, 1974, p.269.

one of the dead Indians as a Mescalero Apache.[140] The Colonel later stated that the slain Mescalero was almost certainly responsible for the killing of Robert Kane, the Ninth Cavalry courier killed near San Jose on 22 March 1880, as this Apache 'was recognized as having in his possession the carbine of the soldier'.[141] Hatch found the remains of 41 wickiups and suspected that there had been many more.[142] He also later stated[143] that his men had found ample evidence (flour sacks, blankets) that their opponents had included a strong force of Mescalero Apaches.[144] This, and his estimation that there had been 200 Apaches involved in the battle, convinced Hatch that the Mescaleros had generally participated in the battle.[145] He also thought that some Comanches had been present, as it was later reported that some of the ponies captured carried Comanche brands.[146]

As a result of his intervention, McLellan, his Sixth Cavalrymen, and his Apache scouts were generally given the credit for saving Carroll's command and driving off the Apaches.[147] Immediately after the fight, Captain Loud, almost certainly passing on a comment made by Hatch, gave the distinct impression that McLellan's command the leading role in this engagement: 'Carroll opened the fight and McLellan closed it last night. Carroll has been roughly handled.'[148] Equally it should be noted that, while McLellan's report gives credit for the victory to Lieutenants Touey, Gatewood and Cruse of the Sixth Cavalry, and Lieutenants Mills[149] and Maney of the Twelfth and Fifteenth Infantry Regiments,[150] Hatch was equally strong in his praise of Captain Carroll, Lieutenants Cusack, Hughes,[151] Conline, and C.B. Taylor of the Ninth Cavalry, and Lieutenant Maney of the

140 Hatch to AAAG SF 8 Apr., 1880, NA, RG393, Part 3, Entry 439, p.17; Hatch to Sheridan 10 Apr., 1880, NA, RG393, Part 1, Entry 2539, Press Copies of Letters and Endorsements Sent, MDoM, Vol. 13, p.155; Platt AAG Fort Leavenworth to Pope, 9 Apr., 1880, 'Victorio Files', NA, RG393, M1495, Roll 14; Sheridan to AG approximately quoting above report, 10 Apr., 1880 in 'Victorio Papers', NA, M666, Roll 526.

141 Hatch to AAG, DoM, Fort Leavenworth, 23 Aug., 1880, NA, RG393, Part 1, Entry 2546, pp.514-520; see also same document in 'Victorio Papers', NA, M666, Roll 527; Same letter in Loud to AAG, DoM, Fort Leavenworth, 23 Aug., 1880 in Letters Sent by '9MD/DNM/DoNM', NA, RG393, M1072, Roll 6, 1880-Aug. 1881, Letter No.433, pp282-285; Stout, p.149.

142 Hatch to Sheridan 10 Apr., 1880, NA, RG393, Part 1, Entry 2539, Press Copies of Letters and Endorsements Sent, MDoM, Vol. 13, p.155; See Loud to AAG Fort Leavenworth, 9 Apr., 1880, Telegrams Sent DoNM, Vol.3, Jan.-Nov. 1880 NA, RG393, Part 3, Entry 431, p.295; Platt AAG Fort Leavenworth to Pope, 9 Apr., 1880, 'Victorio Files', NA, RG393, M1495, Roll 14; Sheridan to AG approximately quoting above report, 10 Apr., 1880 in 'Victorio Papers', NA, M666, Roll 526.

143 This information might be somewhat tainted as this is contained in a letter written in 1886 in response to a claim for compensation by the Mescalero Apaches for their treatment in which they blamed their troubles upon Mescalero renegades and Victorio's Warm Springs Apaches. They also claimed that twenty-five women and children had been killed during Hatch's operation to disarm and dismount them. (See Jose Carrillo to The ColA, 7 Jul., 1885 in 'Victorio Papers', NA, M666, Roll 528).

144 Hatch to AG, U.S. Army, Washington D.C., 3 Apr. 1886 in 'Victorio Papers', NA, M666, Roll 528.

145 See Loud to AAG Fort Leavenworth, 9 Apr., 1880, Telegrams Sent DoNM, Vol.3, Jan.-Nov. 1880 NA, RG393, Part 3, Entry 431, p.295; Hatch to Sheridan 10 Apr., 1880, NA, RG393, Part 1, Entry 2539, Press Copies of Letters and Endorsements Sent, MDoM, Vol. 13, pp.154-155; See also Hatch to AAG, HQ, MDoM, Chicago, 13 Apr., 1880, NA, RG393, Part 1, Entry 2546, p.394.

146 Loud to AAG Fort Leavenworth, 12 Apr., 1880, Telegrams Sent DoNM, Vol.3, Jan.-Nov. 1880 NA, RG393, Part 3, Entry 431, p.300.

147 Willcox, General Orders No. 10, 4 Jun. 1880, NA, RG393, Part 1, Entry 183; Report of Col. E.A. Carr, 11 Sept., 1880, in AR-WD 1880, NA, M997, Roll 35, 1880 Vol. I, p.217.

148 See Loud to AAG Fort Leavenworth, 9 Apr., 1880, Telegrams Sent DoNM, Vol.3, Jan.-Nov. 1880 NA, RG393, Part 3, Entry 431, p.295.

149 See also Personal File Stephen C. Mills, NA, RG94, Entry 297, Box 829.

150 McLellan to Post Adjutant, Fort Bowie, 16 May, 1880 in 'Victorio Papers', NA, M666, Roll 527.

151 See also Personal File Martin B. Hughes, NA, RG94, Entry 297, Box 483.

Fifteenth Infantry.[152] McLellan's report could be interpreted as trying to divert attention away from the active participation of African-American troops throughout the battle. This may be true; but if McLellan's and Hatch's reports are viewed as praising officers directly under their command, then it is Hatch who perhaps comes across as giving less credit than was due to the troops from Arizona. Nevertheless, when later summarizing the campaign from February to May 1880, Hatch was fulsome in his praise of Captain McLellan and Lieutenants Gatewood and Mills for their part in the Hembrillo Canyon battle.[153] Hatch's report for the Annual Report of the Secretary of War records the intervention of both McLellan and Cusack in the relief of Carroll's detachment.[154] (See document file no. 56.)

A Close Run Affair: Luck Plays Into Victorio's Hands

The most unfortunate incident concerning the Hembrillo Canyon fight, at least from the US army's point of view, was about to occur. Until receipt of the news of the fighting in Hembrillo Canyon, the story was that Hatch had been ascending a path into the San Andres Mountains. According to Cruse's memoirs, Hatch had taken the Ninth Cavalry element of the battalion across the San Andres Mountains on a route to the south of that taken by McLellan. If one believes that Hatch knew the location of the Victorio's camp, this would make sense. If McLellan attacked first from the north-east while Hatch moved up from the south, Victorio would be caught in between. Concerned that he had a disaster on his hands, Hatch elected to return to the level ground on the western side of the mountains and hurry his command to the scene of the action.[155] Descending the very same trail were Victorio and Nana, with some warriors who were escorting their families out of the mountains while the rest of the warriors covered their retreat by prolonging the skirmishing in Hembrillo Canyon. The soldiers' 'about face' proved to have been an extremely lucky escape for Victorio's people. The Apaches had spotted them, and Nana later recounted that they had had 'a bad fifteen minutes'[156] until the command suddenly turned aside and hurried north.

Laumbach doubts the veracity of this version of events. He argues that, as Morrow did not finally leave Aleman till about 1:00 p.m., this makes it more likely that Hatch's troops were following up McLellan's route into the mountains. Laumbach notes that it is only Cruse who mentions Hatch going to the south-east before entering the San Andres. He also, quite rightly, points that there is no indication in Kaywaykla's account that the retreating Apaches were fleeing southwards. On retreating out of the southern end of Hembrillo Basin, they could have quickly swung round to the west and almost blundered into the battalion as it moved directly towards the San Andres Mountains:

> Cruse is the only one to mention couriers. If McLellan sent couriers soon after the battle was joined or even as late as 11:00 am and if Morrow is correct that Hatch didn't leave Aleman

---

152 Hatch, General Order No. 5, 4 Aug., 1880, General Orders, Circulars and Court Martial Orders 1870-1881, NA, RG393, Part 1, Entry 183; See also General Order No.5, 4 Aug., 1880, Printed Special Orders 1869-1888, DoNM, NA, RG393, Part 3, Entry 446.

153 Hatch to AAG, DoM, Fort Leavenworth, 5 Aug., 1880 in Letters Sent by '9MD/DNM/DoNM', NA, RG393, M1072, Roll 6, 1880-Aug. 1881, Letter No.407, pp.260-268.

154 Hatch in Report to The Secretary of War for 1880, cited in Sonnichsen, p.196; see also Hatch to AAAG SF 10 Apr., 1880, NA, RG393, Part 3, Entry 439, p.66; Hatch to AAG, HQ, MDoM, Chicago, 13 Apr., 1880, NA, RG393, Part 1, Entry 2546, p.394; Personal File Patrick Cusack, NA, RG94, Entry 297, Box 49.

155 Cruse, 1987, p.76.

156 Thrapp, 1967, p.196: 1974, p.270; Stout, p.132; Utley. 1973, p.361; Worcester, p.226; Haley, 1981, p.326.

> until 1pm, then Hatch would not have had time to do all this manoeuvring before the couriers reached him.[157]

Indeed, while couriers were sent by McLellan, it was from Aleman that Hatch sent a telegram[158] to Acting Assistant Adjutant General, Santa Fé, giving the first news of the fight in Hembrillo Canyon:

> Courier just in from front Indians are there in force we are bound to get a fight out of them already captured some of their animals leave with rest of command in a few minutes.[159]

It would be much more likely that Hatch would have set out from Aleman following his advance guard. Indeed, James Kaywaykla gives the Apache version of events, in which he states that Nana, unaccompanied by Victorio, was guiding the women and children away from Hembrillo Canyon towards the Jornada del Muerto when they encountered Hatch's force. However, he makes it clear that, rather than turning aside, the Apache scouts with the troops failed to note their hastily concealed trail and passed their hiding place.[160] It should be noted that, by this point, Hatch's force would not have included Apache scouts, as these were already fighting in Hembrillo Basin. Kaywaykla assumed that Hatch was accompanied by such scouts; but their absence further explains the failure to spot the hidden Apaches.

As the fighting in Hembrillo Canyon died down, the Apaches split up. Many Mescalero Apaches took to their horses and departed eastwards towards their reservation. Sonnichsen implies that Victorio's Mescalero allies slipped back to the reservation that night. George Sligh, a boy at the time, recalls accompanying his father as he drove a wagonload of liquor from El Paso to the troops at the Tulerosa Agency.[161] They had to drive off the road and hide in the darkness when they suddenly found themselves caught between at least two parties of torch-bearing Apaches making for the Mescalero reservation. The torch bearing sounds a bit conspicuous for Apaches, but Sligh reported to Sonnichsen that they heard Apache voices as well.[162] Laumbach thinks that the groups Sligh encountered were Mescalero women and children. He cites a report of a movement of 50–60 Apache warriors east out of the mountains on 8 April 1880.[163] These are probably the 50–60 Apaches spotted by Lieutenant Finley, guarding the water wagons. These Apaches left the San Andres Mountains approximately 10 miles to the south of Finley's location and made for the Mescalero reservation. Finley could only record his frustration at having only five men with him on four broken-down horses. 'If I had had fifty men on good horses I could have captured their stock and killed a good many of them.'[164]

Victorio's group, separate from Nana's party, and made up principally of warriors, had proceeded south and, once they had lost their pursuers, doubled back to Aleman, watered their horses and

157 Laumbach email, 27/12/2002.

158 It has to be noted that in the heat of the moment, many of the telegrams rec'd are not very clearly dated. But this telegram surely suggests that Hatch had not moved from Aleman by the time a courier reached him informing him of contact with the Apaches.

159 Hatch to AAAG SF Date unclear but looks to be 7 Apr. NA, RG393, Part 3, Entry 439, p.18; Loud to AAG Fort Leavenworth 7 Apr., 1880, Telegrams Sent DoNM, Vol.3, Jan.-Nov. 1880 NA, RG393, Part 3, Entry 431, p.291.

160 Ball, 1970, p.85.

161 Troops had been stationed at Tulerosa and at La Luz midway between Tulerosa and the Mescalero Reservation in 1878 in an effort to stop the selling of alcohol to the Apaches. (Reeve, 1938, p.275).

162 Sonnichsen, 1973, pp.197-198.

163 Laumbach email, 27/12/2002; Laumbach, 2001, p.241.

164 Letter dated Tularosa [Tulerosa] N.M., 18 Apr., 1880 in The Walter Lowry Finley Collection.

departed for their old Black Range haunts.[165] There is even reason to believe that some of the Apaches used the tracks left by Hatch's battalion to hide their movement back towards Aleman Well. Nana's near brush with Hatch may have occurred as this group of Apaches also attempted to use McLellan's trail to hide their westward movement out of the San Andres Mountains, unexpectedly encountering the Ninth Cavalry in the process. Nana and Victorio, following standard practice, probably agreed to rendezvous at Aleman before they left Hembrillo Basin; the former leaving as soon as it became clear that a large reinforcement of troops and Apache scouts had arrived; the latter leaving after delaying these new opponents for most of the day.

Hembrillo Canyon Controversies

The key controversy concerning the Hembrillo Canyon operation relates to the way in which it was reported after the fighting was over. So far, no detailed account by any of the participants in the siege of Carroll's command on 6 and 7 April has emerged. This is particularly surprising as such an event would surely have warranted a report from Captain Carroll. This is also in direct contrast with a detailed report made by Captain Carroll of a very inconclusive running battle with Juh's Chiricahua Apaches on 4 October 1881, near the Dragoon Mountains in Arizona.[166] The engagement in Hembrillo Canyon was a very close run affair, where the fate of Captain Carroll and two companies of Ninth Cavalrymen hung in the balance. Yet the Captain does not seem to have submitted a report. Hatch gave his superiors the distinct impression that he expected this report to be made:

> I have had no report of the number of Indians killed at San Andreas; personally know of only three, the scouts report twenty, not verified by an officer. The fighting was over some three miles of ground. The troops were withdrawn for water this evening. Resuming **the fight in the morning when the Indians broke for the Mescalero Agency Capt Carroll's report is not in**:– he had killed twenty five horses and mules from account received.[167]

The *Army & Navy Journal* of 24 April 1880 cited a 9 April report in the *New Mexican* which maintained that Colonel Hatch had received news from his scouts at Aleman, on 6 April, that the Apaches were concentrated in a specific location in the San Andres Mountains. The article gives the impression that Captain Carroll had led the advance from Aleman backed up by Captain McLellan's command.[168] The *New Mexican* would later be dismissed as a tame Santa Fé mouthpiece for Hatch by *Thirty-Four* and the *Grant County Herald*, so there are grounds to suspect that this report originated from Hatch.

It was clearly in Colonel Hatch's interests to see that the problems experienced in attempting to coordinate the three battalions prior to the battle did not become general knowledge. As we have

165 Ball, 1970, p.85; Thrapp, 1974, p.270; Thrapp, 1967, pp.196-197; Stout, 1974, p.132; Utley, 1973, p.362; Worcester, 1979, pp.226-227; Haley, 1981, p.326.

166 See Letters and Telegrams sent by the Battalion on the Southern Pacific Railroad at Separ NM Aug., 1880/ Nov. 1881, NA, RG391, Entry 921; Letters and Telegrams Received by the Battalion on the Southern Pacific Railroad at Separ NM Aug., 1880/Nov. 1881, NA, RG391, Entry 922; Orders Issued by the Battalion on the Southern Pacific Railroad at Separ NM Aug., 1880/Nov. 1881, NA, RG391, Entry 923; Carroll to AAAG, DoNM, SF, N.M. 17 Oct., 1881, DoM, Letters Received, 7266 DoM 1881.

167 Hatch to AAG, 16 Apr., 1880, NA, RG393, Part 1, Entry 2546, p.412; Loud to AAG Fort Leavenworth, 18 Apr., 1880, Telegrams Sent DoNM, Vol.3, Jan.-Nov. 1880 NA, RG393, Part 3, Entry 431, p.318.

168 'Indian Affairs' *Army & Navy Journal,* Vol.17, 24 Apr., 1880, p.773.

already seen, a hint that Captain Carroll was not aware of the change in the overall schedule did appear in at least one newspaper story. Luckily for Hatch, this story was not further investigated by the territorial press. This is the most important point: Hatch was already under a media spotlight before the Hembrillo Canyon operation commenced. By the time it was over, he had failed to visit anything remotely resembling a defeat on Victorio. The reasons for the delay – logistic inefficiency leading to failure to keep to the timetable – were responsible for operational failure. What is more, Captain Carroll could probably have proved this to be the case. Therefore, Hatch kept a firm grip on how the battle was reported. Carroll's severe wound played into his hands in the short-term; a severely wounded officer can hardly be expected to write a battle report. Yet there was no reason why his junior officers, particularly the officer who assumed command when Carroll was wounded, could not have been asked to submit their reports. In the longer term, there was nothing to prevent Carroll submitting a report. Yet, there appears to exist no primary record of events recorded by any member of D or F Companies, trapped overnight with Carroll. Apart from Lieutenant Conline, who concentrated on his own skirmish and was not trapped overnight with Carroll, none of the officers with Carroll's battalion appears to have seen fit to leave an account of the siege. One suspects that it was quietly agreed that it was in nobody's interests to embroil their regimental commander in further controversy.

'Dihydrogen Monoxide' Takes its Toll

This contemporary controversy has been further obscured by a subsequent myth, probably initiated by Lieutenant Cruse in memoirs written long after the event. This has it that Carroll entered the fray too early, and for reasons completely outside his control. Prior to the battle, his battalion had drunk water tainted with gypsum and, suffering as a result from severe diarrhoea, they had no choice but to seek water in Hembrillo Canyon, thereby initiating the battle too early.

Hatch's report, written in the immediate aftermath of the battle, states that, 'Carroll's command was badly used up being nearly three[169] days without water.'[170] This refers to the events of 6–9 April where, as we have seen, Carroll's men were trapped overnight without water; but they, and the rest of Hatch's two battalions, also ran short of water on the march over the White Sands to the Mescalero reservation.

One of the critical contributions of Laumbach's study has been to directly challenge this story by making the discovery that Carroll's battalion had water wagons. This completely undermines the drinking of gypsum water as an explanation for the failure of the Hembrillo Canyon operation. While this explanation makes it clear that Hatch was more than capable of taking control of how this battle was reported, it is doubtful that the poisoned water thesis has any substance. No primary source from April 1880 mentions it. More importantly, had the story been true, it would have provided the perfect means for Hatch to explain away the failure of this operation, and the District Commander made no mention of this story.

The first mention of this story appears in Cruse's memoirs, *Apache Days and After*, published in 1940, and this has been accepted as the correct version of history ever since.

Hatch may have successfully deflected attention away from the reasons why the operation failed; but claims that a major victory had been achieved over the Apaches garnered a mixed reception. Surgeon MacPherson was convinced that they had administered 'a good thrashing' to the

169 Hatch, Tulerosa to AAAG SF, 10 Apr., 1880, mentions Carroll's command having been without water for two days in 'DoNM/GSFO/L&T', NA, RG393, Part 3, Entry 475, Vol. 5, pp.387-388).

170 Hatch to AAAG SF 10 Apr., 1880, NA, RG393, Part 3, Entry 439, p.68; Hatch to AAG, HQ, MDoM, Chicago, 13 Apr., 1880, NA, RG393, Part 1, Entry 2546, p.394.

Apaches.[171] Hatch also claimed a victory, using such terms as 'thoroughly whipped'[172] and 'the pounding the Indians rec'd'.[173] He was accorded a congratulatory telegram by General Sherman; but this praise immediately provoked controversy, even within army circles.[174] Sherman's accolade provoked Colonel Carr to claim that the key role in this 'victory' had been played by troops from his regiment.[175]

The *Grant County Herald* reported various rumoured versions of the Hembrillo Canyon battle on 17 April 1880.[176] These version ranged from the fairly accurate (Carroll wounded twice, with another seven troopers wounded), to the wildly inaccurate, including 23 soldiers killed and 26 Apache scouts deserting to Victorio.[177] It was further reported that Carroll had been forced to retreat, abandoning his camp to the Apaches.[178] Carroll was stated to have been decoyed into an ambush and pinned down overnight. Captain Cusack was also given qualified credit[179] for joining the relief operation in conjunction with McLellan's men.[180]

However, the newspaper's editorials were savage: it lost no time in dismissing Hatch's claims as fiction. It incorrectly reported a mass desertion by Apache scouts, attributing this to their disgust at the inferiority of the 'buffalo soldiers' and a desire to join the winning side.[181] The only reason that disaster had been avoided was stated to be the arrival of the Sixth Cavalry.[182] The thrust of the paper's analysis was to repeat and reinforce its claims that Hatch was continuing to misrepresent the truth to Washington DC, that 'African' troops were useless, and that the 'right kind of troops', in other words, white troops, should be deployed against the Apaches.[183] The *Herald* also claimed that, after Hembrillo Canyon, Hatch's downfall was imminent, for he would no longer be able to conceal the true state of affairs from his superiors in Washington.[184] General Pope was said to have seen through Hatch and to be intending to remove 'this mass of bombast and incompetency'.[185] The press reporting of the events in Hembrillo Canyon also marked the beginning of press criticism of another newspaper, the *New Mexican*, when its version – Carroll leading a surprise attack and driving the Apaches into McLellan – was widely derided.[186] Such mockery would soon change to

171 MacPherson Letter 10 Apr., 1880.

172 Hatch to AAAG SF 8 Apr., 1880, NA, RG393, Part 3, Entry 439 p.16; Loud to AAG Fort Leavenworth, 9 Apr., 1880, Telegrams Sent DoNM, Vol.3, Jan.-Nov. 1880 NA, RG393, Part 3, Entry 431, p.294; Platt AAG Fort Leavenworth to Pope, 9 Apr., 1880, 'Victorio Files', NA, RG393, M1495, Roll 14; Sheridan to AG approximately quoting above report, 10 Apr., 1880 in 'Victorio Papers', NA, M666, Roll 526.

173 Hatch to AAAG, 10 Apr., 1880 in NA, RG393, Part 3, Entry 439, p.69; Loud to AAG Fort Leavenworth, 12 Apr., 1880, Telegrams Sent DoNM, Vol.3, Jan.-Nov. 1880 NA, RG393, Part 3, Entry 431, p.301; Pope to AAG, MDoM13 Apr., 1880 in 'Victorio Papers', NA, M666, Roll 526.

174 Sherman to AAAG DoNM SF, 13 Apr., 1880, NA, RG393, Part 3, Entry 439, p.22; Laumbach pp.247-248.

175 Carr 21 May, 1880 in 'Victorio Papers', NA, M666, Roll 527; Report of Col. E.A. Carr, 11 Sept., 1880, in AR-WD 1880, NA, M997, Roll 35, 1880 Vol. I, p.217; Hart, p.47.

176 See entries in 'Town and County', 'By Telegraph', 'Correspondence' and 'Victory', the *Grant County Herald*, 17 Apr., 1880.

177 See entries in 'Town and County', 'By Telegraph', 'Correspondence' and 'Victory', the *Grant County Herald*, 17 Apr., 1880.

178 The *Grant County Herald*, 24 Apr., 1880.

179 Cusack being said to have managed to get himself lost the previous day.

180 'Regarding that 'Victory'' and Leading Article, the *Grant County Herald*, 24 Apr., 1880.

181 'Correspondence', the *Grant County Herald*, 17 Apr., 1880.

182 'Victory?', the *Grant County Herald*, 17 Apr., 1880; 'Regarding that 'Victory'', the *Grant County Herald*, 24 Apr., 1880.

183 'Victory?' and 'The Outlook', the *Grant County Herald*, 17 Apr., 1880.

184 'The Outlook', the *Grant County Herald*, 17 Apr., 1880.

185 'Town and County', the *Grant County Herald*, 17 Apr., 1880.

186 The *Grant County Herald*, 24 Apr., 1880.

accusations that the *New Mexican* was merely the Santa-Fé-based mouthpiece for 'General' Hatch's propaganda. Again, no matter how wild the reportage, no mention of troops drinking poisoned water is made. Carroll is only said to have run short of water while pursuing the Apaches.[187]

Therefore, while Hatch managed to deflect attention from the true reasons for the failure of the Hembrillo Canyon operation, the territorial press were not going to let Hatch slip away unscathed. While the press were wrong about many things concerning the army in general, and Hatch in particular, they were not wrong in saying that Hatch was misrepresenting the prosecution of the war against Victorio. The problem was that, while coming close to pinpointing the very reasons for failure, they were all too prone to 'bombast and incompetency' in their own reporting of the campaign.

Nevertheless Victorio had nearly inflicted another humiliating defeat on the Ninth Cavalry, and Hatch could count himself lucky that his overall plan had at least driven Victorio off the field. The battle in Hembrillo Canyon did provide clear evidence that Mescalero Apache warriors were leaving their reservation and allying themselves with Victorio. Laumbach argues that Hembrillo Canyon, while not decisive, proved a turning point in the Victorio Campaign.[188] As we shall see, the operation to close down the Mescalero reservation did have a decisive long-term effect on Victorio's operations. However, beyond dispersing what had been a concentration of Apache warriors, it is difficult to see just what impact the battle had on the Apaches. To describe Victorio as gathering a small army of Apaches is perhaps to misinterpret the management of events by the Apaches themselves. The offensive direction of Apache warriors would have been geared towards raiding, and it is quite clear that the Apaches had hit the Rio Grande valley with a number of raiding parties prior to Hembrillo Canyon. But this is no different from their activities throughout the campaign so far. All Hatch managed to do in his Hembrillo Canyon operation was to shift the Apaches' raiding activities westwards. Hembrillo Canyon may be one of the most interesting episodes of the Victorio campaign; but this is primarily due to its being, probably, the biggest battle of the campaign in terms of numbers involved, and because it was such a close-run affair. This battle rested on a knife-edge, and Victorio came close to winning it; yet it was not a turning point in the campaign.

On the morning of 8 April 1880, Colonel Hatch organized the available Apache scouts and troops and scoured the San Andres Mountains to the south of Hembrillo Canyon, but encountered no Apaches.[189] For the moment, Victorio had disappeared yet again. But the Army was now preparing to execute phase two of the operation: a move in force onto the Mescalero reservation.

187 Leading Article, the *Grant County Herald*, 24 Apr., 1880.
188 Laumbach, 2001, p.248.
189 McLellan to Post Adjutant, Fort Bowie, 16 May, 1880 in 'Victorio Papers', NA, M666, Roll 527.

6

The Mescaleros 'Disarmed and Dismounted', April 1880

> Convey to Gen. Hatch my congratulations on his successful blow to the hostile Apaches and that I want him to go on patiently and persistently to make if possible an end to these annual outbreaks. In pursuing hostiles he need pay no regards to boundaries of Departments & must not allow his enemy to claim a safe refuge in an Indian reservation. He may treat them as hostiles wherever found and when made captive they should be deprived of arms and horses and held as prisoners of war. Such as can be identified with murders and robberies will be surrendered to the civil authorities for trial and punishment. The rest after a fair investigation will probably be sent to work in the stone quarries at Ft Leavenworth.
>
> General Sherman's congratulatory telegram to Colonel Hatch received Santa Fé, 13 April 1880[1]

Hatch and his troops arrived at the Mescalero reservation on 11 April 1880. McLellan reported that they left Hembrillo Canyon for Tulerosa at 4:00 p.m. on 8 April, but managed to get lost in the White Sands due to the absence of a qualified guide. By the time they found water, on the morning of 9 April, their mounts, having been without water for 72 hours, were in poor condition. They finally reached Tulerosa on 11 April 1880.[2] One of Hatch's first acts was to issue orders that forage agents from La Mesilla and Las Cruces should have their contracts revoked.[3] Though only circumstantial, this evidence further suggests that unanticipated delays in the provision of forage had delayed Hatch's proposed timetable for attacking the Apaches in the San Andres Mountains. Hatch also issued instructions to the commander of Fort Bliss to direct supplies to Ojo Caliente for anticipated future operations against the Warm Springs Apaches.[4] These instructions suggests that, while Hatch publicly claimed a major victory over the Apaches, he at least was not a victim of his own propaganda, and was already preparing for further operations against Victorio. Having arrived at the Mescalero reservation a day earlier than originally planned (which in itself suggests

1 Sherman to Pope 12 Apr., 1880, NA, RG393, Part 1, Entry 2539, Press Copies of Letters and Endorsements Sent, MDoM, Vol. 13, p.159-161; See also Sherman to AAAG DoNM SF, 13 Apr., 1880, NA, RG393, Pt 3, Entry 439, p.22; Hatch (acknowledging receipt of Sherman's Telegram) to AAG, 18 Apr., 1880, DoNM/GSFO/L&T, NA, RG393, Part 3, Entry 475, Vol. 5, pp.178-180; Loud to General Hatch, Aleman (operator to forward by first opportunity) 13 Apr., 1880, Telegrams Sent DoNM, Vol.3, Jan.-Nov., 1880 NA, RG393, Part 3, Entry 431, pp.304-305; Sherman to Sheridan, 12 Apr., 1880, 'Victorio Files', NA, RG393, M1495, Roll 14; Sherman to Sheridan, 12 Apr., 1880 in 'Victorio Papers', NA, M666, Roll 526.

2 McLellan to Post Adjutant, Fort Bowie, 16 May, 1880 in 'Victorio Papers', NA, M666, Roll 527; Report of Capt. C.B. McLellan, 16 May, 1880; Hatch, Tulerosa, to AAAG, SF, 10 Apr., 1880, DoNM/GSFO/L&T, NA, RG393, Part 3, Entry 475, Vol. 5, pp.387-388; See also MacPherson Letter, 10 Apr., 1880; See also Special Field Order No. 19, 11 Apr., 1880, NA, RG393, Part 3, Entry 450; Pope's Annual Report Year ending 22 Sept., 1880, NA, RG393, Part 1, Entry 2546, p.612.

3 Hatch to Loud, 11 Apr., 1880, DoNM/GSFO/L&T, NA, RG393, Part 3, Entry 475, Vol. 5, p.145.

4 DoNM/GSFO/L&T, NA, RG393, Part 3, Entry 475, Vol. 5, p.144.

that Hatch had planned for the 'known unknowns' which can frustrate any military endeavour, even though he could not predict what actually went wrong), all that was needed before he tried to disarm and dismount the Mescalero Apaches was the arrival of Colonel Grierson's battalion of Tenth Cavalrymen.

Grierson had set off from Fort Concho on 23 March 1880, having received instructions to move towards Fort Stanton and the Mescalero reservation on 18 March.[5] Having left Fort Concho, he proceeded to Fort Stockton, where he received instructions from General Pope that he was not to arrive at the Mescalero reservation in advance of 12 April 1880. This would, it was hoped, avoid giving premature warning of the intended concentration of New Mexico and Texas troops at the Mescalero reservation.[6] Grierson was accompanied by five companies of the Tenth Cavalry and a small detachment of Twenty-Fifth Infantrymen.[7] The orders to march upon the Mescalero reservation must have been received with some anticipation. As we have seen, small Tenth Cavalry detachments had been sparring occasionally with small Mescalero raiding parties for two years. It would have appeared to the troops that they were finally moving in strength to deal decisively with their Mescalero opponents. Even as Grierson's battalion set out, Mescaleros attacked and killed a 19-year-old Mexican and captured a Mexican boy near Russell's Ranch in Texas. Despite a pursuit mounted by a party of Mexicans led by the boy's father, and detachments led by Lieutenant John L. Bullis and Lieutenant W.H. Beck, the Apaches, by splitting into two groups, evaded their pursuers.[8]

Most of Grierson's battalion was instructed to rendezvous at Pecos Falls on 31 March,[9] though L Company, under Captain Thomas Lebo, did not join until 5 April, at Black River Falls in the Guadalupe Mountains.[10] In fact, Lebo's company had been sent towards the Guadalupe Mountains earlier that month. Once Lebo had established a camp, he was to thoroughly scout the New Mexico-Texas boundary between Waco Tanks, to the west of the Guadalupes, and Dug Springs, east of the Pecos River. Lebo was given explicit instructions to attack and destroy any Apaches he encountered. He was also authorised to pursue such raiders onto their reservation. This reflected the belief that most of the Mescalero Apaches were absent from their reservation, and that numerous small raiding parties were at large.[11]

Indeed, Apache raiders had struck the area around Pecos Falls on 30 March. On his arrival, the following day, Grierson charged Lieutenant C. Esterly and a detachment from F and L Companies with their pursuit. According to the regimental return for the Tenth Cavalry, after three days they surprised a Mescalero raiding party under cover of a sandstorm and killed one Mescalero Apache on 3 April 1880.[12] The bi-monthly return tells a slightly different story. The pursuit managed to

9 Smither to Keyes, CO Company, K, 25th Infantry, CO, Co. E, 10th Cavalry, all based at Grierson's Springs, 26 Mar., 1880 & Smither to Kennedy, Fort Stockton, 28 Mar., 1880 in Letters Sent 19 Sept., 1879-11 Aug., 1880, HQ Records DoP 1878-1881, NA, RG393, M1381, Roll 1 Letter No.'s 42; 43, 44; &47; Record of Events Mar. 1880 in Returns From Regular Army Cavalry Regiments 1833-1916, 10th Cavalry Regimental Returns 1873 to 1880, NA, M744, Roll 96; Bi-Monthly Company Muster Rolls for Company's D, E, F, 10th Cavalry, Mar./Apr., 1880 in NA, RG94; 'Indian Affairs' *Army & Navy Journal*, Vol.17, 27 Mar., 1880, p.693.

10 Bi-Monthly Company Muster Rolls for Company K, 10th Cavalry, Mar./Apr., 1880 in NA, RG94.

11 Smither to CO, Co. L, 10th Cavalry, 14 Mar., 1880 in Letters Sent 19 Sept., 1879-11 Aug., 1880, HQ Records DoP 1878-1881, NA, RG393, M1381, Roll 1, Letter No. 37; See also Smither to Lebo, 25 Mar., 1880 in Telegrams Sent 24 Apr., 1879-22 Jun., 1880, HQ Records DoP 1878-1881, NA, RG393, M1381, Roll 1, pp,232-233 Letter No.120.

12 Record of Events Apr., 1880 in Returns From Regular Army Cavalry Regiments 1833-1916, 10th Cavalry Regimental Returns 1873 to 1880, NA, M744, Roll 96; See also Grierson's Report of his Expedition to the Mescalero Agency Mar. – May 1880: submitted 21 May, 1880 (Hereafter referred to as 'Grierson's Report – May 1880'; NA, RG393, Part 1, Entry 2546, p.634; Grierson to AAG, DoTx, 21 May, 1880 in Letters Sent 19 Sept., 1879-11 Aug., 1880, HQ Records DoP 1878-1881, NA, RG393,

get within firing distance of the Mescaleros, but the latter, having remounts, were able to outrun their pursuers. No Mescalero casualties were mentioned in F Company's bi-monthly return, and I Company claimed that only one Mescalero was wounded in the affray.[13]

Colonel Benjamin H. Grierson. Commander of the Tenth Cavalry and the District of the Pecos. Accompanied by a battalion of troops from his regiment, he helped Colonel Hatch in the latter's less than successful attempt to disarm and dismount the Mescalero Apaches. He and his men would later engage Victorio's warriors at Tinaja de Las Palmas and Rattlesnakes Springs, July/August 1880, in a difficult mini-campaign of manouevre. (See Chapters 9-11 this volume) (National Archives)

Grierson expected to concentrate his battalion of approximately 250 men at Pope's Crossing on the Rio Pecos on 5 April 1880.[14] He also established a supply camp on the Black River three to four miles above where it joined the Pecos. This was 17–18 miles north of the Delaware River and approximately 25 miles from Pope's Crossing. This camp was to supply Grierson's command when it returned from the Mescalero reservation. Grierson left his detachment of Twenty-Fifth Infantrymen to guard this camp, warning them to be vigilant and not to herd the stock at night. Grierson estimated that he would return with his battalion on 25 April, but anticipated that he might be delayed. If so, the detachment would be contacted by courier. In anticipation of this delay, the garrison was to reduce the forage issued to their animals from approximately nine to seven pounds a day.[15]

Grierson spread his command to patrol an area 50 miles wide as they moved towards the Mescalero reservation, in an attempt to sweep up any raiding parties currently active in the area.[16] Having joining Grierson on 5 April, Lebo's company was ordered to scout through the Guadalupe Mountains via Guadalupe Creek, and then by either Blue Water or Crow

M1381, Roll 1, Letter No.79; Record of Engagements, p.94; Chronological List, p.49; Webb, 1976, p.88; Matthews, 1993, p. 35; Rister, 1928, pp.193-194.

The bi-monthly return for Company L stated that the skirmish took place on the 2 of Apr. 'on staked plains, half way between White Sand Hills & Pecos River. (Bi-Monthly Company Muster Rolls for Company L, 10th Cavalry, Mar./Apr. 1880 in NA, RG94).

13 Bi-Monthly Company Muster Rolls for Company F & L, 10th Cavalry, Mar./Apr. 1880 in NA, RG94.

14 Grierson to AAG, San Antonio, Texas, 30 Mar., 1880 in Telegrams Sent 24 Apr., 1879-22 Jun., 1880, HQ Records DoP 1878-1881, NA, RG393, M1381, Roll 1, p.237, Letter No.128; Ord to AAG Fort Leavenworth, 1 Apr., 1880, Telegrams Sent DoNM, Vol.3, Jan.-Nov., 1880 NA, RG393, Part 3, Entry 431, p.271; See also Grierson to AAG, DoTx, 21 May, 1880 in Letters Sent 19 Sept., 1879-11 Aug., 1880, HQ Records DoP 1878-1881, NA, RG393, M1381, Roll 1, Letter No.79; See also Tenth Cavalry Bi-Monthly Company Muster Rolls, NA, RG94.

15 Smither to Lane, 6 Apr., 1880 in Letters Sent 19 Sept., 1879-11 Aug., 1880, HQ Records DoP 1878-1881, NA, RG393, M1381, Roll 1, Letter No. 52.

16 'Grierson's Report – May 1880'; NA, RG393, Part 1, Entry 2546, p.635.

Creek to reach the settlement of Penasco on 10 April and rejoin Grierson at that point.[17] The rest of Grierson's command followed the Pecos River to the Seven Rivers, before turning west and making for Penasco.[18] On 9 April, Captain Lebo's company surprised a raiding party encamped at Shakehand Spring (40 miles south of the Penasco River[19]), killing (and burying) a Mescalero warrior, capturing four women, recovering a kidnapped Mexican boy and capturing 21 horses and mules. The Apaches had been preparing about 3,000 pounds of meat and 500 pounds of dried mescal before Lebo's command found and destroyed the camp where they were doing this.[20] The Mexican boy turned out to be the same boy taken near Russell's Ranch, and he was ultimately reunited with his father when Grierson's battalion returned to Texas.[21]

The Tenth Cavalry battalion, having rendezvoused with Lebo again at Penasco, marched via Silver and Elk Springs, and on past the headwaters of the Penasco River,[22] to reach the Mescalero reservation on or around 12 April, as instructed.[23] In fact, Colonel Grierson had followed numerous trails through the Sacramento Mountains and was preparing to surround and attack a large camp of Mescalero Apaches camped near the 'head of the Tulerosa' when he was contacted by Agent Russell and informed that these Apaches had camped there at the agent's request.[24]

In relative terms, the US force which attempted to disarm the Mescaleros was huge. Five companies of the Tenth Cavalry (D, E, F, K, and L) were combined with the three Ninth Cavalry field battalions, bringing the total to 400 cavalry, 75 Indian scouts and 60 infantry.[25] The Second Battalion, New Mexico Troops left at Tulerosa with orders to send their wounded up to Fort

17 Smither to Lebo 5 Apr., 1880 in Letters Sent 19 Sept., 1879-11 Aug., 1880, HQ Records DoP 1878-1881, NA, RG393, M1381, Roll 1, Letter No.50.

18 Grierson to AAG, DoTx, 21 May, 1880 in Letters Sent 19 Sept., 1879-11 Aug., 1880, HQ Records DoP 1878-1881, NA, RG393, M1381, Roll 1, Letter No.79.

19 Lebo described Shakehand Spring (without naming it as such) as lying between the Guadalupe and Sacramento Mountains. (Bi-Monthly Company Muster Rolls for Company K, 10th Cavalry, Mar./Apr. 1880 in NA, RG94) It is named as Shake Hand Spring in the Guadalupe Mountains (Grierson, 20 May 1880 in Endorsements Sent 24 Feb., 1878-21 Feb., 1881, HQ Records DoP 1878-1881, NA, RG393, M1381, Roll 1, p.238).

20 'Grierson's Report – May 1880'; NA, RG393, Part 1, Entry 2546, p.635; Bi-Monthly Company Muster Rolls for Company K, 10th Cavalry, Mar./Apr. 1880 in NA, RG94; Personal File Samuel L. Woodward, NA, RG94, Entry 297, Box 426; Leckie, 1967, p.217; Chronological List, p.49; Webb, 1976, p.88; Record of Engagements, p.94; O'Neal, 1991, p.156; Matthews, 1993, pp.35-36; Rister, 1928, pp.194-195.

21 Grierson to AG, MDoM, 20 May, 1880, NA, RG393, Part 1, Entry 2546, pp.448-449; 'Grierson's Report – May 1880'; NA, RG393, Part 1, Entry 2546, p.635; List of Persons Killed, Wounded, or Captured, by Indians, &c., in the Department of Texas, since Sept. 30, 1879, officially reported by post commanders. NA, RG393, Part 1, Entry 2546, p.633; Correspondence from Newman (Editor of *Thirty-Four*) concerning Hembrillo Canyon and the Disarming of the Mescaleros published in *Thirty-Four* 21 Apr., 1880.

22 Grierson to AAG, DoTx, 21 May, 1880 in Letters Sent 19 Sept., 1879-11 Aug., 1880, HQ Records DoP 1878-1881, NA, RG393, M1381, Roll 1, Letter No.79.

23 'Grierson's Report – May 1880'; NA, RG393, Part 1, Entry 2546, p.635; Hatch to AAG, 12 Apr., 1880, DoNM/GSFO/L&T, NA, RG393, Part 3, Entry 475, Vol. 5, p.201; Leckie, 1967, p.217; Chronological List, p.49; Webb, 1976, p.88; Record of Engagements, p.94; O'Neal. p.156; Matthews, 1993, pp.35-36; Rister, pp.194-195; Personal File Samuel L. Woodward, NA, RG94, Entry 297, Box 426.

24 Russell to CO in charge of troops that may be coming to this Agency by the way up the Rio Tulerosa [Tulerosa] Canon,12 Apr., 1880 in Letters Rec'd File 19 Mar., 1878-14 Feb., 1881, HQ Records DoP 1878-1881, NA, RG393, M1381, Roll 2; 'Grierson's Report – May 1880'; NA, RG393, Part 1, Entry 2546, p.635

25 Hatch to AAAG SF, 12 Mar., 1880, NA, RG393, pt 3, Entry 439, p.41; Thrapp, 1974, p.271; Leckie, 1967, p.217; Matthews, 1993, p.35.

Stanton, and for the remainder to refit for imminent field service.[26] The rest of the troops in Hatch's force were to set out for the Mescalero agency between 5:00 a.m. and 6:00 a.m. on 12 April.[27] Hatch also specifically ordered that the Apache scouts were to 'be kept well in hand and will not be permitted to advance in front of the Companies of the Ninth Cavalry belonging to the First Battalion.'[28]

Hatch, having contacted Russell on 23 March, requested that all Mescaleros be gathered together at the agency with all their animals by 12 April. On Hatch's arrival on the reservation Agent Russell was emphatic that the Mescalero Apaches encamped on the reservation were peaceful. Russell admitted that 'a few' Mescaleros were acting with Victorio, and that many more passively supported the Chihenne Apache leader; but this did not amount to a majority of the Mescalero Apaches. Hatch would have none of this, concluding that the Mescalero Apaches were largely colluding with Victorio at Hembrillo Canyon. He also pointed out that the Mescalero reservation had, for at least a year, been used as a safe haven for renegade Apaches and the illegal trading of stolen goods for guns and ammunition.[29] In view of this conduct, the Mescalero Apaches were to report with arms and stock to the immediate vicinity of the agency or be considered hostile. Hatch also informed Russell that there were more than enough Apache scouts to hunt down those Mescaleros who chose to remain at large on the reservation.[30] In response, Agent Russell stated that all the Mescalero Apaches were camped above the Agency. 'Any Mescalero's that your force may come in contact with in passing through the reservation from Tulerosa in any direction to this place will merit any punishment you may inflict as they all had timely warning of your coming.'[31]

By 13 April, Hatch informed his superiors that over 400 Mescaleros had reported to the agency.[32] Only 65 warriors had been counted at the agency, with Hatch believing that most of the warriors were with Victorio, led by Caballero 'head chief of Mescaleros'.[33] However, bad weather intervened and frustrated Hatch's intention of disarming the Mescalero Apaches on the morning of 15 April 1880. The inclemency of the weather forced the Mescaleros to delay their congregation at the agency. Accordingly, Hatch delayed his attempt to disarm and dismount the Mescalero Apaches until the afternoon of 16 April. The Mescaleros were thoroughly alarmed by the huge US army profile. While some came in reluctantly, others, whether allied with Victorio or not, remained in far-flung corners of the reservation. It was also reported that Victorio had sent emissaries to

26 Special Field Order No.19 para.3, 11 Apr., 1880, NA, RG393, Part 3, Entry 450; See also DoNM/GSFO/L&T, NA, RG393, Part 3, Entry 475, Vol. 5, p.322.

27 Special Field Order No.19 paras.1&2, 11 Apr., 1880, NA, RG393, Part 3, Entry 450; See also DoNM/GSFO/L&T, NA, RG393, Part 3, Entry 475, Vol. 59, p.322.

28 Special Field Order No.19 para.2, 11 Apr., 1880, NA, RG393, Part 3, Entry 450.

29 Hatch to Russell, 11 Apr., 1880, DoNM/GSFO/L&T, NA, RG393, Part 3, Entry 475, Vol. 5, p.140; Hatch to AAG, DoM, Fort Leavenworth, 23 Aug., 1880, NA, RG393, Part 1, Entry 2546, pp.514-520; see also same document in 'Victorio Papers', NA, M666, Roll 527; Same letter in Loud to AAG, DoM, Fort Leavenworth, 23 Aug., 1880 in Letters Sent by the 9MD/DNM/DoNM, NA, RG393, M1072, Roll 6, Jan., 1880-Aug. 1881, Letter No.433, pp282-285.

30 Hatch to Russell, 11 Apr., 1880, DoNM/GSFO/L&T, NA, RG393, Part 3, Entry 475, Vol. 5, p.140; See also Hatch to AAG, DoM, Fort Leavenworth, Kas, 23 Aug., 1880, NA, RG393, Part 1, Entry 2546, pp.514-520; See also same document in 'Victorio Papers', NA, M666, Roll 527; Same letter in Loud to AAG, DoM, Fort Leavenworth, 23 Aug., 1880 in Letters Sent by the 9MD/DNM/DoNM, NA, RG393, M1072, Roll 6, Jan., 1880-Aug. 1881, Letter No.433, pp282-285.

31 Russell to Hatch, 11 Apr., 1880 in 'Victorio Papers', NA, M666, Roll 527.

32 Hatch to AAG, HQ, MDoM,, Chicago, 13 Apr., 1880, NA, RG393, Part 1, Entry 2546, p.400; Loud to AAG Fort Leavenworth, 16 Apr., 1880, Telegrams Sent DoNM, Vol.3, Jan.-Nov., 1880 NA, RG393, Part 3, Entry 431, pp.308-309.

33 Hatch to Platt AAG, 15 Apr., 1880, NA, RG393, Part 1, Entry 2546, pp.403-404.

Plate 6.1. The Sacramento Mountains seen from the vicinity of Fort Stanton. (Photo: Author)

Plate 6.2. Another view of the Sacramento Mountains. These mountains rise almost vertically out of the plain and are riven by a number of steep canyons which lead into the thickly forested inner heights. It was this terrain which provided the Mescalero Apaches with their home. The rugged terrain also provided the opportunity for Victorio and Nana to trade for munitions with little danger of intervention by US authorities, whether civil or military. (Photo: Author)

the Mescaleros, warning them that they were to be removed to San Carlos.[34] Hatch had almost certainly misjudged the political situation on the reservation, believing his immediate assessment of the outcome of the Hembrillo Canyon battle: 'I move from here to the Mescalero Agency. Think the punishment the Indians have received here will have effect to bring the Indians to terms.'[35] Subsequent events would disprove this suggested inclination towards defeat among the Mescalero Apaches. Agent Russell argued that the large numbers of soldiers suddenly appearing on the reservation had made the Mescaleros very nervous, and that, fearing an en masse removal to San Carlos, they had scattered into the more remote parts of their reservation. Russell had only managed to make contact with Nautzilla, and it had taken much persuasion his part to persuade Nautzilla to meet with Hatch, who gave him assurances that the Mescaleros were not being threatened. It was only after this meeting that Hatch told Agent Russell that a full disarming and dismounting of the Mescalero Apaches was intended.[36] Russell already suspected that the disarming and dismounting of the Mescaleros was intended, and refused to sanction such deception. He then agreed with Hatch that the Mescalero Apaches would surrender their arms and horses to their agent.[37] It should be noted that Grierson thought that Hatch had been too focused on preventing trouble with the Office of Indian Affairs and the Interior Department. Moreover, Grierson judged that Hatch had perhaps relied too much upon Russell's ability to bring in the Mescalero Apaches. Grierson also noted that, no matter what course Hatch adopted, it would expose him to criticism from some quarter.[38]

However, Hatch was not complacent. On 15 April, he ordered that the men of his command be issued with 200 rounds of ammunition, and that ten days' rations be carried by pack mules. Any extraneous equipment or supplies were to be left in the care of Lieutenant Gustavus Valois, the expedition's quartermaster.[39] He ordered Morrow's battalion to the south in search of a camp rumoured to be in Dog Canyon or Alamo Canyon. He also sent Carroll's battalion to block this camp's exit to the south.[40] The latter was ordered to remain outside the canyon entrances and block any attempted escape out onto the plains.[41]

In the meantime, Victorio also had to be tracked down. On 14 April, Hatch detached from Morrow's battalion Companies B, H and M, Ninth Cavalry, under Captain Purington, to pursue

34 Correspondence from Newman (Editor of *Thirty-Four*) concerning Hembrillo Canyon and the Disarming of the Mescaleros published in *Thirty-Four* 21 Apr., 1880.

35 Hatch to AAAG SF, 8 Apr., 1880, NA, RG393, Pt 3, Entry 439, pp.16-17; Se also Hatch to AAG, HQ, MDoM,, Chicago, 13 Apr., 1880, NA, RG393, Part 1, Entry 2546, p.394.

36 Report of the ColA, DoI, OIA, Washington, 1 Nov., 1880, pp.251-252; See also sworn statement by George N. Maxwell, Sept. 30 1880 in Report of Inspector Mahan in 'Victorio Papers', NA, M666, Roll 528.

37 R.E. Trowbridge, Commissioner to The Secretary of the Interior, 5 May, 1880 with attached correspondence from Agent Russell in 'Victorio Papers', NA, M666, Roll 527; Russell to Mahan, U.S. Indian Inspector, 27 Sept., 1880 in 'Victorio Papers', NA, M666, Roll 528.

38 'Grierson's Report – May 1880'; NA, RG393, Part 1, Entry 2546, p.635-637; see also identical document in 'Victorio Papers', NA, M666, Roll 527.

39 Special Field Order No. 22, 15 Apr., 1880, para's.2 ,3 & 5, NA, RG393, Part 3, Entry 450.

40 Hatch Mescalero Agency 13 Apr., 1880, DoNM/GSFO/L&T, NA, RG393, Part 3, Entry 475, Vol. 5, pp.149-150; Hatch to Platt AAG, 15 Apr., 1880, NA, RG393, Part 1, Entry 2546, p.403; Loud to AAG Fort Leavenworth, 17 Apr., 1880, Telegrams Sent DoNM, Vol.3, Jan.-Nov., 1880 NA, RG393, Part 3, Entry 431, pp.311-312; Hatch to Pratt 15 Apr., 1880 in 'Victorio Papers', NA, M666, Roll 526.

41 Hatch Mescalero Agency 13 Apr., 1880, DoNM/GSFO/L&T, NA, RG393, Part 3, Entry 475, Vol. 5, pp.149-150.

Victorio.[42] Purington was ordered to commence his scouting between Las Palomas and San Jose.[43] On paper, this detachment looked impressive; yet it only mustered 62 men.[44] A trail that suggested almost 250 Apaches was reported to Purington, and he followed this trail to the Rio Grande. Here, however, he had to break off his pursuit to collect additional supplies which had been delivered to Fort McRae. His horses were also reported to be exhausted.[45] The Captain subsequently followed a trail that led westwards across the Rio Grande and into the San Mateo Mountains. His detachment stopped at Ojo Caliente between 26 and 28 April 1880,[46] no doubt to replenish their supplies before setting out after the Apaches once more. By the end of the month, Purington was able to report to Hatch that a number of trails had been discovered moving into the San Mateos.[47]

Heavy-Handed Operation to Disarm the Mescalero Apaches (See document file no. 57.)

As noted earlier, Major Morrow's now reduced battalion had been ordered to scout Dog Canyon and Alamo Canyon. Early on 16 April 1880, McLellan's company, with Gatewood's scouts, moved off in advance of the rest of the battalion. Within two hours of setting out, heavy gunfire was heard at the agency.[48] McLellan's advance party had encountered a group of Mescaleros apparently running off some horses, and two of them were shot dead by Gatewood's Apache scouts. Hatch claimed that Gatewood was attacked by the Mescaleros, arguing that the reports of Winchester rifles could be clearly distinguished from the Apache scouts' Springfield rifles.[49] The Mescaleros later claimed that they had been gathering in their own stock.[50] Russell stated that this incident caused additional consternation, as one of the Mescaleros killed was Nautzilla's father. Russell added that, even as he tried to calm the situation down, some Mescalero's disappeared.[51] The flight of some of the Mescalero Apaches was later used by Hatch to claim that the Mescaleros had acted

42 Purington was accompanied by Captains Dawson and Rucker and Lt. Hugo. (Correspondence from Newman (Editor of *Thirty-Four*) concerning Hembrillo Canyon and the Disarming of the Mescaleros published in *Thirty-Four* 21 Apr., 1880).

43 Hatch, Mescalero Agency, 13 Apr., 1880, DoNM/GSFO/L&T, NA, RG393, Part 3, Entry 475, Vol. 5, p.147; Correspondence from Newman (Editor of *Thirty-Four*) concerning Hembrillo Canyon and the Disarming of the Mescaleros published in *Thirty-Four* 21 Apr., 1880.

44 Correspondence from Newman (Editor of *Thirty-Four*) concerning Hembrillo Canyon and the Disarming of the Mescaleros published in *Thirty-Four* 21 Apr., 1880; Report from Andrew Kelley concerning illegal trade with Apaches at Canada Alamosa as reported in *Thirty-Four*, 5 May, 1880.

45 Report from Andrew Kelley concerning illegal trade with Apaches at Canada Alamosa as reported in *Thirty-Four*, 5 May, 1880.

46 Return for Apr., 1880 in Returns From U.S. Military Posts 1800-1916 Ojo Caliente, New Mexico, May 1879-Mar. 1882, NA, M617, Roll 877.

47 Hatch to Loud AAA Genl, SF, 1 May, 1880, NA, RG393, Pt 3, Entry 439, pp.449-450. In his telegram of the 1 of May, 1880, Hatch does not make it clear when he dispatched Purington. The implication given in the telegram is that Purington's detachment was sent out from the Mescalero Reservation as a separate detachment from Morrow, Hatch and McLellan.

48 Correspondence from Newman (Editor of *Thirty-Four*) concerning Hembrillo Canyon and the Disarming of the Mescaleros published in *Thirty-Four* 21 Apr., 1880.

49 Hatch to AAG, DoM, Fort Leavenworth, Kas, 23 Aug., 1880, NA, RG393, Part 1, Entry 2546, pp.514-520; see also same document in 'Victorio Papers', NA, M666, Roll 527; Same letter in Loud to AAG, DoM, Fort Leavenworth, 23 Aug., 1880 in Letters Sent by the 9MD/DNM/DoNM, NA, RG393, M1072, Roll 6, Jan., 1880-Aug. 1881, Letter No.433, pp282-285.

50 'Grierson's Report – May 1880'; NA, RG393, Part 1, Entry 2546, p.635-637; see also identical document in 'Victorio Papers', NA, M666, Roll 527; Correspondence from Newman (Editor of *Thirty-Four*) concerning Hembrillo Canyon and the Disarming of the Mescaleros published in *Thirty-Four* 21 Apr., 1880.

51 Report of the CoIA, DoI, OIA, Washington, 1 Nov., 1880, p.252.

in bad faith, and that this invalidated the agreement to hand over surrendered arms and mounts to Russell.[52] One suspects that Hatch had no intention of keeping to this agreement, and the skirmish gave him all the pretext he needed to disown the 'compact' with Russell.

The physical disarming and dismounting of the Mescaleros was to be carried out by Captain Steelhammer's company of Fifteenth Infantrymen. They were to march to the agency at 1:00 p.m., and at 2:00 p.m. were to commence the disarming of the Mescaleros. However, Grierson thought that this would not be so easily accomplished:

> The Agency Buildings, are situated on the north side of the Tulerosa and the Indians as they arrived, instead of being brought directly there were placed in camp by the agent on a timbered ridge at the base of the mountains, on the opposite side of the stream and valley, fully half a mile distant with a boggy bottom between them and the Troops. I think that this arrangement was a mistake, as it left the Indians on the outside and too far away to be sufficiently under control of the military.[53]

Grierson suggested that Steelhammer be directly supported by the Tenth Cavalry; but both Steelhammer and Russell argued that this move would be counter-productive, and Hatch agreed.[54] However, if assistance was required, three shots would be fired to summon the Tenth Cavalry.[55] According to Grierson, watching from a distance with Hatch, Steelhammer's company reached the Mescalero camp without causing a stampede and commenced disarming the Mescaleros.[56] This situation soon changed. Grierson spotted a number of Mescaleros, mounted and dismounted, including Nautzilla, moving away from their camp up the opposite slope, and he urged Hatch to intervene.[57] Hatch demurred, thinking that Nautzilla was trying to prevent this exodus. At the same time, signs of a commotion were observed within the Mescalero camp itself and, at approximately 2:30 p.m., the three signal shots were fired and the Tenth Cavalry battalion sprang into action.[58] They attempted to surround the camps on the other side of the Tulerosa River, but failed to prevent between 30 and 50 Mescalero Apaches from escaping into the mountains. A number of running fights developed and Grierson reported that the gunfire, at times, became very heavy.[59] According to Hatch, as the Mescalero Apaches fled towards the hills, they opened fire on Steelhammer's infantrymen, who apparently held their fire until the warriors were clear of the women and children before returning that fire. Hatch also claimed that none of the warriors would

---

52 R.E. Trowbridge, Commissioner to The Secretary of the Interior, 5 May, 1880 with attached correspondence from Agent Russell in 'Victorio Papers', NA, M666, Roll 527.

53 Grierson to AAG, DoTx, 21 May, 1880 in Letters Sent 19 Sept., 1879-11 Aug., 1880, HQ Records DoP 1878-1881, NA, RG393, M1381, Roll 1, Letter No.79.

54 'Grierson's Report – May 1880'; NA, RG393, Part 1, Entry 2546, p.635-637; see also identical document in 'Victorio Papers', NA, M666, Roll 527; Grierson to AAG, DoTx, 21 May, 1880 in Letters Sent 19 Sept., 1879-11 Aug., 1880, HQ Records DoP 1878-1881, NA, RG393, M1381, Roll 1, Letter No.79.

55 'Grierson's Report – May 1880'; NA, RG393, Part 1, Entry 2546, p.635-637; see also identical document in 'Victorio Papers', NA, M666, Roll 527.

56 'Grierson's Report – May 1880'; NA, RG393, Part 1, Entry 2546, p.635-637; see also identical document in 'Victorio Papers', NA, M666, Roll 527; Grierson to AAG, DoTx, 21 May, 1880 in Letters Sent 19 Sept., 1879-11 Aug., 1880, HQ Records DoP 1878-1881, NA, RG393, M1381, Roll 1, Letter No.79.

57 'Grierson's Report – May 1880'; NA, RG393, Part 1, Entry 2546, p.635-637; see also identical document in 'Victorio Papers', NA, M666, Roll 527.

58 Ibid.

59 'Grierson's Report – May 1880'; NA, RG393, Part 1, Entry 2546, p.635-637; see also identical document in 'Victorio Papers', NA, M666, Roll 527; Grierson to AAG, DoTx, 21 May, 1880 in Letters Sent 19 Sept., 1879-11 Aug., 1880, HQ Records DoP 1878-1881, NA, RG393, M1381, Roll 1, Letter No.79.

have escaped if their women and children had not been in the way.[60] Even so, the only casualty inflicted was a Mescalero woman who subsequently died of her wounds.[61]

Over the next few days, as the troops and Apache scouts pursued those who had escaped into the mountains, some 10 to 14[62] Mescaleros were killed.[63] Grierson claimed that about 250 Mescalero Apaches, men women and children, had been detained, and that approximately 400 horses had been rounded up. The number of weapons taken was rather disappointing, with only 20 to 30 rifles and revolvers, 'good, bad and indifferent', being recovered.[64]

This version of events was contested by Russell. He argued that Hatch had 'let loose' his Apache scouts on the Mescalero Apaches early on 16 January, and that they had killed two Mescaleros just after daylight. These scouts went on to kill a further seven Mescaleros that day.[65] Russell is not specific, but one presumes that this was in the aftermath of the failed attempt to disarm the Mescalero Apaches that afternoon. Of the events leading up to the effort to disarm and dismount the Mescalero Apaches, Russell stated that:

> I called the Indians around me, and after a brief talk told them that the commandant had orders to disarm them, but that he had consented that they might give their arms and horses to me; that I would give each a receipt for their guns and return them after the trouble was over. On this announcement some of those on the outskirts commenced gradually to withdraw, others handed me their guns. Captain Steelhammer and I both appealed to them not to leave; Nautzilla, the principal chief, went out among them and endeavoured to get them to come back again. Very soon it became evident that those who had left would not return, and the troops opened fire on them. The Indians did not return the fire, and none were hurt by the military.[66]

60 Pope to AAG, HQ MDoM,, Chicago 22 Apr., 1880, citing telegram from Hatch dated 18 Apr., 1880, NA, RG393, Part 1, Entry 2546, p.413 & p.414; Loud to AAG Fort Leavenworth, 21 Apr., 1880, Telegrams Sent DoNM, Vol.3, Jan.-Nov., 1880 NA, RG393, Part 3, Entry 431, p.324.

61 R.E. Trowbridge, Commissioner to The Secretary of the Interior, 5 May, 1880 with attached correspondence from Agent Russell in 'Victorio Papers', NA, M666, Roll 527.

62 Hatch's first report states ten killed, a few days later, after a skirmish with fleeing Mescaleros he places the number now killed at fourteen. (Pope to AAG, HQ, MDoM,, 22 Apr., 1880, citing telegram from Hatch dated 19 Apr., 1880, NA, RG393, Part 1, Entry 2546, p.415 & 416; Pope's Annual Report Year ending 22 Sept., 1880, NA, RG393, Part 1, Entry 2546, p.613; See also Sheridan to Townsend, 23 Apr., 1880 in 'Victorio Papers', NA, M666, Roll 527).

63 Hatch to AAAG SF, 16 Mar., 1880, NA, RG393, Part 3, Entry 439, p.58; Whipple to Ord, 20 Apr., 1880, NA, RG393, Part 1, Entry 2539, Press Copies of Letters and Endorsements Sent, MDoM, Vol. 13, p.178; Telegram from Hatch to AAAG SF, DoNM, 19 Apr., 1880, found between pages 199 & 200 in DoNM/GSFO/L&T, NA, RG393, Part 3, Entry 475, Vol. 5.

Surgeon MacPherson describes a fight near the Mescalero Reservation in which he estimated that between 10 and 15 Apaches were killed. While he dates this to the 13 March, 1880 it is probable that he is referring to events on the 17 April, 1880. It is clear from the letter, dated the 26 April, 1880 that MacPherson had just arrived at Aleman Well and had written in haste. A slip of the pen is more than likely.

64 'Grierson's Report – May 1880'; NA, RG393, Part 1, Entry 2546, p.635-637; see also identical document in 'Victorio Papers', NA, M666, Roll 527; Grierson to AAG, DoTx, 21 May, 1880 in Letters Sent 19 Sept., 1879-11 Aug., 1880, HQ Records DoP 1878-1881, NA, RG393, M1381, Roll 1, Letter No.79.

65 R.E. Trowbridge, Commissioner to The Secretary of the Interior, 5 May, 1880 with attached correspondence from Agent Russell in 'Victorio Papers', NA, M666, Roll 527; Russell to Mahan, U.S. Indian Inspector, 27 Sept., 1880 in 'Victorio Papers', NA, M666, Roll 528.

66 Report of the CoIA, DoI, OIA, Washington, 1 Nov., 1880, p.252; See also R.E. Trowbridge, Commissioner to The Secretary of the Interior, 5 May, 1880 with attached correspondence from Agent Russell in 'Victorio Papers', NA, M666, Roll 527; See also Russell to Mahan, U.S. Indian Inspector, 27 Sept., 1880 in 'Victorio Papers', NA, M666, Roll 528.

Russell argued that the subsequent treatment of those Mescaleros who did not attempt to leave, being confined to the agency under guard, was an unwarranted punishment of the innocent.[67] He suspected some of the troops of plundering the Mescalero camp while ostensibly seeking concealed weapons;[68] and he also protested the removal of the confiscated horses to Fort Stanton.[69] As noted earlier, Hatch regarded the attempt to flee as an act of bad faith by the Mescalero Apaches, since they had promised to surrender their arms and horses peacefully. As far as he was concerned, those held were 'not entitled to any consideration except that of being held prisoners.'[70] Indeed, Hatch made it quite clear that the ponies taken from the Mescaleros and held at Fort Stanton were, under no circumstances, to be returned to the Apaches.[71] On 17 April, an irate Russell wrote to Hatch to complain about the sudden removal of these horses from the agency to Fort Stanton. Hatch responded that this move had been prompted by the suspected attempts made by Mescalero Apaches to recover their horses from the agency corral.[72] Russell's protests were in vain, as the Secretary of War argued that the army had, for some time, had evidence that the Mescalero reservation was a base for raiding and illegal trading in plundered goods.[73]

Finally, Russell also objected to the conditions imposed on the captive Mescaleros, as outlined by N.J. Carter, the agency physician:

> I have the honor to submit the following Special Sanitary Report of the Mescalero Apache Indians, now held as prisoners of war at this place. Some five days ago these captives to the number of over two hundred and forty (240) men women and children were huddled together into a cowpen or corral containing about one fourth of an acre of ground covered to a depth of from two (2) to five (5) inches of half rotted manure and other debris, the decomposition of which under the warm sun of the past days is producing an atmosphere, in connection with the body excrements inseparably connected with crowding together so many little children, very injurious to health, as is shown by an unusual number on sick list during the past few days – one case proving rapidly fatal.
>
> On view of the foregoing facts, as well as a fear of an increase in sickness and mortality, I, respectfully submit the propriety of removing at once the captives to a more healthful location, giving them more space, and where better sanitary measures can be enforced.[74]

---

67 See for instance comments made by Russell about 'peaceable Indians' being held as prisoners in CoIA to the secretary of the Interior, 19 Apr., 1880 in Special Orders No. 109, 'Victorio Papers', NA, M666, Roll 527; R.E. Trowbridge, Commissioner to The Secretary of the Interior, 5 May, 1880 with attached correspondence from Agent Russell in 'Victorio Papers', NA, M666, Roll 527.

68 R.E. Trowbridge, Commissioner to The Secretary of the Interior, 5 May, 1880 with attached correspondence from Agent Russell in 'Victorio Papers', NA, M666, Roll 527; Russell to Mahan, U.S. Indian Inspector, 27 Sept., 1880 in 'Victorio Papers', NA, M666, Roll 528.

69 Report of the CoIA, DoI, OIA, Washington, 1 Nov., 1880, p.252; R.E. Trowbridge, Commissioner to The Secretary of the Interior, 5 May, 1880 with attached correspondence from Agent Russell in 'Victorio Papers', NA, M666, Roll 527.

70 Hatch to AAG, DoM, Fort Leavenworth, Kas, 23 Aug., 1880, NA, RG393, Part 1, Entry 2546, pp.514-520; see also same document in 'Victorio Papers', NA, M666, Roll 527; Same letter in Loud to AAG, DoM, Fort Leavenworth, 23 Aug., 1880 in Letters Sent by the 9MD/DNM/DoNM, NA, RG393, M1072, Roll 6, Jan., 1880-Aug. 1881, Letter No.433, pp282-285.

71 Hatch to Steelhammer and Russell, 17 Apr., 1880, DoNM/GSFO/L&T, NA, RG393, Part 3, Entry 475, Vol. 5, p.165 & 166.

72 R.E. Trowbridge, Commissioner to The Secretary of the Interior, 5 May, 1880 with attached correspondence from Agent Russell in 'Victorio Papers', NA, M666, Roll 527.

73 See Chief Clerk for the Secretary of War to the Secretary of the Interior, 27 Apr., 1880 in Special Orders No. 109, 'Victorio Papers', NA, M666, Roll 527.

74 R.E. Trowbridge, Commissioner to The Secretary of the Interior, 5 May, 1880 with attached correspondence from Agent Russell in 'Victorio Papers', NA, M666, Roll 527.

In fact, both parties were correct in their statements. Yet neither was willing to acknowledge the element of truth in the other's position. Russell was quite right to point out that some of the Mescalero Apaches had not been involved in any hostile activity. However, Russell was very unwilling to accept that any Mescaleros *had* been involved in these activities, and usually agreed only when confronted by the most unequivocal evidence. Equally, the US army, from the top down, was absolutely convinced that the Mescalero reservation was a hotbed of disloyalty and sedition,[75] and that, despite the presence of some possibly innocent parties, the only solution was to declare martial law. Grierson thought that Russell was an honest man trying to achieve the impossible. The Agent, he observed, did not have the means to supervise the Mescalero Apaches, let alone keep a vaguely accurate account of their numbers or movements on or off the reservation. This, Grierson strongly argued, could be put down to the rugged nature of the terrain selected for the reservation. This allowed the Apaches to carry on with their existing way of life and allowed unscrupulous US citizens to carry on a lucrative trade in liquor, weapons and ammunition in exchange for stolen stock. The Tenth Cavalry's commander recommended that the Mescaleros be removed to a more suitable location.[76]

About 50 warriors, including Cab-al-es-so, fled the reservation,[77] some of them later joining Victorio. Hatch reported that most of the Mescaleros held in captivity were women and children. He also stated that as most of them had been allied with Victorio and were 'probably under the impression when made prisoner they were going to be tried & hung'.[78] These prisoners were placed under a 'strong guard' commanded by Captain Steelhammer.[79] Hatch instructed the commander of Fort Bliss to send all the dismounted men of L Company, Ninth Cavalry, and G Company, Fifteenth Infantry, to the agency to provide this guard detail.[80] Twenty dismounted troopers from Carroll's battalion were also sent to join this detail on 23 April.[81]

In what was a small illustration of the on-going mutual mistrust between the War Department and the Office of Indian Affairs, when Colonel Hatch telegraphed his intention to hand over confiscated weapons to the Mescalero Indian Agent on 19 April,[82] he received instructions from

75 See 'Grierson's Report – May 1880'; NA, RG393, Part 1, Entry 2546, p.635-637; see also identical document in 'Victorio Papers', NA, M666, Roll 527.

76 'Grierson's Report – May 1880'; NA, RG393, Part 1, Entry 2546, p.635-637; see also identical document in 'Victorio Papers', NA, M666, Roll 527; Grierson to AAG, DoTx, 21 May, 1880 in Letters Sent 19 Sept., 1879-11 Aug., 1880, HQ Records DoP 1878-1881, NA, RG393, M1381, Roll 1, Letter No.79.

77 Hatch to Loud AAAG SF, 1 May, 1880, NA, RG393, Pt 3, Entry 439, pp.450-451; Hatch to AAG, 15 Apr., 1880, DoNM/GSFO/L&T, NA, RG393, Part 3, Entry 475, Vol. 5, p.204 & p.205; Loud to AAG Fort Leavenworth, 3 May (citing Report by Hatch, Ojo Caliente, 1 May, 1880, rec'd Fort Craig 3 May, 1880), Telegrams Sent DoNM, Vol.3, Jan.-Nov., 1880 NA, RG393, Part 3, Entry 431, pp.364-365; Correspondence from Newman (Editor of *Thirty-Four*) concerning Hembrillo Canyon and the Disarming of the Mescaleros published in *Thirty-Four* 21 Apr., 1880.

78 Hatch to Platt AAG, 16 Apr., 1880, NA, RG393, Part 1, Entry 2546, p.406; Hatch to AAAG SF, 16 Mar., 1880, NA, RG393, Part 3, Entry 439, p.59; Whipple to Ord, 20 Apr., 1880, NA, RG393, Part 1, Entry 2539, Press Copies of Letters and Endorsements Sent, MDoM, Vol. 13, p.178; Loud to AAG Fort Leavenworth, 15 Apr., 1880, Telegrams Sent DoNM, Vol.3, Jan.-Nov., 1880 NA, RG393, Part 3, Entry 431, pp.318-319; Sheridan to Townsend, 20 Apr., 1880 in 'Victorio Papers', NA, M666, Roll 526.

79 Hatch to Loud AAAG SF, 1 May, 1880, NA, RG393, Pt 3, Entry 439, p.448; Loud to AAG Fort Leavenworth, 3 May (citing Report by Hatch, Ojo Caliente, 1 May, 1880, rec'd Fort Craig 3 May, 1880), Telegrams Sent DoNM, Vol.3, Jan.-Nov., 1880 NA, RG393, Part 3, Entry 431, pp.364-365.

80 Hatch, Mescalero Agency, 14 Apr., 1880, DoNM/GSFO/L&T, NA, RG393, Part 3, Entry 475, Vol. 5, p.152.

81 Hatch to Steelhammer from San Nicholas Springs, 23 Apr., 1880, DoNM/GSFO/L&T, NA, RG393, Part 3, Entry 475, Vol. 5, p.181.

82 Hatch to AAAG SF, 17 Mar., 1880, NA, RG393, Part 3, Entry 439, p.60; Hatch to Platt AAG, 17 Apr., 1880, NA, RG393, Part 1, Entry 2546, p.407; (Loud to AAG Fort Leavenworth, 19 Apr., 1880,

the War Department on 23 April not to leave confiscated weapons with the Indian Agent, but to place them in secure storage at Fort Stanton.[83] Concerning the confiscated horses and other items recognised as having been stolen from Texas, Hatch also authorised Colonel Grierson to take such animals with him when the Tenth Cavalry battalion returned to Texas.[84] The unclaimed mules were, if suitable, recruited into the US army, and unclaimed horses were distributed to the Apache scouts.[85]

A more significant issue were the accusations levelled by the Office of Indian Affairs, through the Department of the Interior, that Hatch had acted with 'unnecessary cruelty'. (See document file nos. 57.2 and 57.3.) Sherman ordered Sheridan to investigate the matter.[86] 'Acts of unnecessary cruelty' is the phrase used by the Adjutant General's Office on 7 December 1880, when passing on instructions from the Secretary of War to the General of the Army to investigate Russell's and Mahan's reports. In response, the General of the Army referred to General Hatch's report of 23 August 1880,[87] which stated that all but one of the Mescaleros killed had been outside the boundaries agreed before the operation and had been considered hostile. Further action was not necessary 'unless specific charges and specifications are preferred by some responsible party and a general court martial ordered by the President.'[88] Grierson's evaluation of Russell as an honest man seems to be broadly correct. What is also apparent is that Russell's immediate superior, J.R. Mahan, Indian Inspector, New Mexico, would spare no effort to attribute to Hatch's actions the darkest of motives. (See document file no. 57.2.)

The Ninth and Tenth Cavalry Pursue the Fugitive Mescalero Apaches

In the short term, the operation to disarm and dismount the Mescalero Apaches was botched. It did not succeed in dismounting or disarming those Mescaleros inclined to resist the US army; and it provided Victorio with some new recruits. Whatever feelings he voiced on the matter publicly, Hatch was well aware of the implications of the attempt to disarm the Mescaleros. On 18 April 1880, he reported that Agent Russell estimated that 35 Mescalero warriors had joined Victorio (an underestimation in Hatch's opinion). However, in the longer strategic term, the reservation's role as a source of reinforcements and trade (particularly in guns and ammunition) for Victorio, was seriously undermined.[89]

Telegrams Sent DoNM, Vol.3, Jan.-Nov., 1880 NA, RG393, Part 3, Entry 431, p.321.

83 Platt AAG Ft Leavenworth to AAAG DoNM 23 Apr., 1880, NA, RG393, Pt 3, Entry 439, p.23; Loud to Hatch (Operator at Mesilla will send by mail to Paraje and hold duplicate to be sent to General Hatch when his address is known), 24 Apr., 1880, Telegrams Sent DoNM, Vol.3, Jan.-Nov., 1880 NA, RG393, Part 3, Entry 431, pp.330-331.

84 Hatch to Platt AAG, 17 Apr., 1880, NA, RG393, Part 1, Entry 2546, p.408; Platt to AAG HQ MDoM, 20 Apr., 1880 in 'Victorio Papers', NA, M666, Roll 527.

85 Hatch to Platt AAG, 17 Apr., 1880, NA, RG393, Part 1, Entry 2546, p.410; Loud to AAG Fort Leavenworth, 19 Apr., 1880, Telegrams Sent DoNM, Vol.3, Jan.-Nov., 1880 NA, RG393, Part 3, Entry 431, pp.320-321; Whipple to AAG H.Q. MDoM, 20 Apr., 1880 in 'Victorio Papers', NA, M666, Roll 526.

86 Sherman to Sheridan, 11 Jun. 1880 in 'Victorio Papers', NA, M666, Roll 527.

87 Hatch to AAG, DoM, Fort Leavenworth, Kas, 23 Aug., 1880, NA, RG393, Part 1, Entry 2546, pp.514-520; see also same document in 'Victorio Papers', NA, M666, Roll 527; Same letter in Loud to AAG, DoM, Fort Leavenworth, 23 Aug., 1880 in Letters Sent by the 9MD/DNM/DoNM, NA, RG393, M1072, Roll 6, Jan., 1880-Aug. 1881, Letter No.433, pp282-285.

88 Secretary of War to the General of the Army, 7 Dec., 1880 in 'Victorio Papers', NA, M666, Roll 528.

89 See Thrapp, 1974, p271-273; Worcester, 1979, pp.227-228; Leckie, 1967, pp. 217-219; Haley, 1981, p.327.

The fleeing Mescaleros scattered southwards with detachments of the Ninth and Tenth Cavalry in hot pursuit. Hatch issued clear instructions to his officers that all Apaches not surrendered and held at the agency were to be considered hostile.[90] Hatch first sent Morrow on a sweep southwards through the Sacramento Mountains, while McLellan and the Apache scouts scoured the White Mountains to the north.[91] The Apache scouts commanded by Lieutenant Mills, attached to Morrow's battalion, caught up with some of the Mescalero warriors, in Dog Canyon in the southern reaches of the Sacramento Mountains on 17 April. Lieutenant Mills's detachment of Apache scouts exterminated 'a small party of Indians. Killed three got their arms and twenty head of stock.'[92] Van C. Smith, serving with Mills's detachment, was apparently credited with taking one of the Mescalero's scalps. Smith stated that the three Mescaleros had been fleeing towards the San Andres.[93]

Hatch's longer-term plan was to send the Ninth Cavalry after Victorio, while the Tenth Cavalry helped to mop up the fugitive Mescaleros.[94] As other Mescaleros were thought to be fleeing southwards, towards the Guadalupe Mountains, Hatch ordered Grierson to pursue them,[95] tasking the Tenth Cavalry battalion with scouring the Guadalupe Mountains until 1 May, at which point the battalion would return to Texas.[96] On 20 April, a detachment of L Company, Tenth Cavalry, under the command of Lieutenant Maxon, scattered five Mescaleros, killing one and capturing five horses, between the Rio Fresnal and the Rio Alamo.[97] Grierson's command spent some days scouting the

90 Hatch, Mescalero Agency, to Grierson, 17 Apr., 1880, DoNM/GSFO/L&T, NA, RG393, Part 3, Entry 475, Vol. 5, p.161; Hatch to Grierson, 17 Apr., 1880 in Letters Rec'd File 19 Mar., 1878-14 Feb., 1881, HQ Records DoP 1878-1881, NA, RG393, M1381, Roll 2.

91 Hatch to AAAG SF, 18 Apr., 1880, NA, RG393, Part 3, Entry 439, p.61-62; Hatch to Loud AAAG SF, 1 May, 1880, NA, RG393, Pt 3, Entry 439, pp.448-449; Hatch, Mescalero Agency, to Morrow 17 Apr., 1880, DoNM/GSFO/L&T, NA, RG393, Part 3, Entry 475, Vol. 5, pp.160; Hatch to AAG, 18 Apr., 1880, DoNM/GSFO/L&T, NA, RG393, Part 3, Entry 475, Vol. 5, p.210; Loud to AAG Fort Leavenworth, 21 Apr., 1880, Telegrams Sent DoNM, Vol.3, Jan.-Nov., 1880 NA, RG393, Part 3, Entry 431, p.325.

92 McLellan to Post Adjutant, Fort Bowie, 16 May, 1880 in 'Victorio Papers', NA, M666, Roll 527; See also Report of Capt. C.B. McLellan, 16 May, 1880. Telegram from Hatch to AAAG SF, DONM, 19 Apr., 1880, found between pages 199 & 200 in DoNM/GSFO/L&T, NA, RG393, Part 3, Entry 475, Vol. 5; Pope to AAG, HQ. MDoM,, 22 Apr., 1880, citing telegram from Hatch dated 19 Apr., 1880, NA, RG393, Part 1, Entry 2546, p.415 & 416; Hatch to AAAG SF, 19 Apr., 1880, NA, RG393, Part 3, Entry 439, p.63; Loud to AAG Fort Leavenworth, 21 Apr., 1880, Telegrams Sent DoNM, Vol.3, Jan.-Nov., 1880 NA, RG393, Part 3, Entry 431, pp.325-326; Sheridan to Townsend 23 Apr., 1880, NA, RG393, Part 1, Entry 2539, Press Copies of Letters and Endorsements Sent, MDoM, Vol. 13, pp.190-191; Sheridan to Townsend, 23 Apr., 1880, in 'Victorio Papers', NA, M666, Roll 527; Leckie, 1967, p.220; Thrapp, 1974, p273; Chronological List, p.49; Webb, 1976, p.89; Record of Engagements, p.95; O'Neal, 1991, p.177; Beyer & Keydal (vi), p.376; Sonnichsen, 1973, p.202 Sonnichsen quotes but does not cite his source.

93 *Thirty-Four*, 28 Apr., 1880.

94 Pope to Sheridan, 27 Apr., 1880, 'Victorio Files', NA, RG393, M1495, Roll 14.

95 Pope to AAG, HQ, MDoM,, 22 Apr., 1880, citing telegram from Hatch dated 19 Apr., 1880, NA, RG393, Part 1, Entry 2546, p.415 & 416; Hatch to AAAG SF, 19 Apr., 1880, NA, RG393, Part 3, Entry 439, pp.63-64; Telegram from Hatch to AAAG SF, DoNM, 19 Apr., 1880, found between pages 199 & 200 in DoNM/GSFO/L&T, NA, RG393, Part 3, Entry 475, Vol. 5; Loud to AAG Fort Leavenworth, 21 Apr., 1880, Telegrams Sent DoNM, Vol.3, Jan.-Nov., 1880 NA, RG393, Part 3, Entry 431, pp.325-326; Sheridan to Townsend 23 Apr., 1880, NA, RG393, Part 1, Entry 2539, Press Copies of Letters and Endorsements Sent, MDoM, Vol. 13, pp.190-191; Telegram from Hatch to AAAG SF, DoNM, 19 Apr., 1880, found between pages 199 & 200 in DoNM/GSFO/L&T, NA, RG393, Part 3, Entry 475, Vol. 5.

96 Hatch to Loud AAA Genl SF, 1 May, 1880, NA, RG393, Pt 3, Entry 439, p.448.

97 'Grierson's Report – May 1880'; NA, RG393, Part 1, Entry 2546, p.637; Bi-Monthly Company Muster Rolls for Company L, 10th Cavalry Mar./Apr., 1880 in NA, RG94; Record of Engagements, p.95;

Sacramento and Guadalupe mountains, rendezvousing on the Penasco River. Here they found the local settlers in a state of panic over widespread rumours of vengeful Mescalero raiders, most of which proved to be false.[98] The next eight days were spent scouting from the Penasco country to the Black River, but the Tenth Cavalry battalion encountered no further Apaches. Grierson arrived at Fort Davis on 8 May 1880,[99] and by 16 May was back at Fort Concho, having covered approximately 1,500 miles with his cavalrymen.[100]

Most importantly, Grierson, while in the process of returning to Texas, redeployed part of his battalion in anticipation of further encounters with Apaches. L Company, Tenth Cavalry, was tasked with picketing the Guadalupe Mountains around Mansanita Springs, while F Company was left to guard the Black River Falls. These detachments were left with supplies to last until 30 June, and orders to patrol the country between the Pecos and El Paso, and, if necessary, north to Fort Stanton.[101] D Company was ordered to Grierson's Springs to continue scouting duties from that point.[102] On his return to Fort Concho, Grierson also ordered H Company, under Captain Carpenter, to occupy Eagle Springs. M Company, already stationed at the headwaters of the North Concho River, was to maintain vigorous patrols in all directions.[103] While these deployments were a tacit admission of the failure of the US army to disarm the Mescalero Apaches,[104] some of them would become key components of Grierson's defence of western Texas in July and August 1880. (See Chapters 9-11.)

Within days of the US Army's attempt to disarm and dismount the Mescalero Apaches, the latter retaliated. Bill Smith a freighter, was killed at Penasco on 18 April, and a second freighter, Sam Smith, was killed near Las Vegas on 21 April. Both their wagons were ransacked. Sheepherders Juan Chavez, Trujillo and one other were also reported to have been killed by Mescaleros. In

Record of Events Apr., 1880 in Returns From Regular Army Cavalry Regiments 1833-1916, 10th Cavalry Regimental Returns 1873 to 1880, NA, M744, Roll 96; Sonnichsen, pp.210-202; Chronological List, p.49; Webb, 1976, p.89; Matthews, 1993, p.36.

98 'Grierson's Report – May 1880'; NA, RG393, Part 1, Entry 2546, p.637.

99 Grierson to AAG, San Antonio, Texas, 9 May, 1880 in Telegrams Sent 24 Apr., 1879-22 Jun., 1880, HQ Records DoP 1878-1881, NA, RG393, M1381, Roll 1, p.242, Letter No.137.

100 'Grierson's Report – May 1880'; NA, RG393, Part 1, Entry 2546, pp.637-638; Matthews, 1993, p.37.

101 Smither to CO, Co. L & F, 10th Cavalry & Smither to CO, Fort Stockton, 3 May, 1880 in Letters Sent 19 Sept., 1879-11 Aug., 1880, HQ Records DoP 1878-1881, NA, RG393, NA, RG393, M1381, Roll 1, Letter No.58, 61 & 62; Vincent (in the absence of General Ord) to the AG, Chicago Illinois, 11 May, 1880, 'Victorio Files', NA, RG393, M1495, Roll 14; Loud to Hatch, (Care of CO Bayard who will forward to General as soon as his whereabouts are known), 14 May, 1880, Telegrams Sent DoNM, Vol.3, Jan.-Nov., 1880 NA, RG393, Part 3, Entry 431, pp.400-401; Grierson to AAG DoTx, 9 May, 1880 in 'Victorio Papers', NA, M666, Roll 527; Telegram rec'd 10 May, 1880 (unclear from whom to whom) in Letters Received by HQ DoNM, Sept. 1865-Aug. 1890, NA, RG393, M1088, Roll 40, Jan.-Jun. 1880; Grierson to AAG, DoTx, 21 May, 1880 in Letters Sent 19 Sept., 1879-11 Aug., 1880, HQ Records DoP 1878-1881, NA, RG393, M1381, Roll 1, Letter No.79; Record of Events May 1880 in Returns From Regular Army Cavalry Regiments 1833-1916, 10th Cavalry Regimental Returns 1873 to 1880, NA, M744, Roll 96; Matthews, 1993, p.36.

102 Smither to CO, Co. D, 10th Cavalry, 3 May, 1880 in Letters Sent 19 Sept., 1879-11 Aug., 1880, HQ Records DoP 1878-1881, NA, RG393, M1381, Roll 1, Letter No.57; Grierson to AAG, DoTx, 21 May, 1880 in Letters Sent 19 Sept., 1879-11 Aug., 1880, HQ Records DoP 1878-1881, NA, RG393, M1381, Roll 1, Letter No.79.

103 Smither to CO, Co. M, 10th Cavalry, 25 May, 1880 in Letters Sent 19 Sept., 1879-11 Aug., 1880, HQ Records DoP 1878-1881, NA, RG393, M1381, Roll 1, Letter No.72; See also Matthews, 1993, p.37.

104 See for instance comment that large numbers of Apaches were thought to be at large from the Mescalero Reservation in Smither to CO, Co. F, 10th Cavalry, 3 May, 1880 in Letters Sent 19 Sept., 1879-11 Aug., 1880, HQ Records DoP 1878-1881, NA, RG393, M1381, Roll 1, Letter No. 62.

the same area, 16 mules were reported stolen by members of Victorio's band.[105] By 20 May, 14 Mescalero Apaches, who were suspected of being those who had killed Sam Smith, had killed five cattle and stole 13 horses from Catron Ranch, only 30 miles from Fort Stanton.[106]

By the middle of May, Captain Steelhammer reported that, while he had under guard 42 Mescalero men, 124 women, 70 children and 20 infants:[107]

> quite a number of small bands of Mescaleros, who evidently have no intention of joining Victorio are scattered over the country and issuing from their various hiding places continually committing serious depredations.[108]

Steelhammer argued that these Mescaleros had had ample time to surrender, and when enough troops could be spared, these bands should be hunted down, punished and forced onto the reservation.[109] Reports of continuing depredations led to demands that a detachment of troops be stationed at Three Rivers.[110] By 27 May, a leading Mescalero, four warriors, four women and one child had also surrendered. Steelhammer now estimated that there were not more than 400 Mescalero Apache in total, and he thought that most of the remainder were now with Victorio. He guessed that the rest would steadily trickle into the agency and surrender.[111]

The Ninth Cavalry Renews its Pursuit of Victorio

In the meantime, the New Mexico Troops returned to the search for Victorio. Hatch ordered Morrow to take the Second and Third Battalions towards the Black Range and San Mateo Mountains, while he himself took the Indian scouts and McLellan's Sixth Cavalrymen back through the San Andres and Soledad Mountains in search of Victorio's trail.[112] Up to that point, Hatch admitted,

105 *Thirty-Four*, 5 May, 1880; 'By Telegraph', the *Grant County Herald*, 8 May, 1880; See also John B. Wilson to CO Fort Stanton, 22 Apr., 1880 in Letters Received by HQ DoNM, Sept. 1865-Aug. 1890, NA, RG393, M1088, Roll 40, Jan.-Jun. 1880.

106 'By Telegraph', the *Grant County Herald*, 22 May, 1880.

107 Steelhammer to AAAG, DoNM, 14 May, 1880 in Letters Received by HQ DoNM, Sept. 1865-Aug. 1890, NA, RG393, M1088, Roll 40, Jan.-Jun. 1880; Loud to Hatch, Tularosa (Old Fort Tularosa) (Operator at Craig will forward by first opportunity), 19 May, 1880, Telegrams Sent DoNM, Vol.3, Jan.-Nov., 1880 NA, RG393, Part 3, Entry 431, p.409.

108 Loud to Hatch, Tularosa (Old Fort Tularosa) (Operator at Craig will forward by first opportunity), 19 May, 1880, Telegrams Sent DoNM, Vol.3, Jan.-Nov., 1880 NA, RG393, Part 3, Entry 431, p.409; Steelhammer to AAAG, DoNM, 14 May, 1880 in Letters Received by HQ DoNM, Sept. 1865-Aug. 1890, NA, RG393, M1088, Roll 40, Jan.-Jun. 1880.

109 Loud to Hatch, Tularosa (Old Fort Tularosa) (Operator at Craig will forward by first opportunity), 19 May, 1880, Telegrams Sent DoNM, Vol.3, Jan.-Nov., 1880 NA, RG393, Part 3, Entry 431, p.409; Steelhammer to AAAG, DoNM, 14 May, 1880 in Letters Received by HQ DoNM, Sept. 1865-Aug. 1890, NA, RG393, M1088, Roll 40, Jan.-Jun. 1880; Loud to Hatch (Lt. Plummer at Craig will forward as soon as possible) 23 May, 1880, Telegrams Sent DoNM, Vol.3, Jan.-Nov., 1880 NA, RG393, Part 3, Entry 431, pp.424-425.

110 F.C. Godfrey, Tulerosa to Steelhammer, Fort Stanton, 17 May, 1880 in Letters Received by HQ DoNM, Sept. 1865-Aug. 1890, NA, RG393, M1088, Roll 40, Jan.-Jun. 1880.

111 Steelhammer to AAAG, DoNM, 27 May, 1880 in Letters Received by HQ DoNM, Sept. 1865-Aug. 1890, NA, RG393, M1088, Roll 40, Jan.-Jun. 1880.

112 Hatch to AAAG SF, 20 Apr., 1880, NA, RG393, Part 3, Entry 439, pp.54-56; See also Special Field Order No. 25 para.2, 23 Apr., 1880, NA, RG393, Part 3, Entry 450; Hatch, San Nicholas Springs, to AAG, SF, 24 Apr., 1880, DoNM/GSFO/L&T, NA, RG393, Part 3, Entry 475, Vol. 5, p.217; Loud to AAG Fort Leavenworth, 26 Apr., 1880, Telegrams Sent DoNM, Vol.3, Jan.-Nov., 1880 NA, RG393,

his troops had been unable to find Victorio; but he claimed that US troops had 'killed about forty bucks and captured about two hundred & fifty head of stock.'[113] He also issued a general instruction to the 'quartermaster and commissary of the dist. to keep the supplies of this department at each post up ... arrangements should be made in time to supply the stores thus exhausted.'[114] Going by previous experience, Hatch was obviously anticipating a long pursuit that must not be hampered by any inability of army posts or forage agents to quickly resupply his columns.

Morrow crossed the White Sands and the San Andres Mountains by way of the San Augustin Pass, and then went on to Santa Barbara, before turning north.[115] On 25 April, with McLellan's detachment, he proceeded to St Nicholas Spring, and crossed the San Andres Mountains, arriving at Aleman on 26 April.[116] He reported that, by this time, the Apache scouts had shot about 200 of the captured horses, as they were totally broken down.[117] This strongly suggests that at least half of the confiscated horses had been handed over to the Apache scouts. This would explain the apparent discrepancy between the number of horses taken and the number handed over at Fort Stanton.[118] Hatch's command then crossed the Rio Grande at San Jose.[119] Crossing the Rio Grande at Fort Selden,[120] Morrow's command rejoined McLellan's detachment, the latter still, presumably, accompanying Hatch, via San Jose to Las Palomas, on 29 April, and the whole command returned to Canada Alamosa on the following day. In response to Captain Purington's discovery of a number of trails leading into the San Mateo Mountains, Van C. Smith, with Apache scouts, was ordered to scout the San Mateo Mountains and rejoin the command at Canada Alamosa.[121] Morrow's and Hooker's battalions were then ordered to scout that range and the Black Range for signs of the

Part 3, Entry 431, pp.333-334; Pope to AAG MDoM, 27 Apr., 1880 in 'Victorio Papers', NA, M666, Roll 527.

113 Pope to AAG, HQ MDoM,, Chicago, 27 Apr., 1880, NA, RG393, Part 1, Entry 2546, p.386 & pp.387-388; Loud to AAG Fort Leavenworth, 26 Apr., 1880, Telegrams Sent DoNM, Vol.3, Jan.-Nov., 1880 NA, RG393, Part 3, Entry 431, pp.333-334.

114 Hatch to AAAG SF, 21 Apr., 1880, NA, RG393, Part 3, Entry 439, p.65.

115 Hatch to Loud AAA Genl SF, 1 May, 1880, NA, RG393, Pt 3, Entry 439, p.449.

116 Hatch to Loud AAAG SF, 26 Apr., 1880, NA, RG393, Part 3, Entry 439, p.56; Hatch to Loud AAA Genl SF, 1 May, 1880, NA, RG393, Pt 3, Entry 439, p.449; McLellan to Post Adjutant, Fort Bowie, 16 May, 1880 in 'Victorio Papers', NA, M666, Roll 527; Report of Capt. C.B. McLellan, 16 May, 1880.

117 Loud to AAG Fort Leavenworth, 27 Apr., 1880, Telegrams Sent DoNM, Vol.3, Jan.-Nov., 1880 NA, RG393, Part 3, Entry 431, pp.337-338.

118 The four hundred horses confiscated during the operation were supposedly sent to Fort Stanton escorted by Co. E, Tenth Cavalry though Captain Kelley was given a receipt for one hundred and forty one ponies, ten colts and twenty-one mules by Lt. Clark at Fort Stanton. (Smither to Kelley, 17 Apr., 1880 in Letters Sent 19 Sept., 1879-11 Aug., 1880, HQ Records DoP 1878-1881, NA, RG393, M1381, Roll 1, Letter No.53; Grierson to AAG, DoTx, 21 May, 1880 in Letters Sent 19 Sept., 1879-11 Aug., 1880, HQ Records DoP 1878-1881, NA, RG393, M1381, Roll 1, Letter No.79; Lt. Clark, Fort Stanton, 18 Apr., 1880 in Register of Letters Rec'd 23 Mar., 1878-30 Jan., 1881, HQ Records DoP 1878-1881, NA, RG393, M1381, Roll 2, p.29, Letter No.35; Kelley to AG, DoP, 22 Apr., 1880 in Letters Rec'd File 19 Mar., 1878-14 Feb., 1881, HQ Records DoP 1878-1881, NA, RG393, M1381, Roll 2) An additional fifteen ponies were handed over to officers in command of the Apache scouts as ordered by Hatch and eleven animals being so broken down as to be deemed worthless were shot enroute to Fort Stanton. (Kelley to AG, DoP, 22 Apr., 1880 in Letters Rec'd File 19 Mar., 1878-14 Feb., 1881, HQ Records DoP 1878-1881, NA, RG393, M1381, Roll 2).

119 Hatch to Loud AAA Genl SF, 1 May, 1880, NA, RG393, Pt 3, Entry 439, p.450.

120 Hatch to Loud AAAG SF, 26 Apr., 1880, NA, RG393, Part 3, Entry 439, p.56; Loud to AAG Fort Leavenworth, 27 Apr., 1880, Telegrams Sent DoNM, Vol.3, Jan.-Nov., 1880 NA, RG393, Part 3, Entry 431, p.337.

121 Van C. Smith Letter dated 28 Apr., 1880, San Jose in *Thirty-Four*, 5 May, 1880.

Apaches.[122] Captain Purington's detachment also joined the command at this point. It was noted that the supply of forage was still very low as 'men cannot be hired to cut hay',[123] which did not bode well for Hatch's need for fresh forage for future operations.

During this movement of troops, there was a minor panic in the region of San Augustin when Morrow's Apache scouts were mistaken for Apaches and, despite there being no gunfire, reports came in concerning a major battle between the army and Apaches. The editor of *Thirty-Four* admonished citizens not to spread false rumours, and to report only accurate intelligence.[124]

Of more immediate import, McLellan's detachment, including Lieutenant Mills's and Lieutenant Gatewood's companies of Apache scouts and Sixth Cavalrymen, received orders to return to Arizona on 1 May, and had returned by 13 May. The Apache scouts returned to Fort Thomas via the Gila; and McLellan was ordered to march straight for Fort Bowie.[125]

The return of the Apache scouts to Arizona, at first glance, seems ill-advised, as Victorio had not yet been caught. However, by 27 April,[126] Hatch had received orders from General Willcox that all Arizona troops were to return to their stations.[127] By this time, Hatch had also received reports that Victorio was moving towards San Carlos, and concluded that the Arizona troops should be sent back to counter this threat.[128] Indeed, Hatch appears to have anticipated a pursuit of Victorio into Arizona Territory. On 26 April, his request for six copies of a map of this area to be furnished him from District Headquarters produced only two copies.[129]

Colonel Hatch also used the recall of the Apache scouts to underline yet again to his own superiors the critical necessity and 'economy' of immediately recruiting equivalent Apache scouts specifically for service in New Mexico. He proposed two companies of 50 Apache scouts, each supported by a company of cavalry and a mule train of 25 mules:[130] 'for this mountain warfare [I]

122 Hatch, San Nicholas Springs, to AAG, SF, 24? Apr., 1880, DoNM/GSFO/L&T, NA, RG393, Part 3, Entry 475, Vol. 5, p. 217.

123 Van C. Smith Letter dated 28 Apr., 1880, San Jose in *Thirty-Four*, 5 May, 1880.

124 *Thirty-Four*, 28 Mar., 1880.

125 Carr to CO Fort Bayard, 7 May, 1880, Troops in Southeastern Arizona, DoAz, NA, RG393, Part 1, Entry 232, Vol.6, 7 May-18 May,1880, p.7; Hatch, General Field Orders No. 4, 1 May, 1880. NA, RG393, Part 1, Entry 183; General Field Orders No.4, 1 May, 1880, Printed Special Orders 1869-1888, DoNM, NA, RG393, Part 3, Entry 446; Hatch to McLellan 1 May, 1880, DoNM/GSFO/L&T, NA, RG393, Part 3, Entry 475, Vol. 5, p.189; Special Field Order No.27, para.6, 1 May, 1880, NA, RG393, Part 3, Entry 450; McLellan to Post Adjutant, Fort Bowie, 16 May, 1880 in 'Victorio Papers', NA, M666, Roll 527; Report of Capt. C.B. McLellan, 16 May, 1880

126 In acknowledging these orders, Hatch's AAAG, Captain Loud at SF, informed his counterpart in Arizona that Hatch's exact location was not currently known 'as he is changing positions every day. Operators at Mesilla instructed to forward dispatch wherever he can reach him. It is thought your dispatch will reach him today. (Loud to Martin, AAG, Whipple Barracks, Arizona, 22 Apr., 1880, Telegrams Sent DoNM, Vol.3, Jan.-Nov., 1880 NA, RG393, Part 3, Entry 431, p.327).

127 Loud to Hatch, (Operator Mesilla will forward to General Hatch wherever he can reach him), 22 Apr., 1880, Telegrams Sent DoNM, Vol.3, Jan.-Nov., 1880 NA, RG393, Part 3, Entry 431, pp.325-326; Hatch, Aleman, to AAG SF, 27 Apr., 1880, DoNM/GSFO/L&T, NA, RG393, Part 3, Entry 475, Vol. 5, p.225.

128 Hatch to McLellan 1 May, 1880, DoNM/GSFO/L&T, NA, RG393, Part 3, Entry 475, Vol. 5, p.189. It should also be noted that General McDowell commanding the Division of the Pacific had requested the return of the Arizona Apache scouts to help deal with Indian 'difficulties' on the Colorado River. (McDowell to Commanding General, MDoM, Chicago, 28 Apr., 1880, NA, RG393, Part 1, Entry 2546, p.417).

129 Loud to Hatch, Aleman (Maps mailed to Paraje), 26 Apr., 1880, Telegrams Sent DoNM, Vol.3, Jan.-Nov., 1880 NA, RG393, Part 3, Entry 431, p.335.

130 Hatch to AA General, DoM, Ft. Leavenworth, 18 Apr., 1880 in 'Victorio Papers', NA, M666, Roll 527 & Hatch to AAG, DoM, Ft. Leavenworth, 18 Apr., 1880 in Letters Sent by the 9MD/DNM/DoNM, NA, RG393, M1072, Roll 6, Jan. 1880-Aug. 1881, Letter No.207, p.142.

should prefer one hundred Indians with fifty soldiers to five hundred soldiers alone.'[131] He also repeated his advice that if these could not be entered as scouts, they should be designated as guides or packers.[132] This was wholeheartedly supported by General Pope.[133] (See document file no. 58.)

This conclusion to the Hembrillo Canyon and Mescalero reservation operations heralded the start of another period of gruelling and largely fruitless pursuit of the elusive Victorio. Publicly, Hatch claimed that 41 Apaches had been killed during the army's operations in April.[134] This claim was dismissed by the editor of *Thirty-Four*, who claimed that the Colonel was misrepresenting the true situation in trying to portray the fighting in Hembrillo Canyon as a victory.[135]

At the end of April, General Pope complained to Hatch that information concerning his campaigning was not reaching Department Headquarters, and implied that Hatch was not using all of the infantry units at his disposal to help protect the area being attacked by the Apaches.[136] An exasperated Hatch pointed out that he had deployed every available man, but that these deployments could not protect railroad construction and the burgeoning ranching and mining enterprises in southern New Mexico.[137] Ultimately, Hatch's request for two Apache scout companies became entangled with army bureaucracy. The entire Department of the Missouri was allowed 200 scouts, and the District of New Mexico had a quarter of that complement.[138] Both Sheridan and Sherman rejected the request for additional scouts on these grounds, overruling the recommendation of General Pope.[139]

Victorio had stolen a decisive march on his enemies. He had gained almost three weeks (nineteen days) respite, allowing his people to rest and recuperate, whilst Hatch concentrated his efforts on the Mescalero reservation. Hatch had to contend with difficulties concerning the maintenance of efficient communication between his headquarters and that of his commander, General Pope. More importantly, even with no direct contact with Victorio, Hatch found that his military resources remained strained. The New Mexico Troops, having been on field service since the beginning of April, needed to rest both men and horses, and to be resupplied. The need for resupply was so great that some posts were authorised to purchase supplies on the open market.[140] At San Jose, on 30 April, B, H, L and M Companies, Ninth Cavalry, all received varying numbers of replacement

131 Hatch to AAAG SF, 18 Apr., 1880, NA, RG393, Pt 3, Entry 439, pp.24-25.

132 Hatch 27 Apr., 1880, Telegrams Sent DoNM, Vol.3, Jan.-Nov., 1880 NA, RG393, Part 3, Entry 431, p.342.

133 Pope to AAG HQ MDoM, 28 Apr., 1880, 'Victorio Files', NA, RG393, M1495, Roll 14; See Pope to AAG HQ MDoM, 28 Apr., 1880 in 'Victorio Papers', NA, M666, Roll 527; See Hatch's original letter in Hatch to AA General, DoM, Ft. Leavenworth, 18 Apr., 1880 in 'Victorio Papers', NA, M666, Roll 527 & Hatch to AAG, DoM, Ft. Leavenworth, 18 Apr., 1880 in Letters Sent by the 9MD/DNM/DoNM, NA, RG393, M1072, Roll 6, Jan. 1880-Aug. 1881, Letter No.207, p.142.

134 Hatch to Loud AAAG SF, 26 Apr., 1880, NA, RG393, Part 3, Entry 439, pp.56-57.

135 *Thirty-Four*, 28 Apr., 1880.

136 Pope to Hatch, via Loud, AAAG, DoNM, 30 Apr., 1880, Telegrams Sent DoNM, Vol.3, Jan.-Nov., 1880 NA, RG393, Part 3, Entry 431, pp.351-352 & pp.355-356.

137 Loud to AAG Fort Leavenworth, 3 May (citing Report by Hatch, Ojo Caliente, 1 May, 1880, rec'd Fort Craig 3 May, 1880), Telegrams Sent DoNM, Vol.3, Jan.-Nov., 1880 NA, RG393, Part 3, Entry 431, pp.364-365.

138 Thrapp, 1974, P.273-274.

139 AG, Washington DC to The Commanding General, MDoM, 5 May, 1880, 'Victorio Files', NA, RG393, M1495, Roll 14; Drum to Comdg. General, MDoM,, 5 May, 1880 in Letters Received by HQ DoNM, Sept. 1865-Aug. 1890, NA, RG393, M1088, Roll 40, Jan.-Jun. 1880; Thrapp, 1974, pp.273-274.

140 Loud to CO Fort Bayard, 20 Apr., 1880, Telegrams Sent DoNM, Vol.3, Jan.-Nov., 1880 NA, RG393, Part 3, Entry 431, pp.321-322.

horses and horse furniture.[141] The following day, A, C, D, F and G Companies, based at Canada Alamosa, received the same.[142]

Hatch concentrated his three battalions at Las Palomas, Canada Alamosa and Ojo Caliente,[143] and recruits for E, I and K Companies were ordered to their respective companies at Ojo Caliente.[144] Further remounts and recruits were delivered to the Second Battalion at Las Palomas.[145] Once it had taken delivery, this battalion was ordered to return to Fort Stanton 'for scouting purposes'.[146] This was in response to the news that there were virtually no troops left at Fort Stanton to guard 200 captured ponies. The continued activities of independent Mescalero Apaches might include a raid on the Fort to recover their mounts.[147] Hatch went so far as to instruct his own headquarters in Santa Fé that if any troops were needed to provide the paymaster with an escort, these should be taken from Fort Union's garrison.[148] Hatch's forces were fully stretched; and Victorio was about to launch a new offensive which would test the Ninth Cavalry to the limits.

141 Special Field Order No.26, para.1, 30 Apr., 1880, NA, RG393, Part 3, Entry 450.
142 Special Field Order No.27, para.1, 1 May, 1880, NA, RG393, Part 3, Entry 450.
143 Hatch, San Nicholas Spring to Morrow, 23 Apr., 1880, DoNM/GSFO/L&T, NA, RG393, Part 3, Entry 475, Vol. 5, p.215.
144 Special Field Order No.27, para.2, 1 May, 1880, NA, RG393, Part 3, Entry 450. These replacements were under the command of Sergeant Jordan Co. K, Ninth Cavalry.
145 Special Field Order No.27, para.7, 1 May, 1880, NA, RG393, Part 3, Entry 450.
146 Special Field Order No.27, para.8, 1 May, 1880, NA, RG393, Part 3, Entry 450; Hatch, Canada Alamosa, to Cusack, 1 May, 1880, DoNM/GSFO/L&T, NA, RG393, Part 3, Entry 475, Vol. 5, p.186.
147 Loud to Hatch, Fort Craig, 29 Apr., 1880, Telegrams Sent DoNM, Vol.3, Jan.-Nov., 1880 NA, RG393, Part 3, Entry 431, p.348.
148 Hatch Ojo Caliente to AAA Genl SF, 2 May, 1880, NA, RG393, Pt 3, Entry 439, p.457.

7

There and Back Again: The Ninth Cavalry Dismounted in the Mogollon Mountains and San Francisco Valley, April–May 1880

> I have not seen a hostile Indian in this camp in three years. Victorio's men know some of the men in this camp as well as those men know Victorio.
>
> James Cooney[1]

The Apaches Raids Intensify, April–May 1880

While Victorio and his followers had successfully evaded the US army in the aftermath of Hembrillo Canyon, not everything was playing out to their advantage. In the short term, Victorio had most of February and March to replenish his arms and ammunition through trading and raiding. Much of the trading was probably done through contacts in or around the Mescalero reservation. Now that the army had taken over the reservation, it would be more difficult to arrange clandestine meetings with illicit traders.

This was not the only source of munitions which was now being put under pressure. Victorio seems to have had a falling out with at least some of the people from the town of Canada Alamosa. By the end of March 1880, Hatch informed the Governor of New Mexico that a detachment of volunteers from the hamlet of San Jose and the surrounding area had formed a militia for their own protection. Hatch recommended that they be given arms and ammunition. All of the volunteers were clearly of Mexican descent.[2] There is a story that one, Maximiliano Madrid, had watched as Victorio delivered an ultimatum to the people of Canada Alamosa, threatening that if they helped the troops, he would destroy the town.[3] A raid near Canada Alamosa, reported in *Thirty-Four* on 5 May 1880, took 40 head of horses and thus dismounted half of its citizens.[4] The Apaches, said to have been Mescaleros, were led by Sanchez and Vicente, who were Warm Springs Apaches.[5] One Clem Hightower stated that:

1 *Grant County Herald*, 14 Feb. 1880.

2 Jose Roman Romero (Captain) 1. Anicita Archuleta, 2. Jose Ma Lucero, 3. Bernardo Parras, 4. Heginio Achuleta, 5. Jose Romero, 6. Malio Baca, 7. Julian, Archuleta, 8. Peliz Lucero, 9. Jesus Baca, 10. Siboricie Duran, 11. Mateo Miranda, 12. Fransten Gallego, 13. Feliz Bernal, 14. Josi Francisco Romero, 15. Juan Andreas Sadillo, 16. Anservio Ruvio, 17. Basitio Chavez, 18. Padros, Bayegos, 19. Juan Lopez, 20. Juan Torre, 21. Juan Velirde, 22. Juan Perria, 23. Bernardino Bayegos, 24. Bartolo Perria, 25. Savi Sanchea, 26. Juan Sanchez, 27. Juan Armjo Ysti, 28. Aristu Crispin, 29. Juan Jaramillo, 30. Jose Jaramillo, 31.Vicente Rives. (Hatch to Lew Wallace, 27 Mar., 1880 in Letters Sent by '9MD/DNM/DoNM', NA, RG393, M1072, Roll 6, Jan. 1880-Aug. 1881, Letter No.171 pp.123-124).

3 Bryan, 1998, pp.124-125 .

4 *Thirty-Four*, 5 May, 1880.

5 Report from Andrew Kelley in *Thirty-Four*, 5 May, 1880.

> P.H. Kelley is the only man in the valley who saved his stock. Fred Sanders lost four; Pat Higgins, one; Jose Lopez, two; Luz Chavez, four; Jose Lieba, one; Luis Encinias, two; and your humble servant, three. They started to drive off two of Kelley's colts and one of his renters, a Mexican from Canada Alamosa told them they belonged to him and they let them go.[6]

On 22 April, Apaches killed Basilio Lobato, Ricardo Jaramillo and Jesus Maria Gonzalez, who were herding sheep and cattle in the vicinity of Canada Alamosa. Juan Jose Moreno was also missing, presumed tortured to death. A letter to *Thirty-Four*, dated 24 April, from Canada Alamosa, openly admitted a past bad association with the Apaches, but claimed to have turned over a new leaf by raising a company of volunteers. It also stated that:

> We have made up our minds that the cottonwoods in this vicinity shall bear fruit if there are any midnight meetings between Victorio's men and some of the persons of this town.[7]

A second letter to *Thirty-Four* from Andrew Kelley informed the paper that some of the illegal traders had joined this company of volunteers, but were being closely watched.[8] (See document file no. 60.) It may be that there was a newer influx of Anglo-American immigrants to the area who, culturally, would have felt no need to reach any accommodation with those they regarded as mere savages. This sort of immigrant would have been very hostile towards anybody, Mexican or otherwise, who traded with Apaches.

Victorio's Raid on the Mogollon and San Francisco Mountains

Even as Hatch was reporting, on 1 May 1880, that he was about to follow trails into the San Mateo Mountains,[9] Victorio and his warriors had already launched a series of raids from the Rio Grande westwards through the Black Range and along the southern reaches of the Mogollon Mountains. This part of the country had not seen Apaches for almost a year and was caught unawares by Victorio's sudden descent. As recently as February 1880, James Cooney, a miner and prospector, had extolled the virtues of this particular section of the Mogollons for mining and settlement. He dismissed the dangers of Apaches: 'I have not seen a hostile Indian in this camp in three years. Victorio's men know some of the men in this camp as well as those men know Victorio.'[10]

Thirteen Mexican sheepherders were reported as slain near San Jose on the Rio Grande, and 5,000 sheep were scattered far and wide.[11] Three 'civilians' were slaughtered near Ojo Caliente on 27 April. A further six were killed near the headwaters of the Rio Gilitfe [Gilita Creek] the next day.[12]

With these actions, Victorio launched a sustained attack on the mining and ranching settlements in the Mogollon[13] and San Francisco Mountains in late April and early May 1880. (See Map 7.1.) According to local tradition, his raid was originally provoked by the ambushing and slaying of four

6 *Thirty-Four*, 5 May, 1880.
7 *Thirty-Four*, 28 Apr., 1880.
8 Report from Andrew Kelley in *Thirty-Four*, 5 May, 1880.
9 Hatch to Loud AAAG SF 1 May, 1880, NA, RG393, Part 3, Entry 439, p.450.
10 'A Communication from the Mogollons', the *Grant County Herald*, 14 Feb., 1880.
11 'Hatch and his Indians', the *Grant County Herald*, 1 May, 1880.
12 See entries in the Chronological List, p.49; Webb, 1976, p.89.
13 Cooney himself reported that by December 1879, there were fifteen mine workings started in his district of the Mogollon Mountains. ('Town and County', the *Grant County Herald*, 13 Dec., 1879).

Apache warriors by local settlers and miners.[14] As noted in Volume One of this trilogy, this is probably the incident where four Apaches were killed just prior to Captain Beyer's fight with Victorio in late May 1879.[15] Writing to the *Grant County Herald*, a correspondent who visited the San Francisco Valley in February 1880, approximately ten months after the four warriors were killed, noted that the settlers were still living in fear of retaliation by Victorio. This prompted an appeal for US troops to be stationed locally to protect the scattered farms from attack.[16] Two months later the Chihenne Apaches returned to exact vengeance for their losses.

Eyewitness testimony, some of which was recorded in the 1930s, stated that the Apaches struck Cooney's mining camp, killing two to three men and wounding a fourth man named Taylor.[17] The latter managed to escape from the Apaches despite a severe leg wound by hiding in a 'prospect hole'. He was attacked between Copper and Mineral Creeks, and ran some distance on his wounded leg before reaching his hiding place. Just before he took cover, he ran past the opening of the Williams mine working and his hat blew off and landed in the tunnel entrance. The pursuing Apaches assumed that he had taken refuge in the mine and rolled some rocks into the passage but did not venture into the mine. Taylor watched the Apaches for some time before being able to slip away to safety.[18] In fact Cooney's mining camp may be better described as a mining campus. The Apaches struck this collection of diggings, catching and killing some of the miners, but the shots fired alerted other prospectors and miners to their danger. Parson Williams and some others were ambushed in a ravine above the mining district, but escaped without loss, having been alerted by hearing three earlier shots. Some of these men raised the alarm in the mining camps and beyond.[19]

Cooney's camp was apparently forewarned of danger by the ambush of four prospectors on Mineral Creek on 28 April. Two escaped to warn Cooney's camp.[20] Leaving two miners named John Lambert and George Doyle[21] concealed, watching over the camp, the rest of the camp scattered to warn the other mining communities and camps in the area. Lambert reported that during the night the two men heard Apaches on the prowl but they were not discovered.[22] The two miners saw several groups of heavily armed Apaches arrive and depart during 29 April, including a sighting of Victorio 'a medium-sized, spare looking Indian, mounted on a fine-looking bay horse.'[23] He was accompanied by a small group of warriors with some women and children driving a pack horse and mule train.[24] The camp was thoroughly pillaged, the loot being carried off on pack animals; and the camp was then burned.[25] James Cooney was not killed in this attack but managed to escape with one Jack Chick. The pair moved westwards to warn the settlements near Alma.[26] Cooney and

---

14 Jones, 1970, pp.32-33; See also Misc.3 Document.

15 See Watt, 'I Will Not Surrender the Hair of a Horse's Tail: The Victorio Campaign 1879', Chapter 6, p.141 & document file no. 4.

16 'From the Fresco 6 Feb., 1880', the *Grant County Herald*, 21 Feb., 1880.

17 American Life Histories webpage – Mogollons of the Early days & The Alms/Alma Massacre testimony.

18 'Williams Ranche on the Fresco May 4th 1880' the *Grant County Herald*, 8 May, 1880.

19 Ibid

20 Humphries, 1988, pp.158-159; See also Rakocy & Jones p.69.

21 Humphries, 1988, pp.158-159. Humphries reconstructed his account from an interview with John Lambert.

22 Ibid. p.159.

23 Ibid. p.159.

24 Ibid. pp.159-160.

25 See 'Massacre in the Mogollon Mining District and Upper Fresco Valley – Letter from Meader, Keller, Meadows & Foster', the *Grant County Herald*, 8 May, 1880; American Life Histories webpage – Mogollons of the Early days & The Alms/Alma Massacre testimony; Humphries, 1988, p.160; Jones, 1970, p.33; Rakocy & Jones, pp.69-71.

26 Small settlement was named Alma in 1878 though the site had been settled for a number of years prior to this date. (See Alma Website).

Chick apparently homed in on the settlement of Alma by howling to provoke a response from the setters' dogs. They had already discovered another two prospectors ambushed and slain as they attempted to reach the settlement.[27] Having successfully warned the settlers of the presence of Apaches, Cooney and Chick attempted to return to their mining camp. Both were ambushed and killed by Victorio's warriors. It was less than three months since Cooney had dismissed the dangers of Apaches in the pages of the *Grant County Herald.*

The return of Cooney and Chick's riderless horses with bloodstained saddles[28] alerted the settlement to the immediate danger, and the settlers attempted to fort up at the Roberts family home.[29] Bullets were moulded and attempts were made to gather up their loose stock. Two settlers, Mutsinger and Potter, set out to render assistance to Cooney and Chick but were ambushed in turn, though they managed to escape.[30] One James Keller, 'who participated in the fighting previous to gathering the families together', and a man named Carpenter reached Silver City to raise the alarm, having escaped from the area at night.[31] The Meader Family were pursued by the Apaches as they approached the Roberts house and had to run from their wagon to the house under fire.[32] Five men, including a Mr Coates, were blasting away at the Apaches on the hill opposite, until shot at from behind. They were forced to take cover in the Roberts cabin, but Coates abandoned his revolver and cartridge belt in the confusion.[33] The Apaches then surrounded the house and a day-long exchange of gunfire ensued. The Apaches tried to panic the settlers with their skirmishing tactics without committing themselves to a full assault as long as the settlers held their nerve:

> The Indians were able to keep up a constant fire as fifteen warriors would drive up and fire then drop back to reload their guns and another fifteen would take their place thereby keep up a constant fire as they were always moving in a circle. There were two-hundred thirteen warriors counted.[34]

Even if they failed to panic the defenders, such tactics gave the impression of far greater numbers of Apache raiders than were actually present.

Only one settler, Willcox, was killed, and another, Murray, was wounded, with one or two Apaches warrior being hit in return.[35] Willcox had unwisely risen up to take a look outside and was

---

27 Humphries, 1988, p.160; Jones 1970, p.34. Humphries reconstructed his account from a 1915 article in the *Mogollon Mining Journal* which had interviewed a number of participants.

28 'Massacre in the Mogollon Mining District and Upper Fresco Valley – Letter from Meader, Keller, Meadows & Foster', the *Grant County Herald*, 8 May, 1880; Humphries, 1988, p.161.

29 Lt Buchanan Silver City to Officer in Charge SF 2 May, 1880, NA, RG393, Part 3, Entry 439, p.445; See also Jones, 1970, pp.34-35; Rakocy & Jones, p.71.

30 'Massacre in the Mogollon Mining District and Upper Fresco Valley – Letter from Meader, Keller, Meadows & Foster', the *Grant County Herald*, 8 May, 1880; 'Williams Ranche on the Fresco May 4 1880' the *Grant County Herald*, 8 May, 1880; American Life Histories webpage-The Alma/Alms Massacre testimony; Humphries 1988, p.161; Jones, 1970, p.34; Rakocy & Jones, p.71.

31 Lt Buchanan to Officer in Charge SF, NA, RG393, Part 3, Entry 439, p.446; 'Massacre in the Mogollon Mining District and Upper Fresco Valley – Letter from Meader, Keller, Meadows & Foster', the *Grant County Herald*, 8 May, 1880; 'Williams Ranche on the Fresco May 4th 1880' the *Grant County Herald*, 8 May, 1880.

32 'Massacre in the Mogollon Mining District and Upper Fresco Valley – Letter from Meader, Keller, Meadows & Foster', the *Grant County Herald*, 8 May, 1880; American Life Histories webpage-The Alma/Alms Massacre testimony; Jones, 1970, p.35.

33 Humphries 1988, p.161.

34 American Life Histories webpage-The Alma/Alms Massacre testimony; See also Jones, 1970, pp.34-35.

35 'Massacre in the Mogollon Mining District and Upper Fresco Valley – Letter from Meader, Keller, Meadows & Foster', the *Grant County Herald*, 8 May, 1880; 'Williams Ranche on the Fresco May 4th 1880' the *Grant County Herald*, 8 May, 1880; *Thirty-Four*, 5 May, 1880.

shot dead.[36] The one Apache who was killed during the fight had managed to work his way close to a horse near to the cabin and was shot by Jim Keller as he rose up in an attempt to steal the horse.[37] The settlers recovered Coates' revolver and cartridge belt from the body of the Apache, but during the night the Apaches managed to recover the body.[38] At nightfall, the Apaches withdrew some distance and held what was taken to be a celebration, but in the morning the settlers could see no sign of them. It was not until the following morning that Captain Madden, with a mixed group of Sixth Cavalrymen and volunteers[39] from Silver City, arrived to relieve the settlers, having set out on the morning of 4 May.[40]

While we have quite a lot of detail about these attacks, the exact dates are unclear. Cooney's camp is widely dated as being destroyed on the 29 April 1880. Yet, if the above dates are correct, Cooney was actually killed on either 1 or 2 May 1880.

Madden had informed his superiors of the situation in the Mogollons and had been granted permission to make a detour to aid the settlers before he adhered to his original orders (See Chapter 6.) to return to Fort Bowie.[41] The arrival of Madden's Sixth Cavalry detachment was very fortunate, as Fort Bayard only had 11 men present for duty.[42] On being requested to intervene to relieve the besieged settlers,[43] Captain A.A. Humphreys responded: 'I do not consider I am in condition to render any assistance unless authority is granted me to abandon post and let it look out for itself.'[44] Captain Madden's detachment of 27 men[45] and the Silver City volunteers continued into the Mogollon Mountains, where they discovered and buried Cooney,[46] 'horribly mutilated', Chick, and a third man named Buhlman.[47]

Madden reported that Victorio was commanding 200 warriors and accompanied by 80 squaws.[48] The bodies of some Mexican shepherds and their families were discovered on 7 and 8 May, as Madden and his group tracked the Apaches.[49] By 9 May, Captain Madden had reached Bush

41 Madden to AAAG, Forces in the Field SE Arizona, 26 May, 1880 in 'Victorio Papers', NA, M666, Roll 527; For a brief summary of Madden's movements see Record of Events May, 1880 in Returns From Regular Army Cavalry Regiments 1833-1916, 6th Cavalry Regimental Returns 1875 to 1880, NA, M744, Roll 63

42 Lt Humphrey Bayard to Hatch Ft Craig, Carr Ft Lowell & AAAG SF 3 May, 1880, NA, RG393, Part 3, Entry 439, p.460

43 Loud to CO Fort Bayard, 3 May, 1880, & Loud to Hatch (Operator Fort Craig will send by courier at once), 3 May, 1880, Telegrams Sent DoNM, Vol.3, Jan.-Nov. 1880, NA, RG393, Part 3, Entry 431, pp.361-363 see also p.70.

44 Lt Humphrey Bayard to AAAG, 4 May, 1880, NA, RG393, Part 3, Entry 439, pp.461-462; Humphreys, Captain 15th Infantry to AAAG, DoNM, SF, NM, 3 May, 1880, NA, RG393, Part 3, Entry 440, pp.82-83; Loud to General Hatch (Operator at Craig will forward by first opportunity) 5 May, 1880, Telegrams Sent DoNM, Vol.3, Jan.-Nov. 1880, NA, RG393, Part 3, Entry 431, pp.377-378.

45 Madden, Camp at Roberts & Keller's Ranch to Carr, Lowell, 5 May, 1880, NA, RG393, Part 1, Entry 235, pp.50-51.

46 James Cooney's grave is sealed under a huge boulder marking the spot where he fell. The site of this skirmish is seven miles north and five miles west of Glenwood New Mexico. (See Cooney and Glenwood websites) His brother Michael, no relation to Captain Michael Cooney, then serving in the Ninth Cavalry, a former customs inspector, took over his brother's prospecting business. Finding a huge boulder he carved out his brother's tomb. (See Thrapp, 1988, p.318 & 319; Misc. 3 Document.) He was also to report that in the aftermath of Victorio's attack upon the mining district that there had been attempts to 'claim jump' various deserted miles by unscrupulous parties. (Cooney to Hatch, 21 Jun., 1880 in Letters Received by HQ DoNM Sept. 1865-Aug. 1890, NA, RG393, M1088, Roll 40, Jan.-Jun. 1880).

47 Loud to CO Fort Bayard, 6 May, 1880, Telegrams Sent DoNM, Vol.3, Jan.-Nov. 1880, NA, RG393, Part 3, Entry 431, p.387.

48 Madden, Camp at Roberts & Keller's Ranch to Carr, Lowell, 5 May, 1880, NA, RG393, Part 1, Entry 235, p.50.

49 'Williams Ranche on the Fresco May 4th 1880' the *Grant County Herald*, 8 May, 1880; Jones, 1970, p.55.

Valley at the head of the San Francisco Valley, after three days' pursuit of the Apaches. He estimated that they were one day behind Victorio, whose warriors had stolen 20 horses from the area the previous night. Madden had left Silver City on 4 May, with four days' rations. His command was relying upon whatever local citizens could supply, and his horses were worn out.[50] George W. Helde, one of the Silver City volunteers with Captain Madden, kept a diary (see document file no. 62) of this expedition, and he lists the recovery of 16 bodies by this detachment. Captain Madden's official report (see document file no. 63) also records the recovery of the bodies of four Anglo-Americans and 12 Mexicans, including two women and four children.

Captain Daniel Madden, Sixth Cavalry. Madden led his company on a long but ultimately fruitless pursuit of Victorio in the Mogollon Mountains in May 1880. He would later lose his son to those same Apache warriors when they ambushed a stagecoach in September 1880. (See Chapter 14 this volume) (Carlisle Barracks)

A detachment of 19 Fifteenth Infantrymen was finally cobbled together from the Fort Bayard garrison. Commanded by Captain Humphreys, it was ordered to scout the Mogollon Mountains, leaving Fort Bayard on 12 May 1880. Humphreys camped in the area between 15 and 18 May, but estimated that the Apaches had already departed to the north. Overall, Humphreys estimated that about 40 citizens, mainly Mexicans, had been killed, and that much private property had been badly damaged.[51]

The raiding continued with seven 'civilians' being killed near the San Francisco River[52] and a further six being slain near Las Lentas on 2 and 4 May 1880 respectively.[53] Felipe Chavez notified District Headquarters that 'Melquiade Chavez, Jose Maria Sanchez & about ten men thus far killed by Apaches in the vicinity of Old Fort Tulerosa [Tularosa].'[54] Two of these men were said to have been burned, 'whether before or after death, could not be discovered.'[55] Chavez also reported that approximately 100,000 sheep had been driven off by the Apaches.[56] In response to

50 Madden to Col. E.A. Carr, Ft. Lowell, 9 May, 1880, (Rec'd Lowell 17 May, 1880) NA, RG393, Part 1, Entry 235, pp.93-95.

51 Humphreys to AAAG, DoNM, 23 May, 1880 in Letters Received by HQ_DoNM Sept. 1865-Aug. 1890, NA, RG393, M1088, Roll 40, Jan.-Jun. 1880.

52 The settlement centring upon Parson Williams Ranche in the San Francisco Valley was described in Feb. 1880 as consisting of twenty one well fenced farms. ('From the Fresco', the *Grant County Herald*, 21 Feb., 1880.

53 Chronological List, p.49; Webb, 1976, p.89.

54 Felipe Chavez to CO DoNM date unclear 1 May, 1880?, NA, RG393, Part 3, Entry 439, p.447.

55 Pollack to AAAG, DoNM, 8 May, 1880 in Letters Received by HQ_DoNM Sept. 1865-Aug. 1890, NA, RG393, M1088, Roll 40, Jan.-Jun. 1880.

56 Chavez to AAAG SF 4 May, 1880? NA, RG393, Part 3, Entry 439, pp.647-648; Loud to Hatch Fort Craig (Operator will send to General by first opportunity), 1 May, 1880, Telegrams Sent DoNM, Vol.3,

Plate 7.1. View of one of the hills occupied by the Apaches during the attack on the Roberts Ranch. The hill in question is in the middle distance at the centre of the photograph, just above and to the left of the grove of lighter coloured trees. The Mogollon Mountains march along the horizon. (Photo: Author)

Plate 7.2. A closer view of the Mogollon Mountains to the north of the Roberts Ranch. The photo gives an idea of the ease with which small groups of miners could be picked off by Apaches. Victorio's warriors could conceal themselves in the minimum of cover, so the foothills in the foreground provided abundant concealment. The deeper they travelled into the mountains, the more vulnerable the prospectors would be to attack. (Photo: Author)

their appeals for Hatch to come to their assistance, District Headquarters had to inform Chavez that they did not know the Colonel's current location but believed that he was in the San Mateo Mountains.[57] However, they did assure Chavez that Hatch was personally in the field 'doing everything possible with the Troops he has to afford protection to the people.'[58] The next day, Chavez was contacted again and was informed that US troops were now making their way towards the Mogollon Mountains.[59]

Other casualty reports filtered in. A citizen named Kinnear informed the military authorities that Victorio had slaughtered 19 people 'between Las Valles and Bush Valley', with a further 27 sheep herders reported missing.[60] A prospector by the name of Friend was supposed killed, having fitted himself out in Albuquerque for a prospecting trip to the Mogollons just before Victorio's raid.[61] Over two months later, the *Grant County Herald* reported the discovery of thousands of dead sheep and 'many' slain Mexicans recently discovered by a patrol led by Captain Kramer,[62] Sixth Cavalry, in the Gilitfe Valley.[63]

Did the targeting of isolated Mexicans reflect the loss of the Mescalero reservation and such hamlets as Canada Alamosa as supply depots? Had this forced the Apaches to rely increasingly on raiding former allies to replenish ammunition stocks? The *Grant County Herald* notes, with grim satisfaction, that the Mexican settlements at Piedras Negras and Canada Alamosa, which had previously had good relations with the Apaches, had to organise their own defences as it was now unsafe to step beyond their limits.[64] However, the account of Patrocinio Martinez suggests that Victorio himself did not, even in April–May 1880, indiscriminately target Mexicans. He recalls that his father and brother were out in the mountains looking for stray oxen 'in the spring of 1880':

> Victorio, who was a good friend of my father, warned him and my brother that they had better return home because the Indians might kill them. For some unaccountable reason, Victorio gave my father thirty dollars.

Martinez said that his brother returned home, but that his father ignored Victorio's warning and continued searching for his oxen. He was killed by Apaches shortly afterwards, he said, and the 30 dollars Victorio had given him was found on his body.[65]

At least one Apache raiding party may have moved southwards at the same time as the mining communities were struck in the Mogollon Mountains to the west. On 4 May 1880,[66] Francisco Montoya's freight train was struck near Cooke's Spring, presumably near Fort Cummings and inside Cooke's Range. He submitted a claim for losses of '112 Oxen, 5 Mules, 2 American Mules

---

Jan.-Nov. 1880, NA, RG393, Part 3, Entry 431, pp.358-359; Thrapp, 1967, p.198; Thrapp, 1974, p.276; Stout 1974, p.137 & p.139; Sonnichsen, 1973, p.207; Leckie, 1967, p.220; Haley, 1981, p.327.

57 Loud to Francisco Chavez, 2 May, 1880, Telegrams Sent DoNM, Vol.3, Jan.-Nov. 1880, NA, RG393, Part 3, Entry 431, pp.360-361.

58 Loud to Chavez, Albuquerque, 4 May, 1880, Telegrams Sent DoNM, Vol.3, Jan.-Nov. 1880, NA, RG393, Part 3, Entry 431, pp.371-372.

59 Loud to Felipe & Fransisco Chavez, Albuquerque, 5 May, 1880, Telegrams Sent DoNM, Vol.3, Jan.-Nov. 1880, NA, RG393, Part 3, Entry 431, p.378; See also Loud to AAG Fort Leavenworth, 5 May, 1880, Telegrams Sent DoNM, Vol.3, Jan.-Nov. 1880, NA, RG393, Part 3, Entry 431, p.379.

60 Cochran, NA, RG393, Part 1, Entry 235, p.96.

61 The *Grant County Herald*, 29 May, 1880.

62 Spelled 'Cramer' in the original text.

63 The *Grant County Herald*, 31 Jul., 1880.

64 Ashenfelter Editorial, the *Grant County Herald*, 8 May, 1880.

65 Cited in Bryan, 1998, pp.156-157.

66 The supporting statement of Jose Abatos, claims that the attack occurred on the 8 of May, 1880.

and 1 American Horse.' He lost one freighter killed in the attack.[67] A small wagon train was also reported destroyed between Pueblo Viejo and Las Cruces.[68]

This period of intense raiding may also be the inspiration for the 'Victorio indulging in an orgy of cruelty' narrative. The indiscriminate killing of Mexican shepherds does mark a change in tactics for Victorio, as he normally maintained good relations with these people.[69] Thrapp speculated that Victorio's Mescalero allies might not have had such relations, and might have been the culprits of such attacks.[70] The attacks on Canada Alamosa suggest a wider problem for Victorio, in that relations between the two communities had become strained to the point of open hostility. It was not safe for the inhabitants of Canada Alamosa or Las Palomas to continue their trade with the Apaches; but it was equally dangerous for them to cease trading with Victorio. Whilst the calculation of relative safety had passed a tipping point in favour of the USA, the Apaches were still powerful enough to retaliate with consequences so dreadful that they are still remembered in southern New Mexico even today.

By the end of May, the *Grant County Herald* (see document file no. 66) claimed that 78 people had been killed by Apaches in Valencia County;[71] but the same edition stated that 63 people had been killed in Victorio's foray into the Mogollon and San Francisco Mountains.[72] As far as can be determined, Victorio had not operated in the Mogollons or San Francisco Mountains since April–May 1879. Single and small groups of miners and prospectors, shepherds and settlers would have been incredibly vulnerable to the sudden appearance of several Apache war parties. The Mescalero warriors with Victorio may have wished to avenge their recent losses, and there certainly appear to be grounds for suspecting that Victorio had a deeply personal reason for revenge attacks. Yet the reality is surely more complex.

First, as we shall shortly see, Victorio had embarked on his usual tactic of conducting a long-range raid, to exhaust his US cavalry pursuers by engaging them in a drawn-out pursuit over rough terrain. Second, a surprise attack on an area which had not been visited for about a year would yield rich hauls of loot from people who had dropped their guard. Cooney's letter to the *Grant County Herald* advances this theory. It also suggests that Victorio may have deliberately targeted different regions at different times to take advantage of such complacency. The large numbers of miners and prospectors killed would have provided a number of modern weapons and good supplies of ammunition, without which most of these men would not have ventured into the wilderness. Finally, the revenge motive is almost certainly a factor, but was probably more general and long-term than specific and immediate in its motivation. The Warm Springs Apaches had originally gone to war with the United States as a result of their contacts with Anglo-American miners in this very area, in the early 1860s. A number of long-term scores may have been addressed by the Apaches in their raid of April–May 1880, not to mention more recent losses sustained in May 1879. (See document file no. 4.) Indeed, the most common invaders of their territory in general had been Anglo-American miners and prospectors.

From the 1860s on, it was widely acknowledged that certain areas north and west of Hillsboro, particularly the Black Range and the San Mateos, were held by the Apaches. As late as December 1880, it was acknowledged that any prospectors venturing into these lands 'took their life in their

67 Misc.5 Document; See also 'Would not the Truth do?', the *Grant County Herald*, 5 Jun., 1880.
68 'Would not the Truth do?', the *Grant County Herald*, 5 Jun., 1880.
69 Thrapp, 1974, p.276.
70 Thrapp, 1967, p.199.
71 'Indian Depredations', the *Grant County Herald*, 29 May, 1880.
72 The *Grant County Herald*, 29 May, 1880.

hands.'[73] One Harry Pie[74] survived one trip and told of discovering a rich deposit of precious metal. Returning in 1879, he and a Mexican companion were never seen again, and the skeleton of a white man was later found near the supposed site of Pie's strike.[75] Thus, it can be seen that individual and small parties of prospectors and miners were incredibly vulnerable to the Chihennes, who had viewed them as a threat from the beginning. We will probably never know just how many intrepid men seeking their fortune disappeared into these mountains never to return. There may yet be remains of such unfortunates awaiting discovery.

The fact remains that, in this area of New Mexico, there is the lingering memory of a devastating raid commanded by Victorio. With memory comes exaggeration of numbers and atrocity, reinforced by the official recriminations of the US authorities. Victorio's reputation for personal cruelty probably largely, but not wholly, derives from such a historical memory process. However, the gist of this story of a sudden series of raids with a high fatality rate is probably accurate. The actual numbers killed by the Apaches in late April and early May 1880 will never be quantified.

Logistics, Communication and Miscommunication

Having encountered this tale of havoc and destruction, the reader may quite legitimately enquire as to the whereabouts of Colonel Hatch and his two battalions of Ninth Cavalrymen. In fact, Hatch's forces, having been in the field since the beginning of the Hembrillo Canyon campaign, were not really in a position to mount an effective pursuit.

Lieutenant S.C. Plummer, Fifteenth Infantry, left in charge of detachments of Infantry at San Jose and Canada Alamosa that were intended to act as pickets and escorts,[76] found his men 'need ammunition please have me sent two thousand rounds.'[77] Once again certain local contractors were willing to take advantage of the situation and charge high rates for their goods. District Headquarters contacted Hatch over a grain contract with the Lynch Brothers of El Colorado to complain that the army had been charged seven cents a pound when the 'authorized' rate was four cents a pound. It enjoined Hatch to remind officers to keep to the authorized rates and recommended that the Lynch Brothers' bill be 'disallowed'.[78]

The monthly and bi-monthly returns for the Ninth Cavalry Regiment also show a continuing decline in the numbers of serviceable horses, a steady increase in the numbers of unserviceable horses, and a small increase in the numbers of horses lost during the month of April. (See Table 7.1.) This is despite the arrival of Lieutenant Schaeffer with at least 96 replacement horses for the Ninth Cavalry.[79] This shows that Hatch's attempt to rest his regiment may have had some effect, in that there was a small rise in the number of serviceable horses during March. It also shows that this rise was probably more down to the arrival of replacement horses, as the number of unserviceable horses continued to rise between January and April. The effect of returning the regiment to active service during April is clearly underlined by the large decrease in serviceable horses and the increase in both unserviceable and lost horses.

73 'The Black Range', the *Grant County Herald*, 18 Dec., 1880.
74 Also spelt 'Pye'.
75 'The Black Range', the *Grant County Herald*, 18 Dec., 1880.
76 Lt Davenport AAAG in field Ojo Caliente to Loud AAAG SF 1 May, 1880, NA, RG393, Part 3, Entry 439, p.456.
77 Plummer to Capt Loud AAAG SF 4 May, 1880, NA, RG393, Part 3, Entry 439, p.464.
78 Loud to Hatch, Tularosa (Operator at Craig will forward at first opportunity) 20 May, 1880, Telegrams Sent DoNM, Vol.3, Jan.-Nov. 1880, NA, RG393, Part 3, Entry 431, p.414.
79 *Army & Navy Journal*, Vol.17, 22 May, 1880, p.854.

Table 7.1 Ninth Cavalry, Roster of Horses, 1880.[80]

	Serviceable Horses	Unserviceable Horses	Horses Lost in Action, Died, etc.
January	438	103	36
February	425	129	34
March	441	140	10
April	345	213	54

Table 7.2 Available Men to Serviceable Horses, January–April 1880.[81]

Company	Available Men, January–February 1880	Serviceable Horses, January–February 1880	Available Men, March–April 1880	Serviceable Horses, March–April 1880
A	55	No Entry	21	18
B	55	17	58	22
C	59	No Entry	47	16
D	60	40	26	15
E	37	25	46	29
F	46	34	27	7
G	54	35	66	40
H	54	17	57	No Entry
I	49	57	54	20
K	61	63	55	50
L	57	34	57	30
M	53	12	67	No Entry

Table 7.2 shows that there was often, but not always, a decrease in serviceable horses between the January–February and the March–April bi-monthly muster rolls. If we examine the experience of two companies which did not take part in Morrow's January–February campaign, but did participate in the Hembrillo Canyon operation and beyond, the decrease is obvious. Both companies start with more serviceable horses than available men. Yet by the end of April, I Company has dropped from 57 serviceable horses to 20 and K Company has recorded a reduction from 63 to 50 serviceable horses. Despite covering much ground in April 1880, neither company had fought any Apaches.

Hatch had no choice but to attempt to engage the Apaches, due to the mounting pressure from the New Mexican citizenry and his own superiors. However, these figures show that the Ninth Cavalry had already sustained heavy horse casualties. If they remained in the field in pursuit of Victorio, the situation could only get worse. These difficulties were further compounded by communication problems. Once troops had left established courier or telegraph routes, they could become difficult if not impossible to contact. On 5 May 1880, District Headquarters, Santa Fé, informed Lieutenant Humphreys, at Fort Bayard, that the current location of Hatch's forces was unknown, despite Humphreys' possession of important information for whoever was in command of the Indian scouts.[82] Two days later, District Headquarters still knew nothing as to Hatch's loca-

80 Derived from Returns From Regular Army Cavalry Regiments 1833-1916, 9th Cavalry 1873-1880, NA, M744, Roll 88

81 Derived Bi-Monthly Company Muster Rolls for Jan./Feb. & Mar./Apr. 1880, 9th Cavalry in NA, RG94

82 Humphrey Bayard to AAAG SF 5 May, 1880, NA, RG393, Part 3, Entry 439, pp.465-466.

tion.[83] This lack of knowledge reflects the fact that Hatch had put his forces in motion but, in doing so, had moved out of easy courier and telegraph communication.

It also did not help that, initially, the US army was sceptical as to the reliability of the first reports concerning Victorio's onslaught in the Mogollon Mountains.[84] While it was true that many exaggerated and false reports of Apache raiding had been, and would be, received throughout the campaign, in this case some of these reports were fairly accurate. (See document file no. 64.) Even so, District Headquarters was bombarded by reports of 500 Apaches on the loose.[85] By 7 May 1880, Santa Fé could only confirm the attack on Cooney's Mining camp.[86] Later that day, they were able to confirm some of the other details that, when first received, had been considered of doubtful reliability.[87] On 7 May, Lieutenant Plummer, as CO Fort Craig, received information that Victorio was in the San Mateo Mountains and that Nana, described as Victorio's second chief, and Tomas had recently been killed fighting US troops.[88] Humphreys, at Fort Bayard, also noted that he had received reports that the Apaches numbered between 150 and 250 strong, with estimates even as high as 450 warriors being received. He also had heard nothing from Captain Madden's command.[89] Humphreys could only guess that Hatch and his forces would reach the scene of the fight on the evening of 7 May. He also remained unsure as to the location of Gatewood's and Mills's Apache scout detachments[90] and McLellan's company. If any of these detachments passed through Fort Bayard, he suggested, they would be 'of great assistance'.[91] By 12 May, District Headquarters had still received no news from Colonel Hatch, though they presumed he was in the Mogollon Mountains.[92] Word of Hatch was finally received on 15 May, but was already four days out of date. Hatch estimated that he was 90 miles from Fort Bayard, following a trail of approximately 500 Apaches.[93] This trail was heading towards the White Mountains in Arizona.[94] Despite the time lag, the troops in Arizona were sent the alarm.[95]

83 Loud AAAG to AAG, Fort Leavenworth, Kansas, 7 May, 1880, NA, RG393, Part 1, Entry 2546, p.442.
84 Pope to Col. W.D. Whipple, AAG, Chicago, 5 May, 1880, NA, RG393, Part 1, Entry 2546, pp.428-438.
85 Loud to CO Fort Bayard, 6 May, 1880, Telegrams Sent DoNM, Vol.3, Jan.-Nov. 1880, NA, RG393, Part 3, Entry 431, p.387.
86 Loud AAAG to AAG, Fort Leavenworth, Kansas, 7 May, 1880, NA, RG393, Part 1, Entry 2546, pp.439-440.
87 Loud AAAG to AAG, Fort Leavenworth, Kansas, 7 May, 1880, NA, RG393, Part 1, Entry 2546, pp.442-443.
88 Loud to Hatch (CO Fort Bayard will forward to General as soon as his whereabouts are known), 7 May, 1880, Telegrams Sent DoNM, Vol.3, Jan.-Nov. 1880, NA, RG393, Part 3, Entry 431, p.388.
89 Humphreys, Commanding Fort Bayard to AAAG, SF N.M., 7 May, 1880, NA, RG393, Part 1, Entry 2546, pp.441-442; Loud to AAG Fort Leavenworth, 7 May, 1880, Telegrams Sent DoNM, Vol.3, Jan.-Nov. 1880, NA, RG393, Part 3, Entry 431, pp.389-390 & pp.394-395.
90 Humphreys, Bayard to C[arr], Lowell, 7 May, 1880, NA, RG393, Part 1, Entry 235, p.53.
91 Ibid.
92 Loud to AAG Fort Leavenworth, Telegrams Sent DoNM, Vol.3, Jan.-Nov. 1880, NA, RG393, Part 3, Entry 431, p.396.
93 Perhaps the citizens of New Mexico were not the only individuals capable of exaggerating the numbers of Apaches.
94 Loud , citing Hatch telegram, San Francisco River, 11 May, 1880 to AAG Fort Leavenworth, 15 May, 1880, Telegrams Sent DoNM, Vol.3, Jan.-Nov. 1880, NA, RG393, Part 3, Entry 431, pp.401-402.
95 Loud to CO Fort Bowie and Col Carr, Fort Lowell, 15 May, 1880, Telegrams Sent DoNM, Vol.3, Jan.-Nov. 1880, NA, RG393, Part 3, Entry 431, pp.402-403.

Hatch Moves his Forces into the Mogollon Mountains

As noted in the previous chapter, almost 100 Apaches scouts, accompanied by Henry Parker, Sam Bowman and Van C. Smith, left San Jose on 29 April, to scout the San Mateo Mountains. They spent two days in these mountains but found no recent signs of Apaches. When they emerged, on the south-western side of the mountains, they discovered two large trails estimated to be a week old. The trails quickly joined, moving north along the western edge of the San Mateo Mountains, before turning west for the Mogollon Mountains. One trail, believed to be Victorio's, had come up from the Black Range, while the second trail, believed to be Mescaleros travelling to join Victorio, had come from the east. The latter had crossed the Rio Grande, ten miles south of the San Jose party. These Apaches raided the ranch of Donaciano Montoya, killing some cattle and taking 17 horses.[96] (See document file no. 67.) Having established that the Apaches had left the San Mateo Mountains by 1 May, [97] Hatch's two battalions, the First (Morrow) and Third (Hooker), then refitting as best they could at Ojo Caliente, were sent in the direction of the Mogollon Mountains, on 3 and 4 May respectively. In the meantime, Hatch made it clear that he was relying on the two companies of Sixth Cavalry under Madden and McLellan (the latter then nearing Fort Bayard, on its way back to Arizona) to move into the Mogollon Mountains from the south to protect the threatened citizens.[98]

Morrow's battalion[99] had been ordered into the field with 15 days' rations, accompanied by Lieutenant Maney's Apache scouts, who had been issued with 20 days' rations. Their orders were to proceed to Shaw's Ranch on the North Star Road and follow any trails left by Apaches from that point. The battalion was accompanied by pack mules only, all wagons being left behind at Ojo Caliente.[100] Captain Hooker, with the Third Battalion, was given identical orders and told to make for Shaw's Ranch.[101] It would appear that, despite retaining the battalion formation, individual companies fanned out in an attempt to pick up any signs of the Apaches. An Indian trail was discovered on 7 May near Chase's Ranch by K Company, Ninth Cavalry, and was followed westwards into the Mogollon Mountains.[102]

The apparent tardiness of the Ninth Cavalry's response to Victorio's attacks on the Mogollon Mountain communities did not reflect cowardly or incompetent behaviour. The reason for this inability to respond can be put down to a failure to understand the principles of Apache warfare by more senior US army commanders. Hatch was not getting enough resources, particularly horses and mules and fodder for these, to keep his troops in the field for long periods. Nor was he given the leeway to recruit enough Apache scouts to spearhead his columns. Recognizing the need for

96 Letter from Van Smith to *Thirty-Four*, 7 May, 1880.

97 Loud to AAG Fort Leavenworth, 3 May (citing Report by Hatch, Ojo Caliente, 1 May, 1880, rec'd Fort Craig 3 May, 1880), Telegrams Sent DoNM, Vol.3, Jan.-Nov. 1880, NA, RG393, Part 3, Entry 431, pp.364-365.

98 Hatch Ojo Caliente to AAAG SF 4 May, 1880, NA, RG393, Part 3, Entry 439, pp.467-468 & p.469; See also Pope to Col. W.D. Whipple, AAG, Chicago, 5 May, 1880, NA, RG393, Part 1, Entry 2546, pp.428-438; Hatch, Ojo Caliente to AAAG, SF, 4 May, 1880, Telegrams Sent DoNM, Vol.3, Jan.-Nov. 1880, NA, RG393, Part 3, Entry 431, pp.378-379; Loud to CO Fort Bayard, 5 May, 1880, Telegrams Sent DoNM, Vol.3, Jan.-Nov. 1880, NA, RG393, Part 3, Entry 431, p.380.

99 *Thirty-Four*, 12 May, 1880 stated that Morrow's battalion was accompanied by Captains Purington, Moore, Dawson and Rucker while Hooker was accompanied by Parker Dimmick and Taylor.

100 Special Field Order No. 29 para.3, May 3 1880 (Ojo Caliente), NA, RG393 Part 3, Entry 450.

101 Special Field Order No. 30 para.1, May 4 1880 (Ojo Caliente), NA, RG393 Part 3, Entry 450; Hatch, Ojo Caliente, to AAG SF, 4 May, 1880, 'DoNM/GSFO/L&T', NA, RG393, Part 3, Entry 475, Vol. 5, p.234; *Army & Navy Journal*, Vol.17, 29 May, 1880, front page.

102 Bi-Monthly Company Muster Rolls for Company K, 9th Cavalry, May/Jun. 1880 in NA, RG94.

these, he had sent Lieutenant Emmett to San Carlos to recruit Apache scouts.[103] Yet on 13 May, permission to recruit an additional two companies of Apache scouts was denied 'as an increase in present aggregate number of Indian Scouts cannot be allowed without subtracting an equal number of soldiers from the Army itself.'[104]

Apaches move into Arizona: Ash Creek, 7 May 1880

Ever since Victorio had left members of the Warm Springs Apaches residing on the San Carlos reservation, in 1877–78, the US military authorities had been worried that a rescue attempt would be mounted. With rumours of heavy Apache raiding in the Mogollon Mountains, Colonel Carr realised the danger that Victorio might attack the San Carlos reservation. Captain Chaffee, at San Carlos, was warned to put his scouts on full alert.[105] On 3 May, Carr ordered Lieutenant Blocksom to move his detachment of Apache scouts and Sixth Cavalrymen to join Captain Kramer's E Company, Sixth Cavalry, on Ash Creek.[106] This detachment was to scout east towards the Mogollons in order to detect, and even prevent, any move towards San Carlos.[107] During April, when Kramer was originally ordered to Ash Creek, his detachment was joined by Private John F. Falvey of the Fort Apache Telegraph Station who:

> took with him a key and a relay, and each night, as the trail lay near the line, cut in and placed Captain Kramer in direct telegraphic communication with headquarters. On arrival at Ash Creek he opened a station in a tent, about a quarter of a mile from their camp, and for two weeks transmitted many important messages over the wires.[108]

In effect, Kramer, as long as he stayed close to the telegraph line, was equipped with a 'field telegraph'.

Carr's warning had come none too soon, as a group of warriors under Victorio's son, curiously known as Washington,[109] launched a raid towards San Carlos.[110] The motives for this raid were

103 Hatch to AAAG SF 4 or 5 May, 1880?, NA, RG393, Part 3, Entry 439, p.469; See also Special Field Order No. 30 paras.8&10, May 4 1880 (Ojo Caliente), NA, RG393 Part 3, Entry 450; Hatch, Ojo Caliente, to AAG SF, 4 May, 1880, 'DoNM/GSFO/L&T', NA, RG393, Part 3, Entry 475, Vol. 5, p.237.

104 Loud to General Hatch, (CO Fort Bayard will forward as soon as General's whereabouts are known) 13 May, 1880, Telegrams Sent DoNM, Vol.3, Jan.-Nov. 1880, NA, RG393, Part 3, Entry 431, p.398;R.C. Drum, to Comdg General, MDoM, 5 May, 1880 in Letters Received, DoM 1868-98, RG 393, Entry A1-1 2601, Box 90.

105 Martin to Chaffee, San Carlos, 4 May, 1880, NA, RG393, Part 1, Entry 169, Vol. 10, p.204.

106 Carr, Special Order No.10, 3 May, 1880, Special Orders Oct. 1879-Jan. 1881, DoAz, Vol. 1, NA, RG393, Part 1, Entry 239.

107 Carr to CO Fort Bayard, Madden at Silver City, Captain Kramer and Lt Blocksom, San Carlos, 3 May, 1880, Troops in SE Arizona, DoAz, NA, RG393, Part 1, Entry 232, Vol.5, Dec. 13 1879 – May 7 1880, Letter No.'s 142-145, pp.121-124; See also Loud to AAG Ft. Leavenworth, 6 May, 1880 in 'Victorio Papers', NA, M666, Roll 527.

108 Report of the Chief Signal Officer in AR-WD, NA, M997, Roll 35, 1880 Vol. I-II, p.118.

109 Bourke and Randall report another Apache known as Washington during the peace negotiations in the Sierra Madre in 1883. (Bourke, 2001ii, p.383; Randall, 2001, p.395).

110 It is not clear where this information came from though on 5 June, 1880, Hatch informed Carr that Victorio was not, as first thought, present on this raid but had sent Washington with between forty and fifty warriors. Victorio had, according to Hatch, remained with a larger force near a Cienega in the Sierra Negrito Mountains. (Carr to AG DoAz, 5 Jun., 1880, Troops in SE Arizona, DoAz, NA, RG393, Part 1, Entry 232, Vol.7, 18 May-6 Sept., 1880, Letter No.811, pp.64-67).

threefold: first, they wished to rescue some of their family members from San Carlos; second, they wanted to attack those Apaches at San Carlos who were providing the US army with scouts; and finally, they may have been trying to stir Juh's Chiricahuas back into hostilities with the Americans. The US army was clearly worried about the close proximity of Apaches to the Warm Springs and Chiricahua Apaches then resident on the reservation. Chaffee rounded up Loco's Warm Springs Apaches and marched them in close to the agency.[111] Chaffee remained concerned that if Victorio came too close to the agency, Whoo (Juh) and other Chiricahuas would probably join them.[112] This worry can only have been increased when the Chiricahuas refused Chaffee's orders to move into the agency, responding that as far as they were aware, Victorio was nowhere near the reservation.[113]

However, on Ash Creek, Washington's raiding party were discovered by a group of hunters from San Carlos, and thus lost the element of surprise in the skirmish that followed.[114] Cruse reports that Washington thought that he had bottled the hunters in a cave; however, he had failed to spot two of the hunters, one of whom shadowed the raiders while the other spread the alarm.[115] Chaffee reported that, on 7 May,[116] the Apache raiders had assailed other Apaches on Eagle Creek on the San Carlos reservation, and had killed approximately 12 people. Among the dead was a prominent Apache, 'Captain Killdegoing, and his entire family'.[117]

This attack had critical implications for any peace settlement between Victorio and the United States. It was a continuation of the feud between Victorio's direct following among the Chihennes and the San Carlos Apaches which dated back to their original removal to San Carlos in 1877. It meant that Victorio could not return to the San Carlos reservation, as he could not have hoped to survive reprisals from Apaches who had lost relatives to his warriors and held him directly responsible. By this stage in the campaign, Victorio's only option, apart from fighting to the finish, was winning back the reservation at Ojo Caliente.

Washington did eventually clash with the scouts and cavalrymen of Kramer and Blocksom's commands, in the vicinity of Rocky Canon, Arizona.[118] Kramer and Blocksom had been ordered out in response to reports of an attack on Stevens' Sheep Ranch, 11 miles from Fort Lowell, where several families of Indians were reported to have sustained a number of fatalities.[119] Six Apache scouts from Blocksom's company also spotted the raiders and sped back to Ash Creek to raise the alarm.[120] Victorio's presence was reported by one A.W. Dixon who, with two Apache employees at Stevens' Ranch, discovered Apaches rounding up horses and mules around 11:00 a.m. on 6 May. These Apaches signalled to the Apaches employed by Dixon inside the Ranch. When one of these men went out to talk, he was told that that the warriors were going to ransack the buildings for

111 Stacey, Thomas, Citing message from Capt. Chaffee, to AAAG, Fort Lowell, 8 May, 1880, NA, RG393, Part 1, Entry 235, pp.61-62.

112 Ibid.

113 Stacey, Grant, citing message from Capt. Chaffee, to AAAG, Fort Lowell, 9 May, 1880, NA, RG393, Part 1, Entry 235, p.73.

114 Cruse, 1987, pp.81-82; Worcester, 1979, p.228-229.

115 Cruse, 1987, p.82.

116 Chaffee says on the 11 May that this took place on the previous Friday which the perpetual calendar states to be the 7 May.

117 Chaffee to CoIA 11 May, 1880, 'Victorio Papers', NA, M666, Roll 527.

118 The Chronological List, p.50.

119 Halloran, Rocky Canon Creek to AAAG, Fort Lowell, 7 May, 1880, NA, RG393, Part 1, Entry 235, pp.59-60.

120 Stacey to AG DoAz, 7 May, 1880, Troops in SE Arizona, DoAz, NA, RG393, Part 1, Entry 232, Vol.6, 7 May-18 May, 1880, Letter No.159, p.3) Eleven Coyotero Apaches were said to have been killed by Victorio's warriors on Eagle Creek. (Report of the CoIA. DoI, OIA, Washington, 1 Nov., 1880, p.90.

guns, ammunition and food. Dixon decided to run for his life and was sped on his way by a couple of shots.[121]

On 7 May 1880, hearing the news that Stevenson's[122] sheep camp had been attacked, Kramer, leaving his dismounted Apache scouts to follow him, took his cavalrymen off to the relief of Stevenson's Ranch. Kramer was anxious to render aid as quickly as possible, but forging ahead of his Apache scouts with his Sixth Cavalrymen was unwise. As he approached the location of Stevenson's camp, he was ambushed at close range, losing a number of horses and one man mortally wounded. The Sixth Cavalrymen skirmished with the Apaches until Blocksom's scouts arrived, and the raiders then withdrew, but not before they had seriously wounded an Apache scout. Kramer pursued them for about nine miles before the Apaches made a stand. Kramer ordered a flank attack by the Apache scouts, which once again precipitated a withdrawal. The Apaches were trailed eastwards until dark; then Kramer withdrew to make camp and await the arrival of his mule train. This did not arrive until approximately 9:30 a.m. the following morning. Kramer also reported the discovery of two unknown prospectors and a wounded Mexican shepherd during the pursuit.[123] (See document file no. 68.)

Sergeant Daniel Griffin, a civil-war veteran, died that night.[124] Washington's men had targeted Kramer's mounts in their opening volley and several horses had been killed. Kramer had entered the skirmish with 28 men, but had pursued the Apaches with only 14, which suggests that he had lost up to 12[125] horses killed and wounded.[126] There were no confirmed Apache casualties, despite Colonel Carr's claim that Kramer's force had slain 11 Apaches.[127] Kramer sent a courier to Camp Thomas stating that he was faced by Victorio and 90 warriors.[128]

---

121 Maj. Cochran, 12th Infantry, to AAAG, Fort Lowell, 8 May, 1880, NA, RG393, Part 1, Entry 235, pp.69-70.

122 This probably refers to the Steven's Ranch referred to above. It was not uncommon to have variations of the same location name; for example, McEvers' Ranch is sometimes being referred to as McEverett's Ranch and could sometimes be attributed to individuals mishearing the name.

123 Kramer to Kerr, 8 May, 1880 in 'Victorio Papers', NA, M666, Roll 527; See also Personal File Adam Kramer, NA, RG94, Entry 297, Box 33;See also Personal File Augustus P. Blocksom, NA, RG94, Entry 297, Box 463; Bi-Monthly Company Muster Rolls for Company E, 6th Cavalry, May/Jun. 1880 in NA, RG94; Willcox to AG Presidio, San Francisco, 8 May, 1880, NA, RG393, Part 1, Entry 169, Vol. 10, pp.218-219; Stacey, Thomas to AAAG, Lowell, 7 May, 1880, NA, RG393, Part 1, Entry 235, p.55; Tabular Statement of Scouts and Expeditions of Companies 6th Cavalry from 1 Jul., 1879 to 31 Jul., 1880, NA, RG393, Part 1, Entry 240; Halloran, Rocky Canon to AAAG, Fort Lowell, 8 May, 1880, NA, RG393, Part 1, Entry 235, p.65 & p.66; Record of Events May, 1880 in Returns From Regular Army Cavalry Regiments 1833-1916, 6th Cavalry Regimental Returns 1875 to 1880, NA, M744, Roll 63; Report of Col. E.A. Carr, 29 Aug., 1880, in AR-WD 1880, NA, M997, Roll 35, 1880 Vol. I, p.217; MacPherson Letter 16 May, 1880; 'Indian Affairs', *Army & Navy Journal,* Vol.17, 22 May, 1880, p.855; Cruse, 1987, p.82; Thrapp, 1964, p.216; Thrapp, 1974, p.276; Thrapp, 1967, p.199; Chronological List, p.50; Webb, 1976, p.89; O'Neal, 1991, p.201; Carter, USACMH webpage.

124 Report of The Surgeon General in AR-WD 1880, NA, M997, Roll 35, 1880 Vol. I, p.520.

125 Capt. Stacey at Fort Lowell, reported the arrival of two couriers from Capt. Kramer 'with verbal messages, the first asking assistance which was sent him as promptly as possible. The other messenger both soldiers – whose names I do not know came from Kramer to see whether the first got through. Both men were in the fight which took place about ten miles from Halloran's camp, as near as I am able to ascertain.' (Stacey, Thomas to A.A.A.G. Lowell, 7 May, 1880, NA, RG393, Part 1, Entry 235, p.55).

126 Martin to Carr, 10 May, 1880, NA, RG393, Part 1, Entry 169, Vol. 10, p.220.

127 NA, RG232, Entry 232, 12 May, 1880; See also Comdg Dept. to AAG, Presidio, San Francisco, 12 May, 1880, NA, RG393, Part 1, Entry 169, Vol. 10, p.249; Carr to AG DoAz, 11 May, 1880, Troops in SE Arizona, DoAz, NA, RG393, Part 1, Entry 232, Vol.6, 7 May-18 May, 1880, Letter No.191, pp.19-21; 'Indian Affairs', *Army & Navy Journal,* Vol.17, 15 May, 1880, p.833.

128 Stacey, Thomas to Carr, Lowell, 7 May, 1880, NA, RG393, Part 1, Entry 235, p.57.

Captain Tupper, on joining Kramer the following day, claimed that the latter had successfully repulsed the Apaches.[129] Colonel Carr claimed a victory, stating that Washington's raiders had been 'routed and demoralized'.[130] A basic knowledge of Apache tactics would suggest otherwise. Once again, we see the standard tactic of shooting down their opponents' horses in order to cripple any subsequent pursuit. We can also see an example of a frequent misconception by the army that the Apaches had been routed in a fight when this was not the case. Having crippled their enemies' ability to pursue them, what was there to be gained by entering into a prolonged battle with the pinned-down cavalrymen and arriving Apache scouts?

Captain Adam Kramer.
Captain Adam Kramer, Sixth Cavalry was ambushed by Apache warriors in Ash Canyon, May 1880, when he rashly charged ahead of the Apache scouts accompanying his detachment. (National Archives)

Finally, this spate of raiding underlines the point that Apache warriors could wreak economic chaos, both physically and psychologically, across a wide swathe of territory, in vast disproportion to their actual numbers. For example, Carr felt obliged to station a company of Sixth Cavalrymen in the Dragoon Mountains of south-eastern Arizona. This was to provide visible protection to Tombstone, the surrounding settlements and the Southern Pacific Railroad construction teams then forging eastwards from California. A single foray into Arizona by a small party of raiders had caused a great deal of consternation among US citizens who were relatively far removed from the actual fighting.

Washington's raid into Arizona also stimulated controversy among Kramer's superiors concerning the failure of the troops on the ground to finish off the Apaches. Kramer's skirmish was seen as a lost chance, and all available troops from Fort Lowell were ordered out to join the pursuit, with orders that Victorio should be 'pursued to the bitter end'.[131] In addition, the problems in communicating information quickly up the chain of command caused some confusion and indeed anger at higher levels. The first reports of Kramer's fight noted that he had 36 Cavalrymen and 30 Apache scouts. Willcox subsequently sent off an indignant communication to Carr demanding to know why, if Kramer had 36 men, he had attacked with only 28 men, and why, after that first skirmish 'in which he lost only one man, he moved forward with only fourteen men.'[132] Why Kramer did not first engage the Apaches with the full strength of his detachment is unknown, but could be any combination of factors such as leaving men to guard a mule train or wagons, broken down horses,

129 Tupper to AAAG, Fort Lowell, 8 May, 1880, NA, RG393, Part 1, Entry 235, p.71.
130 Gen. Willcox's General Orders No. 10, 4 Jun., 1880, NA, RG393, Part 1, Entry 183; Martin to AG Military Division of the Pacific, (Hereafter referred to as 'MDoP'), Presidio, San Francisco, 11 Sept., 1880, NA, RG393, Part 1, Entry 169, Vol.10, Letters Sent, DoAz 1880 p.419; Report of Col E.A. Carr, 29 Aug., 1880; Report of Maj. James Biddle 10 Sept., 1880, in AR-WD 1880, NA, M997, Roll 35, 1880 Vol. I, p.213.
131 Martin to ?, Fort Lowell, 8 May, 1880, NA, RG393, Part 1, Entry 169, Vol. 10, p.213.
132 Martin to Carr, 10 May, 1880, NA, RG393, Part 1, Entry 169, Vol. 10, p.220.

stragglers, and so on. The reason he pursued with only 14 men is that the Apaches had killed a number of horses and wounded some of his men. He had also sent back two couriers to call for reinforcements, and such details had not yet reached Department Headquarters. The now-familiar claims that the US army had 'whipped' the Apaches were made without any concrete evidence.[133] Such claims may have been made to counter criticisms that the Arizona troops had not performed as expected. Carr angrily pointed out that a number of his command were on detached service in New Mexico and had not yet returned. Carr felt that, given the shortage of troops, his forces had performed well.[134] A report was passed up to Fort Lowell stating that Blocksom's scouts had not performed as well as could be expected. 'They could not be put in because Kramer did not have enough men to support them.'[135] This may reflect either a misunderstanding of the principles of war followed by Apaches, which did not involve engaging in frontal assaults, or an effort to explain the failure to defeat the Apaches.

It also became clear that Willcox was desperate that Victorio should not wreak the same havoc in Arizona as he had inflicted, and was still inflicting, in New Mexico; and he left his subordinates in no doubt about his desire for a swift victory.[136] His anxiety was fuelled by his belief that certain elements of the US army, based in New Mexico, were not up to the job:

> Entre nous, the fact that the old fellow [Victorio] has been able to do pretty much as he pleased in New Mexico has been pretty generally attributed to color of his opponents in that country. It won't look very well if he should be so in accord with the fourteenth amendment as to make no distinction on account of color when he comes into Arizona.[137]

On receipt of the news of Kramer's fight, reinforcements from Camp Thomas (two officers and 32 men, commanded by Captain Tupper) were sent out to support Kramer.[138] Captain Tupper trailed Washington's raiders for approximately 150 miles.[139] Tupper's immediate concern was that the Apaches would strike the settlements around Clifton.[140] He was relieved to note that the Apaches passed 18 miles to the north-west of Clifton, making for the San Francisco Valley, before veering away north-west, then north, then swerving around to the east and crossing the San Francisco River using the Camp Apache road. He estimated that 48 Apaches had fought Kramer, and after the fight they had ridden 60 miles before taking any rest, abandoning 10–12 horses during that time. On entering the San Francisco Valley, the raiders had scattered briefly, before reforming. They had then slightly altered their course to avoid a collision with Hatch's command marching in from the east, before Tupper had to break off the pursuit.[141] Tupper also thought that, at the first campsite he encountered on entering the San Francisco valley, the raiders had been joined by a larger number of Apaches. At this camp, they found the remains of 18–20 slaughtered cattle. Some of the hides had been removed but little meat had been taken and some of this was found

---

133 Kerr to CO Fort Apache, Troops in SE Arizona, DoAz, NA, RG393, Part 1, Entry 232, Vol.6, 7 May-18 May, 1880, p.11.
134 Carr to AG DoAz, 16 May, 1880, Troops in SE Arizona, DoAz, NA, RG393, Part 1, Entry 232, Vol.6, 7 May-18 May, 1880, Letter No.180. pp.12-14.
135 Stacey, Grant, to AAG, Lowell, 8 May, 1880, NA, RG393, Part 1, Entry 235, p.63.
136 See Martin to Carr, 9 May & 11 May, 1880, NA, RG393, Part 1, Entry 169, Vol. 10, P.218 & p.220.
137 Martin to Carr, 11 May, 1880, NA, RG393, Part 1, Entry 169, Vol. 10 pp.224-225.
138 Stacey, Thomas to AAG Lowell, 7 May, 1880, NA, RG393, Part 1, Entry 235, p.55; Comdg Dept to AG, Presidio, San Francisco, 8 May, 1880, NA, RG393, Part 1, Entry 169, Vol. 10, p.216.
139 Report of Col. E.A. Carr, 29 Aug., 1880, in AR-WD 1880, NA, M997, Roll 35, 1880 Vol. I, p.217.
140 Tupper to Post Adjutant, 23 May, 1880 in 'Victorio Papers', NA, M666, Roll 527.
141 Tupper to Post Adjutant, 23 May, 1880 in 'Victorio Papers', NA, M666, Roll 527.

to be fresh enough to be eaten by Tupper's command.[142] This suggests that the Apaches may have become aware of the close proximity of Tupper and Hatch's commands and abandoned the carcases at short notice. Failing to catch the Apaches, Tupper did manage to contact Hatch on 14 May and pass on information about their quarry.[143] This was not before Tupper had had a narrow escape from Lieutenant Maney's Apache scouts. Tupper's scouts had informed him that the Lieutenant was going into camp less than three miles from Hatch's command:

> I concluded to ride down at daylight. At daybreak next morning Lieut Maney 15th Inf. with 65 Indians marched into my camp & informed me that they had been up all night so as to "jump" the camp at daybreak, as they had seen my scouts the evening before.[144]

Once the two commands joined, Tupper reporting that Hatch was accompanied by eight companies of the Ninth Cavalry, Hatch put his command on the trail of the raiders and seemed confident of meeting the Apaches in battle, a confidence Tupper did not share: 'I did not feel like disregarding representations coming from such high authority.'[145] Tupper remained with Colonel Hatch's command until they had followed the trail to where it crossed the San Francisco River by the road from Fort Wingate to Fort Apache.[146] Tupper had to abandon his pursuit and slowly return to Camp Thomas, due to his horses breaking down and there not being adequate forage in the area to sustain his mounts.[147] Hatch noted that it was on meeting Tupper that he had been informed that the raiding party that had attacked San Carlos and other targets in the area was commanded by Victorio's son, Washington.[148] This suggests that some of Blocksom's scouts may have recognised Victorio's son as the leader.

In the light of Victorio's activities in the Mogollon and San Francisco Mountains, Hatch requested that Colonel Carr station troops in this area. Carr's response was to order two companies of the Sixth Cavalry and an Apache scout company to patrol the area.[149] Carr reported that his contribution to the campaign against Victorio had forced several redeployments of his own command. This included placing the Sixth Cavalry's regimental band on standby for field operations.[150] For the moment, Carr proposed to send two companies of Sixth Cavalry under Captain Hentig to scout up to the head of the San Francisco Valley, as far as the road to Albuquerque. This detachment

---

142 Tupper had to abandon his pursuit and slowly return to Camp Thomas due to his horses breaking down and there not being adequate forage in the area to sustain his mounts.

143 Synopsis of Report of Maj. Morrow June 27, 1880 Concerning March, April & May 80 in Letters Received, Dept. of Missouri 1868-98, RG 393, Entry A1-1 2601, Box 93; Report of Col E.A. Carr, 29 Aug., 1880; See also Loud to AAG Fort Leavenworth, 29 May, 1880, Telegrams Sent DoNM, Vol.3, Jan.-Nov. 1880, NA, RG393, Part 3, Entry 431, p.449; Carr to Haskell, 20 May, 1880 in 'Victorio Papers', NA, M666, Roll 527.

144 Tupper to Post Adjutant, 23 May, 1880 in 'Victorio Papers', NA, M666, Roll 527.

145 Ibid.

146 Ibid.

147 Tupper, Williams Ranche, San Francisco Valley, to AAAG, Fort Lowell, 17 May, 1880, NA, RG393, Part 1, Entry 235, pp.90-92; Carr to Haskell, Aide-de-Camp, Palace Hotel, San Francisco, 20 May, 1880, Troops in SE Arizona, DoAz, NA, RG393, Part 1, Entry 232, Vol.7, 18 May-6 Sept., 1880, Letter No.243, pp.24-25; Carr to Haskell, 20 May, 1880 in 'Victorio Papers', NA, M666, Roll 527.

148 Loud to AAG Fort Leavenworth, 29 May, 1880, Telegrams Sent DoNM, Vol.3, Jan.-Nov. 1880, NA, RG393, Part 3, Entry 431, p.449.

149 Report of Col. E.A. Carr, 29 Aug., 1880, in AR-WD 1880, NA, M997, Roll 35, 1880 Vol. I, p.217; See also Carr to AG DoAz, 5 Jun., 1880, Troops in SE Arizona, DoAz, NA, RG393, Part 1, Entry 232, Vol.7, 18 May-6 Sept., 1880, Letter No.811, pp.64-67.

150 See General Orders No. 1 HQ Troops in the Field in SE Arizona, Fort Lowell A.T., 9 May, 1880, NA, RG393, Part 1, Entry 238; Report of Col E.A. Carr, 29 Aug., 1880 in AR-WD 1880, NA, M997, Roll 35.

would be accompanied by those members of Gatewood's scout company still fit for field service.[151] Surgeon MacPherson also reported that the Sixth Cavalry Regiment, including its musicians, were being mustered at Camp Thomas in preparation for field operations against Victorio. He reported the exhausted state of the soldiers and their horses and mules through incessant pursuit of the Apaches.[152] This convinced Surgeon MacPherson that he should quit military service.[153]

As far as Carr was concerned, an expedition mounted by Arizona troops against Victorio, though he was willing in principle to lead such an expedition, faced several difficulties. First, Carr was still short of troops. Those troops he had deployed to watch the Arizona-New Mexico line he could not move. This left him four companies which could be used, but this would leave south-eastern Arizona unprotected. The increase in freighters and prospectors ranging over Arizona made the task of protecting these citizens even more difficult. Each company was also below strength in men and horses, Carr reporting that he faced a challenge to put in the field more than 40 mounted men per company. Replacement horses and 70 recruits had arrived, and could be used; but both were woefully inexperienced for active field service against Apache guerrillas.[154]

Nor were the Apaches likely to stay in one place long enough for troops to be gathered and an operation planned:

> There have never been any successful operations against these Indians except by surprise. Major Morrow and other troops in New Mexico, with Gen'l Hatch in person have done all that men could do by following and pressing, but the only results have been, either to find the Indians with insufficient force and get badly hurt, or to have rear guard fights among rocks, enabling Victorio to locate the troops and then go elsewhere to work his will.[155]

Carr advocated that an offensive war should be carried out against the Apaches but pointed out that to do this effectively needed an injection of manpower and money.[156] He was keen to make the attempt, but warned that even if additional resources were available, the outcome was not certain, as Victorio 'might beat me. He is both a strategist and a tactician.'[157] Unlike Colonel Hatch, however, the one tactic that Carr did not advocate was the increased use of Apache scouts: 'I think Hatch uses his Indians too hard: making them do too much of the fighting. Their designation of "Indian Scouts" indicates what are their legitimate duties.'[158] In June 1880, Willcox contacted Carr, stating: 'The Dept. Comdr agrees with you that Indian Scouts, should be made to feel that their work is to discover the enemy and the troops to fight.'[159] General Pope was of the same opinion: 'Scouts being responsible not for the fighting but for the trailing.'[160] Later, in September 1880, Carr reiterated his opinion that Indian Scouts were not effective unless backed by the army to do

151 Kerr to Hentig, 17 May, 1880, Troops in SE Arizona, DoAz, NA, RG393, Part 1, Entry 232, Vol.6, 7 May-18 May, 1880, Letter No.223, pp.39-40; See also Bi-Monthly Company Muster Rolls for Company D, 6th Cavalry May/Jun. &Jul./Aug. 1880 in NA, RG94.

152 MacPherson Letter 16 May, 1880.

153 Ibid, 23 May, 1880.

154 Carr to Willcox, 19 May, 1880, Troops in SE Arizona, DoAz, NA, RG393, Part 1, Entry 232, Vol.7, 18 May-6 Sept., 1880, Letter No.242, pp.18-24.

155 Carr to Willcox, 19 May, 1880, Troops in SE Arizona, DoAz, NA, RG393, Part 1, Entry 232, Vol.7, 18 May-6 Sept., 1880, Letter No.242, p.21.

156 Ibid, pp.18-24.

157 Carr to Willcox, 19 May, 1880, Troops in SE Arizona, DoAz, NA, RG393, Part 1, Entry 232, Vol.7, 18 May-6 Sept., 1880, Letter No.242, p.22.

158 Carr to AG DoAz, 5 Jun., 1880, Troops in SE Arizona, DoAz, NA, RG393, Part 1, Entry 232, Vol.7, 18 May-6 Sept., 1880, Letter No.811, p.65.

159 Martin to Carr, 5 Jun., 1880, NA, RG393, Part 1, Entry 169, Vol. 10, p.265.

160 Pope to Buell, 30 Aug., 1880 in Letters Received, DoM 1868-98, RG 393, Entry A1-1 2601, Box 93.

Plates 7.3 and 7.4. Two photos of the Gila Wilderness through which the Ninth Cavalry pursued Victorio in May 1880. (Photos: Author)

the 'heavy fighting'.[161] These ideas were still held at the highest levels of the US army over a year later.[162] This is an excellent example of the complete failure to understand the key lesson (it takes an Apache to fight an Apache) learned by Crook in his Apache Campaigns of 1871–74. Indian scouts had been a feature of both British and American efforts to fight American Indians. However, the tactic generally used was that the Indian scouts found the enemy, then the army spearheaded the assault. If the scouts wished to join the attack, they would be very welcome to do so. Carr's own experience of using Pawnee scouts at Summit Springs in 1869 followed that general principle, though in practice such scouts often ended up spearheading the attacks. Where the Apache Wars were concerned, the European element of the US army (Apache scouts were also part of the US army during their term of service) would have to accept a secondary role in bringing about the end of Apache independence.

Kramer's skirmish at Ash Creek, and Tupper's follow-through, gave Hatch the lead he required. On receipt of news of the fight, and information that the Apaches were heading in his direction, Hatch, on 12 May 1880, moved his command north from Mineral Creek, hoping to find the trail in the San Francisco Valley.[163] Two days later, Hatch sent in word that he was following a day-old trail, but:

> My stock is nearly worn out and am afraid I can't overtake them. The Indians are leaving a good deal of broken down stock on trail. Also killing some. Will be in vicinity of Old Fort Tularosa in three or four days probably.[164]

Hatch also issued instructions to Morrow, dated 12 May 1880, that he should detach a company from the First Battalion to garrison Parson Williams' Ranch and protect 'this section of country as his force will permit.'[165] Hatch ordered that the officer in command of this detachment should take charge of 'all dismounted men belonging to the First and Third Battalions New Mexico Troops and broken down stock.'[166] This implies that the two battalions were working in close conjunction in mid-May 1880. Hatch, Morrow, 360 troops and 65 Apache scouts were reported to have arrived at Keller's Ranch on 10 May.[167] The following day, Hatch sent word by courier, and then by telegraph, that he was following a large trail of 500 Apaches, who appeared to be making for the White Mountains of Arizona. This news did not reach Santa Fé until 14 May 1880.[168] The fact that Hatch felt he had to make available a company of dismounted men to help guard the San Francisco Valley settlements illustrates that, once again, the Apaches' speed and freedom to choose their terrain was inflicting heavy equine casualties.

---

161 Carr to Hatch, 10 Sept., 1880, NA, RG393 Part 3 Entry 439 p.396.
162 Sherman to General Drum 10 Sept., 1881 NA, RG393 Part 1, Entry 181, p.198.
163 Loud (citing Telegram from Hatch dated 12 May, 1880 on Mineral Creek), to AAG Fort Leavenworth, 20 May, 1880, Telegrams Sent DoNM, Vol.3, Jan.-Nov. 1880, NA, RG393, Part 3, Entry 431, p.417.
164 Loud (citing Telegram from Hatch dated 14 May, 1880 no location given), to AAG Fort Leavenworth, 20 May, 1880, Telegrams Sent DoNM, Vol.3, Jan.-Nov. 1880, NA, RG393, Part 3, Entry 431, p.417.
165 Special Field Order No.31, (Mineral Creek) 12 May, 1880, NA, RG393, Part 3, Entry 450; See also Hatch, Mineral Creek, Special Field Order, 12 May, 1880, 'DoNM/GSFO/L&T', NA, RG393, Part 3, Entry 475, Vol. 5, p.237.
166 Ibid.
167 'Town and County', the *Grant County Herald*, 15 May, 1880.
168 Loud to Commanding General, DoAz, 15 May, 1880, NA, RG393, Part 1, Entry 235, pp.88-89.

The 'Juh' Problem

Washington's foray towards San Carlos also rang alarm bells in the Department of Arizona in relation to the presence of the recently arrived Juh and his warriors. On 12 May 1880, Willcox recommended that:

> the best way to keep Hoo [Juh] is to employ him on our side, pay him well, watch him and act accordingly. McIntosh had better be with you, and one or two such Chiricahua as young Cachise [Naiche] and can be trusted. If possible open negotiations with Victorio: tell him he has been out long enough and must come in: and has got your troops to fight as well as Hatch's.[169]

Carr requested permission to recruit Tom Jeffords, as he was held in high regard by the Chiricahuas. He also recommended that immediate steps be taken to 'reassure Hoo and his people as they may think they are to be captured, dismounted or disarmed'.[170] The recent dismounting, disarming and detention of the Mescaleros would not have gone unremarked by the occupants of other Apache reservations. Juh and his warriors were obviously viewed as unknown variables. He was a potential ally, in that he might provide warriors to act as scouts. Equally, he could act as a conduit through Victorio might be persuaded to surrender. However, he had also been reported as having been allied with Victorio in late 1879, so how far could he be trusted? A rumour emerged that Juh's Chiricahuas had been plotting to attack Stevens' Ranch around the same time that Victorio had attacked it. This rumour was from something of a third hand source: 'Our hospital steward saw Mariehilda … [who] has a boy, a half breed, herding for him.' This herder claimed to have been in Juh's camp at the end of April, where he had been closely questioned about the number of people, guns and animals at the Ranch. Captain Stacey reported this 'for what it is worth', but also stated that it showed a possible element of collusion between Juh and Victorio.[171]

Willcox certainly thought that it was worth holding a conference with 'Cochise's son and the Talking Chiefs of the Chiricahuas'.[172] Willcox's letter is vague as to whether he wanted to use the Chiricahuas to open negotiations with Victorio, or to use them as scouts, or both. Willcox was prepared to hire Tom Jeffords at $125 per month, the 'highest price allowed interpreters with the scouting companies'.[173] In addition to Jeffords, Carr was authorised to hire Juh, Naiche and no more than three or four other Chiricahuas to be employed as guides.[174] Willcox also stated that 'in such a negotiation you must seek the cooperation of Hatch, in whose District the Indians are operating.'[175] Willcox also instructed Carr to contact Captain Chaffee, acting Indian Agent at San Carlos, to

169 Gen'l Comdg. To Carr 12 May, 1880, NA, RG393, Part 1, Entry 169, Vol. 10, p.249; NA, RG393, Entry 232, 12 May, 1880, pp.19-20; Carr to AG DoAz, 12 May, 1880, Troops in SE Arizona, DoAz, NA, RG393, Part 1, Entry 232, Vol.6, 7 May-18 May, 1880, Letter No.191, pp.19-21.

170 Carr to AG DoAz & Gen. Willcox , 12 May, 1880, Troops in SE Arizona, DoAz, NA, RG393, Part 1, Entry 232, Vol.6, 7 May-18 May, 1880, Letter No.'s 191 & 192, pp.19-22; NA, RG393, Entry 232, 12 May, 1880, p.20.

171 Stacey, Thomas to Carr, Lowell, 13 May, 1880, NA, RG393, Part 1, Entry 235, pp.83-85.

172 Willcox to Carr, 12 May, 1880, NA, RG393, Part 1, Entry 169, Vol. 10, pp248-249.

173 Carr to AG DoAz, 13 May, 1880, Troops in SE Arizona, DoAz, NA, RG393, Part 1, Entry 232, Vol.6, 7 May-18 May, 1880, Letter No.194, p.25; See also Willcox to Carr, 12 May, 1880, NA, RG393, Part 1, Entry 169, Vol. 10, pp.248-249.

174 Carr to AG DoAz, 13 May, 1880, Troops in SE Arizona, DoAz, NA, RG393, Part 1, Entry 232, Vol.6, 7 May-18 May, 1880, Letter No.194, p.25; Kerr to Jeffords, 18 May, 1880, Troops in SE Arizona, DoAz, NA, RG393, Part 1, Entry 232, Vol.6, 7 May-18 May, 1880, Letter No.232, pp.45-46.

175 Willcox to Carr, 12 May, 1880, NA, RG393, Part 1, Entry 169, Vol. 10, pp.248-249.

make every effort to secure the cooperation of the Chiricahuas.[176] This action was not uncontroversial. Captain Chaffee expressed great doubts as to the wisdom of employing both Jeffords and Archie McIntosh, describing their influence over the Chiricahuas as 'baneful'.[177] Unfortunately for us today, Chaffee did not go into any detail on this issue. Willcox noted that 'Chaffee may be right in his views and will no doubt cooperate in his own way.'[178] Chaffee took the position that, since their arrival, he had treated the Chiricahuas fairly but no better than other Apaches on the reservation. However, he clearly noted that he expected obedience to his instructions and was not impressed with their refusal to move closer to the reservation when so ordered. Jeffords and McIntosh also seem to have clashed with Chaffee over his approach to the newly arrived Chiricahuas.[179] It appears to have been over Chaffee's decision to keep an obvious and close watch on the Chiricahuas after Kramer's skirmish.[180] Nevertheless, it was ultimately concluded that the Chiricahuas had been under close enough supervision to convince the US military of their good faith, which had been 'severely but successfully tested at the time Victorio, or his son, made a raid on San Carlos.'[181]

This potential problem facing Carr seemed to resolve itself when Jeffords reported that young Cachise (presumably Naiche) was disinclined to participate in any form of hostilities, and that Jeffords 'could not tell about the others'.[182] Chaffee had also earlier interviewed Juh and other Chiricahua 'Captains', and received assurances that they did not intend to join Victorio.[183]

Victorio had certainly achieved his usual goal of running the US army into the ground. There were also indications that he was diverting some of the plunder taken in this raiding to be sold down in Mexico. A party of travellers from Janos, arriving at La Mesilla, on 14 May 1880, stated that they had discovered a large and recent trail of horses and mules near Lake Guzman, going towards the Candelaria Mountains.[184] With the Mescalero reservation under US army control and the apparent loss of other trading points such as Las Palomas and Canada Alamosa, it would have made sense for the Apaches to move their plunder down into Mexico for sale in such towns as Galeana.

Morrow's battalion had moved into the San Francisco Mountains and then turned north-eastwards towards the Datil Mountains.[185] It was reported that Apaches had struck Lunas Ranch on 12 May, killing three men, three women and two children, and carrying off two girls. On the same day, Placido Romero lost three herders to the Apaches in the same area. Lunas Ranch was believed to be 60 miles north-west of Old Fort Tularosa, almost on the Arizona border in the Sierra

176 Willcox to Carr, 12 May, 1880, NA, RG393, Part 1, Entry 169, Vol. 10, pp.248-249 Willcox to Carr, 12 May, 1880, NA, RG393, Part 1, Entry 169, Vol. 10, pp.248-249.
177 Chaffee, San Carlos to Carr, Lowell, 13 May, 1880, NA, RG393, Part 1, Entry 235, pp.74-79.
178 Kerr to Jeffords, 18 May, 1880, Troops in SE Arizona, DoAz, NA, RG393, Part 1, Entry 232, Vol.6, 7 May-18 May, 1880, Letter No.232, pp.45-46.
179 Chaffee, San Carlos to Carr, Lowell, 13 May, 1880, NA, RG393, Part 1, Entry 235, pp.74-79.
180 See Carr to AAG DoAz, 30 Jun., 1880, Troops in SE Arizona, DoAz, NA, RG393, Part 1, Entry 232, Vol.7, 18 May-6 Sept., 1880, Letter No.273, pp.104-108.
181 Martin to AG, MDoP, Presidio, San Francisco, 11 Sept., 1880, NA, RG393, Part 1, Entry 169, Vol. 10, p.419; Report of General O.B. Willcox, 11 Sept., 1880, in AR-WD 1880, NA, M997, Roll 35, 1880 Vol. I, p.207; Report of General O.B. Willcox, 11 Sept., 1880, in AR-WD 1880, NA, M997, Roll 35, 1880 Vol. I, p.207.
182 Carr to Willcox, 19 May, 1880, Troops in SE Arizona, DoAz, NA, RG393, Part 1, Entry 232, , Vol.7, 18 May – 6 Sept., 1880. Letter No. 242, p.23.
183 Chaffee, San Carlos to Carr, Lowell, 13 May, 1880, NA, RG393, Part 1, Entry 235, pp.74-79.
184 'Town and County', the *Grant County Herald*, 15 May, 1880.
185 Thrapp, 1974, p.278.

Escudillo.[186] Hatch reported that he had reached the Lunas [Limas] Ranch on or around 15 May, and alleged that the Apaches had killed two women four children and taken two girls captive after finding that the men had abandoned the women and children in the Ranch; which caused Hatch to describe the men as 'simply cowards'.[187] The two girls were later reported to have escaped.[188] Of most interest is the belief that Major Morrow had had a fight with the Apaches on 11 May, 'result not known'.[189] (See document file no. 69.) Lieutenant Hutcheson's short history of the Ninth Cavalry states that in 'May, in the San Francisco Mountains, Troop C and detachment scouts, 2 men killed and one wounded.'[190] There is no record of this skirmish in the Ninth Cavalry's monthly return nor in C Company's bi-monthly roster. However, 'missing official data' concerning unsuccessful engagements with Apache raiders is not unknown. There is also no indication of whether the casualties were Apache scouts, or Ninth Cavalrymen, or both.

Morrow wrote a report of his battalion's activities between March and May 1880, a synopsis of which can be found in the National Archives in Washington DC.[191] The key date, where the next chapter is concerned, is 16 May 1880. It was at this juncture that Morrow detached his Apache scout company of between 50 and 75 Apache scouts under Chief of Scouts H.K. Parker and sent them ahead toward Ojo Caliente.

Enigmatic Skirmish at Old Fort Tularosa, 14 May 1880[192]

On the evening of 13 May 1880, Sergeant George Jordan of K Company, with 25 troopers of K Company,[193] escorting a wagon train of rations, encountered a messenger from Old Fort Tularosa seeking aid.[194] This post should not be confused with the Tulerosa agency on the Mescalero reservation. This was an old army post, which had been abandoned, but had proved to be a focal point for subsequent civilian settlement. In fact, this was the military post, placed on the short-lived Tularosa reservation, which the Mimbres Apaches had been moved to in 1872 and had abandoned in 1874.[195] According to Kayser, the Fort was never properly completed, being a mixture ranging from well-constructed quarters to rough shanty buildings. These varying remains formed a nucleus for civilian settlement after the post's abandonment in late 1874.[196] They lay between the Mogollon Mountains to the south and the Datil Mountains to the north, approximately 50 miles to the west

---

186 Loud to AAG, Fort Leavenworth, 20 May, 1880 & 21 May, 1880, Telegrams Sent DoNM, Vol.3, Jan.-Nov. 1880, NA, RG393, Part 3, Entry 431, p.413 & p.423.

187 Loud (citing communication from Hatch dated Ojo Caliente, 21 May, 1880) to AAG Fort Leavenworth, 23 May, 1880, Telegrams Sent DoNM, Vol.3, Jan.-Nov. 1880, NA, RG393, Part 3, Entry 431, p.426.

188 Loud to Hatch, Ojo Caliente, 23 May, 1880, Telegrams Sent DoNM, Vol.3, Jan.-Nov. 1880, NA, RG393, Part 3, Entry 431, p.429; Loud to AAG, Fort Leavenworth, 23 May, 1880 in 'Victorio Papers', NA, M666, Roll 527.

189 Telegrams Sent DoNM, Vol.3, Jan.-Nov. 1880, NA, RG393, Part 3, Entry 431, p.412 & p.413; Loud to Hatch, Tularosa N.M (Operator at Craig will forward with return of courier), 19 May, 1880, Telegrams Sent DoNM, Vol.3, Jan.-Nov. 1880, NA, RG393, Part 3, Entry 431, p.412.

190 See Copy of Hutcheson's Report written for the 'Journal of the Military Service Institution', Vol. XVI, No. 75, May 1895, on <http://www.vq.com/overview_buffalosoldierhistory_9th_cav.htm> .

191 Synopsis of Report of Maj. Morrow June 27, 1880 Concerning March, April & May 80 in Letters Received, Dept. of Missouri 1868-98, RG 393, Entry A1-1 2601, Box 93.

192 This is the modern-day settlement of Aragon (see Aragon webpage).

193 Thrapp argues that the detachment comprised a composite mix from troopers of E, I and K companies. (1988, p.745).

194 Schubert, 1997, p.74: Leckie, 1967, pp.220-221; O'Neal, 1991, p.149.

195 See Watt, 'I Will Not Surrender the Hair of a Horse's Tail: The Victorio Campaign 1879', Chapter 4.

196 Kayser, 1973ii, p.26.

of Ojo Caliente.[197] Sergeant Jordan's own testimony stated that he had already been ordered to march to Old Fort Tularosa with a supply train to replenish 'the rest of the regiment, which was pursuing Victoria's band of Apaches.'[198]

Apparently Victorio and a large group of warriors had been spotted in the vicinity, and the settlers felt vulnerable to attack. Jordan immediately gathered up his wagons and escort and they made a night march to the settlement, reaching their destination at about 6:00 a.m. on 14 May.[199] There had been no attack,[200] and after some rest the men proceeded to fortify a part of the hamlet. With the civilians placed inside the works, and the troops deployed around them, everyone waited for the Apaches to attack.[201] As evening drew on, the settlement came under intense gunfire as the Apaches closed in on foot. Some of the wagon teamsters and troopers, guarding the animals in a corral, were cut off. The Apaches launched two attacks in the fading light, but were unable to break into the main defences.[202] They then turned their attention to the corral, in an attempt to run off the horses and cattle. Sergeant Jordan sent out 10 troopers to rescue the men in the corral,[203] and following this move the Apaches broke off their attack.[204] Jordan estimated that Victorio had been leading at least 100 warriors in the attack.[205] The following morning, Hatch and the rest of his battalion arrived at Old Fort Tularosa, much to the relief of all concerned.[206] On 7 May 1890, Sergeant George Jordan was awarded the Congressional Medal of Honor for his actions at Old Fort Tularosa on 13-14 May 1880.[207]

However, this skirmish was an anomaly where the Victorio campaign overall was concerned. The two main secondary sources for the campaign, Thrapp and Stout, make no mention of it at all, which implies that the skirmish is not particularly significant as far as the overall campaign is concerned. The Chronological List records an encounter with Apaches at Tularosa (Old Fort) on 14 May. No casualties at all are recorded on either side.[208] Indeed, only a few days after this battle, Hatch, then at Old Fort Tularosa, stated that there had been 'some light skirmishing with detachment here.'[209] The only other comment from Hatch was that the ranch at Old Fort Tularosa had been attacked and this had been repelled by a Ninth Cavalry detachment.[210] Given the pressure upon Hatch to achieve a success over the Apaches, and his past habit of claiming major victories, suggests that a major assault had not occurred.

From the Apache point of view, the first question we have to ask ourselves is: what did the Apaches have to gain from such an attack? The suspicion would be that the attacks by Victorio's

197 Schubert, 1997, p.74.
198 Beyer & Keydal vi, p.376.
199 Schubert, 1997, p.74-75; Billington, 1991, p.96.
200 O'Neal reports that Sergeant Jordan arrived to find that one 'civilian' had been killed working in a cornfield. (1991, p.149; see also Beyer & Keydal vi, p.377).
201 Schubert, 1997, p.75; O'Neal, 1991, p.149.
202 Schubert, 1997, p.75; Leckie, 1967, p221; Billington, 1991, p.96; O'Neal, 1991, p.149; Beyer & Keydal vi, p.377.
203 Schubert, 1997, p.75; Burton. 1999, p.160; O'Neal, 1991, p.149; Beyer & Keydal vi, p.377.
204 Schubert, 1997, p.75; Leckie, 1967, p.221; Beyer & Keydal vi, p.377.
205 Schubert, 1997, p.75; Burton,1999, p.160; Beyer & Keydal vi, p.378.
206 Leckie, 1967, p.221: Schubert, 1997, p.75.
207 Schubert, 1997, p.pp.75-76; Leckie, 1967, p.221.
208 Chronological List, p.50.
209 Loud to AAG, Fort Leavenworth, 19 May, 1880, NA, RG393, Part 1, Entry 2546, p.650; Hatch to AAAG, 17 May, 1880, 'DoNM/GSFO/L&T', NA, RG393, Part 3, Entry 475, Vol. 5, p.264; (Loud to AAG Fort Leavenworth, 19 May, 1880, Telegrams Sent DoNM, Vol.3, Jan.-Nov. 1880, NA, RG393, Part 3, Entry 431, pp.410-411; Loud to AAG Fort Leavenworth, 19 May, 1880 in 'Victorio Papers', NA, M666, Roll 527
210 Hatch to AAG, DoM, Fort Leavenworth, 5 Aug., 1880 in Letters Sent by '9MD/DNM/DoNM', NA, RG393, M1072, Roll 6, Jan. 1880-Aug. 1881, Letter No.407, pp.260-268.

warriors were intended to panic the defence into fleeing. Therefore, as long as the defenders held their ground, they were, in fact, relatively safe. The Apaches would not have closed with an entrenched enemy, as this would almost certainly have resulted in unnecessary fatalities. What did they have to gain? It is easier, and more important, to see what they had to lose in mounting this attack. The relatively large number of Apache warriors said to have been involved in the skirmish is open to question. The attack was mounted in conditions of poor visibility, once again giving the Apaches, through a prodigious consumption of ammunition and constant movement, the chance to create the impression of far greater numbers than were actually present. From a tactical point of view, the timing of the attack appears strange as well. There was enough time, from when the citizens of Fort Tularosa first felt threatened to the point of attack, to summon relief and then fortify the place. The Apaches worked by stealth and speed. Why give such an early warning to the settlers? This seeming lack of logic does in fact hint at a possible reason why the Apaches attacked Old Fort Tularosa. By drawing attention to their presence, they pressured the Ninth Cavalry into maintaining a pursuit which would simply cripple and kill even more of their horses and mules.

This attack has all the hallmarks of a small Apache raiding party tactically probing the settlement's defences. They failed to panic the defenders into flight and did not succeed in running off the livestock. The raiding party then cut their losses and withdrew. What they had succeeded in doing was keeping Hatch on their trail.

In the meantime, Victorio and his men turned towards the Black Range. On 17 May, from Old Fort Tularosa, Hatch reported that his command's stock was worn out, due to the singular lack of forage in that quarter.[211] For this reason, he was going to leave his worn-out horses under guard at that point and continue the pursuit of Victorio on foot. Hatch acknowledged that Victorio might be able to evade him, even though he stated that the Apaches were also 'nearly dismounted'.[212] He also estimated that Victorio had approximately 200 warriors, and he thought it was 'possible he is going east.'[213] Hatch guessed that Victorio was making for the San Mateo Mountains, with the ultimate destination being the Mescalero reservation.[214] This information was gleaned from the number of dead horses left on Victorio's trail and information supplied by some captives taken by the Apaches who had then escaped. The captives reported having overheard Victorio stating his intention to make for the Mescalero reservation. They also stated that Victorio had some Comanche allies with him,[215] although these were more likely Mescalero Apaches. There is a photo of Mescalero Apache scouts taken in the 1880s where some Mescalero warriors are wearing their hair in braids. Hatch also sent instructions to Lieutenant Payne, Fifteenth Infantry, commanding at Ojo Caliente, to send out rations and fodder for his men and horses. Hatch also warned Payne to watch out for a repeat raid on Ojo Caliente's horse herd.[216] Hatch informed District Headquarters that he had

211 Hatch to AAAG, 17 May, 1880, 'DoNM/GSFO/L&T', NA, RG393, Part 3, Entry 475, Vol. 5, p.264; Loud to AAG Fort Leavenworth, 19 May, 1880 in 'Victorio Papers', NA, M666, Roll 527.

212 Loud to AAG, Fort Leavenworth, 19 May, 1880, NA, RG393, Part 1, Entry 2546, p.650; Hatch to AAAG, 17 May, 1880, 'DoNM/GSFO/L&T', NA, RG393, Part 3, Entry 475, Vol. 5, p.264; Loud to AAG Fort Leavenworth, 19 May, 1880 in 'Victorio Papers', NA, M666, Roll 527.

213 Loud to AAG Fort Leavenworth, 19 May, 1880 in 'Victorio Papers', NA, M666, Roll 527.

214 Loud to AAG, Fort Leavenworth, 19 May, 1880, NA, RG393, Part 1, Entry 2546, pp.650-651; Hatch to AAAG, 17 May, 1880, 'DoNM/GSFO/L&T', NA, RG393, Part 3, Entry 475, Vol. 5, p.264; Hatch to AAAG, 17 May, 1880, 'DoNM/GSFO/L&T', NA, RG393, Part 3, Entry 475, Vol. 5, p.264.

215 Loud to AAG, Fort Leavenworth, 19 May, 1880, NA, RG393, Part 1, Entry 2546, pp.650-651; Hatch to AAAG, 17 May, 1880, 'DoNM/GSFO/L&T', NA, RG393, Part 3, Entry 475, Vol. 5, p.264; See also Pope (citing Hatch Telegram of 17 May from Tularosa) to Whipple 20 May, 1880, 'Victorio Files', NA, RG393, M1495, Roll 14.

216 Hatch to Payne, 17 May, 1880, 'DoNM/GSFO/L&T', NA, RG393, Part 3, Entry 475, Vol. 5, p.250.

sent his scouts in advance in the hope of intercepting the Apaches in the San Mateo Mountains.[217] This was the company mentioned earlier as having left Morrow's battalion on the San Francisco River. The news that Victorio had probably managed to evade his pursuers once again, and was now moving eastwards, prompted General Pope to request that Grierson be sent back to Fort Stanton with his Tenth Cavalrymen. General Sheridan responded by issuing instructions that, as soon as three companies of the Tenth Cavalry had arrived in Texas from Fort Sill, Grierson should be ordered out with five companies of Tenth Cavalry to Fort Stanton to cooperate with Hatch.[218] Pope felt that he could not spare any more troops from within the Department of the Missouri without leaving other parts of the frontier open to attack.[219]

In the meantime, Hatch had arrived at Ojo Caliente on 21 May, having pushed ahead of his command with a small detachment of ten men.[220] He noted that Parker's Apache scouts had trailed Victorio to a few miles to the south, before making for Ojo Caliente. Hatch sent them back out in pursuit, but he was not optimistic that the rest of his command could catch up with their quarry.[221] He estimated that Major Morrow was still one day from Ojo Caliente, and Captain Hooker's battalion was three days away.[222] Hatch blamed the faltering pursuit on distance and the nature of the terrain over which they had followed Victorio. He pointed out that his pursuit had taken him over the Mogollon Mountains and on into Arizona before he had turned back, commenting that their horses were too 'fine' for such arduous service.[223] He also noted that the Ninth Cavalry's mounts had been further weakened by lack of water and a scarcity of grass, the latter resource having been eaten down by the large number of sheep being raised in that part of New Mexico. He estimated that his regiment would soon be dismounted, though he comforted himself that Victorio's following were in the same condition, having abandoned many horses and mules.[224] That

217 Loud to AAG, Fort Leavenworth, 19 May, 1880, NA, RG393, Part 1, Entry 2546, p.650; Hatch to AAAG, 17 May, 1880, 'DoNM/GSFO/L&T', NA, RG393, Part 3, Entry 475, Vol. 5, p.264.

218 Pope to AAG, MDoM, 20 May, 1880, & Sheridan to Pope, 22 May, 1880, NA, RG393, Part 1, Entry 2546, pp.651-652; See also Pope (citing Hatch Telegram of 17 May from Tularosa) to Whipple 20 May, 1880, 'Victorio Files', NA, RG393, M1495, Roll 14; Sheridan to Townsend 22 May, 1880 in 'Victorio Papers', NA, M666, Roll 527.

219 Pope to Loud 20 May, 1880, Telegrams Sent DoNM, Vol.3, Jan.-Nov. 1880, NA, RG393, Part 3, Entry 431, p.419; see also See also Pope to Whipple 21 May, 1880, 'Victorio Files', NA, RG393, M1495, Roll 14.

220 Loud to AAG Fort Leavenworth, 29 May, 1880, Telegrams Sent DoNM, Vol.3, Jan.-Nov. 1880, NA, RG393, Part 3, Entry 431, p.448.

221 Hatch, Ojo Caliente, to AAAG, SF, 21 May, 1880, in 'DoNM/GSFO/L&T', NA, RG393, Part 3, Entry 475, Vol. 5, p.266; See also Loud (citing Hatch, Ojo Caliente, 21 May, 1880) to AAG Fort Leavenworth, 23 May, 1880, Telegrams Sent DoNM, Vol.3, Jan.-Nov. 1880, NA, RG393, Part 3, Entry 431, p.427; Pope to AAG MDoM, 25 May, 1880, 'Victorio Files', NA, RG393, M1495, Roll 14; See also similar but more difficult to decipher letter NA, RG393, Part 3, Entry 475, Vol. 5, p.265; see also the *Grant County Herald*, 29 May, 1880; Hatch makes similar comments two days earlier from Old Fort Tularosa, 19 May, 1880, Telegrams Sent DoNM, Vol.3, Jan.-Nov. 1880, NA, RG393, Part 3, Entry 431, pp.410-411.

222 Loud to AAG Fort Leavenworth, 29 May, 1880, Telegrams Sent DoNM, Vol.3, Jan.-Nov. 1880, NA, RG393, Part 3, Entry 431, p.448; 'Indian Affairs', *Army & Navy Journal*, Vol. 17, 19 Jun., 1880, p.940

223 Hatch, Ojo Caliente, to AAAG, SF, 21 May, 1880, in 'DoNM/GSFO/L&T', NA, RG393, Part 3, Entry 475, Vol. 5, p.265; Loud to AAG Fort Leavenworth, 31 May, 1880, Telegrams Sent DoNM, Vol.3, Jan.-Nov. 1880, NA, RG393, Part 3, Entry 431, pp.451-452.

224 Hatch, Ojo Caliente, to AAAG, SF, 21 May, 1880, in 'DoNM/GSFO/L&T', NA, RG393, Part 3, Entry 475, Vol. 5, p.266; See also Loud (citing Hatch, Ojo Caliente, 21 May, 1880) to AAG Fort Leavenworth, 23 May, 1880, Telegrams Sent DoNM, Vol.3, Jan.-Nov. 1880, NA, RG393, Part 3, Entry 431, p.427; Pope to AAG MDoM, 25 May, 1880, 'Victorio Files', NA, RG393, M1495, Roll 14; See also similar but more difficult to decipher letter NA, RG393, Part 3, Entry 475, Vol. 5, p.265; see also the *Grant County Herald*, 29 May, 1880; Hatch makes similar comments two days earlier from Old Fort

Mescalero Apache Scouts.
Throughout the campaign against Victorio there were reports of large numbers of 'renegade' Comanches and Kiowas joining Victorio. There may have been a very small number of such individuals but these were more likely to have been Mescalero Apaches. This photograph shows a group of Mescalero Apache scouts a few years after the campaign where the influence of the Plains Indians living to the east and north of the Mescalero Apaches can be clearly seen, particularly the practice of braiding their hair. It was this influence which probably led rise to the rumours that a large number of Comanches had joined Victorio. (National Archives)

the Apaches did not utilise horses and mules in the same way as the US army did either appears to have escaped the Colonel, or he was attempting to glean anything positive he could to include in his reports.

The state of Hatch's command can be gauged by his urgent requests for fresh mules to be sent to Ojo Caliente from Fort Craig, as well as new boots, shoes and clothing for the men ('a pair of boots will not last in the mountains a month'), hay for 'stuffing aparejos', and additional rations as the post at Ojo Caliente was now denuded of food.[225] To be fair to District Headquarters, while Hatch was away on campaign, they had made sterling efforts to ensure that the Ninth Cavalry could remain in the field:

> Eight thousand rations are en-route and should now be at Ojo Caliente, they left on first instant. Chief Q.S. will ship fifteen thousand more rations to Craig this week. The mules you ordered to Craig to be distributed south arrived at Craig yesterday and are with Lt. Valois. The wagons with them are loaded with corn, as you ordered. Have instructed Chief Quartermaster relative to boots and shoes for Ojo Caliente and hay for Aparejos. Ten bales of Hay was sent with the mules to Craig and which Lt Valois now has. Have telegraphed Commanding Officer

Tularosa, 19 May, 1880, Telegrams Sent DoNM, Vol.3, Jan.-Nov. 1880, NA, RG393, Part 3, Entry 431, pp.410-411.

225 Hatch, Ojo Caliente, to AAAG, SF, 21 May, 1880, in 'DoNM/GSFO/L&T', NA, RG393, Part 3, Entry 475, Vol. 5, p.267.

> Bayard to at once repeat to Craig all telegrams sent you in his case to be forwarded to you at Ojo Caliente and your mail to Paraje ... Every endeavor to get supplies promptly from here to you has been made with means of doing so available here. So far as I can learn we continue to find contract transportation is hardly to be relied upon for the prompt transportation of stores. Lieut Valois telegraphed me that he left Craig for Ojo Caliente this morning, he must with him mules, corn and hay. Clothing[226] for Ojo Caliente was shipped some days ago and Quartermaster informs me is now at Albuquerque awaiting arrival of corn to be shipped to you. Contract team will start with the corn and clothing about Wednesday. Railroad has been washed out causing some delays. Think we need a Quartermaster Agent at Railroad terminus to ship stores and attend to them, someone has now to go from here each time to do it ... Chief Q.S. states he thought the eight thousand rations were at Ojo Caliente and requested Q.M. two days ago upon finding they had not arrived to hurry them up, they should have arrived by this time.[227]

Hatch expressed disappointment that he had been unable to bring Victorio to a decisive battle,[228] and noted that he needed 10 more companies of infantry to help protect the increasing number of ranchers and prospectors entering southern New Mexico. He also strongly recommended the recruiting of 200 Apache scouts to hunt down Victorio. If he was given these additional men the Apaches would be hunted down and destroyed in a matter of months.[229]

It will come as no surprise that Hatch's failure to bring the war to an end once again raised much adverse comment on the part of the press. Hatch was accused of deliberately making his command conspicuous so as to avoid any confrontation with the Apaches. He was also strongly criticized for failing to support Captain Madden, and for insulting ordinary citizens who had volunteered to serve in the Mogollon Mountains.[230] (See document file no. 70.) A petition from the citizens of Silver City to President Hayes stated that the army had proved it could neither defeat the enemy nor protect the citizens of New Mexico. It also stated, without actually naming Hatch, that the situation had been misrepresented 'through military or official channels'. General Pope countered that there were more than enough troops to deal with the Apaches, though the latter's mode of warfare made this a difficult task to complete in the short-term. He also angrily pointed out that many reported depredations were at best exaggerated and at worst fictitious.[231] (See document file no. 71.)

Morrow's command reached Ojo Caliente on 22 May, and Hatch duly reported that Morrow 'considers it important we secure more of the foot indians from San Carlos as actual economy,'[232] in a further attempt to solicit more Apache scouts from his superiors. He also reiterated his desire

226 This included 500 blouses, 400 Campaign hats, 600 Trousers (Cavalry), 150 Trousers (Infantry), 600 Flannel Shirts, 800 Drawers, 1200, Stockings, 800 Boots. (Loud to Hatch, 26 May, 1880, Telegrams Sent DoNM, Vol.3, Jan.-Nov. 1880, NA, RG393, Part 3, Entry 431, p.435)

227 Loud to Hatch, (Lieut Plummer at Fort Craig will forward by return courier) Ojo Caliente, 23 May, 1880, Telegrams Sent DoNM, Vol.3, Jan.-Nov. 1880, NA, RG393, Part 3, Entry 431, p.429.

228 Hatch, Ojo Caliente, to AAAG, SF, 21 May, 1880, in 'DoNM/GSFO/L&T', NA, RG393, Part 3, Entry 475, Vol. 5, p.265; Loud (citing communication from Hatch, Ojo Caliente, 21 May, 1880) to AAG Fort Leavenworth, 23 May, 1880, Telegrams Sent DoNM, Vol.3, Jan.-Nov. 1880, NA, RG393, Part 3, Entry 431, pp.425-426.

229 Loud (citing communication from Hatch, Ojo Caliente, 21 May, 1880) to AAG Fort Leavenworth, 23 May, 1880, Telegrams Sent DoNM, Vol.3, Jan.-Nov. 1880, NA, RG393, Part 3, Entry 431, p.425-426; See also Hatch, Ojo Caliente, to AAAG, SF, 21 May, 1880, in 'DoNM/GSFO/L&T', NA, RG393, Part 3, Entry 475, Vol. 5, p.265.

230 'The Mogollon Campaign', the *Grant County Herald*, 22 May, 1880.

231 Citizens Bailey etc. to President RB Hayes, Washington D.C., 10 May, 1880, 'Victorio Files', NA, RG393, M1495, Roll 14; See also correspondence in 'Victorio Papers', NA, M666, Roll 527.

232 Hatch to Loud AAAG 22 May, 1880, NA, RG393, Part 3, Entry 439, p.72.

for those Warm Springs women and children based at San Carlos to be transferred to his control if the Apaches were going to be successfully fought;[233] and he repeated his earlier argument that the dependents of the Warm Springs Apache should be escorted by 'two Indian police companies,' who could then be deployed to hunt down the Apaches.[234]

Hatch also stated that the Apache raiding parties had remained scattered, and that he thought that they might reunite in the San Andres Mountains.[235] This prediction may have been prompted by the fact that 'Montzilla [Nautzilla] principal Mescalero Chief with four warriors four squaws and one child' surrendered at the Mescalero agency on 20 May 1880, having crossed the Rio Grande on 19 May,[236] indicating that some Mescaleros had split away from Victorio as the latter returned to the Black Range. Hatch also reiterated his claim that American Indians from Indian Territory had also joined Victorio. 'A large fat indian killed on the San Francisco River was a Commanche possibly a sub chief.'[237] Unfortunately, Hatch adds no further detail to this bald statement. Finally, he also sent a message to Fort Bayard asking that the settlements in the Mimbres Valley be alerted to the danger that Apache raiders from Victorio's following might be about to descend on them.[238]

The pursuit of Victorio was so gruelling that Hatch decided to reorganise his battalions. A dismounted battalion was to be deployed into the Black Range, while two companies with horses were to be sent to Fort Stanton to create a mounted battalion of four companies ready for field service.[239] Despite his doubts about the condition of Morrow's command, Hatch ordered it to proceed from Ojo Caliente to Beyer's camp near Hillsboro.[240]

In reality, the Ninth Cavalry was at the end of its tether. Hatch had to admit that if the Tenth Cavalry and extra Apache scouts were not forthcoming, he could only guard fixed points and would not be able to mount the active field operations demanded by General Sherman.[241] Earlier in this chapter it was argued that, at the beginning of May, the Ninth Cavalry Regiment was not in a fit state to operate against the Apaches. By the end of May, it was clear that the pursuit of Victorio from Ojo Caliente through the Mogollon and San Francisco Mountains and back to Ojo Caliente had effectively dismounted the Ninth Cavalry. Table 7.3 shows that by the end of May, the Ninth Cavalry's horse casualty rates had increased from 54 horses lost in April to 62 horses lost in May.

Table 7.3 also shows that the regiment was now carrying more unserviceable than serviceable horses. Effectively, the Ninth Cavalry had run three mini-campaigns against the Apaches between January and the end of May 1880. During March 1880, there had been insufficient time for Hatch

233 Hatch to Loud AAAG 22 May, 1880 NA, RG393, Part 3, Entry 439, p.73 & Hatch to Loud AAAG 26 May, 1880, NA, RG393, Part 3, Entry 439, p.75.

234 Hatch to Loud AAAG 26 May, 1880, NA, RG393, Part 3, Entry 439, p.76.

235 Hatch to Loud AAAG 22 May, 1880, NA, RG393, Part 3, Entry 439, p.73.

236 Hatch, Fort Craig, to Morrow, Capt Beyer's Camp near Hillsborough 27 May, 1880, 'DoNM/GSFO/L&T', NA, RG393, Part 3, Entry 475, Vol. 7, p.496; Hatch to AAG Ft Leavenworth, 28 May, 1880, NA, RG393, Part 3, Entry 439, p.421; Loud to Hatch, Fort Craig, 27 May, 1880, Telegrams Sent DoNM, Vol.3, Jan.-Nov. 1880, NA, RG393, Part 3, Entry 431, pp.441-442; Steelhammer to A.A.A.G., DoNM, 27 May, 1880, 'Victorio Files', NA, RG393, M1495, Roll 14; Hatch to AAG Mil. Div. Mo., 28 May, 1880 in 'Victorio Papers', NA, M666, Roll 527.

237 Hatch, Ojo Caliente, to CO Fort Bayard, 22 May, 1880, in 'DoNM/GSFO/L&T', NA, RG393, Part 3, Entry 475, Vol. 5, p.268.

238 Ibid.

239 Hatch to Loud AAAG 22 May, 1880, NA, RG393, Part 3, Entry 439, p.74.

240 Hatch to Morrow, 24 May, 1880, 'DoNM/GSFO/L&T', NA, RG393, Part 3, Entry 475, Vol. 5, pp.253-254.

241 Loud (citing Hatch, Ojo Caliente, 22 May, 1880) to AAG Fort Leavenworth, 23 May, 1880, Telegrams Sent DoNM, Vol.3, Jan.-Nov. 1880, NA, RG393, Part 3, Entry 431, p.428; Pope to AAG, MDoM, 25 May, 1880, 'Victorio Files', NA, RG393, M1495, Roll 14.

to rest as many of his men and horses as possible, because of severe provocation from Apache raiding parties during that month.

The regiment's return to active operations against the Apaches in April and May had had a catastrophic effect on the Ninth Cavalry's ability to operate as a mobile unit theoretically capable of confronting the Apaches. What we see here is the effect of Victorio's strategy of killing and crippling horses and mules by enticing the Ninth Cavalry into long pursuits over difficult terrain and targeting horses in the opening volley of any engagement with the US army. If we examine the monthly regimental return for the Ninth Cavalry (Table 7.4), we can see that, by individual company, the regiment was in very poor shape for field operations by the end of May. By the end of April, most companies were finding it difficult to mount more than 50 percent of the available men. Those companies that were still able to do so (Companies E, G, I and L) were no longer able to do so by the end of May.

According to the monthly return, 339 men out of an available 668 could be mounted and put into the field at the beginning of May. By the end of that month 240 men still had a serviceable horse out of an overall strength of 668 men. In percentage terms, the cavalrymen available to Colonel Hatch at the beginning of May had dropped from 51 to 36 percent of the men available for duty.

However, this dire situation was about to be dramatically changed by the intervention of the Apache scout company led by Henry K. Parker. Hatch ordered that a wagon carrying 8,000 rounds of ammunition for Morrow's command be sent from San Jose to Canada Alamosa on 26 May, with a two-man escort. From Canada Alamosa a larger escort of dismounted men should escort the wagon on to Major Morrow by 27 May.[242] Hatch stated that this ammunition was for Lieutenant Maney,[243] and was to re-supply the Apache scouts commanded by Parker, who had fought a major battle with the Apaches near the head of the Rio Palomas on 24 May 1880.

242 Special Field Order No.33 25 May, 1880, NA, RG393, Part 3, Entry 450; See also 'DoNM/GSFO/L&T', NA, RG393, Part 3, Entry 475, Vol. 5, p.248.

243 Hatch, Fort Craig, to Morrow, Capt. Beyer's Camp near Hillsborough, 27 May, 1880 'DoNM/GSFO/L&T', NA, RG393, Part 3, Entry 475, Vol. 7, p.496.

Table 7.3 The activities of Morrow and his battalion, April–May 1880.

30 April	Canada Alamosa.
2 May	Ojo Caliente.
3–4 May	March via Shaw's Ranch and Sherman's Cienega.
7 May	Reach the Gileta [Gilita] River. Joined by Hatch with Hooker's Third Battalion.
8 May	Proceed into Mogollon Mountains.
9 May	Reach Cooney's Mining Camp.
11 May	Arrive at Kellar's Ranch. Detach Purington to command dismounted men at Parson Williams Ranch.
14 May	Encounter Tupper's Command on Pueblo Creek. Follow Apache trail to the north-east.
15 May	Continue on trail to the north-east.
16 May	Tupper leaves with his command. Bodies found at Las Lentes. Parker with K Company sent to follow trail from that point. Rest of Battalion follows on Parker's left flank. March down Apache Creek to Tulerosa [Tularosa] Road and on into the Tulerosa [Tularosa] Mountains. Hear of fight between Ninth Cavalry detachment and Apaches at Kelly's Ranch. March to that place and follow trail to Patterson's Cienega on road to Ojo Caliente. Trail leads either toward Ojo Caliente or the San Mateo Mountains. Horses broken down and out of rations. Hatch orders march to Ojo Caliente.
22 May	Arrive Ojo Caliente.
24 May	Reach Canada Alamosa. Rceive news of Parker Fight (see next chapter).
30 May	Arrive Camp French via Cuchillo Negro and Las Palomas.
31 May	March to Fort Cummings.

Table 7.4 Ninth Cavalry, Roster of Horses January–May 1880.[244]

	Serviceable Horses	Unserviceable Horses	Horses Lost in Action, Died, etc.
January	438	103	36
February	425	129	34
March	441	140	10
April	345	213	54
May	244	277	62

244 Derived from Returns From Regular Army Cavalry Regiments 1833-1916, 9th Cavalry 1873-1880, NA, M744, Roll 88

Table 7.5 Serviceable, Unserviceable and Lost Horses to Available Men, Ninth Cavalry, April–May 1880.[245]

Company	Month	Serviceable Horses	Unserviceable Horses	Lost Horses	Available Men
A	April	18	20	13	40
	May	18	19	3	44
B	April	22	18	0	56
	May	22	18	0	51
C	April	16	17	5	48
	May	21	17	0	51
D	April	16	23	9	46
	May	16	23	0	48
E	April	29	20	7	58
	May	1	36	12	54
F	April	20	6	12	43
	May	12	20	7	44
G	April	40	10	1	67
	May	30	20	0	68
H	April	24	34	3	60
	May	24	32	2	59
I	April	40	17	3	59
	May	30	14	7	58
K	April	50	14	4	60
	May	13	40	9	61
L	April	34	5	0	64
	May	23	16	15	64
M	April	30	29	0	67
	May	30	22	7	66

245 Derived from Returns From Regular Army Cavalry Regiments 1833-1916, 9th Cavalry 1873-1880, NA, M744, Roll 88

8

Victorio Defeated on the Palomas River, 24–25 May 1880

As noted earlier, H.K. Parker was accompanied by between 50 and 75[1] Apaches scouts. This was the Apache scout company recruited for service in the District of New Mexico, as opposed to the Apache scouts on loan from the Department of Arizona. On recruiting this company in March 1880, Lieutenant Maney had nominated one Apache known as 'Jim' as first sergeant and three others as sergeants, one of whom was known as 'Jack Long'.[2] Both Jim and Jack Long would play a leading role in the events which followed.

The number of Apache scouts recruited suggests that Colonel Hatch, having been, so far unsuccessful in his requests for additional Apache scouts, had resorted to subterfuge. It would appear that 65 Apache scouts had been recruited by Lieutenant Maney in March 1880, when the District of New Mexico had only been allocated 37.[3] What had happened was that Lieutenant Maney had recruited 37 Apache scouts, while an additional 28 Apaches had been hired as mule packers. This, according to Maney, had been in compliance with a direct order from Colonel Hatch:

> I was authorized by instructions from Gen. Hatch to enlist thirty seven Indian scouts and directed by Genl. Hatch to employ additional Indians as Packers. The Post Quartermaster at Bayard being directed to tally up such packers as I designated.[4]

Certainly, the July 1880 Fort Bayard returns show that 63 Apache scouts arrived at Fort Bayard on 27 March 1880.[5] However, at the end of September, Hatch himself queried the authority granted to recruit 65 scouts when the district was only authorised to have a little over half that number. One detects a 'political' smoke screen being created by Hatch to muddy the waters in preparation for later queries from his superiors when the apparent discrepancy in scout numbers became apparent. This, at first glance, appears quite innocuous; until one realises that Hatch could easily have been accused of acting unconstitutionally by flouting Congress's control over the numbers recruited into the US army. Ultimately, Hatch appears to have deflected the blame for unauthorized recruitment

1 It would appear that the scouts recruited numbered 65. One assumes that the addition of Parker and possibly as many as nine civilian packers could bring this number up to 75.

2 Maney to AAAG, DoNM, 20 Mar., 1880 in Letters Received by HQ DoNM Sept. 1865-Aug. 1890, NA, RG393, M1088, Roll 40, Jan.-Jun. 1880.

3 Maney, Fort Stanton 10 Nov., 1880 in Letters Received by HQ DoNM Sept. 1865-Aug. 1890, NA, RG393, M1088, Roll 41, Jul.-Dec. 1880.

Hatch mentions the figure of thirty-six authorised scouts (Hatch to CO Troops in the Field, Fort Cummings, 29 Sept., 1880 in Letters Received by HQ DoNM Sept. 1865-Aug. 1890, NA, RG393, M1088, Roll 41, Jul.-Dec. 1880).

4 Maney, Fort Stanton, N.M. 10 Nov., 1880 in Letters Received by HQ DoNM Sept. 1865-Aug. 1890, NA, RG393, M1088, Roll 41, Jul.-Dec. 1880.

5 Return for Jul. 1880 in Returns From U.S. Military Posts 1800-1916, Fort Bayard, New Mexico Jan. 1880-Dec. 1894, NA, M617, Roll 88.

onto Colonel George P. Buell, Commander of the Fifteenth Infantry Regiment. Buell was brought in to command field operations against the Apaches in New Mexico during the summer of 1880. As we shall see, he had a habit of acting unilaterally where field operations were concerned. Buell's unauthorised recruitment of citizen guides allowed Hatch the opportunity to pass the blame onto Buell.[6] (See Chapter 15) For the moment, the important point is that, by the time Hatch's creative recruitment came to light, it had already paid a massive dividend.

Disaster for the Apaches on the Palomas River, May 24–25 1880[7]

Parker's scouts were supplied with four days' rations and eight pack mules when they left Morrow's command on the San Francisco River, on 17 May 1880. On the following day the exhausted pack mules collapsed.[8] The Chief of Scouts ordered the rations distributed among the Apache scouts and carried on regardless, arriving on 21 May at Ojo Caliente, where he met Hatch's small detachment. With another three days' rations issued, Hatch ordered Parker and his scouts back on the trail.[9] The scouts moved down the east side of the Black Range. On 23 May 1880, they located Victorio's camp on the Palomas River.

Parker himself used some ambiguous and cryptic language; but having visited the area, we[10] are confident that the location we have identified is accurate. The camp was situated on the north side of the river, where the river runs through a narrow gorge. Victorio may have assumed that he had outrun his pursuers, for this was not a good defensive position. On the southern side of the gorge, opposite the camp, was a hill covered in bushes and rocks which dominated the campsite. To the west, as the trail dropped down to the canyon floor, there was a low ridge which dominated the camp from that direction. A mile or so behind this ridge rose steep dark cliffs topped with pine trees. To the east of the camp, a rocky ridge rose up and joined the mountains at a point north-west of the camp. From this junction there rose a cliff face which extended for no more than 100 yards to the north-west, before resolving itself into a rocky ridgeline which extended out of sight to the west. At the base of this cliff was a steep slope running down to the camp. The bottom of this slope was strewn with large boulders.[11]

Parker's command managed to remain undetected by stealthily moving off the trail and into the mountains. Parker sent out small groups of scouts to check the lie of the land. These returned

6 If the reader thinks that this is a somewhat underhand tactic on the part of Colonel Hatch one can, up to a point, agree with this sentiment. However, one is also inclined to judge Buell in the light of his vindictive nature when dealing with subordinate officers. One cannot help but think that Buell was given a taste of 'just desserts' by Hatch's political manoeuvrings.

7 Hatch does state that this battle took place on the 23 May, 1880 in a letter to the AAG Fort Leavenworth, 29 May, 1880 in 'Victorio Papers', NA, M666, Roll 527 but this appears to have been a mistake.

8 'The Fight on the Headwaters of the Palomas', the *Grant County Herald*, 29 May, 1880; Thrapp, 1974, p.279; Thrapp, 1967, p.200; Thrapp, 1988, p.1111; Stout p.139.

9 'The Fight on the Headwaters of the Palomas', the *Grant County Herald*, 29 May, 1880; Thrapp, 1974, p.279; Thrapp, 1967, p.200; Thrapp, 1988, p.1111; Stout pp.139-140; Haley, 1981, p.328.

10 Dan Aranda, Emilio Tapia and myself visited this site on the 30 June, 2007 and were initially sceptical about the site as there was a rather large gorge which had not been mentioned in Parker's report which effectively bisected the battlefield. Otherwise the area looked very good from the reports left by Parker.

11 Author's survey of this site on 30 June, 2007. Berndt Kuhn of Sweden discovered a contemporary newspaper article which pinpointed the location. Emilio Tapia and Dan Aranda suspected that they knew where this was and Emilio knew the landowner and got permission to visit the site. The Diagrams in this chapter were the author's attempt to reconstruct the battle.

by nightfall and reported that a careful approach during the night would make a dawn assault feasible.[12]

Parker and the Apache Scouts quietly closed in on Victorio's camp from three sides. It would appear that Parker's command approached from the west, down the Palomas River, before splitting into three groups. (See Map 8.1.) These manoeuvres were completed without Parker's men being detected by their quarry. (See document file no. 72.) Parker sent 30 Apache scouts under Sergeant Jim to his right, to occupy the hill to the south of the camp. They were to initiate the attack by firing down into the camp. Parker took 11 warriors to his left and occupied positions in a line to the north-west of the camp. Sergeant Jack Long (an Apache scout who had been in Gatewood's detachment and had been wounded in the battle of 27–28 October 1879 in Mexico) was sent to the other side of the camp and occupied the ridge to the east of it. This effectively cut off any escape down the canyon. To reach his position, Jack Long probably passed round the southern side of the hill occupied by Sergeant Jim, and crossed the Rio Palomas River some distance below their target, before moving back up the canyon to occupy his position.

Parker left the Apache tracks leading to the camp free, as he was confident that no Apaches would attempt to escape along the very route they had taken to reach their encampment.[13] He hoped that the Apaches would assume that this route would be blocked by their opponents. Parker calculated that the Apaches would think that their own trail into their camp was the very means by which their enemy had discovered them.

At dawn, the Apache scouts launched a devastating attack on Victorio's camp. (See Map 8.2.) Sergeant Jim's detachment spotted an Apache sentry as they were taking up position. It is not exactly clear where this sentry was placed, beyond the fact that he was stationed 'on the side next to Jim's position'.[14] If he was placed on the hill occupied by Sergeant Jim's detachment, at first glance, it is truly amazing that he did not detect the scouts as they closed in. From Victorio's camp, the hill occupied by Sergeant Jim and his men looks quite steep and rounded. However, there is a shelf which tapers out into the gorge as it passes opposite the camp. (See maps.) One suspects that the Apache scouts crept round the hill along this shelf below the sentry. It was still a prodigious feat of stealth, and it does raise the possibility that the Apache sentry had dozed off. At dawn, this man was killed either by a carefully aimed shot or effectively executed from point blank range. The rest of Sergeant Jim's detachment fired into the camp, killing a number of men, women and children.

Parker's deployment was, from an Apache point of view, perfect. He had managed to place half his force undetected upon a hill which dominated Victorio's camp. This meant that, in the opening volley, the scouts would be able to take their time in setting up their first shots and make the most of the surprise before smoke and fleeing targets made their job more difficult. The fact that there was a deep ravine between the Apache scouts and the encampment meant that, even if Victorio's men rallied, they would not be able to launch a counterattack: they would neither be able to move directly against the scouts, because of the ravine, nor would they be able to outflank them, because of the two blocking parties. Today, this ravine is very deep, but can be scrambled down from the site of the camp, though the southern side is much more precipitous, and parts of it overhang the river below. Thus Sergeant Jim's detachment was ideally placed to inflict the maximum damage for the minimum loss, and their fire caused chaos in the camp. The Apaches fled towards Parker's detachment, which covered the easiest escape route from the punishment handed out by Sergeant Jim, whilst the latter waited until the last minute before opening fire. This drove the Apaches back down the canyon until they reached a point where they could be driven back by Sergeant Jack

12 'The Fight on the Headwaters of the Palomas', the *Grant County Herald*, 29 May, 1880; Thrapp, 1974, p.277 & 279;Stout, p.140; Billington, 1991, p.96; Sonnichsen, p.208.

13 Parker's Report as cited in the AR-WD, 1880, pp.99-100; Thrapp, 1974, p.277.

14 'The Fight on the Headwaters of the Palomas', the *Grant County Herald*, 29 May, 1880.

Long's detachment. Suffering casualties each time, they fled back to their original camp site and eventually entrenched themselves in some rocks and boulders.[15]

Once they had their quarry cornered, Parker's Apache scouts possibly drew their noose tighter. (See Map 8.3.) This could easily have been accomplished, as Parker's detachment could have worked their way closer to the to the trapped Apaches. Sergeant Jack Long's detachment could also have worked their way down from their positions to increase the pressure on the trapped Apaches.

Victorio was reported to have been shot in the leg at some point during the battle,[16] though scouts calling on the women to surrender were met with a barrage of derision. This included their allegedly threatening to eat Victorio if he died, so that no enemy would touch him.[17] Victorio himself is reported to have spent much of his time urging the Apache scouts to change sides.[18] Given the history of animosity between Victorio's followers and the San Carlos Apache scouts, it is more likely that, punctuated by regular gunfire, both sides exchanged insults, with Parker's men letting Victorio know exactly what would happen to him if they got him, and Victorio and his followers, men and women, hurling their defiance back at the scouts.

The Apache scouts kept the Warm Springs Apaches pinned down for most of the day, but Parker realised that he might have to withdraw if he ran out of ammunition and sent a Mexican mule packer to Ojo Caliente to ask for both reinforcements and ammunition. By the late afternoon, Parker found that his men were down to their last rounds and, with no sign of ammunition or reinforcements, he withdrew them to the nearest water and waited for two nights and a day. Once again, the army failed to show up and he suspected that his messenger had been killed.[19] The only defeat so far inflicted upon Victorio in the United States had been carried out by approximately 60 Apache scouts and a single Anglo-American scout.[20]

Parker then moved back to Ojo Caliente, where he learned that his courier had arrived, and that nobody could explain the failure to send out more ammunition. His messenger had been attached to Lieutenant Maney's pack train and sent to Camp French. Proceeding to this latter point some days later, Parker finally contacted his courier, who informed him that he had arrived at Ojo Caliente to be told that Hatch was at Canada Alamosa. The courier had made his way to that point, and had delivered his message in person to Hatch. In the meantime, at some point during 25 or 26 May, Parker himself made for Canada Alamosa and linked up with Morrow,[21] who had at last arrived there with his command.[22]

It was then alleged by the *Grant County Herald* that Hatch had immediately made for Fort Craig to announce that his command had scored a victory over the Apaches.[23] Hatch had indeed sent word to District Headquarters, from Canada Alamosa, on 25 May, that 'Our scouts and few men with them attacked camp of hostiles at daylight yesterday morning on head of the Palomas River. Chief of Scouts reports officially killing thirty our men and scouts in the fight claim to have killed fifty

---

15 Parker's Report as cited in the AR-WD, 1880, pp.99-100; 'The Fight on the Headwaters of the Palomas', the *Grant County Herald*, 29 May, 1880.

16 Parker's Report as cited in the AR-WD, 1880, pp.99-100; Thrapp, 1974, p.280.

17 This particular story is recounted by Thrapp but while he quotes a passage he does not source this incident. Thrapp, 1974, p.280.

18 Parker's Report as cited in the AR-WD, 1880, pp.99-100; Thrapp, 1974, p.280.

19 'The Fight on the Headwaters of the Palomas', the *Grant County Herald*, 29 May, 1880.

20 'The Fight on the Headwaters of the Palomas', the *Grant County Herald*, 29 May, 1880; See also Thrapp, 1974, p.277-281 for a full account of Parker's operation; *Thirty-Four*, 2 Jun., 1880; Thrapp, 1967, pp.199-202; Thrapp, 1988, p.1112; Stout, 1974, p.139-141; Worcester, 1979, p.229-230; Roberts, 1998, p.185; Leckie, 1967, pp.221-222; Billington, 1991, p.96; Haley, 1981, p.328.

21 Hatch to AAG Fort Leavenworth, 29 May, 1880 in 'Victorio Papers', NA, M666, Roll 527.

22 Morrow's command is described as 'out of rations, tired, footsore, hungry and without clothing.' ('Gen. Hatch has a Fight with the Indians', the *Grant County Herald*, 29 May, 1880).

23 'The Fight on the Headwaters of the Palomas', the *Grant County Herald*, 29 May, 1880.

Plate 8.1. The view over Victorio's camp from a position high on the hill occupied by Sergeant Jim's detachment. These Apache scouts probably opened fire from lower down the hill, but the small outcrop of rock would have provided good cover for a marksman firing into the camp during the day. Immediately beyond this position one can see the upper edge of the gorge as the river carved its way round this hill. Beyond this are the scattered boulders and bushes where Victorio's followers took refuge. Above that is a boulder- and rock-strewn slope leading up to the base of the impassable cliff face. (Photo: Author)

Plate 8.2. The deep gorge between Sergeant Jim's position and Victorio's camp. (Photo: Author)

Plate 8.3. The view up the impassable cliffs from the perspective of the trapped Chihenne Apaches. These cliffs are clearly not impossible to climb, but this would not be an attractive option under fire. (Photo: Author)

five.'[24] (See document file no. 73.) Bar the erroneous use of 'few men' and 'our men', this is hardly claiming credit for the Ninth Cavalry or himself.[25] Rumours even reached the District of the Pecos that Hatch had been killed in the fight.[26] Therefore, accusations that Hatch had tried to take undue credit may have come from the very rumour mill which fuelled the constant press attacks that had been made on him since he took over direction of the campaign in February 1880. However, Hatch did later state that he had had, 'with great difficulty', to order Parker to take his Apache scouts out after their arrival at Ojo Caliente, which could be construed as an attempt to at least garner indirect credit for the whole affair.[27] Hatch stated that his rapid departure for Fort Craig was to coordinate the movements of troops on the east side of the Rio Grande in the on-going campaign against Victorio.[28] He had also issued orders for Morrow's command to follow up and support the Apache scouts,[29] but Morrow's command was in no fit state to rapidly exploit the success of the Apache

24 Hatch to AAAG, SF, 25 May, 1880, in 'DoNM/GSFO/L&T', NA, RG393, Part 3, Entry 475, Vol. 5, p.270; See also Telegrams Sent DoNM, Vol.3, Jan.-Nov., 1880, NA, RG393, Part 3, Entry 431, p.436; Hatch to AAG, HQ MDoM, 27 May, 1880, 'Victorio Files', NA, RG393, M1495, Roll 14; 'Indian Affairs', *Army & Navy Journal*, Vol. 17, 29 May, 1880, p.884.

25 The Record of Engagements merely records a 'fight' in which 55 Apaches were killed. (p.95) However, in seeking to pin the blame for failing to defeat Victorio, the *Grant County Herald*, 29 May, 1880 states that the Apache 'scouts and advance of Gen. Hatch's column' are given the credit for the victory may have fostered the popular belief that Hatch had been in command during this engagement. This version is still in circulation today. The Konstantin webpage entry for 24 May, 1880 stated that: 'Col. Edward Hatch, and a large contingent of cavalry, have been searching for Victorio, and his followers, for some time. Today, they fight a battle near the source of the Palomas River, in New Mexico. The army reports 55 Indians are killed in this battle.'

26 Kennedy, camp on Black River to AAAG, DoP, 18 Jun., 1880 in Letters Rec'd File, 19 Mar., 1878-14 Feb., 1881, HQ Records DoP 1878-1881, NA, RG393, M1381, Roll 2.

27 Hatch to AAG, DoM, Fort Leavenworth, 5 Aug., 1880 in Letters Sent by '9MD/DNM/DoNM', NA, RG393, M1072, Roll 6, 1880-Aug. 1881, Letter No.407, pp.260-268.

28 Hatch to AAAG, SF, 25 May, 1880, in 'DoNM/GSFO/L&T', NA, RG393, Part 3, Entry 475, Vol. 5, p.270; See also Telegrams Sent DoNM, Vol.3, Jan.-Nov., 1880, NA, RG393, Part 3, Entry 431, p.436; Hatch to AAG, HQ MDoM, 27 May, 1880, 'Victorio Files', NA, RG393, M1495, Roll 14.

29 Hatch to AAAG, SF, 25 May, 1880, in 'DoNM/GSFO/L&T', NA, RG393, Part 3, Entry 475, Vol. 5, p.270; See also Telegrams Sent DoNM, Vol.3, Jan.-Nov., 1880, NA, RG393, Part 3, Entry 431, p.436;

scouts straight away.[30] Meanwhile, Hatch rapidly lost touch with Morrow and could only assume that the latter was on the trail of the Apaches.[31]

Everything indicates that there had been a major blunder in the failure of troops based at Ojo Caliente or Canada Alamosa to send out further support, though how quickly they could have arrived at the scene is open to question. Hatch, being in overall charge, was to be held responsible; and his many friends in the territorial press were quick to level more accusations of incompetence at him.[32]

Yet Parker may not have been as forthcoming as he might about this battle. He admitted in his report to Hatch that '[t]here is other things concerning fight which I fail to mention.'[33] One obvious omission would appear to be the killing of quite a large number of women and children. Also interesting is the failure to mention that he had placed half of his command on the other side of an impassable ravine. As noted earlier, from an Apache point of view, this was an excellent deployment. However, it would have been judged a very poor deployment by US army officers, who did not understand Apache tactics. To them it would have seemed that the ravine prevented a charge that, in all probability, would have finished Victorio off. The absence of accompanying US cavalry and infantry thus becomes of critical importance to this battle. An immediate follow-up charge into a surprised camp was not necessarily unknown, but was not a favoured tactic for Apaches, who preferred to avoid unnecessary casualties. However, it was an effective tactic deployed by the US army when attacking American Indian camps. The Apache scouts had pinned Victorio and a group of his followers into a difficult position by careful manoeuvring. Yet this position would only have become untenable if it had been directly assaulted. The Apache scouts had patently been unwilling to do this, as they would have known they would sustain unnecessary casualties. Had a detachment of US cavalry or infantry been present, there is a good chance they would have been willing to risk a number of fatalities to finish off Victorio. Parker, with knowledge of both Apache and US army principles of warfare, had good reason to deliberately omit any reference to the ravine, to avoid criticism of his deployment. This is before one takes into account the storm of criticism levelled at the US army in the immediate aftermath of Parker's victory. Parker may have realised that, if he submitted a full report, it could give Hatch some ammunition, no matter how misguided, to deflect some of this censure onto him and his scouts. Even had Hatch been aware that Apache scouts would not have assaulted a defended emplacement, he probably would not have passed up the opportunity to censure the conduct of Parker's attack.

As for Victorio, once the scouts had withdrawn, he and the survivors of the battle made a quick retreat. The Palomas site was later described as being covered in blood and human remains. There were some hurried attempts to bury the slain but the 'wagonloads of utensils and dried meat' abandoned suggest a precipitate retreat.[34] Despite this defeat, Victorio did not consider surrender. He allegedly released a Mexican captive with the message that, 'Victorio was not dead and would not surrender until the last man was killed.'[35]

Hatch to AAG, HQ MDoM, 27 May, 1880, 'Victorio Files', NA, RG393, M1495, Roll 14; Hatch to AAG, Fort Leavenworth, 7 Jun., 1880 in 'Victorio Papers', NA, M666, Roll 527.

30 Loud (citing Hatch, Fort Craig, 29 May, 1880) to AAG Fort Leavenworth, 29 May, 1880, Telegrams Sent DoNM, Vol.3, Jan.-Nov., 1880, NA, RG393, Part 3, Entry 431, pp.448-449; Thrapp, 1974, note 20 pp.370-371.

31 Loud to AAG Fort Leavenworth, 29 May, 1880, Telegrams Sent DoNM, Vol.3, Jan.-Nov., 1880, NA, RG393, Part 3, Entry 431, pp.448-449.

32 *Thirty-Four*, 2 Jun., 1880.

33 Parker's Report as cited in the AR-WD, 1880, pp.99-100; Thrapp, 1974, p.278.

34 The Battle Ground', the *Grant County Herald*, 12 Jun., 1880

35 Ibid.

Nevertheless, Victorio had been clearly, and heavily, defeated for the first time in this campaign. Parker reported that his detachment[36] had killed 31 Apache men and had killed 55 altogether.[37] Hatch reckoned that Parker's initial report of 31 killed had not included 'non-combatants'. This comment implies that Hatch understood that Parker had chosen not to go into too much detail concerning the killing of what many Europeans would have seen as non-combatants.[38] Lieutenant Cruse commented on the 10–11 warriors killed, though he stated that this battle took place in July 1880.[39] Later in the summer of 1880, in response to an inquiry concerning the particulars of this battle, it was argued[40] that the casualty list might have been somewhat inflated, and it was concluded that only three or four Apache warriors had been killed.[41] (See document file no. 74.) Even if the warrior fatalities were as low as the last figure, with rarely more than 100–150 warriors in his following at any one time, this would have been a devastating setback for Victorio. Even when he was in alliance with Juh, earlier in the campaign, or with Mescalero allies, it would be surprising if that figure had ever exceeded 200 warriors.

We can speculate about casualties forever, but what is clear is that Victorio had been roundly defeated for the first time in the campaign, by Apache scouts with no support from US troops.[42] Thrapp[43] describes the Palomas River battle as one of the most decisive engagements of the Apache Wars, with Victorio being deprived of several of his best warriors and his band being forced to scatter and flee as best they could to Mexico.

Flight into Mexico, May–June 1880

The Warm Springs Apaches and their allies scattered into the Black Range. Apart from those Apaches too wounded to travel, at least three groups went south down the Black Range, making for Mexico.[44] One of the fleeing Apache bands killed one Lyons[45] and four other men on 29 May,

---

36 Parker later commissioned medals for his Apache Sergeants and himself received a watch from the grateful citizens of Grant County on the 16 Jul., 1880. ('Town and County', the *Grant County Herald*, 3 Jul., 1880; the *Grant County Herald*, 17 Jul., 1880) 'The five silver medals which Capt. Parker ordered for Indian Sergeants Peltay, Jim, Loco Jim, Jonny and Jack Long will be presented at Ft Bayard to-morrow. They are about the size of a silver dollar, and are engraved. Presented to Sg't (Name) by Capt. H.K. Parker, for bravery in fight on Palomas River, May 24, 1880' ('Town and County' the *Grant County Herald*, 17 Jul., 1880).

37 Sheridan to Townsend, 27 May, 1880, NA, RG393, Part 1, Entry 2539, Press Copies of Letters and Endorsements Sent, MDoM, Vol. 13, pp.281-283; the *Grant County Herald*, 29 May, 1880; Hatch to AAG Fort Leavenworth, 29 May, 1880 in 'Victorio Papers', NA, M666, Roll 527.

38 Hatch to AAG Fort Leavenworth, 29 May, 1880 in 'Victorio Papers', NA, M666, Roll 527.

39 Cruse, 1987, p.84; Thrapp, 1974, p.280; Sonnichsen, 1973, p.208; Chronological List, p.50; Webb, 1976, p.89.

40 Probably by Lt. Col. Dudley of the Ninth Cavalry.

41 Letter dated Fort Cummings, 1 Aug., 1880 and signed Lt. Col. 9th Cavalry Commanding in Letters, Telegrams, and Endorsements Sent; and General and Special Orders and Circulars Issued by a Battalion Jul./Sept. 1880, NA, RG391 Entry 920, p.3-4.

42 Thrapp, 1974, p.280.

43 Thrapp, 1974, pp.280-281; 1967, p.202.

44 Thrapp, 1974, p.281.

45 According to Lt. Col. Dudley, Ninth Cavalry, writing in 1881, Lyons had been an unofficial trader based at the deactivated Fort Cummings with his Mexican wife for a period of six to seven years before being killed by Apaches. (Dudley, 25 Mar., 1881 (0778-0779) in Endorsements Sent, Volume 5, 5 Jan., 1881-7 Apr., 1881, HQ Records of Fort Cummings, New Mexico, 1863-1873 & 1880-1884, NA, RG393, M1081, Roll 2).

at the western end of Cooke's Canon.[46] It was noted that the bodies had been burned and the trail of their ambushers led towards the Florida Mountains.[47] The western end of Cooke's Canyon is wide and flat. However, there are a number of small watercourses which pass close to, or even cross, the track. When viewed today, these runnels are four to six feet deep and are often very difficult to spot until one is almost on top of them. It would have been very easy for the Apaches to remain concealed until the Lyons party was within point blank range. The *Daily Southwest* for 31 May 1880 and 1 June 1880[48] reported the ambush of two mounted men and three wagons in Cooke's Canyon. Two of the wagons were carrying goods to Las Cruces for a Mr Solomon of Solomonville, driven by two men, Hildebrand and Carson. They, along with the third driver, name unknown, were found burned with their wagons. Two other men, Lyons and Vijil or Vejil, apparently mounted, managed to escape the opening volley but were hemmed in and took cover on a low hillock a short distance away. They had time to make breastworks and apparently, from the cartridge cases later discovered, made a spirited defence before being killed.[49] The probable site (see Figure 8.1) suggests two possible variations on the Apache 'roadside bomb' technique. An arroyo runs parallel to, then crosses, the wagon road and the Apaches could have concealed themselves close to the road and shot the men from point-blank range. An alternative scenario would have the Apaches in the arroyo closing the trap behind the wagons after they had passed and the convoy being attacked from the excellent cover afforded by the rocks along a low but steep bluff which the wagon road passed around. Both scenarios also easily allow concealed mounted Apaches to emerge from good cover and cut off the escape of any survivors.

Lieutenant Smith, with a detachment of H Company, Ninth Cavalry, was the first on the scene after the attack and concluded that the Lyons party had simply been in the wrong place at the wrong time.[50] Lieutenant Maney, with the Apache scouts, estimated that there were 100 warriors in the party, and that, in consideration of their wounded, they were making directly for Mexico. The size of the party led Maney to conclude that this was Victorio's main party.[51] Captain Loud, in

46 Sherman to Townsend, 3 Jun., 1880, NA, RG393, Part 1, Entry 2539, Press Copies of Letters and Endorsements Sent, MDoM, Vol. 13, p.316; Loud to Hatch, 30 May, 1880, Telegrams Sent DoNM, Vol.3, Jan.-Nov., 1880, NA, RG393, Part 3, Entry 431, p.450; Sheridan to Townsend, 3 Jun., 1880 in 'Victorio Papers', NA, M666, Roll 527; 'Fighting at Fort Cummings – Cooks Canon Full of Indians – Raid on Hillsboro', the *Grant County Herald*, 5 Jun., 1880; Pope to AAG HQ MDoM, 2 Jun., 1880, 'Victorio Files', NA, RG393, M1495, Roll 14; See also Thrapp, 1974, p.282; Stout, p.145; Chronological List, p.50; Webb, 1976, p.89.

As noted by Lt Cruse, in Chapter 1, Cooke's Canon was a popular ambush site. In 1880, Hastings recalls seeing 17 graves from those killed when a wagon train was ambushed. (p.295) In the same year Wasson records that Cooke's Canyon: 'is lined with graves.' (p.271) Myers notes that it was four miles long, running east to west and was such a favourite ambush spot that Fort Cummings was located at its eastern entrance at Cooke's Spring. (Myers, 1966i, p.303, note 7; 1966ii, p.56, note 19; 1968, pp.29-30) In 2005 there were a few graves still visible in the eastern section of the canyon.

47 Lt. Smith, Cummings to AAAG, SF, 31 May, 1880, Telegrams Sent DoNM, Vol.3, Jan.-Nov., 1880, NA, RG393, Part 3, Entry 431, p.455; See also Loud to AAG Fort Leavenworth, 2 Jun., 1880, Telegrams Sent DoNM, Vol.3, Jan.-Nov., 1880, NA, RG393, Part 3, Entry 431, p.464.

48 Thank you to Daniel D. Aranda, Las Cruces, New Mexico for this information.

49 *Daily Southwest*, 31 May & 1 June, 1880.

50 Loud to AAG Fort Leavenworth, 2 Jun., 1880, Telegrams Sent DoNM, Vol.3, Jan.-Nov., 1880, NA, RG393, Part 3, Entry 431, p.464; Pope to AAG HQ MDoM, 2 Jun., 1880, 'Victorio Files', NA, RG393, M1495, Roll 14.

51 Maney, Fort Cummings to Hatch, Fort Craig, 31 May, 1880, Telegrams Sent DoNM, Vol.3, Jan.-Nov., 1880, NA, RG393, Part 3, Entry 431, pp.458-459; Pope to AAG HQ MDoM 1 Jun., 1880 in 'Victorio Papers', NA, M666, Roll 527.

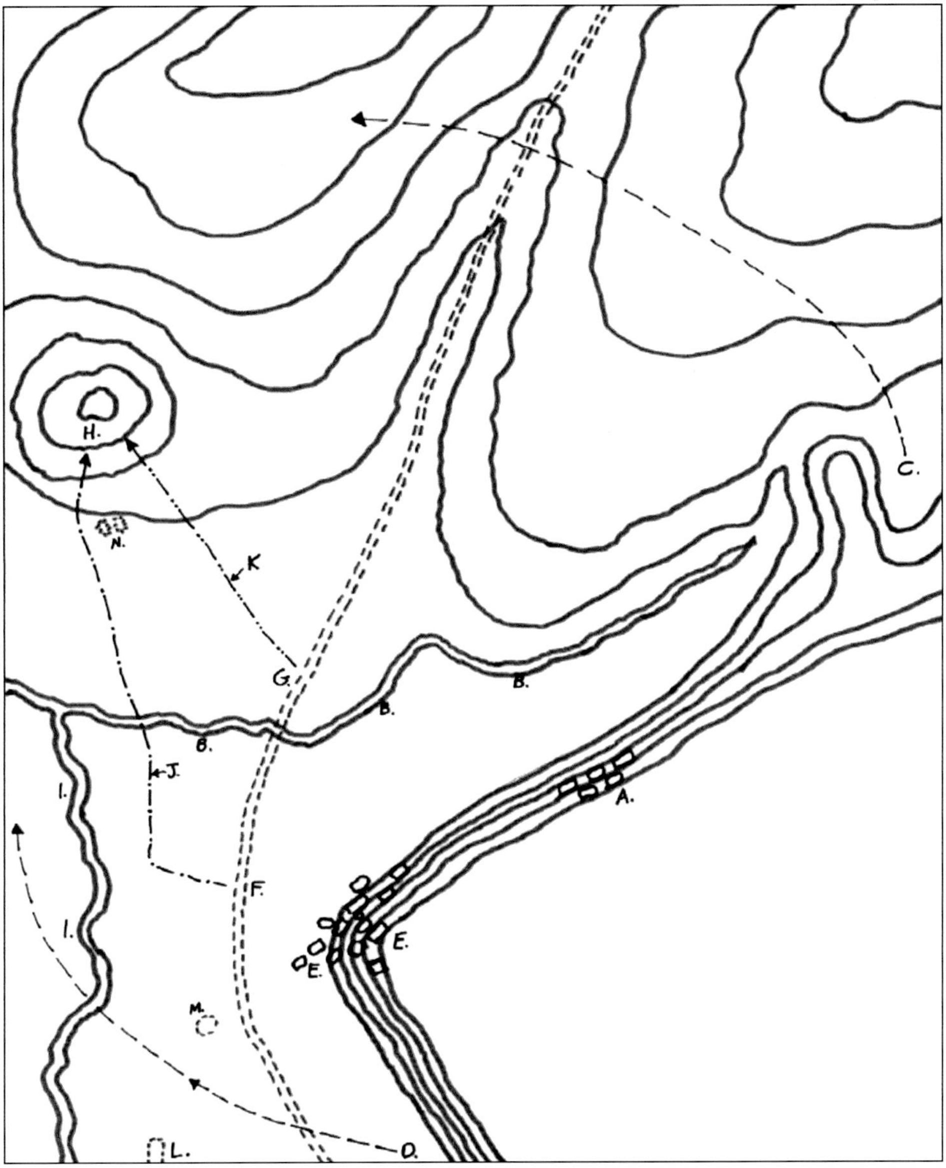

Map 8.4 Lyons Ambush, 29 May 1880.

KEY: A. Apache 'command' position. B. Arroyo paralleling, then crossing, wagon road. Close range hidden Apache positions. C. Possible hiding place for mounted Apaches to ride out and cut off any retreat. D. As C. E. Very rocky outcrops providing excellent cover for Apache warriors. F. Probable location of the attack on the three wagons from Apaches positioned in B and E. G. Possible position of the ambush where Apaches hidden in the arroyo deliver the main attack from point blank range. H. Hillock where the two mounted men fled and dug in when they were cut off. I. Arroyo giving further potential hiding for Apache warriors. These might have blocked the two mounted fugitives and turned them towards H. J. Probable route taken by the two mounted men to H, if the ambush was sprung at F. K. As above, but if the ambush was sprung at G. L. Large grave site not associated with this ambush. M. Probable graves of the three wagon drivers. Given the condition in which they were discovered, it is probable that they were buried very close to where they were found. This makes F. the more likely of the two possible ambush scenes. N. Probable graves of the two men killed on the hillock H.

Santa Fé, thought these must be Mexican Indians but also concluded that the damage done by the scouts at the Palomas River was 'more serious to the hostiles than first supposed'.[52]

Hatch reported that his troops and scouts had had another clash with the Apaches on 27 May, but no particulars of this clash have come to light.[53] Shepherds were rumoured to have been shot at by Apaches on the Mimbres River.[54] As they moved south, the Apaches raided ranches near Hillsboro, even reportedly stealing horses from Hillsboro itself.[55] Rumours were also received that the San Carlos reservation had been attacked, though the latter story was quickly scotched.[56] Such rumours, combined with local press reaction, prompted Headquarters, Department of the Missouri, to request confirmation of 'raids and fights near Cummings', though by this stage in the campaign their primary concern was that accurate and regular situation reports be quickly transmitted to them.[57]

In reality, the Apaches had once again managed to evade their enemies and most had fled towards Mexico. Those Apaches left behind scattered into the Black Range and hid out in its abundant cover, to recover, or not, from their wounds.[58] Such scattered survivors would have been very difficult to find and were more than capable of fending for themselves.

Moreover, problems with logistics had once again intervened to hamper the efficient pursuit of the fleeing Apaches. For example, on 30 May, in reaction to reports that the Apaches had fled east towards the Rio Grande after a fight near Fort Cummings, Captain Charles Parker was ordered to move his command from Canada Alamosa to Las Palomas. If he discovered any traces of the fugitives to the south of Palomas, he was to give pursuit.[59] Captain Parker was told to send a courier to Camp French to instruct a supply train bound for Fort Craig to drop enough rations off for his command at Palomas. He was also told to 'take what grain you can with you from Canada [Alamosa]'.[60] The wagon train, with 8,000 rations for the troops, was found stalled near Fort Craig with both 'wagons and teams broken down'.[61] Hatch had sent out wagons to take some 1,500 rations to Morrow's command, now based at Camp French, with the balance to be sent to Ojo Caliente to replenish its empty stores. He had also sent an urgent request to his chief quartermaster concerning the whereabouts of a batch of requisitioned footwear supposed to have been dispatched to his troops, because 'our men are nearly barefoot.'[62] Hatch also complained that 30 *aparejos* sent from Indian Territory, destined for his mule trains, were not fit for purpose.[63]

---

52 Loud to AAG Fort Leavenworth, 31 May, 1880, Telegrams Sent DoNM, Vol.3, Jan.-Nov., 1880, NA, RG393, Part 3, Entry 431, p.458; Pope to AAG HQ MDoM 1 Jun., 1880 in 'Victorio Papers', NA, M666, Roll 527.

53 Hatch to Head Quarters, MDoM, 29 May, 1880, NA, RG393, Part 1, Entry 2546, p.473 & p.474; Pope to AAG, HQ MDoM, 29 May, 1880, 'Victorio Files', NA, RG393, M1495, Roll 14; Loud to AAG Fort Leavenworth, 28 May, 1880, Telegrams Sent DoNM, Vol.3, Jan.-Nov., 1880, NA, RG393, Part 3, Entry 431, pp.444-445.

54 'Town and County', the *Grant County Herald*, 29 May, 1880.

55 'Fighting at Fort Cummings – Cooks Canon Full of Indians – Raid on Hillsboro', the *Grant County Herald*, 5 Jun., 1880.

56 Loud to Hatch, 29 May, 1880, Telegrams Sent DoNM, Vol.3, Jan.-Nov., 1880, NA, RG393, Part 3, Entry 431, p.446.

57 Pope to Captain Loud, SF, New Mexico, 1 Jun., 1880, NA, RG393, Part 3, Entry 440, p.30.

58 Thrapp, 1974, p.282.

59 Lt. Davenport AAAG In the Field, Fort Craig to Captains Charles Parker, Canada Alamosa, 30 May, 1880, 'DoNM/GSFO/L&T', NA, RG393, Part 3, Entry 475, Vol. 7, p.9.

60 Ibid.

61 Hatch to AAG SF, 26 May, 1880, 'DoNM/GSFO/L&T', NA, RG393, Part 3, Entry 475, Vol. 5, p.272

62 Hatch to Chief Quartermaster, SF, 26 May, 1880, 'DoNM/GSFO/L&T', NA, RG393, Part 3, Entry 475, Vol. 5, p.274.

63 Hatch to Loud, 27 May, 1880 in Letters Received, DoM 1868-98, RG 393, Entry A1-1 2601, Box 90.

Plate 8.4. Accounts of the battle tell of some of the Chihenne Apaches taking shelter between two large sides of split rock. These two rocks are the only clear candidates on the site. While they offer cover from the three different positions occupied by the Apache scouts, these boulders would not have sheltered many Apaches. Nevertheless there are many 'nooks and crannies' in the scattered rocks below the cliff face which would have sheltered individual Apaches. (Photo: Author)

Plate 8.5. View over the Lyons ambush site from the Apache 'Command Post' (Point A on the map). A man can stand fully upright behind these boulders and not be visible to anybody below. The arroyo can be seen running diagonally upwards from the middle right of the picture. The small hill where the two survivors attempted to hold off the Apaches can be seen just below and to the right of the three distinctive peaks on the left horizon. (Photo: Author)

Hints as to the flexibility required of the officers in command of various cavalry and Indian scout detachments in the field can be seen in Special Field Orders, Number 36, issued on 30 May 1880. Such flexibility also had to be exhibited when dealing with the accounting and finance elements of US army bureaucracy.

1. 1st Lieut G. Valois R.Q.M. 9 Cavalry, A.A.Q.M. In the Field will transfer to 2nd Lieut. J.A. Maney. 15th Infantry on proper Invoices and Receipts two Government mules for which he is responsible and which are now in Lieut. Maney's Pack train.
2. 1st Lieut. G.A. Stedman, Adjt. 9 Cavy. A.A.Q.M. Santa Fé, will transfer to 2nd Lieut G.A. Maney 15th Inf. on proper Invoices and Receipts three Government mules for which he is responsible taken from Nichols train and now in Lieut. Maney's Pack train.
3. 1st Lieut. G.A. Stedman, Adjt. 9 Cavy. A.A.Q.M. Santa Fé, N.M., will transfer to Post Quartermaster Fort Bayard on proper Invoices and Receipts three Government mules for which he is accountable taken from Nichols train and now in Major Morrow's Pack train.[64]

Shortages of supplies were no longer confined to the US army. The economic effect of the sustained guerrilla warfare in south-western New Mexico had started to affect the wider population. By the end of May, the citizens of Shakespeare informed the Governor that there was a severe shortage of supplies, due to the Apaches killing or driving off freighters, and they requested him to call out the militia.[65] Acting Governor Ritch, obviously unaware of the logistical problems facing the District of New Mexico, tactlessly contacted Captain Loud, stating that if US troops could not protect the region, they should send supplies to enable the militia 'to take the field'.[66]

The Ninth Cavalry, or at least those elements of that regiment still capable of action, were forced to fan out in an attempt to track down the Apaches. Morrow's command had worked its way south to Fort Cummings, arriving there on 2 June 1880. By 4 June, Morrow was able to inform Hatch that the Apache trail from Cooke's Range made for the Mexican line in the direction of Lake Palomas, and that he had followed the trail to within seven miles of the international line.[67] Morrow also confirmed that a trail of 25 Apaches in the Goodsight Mountains, which was being followed by another detachment of troops, had also crossed into Mexico.[68] Morrow was instructed to scour the area for any small parties of Apaches that might remain in the area.[69]

Once again, Hatch underlined the need for the additional 50 Apache scouts he had requested to be authorised, as small parties of warriors would otherwise be impossible to hunt down.[70] An

64 Special Field Orders No. 36, HQ DoNM, In the Field, Fort Craig N.M. 30 May, 1880, 'DoNM/GSFO/L&T', NA, RG393, Part 3, Entry 475, Vol. 7, p.10.

65 Citizens from Shakespeare to Lew Wallace, 31 May, 1880 in Letters Received by HQ DoNM Sept. 1865-Aug. 1890, NA, RG393, M1088, Roll 40, Jan.-Jun. 1880.

66 Ritch to Loud, 1 Jun., 1880 in Letters Received by HQ DoNM Sept. 1865-Aug. 1890, NA, RG393, M1088, Roll 40, Jan.-Jun. 1880.

67 Loud to AAG Fort Leavenworth, 4 Jun., 1880, Telegrams Sent DoNM, Vol.3, Jan.-Nov., 1880, NA, RG393, Part 3, Entry 431, p.475; Pope to AAG, HQ MDoM, 5 Jun., 1880 in 'Victorio Papers', NA, M666, Roll 527; Hatch to AAG Fort Leavenworth, 7 Jun., 1880, 'Victorio Papers', NA, M666, Roll 527. Rasch states that Palomas Lake is 12 miles south of Columbus. (1960, p.9) On modern maps the Laguna would appear to be approximately ten to fifteen kilometres south of Columbus. See NH 13-1 – El Paso (USGS) & H13-1-Cuidad Juarez (INEGI).

68 Loud to AAG Fort Leavenworth, 5 Jun., 1880, Telegrams Sent DoNM, Vol.3, Jan.-Nov., 1880, NA, RG393, Part 3, Entry 431, p.478.

69 Hatch, Fort Craig to AAAG SF, 7 Jun., 1880, Telegrams Sent DoNM, Vol.3, Jan.-Nov., 1880, NA, RG393, Part 3, Entry 431, p.490.

70 Hatch to AAG Fort Leavenworth, 7 Jun., 1880, 'Victorio Papers', NA, M666, Roll 527.

additional problem was that communications between Morrow and Hatch had been undermined by the 'impatience and bad sending'[71] of the telegraph operator at Fort Cummings, and the man was replaced as quickly as possible.[72] Lieutenant Allen, in charge of the telegraph lines, thought that this episode could in fact be blamed on the 'impatience and bad sending' of the operator at Craig.[73] Apparently, there was some animosity between the operators at Fort Cummings and Fort Craig. As part of this infighting, the operator at Fort Craig had informed Hatch that the Fort Cummings operator, on being told that Hatch was awaiting a reply to a telegram, had told him to tell the Colonel to 'go to hell'.[74] Later that summer, further neglect of duty was reported by Captain Bean, Commanding Officer, Fort Craig, concerning the operators at Fort Craig and Socorro. Lieutenant Allen recorded that the operator at Socorro had been relieved, and that the operator at Fort Craig would be replaced. Allen also noted that Captain Bean's specific charges were being investigated.[75] This extraordinary behaviour was a completely unnecessary addition to the list of obstacles confronting the US army's attempts to prosecute a successful war against Victorio.

On or around 5 June, Major Morrow was finally rewarded for his enduring pursuit of the Apaches, when some of his battalion caught up with one small group between Cooke's Range and the Mexican border. However, the exact details of this skirmish or skirmishes are not clear. Two Apaches were killed and three wounded, and their livestock was captured.[76] The first clash developed into a running battle as the Apaches made for the Mexican border south of Fort Cummings. The original US army reports mention catching a small party in Cooke's Range, and that one of the two killed was Victorio's son. Washington was recognised by Apache scouts from Parker's command, and it was apparent that Parker's scouts had done most, if not all, of the damage in this encounter.[77] Hutcheson states that L Company, Ninth Cavalry, lost two troopers in a clash in 'Cooke's Canon' on 5 June.[78] Interestingly, the *Army & Navy Journal* reported that the pursuit of the Apaches from Cooke's Canyon was undertaken by L Company and the Apache scouts.[79] It is possible that the cavalry and scouts were ambushed by an Apache rear-guard in Cooke's Canyon before the running fight in the direction of Palomas Lake developed. Overall, the Ninth Cavalry detachment claimed to have killed 10 Apaches.[80] We are not informed whether the Apache

---

71 Buchanan (temporarily in charge of Signals, DoNM to Loud, 5 Jun., 1880 in Letters Received by HQ DoNM Sept. 1865-Aug. 1890, NA, RG393, M1088, Roll 40, Jan.-Jun. 1880.

72 Buchanan to AAAG, DoNM, 6 Jun., 1880 in Letters Received by HQ DoNM Sept. 1865-Aug. 1890, NA, RG393, M1088, Roll 40, Jan.-Jun. 1880.

73 Loud to Hatch, Fort Craig, 5 Jun., 1880, Telegrams Sent DoNM, Vol.3, Jan.-Nov., 1880, NA, RG393, Part 3, Entry 431, p.479.

74 Hatch to Buchanan, 12 Jun., 1880 in Letters Received by HQ DoNM Sept. 1865-Aug. 1890, NA, RG393, M1088, Roll 40, Jan.-Jun. 1880. A livid Hatch promised to deal with the culprit but so far no indication of the outcome of the investigation into such a puerile situation has come to light.

75 Allen to Bean, 4 Aug., 1880 in Letters Received by HQ DoNM Sept. 1865-Aug. 1890, NA, RG393, M1088, Roll 41, Jul.-Dec. 1880.

76 Hatch to Loud, 5 Jun., 1880, Telegrams Sent DoNM, Vol.3, Jan.-Nov., 1880, NA, RG393, Part 3, Entry 431, p.480; Sheridan to Townsend, 8 Jun., 1880 in 'Victorio Papers', NA, M666, Roll 527; Hatch to AAG Fort Leavenworth, 7 Jun., 1880, 'Victorio Papers', NA, M666, Roll 527; Bi-Monthly Company Muster Rolls for Company B, 9th Cavalry May/Jun. in NA, RG94 stated that 'had one Engagement with hostile Indians Jun. 5 1880,'.

77 The *Grant County Herald*, 12 Jun., 1880.

78 See web article The Ninth Regiment of Cavalry by Lt G. Hutcheson. Hutcheson also reports a skirmish between Company B, Ninth Cavalry and presumably Apaches on the 11 and 12 of Jun. close to Fort Cummings but records no casualties.

79 'Indian Affairs', *Army & Navy Journal*, Vol. 17, 12 Jun., 1880, p.920.

80 Hatch to Loud, 5 Jun., 1880, Telegrams Sent DoNM, Vol.3, Jan.-Nov., 1880, NA, RG393, Part 3, Entry 431, p.480; Sheridan to Townsend, 8 Jun., 1880 NA, RG393, Part 1, Entry 2539, Press Copies of Letters and Endorsements Sent, MDoM, Vol. 13, p.328; Letter dated Aleman N.M. 6 Jun., 1880 in The

casualties were men, women or children. Two scalps of Apaches killed near Cooke's Canyon were put on display at the Centennial Hotel in Silver City.[81]

Once across the border, the Apaches were not pursued. Hatch, strongly backed by General Pope,[82] appealed for permission to pursue the Apaches into Mexico, in order to maintain a relentless pressure on them.[83] Hatch also confidently stated that he could 'obtain the consent of the State of Chihuahua to pursue them'.[84] (See document file no. 75.)

> Mr Ayers informed me last night that while in Chihuahua some time ago Governor Terrasas said the state was too poor to support Troops to hunt Victorio's Indians, but that he could and would willingly make a treaty or arrangements by which our Troops could come in to the State of Chihuahua to get the Indians. I repeat the information to you for what it is worth.[85]

Quite what resources Hatch would have used to maintain this relentless pressure, given the reported state of the Ninth Cavalry by the end of May 1880, is an interesting question.

The State Department acknowledged Hatch's request and contacted the Federal Mexican Government.[86] On 22 June 1880, the Federal Mexican Government informed the United States that it would not allow troops to enter its territory in pursuit of Apaches.[87] For the moment, Lieutenant Maney, based at Fort Cummings, with his Apache scout company, was instructed: 'Hold your Indians well in hand and watch the trails.'[88]

Walter Lowry Finley Collection; Pope's Annual Report Year ending 22 Sept., 1880, NA, RG393, Part 1, Entry 2546, p.613; *Thirty-Four*, 2 Jun., 1880; Thrapp, 1974, p.281 &p.282; Thrapp, 1967, pp.202-203; Stout, p.145; Billington, 1991, p.96; Chronological List, p.50; Record of Engagements, p.95; Webb, 1976, p.89; O'Neal, p.177; Smith, 1994, p.164. The Army & Navy Journal also reported that Victorio's son was killed but names him as 'Mennolito'. ('Indian Affairs', *Army & Navy Journal*, Vol. 17, 12 Jun., 1880, p.920).

81 *Thirty-Four*, 2 Jun., 1880; 'Town and County', the *Grant County Herald*, 12 Jun., 1880.

82 Pope to AAG HQ MDoM 14 Jun., 1880 in 'Victorio Papers', NA, M666, Roll 527; Pope to AAG, HQ MDoM, 14 Jun., 1880, 'Victorio Files', NA, RG393, M1495, Roll 14.

83 Loud (citing Telegram from Hatch, Fort Craig, 31 May, 1880) to AAG Fort Leavenworth, 1 Jun., 1880, Telegrams Sent DoNM, Vol.3, Jan.-Nov., 1880, NA, RG393, Part 3, Entry 431, p.459; Hatch, Fort Craig to AAG, DoM, Fort Leavenworth, 10? Jun., 1880; 'DoNM/GSFO/L&T', NA, RG393, Part 3, Entry 475, Vol. 7, p.34; Hatch to AAG, DoM, 10 Jun., 1880 in Letters Received, DoM 1868-98, RG 393, Entry A1-1 2601, Box 91; Hatch to AAAG, SF, 12 Jun., 1880, 'DoNM/GSFO/L&T', NA, RG393, Part 3, Entry 475, Vol. 7, p.338.

84 Hatch to AAAG, SF, 12 Jun., 1880, 'DoNM/GSFO/L&T', NA, RG393, Part 3, Entry 475, Vol. 7, p.338; Loud to AAG Fort Leavenworth, 13 Jun., 1880, Telegrams Sent DoNM, Vol.3, Jan.-Nov., 1880, NA, RG393, Part 3, Entry 431, p.515; Pope to AAG, HQ MDoM, 14 Jun., 1880, 'Victorio Files', NA, RG393, M1495, Roll 14.

85 Loud to Hatch, Fort Craig, 13 Jun., 1880, Telegrams Sent DoNM, Vol.3, Jan.-Nov., 1880, NA, RG393, Part 3, Entry 431, p.517; See also Hatch to AAAG, SF, 12 Jun., 1880, 'DoNM/GSFO/L&T', NA, RG393, Part 3, Entry 475, Vol. 7, p.338.

86 Drum, AG to Commanding General, MDoM, 19 Jun., 1880, 'Victorio Files', NA, RG393, M1495, Roll 14; AG to Gen. Pope 19 Jun., 1880, NA, RG393, Part 1, Entry 2539, Press Copies of Letters and Endorsements Sent, MDoM, Vol. 13, p.377; Pope's Annual Report Year ending 22 Sept., 1880, NA, RG393, Part 1, Entry 2546, p.612.

87 Secretary of State to the Secretary of War, Jun. 22 1880, in Papers relating to the Frelinghuysen-Romero Agreement of Jul. 29, 1882, providing for reciprocal crossings of the international boundary by troops of the United States and Mexico in pursuit of hostile Indians, Feb., 1862, Jan.-Jun. 1867; Letters Rec'd by the AGO (Main Series), 1881-1889, NA, M689, Roll 81; Drum, AG to Sheridan, 22 Jun., 1880, 'Victorio Files', NA, RG393, M1495, Roll 14; Drum AG Wash. D.C. to Gen. P.H. Sheridan, 22 Jun., 1880 in Letters Received by HQ DoNM Sept. 1865-Aug. 1890, NA, RG393, M1088, Roll 40, Jan.-Jun. 1880.

88 Instructions to Lt. Maney, Fort Cummings, 10 Jun., 1880'DoNM/GSFO/L&T', NA, RG393, Part 3, Entry 475, Vol. 7, p.365.

Colonel Hatch claimed that, between the start of the Hembrillo Canyon operation and the end of May, approximately 100 Apaches had been killed.[89] He, and to a lesser extent the Ninth Cavalry, received scant praise from the territorial press. General Sherman himself contacted Hatch through General Pope to assure him that he had his continued support, and that the actions of the territorial press carried no weight in Washington.

However, in the same letter, Sherman revealed that there was no further money available to buy extra horses and mules until Congress approved the next appropriation of funds for the army. This money would not be available until 1 July 1880.[90] (See document file no. 76.) Thus we have no less a person than Sherman himself stating that, in effect, Victorio's tactic of constantly engaging his enemies in gruelling pursuits had emptied the US army's coffers for the financial year 1879–80. Sherman had to resort to the emergency measure of ordering the movement of troops and animals that could be spared from other Departments and Divisions.[91] One wonders what Sherman, an advocate of 'economic' warfare, in which the resources of the enemy (the Confederacy, and afterwards the Plains Indians) were targeted as well as their armed forces, made of being forced to take his own medicine from the Apaches. The Apaches had effectively dismounted the Ninth Cavalry, and unless horses and mules could be transferred from other military sources, the regiment could not be remounted until Congress approved the army's 1880–81 budget. Two days later, Sherman reminded General Sheridan that the US army's authorized strength was fixed at 25,000 men. Therefore, if more scouts were to be recruited for service in the District of New Mexico, Sheridan would have to dispense with a similar number of scouts elsewhere within his division. As Sherman succinctly put it, 'We must not exceed the law.'[92] (See document file no. 77.) As we have seen, Hatch had already creatively interpreted the law where the recruitment of extra Apache scouts was concerned.

Sherman's pronouncement on the law came on the same day that Hatch made the most intriguing statement that 'casualties in my command should give me fifty Indian scouts more valuable now than four times the number of recruits.'[93] This clearly implies that Hatch had lost 50 men, but this cannot be correct. If we assume Hatch was referring to the fiscal year July 1879 to the end of June 1880, the District of New Mexico had lost one officer and 20 men (including Indian scouts) killed in action. It is also clear from the regimental and company returns that recruits were steadily trickling in. This is a most ambiguous statement on the part of Hatch, and one wonders whether this was an attempt to bluff his superiors into allowing him to recruit additional scouts. It does also raise the suspicion that one or two skirmishes had either been missed from the official record or that a number of casualties, even fatalities, had gone unrecorded.

The failure to defeat the Apaches brought out the worst in Hatch, who made a statement that was to prove prophetic in the parallel case of the Chiricahua Apaches in 1886:

89 Pope's Annual Report Year ending 22 Sept., 1880, NA, RG393, Part 1, Entry 2546, pp.612.

90 Sherman to Pope, 29 May, 1880, NA, RG393, Part 1, Entry 2539, Press Copies of Letters and Endorsements Sent, MDoM, Vol. 13, pp.290-291; Loud quoting Sherman's letter to Hatch, Fort Craig, 31 May, 1880, Telegrams Sent DoNM, Vol.3, Jan.-Nov., 1880, NA, RG393, Part 3, Entry 431, pp.452-453; Sherman to Sheridan, 28 May, 1880, 'Victorio Files', NA, RG393, M1495, Roll 14.

91 Sherman to Pope, 29 May, 1880 in Press Copies of Letters and Endorsements Sent, MDoM, Vol. 13, NA, RG393, Part 1, Entry 2539, pp.290-291.

92 Sherman to Sheridan, 31 May, 1880, NA, RG393, Part 1, Entry 2546, p.479 & p.480.

93 Hatch to AAG HQ MDoM, 31 May, 1880, 'Victorio Files', NA, RG393, M1495, Roll 14; Pope to AAG HQ MDoM 1 Jun., 1880 in 'Victorio Papers', NA, M666, Roll 527; Hatch to AAG, DoM, 3 Jun., 1880 in Letters Received, DoM 1868-98, RG 393, Entry A1-1 2601, Box 90.

> they must be destroyed or held as prisoners at some remote point from New Mexico. With the present uneasiness of Indian tribes I need not urge the importance of pitting one tribe against the other, and fostering the enmity already existing between them, it is sound policy to do so.[94]

Despite Sherman's support for Colonel Hatch, the press continued to launch deeply personal attacks. One report recounted a fictional combat between Hatch and Victorio where the former was 'unaffected by a shot through the head!'[95] Hatch continued to be the main target, but the black troops were again dismissed as inferior to white troops,[96] though the same paper would also state that a white regiment would be hard pushed to equal the Ninth Cavalry Regiment's performance. This turned out to be a device to present Colonel Hatch as an untruthful blundering incompetent.[97] Sherman was also accused of being complicit with Hatch in misrepresenting the true situation, though the editor of *Thirty-Four*, conveniently forgetting some of his papers own statements, also argued that exaggeration of Hatch's faults would be counter-productive and would serve only to delay his removal.[98] On 4 June 1880, the editor of the *Grant County Herald*, S.M. Ashenfelter, wrote to the Secretary of War repeating these charges and demanding that Hatch be removed from command.[99] (See document file no. 78.1.) The following week, the same paper again attacked Hatch but also dismissed 'negro' soldiers as worthless.[100] (See document file no. 78.2.) *Thirty-Four* also slyly enquired as to the possibility that Hatch might be controlling the telegraph and suppressing bad news from New Mexico.[101] Victorio's prowess as a war leader was acknowledged, but even this was turned into an assault on Hatch, in which it was stated that more troops were needed but also that there needed to be a change in commander.[102] Hatch's request that he be allowed to pursue the Apaches into Mexico was dismissed as an attempt to be close enough to any Mexican victory to falsely claim that victory. As noted earlier, Hatch also stood accused of trying to steal the laurels of Parker's victory on the Palomas River.[103] The paper also noted an effort on the part of the military to discredit Parker, and suggested to its readers that he be referred to as 'Citizen Parker', just in case the army attempted to credit one of the two officers named Parker in the Ninth Cavalry.[104] One Joseph Brown wrote to the Secretary of War accusing Hatch of masterly

94 Hatch to AAG, DoM, 3 Jun., 1880 in Letters Received, DoM 1868-98, RG 393, Entry A1-1 2601, Box 90

95 *Thirty-Four*, 2 Jun., 1880; Hart. 1997, p.48.

96 *Thirty-Four*, 5 May, 1880; On 2 June, 1880 the paper stated that: 'While there are, undoubtedly, exceptions to this rule, yet as a whole, that race loves ease, show and tinsel, and prefers these things to all others. They cannot endure the hardships of mountain warfare, and they lack the ambition necessary to the making of a good soldier.' An article titled 'Fault Finding' in the *Grant County Herald*, 12 June, 1880 stated that 'The negro, as we asserted in our last issue, is unfit for, and not adapted to be, a first class soldier. The campaign of the last ten months shows this clearly: this is not his fault, it is one of the characteristics of the race: the great mistake was in ever enlisting them into the regular army. The years which have elapsed since the war of the rebellion, have been passed by these soldiers in a round of garrison duty, of pleasure, and no fighting. This of itself is demoralizing to any soldier, much more so to the negro. In a fight they have no confidence in themselves, and their officers can have no confidence *in them*.'

97 *Thirty-Four*, 19 May, 1880.

98 *Thirty-Four*, 12 May, 1880.

99 S.M. Ashenfelter to Alexander Ramsey, Secretary of War, 4 Jun., 1880 in 'Victorio Papers', NA, M666, Roll 527; Ashenfelter to Alexander Ramsey, Sec. of War, 4 Jun., 1880 in Letters Received by HQ DoNM Sept. 1865-Aug. 1890, NA, RG393, M1088, Roll 40, Jan.-Jun. 1880.

100 'Fault Finding', the *Grant County Herald*, 12 Jun., 1880.

101 *Thirty-Four*, 2 Jun., 1880.

102 *Thirty-Four*, 19 May, 1880.

103 *Thirty-Four*, 23 Jun., 1880.

104 *Thirty-Four*, 23 Jun., 1880.

inaction at Fort Craig, miles away from the action, and Morrow of being incapacitated by drink at Fort Cummings. Brown clearly implied that Morrow's drunkenness pinned down 200 troops and scouts at Fort Cummings, while only a few miles away the Lyons party was wiped out in Cooke's Canyon.[105]

This anger occasionally manifested itself in verbal exchanges between soldiers and citizens:

> Upon arrival of the Coach from the East, at the Post Office at the Post this morning, the driver addressed the escort, a soldier of Co. "M" 9th Cavalry as follows. "Get down you damned nigger and tell your Company Officer to send a White man as escort"
>
> Inasmuch as the Stage Company has asked for soldiers as escorts, it should see that they are decently treated by its employees and until this assurance can be given, I respectfully request permission to call in all detachments stationed at the mailstations.[106]

Hatch obviously concurred and authorised the withdrawal until the guards were 'treated properly'.[107]

In response to Ashenfelter's charges, Hatch argued that Lieutenant Merritt had been responsible for the breakout in April 1879,[108] and had been court-martialled and cashiered. Hatch also admitted that the number of people killed by Apaches was large, but maintained it was nowhere near as large as stated by the press and denied any form of misrepresentation of the situation.[109] Hatch was quite correct to argue that the numbers killed by Apaches were exaggerated; but he was also too willing to underestimate these numbers. And the allusion to Lieutenant Merritt, who had committed suicide after the court-martial verdict, showed a less edifying side to Hatch, in that he was willing to place culpability on a dead officer. To state that Lieutenant Merritt was responsible for the Victorio War was quite wrong (since Merritt had certainly not been one of the authors of the concentration policy), and represented a thoroughly dishonourable position for Hatch to adopt.[110] Similarly unpleasant was his later accusation that utter cowardice had been demonstrated by the Mexican sheepherders who had survived Victorio's raids in April and May 1880. His accusation that Mexican shepherds had engaged in supplying food and occasional ammunition to Victorio's Apaches (see document file no. 79) had a strong element of truth in it; yet Hatch failed to acknowledge the lack of US army protection for these men when they were confronted by Apache warriors. Hatch, also with some justification, argued that in pursuing the Apaches during April and May 1880, he had had to contend with citizens more concerned with war-profiteering than facilitating the army's pursuit of Victorio. (See document file no. 80.) Thus, while Hatch had a number of legitimate problems which undermined his efforts to defeat Victorio, his acumen in judging these was mixed with political naivety. Hence his relations with the press and most of the citizen they represented were appalling, and his difficulties in this aspect of his job largely self-inflicted.

105 Brown to The Secretary of War, 28 Jun., 1880 in 'Victorio Papers', NA, M666, Roll 527.

106 Capt Purington, Fort Bayard to AAAG, DoNM, 6 Jun., 1880 in Letters Received by HQ DoNM Sept. 1865-Aug. 1890, NA, RG393, M1088, Roll 40, Jan.-Jun. 1880.

107 Loud to Henderson, Agent N.M. Transportation Co. 13 Jun., 1880, Telegrams Sent DoNM, Vol.3, Jan.-Nov., 1880, NA, RG393, Part 3, Entry 431, p.514.

108 See Watt, 'I Will Not Surrender the Hair of a Horse's Tail: The Victorio Campaign 1879' Chapter 5, pp.131-132

109 Hatch to Major J.J. Coppinger 10th Infantry, Acting Assistant Inspector General, DoM, 26 Jun., 1880 in Letters Sent by '9MD/DNM/DoNM', NA, RG393, M1072, Roll 6, Jan. 1880-Aug. 1881, Letter No.309, pp.199-201.

110 In response to Ashenfelter's charges Hatch made the following statements. 'The Officer responsible [Merritt] for the outbreak was brought to trial and dismissed the service and is now dead' (Hatch to Major J.J. Coppinger 10th Infantry, Acting Assistant Inspector General, DoM, 26 Jun., 1880 in Letters Sent by '9MD/DNM/DoNM', NA, RG393, M1072, Roll 6, Jan. 1880-Aug. 1881, Letter No.309, pp.199-201).

Nonetheless, he was aware of the key principles of Apache warfare and knew how to get around army and congressional red-tape to get what was needed: a dangerous game to play, but one he played successfully.

A nine-point resolution was passed in Silver City on 10 June 1880 that is indicative of the general feeling against the troops in New Mexico. This blamed a drunken officer for provoking the war with Victorio, thus indicating that the citizens believed Colonel Hatch's version of events when it suited them. It claimed that in the course of the war almost 300 New Mexicans had been butchered, with much loss in property and the economy. They then passed a number of resolutions roundly accusing the army in general, and the Ninth Cavalry and Colonel Hatch in particular, of incompetence and misrepresentation of the course of events. Only H.K. Parker and Captain Madden of the Sixth Cavalry were given any credit for the prosecution of the war. The citizens also accused Colonel Hatch of trying to claim the credit for Parker's victory, and demanded that he be removed from the command of the District of New Mexico.[111] (See document file no. 81.1.)

Most of the above points can be countered, and Hatch presented a robust rebuttal of these accusations (see document file no. 81.2); but this resolution offered a justifiable criticism in accusing Hatch of misrepresentation. Equally, we have to ask why Hatch felt he had to misrepresent the situation in New Mexico? Did the sheer volume of personal vilification aimed at him, and transmitted to Washington DC by the local press, lead Hatch into misrepresenting events in New Mexico?

It should also be noted that, hidden away in the press coverage of the Victorio Campaign, there was the occasional piece of constructive advice concerning the prosecution of the war against the Apaches. A letter, printed in the *Grant County Herald* on 12 June, noted that the success garnered by Parker was due to his not following the formal procedure of an army expedition, which could easily be monitored and avoided by Apaches. What Parker's command had done was to betray their presence as little as possible, with most of them hiding during the day while a few scouts were sent to spy out the land. The detachment generally only moved at night. The correspondent only regretted that Parker had not had a back-up force of 100 men which 'would soon put an end to Old Vic, and his band of cut-throats'.[112] (See document file no. 82)

Despite the tide of negative public opinion, Hatch was still faced with finishing off the war. He advised that an additional regiment and 100 Apache scouts would be required.[113] He pointed out that:

> Experience certainly advises obtaining them [Apache scouts] in some manner. Troops cannot find Apaches in the mountains without incurring great risks and expense. to be successful they must be hunted in the Indian way keeping the troops off the trail and Indians are best adapted for this service. Since the attack on the San Carlos Agency where a number were killed the best Indians on the Reservation are anxious to go out. I also consider it important to encourage the enmity between the tribes.[114]

111 The *Grant County Herald*, 12 Jun., 1880; See also *Thirty-Four*, 16 Jun., 1880; Copy of said resolution in 'Victorio Papers', NA, M666, Roll 526Hart, 1997, p.48.

112 'How to Fight Apaches', the *Grant County Herald*, 12 Jun., 1880.

113 Hatch to Department HQ, 26 May, 1880, 'DoNM/GSFO/L&T', NA, RG393, Part 3, Entry 475, Vol. 5, p.273.

114 Hatch, Fort Craig to AAAG, SF, 26 May, 1880, 'DoNM/GSFO/L&T', NA, RG393, Part 3, Entry 475, Vol. 5, p.271; Hatch to HQ, MDoM, 26 May, 1880, NA, RG393, Part 1, Entry 2546, p.475, p.476 & p.482; Loud to AAG Fort Leavenworth, 27 May, 1880, Telegrams Sent DoNM, Vol.3, Jan.-Nov., 1880, NA, RG393, Part 3, Entry 431, pp.439-440.

This was once again endorsed by General Pope.[115] Finally, on 7 June 1880, Hatch received permission to recruit 50 Apache scouts in addition to the 25 he was already authorised to recruit.[116] Sheridan had to make a direct request to General Sherman to allow this additional recruitment as 'I cannot change the allotment in this Division to accommodate him [Hatch].'[117] Apparently, as the authorised strength of the US army was at full capacity, Sherman had to reiterate the point that such scouts would have to be found from within Sheridan's Military Division.[118] Hatch estimated that the Apaches could survive for at least two years off the horses and cows to be found scattered over the territory. He also thought that Victorio could be persuaded to surrender 'if promised amnesty and if his families were at Ojo Caliente.'[119]

Nevertheless, Hatch received instructions that Victorio should be hunted down, and that, as part of this operation, a force of Apache scouts should be stationed in the Florida Mountains. It was also suggested that the Mescaleros with Victorio could be persuaded to surrender by the use of the prisoners on the Mescalero reservation.[120] This plan was foiled when the Mescaleros refused to send a runner, reportedly saying that 'they don't care whether Mescaleros with Victorio are killed or not, that they deserve to for joining him.'[121] This was a position they maintained throughout that summer.[122] On 8 June 1880, Hatch also reported that some of the Mescaleros who wished to give up 'were prevented by Victoria',[123] and Russell repeated Hatch's statement to the Commissioner of Indian Affairs two days later.[124] The source or sources of such information is not clear.

Hatch also attempted to estimate the numbers of Apaches still at large and concluded that Victorio had lost approximately 100 men and still had 336 warriors and 160 women and children in his following.[125] (See document file no. 83.) This is a substantial over-estimation of both the casualties sustained by, and the overall numbers of, the Apaches. However, it also clear that, going back to the events of 1876 and 1877, the US authorities had no clear idea of just how many Chiricahua Apaches had settled on the Fort Bowie reservation, nor of how many Warm Springs Apaches had been residing at Ojo Caliente before the closure of both reservations. Indian Agents were also not

---

115 Pope to Lieutenant General P.H. Sheridan, HQ Mil. Division of the Mo., 30 May, 1880, NA, RG393, Part 1, Entry 2546, p.477 7 P.478.

116 Pope to Hatch, 7 Jun., 1880, Telegrams Sent DoNM, Vol.3, Jan.-Nov., 1880, NA, RG393, Part 3, Entry 431, pp.488-489; Platt, AAG to Colonel Hatch, Fort Craig, New Mexico, 7 Jun., 1880, NA, RG393, Part 3, Entry 440, p.18; See also Platt AAG to AAAG, DoNM, 7 Jun., 1880, NA, RG393, Part 3, Entry 440, p.21.

117 Sheridan to Sherman, 31 May, 1880, NA, RG393, Part 1, Entry 2539, Press Copies of Letters and Endorsements Sent, MDoM, Vol. 13, p.300; Sheridan to Sherman 31 May, 1880, NA, RG393, Part 1, Entry 2546, pp.482-483.

118 Sherman to Sheridan, 31 May, 1880, NA, RG393, Part 1, Entry 2546, p.479, p.480 & P.483.

119 Hatch, Fort Craig to Loud, 26 May, 1880, Telegrams Sent DoNM, Vol.3, Jan.-Nov., 1880, NA, RG393, Part 3, Entry 431, pp.440-441; See also Hatch to Pope, 4 Mar., 1880 in Letters Received, DoM 1868-98, RG 393, Entry A1-1 2601, Box 90.

120 Platt, AAG to Colonel Hatch, Fort Craig, New Mexico, 7 Jun., 1880, NA, RG393, Part 3, Entry 440, p.18; (Pope to Hatch, 7 Jun., 1880, Telegrams Sent DoNM, Vol.3, Jan.-Nov., 1880, NA, RG393, Part 3, Entry 431, pp.488-489.

121 McGonnigle, 1 Lt 15th Inf. To Hatch 9 Jun., 1880, Telegrams Sent DoNM, Vol.3, Jan.-Nov., 1880, NA, RG393, Part 3, Entry 431, p.516; Russell to CoIA, 10 Jun., 1880 in 'Victorio Papers', NA, M666, Roll 527.

122 Morrow, CO Fort Stanton to AAG, DoM, 22 Jul., 1880 in Letters Received, DoM 1868-98, RG 393, Entry A1-1 2601, Box 92; Hatch to Buell, 17 Aug., 1880, Telegrams Sent DoNM, Vol.3, Jan.-Nov., 1880, NA, RG393, Part 3, Entry 431, p.748.

123 Hatch to AAG, Fort Leavenworth, 8 Jun., 1880, 'Victorio Files', NA, RG393, M1495, Roll 14.

124 Russell to CoIA, 10 Jun., 1880 in 'Victorio Papers', NA, M666, Roll 527.

125 Loud to General Pope, Fort Leavenworth, 16 Jun., 1880, Telegrams Sent DoNM, Vol.3, Jan.-Nov., 1880, NA, RG393, Part 3, Entry 431, p.525; See also Loud to Pope, 16 Jun., 1880 in 'Victorio Papers', NA, M666, Roll 527; See also Pope to Whipple, 21 Jun., 1880 in 'Victorio Papers', NA, M666, Roll 527.

necessarily willing or able to keep an accurate headcount of the Apaches on their reservations. There is the distinct possibility that a number of these Apaches had escaped the notice of the US authorities. Equally, to suggest that Victorio was directing almost 450 Apache warriors was a significant over-estimation of the numbers of independent Apaches.

Hatch concluded that the Apaches would attempt to cross the Rio Grande around Fort Quitman in an attempt to return to the Mescalero reservation.[126] Morrow reported that if Victorio 'does return he is liable to cross the Rio Grande below Old Fort Quitman he cannot reach Stanton by any other trail that I know of without coming within striking distance of this post and I would certainly hear of him.'[127] Hatch believed that a large number of Mescaleros had attempted to make for their reservation after the Palomas River fight, but had been unable to get across the Rio Grande because of the presence of troops. They had had to abandon their possessions and flee south to Mexico 'with the intention of crossing above Old Fort Quitman and returning to Agency'.[128] By 13 June, Hatch could confidently report that Victorio's people were in the mountains of Mexico and would return as soon as their wounded recovered.[129] This certainly suggests that Hatch had some source of information working south of the border. However, such sources could be extremely unreliable.

Two scouts with typically overstated frontier pseudonyms, 'Hurricane' Bill and 'Cherokee' Jim, returned from a scout into Mexico on 12 July, to pass on information that Victorio had allegedly moved back into New Mexico.[130] Both men were described as 'among the most trustworthy scouts on this frontier' and as 'employed by the military authorities to make the expedition in question'.[131] Both 'Hurricane' Bill and 'Cherokee' Jim were also wrong. For once, Hatch and Morrow were correct in predicting Victorio's next move.

---

126 Hatch, Fort Craig to Grierson, Fort Concho, 9? Jun., 1880, 'DoNM/GSFO/L&T', NA, RG393, Part 3, Entry 475, Vol. 7, p.384 & p.385; Thrapp, 1974, p.282; Thrapp, 1967, p.203.

127 Morrow to loud AAAG 20 Jun.? 1880, NA, RG393, pt 3, Entry 439 pp.12-13.

128 Loud to AAG Fort Leavenworth, 9 Jun., 1880, Telegrams Sent DoNM, Vol.3, Jan.-Nov., 1880, NA, RG393, Part 3, Entry 431, p.496; Hatch to AAG, Fort Leavenworth, 8 Jun., 1880, 'Victorio Campaign, Feb., 1879-Nov. 1880' in 'Victorio Files', NA, RG393, M1495, Roll 14.

129 Loud to AAG Fort Leavenworth, 13 Jun., 1880, Telegrams Sent DoNM, Vol.3, Jan.-Nov., 1880, NA, RG393, Part 3, Entry 431, pp.515-516.

130 The *Grant County Herald*, 17 Jul., 1880.

131 The *Grant County Herald*, 14 Aug., 1880.

9

Grierson Prepares his Forces, June–July 1880

When we last met Colonel Grierson, he had returned to the District of the Pecos after an attempt to disarm and dismount the Mescalero Apaches. (See Chapter 6.) By mid-June, with Victorio in Mexico, and Hatch and Morrow predicting that the Apaches would attempt to return to New Mexico via the District of the Pecos, Grierson knew that he had to prepare an effective defence should the latter's predictions come to pass.

There was some Apache activity in western Texas during May and June 1880, which was probably the result of Mescalero Apaches taking advantage of the turmoil caused by Victorio's uprising, or raiding as a reaction to the US Army's recent operation to disarm and dismount them.[1] On 12 May, eight heavily armed Mescaleros ambushed a party of civilians in Bass Canon, killing a man and a woman (James Grant and Margaret Graham) and wounding two other men. Eight horses were stolen, and it was assumed that the Apaches were intending to ally with Victorio, as they had departed the scene in a south-westerly direction.[2] The survivors managed to reach Van Horn Wells, and from there Fort Davis was alerted late on 14 May.[3] (See document file no. 84.) As the Apaches were reported to have fled towards the Rio Grande, only 25 miles distant,[4] Major McLaughlin thought it futile to pursue the party. Instead, he sent immediate relief in the form of food and clothing, and instructions to help the destitute survivors reach either Ysleta or El Paso.[5]

Grierson had ordered Captain Carpenter's company to Eagle Springs (see Chapter 6) to scout the Eagle and Carrizo Mountains. Carpenter was also instructed to coordinate his company's activities

1 Leckie, 1967, p.223.

2 Dan Murphy, Survivor of the attack, to Major McLaughlin, 10th Cavalry, from Van Horn Station, 13 May, 1880, NA, RG393, Part 1, Entry 2546, pp.463-464; Carpenter to AAAG, DoP, NA, RG393, Part 1, Entry 2546, p.460; Pope to AG, Chicago, Illinois, 17 May, 1880, NA, RG393, Part 1, Entry 2546, pp.444-446; McLaughlen, Fort Davis to AAAG, DoP, 17 May, 1880 in Register of Telegrams Rec'd 11 Oct., 1879-8 Oct., 1880, HQ Records DoP 1878-1881, NA, RG393, M1381, Roll 2, pp.118-119, Letter No.145; Grierson to AAG, DoTx, 18 May, 1880, NA, RG393, Part 1, Entry 2546, p.450; Carpenter to AAAG, DoP, NA, RG393, Part 1, Entry 2546, pp.459-460; Tabular Statement of Expeditions and Scouts against Indians, &c., made in the DoTx, during the Year ending Sept. 30, 1880., NA, RG393, Part 1, Entry 2546, p.628; List of Persons Killed, Wounded, or Captured, by Indians, &c., in the DoTx, since Sept. 30, 1879, officially reported by post commanders. NA, RG393, Part 1, Entry 2546, p.633; 'By Telegraph', the *Grant County Herald*, 22 May, 1880; 'Town and County' the *Grant County Herald*, 29 May, 1880; Record of Engagements, p.95; Leckie, 1967, p.223; Leckie & Leckie, 1984, p.260; See also Baylor, 1996, p.321 note 18; Gillett, 1976, p.202; Thompson, p.165; Webb, 1976, p.89.

3 McLaughlin, Fort Davis, to AAG, DoTx, 17 May, 1880, NA, RG393, Part 1, Entry 2546, pp.462-463 & pp.465-468

4 Dan Murphy, Survivor of the attack, to Major McLaughlin, 10th Cavalry, from Van Horn Station, 13 May, 1880, NA, RG393, Part 1, Entry 2546, pp.463-464.

5 McLaughlin, Fort Davis, to AAG, DoTx, 17 May, 1880, NA, RG393, Part 1, Entry 2546, pp.462-463 & pp.465-468; Smither to AAG, San Antonio, Texas, 18 May, 1880 in Telegrams Sent 24 Apr., 1879-22 Jun., 1880, HQ Records DoP 1878-1881, NA, RG393, M1381, Roll 1, p.251-252, Letter No.150.

with those of Captain Viele's company.[6] The latter had also been ordered into the area from its station in the Chenati Mountains, where it had been conducting regular patrols since late March that year.[7] Carpenter, with his superior knowledge of the local terrain, was given overall command, and he tracked the raiders to the Rio Grande.[8] From the signs he found, Carpenter he estimated there were eight Apaches; and he was certain that these had recently escaped from Fort Stanton. He also reported that the waterholes in the area were dry, and the grass thus very poor. For this reason, any units operating from Eagle Springs should carry their own forage.[9]

In reaction to the attack in Bass Canon, General Pope endorsed Grierson's request that the three remaining companies of Tenth Cavalry stationed at Fort Sill be sent to the Department of Texas.[10] General Sheridan accordingly ordered these companies to join Grierson in western Texas, with instructions to strengthen the defence of the District of the Pecos against Apache incursions from the Mescalero reservation. They were also to cooperate with troops from New Mexico. The lynchpin of this defence was the holding of three companies of Tenth Cavalry in readiness to 'break up and destroy' Victorio's band should they venture into Grierson's district.[11]

During March 1880, in anticipation of future conflict with Mescalero Apaches, Grierson had sent an officer to the Ysleta Mission, close to El Paso, to recruit some Pueblo scouts.[12] Nineteen[13] Pueblo Indians signed on and were formed into a unit under Lieutenant Frank H. Mills of the Twenty-Fourth Infantry.[14] On 11 June, this detachment, in the process of following an Indian trail, was breaking camp in Viejo Pass when it was suddenly attacked by approximately 20 Apaches. Sergeant Simon Olguin, the leading Pueblo scout, and one horse were killed outright, and two horses were later shot and a wounded mule abandoned. Mills's party was not best placed to retaliate, as the US Army had not yet furnished all his scouts with enough weapons.[15] This left Mills with

---

6 Grierson to AAG, DoTx, 18 May, 1880, NA, RG393, Part 1, Entry 2546, pp.450-452; Smither to CO, Fort Davis, 18 May, 1880 in Telegrams Sent 24 Apr., 1879-22 Jun., 1880, HQ Records DoP 1878-1881, NA, RG393, M1381, Roll 1, pp.249-250, Letter No.148.

7 Viele to AAG, DoTx, 28 May, 1880, NA, RG393, Part 1, Entry 2546, pp.500-502; Tabular Statement of Expeditions and Scouts against Indians, &c., made in the DoTx, during the Year ending Sept. 30, 1880., NA, RG393, Part 1, Entry 2546, p.628.

8 Carpenter to AAAG, DoP, NA, RG393, Part 1, Entry 2546, pp.459-461; Carpenter to AAG, DoP, 20 Jun., 1880 in Letters Rec'd File 19 Mar., 1878-14 Feb., 1881, HQ Records DoP 1878-1881, NA, RG393, M1381, Roll 2Tabular Statement of Expeditions and Scouts against Indians, &c., made in the DoTx, during the Year ending Sept. 30, 1880., NA, RG393, Part 1, Entry 2546, p.628.

9 Carpenter to AAAG, DoP, NA, RG393, Part 1, Entry 2546, pp.459-461.

12 Smither to CO Fort Davis, 3 Mar., 1880 in Telegrams Sent 24 Apr., 1879-22 Jun., 1880, HQ Records DoP 1878-1881, NA, RG393, M1381, Roll 1, p.206, Letter No.78.

13 Woodward to AAAG, DoP, 23 Mar., 1880 in Register of Telegrams Rec'd 11 Oct., 1879-8 Oct., 1880, HQ Records DoP 1878-1881, NA, RG393, M1381, Roll 2, p.110, Letter No.122.

Permission to recruit nineteen Pueblo scouts had been authorised on the 19 Feb., 1880. (See Vincent to CO, DoP, 19 Feb., 1880 in Letters Rec'd File 19 Mar., 1878-14 Feb., 1881, HQ Records DoP 1878-1881, NA, RG393, M1381, Roll 2).

14 Report of Indian Scouts serving in the DoTx on Mar. 31. 1880, NA, RG393, Part 1, Entry 2546, p.391; Report of Indian Scouts serving in the DoTx on 31 May, 1880, NA, RG393, Part 1, Entry 2546, p.494; Matthews, 1993, p.37.

15 District HQ were aware of the shortage of equipment and though there is no mention of firearms, on the 3 June, 1880 the CO Fort Davis was instructed to order Lt. Mill's detachment to Fort Davis to supply the Pueblo scouts with their outstanding equipment, noting that while the detachment had 'horses, pack mules, pack saddles, ammunition and canteens, but no cartridge belts nor lariats, and only twelve canteens [carbines?].' (Smither to CO Fort Davis, 3 Jun., 1880 in Telegrams Sent 24 Apr., 1879-22 Jun., 1880, HQ Records DoP 1878-1881, NA, RG393, M1381, Roll 1, pp.273-274, Letter No.183) Another communication gave the above list but clearly stated that the detachment had no revolvers and only twelve carbines. (Vincent to Grierson, 1 Jun., 1880 in Register of Telegrams Rec'd 11 Oct., 1879-8 Oct.,

only 12 men who were armed with carbines.[16] The skirmish lasted about four hours and ended when Mills directed some of his men to seize higher ground, which overlooked the Apache positions. When these men opened fire, the Apaches quickly dispersed. Mills did not mount a pursuit as those members of his detachment who were armed had run low on ammunition.[17] (See document file no. 85.) His superiors were aware of the unit's shortages, and around 3 June he was instructed to march to Fort Davis to supply the Pueblo scouts with their outstanding equipment. The scouts had 'horses, pack mules, pack saddles, ammunition and canteens, but no cartridge belts nor lariats, and only 12 canteens [carbines?].'[18] It would appear that Lieutenant Mills was en route to Fort Davis to pick up these supplies when he picked up the trail of the Apaches and decided to follow them. Lieutenant R. Read led a detachment of 20 Tenth Cavalrymen after the Apaches, but failed to catch them, the trail having been destroyed by heavy rainfall.[19] It was assumed, correctly or otherwise, that these Apaches were scouting the lie of the land on behalf of Victorio.[20]

Other intelligence was received from the authorities in the State of Chihuahua. Roman Aranda, in acknowledging receipt of authority from Governor Terrazas to cooperate with the commanding officer, Fort Bliss, also sent word to the latter that on 6 July, 'five Indians on foot crossed near Ft Quitman[21] on the second inst. into Texas & returned on the fourth. I start at once with fourteen men to scout for these Indians.'[22] Aranda also passed on word that Victorio and his men were 40 miles to the south-west of Gallegos for the purpose of trading with its citizens.[23] At the same time, the Apaches, having regrouped after their defeat on the Palomas River, commenced raiding

1880, HQ Records DoP 1878-1881, NA, RG393, M1381, Roll 2, pp.134-135, Letter No.183). It would appear that Lt. Mills was en-route to Fort Davis when he picked up the trail of the Apaches.

16 Carpenter to Post Adjutant, Fort Davis,, 11 Jul., 1880 in Unregistered Letters 1878-1881, HQ Records DoP 1878-1881, NA, RG393, M1381, Roll 2; Vincent to Grierson, 1 Jun., 1880 in Register of Telegrams Rec'd 11 Oct., 1879-8 Oct., 1880, HQ Records DoP 1878-1881, NA, RG393, M1381, Roll 2, pp.134-135, Letter No.183.

17 Frank H. Mills 1st Lieut, 24th Infantry to Post Adjutant, Fort Davis, Texas, 10 Jun., 1880, NA, RG393, Part 1, Entry 2546, pp.505-507; Mills to Adjutant, Fort Davis, 10 Jun., 1880 in Telegrams Sent 24 Apr., 1879-22 Jun., 1880, HQ Records DoP 1878-1881, NA, RG393, M1381, Roll 1, pp.296-297, Letter No.219 See also Whipple to AG Wash. D.C. 15 Jun., 1880 in 'Victorio Papers', NA, M666, Roll 527; NA, RG393, Part 1, Entry 2539, Press Copies of Letters and Endorsements Sent, MDoM, Vol. 13, p.357; List of Persons Killed, Wounded, or Captured, by Indians, &c., in the DoTx, since Sept. 30, 1879, officially reported by post commanders. NA, RG393, Part 1, Entry 2546, p.633; Record of Engagements, p.95; Leckie, 1967, p.223; Baylor, 1996; p.307 & p.320, note 7; Matthews, 1993, p.37.

18 Smither to CO Fort Davis, 3 Jun., 1880 in Telegrams Sent 24 Apr., 1879-22 Jun., 1880, HQ Records DoP 1878-1881, NA, RG393, M1381, Roll 1, pp.273-274, Letter No.183.

Another communication gave the above list but clearly stated that the detachment had no revolvers and only twelve carbines. (Vincent to Grierson, 1 Jun., 1880 in Register of Telegrams Rec'd 11 Oct., 1879-8 Oct., 1880, HQ Records DoP 1878-1881, NA, RG393, M1381, Roll 2, pp.134-135, Letter No.183)

19 Lt. Col. Yard, Fort Davis to AAG, DoP, 25 Jun., 1880 in Register of Telegrams Rec'd 11 Oct., 1879-8 Oct., 1880, HQ Records DoP 1878-1881, NA, RG393, M1381, Roll 2, p.161, Letter No.251; Tabular Statement of Expeditions and Scouts against Indians, &c., made in the DoTx, during the Year ending Sept. 30, 1880., NA, RG393, Part 1, Entry 2546, p.628.

20 Leckie & Leckie, 1984, p.260.

21 In 1876, Fort Quitman was de-activated as a military establishment. A stage station was built on the site in 1879. In early 1880, Col. Grierson sent Captain Carpenter to investigate its re-establishment. (Vincent to CO Fort Davis 12 Feb., 1880 in Letters Rec'd File 19 Mar., 1878-14 Feb., 1881, HQ Records DoP 1878-1881, NA, RG393, M1381, Roll 2).

22 Brinkerhoff to AAAG 10 Jul., 1880, NA, RG393, Part 3, Entry 439, pp.576-577; Hatch to AAG Fort Leavenworth, 13 Jul., 1880, Telegrams Sent DoNM, Vol.3, Jan.-Nov. 1880, NA, RG393, Part 3, Entry 431, pp.605-606.

23 Hatch to AAG Fort Leavenworth quoted in 'Indian Affairs', *Army & Navy Journal*, Vol. 17, 24 Jul., 1880, p.1048.

Plates 9.1 and 9.2 Two photos taken in Bass Canyon, where James Grant and Margaret Graham were killed in May 1880. These photos were taken on the same day (12 September 2006) and show how quickly the weather can change in the South West. (Photos: Author)

in northern Chihuahua. Even the property of the Governor Luis Terrazas was not safe. His San Lorenzo Ranch was raided, on or around 21 June, and 100 horses lost, their herders slain. The same raiders then moved south and repeated their actions at a ranch near Santa Clara.[24] In just two raids, Victorio managed to remount most or all of his warriors. The Apaches were reported to have raided in an arc about 30 miles out from Chihuahua City and were trading with the inhabitants of the town of Galejos (possibly Galeana).[25]

Attacks by Apaches in western Texas indicated only the possibility that such incidents might represent a shift in Victorio's area of operations. It should also be noted that, while these raids were carried out by Apaches, it does not necessarily mean that these were members of, Victorio's band or allied to it. If we consider the army's treatment of the Mescaleros in April 1880, while attempting to disarm and dismount them, it is small wonder that some Mescaleros may have been provoked into retaliating. Yet it was clear that the US Army was concerned that Victorio should, at all costs, be prevented from returning to the Mescalero Reservation. To this end, Hatch made it clear that if the Tenth Cavalry could be moved to New Mexico, he would have enough men to guard the area to prevent Victorio from trading for guns and ammunition. This would leave him with enough troops to prosecute an active campaign against the Apaches.[26] (See document file no. 86.)

Requests to use the Tenth Cavalry in New Mexico had been made almost from the moment that Grierson's battalion had returned to their stations in Texas.[27] So far, these requests had failed to bear fruit; but such redeployment was being seriously considered. By 26 May, thoroughly alarmed at reports that the Ninth Cavalry were 'about dismounted', Sheridan considered the transfer of five companies of the Tenth Cavalry to Fort Stanton.[28] This request had come from Hatch, who also telegraphed Grierson on 27 May, enquiring how many companies of the Tenth Cavalry would be deployed to Fort Stanton.[29]

Unfortunately, Hatch's appeals for more troops to counter Victorio in New Mexico[30] threatened to disrupt Grierson's own careful strategy. The original instructions, that Grierson should

---

24 Loud to Morrow, Fort Bayard, 30 Jun., 1880, Telegrams Sent DoNM, Vol.3, Jan.-Nov. 1880, NA, RG393, Part 3, Entry 431, p.571; See also Pope to AAG HQ MDoM, 2 Jul., 1880, 'Victorio Files', NA, RG393, M1495, Roll 14; 'By Telegraph', the *Grant County Herald*, 3 Jul., 1880; Thrapp, 1974, pp.285-286.

25 Hatch to AAG Fort Leavenworth, 13 Jul., 1880, Telegrams Sent DoNM, Vol.3, Jan.-Nov. 1880, NA, RG393, Part 3, Entry 431, pp.605-606 Hatch to AAG Fort Leavenworth, 13 Jul., 1880, 'Victorio Files', NA, RG393, M1495, Roll 14; Hatch to AAG Ft Leavenworth, 13 Jul., 1880 in 'Victorio Papers', NA, M666, Roll 527; Hatch to Grierson, 14 Jul., 1880 in Register of Telegrams Rec'd 11 Oct., 1879-8 Oct., 1880, HQ Records DoP 1878-1881, NA, RG393, M1381, Roll 2, p.193, Letter No.329; Thrapp, 1974, p.284; Thrapp, 1967, p.203; Haley, 1981, p.328.

26 Hatch to AAG, SF, 22 May, 1880, in 'DoNM/GSFO/L&T', NA, RG393, Part 3, Entry 475, Vol. 5, p.269.

27 Platt to Captain Loud SF 20 May, 1880, NA, RG393, Part 3, Entry 440, p.74; See also Hatch to Department HQ, 26 May, 1880, 'DoNM/GSFO/L&T', NA, RG393, Part 3, Entry 475, Vol. 5, p.273.

28 Sheridan to Townsend, 26 May, 1880, NA, RG393, Part 1, Entry 2539, Press Copies of Letters and Endorsements Sent, MDoM, Vol. 13, pp.274-275; Sheridan to Ord, 26 May, 1880, NA, RG393, Part 1, Entry 2539, Press Copies of Letters and Endorsements Sent, MDoM, Vol. 13, p.271; Vincent to Grierson, 26 May, 1880 in Register of Telegrams Rec'd 11 Oct., 1879-8 Oct., 1880, HQ Records DoP 1878-1881, NA, RG393, M1381, Roll 2, pp.126-127, Letter No.164.

29 Hatch, Fort Craig, to Grierson, Fort Concho, 27 May, 1880, 'DoNM/GSFO/L&T', NA, RG393, Part 3, Entry 475, Vol. 7, p.494; Hatch to Grierson, 27 May, 1880 in Register of Telegrams Rec'd 11 Oct., 1879-8 Oct., 1880, HQ Records DoP 1878-1881, NA, RG393, M1381, Roll 2, p.130, Letter No.172; Grierson to AAG, San Antonio, Texas, 28 May, 1880 & Grierson to Hatch, 29 May, 1880 in Telegrams Sent 24 Apr., 1879-22 Jun., 1880, HQ Records DoP 1878-1881, NA, RG393, M1381, Roll 1, pp.268-269, Letter No.'s 174 & 175.

30 See for instance Hatch to AAG, SF, 22 May, 1880, in 'DoNM/GSFO/L&T', NA, RG393, Part 3, Entry 475, Vol. 5, p.269.

establish pickets backed by a central reserve of three companies, were soon changed. Grierson was ordered to take a battalion of the Tenth Cavalry to Fort Stanton, thereby allowing Hatch to concentrate his regiment on the western side of the Rio Grande.[31] While in New Mexico, this Tenth Cavalry battalion would be under the direct orders of Hatch.[32] This proposed deployment was complicated by Grierson's commander, General Ord, who tried to insist that while the Tenth Cavalry aided Hatch in the District of New Mexico and Department of Missouri, Grierson's battalion would remain under Department of Texas command.[33] At first, General Sheridan seemed to accept this position stating that Ord could retain control of the Tenth Cavalry battalion, even suggesting that Fort Bliss be transferred to the Department of Texas.[34] Ultimately, Sheridan, suspecting Ord of 'empire-building', was forced to remind him that 'the object is to destroy the indians in New Mexico, and in giving orders to General Grierson you should exercise your discretion as to the best means of accomplishing that end.'[35]

General Edward Otho Cresap Ord. Commander of the Department of Texas, proved to be more interested in internal US Army politic than cooperating with troops outside his Department in the effort to defeat Victorio. (National Archives)

Sheridan's vexation with Ord had had been prompted by a complaint from General Pope that Ord had refused to send any Tenth Cavalry until the three companies of the Tenth Cavalry had been sent from Fort Sill to Texas. Pope was worried that trouble with the Navajo was brewing, which had necessitated the moving of Colonel George P. Buell to Fort Wingate. The perceived urgency of the situation in New Mexico, where the Ninth Cavalry was in effect 'out of action', left Pope facing the possibility of having to move other cavalry units from Indian Territory, leaving that region dangerously undermanned, because of Ord's refusal to act on the moment.[36] Pope also made

31 Sheridan to Pope, 22 May, 1880 in 'Victorio Papers', NA, M666, Roll 527; See also Pope to Whipple, AAG Chicago, 3 Jun., 1880, 'Victorio Files', NA, RG393, M1495, Roll 14; Dinges, 1987, p.87; McChristian, 1982, pp.49-50.

32 Platt to AAAG, DoNM, 31 May, 1880 in Letters Received by HQ DoNM Sept. 1865-Aug. 1890, NA, RG393, M1088, Roll 41, Jul.-Dec. 1880.

33 Vincent to Grierson, 25 May, 1880 & 28 May, 1880, Ord to Grierson, 4 Jun., 1880 in Register of Telegrams Rec'd 11 Oct., 1879-8 Oct., 1880, HQ Records DoP 1878-1881, NA, RG393, M1381, Roll 2, p.124, p.132, & p.137, Letter No.159, 177 & 189; Whipple AAG to Gen. Pope 5 Jun., 1880, NA, RG393, Part 1, Entry 2539, Press Copies of Letters and Endorsements Sent, MDoM, Vol. 13, p.323; Dinges, 1987, p.87; Matthews, 1993, p.37.

34 Sheridan to Ord, 21 May, 1880 in 'Victorio Papers', NA, M666, Roll 527; See also Vincent to Grierson, 28 May, 1880 in Register of Telegrams Rec'd 11 Oct., 1879-8 Oct., 1880, HQ Records DoP 1878-1881, NA, RG393, M1381, Roll 2, pp.131-132, Letter No.176.

35 Whipple to Ord, NA, RG393, Part 1, Entry 2539, Press Copies of Letters and Endorsements Sent, MDoM, Vol. 13, p.339; Whipple to Ord, 11 Jun., 1880, 'Victorio Files', NA, RG393, M1495, Roll 14.

36 Pope to Whipple 22 May, 1880, & Pope to AAG HQ MDoM, 25 May, 1880, 'Victorio Files', NA, RG393, M1495, Roll 14.

it quite clear that this was a temporary measure and that he did not want the Tenth Cavalry transferred and would return them as soon as the Apaches were defeated.[37] Nevertheless, General Ord continued to use the war with Victorio in an attempt to increase the size of his own Department.[38]

This was not the first time that Ord had proposed a redrawing of department boundaries. In January 1880, comments attributed to General Ord were reported in the Texas Press, suggesting that the Fort Stanton and Indian Territory reservations should be transferred to the Department of Texas. This would prevent raids into Texas from these reservations. Pope pointed out to his superiors that Ord had as many troops in Texas as Pope had across the entire Department of the Missouri. He thought that Ord would be well-advised to use some of his considerable forces to counter the raids he talked about and not publicly blame another military department for failing to stop Indian raids.[39] When Ord repeated this suggestion on 11 June 1880,[40] Sheridan concluded that quibbling over command protocol and jealous protection of military resources was not the best means of tackling Apaches. It also showed what could potentially go wrong when attempting to combat Apache guerrillas using three separate headquarters (the Departments of Arizona, Missouri and Texas).

In the meantime, General Pope took the decision to move three companies of the Fourth Cavalry and two companies of Infantry to New Mexico. This, he noted, would leave no garrisons at Forts Gibson, Hays, Lyon, Riley and Wallace; and the rest of the military garrisons in Indian Territory and Kansas were left much weakened. While Pope regarded this as a huge risk, he could see no alternative.[41]

Grierson himself wanted nothing to do with guarding the Mescalero reservation. He believed that his troops would be wasted in fruitless trailing through New Mexico, and would continue to be plagued by responsibilities to both the Interior Department and the War Department which would pull them in different directions. He also thought that a move to Fort Stanton would put undue pressure on the Tenth Cavalry's logistic support. He suggested that a more limited transferral to El Paso and the Guadalupe Mountains, as far north as the Seven Rivers, with the authorisation to scout the Sacramento and White Mountains as far as Fort Stanton, would suffice.[42] Grierson was convinced that a strategy of patrolling or picketing known waterholes, passes and river crossings in western Texas, ground already well-known to the Tenth Cavalry, would be a more effective means of preventing Victorio reaching the Mescalero reservation, if the latter tried to move through western Texas.[43] Having seen what had happened to the Ninth Cavalry in New Mexico, he was certain that this was not the means to defeat Victorio. By the end of May, his regiment was almost in position to achieve this goal:[44] Half the regiment was already in the field and assigned to specific areas between the Pecos River and the Rio Grande. These troops were instructed to patrol their respective areas vigorously. Another three companies were resting and refitting; and

37 Pope to Whipple, 24 May, 1880, 'Victorio Files', NA, RG393, M1495, Roll 14.

38 Ord to AG Chicago, 3 Jun., 1880, 'Victorio Files', NA, RG393, M1495, Roll 14.

39 Pope to Col. W.D. Whipple, AAG, 18 Jan., 1880, NA, RG393, Part 1, Entry 2546, pp310-314.

40 Ord to AG, Chicago, 11 Jun., 1880, NA, RG393, Part 1, Entry 2546, pp.495-496 & p.497.

41 Pope to Sheridan, 26 May, 1880, 'Victorio Files', NA, RG393, M1495, Roll 14; Special Orders No. 113, HQ DoM, Fort Leavenworth, 26 May, 1880 in 'Victorio Papers', NA, M666, Roll 527.

42 Grierson to AAG, San Antonio, Texas, 4 Jun., 1880 in Telegrams Sent 24 Apr., 1879-22 Jun., 1880, HQ Records DoP 1878-1881, NA, RG393, M1381, Roll 1, pp.277-280, Letter No.190.

43 Grierson to Col. Hatch 19 Jul., 1880, NA, RG393, Part 3, Entry 439, pp.551-53; Grierson to AAG, San Antonio, 24 Jun., 1880 in Telegrams Sent 23 Jun.-30 Nov., 1880, HQ Records DoP 1878-1881, NA, RG393, M1381, Roll 1, pp.18-19, Letter No. 249; Grierson's Report of the Campaign in Western Texas, Jul. –Aug. 1880: submitted 22 Sept., 1880 (hereafter referred to as 'Grierson's Report Sept. 1880'); NA, RG393, Part 1, Entry 2546, pp.639-644; Dinges, 1987, p.87; Matthews, 1993, p.37; Temple, 1957, pp.49-50; Temple, 1959, pp.99-100; McChristian, 1982, p.50.

44 Grierson to AAG, San Antonio, Texas, 28 May, 1880 in Telegrams Sent 24 Apr., 1879-22 Jun., 1880, HQ Records DoP 1878-1881, NA, RG393, M1381, Roll 1, pp.267-268, Letter No.173.

the remaining three were marching towards the area of operations. It was hoped that by the end of June the whole of the Tenth Cavalry Regiment would be deployed in this area. As we have already seen (see Volume One of the Victorio Campaign), detachments of the Tenth Cavalry had, between 1877 and 1879, thoroughly scouted and mapped extensive sections of Texas west of the Pecos River. It was knowledge gained from these trips that which allowed Grierson to adopt these tactics.[45]

A cursory glance at the annual reports submitted for 1877–79 shows a mixture of scouting expeditions, some of which lasted two months, and most of which which involved fruitless pursuits of Mescalero Apache raiders.[46] Yet, a serious effort had been made to explore and map the interior, in order ultimately to frustrate raids made by Mescalero Apaches.[47] The first test of Grierson's strategy proved to be a false alarm. Hatch telegraphed Grierson on 9 June, stating that, having been driven out of New Mexico, the Apaches were thought to have crossed the Rio Grande to the south-east of Old Fort Quitman. Grierson alerted his field detachments to be on their guard, but the rumour proved to be groundless.[48]

Throughout June, Grierson struggled to oppose orders to disperse his regiment in support of Hatch in New Mexico.[49] He continued to lobby General Ord on the wisdom of his own plan, and General Sheridan ultimately accepted this alternative on 27 June.[50] General Pope's only concern was that Grierson should guarantee he would continue to picket the country to the east of the Pecos, following a line drawn from Fort Stanton to El Paso.[51] Indeed, on reflection, it looks as though the original orders to re-deploy the Tenth Cavalry battalion to Fort Stanton were more an unthinking response to Hatch's requests for more support than a co-ordinated effort to trap Victorio. However, General Sheridan's instructions were clear on one thing: Grierson was independent of any operations planned by Hatch.[52]

45 See for example Watt, 'I Will Not Surrender the Hair of a Horse's Tail: The Victorio Campaign 1879', pp.119-120 & document file nos. 1.1-1.4, pp.326-344.

46 Tabular Statement of Expeditions and Scouts against Indians & c., made in the DoTx during the Year ending Sept. 30, 1879, NA, RG393, Part 1, Entry 2551, Annual Reports of Departments 1879-1881, MDoM; Col. Grierson's Report for Year ending 31 Dec., 1879, NA, RG393, Part 1, Entry 2546, pp.319-334.

47 Annual Report, DoTx, 1 Oct. 1879, NA, RG393, Part 1, Entry 2551, Annual Reports of Departments 1879-1881, MDoM, p.1 & p.2.

48 Smither to CO Fort Davis & AAG, San Antonio, Texas, 9 Jun., 1880 in Telegrams Sent 24 Apr., 1879-22 Jun., 1880, HQ Records DoP 1878-1881, NA, RG393, M1381, Roll 1, pp.285-287, Letter No.200 & 201.

49 See for example Pope to Whipple 3 Jun., 1880, 'Victorio Files', NA, RG393, M1495, Roll 14.

50 Vincent citing Sheridan's telegram of the 27 Jun., 1880 to Grierson, 28 Jun., 1880 in Register of Telegrams Rec'd 11 Oct., 1879-8 Oct., 1880, HQ Records DoP 1878-1881, NA, RG393, M1381, Roll 2, p.167, Letter No.262; Vincent to Grierson, 28 Jun., 1880 in Telegrams Rec'd, 18 May, 1880-4 Feb., 1881,HQ Records DoP 1878-1881, NA, RG393, M1381, Roll 4; 'Grierson's Report, Sept.1880'; NA, RG393, Part 1, Entry 2546, pp.639-644; Dinges, 1987, p.87; Matthews, 1993, p.37; Temple 1959, p.101; McChristian, 1982, p.50; Haley, 1981, p.329; Haley, 1952, p.331; Rister, 1928, pp.204-206.

51 Pope to Sheridan, 1 Jul., 3 Jul. & 4 Jul., 1880, 'Victorio Files', NA, RG393, M1495, Roll 14.

52 Sheridan to Pope, 4 Jul., 1880, NA, RG393, Part 1, Entry 2539, Press Copies of Letters and Endorsements Sent, MDoM, Vol. 13, p.417; See also Platt to CO, DoNM, SF, 5 Jul., 1880, NA, RG393, Part 3, Entry 440, p.6.

Please see pages viii–xx for detailed notes and captions relating to the maps.

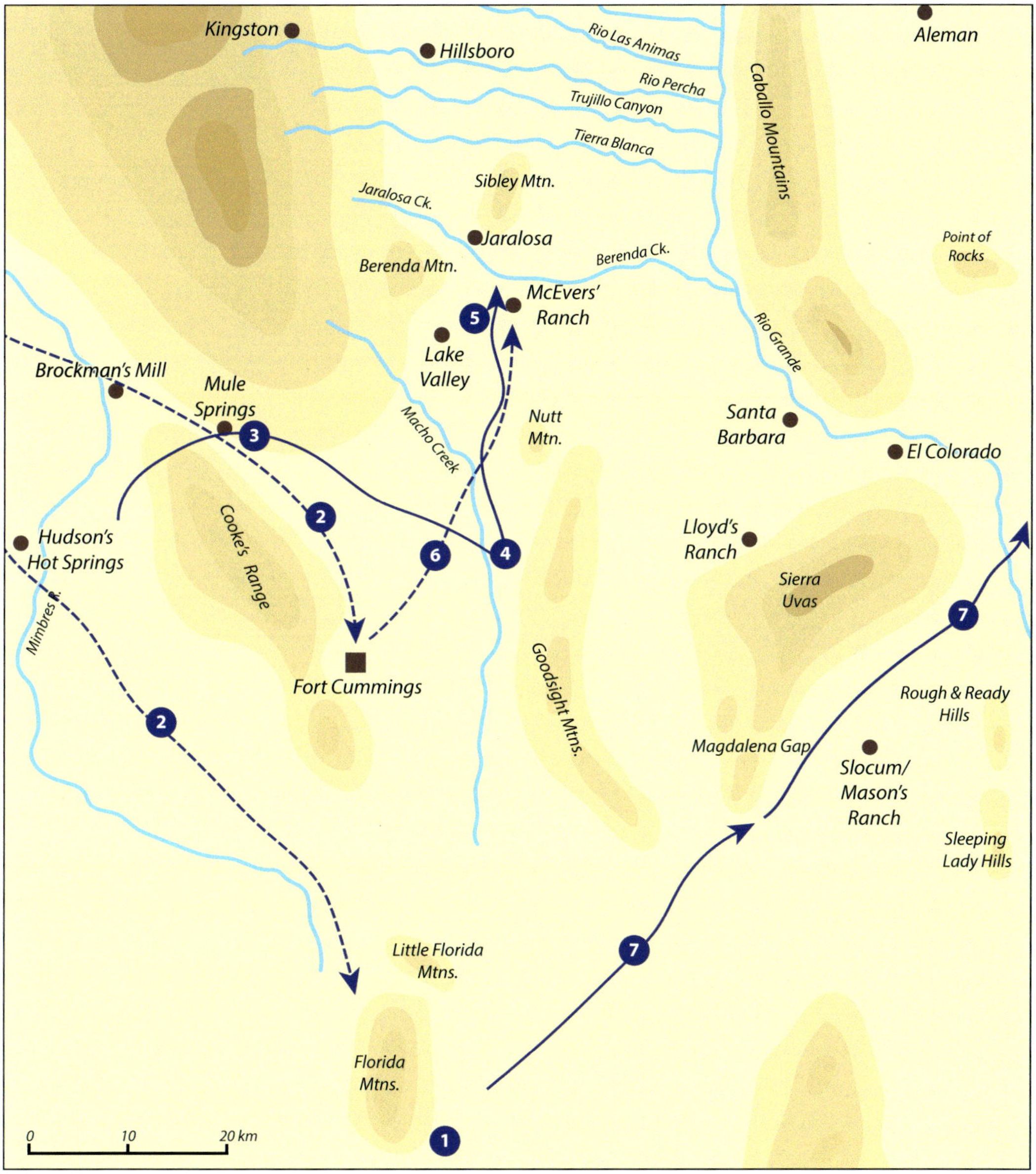

Map 1.1 Morrow's Campaign, January–February 1880.

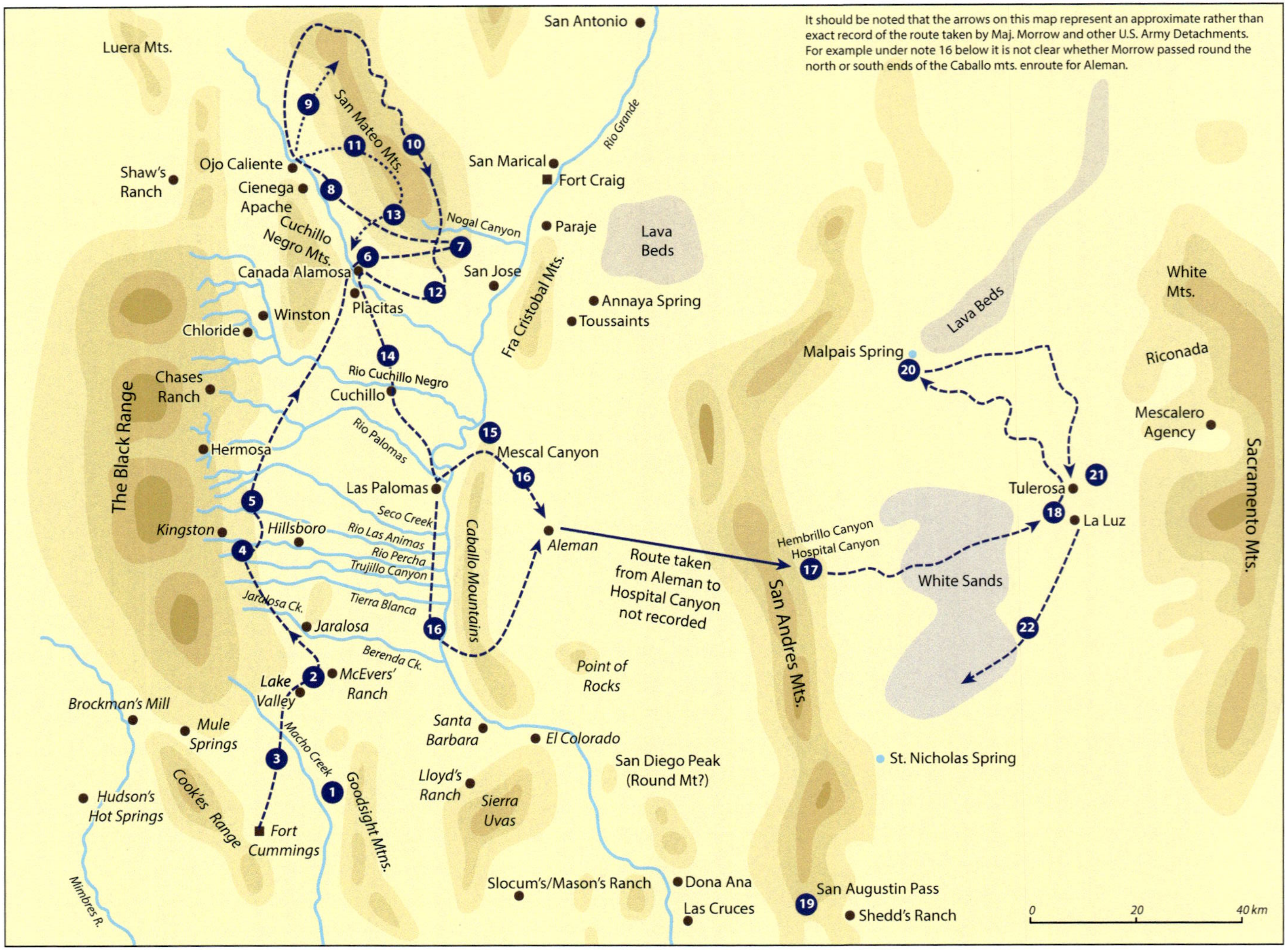

Map 2.1 Morrow's Campaign, January–February 1880.

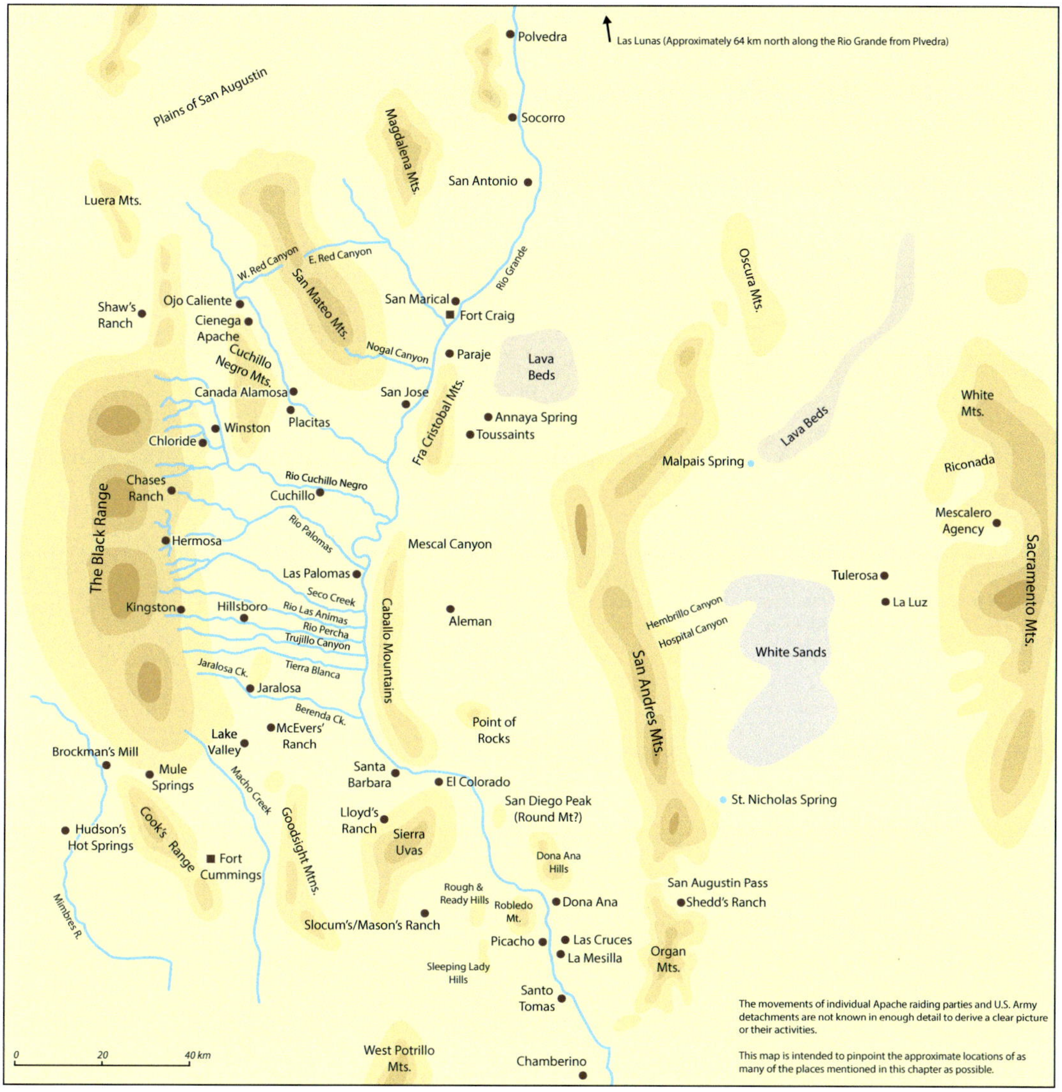

Map 4.1 Victorio raids the Rio Grande valley, March 1880.

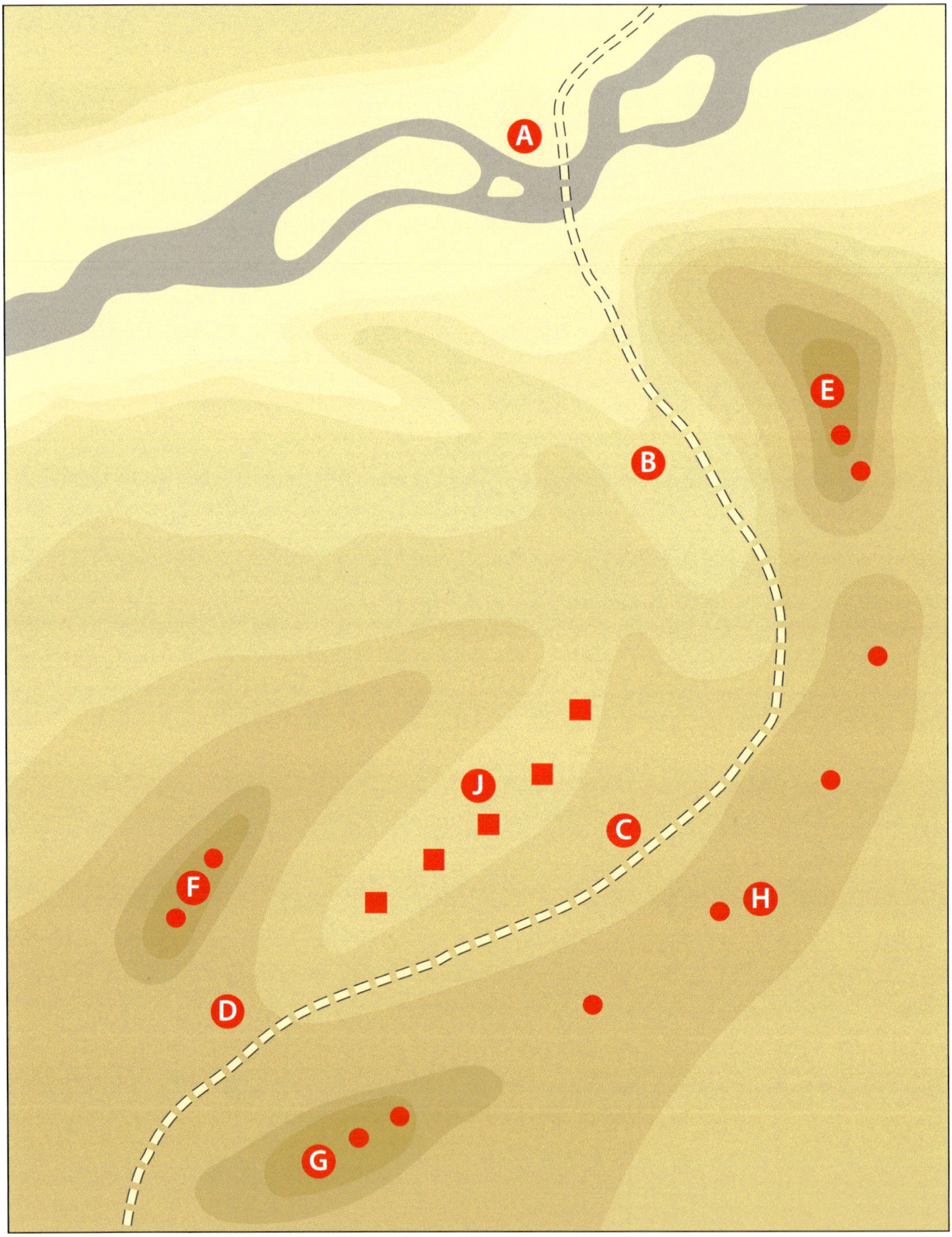

Map 4.2 Ambush site south of Las Palomas, March 1880.

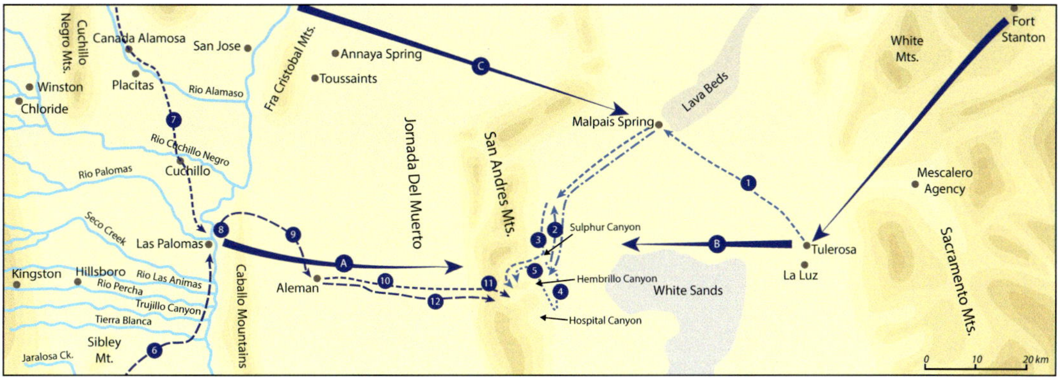

Map 5.1 Hatch's Plan to Trap Victorio: The Hembrillo Canyon Operation, April 1880.

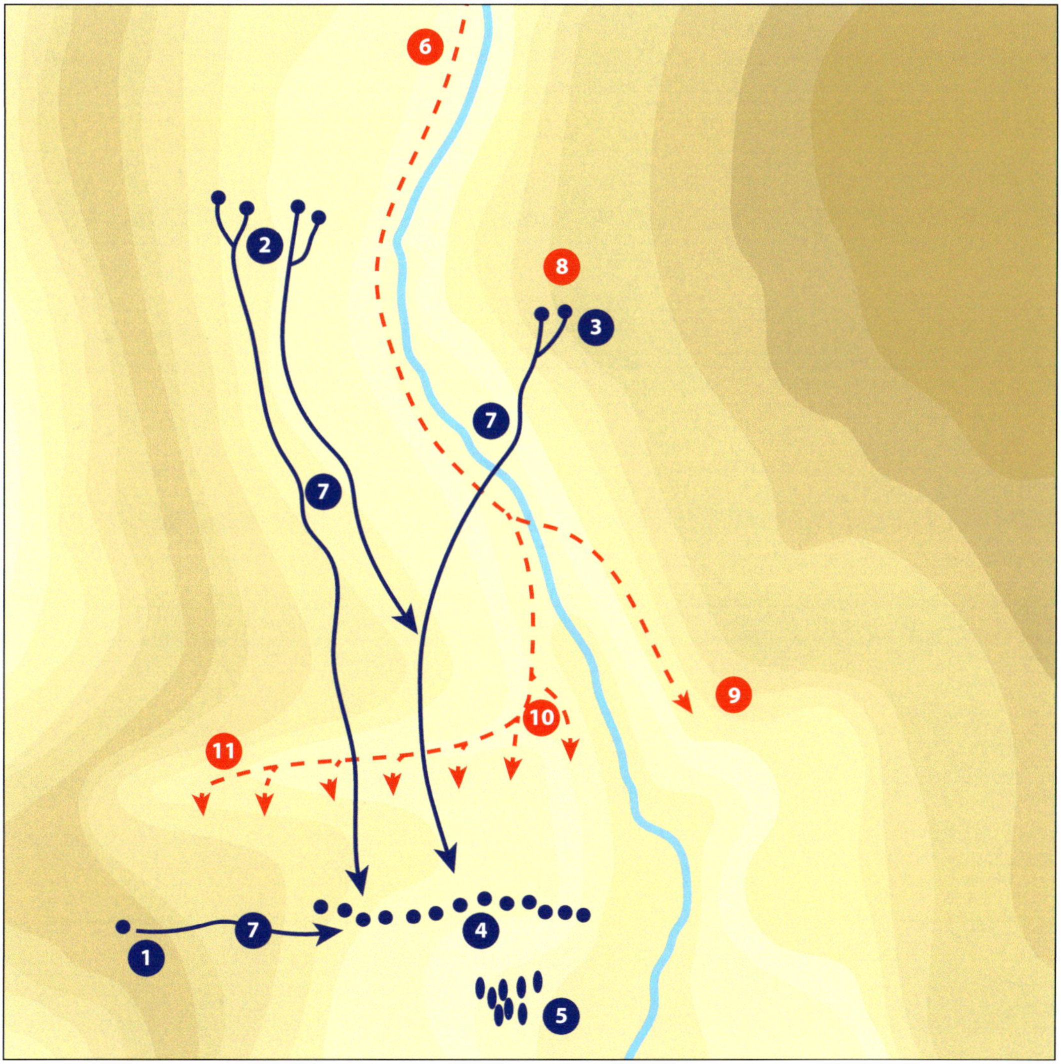

Map 5.2 Conline's Skirmish I, 5 April 1880.

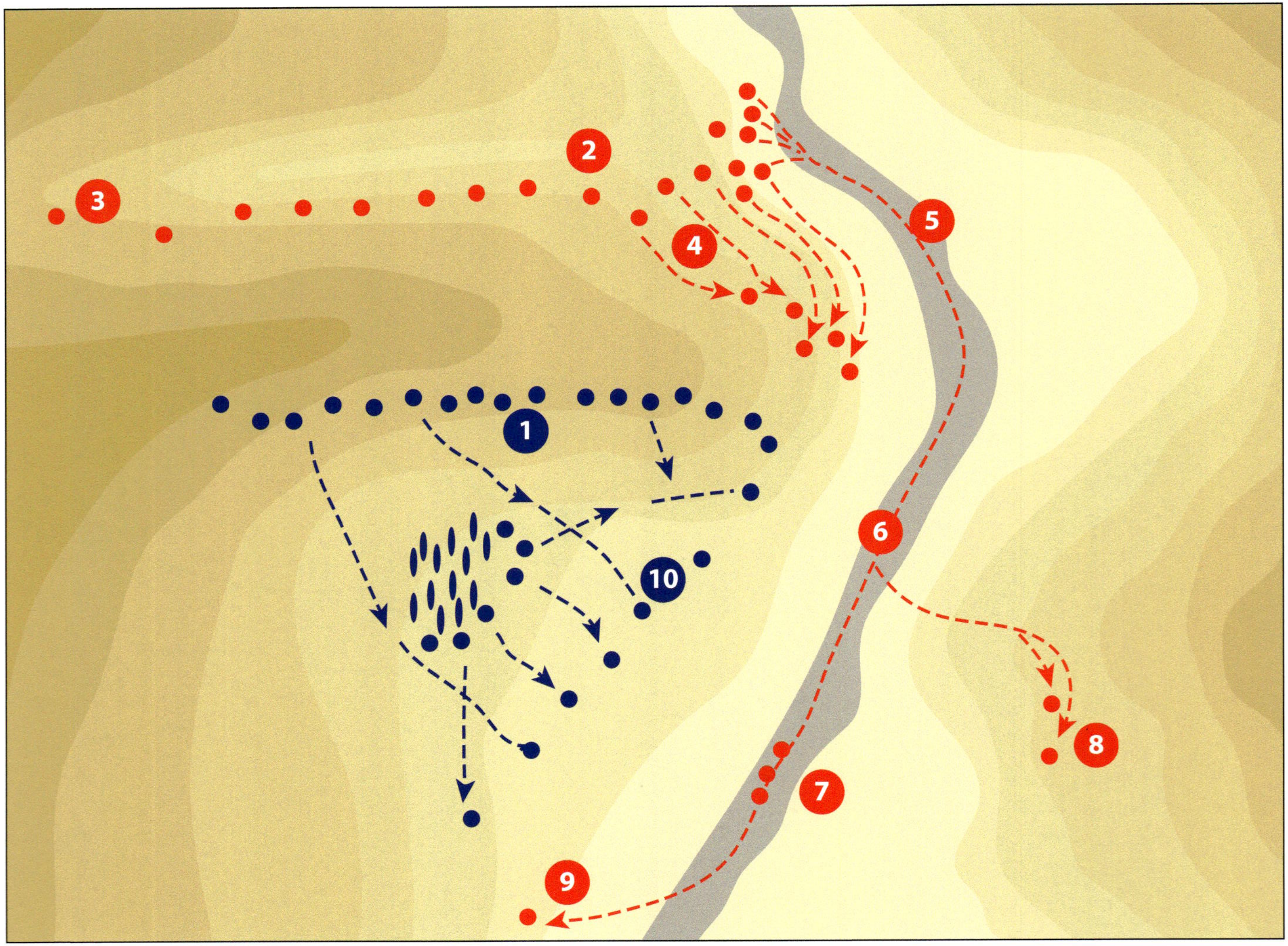

Map 5.3 Conline's Skirmish II, 5 April 1880.

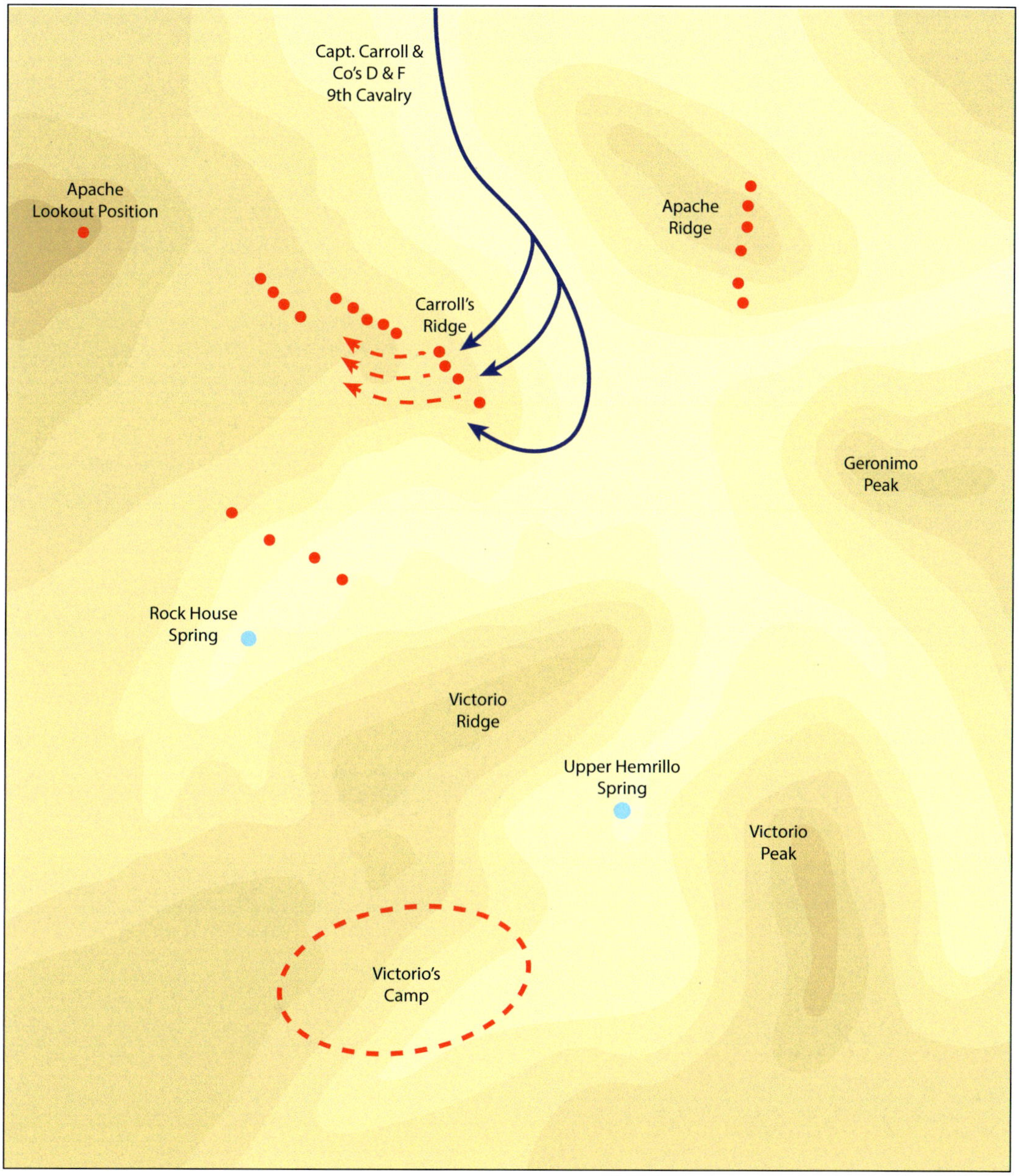

Map 5.4 Hembrillo Canyon Battle I, Evening 6 April 1880.

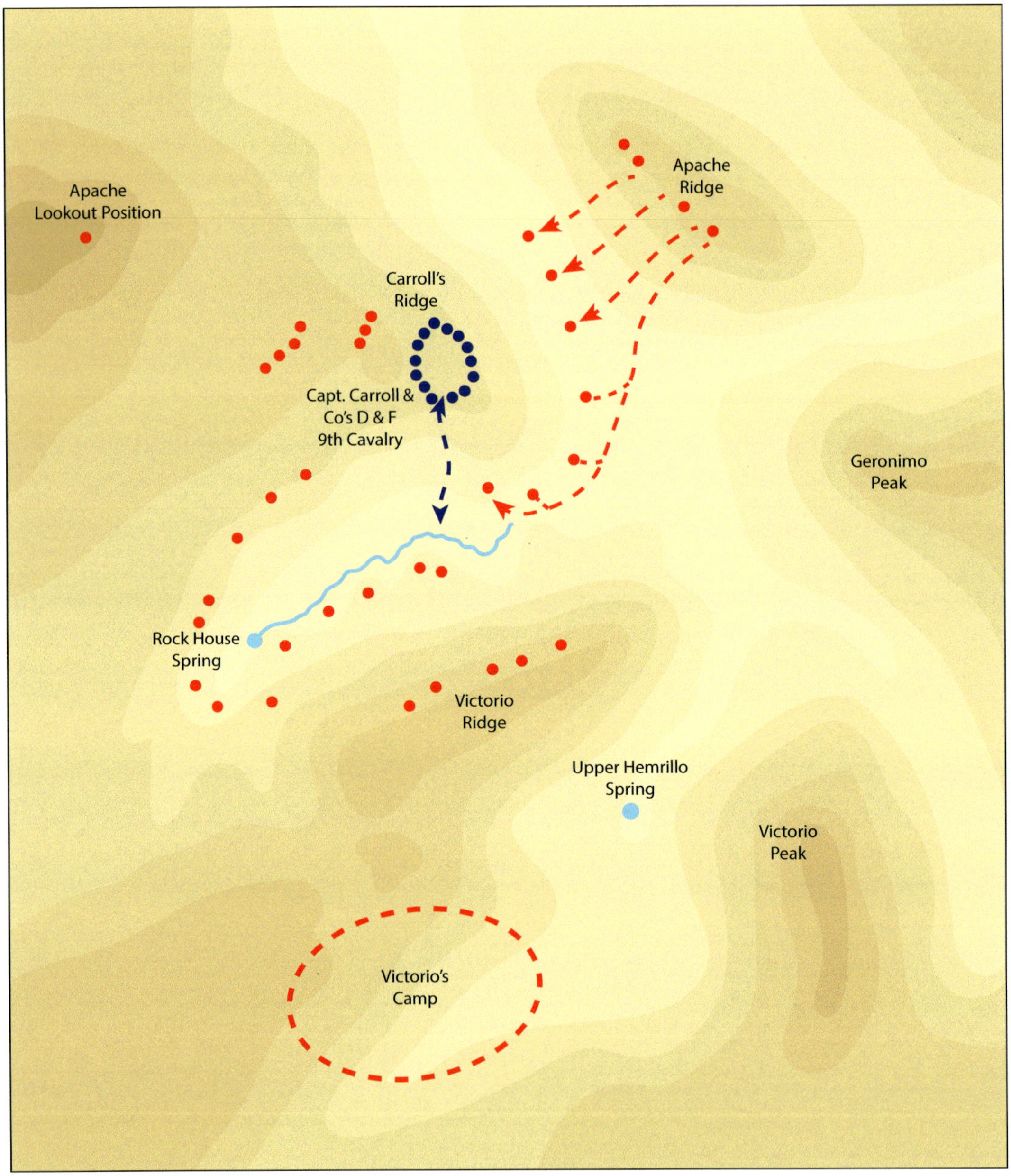

Map 5.5 Hembrillo Canyon Battle II, Night 6–7 April 1880.

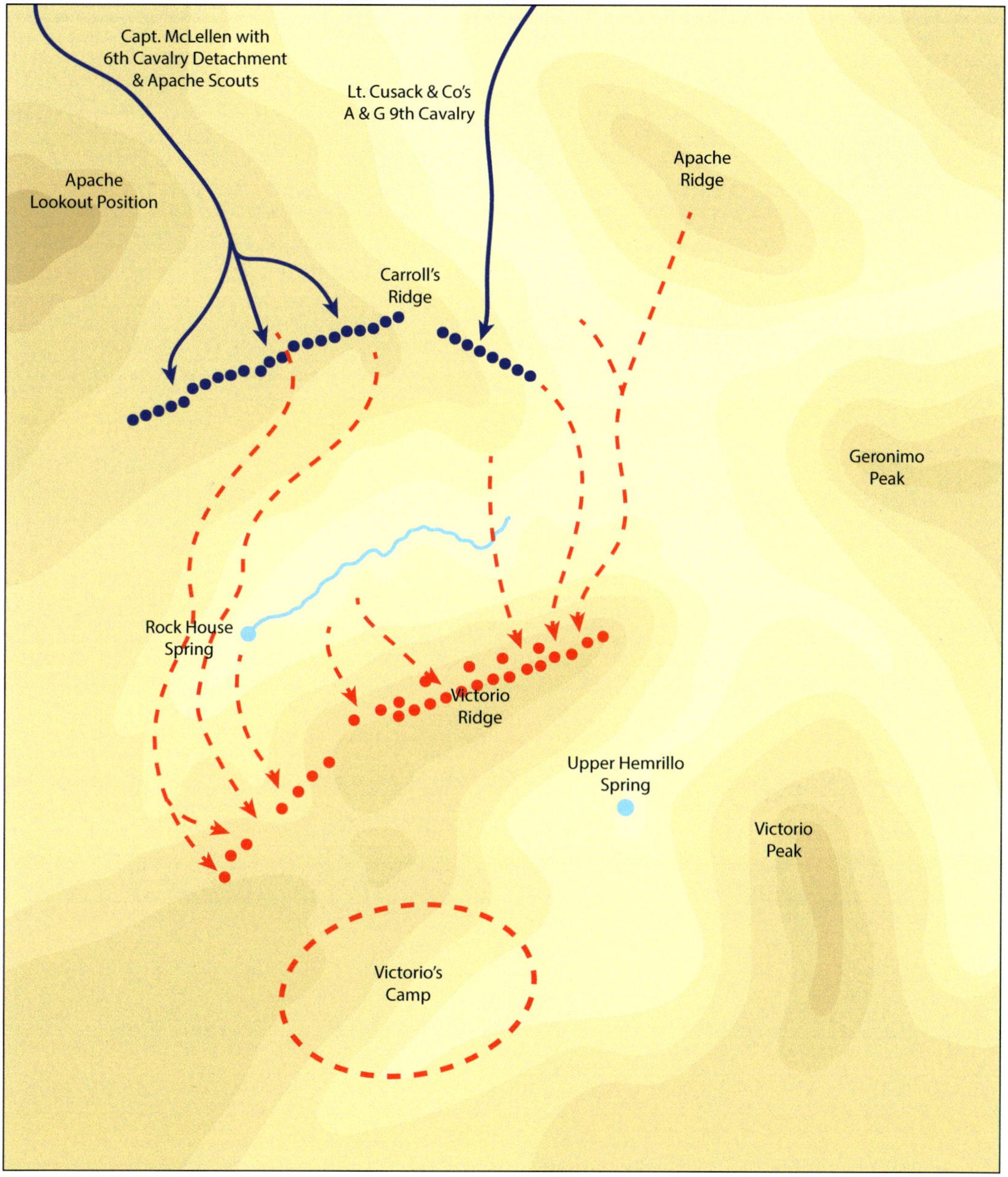

Map 5.6 Hembrillo Canyon Battle III, Early Morning 6-7 April 1880.

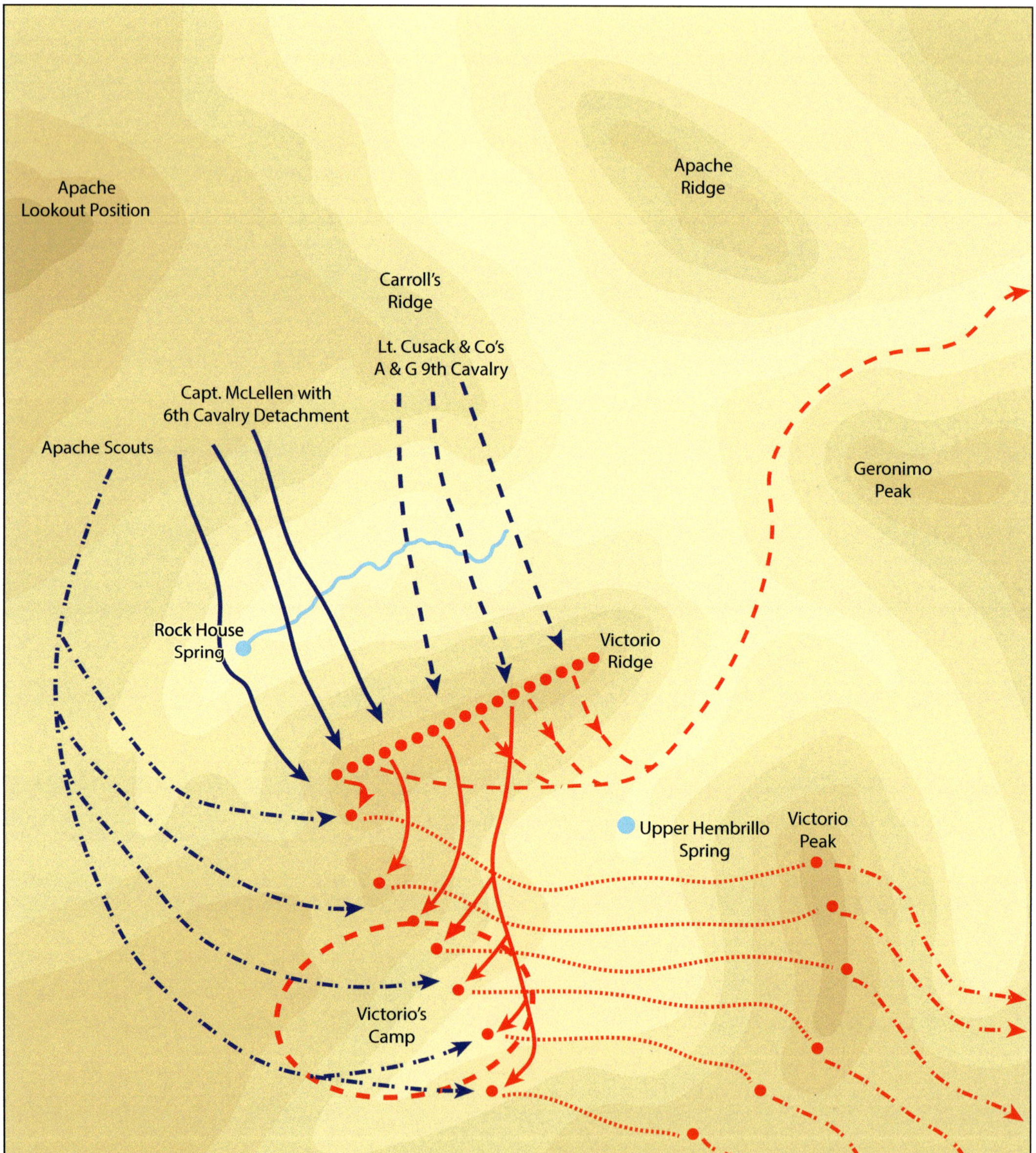

Map 5.7 Hembrillo Canyon Battle III, Early Morning 6-7 April 1880.

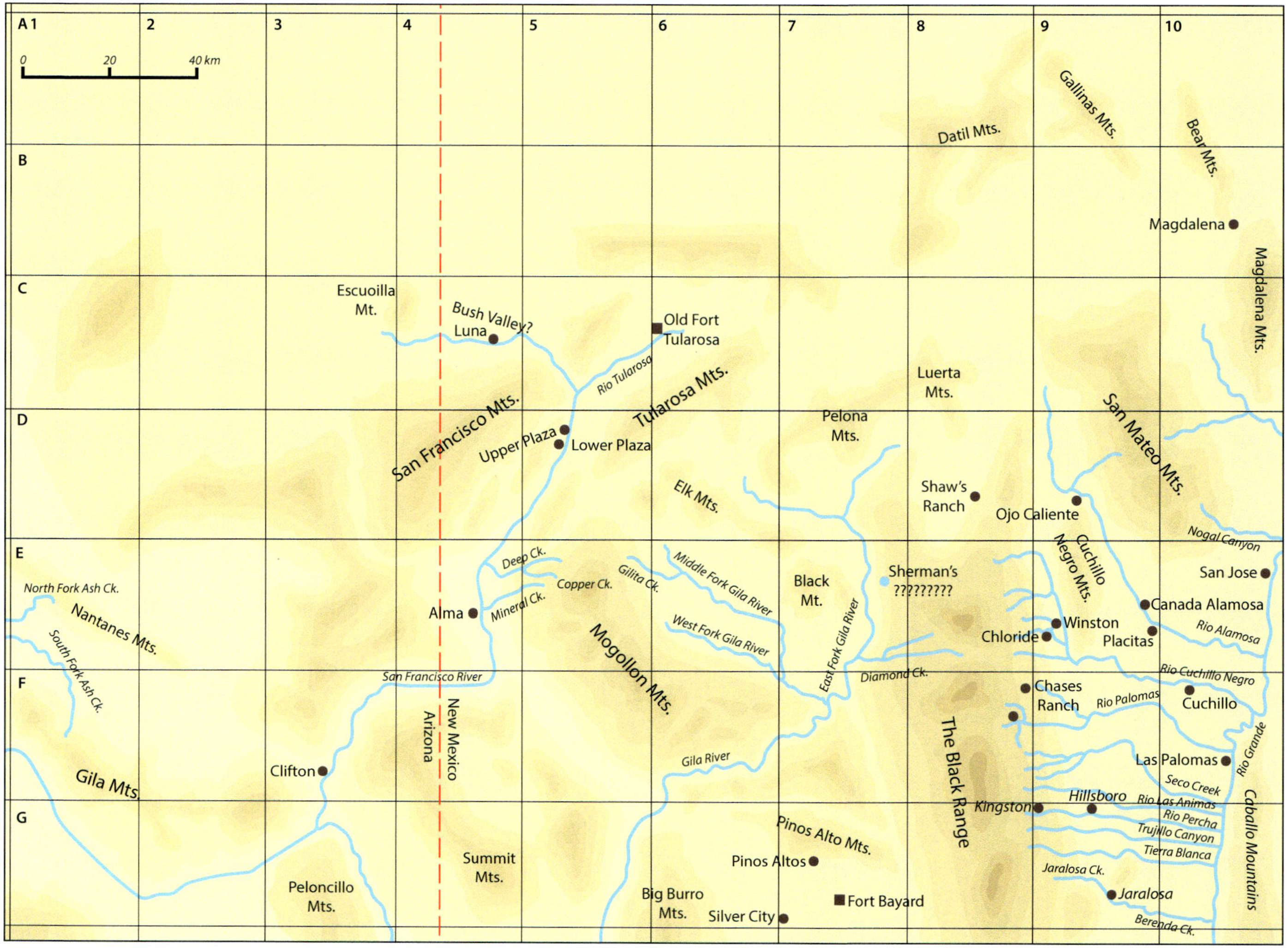

Map 7.1 Hatch's Campaign in the Mogollon Mountains, April–May 1880.

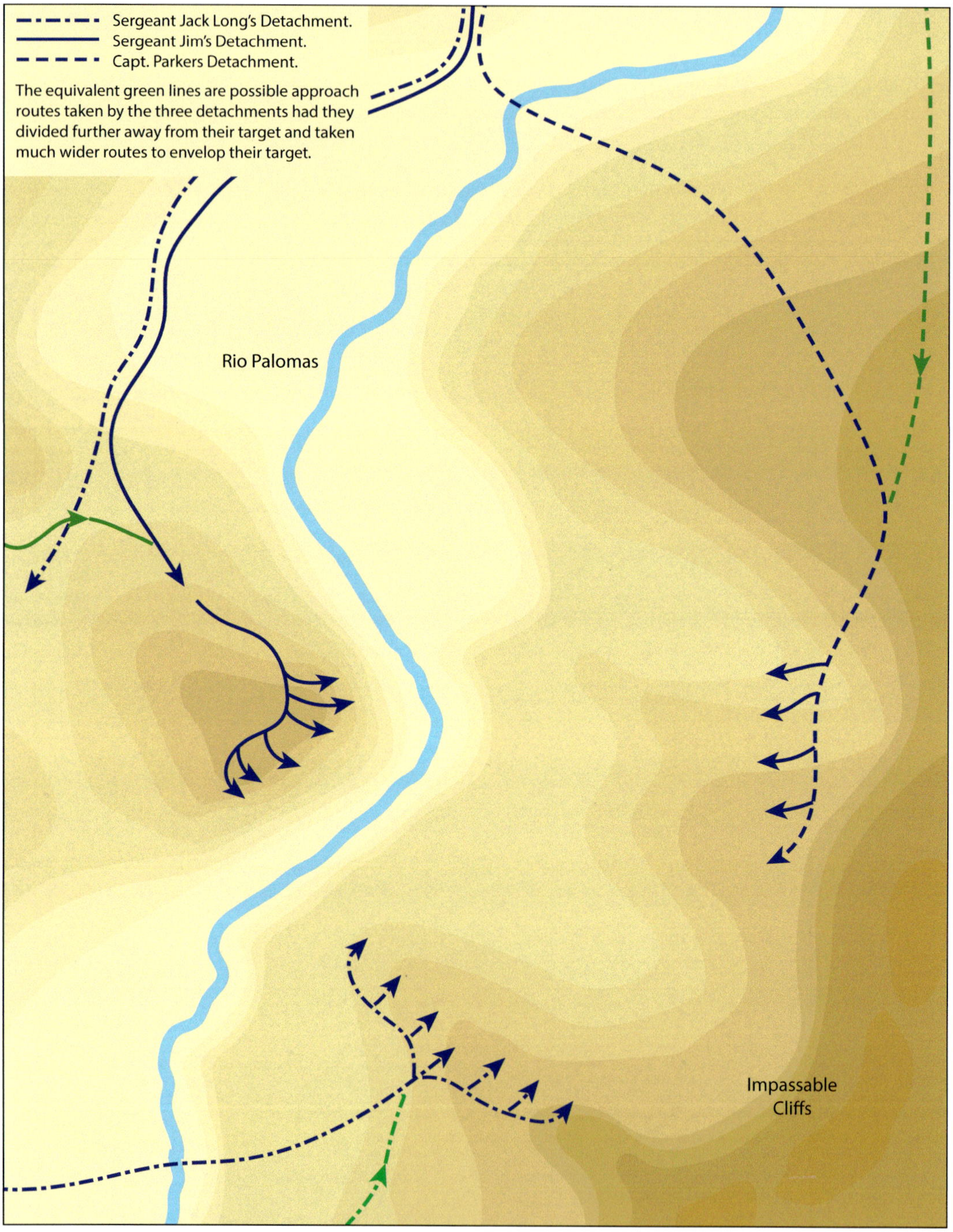

Map 8.1 Parker's Approach, Palomas River, 24 May 1880.

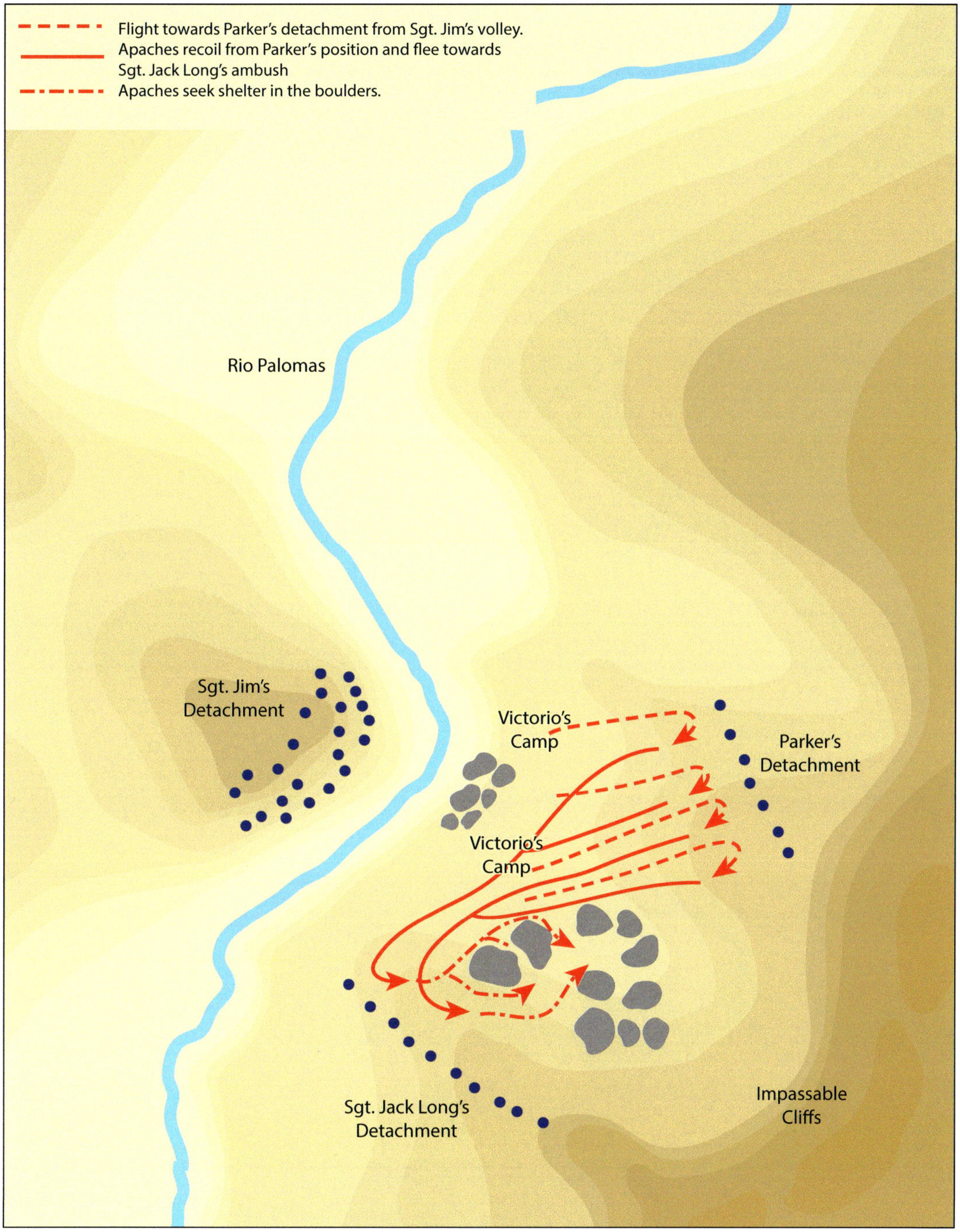

Map 8.2 Victorio Ambushed, Palomas River, 24 May 1880.

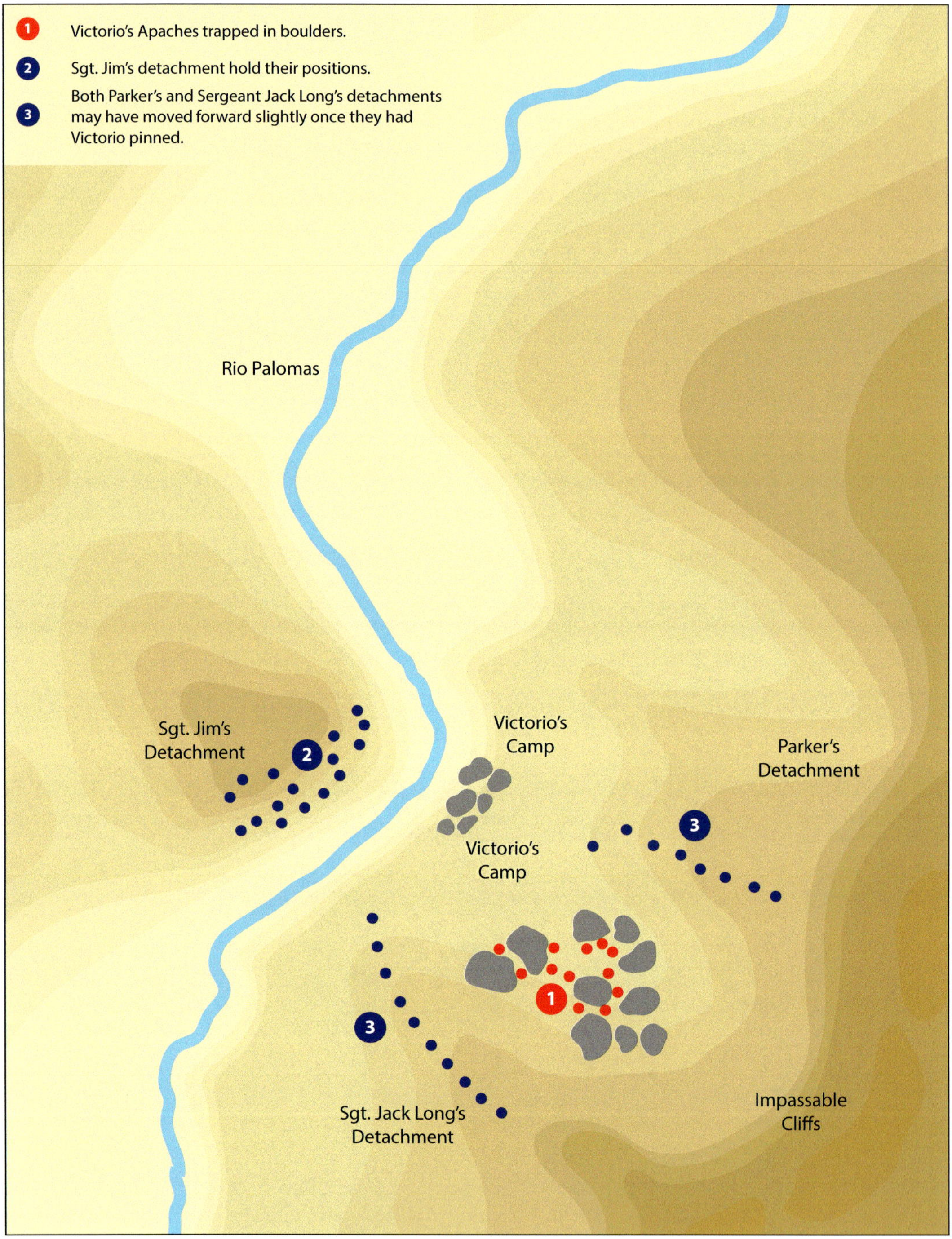

Map 8.3 Victorio Besieged, Palomas River, 24 May 1880.

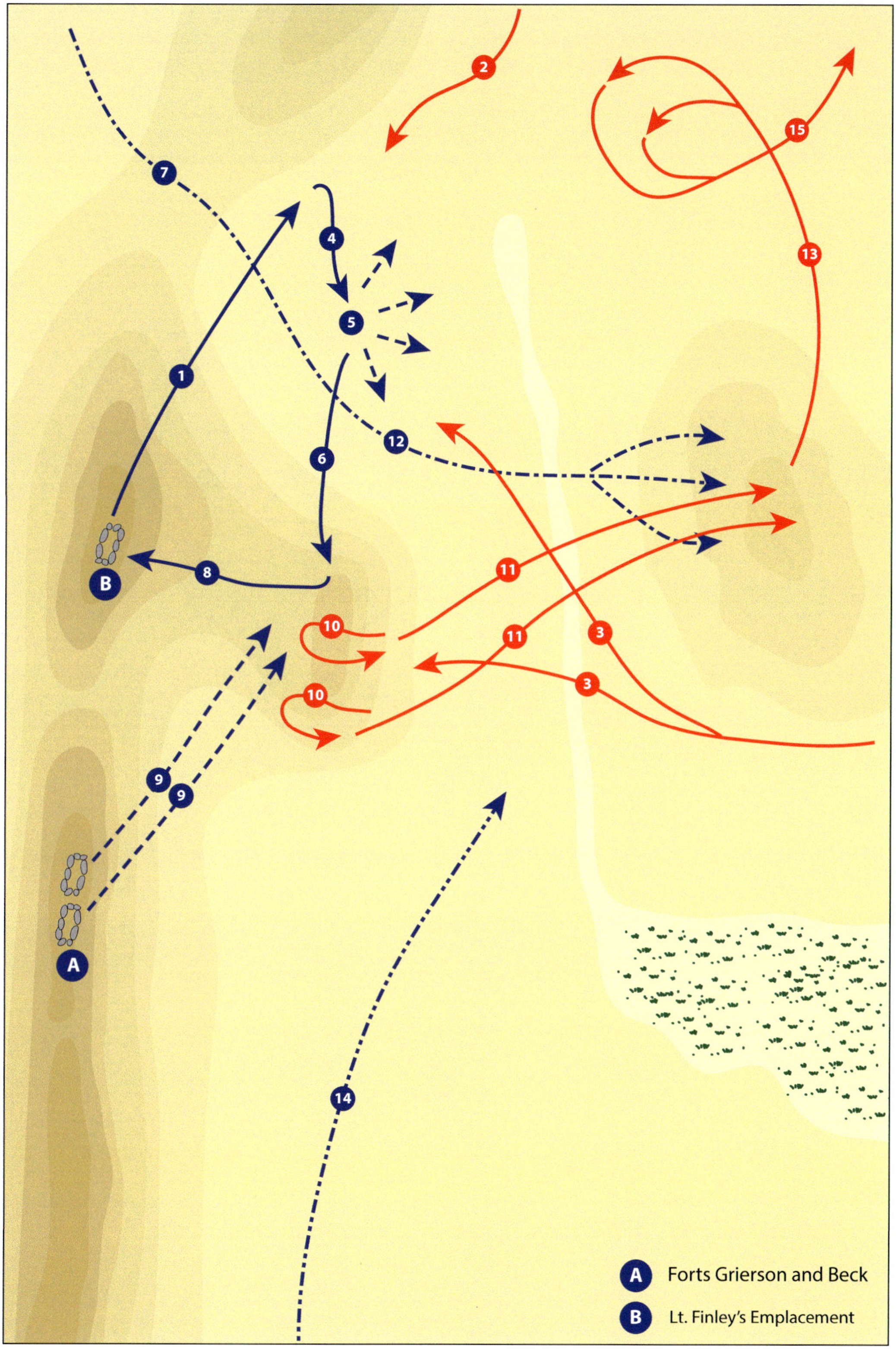

Map 10.1 Tinaja de las Palmas, 30 June 1880.

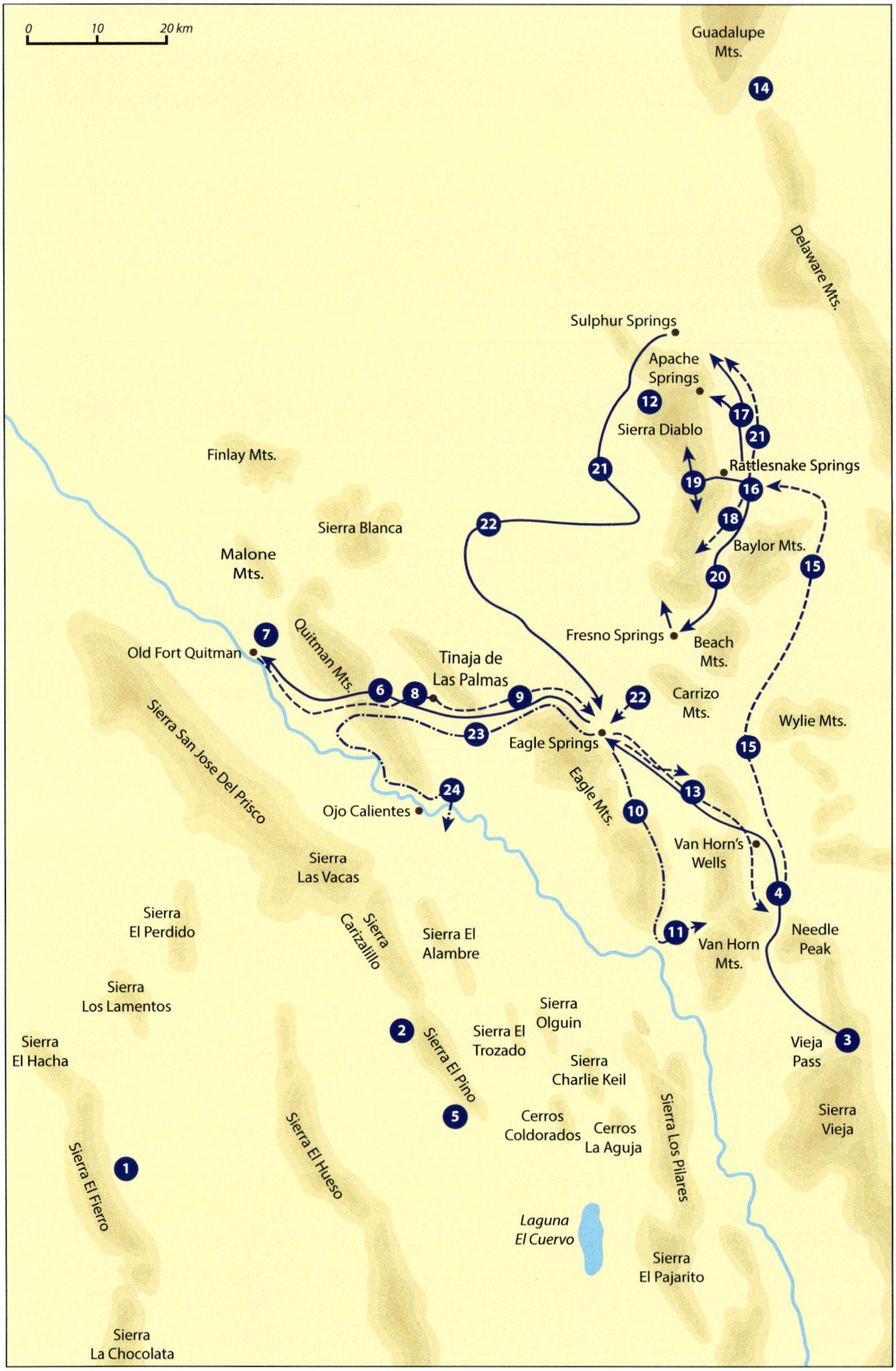

Map 11.1 Grierson's Campaign, July–August 1880.

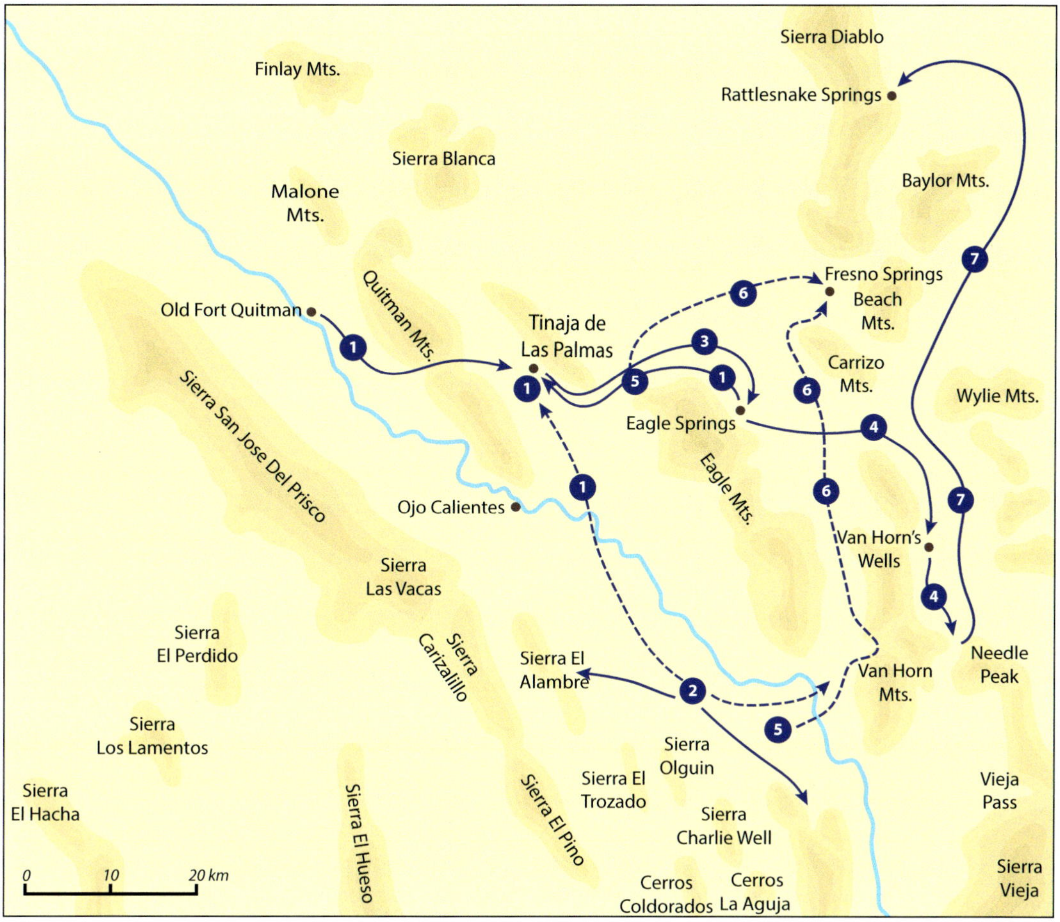

Map 11.2 Victorio's Decoy Strategy, Western Texas, July–August 1880.

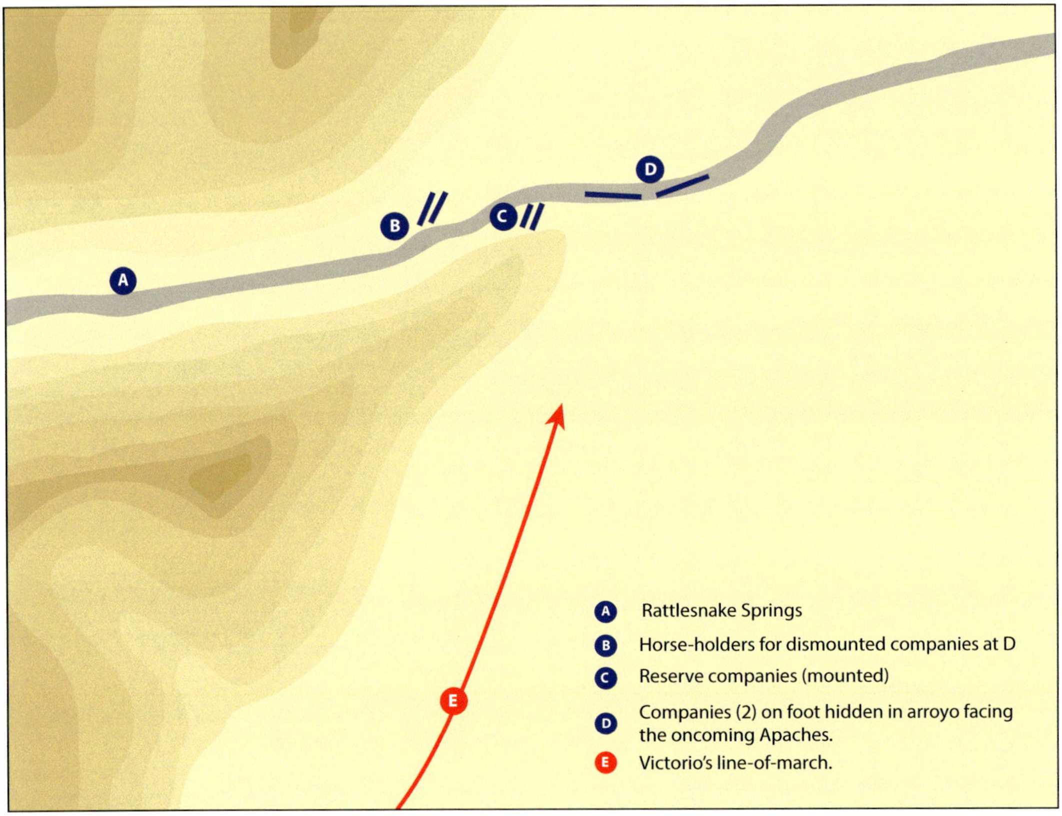

Map 11.3 Grierson's Plan to Ambush Victorio at Rattlesnake Springs, 6 August 1880.

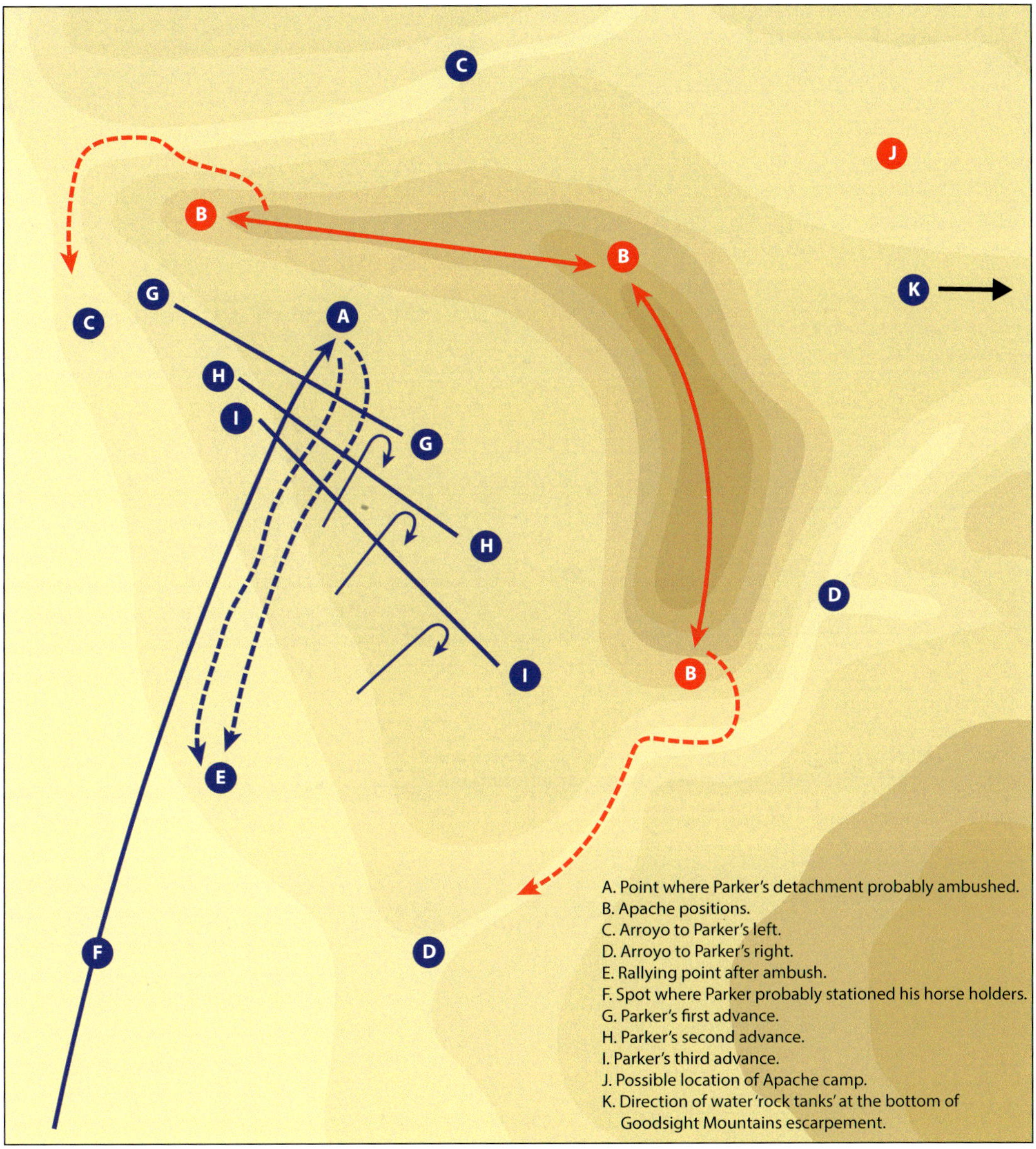

Map 14.1 Captain L.O. Parker's Fight, 7 September 1880.

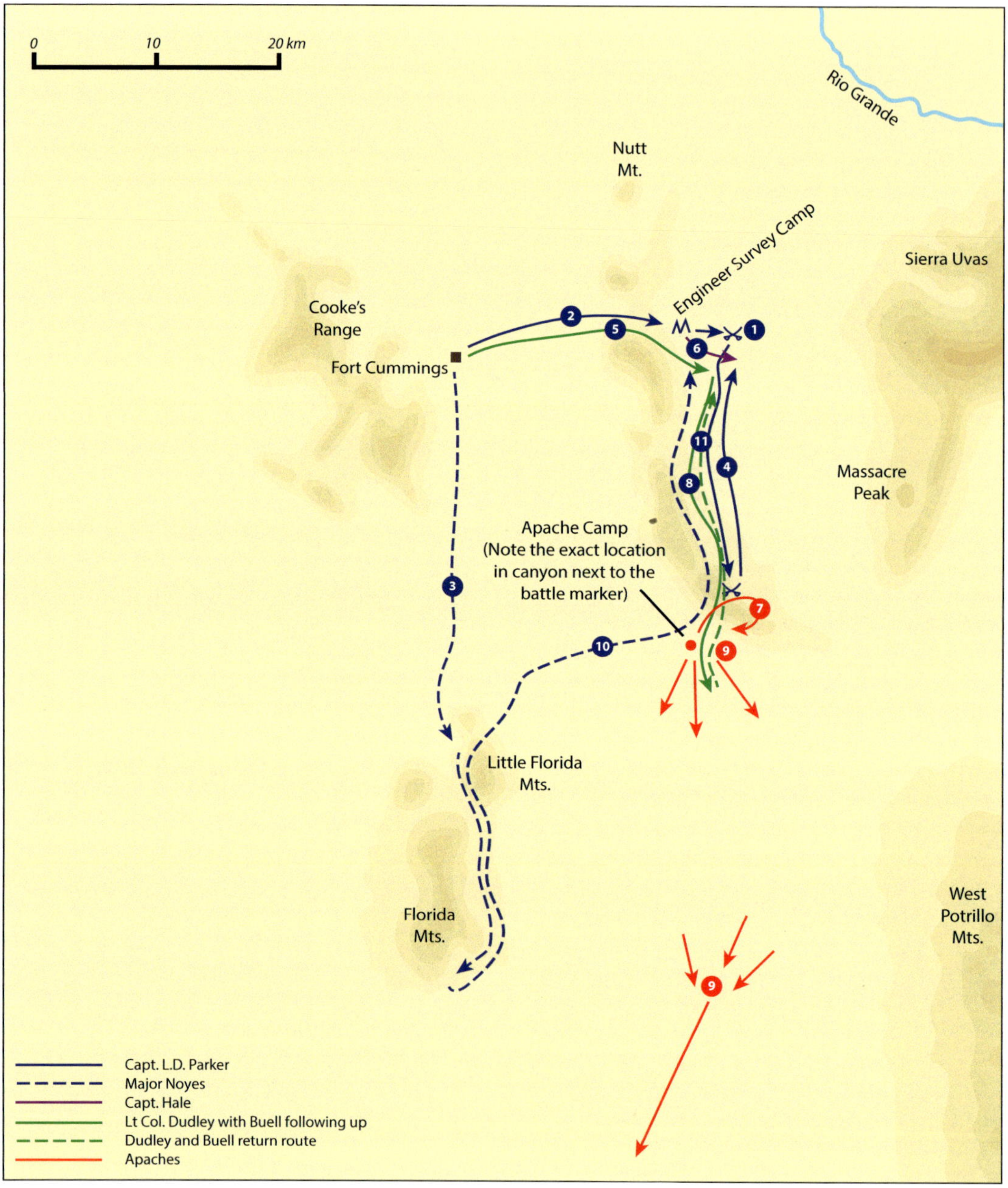

Map 14.2 Buell's Goodsight Mountain Expedition, September 1880.

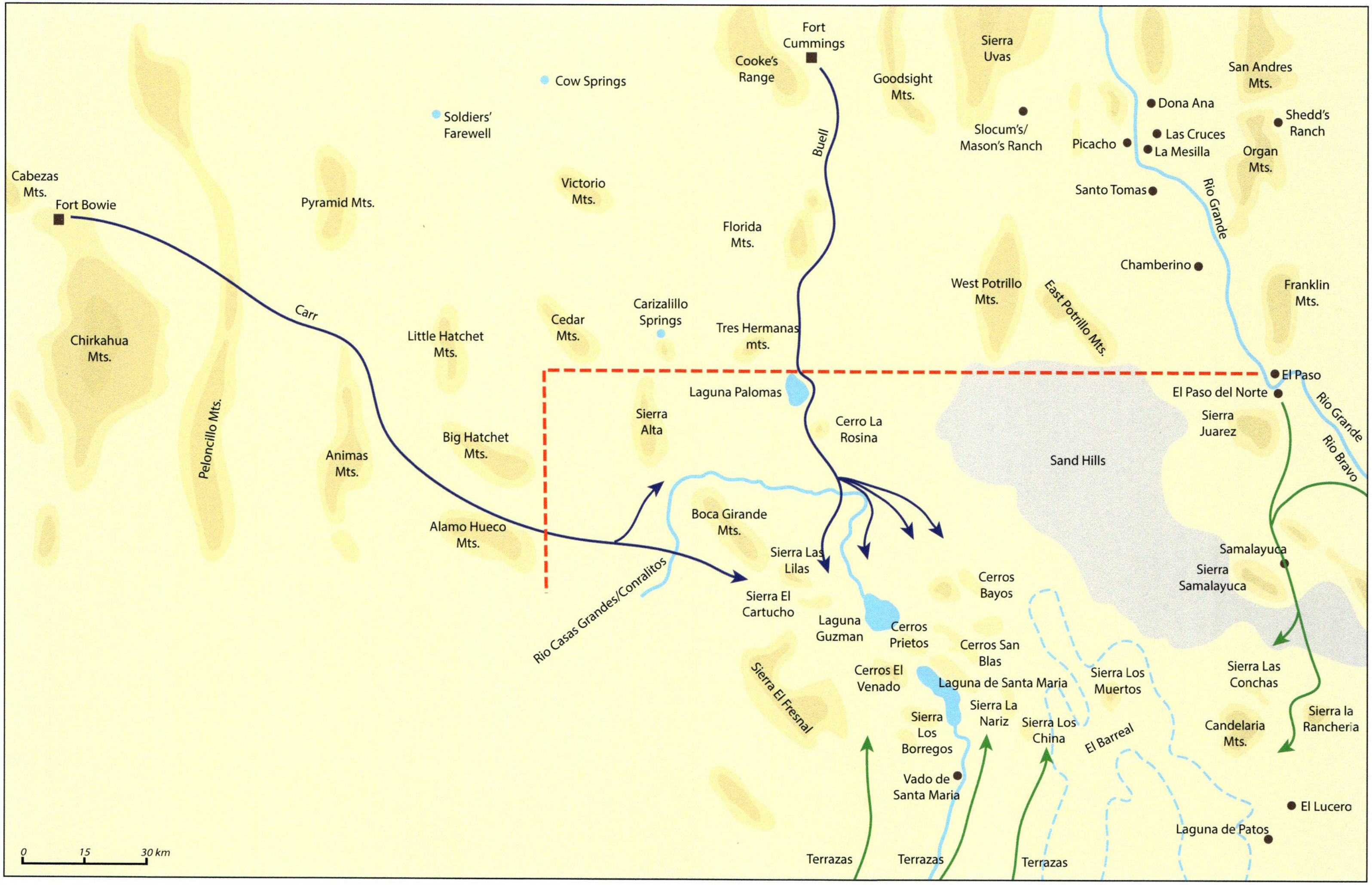

Map 15.1 Buell and Terrazas' Plan to Trap Victorio, September 1880.

Map 15.2 Buell and Terrazas Campaign against Victorio. Part 1: Terrazas' Campaign (Green Arrows) Part 2: Buell's Campaign (Blue Arrows).

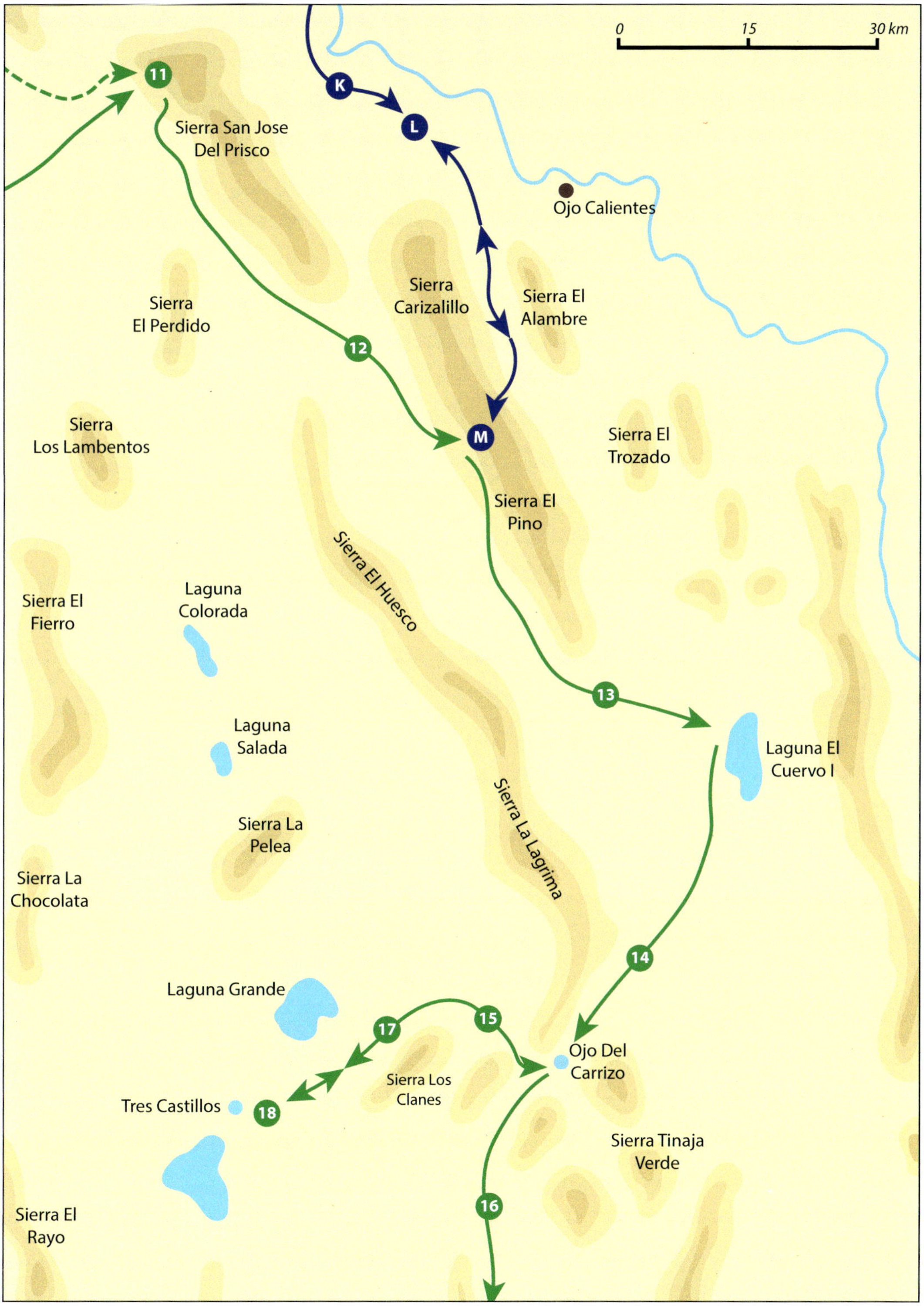

Map 16.1 Terrazas' Campaign, October 1880. Part 1: Terrazas' Campaign (Blue Arrows)
Part 2: Buell's Campaign (Blue Arrows).

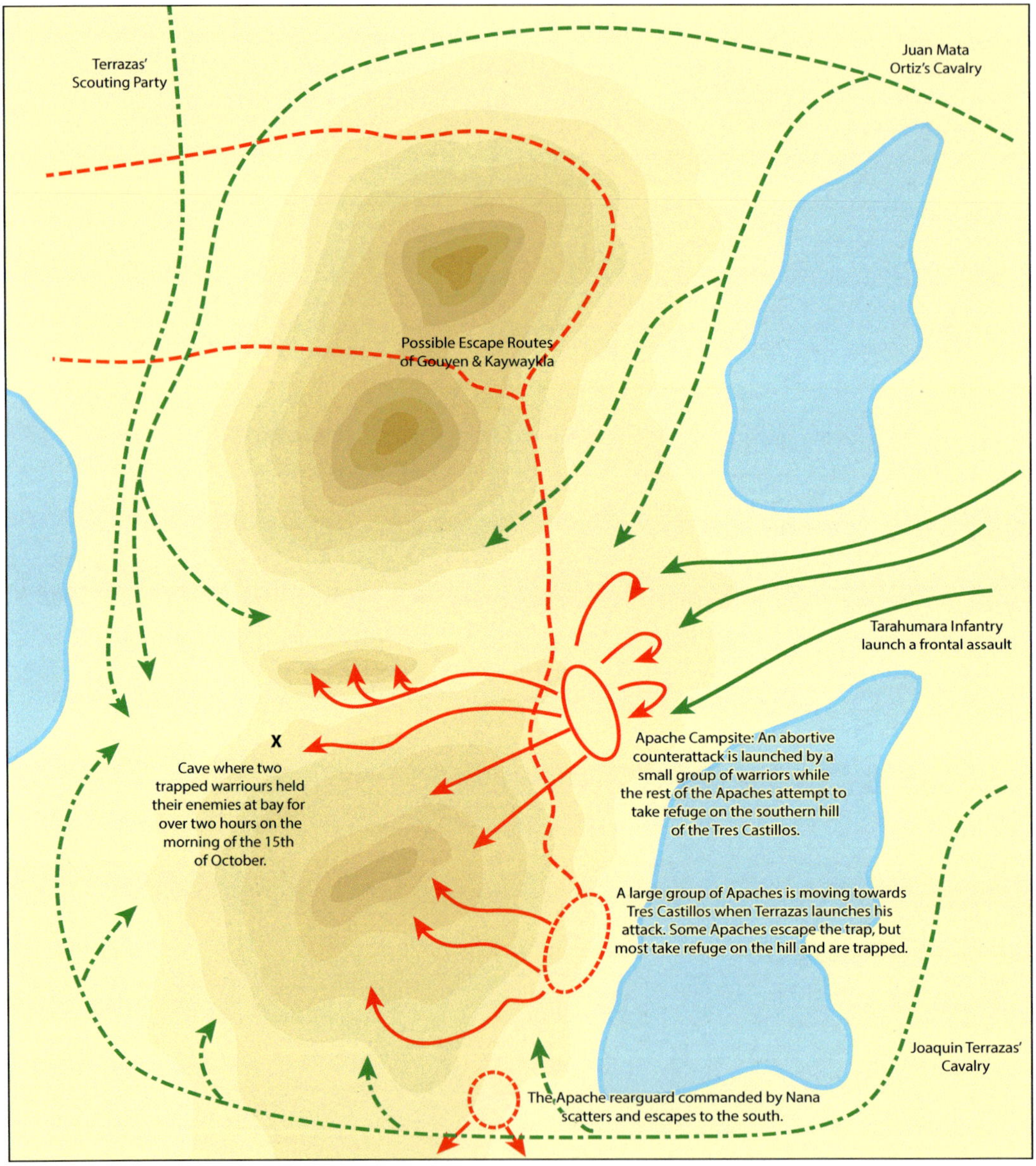

Map 16.2 Tres Castillos, 14–15 October 1880.

Table 9.1 Disposition of Companies of the Tenth Cavalry Regiment, 28 May 1880.[53]

Company	Location	Instructions
A	En route to District from Fort Sill	
B	Chinati [Chenati] Mountains	Scout surrounding countryside
C	Fort Davis	Recuperating but also scouting surrounding country
D	Grierson's Springs	Scout surrounding countryside
E	Fort Stockton	Recuperating but also scouting surrounding country
F	Black River Falls	Scout surrounding countryside
G	En route to District from Fort Sill	
H	Eagle Springs	Scout surrounding countryside
I	En route to District from Fort Sill	
K	Fort Davis	Recuperating but also scouting surrounding country
L	Near Guadalupe Peak	Scout surrounding countryside
M	Head of the North Concho River	Scout surrounding countryside

Grierson Mobilises His Forces[54]

Colonel Grierson set his command in motion in early July, despatching his troops to cover the known passes and waterholes in western Texas.[55] Captain Carpenter, already stationed at Eagle Springs, had earlier reported there was now very little water there. Near the end of June, two large trails were discovered, believed to be Apaches, passing though Viejo Pass. Carpenter was ordered to move his company to that point on 30 June 1880.[56] Lieutenant Mills and his detachment of Pueblo scouts remained stationed at Eagle Springs, as was H Company, Twenty-Fourth Infantry.[57] This would relieve the pressure on the levels of water at Eagle Springs, which Grierson intended to use as his field headquarters if the Apaches attempted to enter western Texas.

Grierson left Fort Concho on 10 July, with his teenage son Robert and a small escort detachment[58] of one NCO and three privates taken from Captain Keyes' company at Grierson's Spring,[59] which

53 Grierson to AAG, San Antonio, Texas, 28 May, 1880 in Telegrams Sent 24 Apr., 1879–22 Jun., 1880, HQ Records DoP 1878-1881, NA, RG393, M1381, Roll 1, pp.267-268, Letter No.173

54 See document file no. 87 for Grierson's overall report of his campaign against the Apaches in Western Texas in July & Aug. 1880 and Robert Grierson's and Lt. Leighton Finley's Diaries kept during this campaign.

55 Ord to CO, DoNM, 22 Jul., 1880, NA, RG393, Part 3, Entry 440, pp.32-33; 'Grierson's Report, Sept.1880'; NA, RG393, Part 1, Entry 2546, pp.639-644; Leckie, 1989, p.130; Matthews, 1993, pp.37-38.

56 in Register of Telegrams Rec'd 11 Oct., 1879-8 Oct., 1880, HQ Records DoP 1878-1881, NA, RG393, M1381, Roll 2, pp.172-173, Letter No.276.

57 Yard, fort Davis to AAAG, DoP, 30 Jun., 1880 in Telegrams Rec'd, 18 May, 1880-4 Feb., 1881,HQ Records DoP 1878-1881, NA, RG393, M1381, Roll 4; McChristian, 1982, p.50.

58 Robert Grierson's Diary, 10 Jul. to 1 Sept., 1880. Copy courtesy of the Fort Davis Museum Archives (hereafter referred to as 'Robert Grierson Diary'); Grierson to AAG, San Antonio, Texas, 8 Jul., 1880 in Telegrams Sent 23 Jun.-30 Nov., 1880, HQ Records DoP 1878-1881, NA, RG393, M1381, Roll 1, p.44, Letter No.295; Leckie, 1989, p.130; Matthews, 1993, p.38; Temple, 1957, p.49; Temple, 1959, p.101; McChristian, 1982, p.50; Haley, 1952, p.332.

59 Smither to Keyes, 9 Jul., 1880 in Telegrams Sent 23 Jun.-30 Nov., 1880, HQ Records DoP 1878-1881, NA, RG393, M1381, Roll 1, p.49, Letter No.304.

the Colonel passed through on the following day.[60] Grierson appointed First Lieutenent Smither as his acting adjutant general to relay information and instructions from Fort Concho. Second Lieutenant William H. Beck was appointed as Grierson's personal aide-de-camp and acting assistant adjutant general in the field.[61] Grierson was also accompanied by a telegraph operator named McCarthy.[62] In fact, Grierson has asked for the services of two telegraph operators. McCarthy was assigned to Grierson, whilst Charles Palmer was sent to set up a telegraph station at Old Fort Quitman.[63] At Old Fort Quitman, Palmer was provided with a small escort of infantrymen from Fort Davis.[64] The Colonel was quite clearly aware that it was not just guarding known waterholes passes that would enable him to successfully combat the sudden appearance of Apache raiders: the waterhole guard detachments were usually large enough to deny the use of these facilities to Apaches, but were not strong enough to decisively defeat them. He also needed to be in a position to concentrate his forces quickly enough to engage and defeat the Apaches.

Grierson travelled westwards visiting his detachments in the field. From Fort Concho, he visited Forts Stockton and Davis, arriving at the latter on 15 July 1880.[65] Following their experience of raids deep into the State of Chihuahua in June, the Mexicans informed the US authorities that between 400 and 500 troops under Colonel Adolfo[66] J. Valle intended to attack Victorio on or around 15 July 1880[67]. Colonel Valle also had permission to pursue the Warm Springs Apaches over the border into the United States.[68] (See document file no. 88.) This information was received

60 'Robert Grierson Diary'. See document file no. 87.2 this volume.

61 General Orders No. 3, 9 Jul., 1880 in General Orders, 28 Jan., 1878-7 Feb., 1881, HQ Records DoP 1878-1881, NA, RG393, M1381, Roll 5; 'Grierson's Report, Sept.1880'; NA, RG393, Part 1, Entry 2546, pp.639-644; See also Smither to CO, Fort Davis, 9 Jul., 1880 in Telegrams Sent 23 Jun.-30 Nov., 1880, HQ Records DoP 1878-1881, NA, RG393, M1381, Roll 1, p.48, Letter No.303.

62 McCarthy, a civilian operator was recorded as having arrived at Fort Concho on the 21 Jan., 1880 (Tingle to Grierson, 21 Jan., 1880 in Register of Telegrams Rec'd 11 Oct., 1879-8 Oct., 1880, HQ Records DoP 1878-1881, NA, RG393, M1381, Roll 2, p.72, Letter No.34).

63 McChristian, 1982, p.50; 'Grierson's Report, Sept.1880'; NA, RG393, Part 1, Entry 2546, pp.639-644; 'Robert Grierson Diary'; See also Smither to CO Fort Davis, 9 Jul., 1880 in Telegrams Sent 23 Jun.-30 Nov., 1880, HQ Records DoP 1878-1881, NA, RG393, M1381, Roll 1, p.49, Letter No.305; Grierson (Eagle Springs to Cols. Hatch and Buell 24 Jul., 1880, NA, RG393, Part 3, Entry 440, p.24; Ord to CO DoNM, SF, 22 Jul., 1880, NA, RG393, Part 3, Entry 440, p.33.

64 Grierson to CO, Fort Davis, 9 Jul., 1880 in Telegrams Sent 23 Jun.-30 Nov., 1880, HQ Records DoP 1878-1881, NA, RG393, M1381, Roll 1, p.49, Letter No.305.

65 'Robert Grierson Diary'; McChristian, 1982, p.51.

66 Referred to as 'Adolpho' in some US State Department correspondence.

67 Brinkerhoff to AAAG SF 14 Jul., 1880, NA, RG393, Part 3, Entry 439, p.539; Brinkerhoff Ft Bliss to AAAG SF, 15 Jul., 1880, NA, RG393, Part 3, Entry 439, pp.542-547; Hatch to AAG Fort Leavenworth, 14 Jul., 1880, Telegrams Sent DoNM, Vol.3, Jan.-Nov. 1880, NA, RG393, Part 3, Entry 431, p.611; Hatch to AAG Fort Leavenworth, 16 Jul., 1880 in 'Victorio Papers', NA, M666, Roll 527; Ord to CO, DoNM, 22 Jul., 1880, NA, RG393, Part 3, Entry 440, p.32; Sheridan to AG Washington D.C. 20 Jul., 1880, NA, RG393, Part 1, Entry 2539, Press Copies of Letters and Endorsements Sent, MDoM, Vol. 13, p.451; Ord to Pope, 22 Jul., 1880, NA, RG393, Part 1, Entry 2539, Press Copies of Letters and Endorsements Sent, MDoM, Vol. 13, pp.460-461; Pope to AAG HQ MDoM, 19 Jul., 1880, & Ord to AG Chicago, 21 Jul., 1880, 'Victorio Files', NA, RG393, M1495, Roll 14; the *Grant County Herald*, 31 Jul., 1880; 'Grierson's Report, Sept.1880'; NA, RG393, Part 1, Entry 2546, pp.639-644.

68 Brinkerhoff to CO, Fort Davis, 15 Jul., 1880 in Telegrams Rec'd by General Grierson in the Field 30 Jun.-14 Sept., 1880 HQ Records DoP 1878-1881, NA, RG393, M1381, Roll 4; Ord to CO, DoNM, 22 Jul., 1880, NA, RG393, Part 3, Entry 440, p.32; Hatch to AAG Fort Leavenworth, 17 Jul., 1880, Telegrams Sent DoNM, Vol.3, Jan.-Nov. 1880, NA, RG393, Part 3, Entry 431, p.629; Sheridan to AG, Washington D.C. 20 Jul., 1880, NA, RG393, Part 1, Entry 2539, Press Copies of Letters and Endorsements Sent, MDoM, Vol. 13, p.451; Ord to Pope, 22 Jul., 1880, NA, RG393, Part 1, Entry 2539, Press Copies of Letters and Endorsements Sent, MDoM, Vol. 13, pp.460-461; Carr to AG DoAz,

at Fort Bliss on 15 July, and passed to both Colonel Hatch and General Ord.[69] Grierson received this information on 18 July, and he promptly sent word to Valle of his troop deployments and of his 'hearty cooperation.'[70]

When General Trevino had taken to the field against Victorio in December 1879, Grierson had been instructed to maintain communication with the Mexican authorities through Dr Mariano Samaniego.[71] Grierson had immediately contacted Samaniego and informed him that the troops based at Forts Stockton and Davis had been instructed to cooperate with Mexican troops and repulse any attempt by the Apaches to cross into Mexico. This would be accomplished by communicating any news concerning the latter to General Trevino via Dr Samaniego.[72] As the historian Bruce J. Dinges points out, the key problem was the slow and unreliable transmission of such information.[73] It took 10 days for General Trevino to respond to Grierson's telegram of 16 December 1879. The information that Trevino's local field commander was Colonel Ponciano Cisneros, 'who had instructions to enter into communication with you' via Dr Samaniego, was not received by Grierson until 4 January 1880.[74] Both Hatch and Grierson maintained this link with Dr Samaniego via the offices of Captain Brinkerhoff, then commanding Fort Bliss, which lay in close proximity to both El Paso and El Paso del Norte.

This unreliable conduit of communication was still the only one available to the US and Mexican forces, and would be utilised to coordinate the movements of Grierson's force with that of the Mexican forces about to move against Victorio in July 1880.[75] In January, Victorio had not elected to cross the border into Texas, thus the problems in communication between Grierson and the Mexican forces had not had any effect upon Morrow's campaign against the Apaches. All the indications in July were that, if Victorio did move into the USA, it would be to cross the Rio Grande into western Texas. The delays in communicating information between the two forces did not bode well for their chances of defeating Victorio should he attempt to cross the border.

Valle's plan was to march the majority of his force (200 cavalry and 120 infantry) directly to the village of Guadalupe on the Rio Grande and close to El Paso Del Norte. Another force of 120 cavalry was to follow Victorio's trail which, at that point, led in the direction of the Sierra del Fierro.[76] Valle intended place a strong force near the Rio Grande in readiness to catch the Apaches as they crossed the river. To ensure that he struck at the right time and place, he had sent the

---

21 Jul., 1880, Troops in SE Arizona, DoAz, NA, RG393, Part 1, Entry 232, Vol.7, 18 May, 1880 – 6 Sept., 1880, p.26; Thrapp, 1974, p.286; Thrapp, 1967, p.204; Stout, 1974, p.152.

69 Brinkerhoff Ft Bliss to AAAG SF 15 Jul., 1880, NA, RG393, Part 3, Entry 439, pp.542-547; See also Pollack Capt. 9th Infantry, AAAG, SF to Col. Buell, CO Fort Cummings, 17 Jul., 1880, Telegrams Sent DoNM, Vol.3, Jan.-Nov. 1880, NA, RG393, Part 3, Entry 431, pp.621-623; See also Ord to AG Chicago, 21 Jul., 1880, 'Victorio Files', NA, RG393, M1495, Roll 14.

70 Grierson to AAG, San Antonio, 20 Jul., 1880 in Telegrams Sent 23 Jun.-30 Nov., 1880, HQ Records DoP 1878-1881, NA, RG393, M1381, Roll 1, pp.63-64, Letter No.330.

71 Vincent, AAG, DoTx to District Commander, Fort Concho, 11 Dec., 1879 in Register of Telegrams Rec'd 11 Oct., 1879-8 Oct., 1880, HQ Records DoP 1878-1881, NA, RG393, M1381, Roll 2, p.43, Letter No.73; Smither to CO's, Fort Davis & Stockton, 16 Dec., 1879 in Telegrams Sent 24 Apr., 1879-22 Jun., 1880, HQ Records DoP 1878-1881, NA, RG393, M1381, Roll 1, pp.135-137, Letter No.'s 290 & 291.

72 Grierson to Samaniego, 16 Dec., 1879 in Telegrams Sent 24 Apr., 1879-22 Jun., 1880, HQ Records DoP 1878-1881, NA, RG393, M1381, Roll 1, pp.137-138, Letter No.292.

73 Dinges, 1987, p.85.

74 Grierson to AAG, San Antonio, Texas, 4 Jan., 1880 in Telegrams Sent 24 Apr., 1879-22 Jun., 1880, HQ Records DoP 1878-1881, NA, RG393, M1381, Roll 1, pp.161-162, Letter No.4.

75 Ord to Pope, 22 Jul., 1880, NA, RG393, Part 1, Entry 2539, Press Copies of Letters and Endorsements Sent, MDoM, Vol. 13, pp.460-461.

76 Brinkerhoff Ft Bliss to AAAG SF 15 Jul., 1880, NA, RG393, Part 3, Entry 439, pp.542-547; See also Pollack Capt. 9th Infantry, AAAG, SF to Col. Buell, CO Fort Cummings, 17 Jul., 1880, Telegrams

Captain Brinkerhoff (bearded officer, middle row, extreme right) As CO Fort Bliss he played a pivotal role as a conduit of information between US field commanders and their Mexican federal and state counterparts in their efforts to combat Victorio on both sides of the border during 1880. Captain Bean, CO Fort Craig, who reported indiscipline amongst some telegraph operators in the last chapter can be seen sitting front row second from the left. (Carlisle Barracks)

120 cavalrymen to follow their trail. This unit would keep Valle informed of the movements of the Apaches by courier to alert him when the time was ripe to attack with his main force. In the meantime, Valle seems to have adopted a similar strategy to Grierson's in picketing known water holes along the border:

> Colonel Valle writes doctor Samaniego July 18th that the Indians are still in the state [of Chihuahua] but ????ing that he had sent troops to intercept them to Tinaja De Victorio to El boracho to El Nino & to El Cerrizeilillo? Col Valle's head qrs will be at the tanks for the present I have requested him to transmit information of his movements & those of the Indians if deemed advisable couriers can be employed here.[77]

As a result of this information, Grierson ordered Lieutenant Mills[78] to deploy his Pueblo scouts along the Rio Grande to provide as early a warning as possible of any incursion.[79] Grierson also warned his field detachments at Viejo Pass, Eagle Springs, Chenati Mountains and the Guadalupe

Sent DoNM, Vol.3, Jan.-Nov. 1880, NA, RG393, Part 3, Entry 431, pp.621-623; See also Ord to AG Chicago, 21 Jul., 1880, 'Victorio Files', NA, RG393, M1495, Roll 14.

77 Brinkerhoff to AAAG SF 19 Jul., 1880, NA, RG393, Part 3, Entry 439, pp.540-541.

78 Lt. Mills appears to be conspicuously absent from the record of Grierson's campaign against Victorio. The reason for this is that the unfortunate Mills fell sick from 'agne' at Eagle Springs and was evacuated to Fort Davis on the 4 Aug., 1880 (Robert Grierson's Diary, 4 Aug., 1880. Copy courtesy of the Fort Davis Museum Archives).

79 Ord to AG Chicago, 24 Jul., 1880, 'Victorio Files', NA, RG393, M1495, Roll 14; 'Grierson's Report, Sept.1880'; NA, RG393, Part 1, Entry 2546, pp.639-644; Rister, 1928, p.208; McChristian, 1982, p.51.

Mountains of these developments. He finally informed Captain Brinkerhoff that Grierson would reach Eagle Springs or Quitman on or around 22 July 1880.[80]

On 21 July, Grierson received a telegram from Colonel Buell informing him that the latter had taken over command of troops in the field against Victorio in New Mexico. Buell asked that Grierson keep him posted concerning any information concerning Victorio and promised to do the same in return.[81]

Additional troops arrived from Fort Sill (A, G and I Companies, Tenth Cavalry) on 17 June 1880, under the command of Captain Nicholas Nolan. Grierson found them to be ill-prepared for the coming campaign, being poorly mounted, equipped and provisioned. He submitted an urgent request for 180 improved Springfield carbines with their associated equipment.[82] Nevertheless on 20 July, before the equipment arrived, these troops were sent into the field, leaving for El Muerto. The following day, Grierson with K Company, left Fort Davis and joined them that night.[83] Grierson also contacted headquarters, Department of Texas, to remind them that the Tenth Cavalry urgently required 100 cavalry mounts and 60 pack mules.[84] The pack mules were particularly required as Grierson wanted to attach them to scouting detachments, as wagons were clearly unable to traverse the terrain.[85]

By 24 July, Grierson received word that no additional horses were to be assigned to the regiment and he issued instructions that every effort be made to ensure that broken-down horses should be allowed to recover rather than being deemed unserviceable.[86] On 1 August 1880, Grierson contacted General Ord to remind him of his own earlier request for 100 additional horses.[87] Once again, budgetary constraints were cited and Sherman informed Sheridan that out of the overall appropriation of $200,000 for remounts, the Division of the Missouri had already received $116,000, and that any further expenditure would have to be taken from the Division of the Pacific's allowance. Sherman concluded that this was 'hardly fair' and suggested[88] that additional remounts for the Department of Texas be diverted from the Department of the Platte.[89] (See document file no. 89.)

It was on 21 July 1880 that Grierson deployed his battalion to meet Victorio should he cross the border. Captain Lebo was sent to occupy Fresno Springs in the Carizzo Mountains[90] and to scout from that point, with a view to denying passage through that section of the country to the

80 Grierson to CO Fort Bliss, 18 Jul., 1880 in Letters Sent 19 Sept., 1879-11 Aug., 1880, HQ Records DoP 1878-1881, NA, RG393, M1381, Roll 1, Letter No.108.

81 Buell (through Capt. Brinkerhoff) to Grierson, 21 Jul., 1880 in Telegrams Rec'd by General Grierson in the Field 30 Jun.-14 Sept., 1880 HQ Records DoP 1878-1881, NA, RG393, M1381, Roll 4.

82 Grierson to AAG, San Antonio, Texas, 26 Jun., 1880 in Telegrams Sent 23 Jun.-30 Nov., 1880, HQ Records DoP 1878-1881, NA, RG393, M1381, Roll 1, pp.21-22, Letter No.253.

83 'Robert Grierson Diary'.

84 Grierson to AAG, San Antonio, 20 Jul., 1880 in Telegrams Sent 23 Jun.-30 Nov., 1880, HQ Records DoP 1878-1881, NA, RG393, M1381, Roll 1, pp.63-64, Letter No.330.

85 Grierson to AAG, San Antonio, 22 Jul., 1880 in Telegrams Sent 23 Jun.-30 Nov., 1880, HQ Records DoP 1878-1881, NA, RG393, M1381, Roll 1, p.65, Letter No.333.

86 Beck to Maj. Mills, Fort Concho, 24 Jul., 1880 in Telegrams Sent 23 Jun.-30 Nov., 1880, HQ Records DoP 1878-1881, NA, RG393, M1381, Roll 1, p.72, Letter No.345.

87 Grierson to AAG, DoTx, 1 Aug., 1880 in Telegrams Sent 23 Jun.-30 Nov., 1880, HQ Records DoP 1878-1881, NA, RG393, M1381, Roll 1, pp.94-95, Letter No.376; Ord to AG, Chicago, Ills. 4 Aug., 1880, NA, RG393, Part 1, Entry 2546, p.568 & 572.

88 One suspects that a suggestion from General Sherman should be interpreted as an instruction.

89 Sherman to Sheridan 9 Aug., 1880, NA, RG393, Part 1, Entry 2546, pp.569-570 & 571.

90 The location of the Springs as being in the Carrizo Mountains is given in Grierson to AAG, San Antonio TX., 14 Jun. 1878 in Telegrams Sent 29 Jan., 1878-21 Apr., 1879, HQ Records DoP 1878-1881, NA, RG393, M1381, Roll 1, p.48.

Plates 9.3 and 9.4 Two shots of Fort Davis, Texas. (Photos: Author)

Apaches.[91] Captain Nolan, with A Company, Tenth Cavalry, was ordered to proceed via Eagle Springs to Old Fort Quitman.[92] Captain Baldwin, with I Company, was directed to march his company to Viejo Pass, while Lieutenant R.S. Colladay was instructed to march G Company, Tenth Cavalry, to Eagle Springs.[93] Three days later, Captain Viele, with C Company, was ordered to proceed from Fort Davis to El Muerto and there to await further orders as to their deployment.[94]

From El Muerto, Grierson proceeded to Captain Carpenter's picket in the Viejo Pass and then proceeded to Eagle Springs, arriving on 23 July.[95] Captain Carpenter was ordered to remain at Viejo Pass and patrol the Rio Grande between the Capote Mountains and Eagle Springs. Carpenter was also ordered to pursue and attack Victorio with vigour, should the Apache leader cross the Rio Grande between these points.[96] Lieutenant Jones, commanding B Company, Tenth Cavalry, was ordered to move from his station in the Chenati Mountains to join Carpenter at Viejo Pass.[97] Grierson also sent word to Colonel Valle that:

> Have established telegraph office at Quitman and have an operator with me at this point. I would be glad to keep up communication with United States and Mexican troops and will thank you for any information you may be able to furnish me relative to the movements and whereabouts of the hostile Indians. Will be pleased to have you forward telegrams to Bliss any communications you may wish to send to Chihuahua, or elsewhere.[98]

When Grierson arrived at Eagle Springs, he received reports that, on 21 July, Valle and Victorio had clashed in the Sierra de Los Pinos. Six Mexican soldiers were killed at Ojo del Pino.[99] The

---

91 Beck to Lebo, 21 Jul., 1880 in Letters Sent 19 Sept., 1879-11 Aug., 1880, HQ Records DoP 1878-1881, NA, RG393, M1381, Roll 1, Letter No.116; See also 'Grierson's Report, Sept.1880'; NA, RG393, Part 1, Entry 2546, pp.639-644; McChristian, 1982, p.52; Leckie & Leckie, p.261.

92 Beck to Nolan, 21 Jul., 1880 in Letters Sent 19 Sept., 1879-11 Aug., 1880, HQ Records DoP 1878-1881, NA, RG393, M1381, Roll 1, Letter No.117; See also 'Grierson's Report, Sept.1880'; NA, RG393, Part 1, Entry 2546, pp.639-644; McChristian, 1982, p.52; Leckie & Leckie, p.261.

93 Beck to Baldwin & Colladay, 21 Jul., 1880 in Letters Sent 19 Sept., 1879-11 Aug., 1880, HQ Records DoP 1878-1881, NA, RG393, M1381, Roll 1Letter No.'s 118 & 119; See also 'Grierson's Report, Sept.1880'; NA, RG393, Part 1, Entry 2546, pp.639-644; Tabular Statement showing Stations, Positions and Movements of Troops operating against Victorio and his hostile Indians, in the DoP, from 1 Jul., 1880 to Sept. 20 1880 in Letters Sent 23 Aug. -31 Dec., 1880, HQ Records DoP 1878-1881, NA, RG393, M1381, Roll 1, McChristian, 1982, p.52.

94 Beck to CO Fort Davis, 24 Jul., 1880 in Telegrams Sent 23 Jun.-30 Nov., 1880, HQ Records DoP 1878-1881, NA, RG393, M1381, Roll 1, p.68, Letter No.337.

95 'Grierson's Report, Sept.1880'; NA, RG393, Part 1, Entry 2546, pp.639-644; 'Robert Grierson Diary'; Temple, 1959, p.101; Matthews, 1993, p.38.

96 Beck to Carpenter 22 & 23 Jul., 1880 in Letters Sent 19 Sept., 1879-11 Aug., 1880, HQ Records DoP 1878-1881, NA, RG393, M1381, Roll 1, Letter No. 120 & 121.

97 Beck to Jones, 23 Jul., 1880 in Letters Sent 19 Sept., 1879-11 Aug., 1880, HQ Records DoP 1878-1881, NA, RG393, M1381, Roll 1, Letter No,122; Beck to CO, Fort Davis, 23 Jul., 1880 in Telegrams Sent 23 Jun.-30 Nov., 1880, HQ Records DoP 1878-1881, NA, RG393, M1381, Roll 1, pp.66-67, Letter No.335

98 Grierson to CO, Mexican Troops, near Quitman, 24 Jul., 1880 in Telegrams Sent 23 Jun.-30 Nov., 1880, HQ Records DoP 1878-1881, NA, RG393, M1381, Roll 1, pp.68-69, Letter No.339.

99 Brinkerhoff to AAAG SF 24 Jul., 1880, NA, RG393, Part 3, Entry 439, p.563; Grierson, Eagle Springs TX, to Col's. Hatch and Buell, 24 Jul., 1880, NA, RG393, Part 3, Entry 440, p.24; Grierson to Hatch & Buell, 24 Jul., 1880 in Telegrams Sent 23 Jun.-30 Nov., 1880, HQ Records DoP 1878-1881, NA, RG393, M1381, Roll 1, pp.69-70, Letter No.341; Ord to AG Chicago, 24 Jul., 1880, 'Victorio Files', NA, RG393, M1495, Roll 14; the *Grant County Herald*, 31 Jul., 1880; Thrapp, 1967, p.204; Thrapp, 1974, p.286; Leckie & Leckie, p.261; Stout, p.153; Hatch to AAG Fort Leavenworth, 28 Jul., 1880, Telegrams Sent DoNM, Vol.3, Jan.-Nov. 1880, NA, RG393, Part 3, Entry 431, pp.659-660; Ord to AG

New York Times reported that there was a long battle, and that the losses of the Apaches were unknown.[100] Reports also came in that Roman Aranda and two other men had been killed in a clash between Valle's advance guard and the Apaches 'thirty miles below Quitman'.[101] The report that Aranda had been killed was false, but does not rule out the possibility that three men had been killed in a skirmish with the Apaches.

A large force of 200 Mexican troops arrived opposite Old Fort Quitman on 23 July, but did not linger, setting out again during the night towards Ojo Del Pino in pursuit of the Apaches.[102] Valle must have decided that when the Apaches entered the Sierra del Fierro, he would try to trap them. While Valle's detachment of 120 cavalry followed Victorio to the southern side of the mountains, the troops briefly seen opposite Fort Quitman were probably part of Valle's larger force, which had earlier marched to the vicinity of the village of Guadalupe and were now advancing to cover the northern edge of the Sierra del Fierro. Brinkerhoff states that there was no major battle as a result of this operation, but that some skirmishes had taken place.[103] He also reported that the Apaches had an abundance of stolen cattle and horses gained over almost a month's raiding in Mexico.[104] As a result, Grierson delayed Captain Nolan's departure for Fort Quitman, holding A Company with him at Eagle Springs until 27 July.[105]

On 25 July, Valle's troops were reported to have fared better. Once again in the Sierra de los Pinos, they claimed to have killed four Apaches for the loss of one Mexican soldier.[106] Three Mexicans were also reported as being wounded with 10 horses being stolen.[107] Valle also sent word

---

Chicago, 24 Jul., 1880 in 'Victorio Papers', NA, M666, Roll 527; 'Indian Affairs', *Army & Navy Journal*, Vol. 17, 31 Jul., 1880, p.1068; 'Punishing Victorio's Band', The New York Times 30 Jul., 1880.

Ojo Del Pino was reported to be opposite Ojo Caliente TX forty miles from Fort Quitman TX. (Hatch to AAG Fort Leavenworth, 28 Jul., 1880, Telegrams Sent DoNM, Vol.3, Jan.-Nov. 1880, NA, RG393, Part 3, Entry 431, pp.659-660; Platt, citing Hatch's report, Fort Leavenworth to AAG, HQ MDoM, 29 Jul., 1880, 'Victorio Files', NA, RG393, M1495, Roll 14.

100 'Punishing Victorio's Band', The New York Times 30 Jul., 1880.

101 Brinkerhoff Ft Bliss to AAAG SF 24 Jul., 1880, NA, RG393, Part 3, Entry 439, p.558; Hatch to AAG Fort Leavenworth, 27 Jul., 1880, Telegrams Sent DoNM, Vol.3, Jan.-Nov. 1880, NA, RG393, Part 3, Entry 431, p.653; See also the *Grant County Herald*, 31 Jul., 1880.

102 Grierson to Hatch & Buell, 24 Jul., 1880 in Telegrams Sent 23 Jun.-30 Nov., 1880, HQ Records DoP 1878-1881, NA, RG393, M1381, Roll 1, pp.69-70, Letter No.341; Brinkerhoff Bliss to AAAG SF 24 Jul., 1880, NA, RG393, Part 3, Entry 439, p.564; Grierson, Eagle Springs TX, to Col's. Hatch and Buell, 24 Jul., 1880, NA, RG393, Part 3, Entry 440, p.24.

103 Brinkerhoff to AAAG 30 Jul., 1880, NA, RG393, Part 3, Entry 439, pp.581-582; Grierson to CO, Fort Bliss, Texas, 26 Jul., 1880, NA, RG393, Part 3, Entry 440, p.68.

104 Ord to AG Chicago, 24 Jul., 1880, 'Victorio Files', NA, RG393, M1495, Roll 14; Thrapp, 1974, p.286

105 Beck to Kennedy, 27 Jul., 1880 in Letters Sent 19 Sept., 1879-11 Aug., 1880, HQ Records DoP 1878-1881, NA, RG393, M1381, Roll 1, Letter No.127; McChristian, 1982, p.53.

106 Hatch to AAG Fort Leavenworth, 28 Jul., 1880, Telegrams Sent DoNM, Vol.3, Jan.-Nov. 1880, NA, RG393, Part 3, Entry 431, pp.659-660; Grierson to CO, Fort Bliss, Texas, 26 Jul., 1880, NA, RG393, Part 3, Entry 440, p.68; Grierson to Col's Hatch & Buell, 26 Jul., 1880 in Telegrams Sent 23 Jun.-30 Nov., 1880, HQ Records DoP 1878-1881, NA, RG393, M1381, Roll 1, pp.74-75, Letter No.349; Grierson to Ord sent via Fort Bliss to General Ord, 29 Jul., 1880, Telegrams Sent DoNM, Vol.3, Jan.-Nov. 1880, NA, RG393, Part 3, Entry 431, pp.668-669; Platt, citing Hatch's report, Fort Leavenworth to AAG, HQ MDoM, 29 Jul., 1880 & Platt to AAG, HQ MDoM, 1 Aug., 1880, 'Victorio Files', NA, RG393, M1495, Roll 14; Hatch to AAG Fort Leavenworth, 29 Jul., 1880 in 'Victorio Papers', NA, M666, Roll 527 Thrapp, 1974, p.286; Rister, 1928, p.208; Haley, 1952, p.332.

107 Translation of Valle's letter to Grierson dated 25 Jul., 1880 at Camp in Sierra Borracho attached to Grierson to AAG, DoTx, 26 Jul., 1880 in Telegrams Sent 23 Jun.-30 Nov., 1880, HQ Records DoP 1878-1881, NA, RG393, M1381, Roll 1, pp.76-78, Letter No.352; Valle to Grierson, 25 Jul., 1880 in Telegrams Rec'd, 18 May, 1880-4 Feb., 1881,HQ Records DoP 1878-1881, NA, RG393, M1381, Roll 4; Grierson to CO, Fort Bliss, Texas, 26 Jul., 1880, NA, RG393, Part 3, Entry 440, p.68; Brinkerhoff to AAAG SF 27 Jul., 1880, NA, RG393, Part 3, Entry 439, pp.559-560; Grierson to Col's Hatch & Buell,

to the United States that he was gearing up to make a full scale attack on Victorio in the Sierra del Fierro and Borracho, and that the US army should occupy the passes north of the international line to prevent the Apaches escaping. Finally, he requested that the US authorities transmit his report to the Governor of Chihuahua, who could then keep the Federal Government of Mexico informed as to his movements.[108] Valle also communicated directly with Grierson informing him that after the fight at Ojo del Pinos, the Apaches had turned southwards and had 'made a stand' in the Sierra del Fierro. This point was estimated to be approximately fifty miles south of Eagle Springs.[109]

On receipt of the first reports of fighting between Valle's *federales* and the Apaches, Grierson sent out two Pueblo scouts to contact Valle. They returned a couple of days later confirming the details of the recent clash in the Sierra de los Pinos. At this point, Grierson estimated that Colonel Valle commanded approximately 600 troops[110] made up of both federal and state troops.[111] The Pueblo scout couriers were stationed at Old Fort Quitman and the telegraph operator, Palmer, described how the two men and their horses returned with dispatches from Valle in a dreadfully exhausted condition, having been in the saddle for a couple of days. He informed Grierson that fresh horses were required at Quitman if this form of communication was to be maintained. Palmer also reported that a Mexican courier from Fort Bliss with urgent dispatches for Colonel Valle had arrived, stating that he needed a horse as his own mount was all in.[112]

On 26 July, with a better idea of the broad location of the Apaches, Grierson issued further orders to his detachments. Captain Lebo was warned that Victorio might be aiming for the Eagle and Carrizo Mountains. Lebo was to fortify his camp and scout the country to the south and south west of Fresno Springs, as far as Van Horn Wells.[113] Captain William B. Kennedy, at Camp Safford in the Guadalupe Mountains, was also instructed to keep his command in readiness and to patrol southwards in the broad direction of Old Fort Quitman.[114] Captain Viele was also ordered to move his company from El Muerto to Eagle Springs. Viele was instructed to follow the telegraph line between El Muerto and Eagle Springs and to repair any damage done to it.[115]

---

26 Jul., 1880 in Telegrams Sent 23 Jun.-30 Nov., 1880, HQ Records DoP 1878-1881, NA, RG393, M1381, Roll 1, pp.74-75, Letter No.349; Brinkerhoff to AAAG SF 29 Jul., 1880, NA, RG393, Part 3, Entry 439, pp.565-566; Dinges, 1987, p.89; Grierson to Ord sent via Fort Bliss to General Ord, 29 Jul., 1880, Telegrams Sent DoNM, Vol.3, Jan.-Nov. 1880, NA, RG393, Part 3, Entry 431, pp.668-669; Platt to AAG, HQ MDoM, 1 Aug., 1880, 'Victorio Files', NA, RG393, M1495, Roll 14.

108 Valle, Camp in Sierra Borracho to Grierson via telegraph at Fort Quitman, 25 Jul., 1880 in Register of Telegrams Rec'd 11 Oct., 1879-8 Oct., 1880, HQ Records DoP 1878-1881, NA, RG393, M1381, Roll 2, pp.198-199, Letter No.339 & in Telegrams Rec'd by General Grierson in the Field 30 Jun.-14 Sept., 1880 HQ Records DoP 1878-1881, NA, RG393, M1381, Roll 4; Brinkerhoff Bliss to AAAG SF 27 Jul., 1880, NA, RG393, Part 3, Entry 439, p.561; Brinkerhoff Bliss to AAAG SF 27 Jul., 1880, NA, RG393, Part 3, Entry 439, p.566.

109 Beck to Kennedy, 27 Jul., 1880 in Letters Sent 19 Sept., 1879-11 Aug., 1880, HQ Records DoP 1878-1881, NA, RG393, M1381, Roll 1, Letter No.127; Grierson to Col's Hatch & Buell, 26 Jul., 1880 in Telegrams Sent 23 Jun.-30 Nov., 1880, HQ Records DoP 1878-1881, NA, RG393, M1381, Roll 1, pp.74-75, Letter No.349.

110 Grierson to CO, Fort Bliss, Texas, 26 Jul., 1880, NA, RG393, Part 3, Entry 440, p.68

111 Grierson to CO, Fort Bliss, Texas, 26 Jul., 1880, NA, RG393, Part 3, Entry 440, p.68; McChristian, 1982, p.52.

112 Palmer to Grierson, Eagle Springs, 26 Jul., 1880 in Telegrams Rec'd by General Grierson in the Field 30 Jun.-14 Sept., 1880 HQ Records DoP 1878-1881, NA, RG393, M1381, Roll 4.

113 Beck to Lebo, 26 Jul., 1880 in Letters Sent 19 Sept., 1879-11 Aug., 1880, HQ Records DoP 1878-1881, NA, RG393, M1381, Roll 1, Letter No.125.

114 Beck to Kennedy, 27 Jul., 1880 in Letters Sent 19 Sept., 1879-11 Aug., 1880, HQ Records DoP 1878-1881, NA, RG393, M1381, Roll 1, Letter No.127.

115 Beck to Viele, 26 Jul., 1880 in Letters Sent 19 Sept., 1879-11 Aug., 1880, HQ Records DoP 1878-1881, NA, RG393, M1381, Roll 1, Letter No.123.

On 26 July, Grierson had informed Fort Bliss that the telegraph line was down to the east of Eagle Springs, and he requested that Captain Brinkerhoff forward information to General Ord via the telegraph line to Santa Fé and beyond.[116] A repairman had been sent eastwards from Fort Bliss, but on reaching Fort Quitman he had wisely refused to proceed further and returned to Fort Bliss.[117] A repair team was also sent out from Fort Davis; but a day later, Robert Grierson noted that the line was still down.[118]

That same day (27 July 1880), Grierson started out from Eagle Springs for Old Fort Quitman, leaving instructions for Captain Nolan to follow with his troop the next day. The following day, Colonel Valle and his command arrived on the opposite bank of the Rio Grande.[119] Having run out of, or lost, their supplies, the Mexican troops were in no position to complete their part of the operation. Grierson gave the Mexicans some provisions, but sent an urgent telegram to Hatch asking if the Mexican troops could be supplied from Fort Bliss.[120] Victorio had apparently managed to cripple Valle's expedition by capturing the bulk of the Colonel's provisions: 'Victorio is evidently holding his own in Mexico. Brinkerhoff telegraphs today from El Paso that Mexican Troops at Quitman report Victorio capturing their supplies.'[121] Palmer and Robert Grierson also mention the capture of the Mexican's supply train.[122] Valle was able to inform Grierson that his scouts had tracked Victorio to the Bosque Bonito or the Carresalillo Mountains, which was roughly opposite a line drawn between Alamo and Vieja Springs on the US side of the border. (See document file no. 90.) This was, as we shall see, a crucial piece of intelligence which helped to point Grierson in the right direction as to the location of the Apaches. Grierson was able to reassure Valle that he had troops covering these points. Valle planned to advance downriver from opposite Fort Quitman to strike Victorio. He also stated his intention to keep the US army informed of developments via courier and telegraph using the stations at Fort Quitman or Eagle Springs.[123] The *federales* were low on provisions and despite Grierson supplying approximately: '2000lbs of flour and grain' and presenting some personal goods for Valle's use, the latter felt that without re-supply by his own government, he might have to terminate his operation.[124] In the meantime, Colonel Grierson

116 Grierson to Col's Hatch & Buell, 26 Jul., 1880 in Telegrams Sent 23 Jun.-30 Nov., 1880, HQ Records DoP 1878-1881, NA, RG393, M1381, Roll 1, pp.74-75, Letter No.349; Grierson to Ord sent via Fort Bliss to General Ord, 29 Jul., 1880, Telegrams Sent DoNM, Vol.3, Jan.-Nov. 1880, NA, RG393, Part 3, Entry 431, pp.668-669.

117 Brinkerhoff Bliss to AAAG 30 Jul., 1880, NA, RG393, Part 3, Entry 439, p.581.

118 'Robert Grierson Diary'; McChristian, 1982, p.52; See also Brinkerhoff to AAAG SF 29 Jul., 1880, NA, RG393, Part 3, Entry 439, pp.567-568.

119 Platt to Comdg Off DoNM 2 Aug., 1880, NA, RG393, Part 3, Entry 439, pp. 47-49; Brinkerhoff to AAAG DoNM 29 Jul., 1880, NA, RG393, Part 3, Entry 439, pp.566-567; Brinkerhoff to AAAG SF 30 Jul., 1880, NA, RG393, Part 3, Entry 439, p.569; 'Grierson's Report, Sept.1880'; NA, RG393, Part 1, Entry 2546, pp.639-644.

120 Hatch to Pope, 31 Jul., 1880, Telegrams Sent DoNM, Vol.3, Jan.-Nov. 1880, NA, RG393, Part 3, Entry 431, p.678; McChristian, 1982, p.53.

121 Hatch to Pope, 31 Jul., 1880, Telegrams Sent DoNM, Vol.3, Jan.-Nov. 1880, NA, RG393, Part 3, Entry 431, p.677; See also Temple,1959, p.102; see also Matthews, p.38; Dinges, 1987, p.89; Miles, 1971, p.21.

122 Palmer to Grierson, Eagle Springs, 26 Jul., 1880 in Telegrams Rec'd by General Grierson in the Field 30 Jun.-14 Sept., 1880 HQ Records DoP 1878-1881, NA, RG393, M1381, Roll 4; Robert Grierson's Diary 28 Jul., 1880. Copy courtesy of the Fort Davis Museum Archives.

123 Grierson to CO Fort Bliss & AAG, San Antonio, Texas, 29 Jul., 1880 in Telegrams Sent 23 Jun.-30 Nov., 1880, HQ Records DoP 1878-1881, NA, RG393, M1381, Roll 1, pp.82-83, Letter Nos. 357 & 358; Brinkerhoff to AAAG SF 31 Jul., 1880, NA, RG393, Part 3, Entry 440, pp.96-97; Brinkerhoff to AAAG SF 30 Jul., 1880, NA, RG393, Part 3, Entry 439, p.569.

124 Brinkerhoff to AAAG SF 30 Jul., 1880, NA, RG393, Part 3, Entry 439, pp.569-570; 'Grierson's Report, Sept.1880'; NA, RG393, Part 1, Entry 2546, pp.639-644; Rister, 1928, p.208; Temple, 1959, pp.101-102; Matthews, 1993, p.38; McChristian, 1982, p.53.

and his officers invited Colonel Valle, Captains Lestrade and Valdez, and Don Juan Terrazas, the Governor of Chihuahua's nephew, to dine in the officer's field mess. The invitation was accepted, and Grierson's son Robert, reported a generous donation to the Mexican Officer's supplies when they left the following morning.[125] It is also noteworthy that Governor Terrazas had placed a nephew on Colonel Valle's staff.

Given the logisitical challenges facing Valle, Grierson was faced with the certainty that Victorio would attempt to cross the Rio Grande without the disadvantage of having Mexican troops in pursuit. It was clear to Grierson that he needed to return to his field headquarters at Eagle Springs to prepare his forces.

Approval for this action was relatively quickly granted at the highest level of the U.S. Army. (See Drum, AG Washington D.C. to the Commanding General of Subsistence, 19 Aug., 1880 in Letters Rec'd File 19 Mar., 1878-14 Feb., 1881, HQ Records DoP 1878-1881, NA, RG393, M1381, Roll 2).

125 'Robert Grierson Diary'.

10

Grierson's Texas Campaign 1: Tinaja de las Palmas, July 1880[1]

Grierson departed Old Fort Quitman for Eagle Springs on 29 July 1880. The other members of his detachment were Lieutenant Beck, one sergeant, five troopers and his son, Robert.[2] Arriving at at Tinaja de las Palmas, they had a brief skirmish with a lone Apache warrior, and Grierson guessed that this insignificant spring was Victorio's destination.[3] Tinaja de las Palmas was located where:

> The road passed at an angle between two small hills paralleling the much larger Devil Ridge to the northeast. The jagged spine north of the road was known as "Rocky Ridge," an appropriate name for it was indeed a solid pile of rock which rose about one hundred twenty five feet above the surrounding desert. A similar but smaller hill stood south of the road.
>
> At the foot of Rocky Ridge, in the natural drainage formed with the adjacent hill, the stage road traversed an area of deep sand bounded on either side by rocky flats.[4]

Grierson sent his sergeant and two men after the warrior, but the latter fled, sped on his way with a couple of shots.[5]

Shortly after the Apache scout had been driven off, couriers from Eagle Springs arrived at Tinaja de las Palmas. They reported that approximately 40 Apache warriors had been spotted across the Rio Grande, opposite Ojo Caliente, Texas. A vidette party, with at least one Pueblo scout, had spotted this group from a hill six miles from the Rio Grande at about 7:00 a.m. on the morning of 29 July. On returning to Eagle Springs to report, they twice exchanged fire with Apaches near the river, but no casualties were inflicted on either side. In the first exchange, they had been fired at by a lone Apache who had fled towards the Rio Grande. A few miles further on, they had skirmished

1 There are slightly differing versions of the prelude of this skirmish. See Appendix One at end of this Chapter.

2 Grierson to Hatch SF 30 Jul., 1880, NA, RG393, Part 3, Entry 439, p.583; See slightly tidied up version quoted in Loud to Hatch, 31 Jul., 1880, Telegrams Sent DoNM, Vol.3, Jan.-Nov. 1880, NA, RG393, Part 3, Entry 431, pp.680-681; Sheridan to AG Wash. D.C. 2 Aug., 1880 in 'Victorio Papers', NA, M666, Roll 527; Whipple to CO DoNM, 2 Aug., 1880 in NA, RG393, Part 3, Entry 439, pp.46-49; Grierson to HQ DoP, 31 Jul., 1880, 'Victorio Files', NA, RG393, M1495, Roll 14; Brinkerhoff to AAAG SF 30 Jul., 1880, NA, RG393, Part 3, Entry 439, pp.569-570; Platt to Comdg Off DoNM 2 Aug., 1880, NA, RG393, Part 3, Entry 439, p.47; 'Town and County', the *Grant County Herald*, 7 Aug., 1880; See also McChristian, 1982, p.53. On reading some of Grierson's reports of this period and his son's own diary, it is clear that his son was not present in an official capacity and if included, the number of men including Col. Grierson originally stationed at Tinaja de Las Palmas would be nine. One suspects that the Colonel was not sure what his superiors may have made of his allowing his son to participate in this skirmish.

3 'Grierson's Report, Sept.1880'; NA, RG393, Part 1, Entry 2546, pp.639-644; Matthews, 1993, p.38; Leckie, 1967, p.224; Temple, 1959, p.102; Haley, 1952, p.332; Miles, 1971, p.21.

4 McChristian, 1982, p.54; Chronological List, p.50.

5 'Robert Grierson Diary', 29 Jul., 1880; McChristian, 1982, p.54.

with four Apaches who also made off towards the river. Captain Gilmore, in charge at Eagle Springs in Grierson's absence, had sent another patrol back to the general area to monitor the situation. One significant piece of information was that the members of the first patrol thought that the Apaches they had encountered had been heading south towards the Rio Grande, away from the Eagle Springs to Fort Quitman road.[6]

Lt. William H. Beck, Tenth Cavalry. Appointed as Grierson's personal aide-de-camp and acting assistant adjutant general in the field for the upcoming campaign against Victorio. As such he was one of the original tiny garrison at Tinaja de Las Palmas. (Carlisle Barracks)

This news, combined with Grierson's encounter with a lone Apache scout on the same day, suggests that Victorio had sent out scouts to discover the location of any US troops stationed between Forts Quitman and Eagle Springs. That evening, Gilmore sent further word that his second patrol had been 'driven' back to Eagle Springs by an estimated 60 Apaches. They also reported finding two camps of 16 and 6 wickiups approximately 16 miles to the south west of Eagle Springs.[7] Captain Nolan, whose detachment had remained on the alert at Old Fort Quitman, had subsequently been informed by his own patrols that over 60 Apaches had crossed the Rio Grande. Captain Gilmore then sent couriers along the route to Fort Quitman, where they encountered Grierson at Tinaja de las Palmas.[8] These couriers confirmed Grierson's suspicions.

Grierson had probably not previously stationed a picket at this point because 'tinaja' (tank), suggests that it was only an irregular resource, where water periodically collected in natural rock tanks.[9] It should be noted, however, that it was also known to the army as 'Eighteen Mile Waterhole', situated about 18 miles equidistant from both Old Fort Quitman and Eagle Springs.[10] This name suggests a more reliable source of water than 'Tinaja de las Palmas'.

6 Gilmore, Eagle Springs to AAAG, DoP, Fort Quitman 12:15 p.m., 29 Jul., 1880 in Telegrams Rec'd by General Grierson in the Field 30 Jun.-4 Sept., 1880, HQ Records DoP 1878-1881, NA, RG393, M1381, Roll 4; See also 'Robert Grierson Diary', 29 Jul., 1880.

7 Gilmore, Eagle Springs to AAAG, DoP, Fort Quitman, 7:00 p.m. 29 Jul., 1880 in Telegrams Rec'd by General Grierson in the Field 30 Jun.-4 Sept., 1880, HQ Records DoP 1878-1881, NA, RG393, M1381, Roll 4.

8 'Robert Grierson Diary', 1 Aug., 1880; 'Grierson's Report, Sept.1880'; NA, RG393, Part 1, Entry 2546, pp.639-644; Leckie & Leckie, pp.261-262; Miles, 1971, p.21 It has been generally assumed that Captain Nolan sent Lt. Henry Ossian Flipper as a courier to Grierson at this point and Flipper's own memoirs suggest that this was the case but on closer reading of Flipper's recollections suggest that this ride took place in October 1880 in the aftermath of an Apache ambush of a Tenth Cavalry picket at Ojo Calientes, Texas on 28 October, 1880 (See Chapter 16 this volume for further comment).

9 McChristian, 1982, p.54.

10 See Bi-Monthly Company Muster Rolls for Company A, 10th Cavalry, Jul./Aug. 1880 in NA, RG94.

The Colonel and his companions took up positions on a part of 'Rocky Ridge' which overlooked the spring.[11] In geological terms, while Rocky Ridge is not particularly high, it is effectively a knife-blade with precipitous sides before sloping more gently towards the level ground.

The small detachment created two emplacements and named them Forts 'Grierson' and 'Beck',[12] These were virtually impregnable being almost as wide as the top of Rocky Ridge. The Apaches would not have risked the loss of unnecessary lives trying to take such a position by a frontal assault. These two emplacements also have a clear line-of fire along the narrow ridge making it very risky for the Apaches to try to take these positions by a flanking attack.[13] Tinaja de las Palmas was on the stage line, which passed through both Eagle Springs and Fort Quitman. Grierson used a stage-coach arriving from Fort Quitman to transmit orders to Captain Viele at Eagle Springs to march his troops to the Tinaja de las Palmas group's immediate support.[14] A second stagecoach travelling out of Eagle Springs delivered a message that Captain Viele was on his way with C Company.[15] During the night, further messages from Old Fort Quitman informed Grierson that the Apaches were camped less than 10 miles away. They had twice skirmished with scout detachments, and one Pueblo scout was reported to have been killed.[16] These messengers were immediately sent back to Old Fort Quitman with orders for Captain Nolan to gather A Company and bring it with due speed to support Grierson.[17]

In the meantime, they finished constructing their forts, Robert Grierson noting that 'The rocks were very rough and we got our hands scratched like everything.'[18] Robert Grierson also noted that their transport and animals were placed behind the ridge[19] and the nature of Grierson's chosen position would certainly place horse drawn vehicles and any horses and mules out of sight of

11 Thrapp, 1974, p.287; Thrapp, 1967, p.204; Record of Engagements, p.95; Stout, 1974, p.153; Leckie, 1967, p.224; Temple, 1959, p.102; McChristian, Handbook of Texas Online; McChristian, 1982, p.54; Bigelow, USACMH webpage; Wellman, 1957, p.169; Miles, 1971, p.21; Longstreet, 1970, p.95.

12 'Robert Grierson Diary', 1 Aug., 1880; Matthews, 1993, 1993, p.39; Temple, 1959, p.102; McChristian, 1982, p.54; McChristian, 1982, p.57.

13 The author got permission to visit Tinaja de las Palmas on 11 June 2018 and comments upon the terrain are based upon personal observation.

14 Grierson to Hatch SF 30 Jul., 1880, NA, RG393, Part 3, Entry 439, p.583; See slightly tidied up version quoted in Loud to Hatch, 31 Jul., 1880, Telegrams Sent DoNM, Vol.3, Jan.-Nov. 1880, NA, RG393, Part 3, Entry 431, pp.680-681; Sheridan to AG Wash. D.C. 2 Aug., 1880 in 'Victorio Papers', NA, M666, Roll 527; NA, RG393, Part 3, Entry 439, pp.46-49; Grierson to HQ DoP, 31 Jul., 1880, 'Victorio Files', NA, RG393, M1495, Roll 14; 'Grierson's Report, Sept.1880'; NA, RG393, Part 1, Entry 2546, pp.639-644; Leckie, 1967, p.224; Leckie & Leckie, 1984, p.262; Rister, 1928, p.209; Temple, 1959, p.102; McChristian, 1982, p.55; McChristian Handbook of Texas Online entry; Stout, 1974, p.153; Haley, 1952, p.332; Miles, 1971, p.21.

15 'Robert Grierson Diary', 1 Aug., 1880; McChristian, 1982, p.55.

16 'Grierson's Report, Sept.1880'; NA, RG393, Part 1, Entry 2546, pp.639-644; Leckie & Leckie, p.262; McChristian, 1982, p.56; McChristian Handbook of Texas Online entry ;Rister, 1928, p.209; Miles, 1971, p.21.

Nineteen Pueblo scouts were originally recruited with Simon Olguin being killed on 12 June. By the end of September seventeen Pueblo scouts were recorded as being in service which would seem to support one of their number being killed at this time. (Tabular Statement showing Stations, Positions and Movements of Troops operating against Victorio and his hostile Indians, in the DoP, from Jul., 1 1880 to Sept. 20, 1880 in Letters Sent 23 Aug.-31 Dec., 1880, HQ Records DoP 1878-1881, NA, RG393, M1381, Roll 1).

17 'Grierson's Report, Sept.1880'; NA, RG393, Part 1, Entry 2546, pp.639-644; Leckie, 1967, pp.224-225; Leckie & Leckie, 1984, p.262; McChristian, 1982, p.56; Temple, 1959, p.102; Rister, 1928, p.209.

18 'Robert Grierson Diary', 1 Aug., 1880. Having descended the ridge from the right of Grierson's position the author can attest that these rocks are very difficult to grasp without inflicting numerous superficial scratches upon one's hands.

19 'Robert Grierson Diary', 1 Aug., 1880

Apaches approaching from the Mexican border on the reverse side of Rocky Ridge. Grierson's son also reported that each fortlet was well supplied with water and other supplies.[20] He also stated that the two emplacements were built up as breastworks on the side facing Tinaja de las Palmas[21] yet the remains of the forts today suggest that they were built for all-round defence.

However, at 4:00 a.m. the following morning, Grierson's plan started to unravel. His orders to Captain Viele had been misinterpreted. Fearing for Grierson's safety, Gilmore had sent a detachment of 15 men of G Company, Tenth Cavalry, led by Lieutenant Finley,[22] to provide an escort back to Eagle Springs.[23] An exasperated Grierson sent two of Finley's troopers back to Eagle Springs with 'peremptory' orders for the balance of the Eagle Springs garrison to march to Tinaja de las Palmas as soon as possible.[24] Grierson immediately reassigned the rest of Finley's detachment to a position lower down the ridge and presumably closer to the water. Finley's men constructed additional rock breastworks for cover.[25] This was placed further down Rocky Ridge as it descended towards the flat ground.

Finley's men found a point where large boulders already protected their front and rear and they constructed walls to close off either flank of their emplacement. This also covered a potential weak point in Grierson's own position. As noted earlier, it would have been difficult to assault Grierson's positions from left or right. Yet the Apaches could have approached to very close range of Grierson's left before exposing themselves to fire from the defenders: the ridge quickly drops down significantly to where Finley constructed his fortlet. Thus, any attempt to try to flank Grierson's left would have been exposed to close-range fire from Finley's men.

20 Ibid.

21 Ibid.

22 On hearing that Leighton Finley had managed to gain a transfer from the 15th Infantry to the Tenth Cavalry, Lt Walter Finley, Ninth Cavalry, commented that 'he will have a pleasant service down in Texas, not much scouting and easy service'. (Letter dated Fort Bayard, 30 Nov., 1879 in The Walter Lowry Finley Collection).

23 Leighton Finley Diary 30 Jul., 1880 entry Special Collections, University of Arizona Library, Tucson. There is some confusion as to the number of men in Finley's detachment though Finley himself states that his command consisted of fifteen men. Some accounts mention ten (Leckie, 1967, p.225; Burton, 1999, p.189) or fifteen (Matthews, 1993, p.39; Temple, 1959, p.102; McChristian, 1982, p.57; McChristian Handbook of Texas Online entry; Leckie & Leckie, 1984, p.262; Wellman, 1957, p.170; Miles, 1971, p.62). Finley's diary is quite clear that he was accompanied by fifteen men to Tinaja de Las Palmas and that ten of those men accompanied him when he charged at Victorio's warriors during the battle. However, The number thirteen seems to be the most likely figure as Grierson quoted this number as being involved in the fight within hours of the event. (See Grierson to Hatch SF 30 Jul., 1880, NA, RG393, Part 3, Entry 439, p.583; See slightly tidied up version quoted in Loud to Hatch, 31 Jul., 1880, Telegrams Sent DoNM, Vol.3, Jan.-Nov. 1880, NA, RG393, Part 3, Entry 431, pp.680-681) However he also makes it clear that prior to the skirmish he had sent two of the fifteen men back to Eagle Springs to summon reinforcements. (See 'Grierson's Report, Sept.1880'; NA, RG393, Part 1, Entry 2546, pp.639-644; 'Robert Grierson Diary', 1 Aug., 1880).

24 'Grierson's Report, Sept.1880'; NA, RG393, Part 1, Entry 2546, pp.639-644; Stout, pp.153-154; Matthews, 1993, p.39; McChristian, 1982, p.57; McChristian Hand Book of Texas Online entry; Miles, 1971, p.62.

25 Leighton Finley Diary 30 Jul., 1880 entry Special Collections, University of Arizona Library, Tucson; 'Robert Grierson Diary', 1 Aug., 1880; Leckie, 1967, p.225; Temple, 1959, p.102; McChristian Handbook of Texas Online entry; Burton, 1999, p.189.

Plate 10.1 One of Grierson's emplacements on the highest point of Rocky Ridge looking east towards the Eagle Mountains on the horizon. Author is seated on the edge of the emplacement for scale. The low range of hills below these mountains and behind the author's head are where the approaching Apaches were first spotted.

Plate 10.2 Finley's larger emplacement looking west along Rocky Ridge. Grierson's two emplacements are just behind the high point at the top right of the photo. The Quitman Mountains can be seen marching along the left-hand horizon.

Tinaja de las Palmas: Skirmish between Victorio's Apaches and Grierson's Tenth Cavalry, 30 July 1880 (see Map 10.1)

Grierson, with between 23 and 25 men, was left to hold Tinaja de las Palmas and await both reinforcements and Apaches. The Apaches arrived first, at about 9:00 a.m. on 30 July 1880.[26] (See document files nos. 87 and 91.) Robert Grieson reported that 'the vedettes holloed: "Here come the Indians!!!" We made for our posts immediately. The Indians came through a canyon in the hills S.E. of camp & got within half a mile before we saw them.'[27] The Apaches were obviously aware that there was a Tenth Cavalry detachment holding the water, either through spotting them as they approached, or through the report of their own scout who had escaped the previous day. It should be noted that, from the Apaches' point of view, that Finley's position is difficult, but not impossible to detect. However, Grierson's breastworks are impossible to spot from this direction.[28]

They apparently swung to the east to avoid a battle with the troops.[29] Grierson sent out Lieutenant Finley with 10 of his men to challenge this manoeuvre.[30] Lieutenant Finley laconically noted that this was his 'first charge'.[31] As the detachment skirmished at long range with the visible warriors, other Apaches infiltrated down through thick vegetation between two hills south of the stage road. Once the Tenth Cavalrymen had passed them, they suddenly opened fire, and Finley's men turned and stood their ground and skirmished with the Apaches for approximately one hour.[32] Robert Grierson noted that the Apaches made more use of their horses than was usual during this campaign. However, their horses were used by the warriors to speed their movement around the battlefield, and they dismounted before firing on their opponents.[33]

26 Grierson to Hatch SF 30 Jul., 1880, NA, RG393, Part 3, Entry 439, p.583; See slightly tidied up version quoted in Loud to Hatch, 31 Jul., 1880, Telegrams Sent DoNM, Vol.3, Jan.-Nov. 1880, NA, RG393, Part 3, Entry 431, pp.680-681; Sheridan to AG Wash. D.C. 2 Aug., 1880 in 'Victorio Papers', NA, M666, Roll 527; Whipple to CO DoNM, 2 Aug., 1880 in NA, RG393, Part 3, Entry 439, pp.46-49; Grierson to HQ DoP, 31 Jul., 1880, 'Victorio Files', NA, RG393, M1495, Roll 14; Grierson's Report on Tinaja de Las Palmas in NA, RG393, Part 1, Entry 2538, p.355; Leckie & Leckie, 1984, p.262; Matthews, 1993, p.39; Miles, 1971, p.62.

27 'Robert Grierson Diary', 1 Aug., 1880.

28 On visiting the site in June 2018, I first passed Finley's position, climbed up to Grierson's position then climbed down Rocky Ridge. Periodically, I took photos from below sighting upon a small bush where I knew Grierson's fortlets were located. I knew they were there but could not spot them.

29 'Grierson's Report, Sept.1880'; NA, RG393, Part 1, Entry 2546, pp.639-644; Leckie, 1967, p.225; Matthews, 1993, p.39; Burton 1999, p.189.

30 'Grierson's Report, Sept.1880'; NA, RG393, Part 1, Entry 2546, pp.639-644; Leighton Finley Diary 30 Jul., 1880 entry Special Collections, University of Arizona Library, Tucson; 'Robert Grierson Diary', 1 Aug., 1880; Record of Engagements, p.95; McChristian Hand Book of Texas Online entry: Stout, 1974, p154; Matthews, 1993, p.39; Thrapp, 1967, p.204; Thrapp, 1988, p.493; Leckie, 1967, p.225; Bigelow, USACMH webpage; Wellman, 1957, p.170; Rister, 1928, p.210; Miles, 1971, p.62.

31 Leighton Finley Diary 30 Jul., 1880 entry Special Collections, University of Arizona Library, Tucson; See also Dinges, 1988, pp.165-166.

32 'Grierson's Report, Sept.1880'; NA, RG393, Part 1, Entry 2546, pp.639-644; 'Robert Grierson Diary', 1 Aug., 1880; McChristian, 1982, p.59.

33 'Robert Grierson Diary', 1 Aug., 1880.

Plate 10.3 Apache view of Finley's position from the south-east. They are just below and to the left of the spiky Yucca plant clearly visible silhouetted on the skyline. While well hidden it is possible to detect this position from a distance.

Plate 10.4 The top of Rocky Ridge from the point of view of any Apache to the south. Until the defenders rose up and opened fire, Grierson's two small emplacements are virtually impossible to detect.

Captain Viele and C Company, and Lieutenant Colladay with part of G Company, arrived around 10:00 a.m.[34] Lieutenant Finley was in the process of dislodging some Apache warriors from behind a rock outcrop[35] when Captain Viele and Lieutenant Colladay came into view:

> When the companies came upon the Indians, Cap. Viele and Lt. Colladay were riding about 300 yds ahead of their troops. As Lt. C was dismounting an Indian shot him in his leg[36] and broke his horse's leg. The Indian then shot at Capt. V. as he was getting off. Capt. V. then got good aim and killed the Indian dead.[37]

Lt. Samuel R. Colladay, Tenth Cavalry. Part of the relief force arriving at Tinaja de Las Palmas from Eagle Springs. Riding ahead of the force with Lt. Viele, he was wounded when they suddenly encountered Apache warriors engaged in the assault upon Grierson's small garrison. (Carlisle Barracks)

At first glance, the actions of Captain Viele and Lieutenant Colladay, riding in advance of their command, may appear to have been somewhat foolhardy. However, Lieutenant Finley noted that Pueblo scouts, commanded by Lieutenant Mills, arrived with Viele and Colladay.[38] Mistaking Finley's detachment for Apaches, the reinforcements volleyed into them and forced them to abandon their stand and ride back to their original positions.[39]

This was not before Lieutenant Finley's men returned fire, assuming that more Apaches had appeared to work their way around their flank.[40] The Apaches took advantage of the mistake to try and close with Finley's retreating detach-

34 Grierson to Hatch SF 30 Jul., 1880, NA, RG393, Part 3, Entry 439, p.583; See slightly tidied up version quoted in Loud to Hatch, 31 Jul., 1880, Telegrams Sent DoNM, Vol.3, Jan.-Nov. 1880, NA, RG393, Part 3, Entry 431, pp.680-681; Sheridan to AG Wash. D.C. 2 Aug., 1880 in 'Victorio Papers', NA, M666, Roll 527; Whipple to CO DoNM, 2 Aug., 1880 in NA, RG393, Part 3, Entry 439, pp.46-49; Grierson to HQ DoP, 31 Jul., 1880, 'Victorio Files', NA, RG393, M1495, Roll 14; Platt to Comdg Off DoNM 2 Aug., 1880, NA, RG393, Part 3, Entry 439, pp. 46-49; 'Grierson's Report, Sept.1880'; NA, RG393, Part 1, Entry 2546, pp.639-644; See also Thrapp, 1974, p.287; McChristian, 1982, p.60; McChristian Hand Book of Texas Online entry; Leckie & Leckie, 1984, p.263; Matthews, 1993, p.39; Stout, 1974, p.154.

35 'Robert Grierson Diary', 1 Aug., 1880.

36 Colladay never recovered from this wound and other privations suffered during his long service in the Tenth Cavalry, remaining present but sick or on sick leave until dying on 14 Jan., 1884 (Personal File Samuel R. Colladay, NA, RG94, Entry 297, Box 66).

37 'Robert Grierson Diary', 1 Aug., 1880; McChristian, 1982, p.60.

38 Leighton Finley Diary 30 Jul., 1880 entry Special Collections, University of Arizona Library, Tucson.

39 'Grierson's Report, Sept.1880'; 'Robert Grierson Diary', 1 Aug., 1880; 'Grierson's Report, Sept.1880';MDoM: Letters Received 1879-1881 NA, RG393, Part 1, Entry 2546, pp.639-644; Matthews, 1993, p.39; McChristian Hand Book of Texas Online entry: Leckie, 1967, p.225; Stout, p.154; O'Neal, p.125; Wellman, 1957, pp.170-171; Rister, 1928, p.210; Miles, 1971, p.62.

40 'Robert Grierson Diary', 1 Aug., 1880.

ment.[41] One trooper, Private Samuel Prescott,[42] was forced to run for his life when his horse was killed and he received a minor graze on one of his fingers. He paused once to discourage close pursuit with his revolver, before he turned and ran. This respite allowed him to reach a point where Grierson and his men on Rocky Ridge could safely open fire.[43] This volley took the Apaches by surprise, as they were apparently unaware of the two emplacements built by Grierson before the arrival of Finley's patrol. Robert Grierson thought that the Apaches had probably assumed that Lieutenant Finley's detachment were the only ones guarding the water.[44] The pursuing Apaches were driven off by this sudden covering fire, and Lieutenant Finley's detachment, including the dismounted Prescott, were able to escape.[45]

Once the reinforcements under Captain Viele had correctly identified the Apaches, they counterattacked. The fighting was now focussed in Viele's detachment, as they attempted to reach Grierson. During this part of the fight, Private Martin Davis had his horse shot from under him. He continued to fight on foot but was shot dead by the Apaches.[46] At this point, some of the Apaches spotted dust to the west announcing the approach of Captain Nolan's company from Fort Quitman.[47] This broke up the Apache attack and they pulled back, allowing Captain Viele's command to link up with Grierson.[48] This gave Grierson the opportunity to send out a courier with orders for Nolan to bring his men on as fast as possible, and they completed the last 10 miles at a 'lope'.[49] Meanwhile, the Apaches returned to the attack, occupying a ridge to the south of the stage road. Captain Viele mounted his men and drove them off the ridge.[50] The Apaches re-grouped and were again attempting to flank their enemies when Captain Nolan with A Company was judged to have come too close for comfort.[51] Lieutenant Henry Ossian Flipper, the first African-American to be commissioned into the army from West Point, noted that they 'got right into it and soon had the Indians on the run … [t]his was the first and only time I was under fire, but escaped without a scratch.'[52] Whereas the reinforcements from Eagle Springs had swept in from the east, these reinforcements were advancing at a forced march from Old Fort Quitman to the west. The reinforcement

41 McChristian Hand Book of Texas Online entry; Stout, 1974, p.154; Leckie, 1967, p.225; Leckie & Leckie, 1984, p.264.

42 Bi Monthly Muster Rolls for Company G, 10th Cavalry, NA, RG94; Record of Events Jul., 1880 in Returns From Regular Army Cavalry Regiments 1833-191610th Cavalry Regimental Returns 1873 to 1880, NA, M744, Roll 96.

43 'Robert Grierson Diary', 1 Aug., 1880; McChristian, 1982, p.61; Miles, 1971, p.62.

44 'Robert Grierson Diary', 1 Aug., 1880; McChristian, 1982, p.61.

45 'Grierson's Report, Sept.1880'; NA, RG393, Part 1, Entry 2546, pp.639-644; 'Robert Grierson Diary', 1 Aug., 1880; McChristian, 1982, p.61; McChristian Hand Book of Texas Online entry; Leckie, 1967, p.225.

46 'Robert Grierson Diary', 1 Aug., 1880; McChristian, 1982, p.61.

47 'Grierson's Report, Sept.1880'; NA, RG393, Part 1, Entry 2546, pp.639-644; McChristian, 1982, p.61.

48 'Robert Grierson Diary', 10 Jul. to 1 Sept., 1880; 'Grierson's Report, Sept.1880'; NA, RG393, Part 1, Entry 2546, pp.639-644; McChristian, 1982, p.61.

49 'Robert Grierson Diary', 1 Aug., 1880; McChristian, 1982, p.61. It is only fair to note that the *Grant County Herald* reported a rather different story which can only be referring to Captain Nolan. A letter alleged to be from 'An Old Sergeant' in the Tenth Cavalry stated 'There was a certain captain in the 10th cavalry ordered to join Gen. Grierson at the time he had first contact with Victorio's warriors. At 9 o'clock the following morning the captain ordered his company to mount, started to join Gen. Grierson at a walk, dismounted and walked his men five or six miles, or until he got in sight of Gen. Grierson, then mounted his company and brought them up at charge, after the Indians had fled; Gen. Grierson having whipped them back with small detachments.' ('A Plea for the Colored Soldier', the *Grant County Herald*, 9 Oct., 1880).

50 'Robert Grierson Diary', 1 Aug., 1880; Leckie, 1967, p.225; Leckie & Leckie, p.264; McChristian Hand Book of Texas Online entry.

51 'Grierson's Report, Sept.1880'; NA, RG393, Part 1, Entry 2546, pp.639-644; McChristian, 1982, p.62.

52 Harris, 1997, p.34.

Plate 10.5 View south-east from Grierson's position. The Ocotillo plant with the very long and thin branches provides excellent pointers for two other positions on the battlefield. The lower branch on the left points to the rocky outcrop which Finley was clearing of Apaches when fired upon by the reinforcements arriving from Eagle Springs. The much taller Ocotillo branch to the right ends just to the right of the small ridge where the Apaches regrouped.

Plate 10.6 A clearer view of the same rocky outcrop and ridge taken from the flat ground some distance from the base of Rocky Ridge.

Plate 10.7 View north-east from the ridge where the Apaches regrouped. There may have been some skirmishing upon the small hill in the distance almost at the centre of the picture. The end of Devil's Ridge can be seen on the left horizon of the photo while the Eagle Mountains dominate the right horizon. The reinforcements from Eagle springs would have arrived on the battlefield from between Devil's Ridge and this small hill. Much of their initial fighting with the Apaches on their immediate arrival from Eagle Springs would probably have occurred in the area around this small hill before they managed to link up with Grierson's force.

Plate 10.8 Western perspective from the top of the same ridge. The Quitman Mountains run along the far horizon. Captain Nolan's company advancing from Old Fort Quitman would be seen coming from this direction at some distance from the fighting. The greenery visible in the middle of the photo indicate where water is located today. In 1880 it was reported that there were natural rock tanks holding water. I could not see where these might have been but in June, when completely dry, these tanks would be difficult to detect.

of Grierson's position at Tinaja de las Palmas had won the day. From the Apaches' point of view, to continue the fight was pointless. Their primary goal was now to evade their enemies and avoid any further casualties. They broke off the engagement and retreated southwards, and it was presumed that they had crossed the Rio Grande and returned to Mexico.[53]

Grierson claimed seven Apache warriors slain, with Private Martin Davis of C Company killed, and Lieutenant Colladay and Private Prescott of G Company wounded.[54] The Tenth Cavalry had also lost 10 horses killed and four horses and a mule wounded.[55] If the Apaches had chosen to return to Mexico, there was nothing to stop them. Colonel Valle's large detachment of *federales*, still in need of supplies, had apparently withdrawn towards El Paso del Norte.[56] Grierson had presumed that Valle's force was, by this point, directly to the south of Eagle Springs, on the opposite bank of the Rio Grande,[57] as Valle had informed Grierson that he was going to march in the direction of

---

53 Grierson to Hatch SF 30 Jul., 1880, NA, RG393, Part 3, Entry 439, p.583; See slightly tidied up version quoted in Loud to Hatch, 31 Jul., 1880, Telegrams Sent DoNM, Vol.3, Jan.-Nov. 1880, NA, RG393, Part 3, Entry 431, pp.680-681; Sheridan to AG Wash. D.C. 2 Aug., 1880 in 'Victorio Papers', NA, M666, Roll 527; Whipple to CO DoNM, 2 Aug., 1880 in NA, RG393, Part 3, Entry 439, pp.46-49; Grierson to HQ DoP, 31 Jul., 1880, 'Victorio Files', NA, RG393, M1495, Roll 14; Platt to Comdg Off DoNM 2 Aug., 1880, NA, RG393, Part 3, Entry 439, pp. 47-49; NA, RG393, Part 1, Entry 2538, p.355; 'Robert Grierson Diary', 1 Aug., 1880: McChristian Hand Book of Texas Online entry; Leckie, 1967, p.225; Leckie & Leckie, p.264; Thrapp, 1967, p.204; Thrapp, 1974, p.287; Stout, 1974, p.154; Burton, 1999, p.189; Wellman, 1957, p.171; Miles, 1971, p.62.

54 Grierson to Hatch SF 30 Jul., 1880, NA, RG393, Part 3, Entry 439, p.583; See slightly tidied up version quoted in Loud to Hatch, 31 Jul., 1880, Telegrams Sent DoNM, Vol.3, Jan.-Nov. 1880, NA, RG393, Part 3, Entry 431, pp.680-681; Leighton Finley Diary 30 Jul., 1880 entry Special Collections, University of Arizona Library, Tucson; Sheridan to AG Wash. D.C. 2 Aug., 1880 in 'Victorio Papers', NA, M666, Roll 527; Whipple to CO DoNM, 2 Aug., 1880 in NA, RG393, Part 3, Entry 439, pp.46-49; Grierson to HQ DoP, 31 Jul., 1880, 'Victorio Files', NA, RG393, M1495, Roll 14; List of Persons Killed, Wounded, or Captured, by Indians, &c., in the DoTx, since Sept. 30, 1879, officially reported by post commanders. NA, RG393, Part 1, Entry 2546, p.633; Bi-Monthly Company Muster Rolls for Company G, 10th Cavalry, Jul./Aug. 1880 in NA, RG94; Record of Events Jul., 1880 in Returns From Regular Army Cavalry Regiments 1833-1916, 10th Cavalry Regimental Returns 1873 to 1880, NA, M744, Roll 96; The Fort Concho Post Return for Aug. 1880 mentions one Tenth Cavalryman killed in action or died of wounds in Returns From U.S. Military Posts 1800-1916, Fort Concho, Texas Jan. 1879-Jun. 1889, NA, M617, Roll 242; Regimental History 1866-98 10th Cavalry, NA, RG391, Entry 933, pp.19-20; NA, RG393, Part 1, Entry 2538, p.355; 'Robert Grierson Diary', 1 Aug., 1880; 'Town and County', the *Grant County Herald*, 7 Aug., 1880; 'Grierson's Report, Sept.1880'; NA, RG393, Part 1, Entry 2546, pp.639-644; See also Record of Engagements, p.95; Leckie, 1967, p.225; Leckie & Leckie, 1984, p.264; Burton, 1999, p.189 McChristian, 1982, p.62; McChristian Hand Book of Texas Online entry; Thrapp, 1974, p286-287; Matthews, 1993, p.39; O'Neal, 1991, p.125; Bigelow, USACMH webpage; Wellman, 1957, p.171; Haley, 1952, p.333; Rister, 1928, p.211; Miles, 1971, p.62.

The Chronological List adds three wounded 'enlisted' men to this total (Chronological List, p.50; Webb, 1976, p.89). There are claims that four troopers were wounded (Stout, p.155) and a suggestion that a second trooper was killed. According to Thrapp Grierson mentions a trooper from E company being killed (Thrapp, 1974, p.287).

55 'Robert Grierson Diary', 1 Aug., 1880.

56 Ord to AG Chicago, 4 Aug., 1880, 'Victorio Files', NA, RG393, M1495, Roll 14; 'Grierson's Report, Sept.1880'; NA, RG393, Part 1, Entry 2546, pp.639-644.

57 Beck to Carpenter, 30 Jul., 1880 in Letters Sent 19 Sept., 1879-11 Aug., 1880, HQ Records DoP 1878-1881, NA, RG393, M1381, Roll 1, Letter No.128; Grierson to Hatch SF 30 Jul., 1880, NA, RG393, Part 3, Entry 439, p.583; See slightly tidied up version quoted in Loud to Hatch, 31 Jul., 1880, Telegrams Sent DoNM, Vol.3, Jan.-Nov. 1880, NA, RG393, Part 3, Entry 431, pp.680-681; Whipple to CO DoNM, 2 Aug., 1880 in NA, RG393, Part 3, Entry 439, pp.46-49; Grierson to HQ DoP, 31 Jul., 1880, 'Victorio Files', NA, RG393, M1495, Roll 14; Sheridan to AG Wash. D.C. 2 Aug., 1880 in 'Victorio Papers', NA, M666, Roll 527.

Ojo Caliente down the Mexican side of the Rio Grande.[58] It was not until 3 August that Grierson discovered that Valle's command had been seen passing Quitman going west on the evening of 2 August. Grierson acknowledging himself completely mystified, and somewhat angered, concluded that Valle's departure had allowed Victorio an easy escape route into Mexico.[59]

The accusation that Valle had abandoned the frontier was not quite accurate. In the short term, he had turned and marched to El Paso del Norte for supplies, although he had already sent word to Grierson on 4 August that he had proceeded down the Rio Grande. His scouts found no signs of Apaches, and Valle assumed that they had all crossed into the United States.[60] Captain Brinkerhoff reported that Valle had contacted him on 9 August, stating that he had been unable to follow up the pursuit of Victorio on 29 July, due to lack of supplies and the Rio Grande being too high. Valle added that he was going to leave 50 troops in El Paso, while he intended to lead 150 men into the vicinity of the Laguna de Guzman Lake. 'Colonel Valle informs me that should it become necessary he will cross into the U.S. under authority given in pursuit of hostile Indians.'[61] Brinkerhoff had received news from Grierson that same day of his engagement with Victorio at Rattlesnake Springs (see Chapter 11) and had obviously transmitted this news to Valle in El Paso del Norte, as he notified District Headquarters, Santa Fé, that at 3:00 p.m., 9 August, Valle was going to take out 200 men in an attempt to intercept Victorio.[62] One day later, Brinkerhoff reported that Colonel Valle was still in the field and awaiting reports from his scouts[63]. Then came the report of a clash between a small group of Mexican irregulars or scouts and a party of Apaches, north of the border, on 10 August 1880. The Mexicans were implied to be scouts sent out from Valle's force,[64] and it is clear that, up to 15 August, Colonel Valle was still in the field.[65] However, this marked, for the moment, the end of Mexican operations against Victorio, and Valle was soon reported to have left the area to seek supplies and additional troops. It was also reported that he had been summoned back to Chihuahua to thwart a threatened internal revolution.[66] In the meantime, at least some of his troops were divided up into detachments to guard Mexican settlements to the east of the

58 Valle in the field 7 miles below Quitman to Grierson, Eagle Springs, 31 Jul., 1880 in Telegrams Rec'd by General Grierson in the Field 30 Jun.-4 Sept., 1880, HQ Records DoP 1878-1881, NA, RG393, M1381, Roll 4.

59 Grierson to AAG, San Antonio, Texas, 3 Aug., 1880 in Telegrams Sent 23 Jun.-30 Nov., 1880, HQ Records DoP 1878-1881, NA, RG393, M1381, Roll 1, pp.79, Letter No.353; 'Grierson's Report, Sept.1880'; NA, RG393, Part 1, Entry 2546, pp.639-644; Dinges, 1987, p.90; McChristian, 1982, p.63.

60 Valle to Grierson, 4 Aug., 1880 in Letters Rec'd File 19 Mar., 1878-14 Feb., 1881, HQ Records DoP 1878-1881, NA, RG393, M1381, Roll 2.

61 Brinkerhoff to AAAG, DoNM, 9 Aug., 1880 in Letters Received by HQ DoNM Sept. 1865-Aug. 1890, NA, RG393, M1088, Roll 41, Jul.-Dec. 1880.

62 Brinkerhoff, citing dispatch rec'd from Grierson, Rattlesnake Springs, rec'd 9 Aug., 1880, to AAAG SF NM 10 Aug., 1880, NA, RG393 Part 3 Entry 440 pp.84-88; AAG, DoTx to AG Chicago, 11 Aug., 1880, 'Victorio Files', NA, RG393, M1495, Roll 14.

63 Brinkerhoff to Buell, 11 Aug., 1880, Telegrams Sent DoNM, Vol.3, Jan.-Nov. 1880, NA, RG393, Part 3, Entry 431, p.725.

64 Brinkerhoff to Buell, 11 Aug., 1880, Telegrams Sent DoNM, Vol.3, Jan.-Nov. 1880, NA, RG393, Part 3, Entry 431, p.725; Platt, citing Brinkerhoff's report, to AAG HQ MDoM, 12 Aug., 1880, 'Victorio Files', NA, RG393, M1495, Roll 14; Whipple to Sheridan 12 Aug., 1880, NA, RG393, Part 1, Entry 2539, Press Copies of Letters and Endorsements Sent, MDoM, Vol. 13, p.506; Whipple to Sheridan, 12 Aug., 1880, NA, RG393, Part 1, Entry 2538, p.360; Sheridan to Whipple, 14 Aug., 1880, NA, RG393, Part 1, Entry 2546, p.580; Hatch to AAG Fort Leavenworth, 12 Aug., 1880 in 'Victorio Papers', NA, M666, Roll 527; Thrapp, 1974, p.288.

65 Hatch (citing telegram from Samaniego to Brinkerhoff) to AAG Fort Leavenworth, 17 Aug., 1880, Telegrams Sent DoNM, Vol.3, Jan.-Nov. 1880, NA, RG393, Part 3, Entry 431, p.749.

66 Whipple to Sheridan, 26 Aug., 1880, NA, RG393, Part 1, Entry 2539, Press Copies of Letters and Endorsements Sent, MDoM, Vol. 13, p.541.

Candelaria Mountains.[67] Finally, on 31 August 1880, Brinkerhoff informed District Headquarters, Santa Fé, that there was a force of 200 *federales* and ranchmen concentrated at Carrizal.[68]

Grierson claimed that he had sent scouts, presumably the Pueblo Indians, to follow Victorio, and that they had reported that Victorio had retreated back to Mexico, where he was camped opposite Ojo del Alamo in the Bosque Bonito.[69] One suspects that Grierson's command was too tired to have sent out scouts, and had merely assumed that the Apaches had fled back to their camp in Mexico. This location had, after all, been reported to him by two separate sources. The Pueblo scouts had pinpointed it and had returned to Eagle Springs to report this on 29 July. The same information had been delivered to Grierson by Colonel Valle, based on intelligence delivered by the latter's own scouts. In the days following the hostilities at Tinaja De Las Palmas, Grierson's scouts confirmed[70] the precise location of this camp. Indeed on the day after the fight there, scouts reported a large camp of Apaches with a large herd of stock camped miles below Quitman on the Mexican side of the border.[71] Grierson certainly sent a message to Valle on 1 August, repeating the information he had given Valle earlier, on 30 July,[72] that the main camp of the Apaches was opposite Ojo del Alamo. Grierson also sent four scouts to Valle to act as couriers.[73] This was prompted by a message from Old Fort Quitman that, while they had received Grierson's information, they could not see anybody to contact on the other side of the river. Palmer, the telegraph operator at Quitman, was instructed to 'Hire a Mexican, make a raft, or go to the river and get someone to come over – show them the paper. Do not fail in getting some one from either side to take the dispatch across at once.'[74] Palmer himself took the dispatch across the river and was later commended for his prompt initiative.[75]

There is some evidence to suggest that the Apaches who fought Grierson at Tinaja de las Palmas did not return to Mexico. When the Mexicans first reported Victorio's move northwards to Grierson, the latter had, as part of his defence efforts, asked the Texas Rangers to help trap and destroy the Apaches.[76] Thus, a small group of 13 Texas Rangers and Ranger Sergeant James B. Gillett departed from their base at Ysleta[77] on 2 August 1880, under the command of Ranger Lieutenant George W. Baylor, responding to Grierson's request that they scout eastwards to Eagle Springs.[78] They arrived at Old Fort Quitman two days later, and Baylor was in the middle of reporting to Colonel Grierson by wire when the Apaches again cut the line between the Fort and Eagle Springs. Following their original orders, the Texas Rangers arrived at 'Eighteen Mile Water

67 Brinkerhoff to Hatch, 19 Aug., 1880, 'Victorio Files', NA, RG393, M1495, Roll 14.

68 Brinkerhoff to AAAG, 31 Aug., 1880, NA, RG393, Part 3, Entry 439, p. 807.

69 'Grierson's Report, Sept.1880'; NA, RG393, Part 1, Entry 2546, pp.639-644; McChristian, 1982, p.62; Rister, 1928, p.211; Miles, 1971, p.62.

70 On 1 August, Robert Grierson observed that 'Scouts are kept out all the time and are coming in often with news. Victorio is on the other side of the river, and Col. Valle, Mexican Army, is moving towards him.' ('Robert Grierson Diary', 1 Aug., 1880).

71 Grierson to CO Mexican Troops opposite Quitman, 31 Jul., 1880 in Telegrams Sent 23 Jun.-30 Nov., 1880, HQ Records DoP 1878-1881, NA, RG393, M1381, Roll 1, p.85, Letter No.360.

72 This message was actually sent on the 31 as noted in Grierson's own correspondence.

73 Grierson to Valle, 1 Aug., 1880 in Letters Sent 19 Sept., 1879-11 Aug., 1880, HQ Records DoP 1878-1881, NA, RG393, M1381, Roll 1, Letter No.131.

74 Beck to Palmer, 31 Jul., 1880 in Telegrams Sent 23 Jun.-30 Nov., 1880, HQ Records DoP 1878-1881, NA, RG393, M1381, Roll 1, p.87, Letter No.362.

75 Beck to Palmer, 1 Aug., 1880 in Telegrams Sent 23 Jun.-30 Nov., 1880, HQ Records DoP 1878-1881, NA, RG393, M1381, Roll 1, p.92, Letter No.372.

76 Gillett, 1976, p.180; Stout, 1974, p.159.

77 Ysleta is approximately 10-15 miles east of El Paso.

78 Baylor, 1996, p.253.

Plate 10.9 Eagle Mountains from the north, in the vicinity of Eagle Springs. (Photo: Author)

Plate 10.10. Eagle Springs. (Photo: Author)

Hole, where General Grierson's troops had had an engagement with Victorio'.[79] Baylor reported seeing bullet and blood marks, dead cavalry horses and Grierson's hasty entrenchments.[80] Having passed beyond Tinaja de las Palmas on Victorio's trail, they spotted the remains of a stagecoach ambushed by the Apaches on 30 July.[81] Frank Wyant, who had been driving the coach, and one of his passengers, E.C. Baker, had been killed. A second passenger, Captain Coldwell, had managed to escape.[82] The Apache warriors:

> had cut the mail sacks open, cut canvass off the buck board & tore the mail matter into shreds- the men were mutilated[83] and papers stuffed in their wounds. Capt. Coldwell escaped by a miracle.[84]

The wreckage had first been discovered by Grierson and his force, presumably when they were on their way back to Eagle Springs on the evening of 30 July. Robert Grierson had noted that a mule had been butchered for steaks and speculated that the Apaches were short of supplies.[85] The following day, the driver and passenger, and Private Davis, had been buried near Eagle Springs stage station.[86]

The Rangers tracked the Apaches south and east as they detoured around the Eagle Mountains, and they discovered that the Apaches had destroyed the telegraph line along a quarter of a mile of its length, smashing what they could not take with them.[87] If the Rangers had followed a trail from Tinaja de las Palmas, they made no mention of it crossing the border. Moreover, if the telegraph line was cut on 4 August, then some or possibly all the Apache warriors had remained in the United States for at least four days. The key questions are: why had they remained in the area; and why had they suddenly cut the wire on 4 August? These actions suggest that Victorio may have deployed his men in an attempt to wrong-foot his opponent. For instance, Coldwell's escape appears to be particularly fortuitous; could Victorio have needed a survivor to draw the army's attention to this particular area? Answers to these questions will be investigated as the next chapter unfolds.

Grierson, with his entire command, had arrived back at Eagle Springs by the evening of 30 July.[88] Once there, he summoned Captain Carpenter from Viejo Pass, with B and H Companies, Tenth Cavalry. Captain Baldwin, with I Company, was left in charge of Viejo Pass.[89] Carpenter was to

---

79 Gillett, 1976, p.180.

80 Stout, 1974, pp.159-160; Baylor, 1996, p.253 & p.257 note 10.

81 'Robert Grierson Diary', 10 Jul. to 1 Sept., 1880. Some sources (List of Persons Killed, Wounded, or Captured, by Indians, &c., in the DoTx, since Sept. 30, 1879, officially reported by post commanders. NA, RG393, Part 1, Entry 2546, p.633; Chronological List, p.50; Record of Engagements, p.95; Baylor, 1996, p.257 note 11) list this attack as having occurred on the 31 July, 1880 but Robert Grierson is clear that it occurred late on the 30 July, 1880.

82 Wellman states that Capt. Coldwell was travelling on the eastbound stage which discovered the wreckage of the westbound stage. (1957, p.169).

83 This is probably hearsay as the site was cleared by a detachment of the Tenth Cavalry as they repaired back to Eagle Springs on the 31 Aug., 1880.

84 Baylor, 1996, p.257 note 11 see also Stout, 1974, p.160.

85 'Robert Grierson Diary', 1 Aug., 1880.

86 Ord to AAG, DoTx, 3 Aug., 1880, NA, RG393, Part 1, Entry 2546, pp.573-574; Leighton Finley Diary 31 Jul., 1880 entry Special Collections, University of Arizona Library, Tucson; 'Robert Grierson Diary', 1 Aug., 1880; McChristian, 1982, pp.62-63; See also Webb, 1976, p.89.

87 Baylor, 1996, p.253; Gillett, 1976, pp.180-181; See also Whipple to Sheridan, 11 Aug., 1880, NA, RG393, Part 1, Entry 2538, p.359.

88 'Robert Grierson Diary', 1 Aug., 1880.

89 Beck to Carpenter, 30 Jul., 1880 in Letters Sent 19 Sept., 1879-11 Aug., 1880, HQ Records DoP 1878-1881, NA, RG393, M1381, Roll 1, Letter No.128; Bi-Monthly Company Muster Rolls for Company I, 10th Cavalry Jul./Aug. 1880 in NA, RG94; Matthews, 1993, p.39.

proceed to Eagle Springs via Van Horn Wells, with a view to contacting Captain Lebo, who had earlier been instructed to scout in that direction, and instructing him to move to Eagle Springs as well.[90] As luck would have it Carpenter failed to contact Lebo, and as we shall see in the next chapter, this failure was to be fortuitous. There was no attempt to pursue Victorio, Grierson being more concerned to concentrate a force to counter the Apaches' next move.[91] Most of the Tenth Cavalrymen involved in the battle had reached Tinaja de las Palmas from Fort Quitman or Eagle Springs at a forced march, and were in no condition to mount an immediate pursuit. At Eagle Springs, Grierson found time to write a letter reassuring his wife of his safety. He characterised his stand at Tinaja de las Palmas as:

> the best thing that could possibly have been done under the circumstances ... If I had not made my stand as I did Victorio and his whole outfit would have gotten through without a fight, and we would have had only the uncertain chance of pursuit.[92]

The key issue, from Grierson's point of view, was that, as far as he was concerned, he had successfully prevented the Apaches from penetrating his defences. In doing so, he had avoided being drawn into the kind of horse-killing pursuit which he had seen cripple the Ninth Cavalry in New Mexico. A number of Grierson's reports state quite categorically that no Apaches had managed to pass his defences and proceed north towards New Mexico.[93] For example, on 2 August, 1880, he sent a report to Hatch where he stated 'the Indians fled rapidly to the Rio Grande - none having gone north.[94] This was a claim he reiterated with vigour on 24 September 1880 in response to reports to the contrary received in New Mexico.[95]

However, at least one communication from Grierson shows that he had failed to block the passage of some Apaches. On 31 July, from Eagle Springs, Grierson had alerted Hatch and Buell that they should send infantry to cover water sources in the Comidas [Cornudas?] and Wind Mountains, particularly San Antonio Springs. He had also recommended that they send cavalry to picket the Sacramento Mountains. While Grierson had two companies of Tenth Cavalry stationed in the Guadalupe Mountains, he did not have the troops to cover the Sacramentos. He noted that such steps were necessary as 'pursuit indicates the hostile Indians will go either there [the Sacramento Mountains] or to the Guadalupes'. This message post-dates Tinaja de las Palmas, as Brinkerhoff mentions that Grierson's 'dispatch of this morning concerning fight with Indians was put through directly request from here'.[96] (See document file no. 92.) Hatch responded that

---

90 Beck to Carpenter, 30 Jul., 1880 in Letters Sent 19 Sept., 1879-11 Aug., 1880, HQ Records DoP 1878-1881, NA, RG393, M1381, Roll 1, Letter No.128.

91 Ibid.

92 Temple, 1959, pp.103-104.

93 Beck to Carpenter, 30 Jul., 1880 in Letters Sent 19 Sept., 1879-11 Aug., 1880, HQ Records DoP 1878-1881, NA, RG393, M1381, Roll 1, Letter No.128; Grierson to Hatch SF 30 Jul., 1880, NA, RG393, Part 3, Entry 439, p.583; See slightly tidied up version quoted in Loud to Hatch, 31 Jul., 1880, Telegrams Sent DoNM, Vol.3, Jan.-Nov. 1880, NA, RG393, Part 3, Entry 431, pp.680-681; Sheridan to AG Wash. D.C. 2 Aug., 1880 in 'Victorio Papers', NA, M666, Roll 527; Whipple to CO DoNM, 2 Aug., 1880 in NA, RG393, Part 3, Entry 439, pp.46-49; Grierson to HQ DoP, 31 Jul., 1880, 'Victorio Files', NA, RG393, M1495, Roll 14; Sheridan to AG, Washington D.C. 2 Aug., 1880, NA, RG393, Part 1, Entry 2539, Press Copies of Letters and Endorsements Sent, MDoM, Vol. 13, pp.483-485.

94 Grierson to Commanding Officer, District of New Mexico, 2 August, 1880, RG303, Pt 3, Entry 440, pp.34-37

95 Grierson to CO Fort Bliss, 24 Sept., 1880 in Telegrams Sent 23 Jun.-30 Nov., 1880, HQ Records DoP 1878-1881, NA, RG393, M1381, Roll 1, pp.169-170, Letter No.504.

96 Grierson to CO Fort Bliss, 31 Jul., 1880 in Telegrams Sent 23 Jun.-30 Nov., 1880, HQ Records DoP 1878-1881, NA, RG393, M1381, Roll 1, pp.85-86, Letter No.361; Brinkerhoff to AAAG SF 31 Jul., 1880, NA, RG393, Part 3, Entry 439, pp.572-574.

he would, for the moment, place the New Mexican troops on the alert. The District Commander was not going to scatter his forces to cover specific points until Buell could be given more specific information concerning the Apaches' movements. The matter was also complicated by the fact that the area was flooded on account of recent and prolonged heavy rain.[97] At a later stage of Grierson's campaign against the Apaches, Buell did move 'his command to the west bank of the Rio Grande'[98] so as to be best placed to move into action should the Apaches penetrate Grierson's defence or retreat into Mexico and attempt to return to New Mexico somewhere between the Florida Mountains and El Paso.

97 Hatch to Grierson, Eagle Springs, and to Col. Buell, Fort Cummings, 1 Aug., 1880, Telegrams Sent DoNM, Vol.3, Jan.-Nov. 1880, NA, RG393, Part 3, Entry 431, pp.685-686.

98 Whipple to Sheridan 12 Aug., 1880, NA, RG393, Part 1, Entry 2539, Press Copies of Letters and Endorsements Sent, MDoM, Vol. 13, p.506; See also Whipple to Sheridan, 12 Aug., 1880, NA, RG393, Part 1, Entry 2538, p.360; Platte to AAG HQ MDoM, 14 Aug., 1880 in 'Victorio Papers', NA, M666, Roll 528; See also 'Town and County', the *Grant County Herald*, 14 Aug., 1880.

11

Grierson's Texas Campaign 2: Rattlesnake Springs, August 1880

(For an overview of Grierson's July-August campaign against Victorio, see Map 11.1)

Grierson now had five companies of Tenth Cavalry (A, B, C, G and H), together with H Company, Twenty-Fourth Infantry, concentrated at Eagle Springs. To the north, K Company, under Captain Lebo, earlier tasked with scouting the area between Van Horn Wells and the Sierras Carrizo and Diablo, commenced their scout on 1 August 1880.[1]

At Eagle Springs, Grierson was informed that a section of 13 miles of the telegraph line between Forts Davis and Stockton was 'down'. While this might have been the work of the Apaches, the extent of the damage suggests adverse weather conditions. A strong detachment had been sent out to repair the line, but in the meantime, Grierson's communications to Fort Stockton would have to be carried by courier.[2] In the immediate aftermath of Tinaja de las Palmas, Grierson suspected that Victorio would try to penetrate his defences further to the east, between the Eagle and Van Horn Mountains.[3] At least some troops were sent out from Eagle Springs on 1 August, to guard Alamo Springs. This small detachment, its members drawn from several companies of the Tenth Cavalry, was commanded by Corporal Asa Weaver.[4]

On 3 August 1880, the Apaches fought a running battle with Weaver's detachment near Alamo Springs,[5] a location described as 'a trickle of water between Eagle Mountains and Van Horn Mountains'.[6] Weaver lost Private Willie Tockes (C Company), whose horse bolted right into the middle of the Apaches;[7] and another trooper, Julius Londin (or London) was wounded.[8]

---

1 Bi-Monthly Company Muster Rolls for Company K, 10th Cavalry, Jul./Aug. 1880 in NA, RG94; 'Grierson's Report, Sept.1880'; NA, RG393, Part 1, Entry 2546, pp.639-644; Fort Davis Museum Webpage.

2 Yard, CO Fort Davis to Grierson, Eagle Springs, 31 Jul., 1880 in Telegrams Rec'd by General Grierson in the Field 30 Jun.-14 Sept., 1880, HQ Records DoP 1878-1881, NA, RG393, M1381, Roll 4

3 Grierson to AAG, San Antonio, Texas, 31 Jul., 1880 in Telegrams Sent 23 Jun.-30 Nov., 1880, HQ Records DoP 1878-1881, NA, RG393, M1381, Roll 1, pp.80-81, Letter No.355.

4 Glass, 1971, p.135.

5 'Grierson's Report, Sept.1880'; NA, RG393, Part 1, Entry 2546, pp.639-644; Record of Events Aug., 1880 in Returns From U.S. Military Posts 1800-1916, Fort Davis, Texas Jan. 1879-Jun. 1891, NA, M617, Roll 298; Record of Engagements, pp.95-96; Leckie, 1967, p.226; Dinges Handbook of Texas Online entry; Leckie & Leckie, p.265; Thrapp, 1967, p.205; Miles, 1971, p.62; Webb, 1976, p.89.

6 Fort Davis Museum Webpage.

7 Regimental History 1866-98 10th Cavalry, NA, RG391, Entry 933, pp.19-20; Leighton Finley Diary 3 Aug., 1880 entry Special Collections, University of Arizona Library, Tucson (Finley named the dead man as Pvt. George Jockoe); Leckie, 1967 p.226; see also Wharfield, p.173. My copy of the Chronological List has a smudge under 'enlisted' men killed but definitely notes a trooper as being wounded in this skirmish. (Chronological List, p.50) The Regimental History of the Tenth Cavalry notes that Tokes remains were not found until 'months afterwards.' (Regimental History 1866-98 10th Cavalry, NA, RG391, Entry 933, pp.19-20).

8 Record of Events Aug., 1880 in Returns From Regular Army Cavalry Regiments 1833-1916, 10th Cavalry Regimental Returns 1873 to 1880, NA, M744, Roll 96.

Robert Grierson recorded that one of Weaver's men had been shot in the foot, and that the 125 Apaches involved had just crossed the Rio Grande with many horses.[9] Weaver received an immediate promotion to sergeant for his conduct in this skirmish.[10] His patrol returned to returned to Eagle Springs at approximately 3:30 p.m. on 3 August, and Weaver reported that the Apaches were to the east of Eagle Springs and were approximately 15 miles south of the road between Eagle Springs and Van Horn Wells.[11]

This skirmish raises a question as to the strategy deployed by Victorio. The Tenth Cavalry detachment cannot have been large, if it was commanded by a corporal, and its small size prompts the question: why did the Apaches choose to fight a running battle? If Victorio and most of his warriors had been present, they should have had the numbers to put out a strong rearguard, thereby stopping Weaver's detachment in its tracks; but if Weaver's detachment had clashed with Victorio's dependants, accompanied only by a few warriors, this would explain why the Apaches did not attempt to drive off such a small detachment.

If the Apaches were operating in two groups, as appears to have been standard practice[12] for Victorio when attempting to move dependents or plunder, they might have made arrangements to rendezvous further to the north. Victorio appears to have designated Fresno Springs, between the Sierra Diablo and the Carrizo Mountains, as the rendezvous.[13] Study of the USGS maps suggests this would have been an ideal spot for both groups to unite in preparation for a move north into New Mexico. The warriors who had confronted Grierson at Tinaja de las Palmas also attacked a stagecoach, leaving a convenient survivor to spread the alarm. This would hopefully draw the Tenth Cavalry detachments westwards from Eagle Springs. The second group of Apaches (families and plunder escorted by a few warriors) would then cross the border, pass between the Eagle and Van Horn Mountains, and make for Fresno Springs, arriving from the south-east. The bulk of the warriors, after creating their diversions, would arrive from the south-west.

Yet the success of this diversionary tactic was threatened from the outset by the reports of Grierson's and Valle's scouts of the large camp 60 miles south-east of Fort Quitman. Grierson would naturally have assumed that the next attempt to penetrate his defences would be made from this location. So, it is important to consider that he had knowledge from two sources of the broad location of the second group of Apaches *before* the first group drew attention to themselves. After Tinaja de las Palmas, the Tenth Cavalry returned to Eagle Springs because, as far as Grierson was concerned, this was the best place from which to counter any further manoeuvring by the Apaches camped opposite Ojo del Alamo in Mexico. Corporal Weaver's skirmish would only confirm his commander's assessment. Weaver's detachment had intercepted the Apaches' dependants travelling with a relatively light escort of older warriors. These Apaches would not have had any other option but to throw out a rearguard that became engaged in a skirmish while the rest made a run for it.

When the telegraph line east from Fort Quitman was cut, on 4 August, this was probably a second attempt to draw the Tenth Cavalry to the west. Victorio appears to have based himself in the Eagle Mountains after Tinaja de las Palmas. One suspects that he was hoping to draw Grierson in pursuit into those mountains, fight a rearguard action or two, then draw the Tenth Cavalry into a horse-killing pursuit. When Grierson failed to take the bait, Victorio was ideally placed to monitor

9 'Robert Grierson Diary', 4 Aug., 1880.

10 Regimental History 1866-98 10th Cavalry, NA, RG391, Entry 933, pp.19-20; Schubert, 1997, p.165; Bigelow, USACMH webpage.

11 'Robert Grierson Diary', 4 Aug., 1880. The Handbook of Texas Online places Van Horn Wells twelve miles to the south of present day Van Horn, Texas. Van Horn Wells was originally established as a small military post on the California Trail sometime between 1859 and 1861. J.J. Van Horn of the 8th U.S. Infantry Regiment the first commander of this post gave his name to the post. (Thrapp, 1988, p.147).

12 See in particular , Chapter 14 for an illustration of this strategy.

13 Fort Davis Museum Webpage.

Tenth Cavalry movements. The Eagle Mountains soar high above Eagle Springs, and it would not have been difficult to station a scout or two on the heights around Grierson's field headquarters. While Grierson could only speculate as to how many Apaches had cut the telegraph line to the west, he had *already* received confirmation of the location of what he assumed to be the main group of warriors. The location of Corporal Weaver's running battle with Apaches, south-east of Eagle Springs, was approximately where Grierson had expected a large party to appear. (See Map 11.2)

The Colonel now had what he thought was a strong lead on a large group of Apaches, and he assumed that this was Victorio's main force of 125–150 warriors. As Weaver had reported that the Apaches had fled to the north-east, towards the Van Horn Mountains, Grierson supposed the party was travelling to Viejo Pass, Van Horn Wells or Bass Canyon, before turning towards the Guadalupe Mountains.[14] His prediction was that Victorio was aiming to pass through Bass Canon,[15] and he marched to Van Horn Wells to block the canyon.[16] On reaching the area and finding no signs of the passing of these Apaches, Grierson concluded that Victorio had continued east along the southern side of the Van Horn Mountains. He therefore sent some of his men south-eastwards to block the passage around the eastern end of the Van Horn Mountains,[17] covering the passage between Needle Peak and the Van Horn Mountains. In their records, A, B and H Companies, Tenth Cavalry, recounted moving beyond Van Horn Wells to what they termed the Devil's Racecourse[18] or Race Track, on 3 August 1880.[19] Grierson himself reported that his command had covered the passes between the Eagle Mountains and Van Horn Wells on the evening of 3 August. By the following morning, some of his troops were picketing the only pass between Bass Canyon and Capote. The Colonel had also received word by courier from Viejo Pass that all was quiet there. He was thus confident that the Apaches had not passed through his picket line.[20] Robert Grierson and Lieutenant Finley stated that, by the time they camped on the evening of 4 August, they were 10 miles to the south-east of Van Horn Wells.[21] Robert Grierson also noted that they had reached a flat plain which stretched away for many miles, but had found no sign that a large group of Apaches had crossed the road.[22] However, Grierson knew Apaches well enough not to make assumptions and, from his camp near Van Horn Wells, he sent out scouting parties southwards towards the border with Mexico, in search of the Apaches.[23]

---

14 Grierson to AAG, San Antonio, Texas, 3 Aug., 1880 in Telegrams Sent 23 Jun.-30 Nov., 1880, HQ Records DoP 1878-1881, NA, RG393, M1381, Roll 1, pp.79, Letter No.353.

15 Ord, Citing Grierson's report of the 3 Aug., 1880, to AG Chicago, 4 Aug., 1880, 'Victorio Files', NA, RG393, M1495, Roll 14; NA, RG393, Part 1, Entry 2538, p.355; 'Grierson's Report, Sept.1880'; NA, RG393, Part 1, Entry 2546, pp.639-644.

16 'Grierson's Report, Sept.1880'; NA, RG393, Part 1, Entry 2546, pp.639-644; Matthews, 1993, p.40; Fort Davis Museum Webpage.

17 'Grierson's Report, Sept.1880'; NA, RG393, Part 1, Entry 2546, pp.639-644.

18 On passing the site of Van Horn Wells in September 2006 enroute to Fort Davis we passed through a long flat grass covered plain running east from that point, which could be described as a race course. In July and August I am reliably informed by my companions that the temperatures at that time of year could be very hot. Hence the Devil's racetrack.

19 Bi-Monthly Company Muster Rolls for Company A & B, 10th Cavalry Jul./Aug. 1880 in NA, RG94; Record of Events Aug., 1880 in Returns From U.S. Military Posts 1800-1916, Fort Davis, Texas Jan. 1879-Jun. 1891, NA, M617 Roll 298; See also Glass, pp.134-135.

20 Grierson to AAG, San Antonio, Texas, 4 Aug., 1880 in Telegrams Sent 23 Jun.-30 Nov., 1880, HQ Records DoP 1878-1881, NA, RG393, M1381, Roll 1, pp.81-82, Letter No.356.

21 'Robert Grierson Diary', 4 Aug., 1880.; Leighton Finley Diary 4 Aug., 1880 entry Special Collections, University of Arizona Library, Tucson.

22 'Robert Grierson Diary', 4 Aug., 1880.

23 Grierson to AAG, San Antonio, Texas, 4 Aug., 1880 in Telegrams Sent 23 Jun.-30 Nov., 1880, HQ Records DoP 1878-1881, NA, RG393, M1381, Roll 1, pp.81-82, Letter No.356.

This time it was the second group of Apaches who anticipated Grierson's response to their discovery. On being discovered by Corporal Weaver's detachment, they had fled to the north-east, to give the impression that they were going to pass east of the Van Horn Mountains. Having thrown off their pursuers, they turned north-west and headed for Fresno Springs pass, to the west of Van Horn Wells.[24] On 4 August, around midnight, Grierson learned that the Apaches had not attempted to pass to the east of the Van Horn Mountains. An east-bound stage, attempting to travel from Eagle Springs to Van Horn Wells, reported that they had seen between 50 and 100 Apaches with about 100 horses. The driver claimed to have identified Victorio at approximately 800 yards. The stage returned to Eagle Springs and tried to pass through again under cover of darkness. They discovered that the telegraph line between Eagle Springs and Van Horn Wells had been ripped up, with some of the poles burned and all of the insulators smashed. The driver thought that he passed within a mile of the Apaches' camp and estimated that they were making for the Guadalupe Mountains.[25] (See document file no. 93.) Grierson also stated that similar information had been delivered to him by one of his scouting detachments that same evening.[26] He immediately alerted his counterparts in New Mexico and advised them to send troops eastwards to cover the Sacramento Mountains.[27]

Hatch alerted Fort Stanton and the detachment stationed at the Mescalero agency; and he approved Buell's movement of forces to the Rio Grande and the sending of scouts into the San Andres Mountains.[28] Major Morrow's command was left intact at Knight's Ranch,[29] with a sufficient garrison left at Fort Cummings to keep a close eye on the Mexican border west of the Rio Grande.[30] This was the last that Hatch heard from Grierson until 10 August 1880. This was a recurring problem throughout the Victorio campaign, as troops moved away from close proximity to the telegraph lines in pursuit of the Apaches.

Subsequent events show that Grierson correctly concluded that Victorio was aiming for Rattlesnake Springs in Salt Flat Valley.[31] For the moment, he had been completely outmanoeuvred by Victorio, and between 11:00 p.m. on 4 August and 3:00 a.m. on 5 August, he concentrated his

---

24 'Grierson's Report, Sept.1880'; NA, RG393, Part 1, Entry 2546, pp.639-644; Thrapp, 1974, p.288; Leckie, 1967 p.226; Matthews, 1993, p.40; Leckie & Leckie, 1984, p.265; Dinges Handbook of Texas Online entry.

25 Loud to Buell, 7 Aug., 1880, Telegrams Sent DoNM, Vol.3, Jan. – Nov. 1880 NA, RG393, Part 3, Entry 431, pp.713-714.

26 Grierson to AAG, DoTx, 8 Aug., 1880 in Telegrams Sent 23 Jun.-30 Nov., 1880, HQ Records DoP 1878-1881, NA, RG393, M1381, Roll 1, pp.99-101, Letter No.384; Brinkerhoff, citing dispatch rec'd from Grierson, Rattlesnake Springs, rec'd 9 Aug., 1880, to AAAG SF NM 10 Aug., 1880, NA, RG393 Part 3 Entry 440 pp.84-88; AAG, DoTx to AG Chicago, 11 Aug., 1880, 'Victorio Files', NA, RG393, M1495, Roll 14; 'Grierson's Report, Sept.1880'; NA, RG393, Part 1, Entry 2546, pp.639-644.

27 Hatch (repeating Grierson's telegram of 4 Aug., 1880) to CO Fort Stanton, 6 Aug., 1880 & AAG Fort Leavenworth, 7 Aug., 1880, Telegrams Sent DoNM, Vol.3, Jan. – Nov. 1880 NA, RG393, Part 3, Entry 431, p.707, 710 &711; Grierson to AAAG SF 4 Aug., 1880 (It is worth noting that this message reached Capt Brinkerhoff at Fort Bliss on the 6 August, 1880 and this information was duly telegraphed to SF) NA, RG393, Part 3, Entry 439, p.128; See also 'By Telegraph', the *Grant County Herald*, 14 Aug., 1880; Hatch to AAG Fort Leavenworth, 7 Aug., 1880, 'Victorio Files', NA, RG393, M1495, Roll 14.

28 Hatch to AAG Fort Leavenworth, 6 Aug., 1880, Telegrams Sent DoNM, Vol.3, Jan. – Nov. 1880 NA, RG393, Part 3, Entry 431, p.711; see also p.710.

29 The refitting and re-deployment of the troops in New Mexico will be covered in the following chapter.

30 Hatch to AAG Fort Leavenworth, 7 Aug., 1880, Telegrams Sent DoNM, Vol.3, Jan. – Nov. 1880 NA, RG393, Part 3, Entry 431, p.711.

31 Fort Davis Museum Webpage. Rattlesnake Springs were approximately 17 miles to the north of Fresno Springs and 10 miles from Apache Springs in the Sierra Diablo. (Capt. Viele to AAAG, DoP, Fort Concho, Texas, 24 Jan., 1879, NA, RG393, Part 1, Entry 2546, pp.25-40).

Plate 11.1. The Van Horn Wells of Grierson's time was a number of miles to the south of the modern town. All that remains at the original site today is a couple of historical markers and some debris. (Photo: Author)

Plate 11.2. The Devil's Racecourse runs south-east from Van Horn Wells and, as the name suggests, it is unusually level and very hot during the summer. (Photo: Author)

battalion 10 miles south-east of Van Horn Wells.[32] This concentration might have been accomplished more rapidly, had not one of his couriers failed to find the cavalry camp south-east of Van Horn Wells in the dark.[33] Grierson had a lot to lose if he let Victorio's Apaches slip through into New Mexico. After all, it had been Grierson who had lobbied his superiors to accept his plan to stop Victorio in western Texas, rather than further north in New Mexico. If the Apaches reached the Mescalero reservation, Grierson would be to blame. The Colonel did not panic, and rather than trying to pick up and pursue the trail, he sought to get ahead of Victorio and head the Apaches off at Rattlesnake Springs.[34] Once again, he refused to be led into a horse-killing pursuit by the Apaches. If successful, this manoeuvre would prevent Victorio deploying most of his warriors as a strong rearguard, if the Tenth Cavalry did manage to catch up with them.

Setting out in the early hours of 5 August, Grierson sent A, B, C, G and H Companies, Tenth Cavalry, numbering 170[35] or over 200[36] troopers, on their way towards Rattlesnake Springs. He and his headquarters staff followed his cavalrymen in two ambulance wagons. This group in turn was followed by a supply wagon train, under Captain Gilmore, with 25 men of the Twenty-Fourth Infantry Regiment.[37]

Grierson marched northwards, keeping out of sight of the Apaches, by moving parallel to them on the east side of the Baylor Mountains.[38] His command swung round the northern end of the Baylor Mountains and marched west across Salt Flat Valley and reached Rattlesnake Springs in the early hours of 6 August 1880. The command had covered an estimated 65 miles,[39] from the camp 10 miles to the south-east of Van Horn Wells to Rattlesnake Springs, in just under 24 hours,[40] an accomplishment in itself. The Tenth Cavalry battalion reached their destination around midnight, with Grierson himself arriving at half past three in the morning.[41] The wagon train, being much slower, was not expected to arrive before the afternoon. Lieutenant Flipper recalled that campfires and use of lamps was strictly forbidden, saddles were left on their horses and the troops had cold food and coffee for their supper.[42]

---

32 'Grierson's Report, Sept.1880'; NA, RG393, Part 1, Entry 2546, pp.639-644.

33 'Robert Grierson Diary', 6 Aug., 1880.

34 Lt. Flipper's memoir states that Victorio's destination was Fresno Spring but then assumes that the destination of their long night march was that location and did not realise that they had arrived at Rattlesnake Springs. While mistaken it does lend credence to the argument that Victorio had used Fresno Spring as the rendezvous point for the two groups of Apaches.

35 Dinges Handbook of Texas Online entry.

36 Fort Davis Museum Webpage.

37 Dinges Handbook of Texas Online entry.

38 'Grierson's Report, Sept.1880'; NA, RG393, Part 1, Entry 2546, pp.639-644; Leckie & Leckie, 1984, p.265; Thrapp, 1974, p.288; 1967, p.204; Stout, 1974, p.155; Miles, 1971, p.62. Thrapp notes that the original despatches are too vague to pinpoint the exact route (Thrapp, 1974, p.288) However, the Fort Davis Museum webpage provides a clear location of Rattlesnake Springs as being just to the west of the Sierra Diablo Mountains and southeast of the opening into Victorio Canyon.

39 Grierson to AAG DoTx, San Antonio, 14 Aug., 1880 in 'Victorio Files', NA, RG393, M1495, Roll 14;See also Whipple to AG Wash. D.C. 13 Aug., 1880 in 'Victorio Papers', NA, M666, Roll 527; Leighton Finley Diary, 5 Aug., 1880 entry Special Collections, University of Arizona Library, Tucson; 'Indian Affairs', *Army & Navy Journal*, Vol. 18, 14 Aug., 1880, p.30.

40 Brinkerhoff, citing dispatch rec'd from Grierson, Rattlesnake Springs, rec'd 9 Aug., 1880, to AAAG SF NM 10 Aug., 1880, NA, RG393 Part 3 Entry 440 pp.84-88; Brinkerhoff to AAAG SF, 13 Aug., 1880, Telegrams Sent DoNM, Vol.3, Jan. – Nov. 1880 NA, RG393, Part 3, Entry 431, p.737; 'By Telegraph', the *Grant County Herald*, 14 Aug., 1880; AAG, DoTx to AG Chicago, 11 Aug., 1880, 'Victorio Files', NA, RG393, M1495, Roll 14; 'Robert Grierson Diary', 7 Aug., 1880. 'Grierson's Report, Sept.1880'; NA, RG393, Part 1, Entry 2546, pp.639-644.

41 'Robert Grierson Diary', 7 Aug., 1880. Dinges Handbook of Texas Online entry; Fort Davis Museum Webpage.

42 Harris. 1997, p.34.

While Grierson thought that his battalion had out-marched the Apaches, he did not immediately know this for sure. This is confirmed by Lieutenant Flipper's account of the troops occupying positions all round Rattlesnake Springs during the night.[43] The following morning, Captain Nolan, with A Company, was sent to scout the Sierra Diablo.[44] It is probable that Grierson dispatched A Company, Tenth Cavalry, to scout across the Sierra Diablo and check that the Apaches had not attempted to pass to the west of the Sierra, thereby avoiding Rattlesnake Springs altogether.

Scouts[45] sent out in the early hours of the morning found the Apaches to the south, confirming that the Colonel had regained the initiative.[46] From these reports, Grierson predicted that Victorio would use Rattlesnake Canyon[47] to reach Rattlesnake Springs. Remaining at the water hole, he delegated command to Captain Carpenter, who deployed C and G companies, under Captain Viele and Lieutenant Ayres respectively, in ambush along Rattlesnake Canyon,[48] though Lieutenant Finley claimed to have effectively commanded C Company during the skirmish.[49] B and H Companies were held in reserve, under the command of Captain Carpenter.[50]

Captain Louis H. Carpenter, Tenth Cavalry. Grierson placed him in direct command of the four companies of Tenth Cavalry which engaged Victorio's warriors at Rattlesnake Springs. (Carlisle Barracks)

43 Ibid.
44 Bi-Monthly Company Muster Rolls for Company A, 10th Cavalry, Jul./Aug. 1880 in NA, RG94; Dinges Handbook of Texas Online entry; See also Thrapp, 1974, pp.288-289; Leckie, 1967, p.226; Leckie & Leckie, 1984, p.265; Thrapp, 1967, pp.204-205; Stout, pp.155-156; Matthews, 1993, p.40; Worcester, 1979, pp.230-231; Rister, 1928, p.212; Miles, 1971, p.62; Fort Davis Museum Webpage; Burton, 1999, p.190; Glass, 1971, p.134.
45 The Pueblo scouts are not mentioned in the accounts of the move to Rattlesnake Springs but Grierson moved the majority of his immediate command from Eagle Springs to Van Horn Wells and on to Rattlesnake Springs and it seems unlikely that he left his Pueblo scouts behind.
46 'Grierson's Report, Sept.1880'; NA, RG393, Part 1, Entry 2546, pp.639-644; 'Robert Grierson Diary', 7 Aug., 1880. Rister, 1928, p.212.
47 The Fort Davis Museum webpage states that today Highway 54 runs through Rattlesnake Canyon.
48 Brinkerhoff, citing dispatch rec'd from Grierson, Rattlesnake Springs, rec'd 9 Aug., 1880, to AAAG SF NM 10 Aug., 1880, NA, RG393 Part 3 Entry 440 pp.84-88; AAG, DoTx to AG Chicago, 11 Aug., 1880, 'Victorio Files', NA, RG393, M1495, Roll 14; 'Grierson's Report, Sept.1880'; NA, RG393, Part 1, Entry 2546, pp.639-644.
49 Leighton Finley Diary 6 Aug., 1880 entry Special Collections, University of Arizona Library, Tucson; Dinges, 1988, p.166.
50 Bi-Monthly Company Muster Rolls for Company A, 10th Cavalry, Jul./Aug. 1880 in NA, RG94; Dinges Handbook of Texas Online entry; See also Thrapp, 1974, pp.288-289; Leckie, 1967, p.226; Leckie & Leckie, 1984, p.265; Thrapp, 1967, pp.204-205; Stout, 1974, pp.155-156; Matthews, p.40;

It should be noted that the contemporary accounts of the deployment of the troops to ambush Victorio are quite ambiguous. Victorio would indeed have to pass along the arroyo in order to enter the canyon leading to Rattlesnake Springs but as the arroyo left the mountains it runs east and slightly north out into the plains. The southern side of the canyon entrance forms a spur which hides the opening from anybody approaching from the south along the edge of the Sierra Diablo. Therefore, the dismounted Tenth Cavalrymen would be concealed along the arroyo facing the approach of the Apaches from the south. In other words, they were not deployed along the arroyo in the canyon but immediately after it left the Sierra Diablo in an attempt to open fire at close range without warning. The intention was to catch the Apaches in the open ground immediately to the south of the arroyo. The spur of the Sierra Diablo would conceal both the horse holders of the two dismounted companies. It would also conceal the two mounted Tenth Cavalry companies poised to charge the Apaches after their comrades opened fire from the arroyo.[51] In theory it was a good plan. (See Map 11.3.)

Rattlesnake Springs, 6 August 1880[52] (See document files nos. 87, 94, 95 and 96.)

In the early afternoon, around 2:00 p.m., Victorio's following was spotted approaching the area.[53] Probably detecting something suspicious, the Apaches stopped well short of the ambush.[54] Indeed, Kaywaykla mentions an episode where Victorio and his band refrained from accessing a water-hole because they detected a 'bluecoat' ambush. His short description of events almost certainly refers to the events around Rattlesnake Springs.[55] On seeing the Apaches draw back, their would-be ambushers fired several volleys at long range, which failed to do any physical damage, but were sufficient to cause the Apaches to take cover.[56] So far, they had only spotted the two companies in ambush. Victorio's warriors regrouped and, using the rough ground to their advantage, they

Worcester, 1979, pp.230-231; Rister, 1928, p.212; Miles, 1971, p.62; Fort Davis Museum Webpage; Burton, 1999, p.190; Glass, 1971, p.134.

51 I visited this site in June 2018. The land is privately owned but I could see the lie of the land from the main road. This, in combination with looking at the area on Google-Earth strongly suggested the above deployment.

52 There is some confusion in some of the records as to whether the skirmish occurred on the 6 or 7 August. 'Robert Grierson Diary' if carefully read shows this to be the 6 of August though the fact that he wrote up two days events on the 7 August can be confusing. One of Grierson's own reports has been obviously changed from the 6 to the 7 August for reasons unknown. (Grierson to AAG, DoTx, 8 Aug., 1880 in Telegrams Sent 23 Jun.-30 Nov., 1880, HQ Records DoP 1878-1881, NA, RG393, M1381, Roll 1, pp.99-101) Until clear evidence comes to the fore the author will remain with the 6 Aug. as the date.

53 Brinkerhoff, citing dispatch rec'd from Grierson, Rattlesnake Springs, rec'd 9 Aug., 1880, to AAAG SF NM 10 Aug., 1880, NA, RG393 Part 3 Entry 440 pp.84-88; AAG, DoTx to AG Chicago, 11 Aug., 1880, 'Victorio Files', NA, RG393, M1495, Roll 14; 'Robert Grierson Diary', 7 Aug., 1880.; 'Grierson's Report, Sept.1880'; NA, RG393, Part 1, Entry 2546, pp.639-644; 'Indian Affairs', *Army & Navy Journal*, Vol. 18, 14 Aug., 1880, p.30; Thrapp, 1974, p.288; Thrapp, 1967, p.205; Leckie, 1967, p.226; Dinges Handbook of Texas Online entry.

54 Leckie & Leckie, 1984, p.266.

55 Ball, 1970, p.76.

56 Brinkerhoff, citing dispatch rec'd from Grierson, Rattlesnake Springs, rec'd 9 Aug., 1880, to AAAG SF NM 10 Aug., 1880, NA, RG393 Part 3 Entry 440 pp.84-88; AAG, DoTx to AG Chicago, 11 Aug., 1880, 'Victorio Files', NA, RG393, M1495, Roll 14; 'Robert Grierson Diary', 7 Aug., 1880.; 'By Telegraph', the *Grant County Herald*, 14 Aug., 1880; 'Grierson's Report, Sept.1880'; NA, RG393, Part 1, Entry 2546, pp.639-644; Thrapp, 1974, p.288; Thrapp, 1967, p.205; Record of Engagements, p.96; Leckie, 1967, p.226; Leckie & Leckie, 1984, p.266; Stout, 1974, p.156; Dinges Handbook of Texas Online entry; Rister, 1928, p.212; Miles, 1971, p.62; Burton, 1999, p.190.

Plate 11.3 Entrance to Victorio Canyon leading to Rattlesnake Springs in the Sierra Diablo as seen from the north-east. In the immediate foreground is the arroyo running down from present-day Victorio Canyon.

Plate 11.4 Closer view of the entrance to Victorio Canyon this time seen from the east. One can see the flat ground to the left over which the Apaches would approach from the south. The spur running out from the Sierra Diablo hiding the entrance to Victorio Canyon can be seen. This would have hidden the two reserve companies of mounted Tenth Cavalrymen from the approaching Apaches.

fanned out and sought to infiltrate their targets' lines, firing as they dodged from cover to cover. By attempting to close with their enemy, they hoped to force the latter away from the spring.[57] However, they had failed to spot the Tenth Cavalrymen held in reserve. Carpenter's B and H Companies flanked and charged the Apaches.[58] Victorio's warriors broke off and took cover in the higher slopes of the Sierra Diablo Mountains. For two hours, the two sides skirmished, with neither gaining any advantage.[59]

Late that afternoon, the supply train, escorted by Captain Gilmore, appeared around the northern end of the Baylor Mountains.[60] The escort of African-American soldiers from H Company, Twenty-Fourth US Infantry, was riding inside the wagons.[61] Though some contemporary accounts claimed this as a cunning ploy, the troops were unaware of the stand-off between Grierson and Victorio.[62] All the Apaches saw was an apparently unescorted wagon train. Two small groups of warriors who launched attacks were completely surprised by the infantrymen jumping out of the wagons and opening fire. At least one Apache was seen to fall from his horse, and others were believed to have been wounded before they could withdraw.[63] Captain Carpenter then intervened, leading his four companies to the rescue.[64] Company A may have returned from the Sierra Diablo, or have been able to see this portion of the battle from the mountains, as Lieutenant Flipper left a brief account which matches this part of the battle.[65]

The Apaches made one final attack on the Tenth Cavalrymen stationed round the water hole in an attempt to panic their pack mules and horses; but the confident defence put up by the troops thwarted this attack.[66] At one point, Victorio feigned a retreat, which triggered a pursuit by three

---

57 'Robert Grierson Diary', 7 Aug., 1880.; 'Grierson's Report, Sept.1880'; NA, RG393, Part 1, Entry 2546, pp.639-644; Dinges Handbook of Texas Online entry; Thrapp, 1974, p.288; Thrapp, 1967, p.205 Stout, 1974, p.156; Leckie, 1967, p.226; Miles, 1971, p.62.

58 Brinkerhoff, citing dispatch rec'd from Grierson, Rattlesnake Springs, rec'd 9 Aug., 1880, to AAAG SF NM 10 Aug., 1880, NA, RG393 Part 3 Entry 440 pp.84-88; AAG, DoTx to AG Chicago, 11 Aug., 1880, 'Victorio Files', NA, RG393, M1495, Roll 14; 'Robert Grierson Diary', 7 Aug., 1880.; 'By Telegraph', the *Grant County Herald*, 14 Aug., 1880; 'Grierson's Report, Sept.1880'; NA, RG393, Part 1, Entry 2546, pp.639-644; Dinges Handbook of Texas Online entry; Leckie, 1967, p.226; O'Neal, 1991, p.67.

59 Brinkerhoff, citing dispatch rec'd from Grierson, Rattlesnake Springs, rec'd 9 Aug., 1880, to AAAG SF NM 10 Aug., 1880, NA, RG393 Part 3 Entry 440 pp.84-88; AAG, DoTx to AG Chicago, 11 Aug., 1880, 'Victorio Files', NA, RG393, M1495, Roll 14; 'Grierson's Report, Sept.1880'; NA, RG393, Part 1, Entry 2546, pp.639-644; 'Indian Affairs', *Army & Navy Journal*, Vol. 18, 14 Aug., 1880, p.30; Thrapp, 1974, pp.288-289; Thrapp, 1967, p.205; Thrapp, 1988, p.744; Stout, 1974, p.156; Leckie & Leckie, 1984, p.266; Matthews, 1993, p.40; Rister, 1928, p.213.

60 'Indian Affairs', *Army & Navy Journal*, Vol. 18, 14 Aug., 1880, p.30; Fort Davis Museum Webpage.

61 Record of Engagements, p.96; Leckie & Leckie, p.266; see also '24th U.S. Infantry at Fort Davis Texas' web-site.

62 Thrapp, 1967, p.205, note 50.

63 Brinkerhoff, citing dispatch rec'd from Grierson, Rattlesnake Springs, rec'd 9 Aug., 1880, to AAAG SF NM 10 Aug., 1880, NA, RG393 Part 3 Entry 440 pp.84-88; AAG, DoTx to AG Chicago, 11 Aug., 1880, 'Victorio Files', NA, RG393, M1495, Roll 14; 'Robert Grierson Diary', 7 Aug., 1880.; 'By Telegraph', the *Grant County Herald*, 14 Aug., 1880; 'Grierson's Report, Sept.1880'; NA, RG393, Part 1, Entry 2546, pp.639-644; Leckie, 1967, pp.226-227; Leckie & Leckie, 1984, p.266; Thrapp, 1967, pp.205-206; Thrapp, 1974, p.289; Stout, 1974, p.156; Dinges Handbook of Texas Online entry; Rister, 1928, p.213; Miles 1971, p.62.

64 Brinkerhoff, citing dispatch rec'd from Grierson, Rattlesnake Springs, rec'd 9 Aug., 1880, to AAAG SF NM 10 Aug., 1880, NA, RG393 Part 3 Entry 440 pp.84-88; AAG, DoTx to AG Chicago, 11 Aug., 1880, 'Victorio Files', NA, RG393, M1495, Roll 14; 'Grierson's Report, Sept.1880'; NA, RG393, Part 1, Entry 2546, pp.639-644.

65 Harris, 1997, p.35.

66 'Grierson's Report, Sept.1880'; NA, RG393, Part 1, Entry 2546, pp.639-644; 'Indian Affairs', *Army & Navy Journal*, Vol. 18, 14 Aug., 1880, p.30; Handbook of Texas Online entry; Leckie, 1967, p.227.

Plate 11.5 The northern end of the Baylor Mountains from behind which Grierson's supply train would appear only to become embroiled in the closing stages of the battle.

Plate 11.6 The Sierra Diablo to the south of Rattlesnake Springs. Victorio and his people approached and retreated from the Tenth Cavalry along this side of the mountain range.

companies led by Captain Carpenter. A hidden group of Apaches then burst out of cover behind the pursuing Tenth Cavalrymen and made for the pack train. However, the troops left on guard held their nerve and averted a minor disaster.[67] The Apaches finally retreated to the south, towards the Carrizo Mountains. A pursuit, led by Captain Carpenter, was terminated by the fading light, and the troopers regrouped and returned to Rattlesnake Springs.[68]

Grierson at first thought that he had suffered no casualties in this engagement,[69] but it was later found that Private Wesley Hardy was missing. He was 'last seen on the day of engagement with Victorio's band of hostile Indians, has not been seen since'.[70] Grierson himself could only say that he knew of four Apaches who had fallen from their horses during the engagement,[71] though it was later claimed that the Apaches might have sustained as many as 30 casualties.[72] A stock US army phrase,[73] 'Carried off their dead and wounded,' was applied to Rattlesnake Springs and indicates that the Tenth Cavalry were unable to confirm Apache casualties for this battle.[74] This event was certainly a setback for Victorio; but we should avoid hyperbole when describing it. The fact that Grierson and his men had managed to prevent Victorio's band from infiltrating through West Texas was an outstanding achievement in itself; accomplished without the aid of Apache scouts, and speaks volumes of the skill of their commander and the discipline of his troops.

It is only fair to record that Grierson himself seems to have been disappointed in the outcome of the battle. His son Robert recorded in his diary hearing, but not seeing, the fighting, and commented:

> I wish Papa had gone with the troops yesterday after the Indians – the movements could've been decidedly better made – a lot of Indians ought to've been captured. Papa wishes he'd gone, but he supposed the movements would be made according to his directions.[75]

If Grierson was disappointed, then he had only himself to blame for not being present at the battle. From the outset, the engagement did not go as planned. The Apaches detected their would-be ambushers in Rattlesnake Canyon, and so Captain Carpenter and his men found themselves facing experienced Apache warriors who were aware of their presence, rather than springing an ambush on a completely unsuspecting foe. Grierson may have committed the cardinal sin of assuming that the Apaches would blithely ride into an ambush. The standard Apache practice of throwing

67 'Grierson's Report, Sept.1880'; NA, RG393, Part 1, Entry 2546, pp.639-644; Leckie & Leckie, p.266; See also Miles, 1971, p.62.

68 Brinkerhoff, citing dispatch rec'd from Grierson, Rattlesnake Springs, rec'd 9 Aug., 1880, to AAAG SF NM 10 Aug., 1880, NA, RG393 Part 3 Entry 440 pp.84-88; AAG, DoTx to AG Chicago, 11 Aug., 1880, 'Victorio Files', NA, RG393, M1495, Roll 14; Fort Davis Museum webpage.

69 Brinkerhoff, citing dispatch rec'd from Grierson, Rattlesnake Springs, rec'd 9 Aug., 1880, to AAAG SF NM 10 Aug., 1880, NA, RG393 Part 3 Entry 440 pp.84-88; AAG, DoTx to AG Chicago, 11 Aug., 1880, 'Victorio Files', NA, RG393, M1495, Roll 14; 'Grierson's Report, Sept.1880'; NA, RG393, Part 1, Entry 2546, pp.639-644; Stout, p.157; see also Chronological List, p.50.

70 Record of Events Aug., 1880 in Returns From Regular Army Cavalry Regiments 1833-1916, 10th Cavalry Regimental Returns 1873 to 1880, NA, M744, Roll 96.

71 Brinkerhoff, citing dispatch rec'd from Grierson, Rattlesnake Springs, rec'd 9 Aug., 1880, to AAAG SF NM 10 Aug., 1880, NA, RG393 Part 3 Entry 440 pp.84-88; AAG, DoTx to AG Chicago, 11 Aug., 1880, 'Victorio Files', NA, RG393, M1495, Roll 14; 'Grierson's Report, Sept.1880'; NA, RG393, Part 1, Entry 2546, pp.639-644.

72 Handbook of Texas Online entry: see also Record of Engagements, p.96; Webb, 1976, p.90; Leckie, 1967, p.227; Stout, 1974, p.157.

73 See comments by Thrapp, in Watt, 'I Will Not Surrender the Hair of a Horse's Tail: The Victorio Campaign 1879', p.52.

74 Thrapp, 1967, p.206.

75 'Robert Grierson Diary', 7 Aug., 1880. Fort Davis Museum webpage.

out scouts well in advance, to the flanks and rear of the main body, clearly led to detection of the ambush and alerted the main body.

In the meantime, Captain Lebo, in command of K Company, Tenth Cavalry, had separately inflicted significant damage on the Apaches. On 1 August,[76] Lebo's company found and captured a supply camp hidden in the Sierra Diablo. The Apaches guarding the camp were alert, spotting the Tenth Cavalrymen in sufficient time to make good their escape. Lebo's men captured some live steers and ponies; and also captured a large stock of dried meat which was assumed to be being prepared in advance of Victorio's arrival.[77] (See document files nos. 95 and 96.) In capturing the camp, K Company had deprived the Apaches of at least some of their provisions.[78] It may have been this loss of supplies, plus his inability to reach Rattlesnake Springs ahead of Grierson's forces, which forced Victorio ultimately to retreat back into Mexico. Captain Lebo attempted to pursue the Apaches, who fled north towards the Guadalupe Mountains, but gave up the chase at a place called Escondido. Lebo's company scouted back down the western side of the Sierra Diablo, arriving at Fresno springs at their southern end and discovering abundant signs of Victorio's having passed north the previous day. This trail was followed north to the point where Lebo made contact with Captain Nolan's company in Rattlesnake Canyon, before the two detachments linked up with Grierson at Rattlesnake Springs on 7 August.[79]

There were two further clashes between the Tenth Cavalry and the Apaches in the Guadalupe Mountains, and these involved detachments belonging to F and L Companies, Tenth Cavalry. On 4 August, Sergeant William Richardson, with 11 men, was caught in a well planned and executed ambush. The detachment was pursuing a trail into a canyon on the south-western side of the Guadalupe Mountains. The Apaches had occupied the higher ground and peaks which dominated the canyon, from where they killed Private William Taylor and forced the rest of the detachment to withdraw from the canyon under a hail of bullets 'necessitating the abandonment of a number

---

76 Leckie and Dinges etc. date this to Aug. 3 1880; Regimental History 1866-98 10th Cavalry, NA, RG391, Entry 933, pp.19-20; Handbook of Texas Online entry; Leckie, 1967 p.227; Leckie & Leckie, 1984, p.266; O'Neal, 1991, p.156; Bigelow, USACMH webpage; see also Haley, 1952, pp.333-334; Miles 1971, p.62; Webb, 1976, p.89). Thrapp, while acknowledging that two of his sources, (The Chronological List and Record of Engagements) list this as occurring on the 3 of Aug., he places it on the 9 of Aug. (Thrapp, 1967, p.206; See also Stout, 1974, p.157; Chronological List, p.50; Record of Engagements, p.96).

There may be a simple explanation for this discrepancy. The Chronological List is quite definite that Captain Lebo attacked the Apaches in the Sierra Diablo, Texas on the 3 August, 1880. (p.50) However, on page 49 of the Chronological List, Captain Lebo's attack, on 9 April, on a party of Mescaleros at Shakehand Springs is listed. Could one author have mistaken the April 1880 entry for the August, 1880 entry while the other just assumed the former was correct? He may also have relied upon Rister's account of this campaign where he argues that Lebo attacked Victorio and captured his supplies a few days after Rattlesnake Springs. (p.214).

77 Bi-Monthly Company Muster Rolls for Company K, 10th Cavalry Jul./Aug. in NA, RG94; See also Record of Events Aug., 1880 in Returns From U.S. Military Posts 1800-1916, Fort Davis, Texas Jan. 1879-Jun. 1891, NA, M617, Roll 298.

78 Brinkerhoff to AAAG SF, 13 Aug., 1880, Telegrams Sent DoNM, Vol.3, Jan. – Nov. 1880 NA, RG393, Part 3, Entry 431, p.737; Thrapp, 1967, p.206; Dinges, Handbook of Texas Online entry; Leckie, 1967, p.227; O'Neal, 1991, p.156.

79 Leighton Finley Diary 3 Aug., 1880 entry Special Collections, University of Arizona Library, Tucson; 'Grierson's Report, Sept.1880'; NA, RG393, Part 1, Entry 2546, pp.639-644; See also Matthews, p.41; Fort Davis Museum Webpage.

The National Archives Wash D.C. contain a succinct summary of the campaign from Tinaja de las Palmas to Rattlesnake Springs. (Regimental History 1866-98 10th Cavalry, NA, RG391, Entry 933, pp.19-20).

of horses[80] & other Government property'.[81] Richardson was thought to have been ambushed a few miles to the north of Bowen Springs.[82] On receipt of this news, Grierson was convinced that this was the same Apache party that had fled from Captain Lebo in the Sierra Diablo.[83] Captain Kennedy, with a detachment drawn from men of both companies, set out after them; but following a five-day pursuit, they had to acknowledge failure, due to the weakening effect of lack of water on their horses.[84] (See document file no. 95.) However, on 6 August, Kennedy stumbled on another party of Apaches, killing a Mescalero woman, and killing one pony and wounding another.[85]

In the aftermath of Rattlesnake Springs, Grierson despatched several detachments to likely waterholes and passes. On 7 August, Captain Carpenter, with Companies G and H, was sent to picket Sulphur Springs. On the following day, a small detachment under Lieutenant Finley was sent to occupy Apache Springs.[86] Grierson was confident that in picketing these three water sources (Rattlesnake, Sulphur and Apache Springs) he had denied access to the only water in this particular section of the county, thus denying the Apaches passage to New Mexico.[87] Yet Lebo's arrival from the south, on 7 August, must have caused Grierson some concern. Lebo's detachment had not encountered any apparent sign of Victorio's withdrawal from Rattlesnake Springs as they moved north towards that location from Fresno Springs.

---

80 Grierson received news of this skirmish on the 9 August while still camped at Rattlesnake Springs and recorded that nine horses had been 'shot' during the attack. (Brinkerhoff, citing dispatch rec'd from Grierson, Rattlesnake Springs, rec'd 9 Aug., 1880, to AAAG SF NM 10 Aug., 1880, NA, RG393 Part 3 Entry 440 pp.84-88; AAG, DoTx to AG Chicago, 11 Aug., 1880, 'Victorio Files', NA, RG393, M1495, Roll 14; 'Grierson's Report, Sept.1880'; NA, RG393, Part 1, Entry 2546, pp.639-644).

81 In all the detachment lost 5 Saddles, 5 Curb Bridles, 2 Watering Bridles, 5 Cavalry Links, 5 Halters & Straps, 4 Surcingles, 5 Saddle Blankets, 4 Lariats, 5 Picket Pins, 3 Side Lines, 3 Nose Bags, 5 Curry Combs, 5 Horse Brushes, 4 Haversacks, 1 Saddle Bag, 5 Meat Cans, 2 Knives, 3 Forks, 3 Spoons, 10, Canteens & Straps, 1 Springfield Carbine, 1 Carbine Sling, 1 Swivel, 1, Cartridge Belt, 1 Jointed Ramrod, 1 Shell Extractor, 1 Colt Pistol, 1 Pistol Holster, 50 Carbine Cartridges, 20 Pistol Cartridges. (Proceedings of a Board of Survey convened at Camp Safford, 21 Aug., 1880 in Unregistered Letters 1878-1881, HQ Records DoP 1878-1881, NA, RG393, M1381, Roll 2) Bi-Monthly Company Muster Rolls for Company F, 10th Cavalry, Jul./Aug. 1880 in NA, RG94).

It was stated in the L Company bi-monthly return that four horses were lost. Whether this refers to L Company or the overall detachment's losses is not made clear. (Bi-Monthly Company Muster Rolls for Company L, 10th Cavalry, Jul./Aug. in NA, RG94) The *Grant County Herald* also stated that the Sergeant also lost four horses but held his ground for two hours. (The *Grant County Herald*, 14 Aug., 1880).

82 'Indian Affairs', *Army & Navy Journal*, Vol. 18, 14 Aug., 1880, p.30.

83 Beck to Kennedy, 11 Aug., 1880 in Letters Sent 19 Sept., 1879 – 11 Aug., 1880, HQ Records DoP 1878-1881, NA, RG393, M1381, Roll 1, Letter No.137; 'Grierson's Report, Sept.1880'; NA, RG393, Part 1, Entry 2546, pp.639-644.

84 Bi-Monthly Company Muster Rolls for Company L, 10th Cavalry, Jul./Aug. 1880 in NA, RG94.

85 Bi-Monthly Company Muster Rolls for Company F, 10th Cavalry Jul./Aug. 1880 in NA, RG94; For a slightly different version of events see Chronological List entries, p.50; Record of Engagements, p.96; Webb, 1976, p.90.

86 'Grierson's Report, Sept.1880'; NA, RG393, Part 1, Entry 2546, pp.639-644. Sulphur Springs were on the eastern side of the Sierra Diablo and to the north of Rattlesnakes Springs. Apache Springs are in the Sierra Diablo, 22 miles from Sulphur Springs and 10 miles from Rattlesnake Springs. (Capt. Viele to AAAG, DoP, Fort Concho, Texas, 24 Jan., 1879, NA, RG393, Part 1, Entry 2546, pp.25-40) Captain Lebo stated that the Apache Springs are located high in the Sierra Diablo and some approximately 9 miles north of Rattlesnake Springs. (Capt. Thomas Lebo to Post Adjutant, Fort Davis, Texas, 16 Feb., 1879, NA, RG393, Part 1, Entry 2546, pp.68-104).

87 Brinkerhoff, citing dispatch rec'd from Grierson, Rattlesnake Springs, rec'd 9 Aug., 1880, to AAAG SF NM 10 Aug., 1880, NA, RG393 Part 3 Entry 440 pp.84-88; AAG, DoTx to AG Chicago, 11 Aug., 1880, 'Victorio Files', NA, RG393, M1495, Roll 14; 'Grierson's Report, Sept.1880'; NA, RG393, Part 1, Entry 2546, pp.639-644; Matthews, 1993, p.41; Rister, 1928, p.214.

That evening K Company, Eighth Cavalry, accompanied by a handful of Lipan Apache scouts, and led by Captain William R. Livermore, arrived at Rattlesnake Springs. A detachment from this company was detailed to scout southwards on the following morning, to follow Victorio's trail from Rattlesnake Canyon.[88] The detachment duly picked up the trail and followed it 'some distance west into the mountains', clearly implying that the Apaches had retreated into the Sierra Diablo.[89] That afternoon, Captain Baylor's detachment of Texas Rangers finally caught up with Grierson at Rattlesnake Springs.[90]

On 9 August, Grierson, with Captain Gilmore's infantry company, and the Pueblo and Lipan scouts, scaled the eastern side of the Sierra Diablo and searched a portion of the range without encountering any Apaches.[91] According to Grierson's son, this force went out in advance of Grierson, who mounted up and followed their trail alone into the Sierra Diablo. On reaching the top, where the land levelled out into a relatively flat mesa, the Colonel spotted a number of men, whom he took for Apaches, and had defensively positioned himself with his back to the cliff before realising that the men were Charles Berger[92] and some Pueblo scouts.[93] Grierson returned to Rattlesnake Springs and on the following day placed Captain Nolan in charge a small battalion made up of the Captain's own A Company, Tenth Cavalry, K Company, Eighth Cavalry, the Lipan Apache scouts and the Texas Rangers, and sent these troops south to Fresno Springs. From there they were to scout the southern reaches of the Sierra Diablo.[94] Captain Lebo's and Captain Gilmore's companies were left to picket Rattlesnake Springs, while Grierson took C Company, Tenth Cavalry, north to Sulphur Springs.[95] On arrival at Sulphur Springs, Captain Carpenter, with B and H Companies, Tenth Cavalry, were dispatched around the northern end of the Sierra Diablo to scout down its western flank, with Grierson remaining at Sulphur Springs with C and G Companies, Tenth Cavalry.[96] This series of manoeuvres was designed to trap the Apaches in the Sierra Diablo or, at the very least, force their withdrawal and allow Grierson to set his forces in pursuit.[97]

Grierson appears to have stated that there was another clash between the Tenth Cavalry and the Apaches, on 11 August; but this report turned out to be erroneous.[98] (See document file no. 97.) The

88 'Grierson's Report, Sept.1880'; NA, RG393, Part 1, Entry 2546, pp.639-644; See also Leighton Finley Diary 7 Aug., 1880 entry Special Collections, University of Arizona Library, Tucson.

89 Ibid.

90 'Grierson's Report, Sept.1880'; NA, RG393, Part 1, Entry 2546, pp.639-644; See also Leighton Finley Diary 7 Aug., 1880 entry Special Collections, University of Arizona Library, Tucson; See also Baylor, 1996, p.253; Temple, 1959, p.106; Haley, 1952, p.334.

91 'Grierson's Report, Sept.1880'; NA, RG393, Part 1, Entry 2546, pp.639-644; See also Leighton Finley Diary 7 Aug., 1880 entry Special Collections, University of Arizona Library, Tucson; See also Record of Events Aug., 1880 in Returns From U.S. Military Posts 1800-1916, Fort Davis, Texas Jan. 1879-Jun. 1891, NA, M617, Roll 298.

92 Berger had come to the attention of Grierson by being on hand to help operator Palmer at Fort Quitman to translate messages from the military authorities in Mexico. Berger expressed a desire to enlist as a scout and Palmer heartily endorsed his recruitment as a man to be 'trusted.' (Palmer to Grierson, 25 Jul., 1880 in Telegrams Rec'd by General Grierson in the Field 30 Jun.-14 Sept., 1880, HQ Records DoP 1878-1881, NA, RG393, M1381, Roll 4).

93 'Robert Grierson Diary', 11 Aug., 1880.

94 'Grierson's Report, Sept.1880'; NA, RG393, Part 1, Entry 2546, pp.639-644

95 Ibid.

96 Ibid.

97 Ibid.

98 'As a result of the fight of the 11 instant, and the activity and disposition of the troops, Victorio and his band have again been driven into Mexico. The trail leads in the direction of Ojo Caliente, and troops are in pursuit with Gillmore's company of Infantry, and Livermore with his scouts and Pueblos.

We climbed the rough and precipitous cliff of the Sierra Diablo, two thousand feet in height, this, with the march of sixty-five miles in one day, and rapidity with which the mountains were encircled, and

only sign of Apaches were the two ponies picked up by Lieutenant Finley between Apache Spring and Rattlesnake Springs on 9 August.[99]

Captain Carpenter finally picked up Victorio's trail on 11 August, and followed it to the west, to a point approximately 45 miles from Fort Bliss, where it turned south towards the Rio Grande.[100] Carpenter sent word to Captain Nolan, who was camped at Carrizo Pass. Carpenter, whose horses were showing signs of exhaustion, then made for Eagle Springs, where he was joined by Captain Nolan in the early hours of the following morning. Nolan pressed on towards Tinaja de las Palmas and picked up the trail two miles before that location.[101] The trail of the Apaches was reported to have reached the Rio Grande, but then to have turned southwards, away from Old Fort Quitman and down towards Ojo Caliente, Texas.[102] A Mexican scout working from Quitman reported having seen some of the Apaches camped on the US side of the river, within five miles of the Fort, on or around 12 August.[103] It was supposed that the Apaches might have hidden in the mountains just north of the river, and Nolan's detachment was reported to be investigating this possibility.[104] On 13 August, Nolan finally confirmed that the Apaches had crossed back into Mexico.[105] It was reported that the hurried manner in which they had torn strips of meat from the dead animals found in their camps indicated a rout rather than a retreat.[106] It was also reported that a group of Colonel Valle's scouts had been attacked on 13 or 14 August, in the mountains across the

the Indians were driven from their stronghold, the haste with which they fled, fully attests the energy, pluck and earnest activity of the troops' (Grierson to AAG DoTx, San Antonio, 14 Aug., 1880 'Victorio Files', NA, RG393, M1495, Roll 14;sSee also Whipple to AG Wash. D.C. 13 Aug., 1880 in 'Victorio Papers', NA, M666, Roll 527; Miles, 1971, p.62) At first glance one would presume Grierson is referring to the fight at Rattlesnake Springs on the 6 August. Yet on reflection it seems difficult to see how Grierson, writing on the 14 August, could mistake the 6 with the 11 August.

However if one consults the same document as recorded as 'Grierson to AAG, DoTx, 12 Aug., 1880 in Telegrams Sent 23 Jun.-30 Nov., 1880, HQ Records DoP 1878-1881, NA, RG393, M1381, Roll 1, p.105, Letter No.389' it becomes clear that Grierson has himself recorded Rattlesnake Springs as happening on the 7 Aug. and the manner in which the '7' has been written in this record it can be misinterpreted as the number '11'.

99 Leighton Finley Diary 9 Aug., 1880 entry Special Collections, University of Arizona Library, Tucson.

100 Whipple to Sheridan, 14 Aug., 1880, NA, RG393, Part 1, Entry 2539, Press Copies of Letters and Endorsements Sent, MDoM, Vol. 13, p.514; 'Grierson's Report, Sept.1880'; NA, RG393, Part 1, Entry 2546, pp.639-644.

101 Carpenter to Beck, AAAG, 16 Aug., 1880 in Unregistered Letters 1878-1881, HQ Records DoP 1878-1881, NA, RG393, M1381, Roll 2.

102 Whipple to Sheridan, 14 Aug., 1880, NA, RG393, Part 1, Entry 2539, Press Copies of Letters and Endorsements Sent, MDoM, Vol. 13, p.514 & Whipple to Sheridan, 15 Aug., 1880, NA, RG393, Part 1, Entry 2539, Press Copies of Letters and Endorsements Sent, MDoM, Vol. 13, p.513.

103 Brinkerhoff, 12 Aug., 1880, Telegrams Sent DoNM, Vol.3, Jan. – Nov. 1880 NA, RG393, Part 3, Entry 431, p.725.

104 Nolan to AAG Fort Leavenworth, 13 Aug., 1880, Telegrams Sent DoNM, Vol.3, Jan. – Nov. 1880 NA, RG393, Part 3, Entry 431, p.735; Whipple to Sheridan, 14 Aug., 1880, NA, RG393, Part 1, Entry 2539, Press Copies of Letters and Endorsements Sent, MDoM, Vol. 13, p.514; Platt to AAG, HQ MDoM, 14 Aug., 1880, 'Victorio Files', NA, RG393, M1495, Roll 14.

105 Brinkerhoff to AAAG, SF, 13 Aug., 1880, Telegrams Sent DoNM, Vol.3, Jan. – Nov. 1880 NA, RG393, Part 3, Entry 431, p.739; Platt to AAG, HQ MDoM, 15 Aug., 1880, 'Victorio Files', NA, RG393, M1495, Roll 14; 'By Telegraph', the *Grant County Herald*, 14 Aug., 1880; 'Grierson's Report, Sept.1880'; NA, RG393, Part 1, Entry 2546, pp.639-644; Record of Engagements, p.96; Leckie, 1967, p.227; Leckie & Leckie, p.266; Thrapp, 1974, p.289; Thrapp, 1988, p.1059; Matthews, 1993, p.41; Haley, 1952, p.335; Miles, 1971, p.62.

106 Grierson, Eagle Springs to AAG, San Antonio, 19 Aug., 1880, 'Victorio Files', NA, RG393, M1495, Roll 14; 'Grierson's Report, Sept.1880'; NA, RG393, Part 1, Entry 2546, pp.639-644.

river from Fort Quitman; though the veracity – let alone the details – of this skirmish remained unconfirmed.[107]

The Texas Ranger company had joined Captain Nolan's company in their pursuit of Victorio, following the Apaches west to Carrizo Springs[108] and then south past Tinaja de las Palmas and on towards Fort Quitman.[109] On returning to the site of Grierson's stand at Tinaja de las Palmas, they discovered what Baylor chose to interpret as a message to Grierson from Victorio:

> When they [the Apaches] got to General Grierson hill they perpetrated a small joke at his expense. They had managed to get a woman's bonnet and dress, probably in the murder of Mrs Graham and old man Grant at Bass Canyon,[110] and they placed it on top of Standemoffski,[111] making a scarecrow of dagger stalks, intending as much to say, " why didn't you come out and fight on open ground and not hide behind rocks, like an old woman?"[112]

This story is potentially corroborated by Robert Grierson. On 25 August, when passing Tinaja de las Palmas on his way towards Fort Quitman, his son Robert described how:

> The Indians had been there & knocked down the walls. Papa found a sort of wrap made of calico & red flannel-we stuck it away up on a dagger bush.[113]

Ironically the Texas Rangers had probably thrown down this scarecrow only to have it effectively reinstated by the Grierson's. In fact, such an overt display of contempt or frustration on the part of the Apaches, is unusual as it did not reflect their own attitudes towards warfare. If this was a message left by the Apaches, it was more likely one of defiance than contempt; they may have been forced back into Mexico, but the fight for their Ojo Caliente reservation was by no means over.

During their move south past Tinaja de las Palmas, the Apaches encountered a stage coach and riddled it with bullets, killing ex-civil war General, J.J. Byrne.[114] The attack occurred on 9 August, and it was initially reported that a passenger had been wounded.[115] The stage's driver,

---

107 Carpenter to Beck, AAAG, 16 Aug., 1880 in Unregistered Letters 1878-1881, HQ Records DoP 1878-1881, NA, RG393, M1381, Roll 2.

108 Presumably in or by the Carrizo Mountains. (See Leckie, p.156) According to Baylor's Editor these springs are approximately: "seven miles northwest of present-day Van Horn" (1996, note 14, p.257).

109 Gillett, 1976, p.181.

110 See Chapter 9. If Baylor is correct then this attack was probably carried out by Mescalero raiders who subsequently allied with Victorio's band. On May 12 1880 Victorio and his people seem to have been operating in New Mexico. See chapters 7 and 8.

111 Baylor seems to have nick-named Grierson's Hill 'Standemoffski' for it's defensive qualities. On the 13 of September 1861 five Texans had held off a large Apache warparty from the same hill. (Baylor, 1996, pp.250-252 & p.256 note 4).

112 Baylor, 1996, p.254; Baylor 1925, pp.12-13.

113 Robert Grierson's Diary, 24 August 1880. Copy courtesy of the Fort Davis Museum Archives; Temple, 1959, p.106.

114 'By Telegraph', the *Grant County Herald*, 14 Aug., 1880; Thrapp, 1974, p.290; Stout, pp.158-159; Baylor, 1996, p254; Temple, 1959, p.107; Cutrer, Handbook of Texas Online entry

115 Hatch to AAG Fort Leavenworth, 10 Aug., 1880, Telegrams Sent DoNM, Vol.3, Jan. – Nov. 1880 NA, RG393, Part 3, Entry 431, p.724; List of Persons Killed, Wounded, or Captured, by Indians, &c., in the DoTx, since September 30, 1879, officially reported by post commanders. NA, RG393, Part 1, Entry 2546, p.633; Gillett, 1976, p.181; Leckie & Leckie, 1984, p.268; Webb, 1976, p.90.

Some reports suggested that the attack had occurred on the following day. (Whipple to Sheridan, 11 Aug., 1880, NA, RG393, Part 1, Entry 2538, p.359; See also Cutrer, Handbook of Texas Online entry.) Others suggested the attack may have occurred as late as the 19 August. Thrapp, (1974, p.372 note 56) notes that Col Grierson reported this attack on the 19 August (Grierson, Eagle Springs to AAG, San

Ed Walde, had suddenly found himself confronted by a large dismounted group of Apaches in Quitman Canyon. He managed to swing his team around, but the Apaches had immediately opened fire, hitting Byrne in the side. The Apaches mounted their horses and charged after the fleeing coach. During the chase, an Apache warrior who had caught up with the coach fired a bullet and it smashed Byrne's hip. Byrne was unarmed, and Walde only had an old Spencer carbine with one bullet. According to Walde, he handed the gun to Byrne who, despite his injuries, managed to badly wound one of the following Apaches. Walde eventually succeeded in getting away and returned to Fort Quitman; but Byrne died of his wounds on 13 August.[116] (See document files nos. 98 and 99.) Gillett reports that driver Walde (or the name may have been West) joined the Rangers, so eager was he to exact revenge on the Apaches.[117] The Texas Ranger detachment came across the signs of the attack as they 'passed through the worst part of Quitman Canyon and beyond what was known as the Apache Post Office, where the Indians had some hieroglyphics on the rocks'.[118] Gillett was able to examine the stagecoach at Fort Quitman a few days later, and reported:

> I examined the little canvas-topped stage and found it literally shot to pieces. I noticed where a bullet had glanced along the white canvas, leaving a blue mark a foot long before it passed through the top. Three of the spokes of the wheels were shot in two and there were fifteen to twenty bullet marks on and through the stage.[119]

The same raiders then carried on to kill a Mexican herder on a ranch belonging to Jesus Cota and made off with 140 cattle.[120] The Apaches then finally crossed the Rio Grande into Mexico.[121] (See document file no. 99.) The Texas Rangers, following up, found approximately 40 cattle mired in the mud of a riverbank. Some of the trapped cattle had had chunks of meat torn from them before being abandoned by the Apaches. Some of these unfortunate animals were still alive when the Texas Rangers found them.[122] Gillett interpreted this as heartless savagery; but Grierson was closer to the truth when he interprets this as starvation on the part of the Apaches, having lost a significant proportion of their provisions to the Tenth Cavalry in the Sierra Diablo, combined with a desperate need to keep moving in an effort to evade pursuit.[123]

As a final comment, it should be noted that the Apaches had, in shooting retired General Byrne, killed a severe critic of the Ninth and Tenth Cavalry Regiments and their commanders. Only days before he was killed, Byrne had written to a Texas congressman:

Antonio, 19 Aug., 1880, 'Victorio Files', NA, RG393, M1495, Roll 14) and suspects that the attack took place on or around that date. However, Grierson did not receive this information for some days as he was still in the field coordinating his regiment's pursuit of the Apaches.

116 'The Driver's Account of how Gen. J.J. Byrne was Killed', the *Grant County Herald*, 9 Oct., 1880; See also Gillett, 1976, pp.181-182; Thrapp, 1988, p.203Stout, pp.158-159; Baylor, 1996, pp.257-258; Ruhlen, 1971, p.112. Cutrer names the driver as Charles D West and adds that Byrne was not carrying a weapon and that West had only two bullets for his Winchester. He also states that Byrne died of his wounds on the 14 Aug., 1880. (Cutrer, Handbook of Texas Online entry; see also Thrapp, 1988, p.203).

117 Gillett, 1976, p.182.

118 Baylor, 1996, p.254 see also Cutrer, Handbook of Texas Online entry; Smith, 1994, p.185.

119 Gillett, p.182.

120 'Indian Affairs', *Army & Navy Journal*, Vol. 18, 28 Aug., 1880, p.62; Gillett, 1976, p.182; Stout, p.189.

121 Whipple to Sheridan, 26 Aug., 1880, NA, RG393, Part 1, Entry 2539, Press Copies of Letters and Endorsements Sent, MDoM, Vol. 13, pp.540-541.

122 Gillett, 1976, p.182; Stout, 1974, p.159.

123 Grierson, Eagle Springs to AAG, San Antonio, 19 Aug., 1880, 'Victorio Files', NA, RG393, M1495, Roll 14; 'Indian Affairs', *Army & Navy Journal*, Vol. 18, 28 Aug., 1880, p.62; Gillett, 1976, p.182; Stout, 1974, p.159.

> For God's sake … have some other soldiers sent … besides Negroes, and another commander, MacKenzie, Merritt, Davidson – anybody but Grierson or Hatch.[124]

He also somewhat misrepresented Grierson's conduct, presumably at Tinaja de las Palmas, by castigating the Colonel for fleeing 'to an almost impregnable mountain fortress when Victorio appeared'.[125] Unfortunately, the death of a retired general who had fought for the Union in the Civil War was an event which distracted public attention away from the Tenth Cavalry's success in forcing the Apaches back into Mexico. It must have provided critics of the Ninth and Tenth Cavalry Regiments with yet another small piece of ammunition for their attacks. Byrne's widow even wrote to Grierson on 24 October 1880 accusing him of refusing to provide:

> a few **negro** soldiers – some of them probably having been slaves of mine – to protect the body of him who was **murdered** on a frontier that is supposed to be protected by you.[126]

In the weeks following the campaign, the Tenth Cavalry's regimental adjutant, Lieutenant Robert G. Smither, robustly rebutted these criticisms, going so far as to describe the reports of one Judge Blacker as coming 'from his soggy and alcoholic brain or, they are the wild imaginations of a scared man'.[127] Yet such reports clearly illustrate the hostility faced by the Ninth and Tenth Cavalry from the very people they were trying to protect, in addition to the very real threat posed by Apaches.

Gillett and Baylor also portray the often contradictory relations between Anglo-Americans and Mexicans. As we have seen, and shall see, the Texas Rangers were happy to ally with, and indeed had great respect for, those Mexicans pursuing the Apaches south of the border. Yet their comment, on finding the slain Mexican herder, betrays a casual contempt for Mexicans north of the border:

> The redskins, with a freakish sense of humor, perpetrated a grim joke on the murdered herder. He was rendering tallow when surprised and killed, so the murderers rammed his head into the melted tallow to make him a greaser.[128]

We must, of course, remind ourselves to refrain from applying today's morality to past events; but one wonders whether Gillett or Baylor would have seen anything humorous in the victim's end if he had been an Anglo-American cowboy? However, it also has to be acknowledged that Baylor had made sterling efforts to reduce ethnic tensions across the Rio Grande between Texan and Mexican.[129] Having originally set out to hunt for Victorio on 2 August, the Rangers, after covering a distance of approximately 500 miles, returned to their base at Ysleta on, or around, the 22 August 1880.[130]

---

124 'General Byrne's Last Letter', the *Grant County Herald*, 11 Sept., 1880; Leckie & Leckie, 1984, p.268

125 'General Byrne's Last Letter', the *Grant County Herald*, 11 Sept., 1880; Leckie & Leckie, 1984, p.268; Temple, 1959, p.107. As noted in the previous chapter, Grierson's position was undoubtedly impregnable but can hardly be described as the top of a mountain.

126 Temple, 1959, p.107. From the language used it is somewhat unclear as to whether Mrs Byrne's is referring to Grierson as directly responsible for her husband's death by refusing to provide an escort through Quitman Pass or whether Grierson had refused to provide an escort for her husband's body.

127 Smither to Gen. Tho. M. Vincent, San Antonio, TX., 22 Aug., 1880 in Letters Sent 19 Sept., 1879 – 11 Aug., 1880, HQ Records DoP 1878-1881, NA, RG393, M1381, Roll 1, Letter No.136; Temple, 1959, pp.105-107.

128 Gillett, pp.182-183; see also Baylor, 1996, p.254.

129 See Thompson's comments in the introduction to Baylor's works 1996, p.21.

130 Baylor, 1996, p.258 note 17.

If we take an overview of the campaign in western Texas during July and August, it can be argued that much of the US success can be put down to the able direction of the Tenth Cavalry by their commander.

Most importantly, Grierson had not been tempted into a futile pursuit of his enemy; and this was his stated intention *before* Victorio made any attempt to pass through western Texas. At the critical point, at Rattlesnake Springs, Grierson had held off Victorio by getting in front of him. Had Grierson, from Van Horn Wells, followed the trail of the Apaches and come up from behind, Victorio would have been able to hold him off with ease while his families and plunder were got safely away to the Guadalupe Mountains. By that point, Kennedy had been drawn into a fruitless pursuit north against a group of Apaches who had penetrated Grierson's picket lines undetected, until surprised by Lebo in the Sierra Diablo. The way would have been clear for Victorio. The only other company in the area, Lebo's, was scouting down the western side of the Sierra Diablo, and did not detect the fighting that occurred at Rattlesnake Springs. Therefore, Grierson's knowledge of Apache strategy and tactics played a part in his victory.

Key to Grierson's strategy was the fact that he had been alerted, first by the Mexicans, and then by his own scouts, to the approximate location of the second group of Apaches, before the first group of Apaches attempted to distract him. This meant that he never really lost sight of the very group of Apaches whom Victorio hoped to conceal from him. This is all the more important as it is clear that none of Victorio's opponents had realised what the Apache leader was trying to accomplish. For example, Colonel Hatch, a more effective Apache campaigner than most give him credit for, in October 1880, would state that: 'The Apache is crafty enough to lead the main column as far away as possible while his small parties are sent out to the war.'[131] This observation is reasonably accurate under some circumstances. When the Apaches thought that their dependents and plunder were safely hidden, or did not need to be moved, they would adopt such techniques. This is exactly how Victorio operated in March 1880 when the Rio Grande valley was raided. However, it was not how Victorio would move dependents or plunder from one location to another in the presence of hostile forces.

Grierson also benefitted from being able to rely on his officers and men to react swiftly to his orders as intelligence reached headquarters. Some of these orders were transmitted by telegraph and, as chance allowed, via stagecoach. Yet by implication, much of the communication between Grierson and his detachments was carried by hard-riding couriers who knew the country.

The strategy of picketing passes and waterholes was an important one, and the factor most highlighted in contemporary sources, and indeed by history. As early as 14 August 1880, the *Grant County Herald* argued that Grierson's occupation of known water sources had frustrated Victorio's attempt to return to New Mexico and was forcing a retreat into Chihuahua.[132] Yet this tactic only provided the foundation from which Grierson achieved his success. It was the use of small active patrols and scouts, plus close cooperation with Mexican forces from these bases, which was the key to his success.

Most US army successes against Apaches were spearheaded by Chiricahua or Western Apache scouts. However, the Tenth Cavalry managed to defeat one of the most successful Apache leaders without the aid of such scouts. It is true that Pueblo scouts were involved in confirming the intelligence received from Colonel Valle. But the Pueblo scouts also failed to find the Apaches after Rattlesnake Springs, when Grierson lost track of the latter for almost five days. This is something previous accounts of Grierson's campaign against Victorio have not commented upon. It would appear that Victorio's following spent almost two days somewhere in the Sierra Diablo and hints

131 Hatch to AAG, DoM, 6 Oct., 1880 in Letters Received, DoM 1868-98, RG 393, Entry A1-1 2601, Box 94.

132 'By Telegraph', the *Grant County Herald*, 14 Aug., 1880.

that there was at least one water source which had not been discovered by the Tenth Cavalry when they were surveying the Trans-Pecos Region 1878-1879. If there had been a Chiricahua or Western Apache scout company with Grierson at this point, it is unlikely that the Apaches could have remained hidden in the Sierra Diablo for at least two days. It is even possible that, with six companies of Tenth Cavalry in and around the Sierra Diablo, the presence of an Apache scout company might have brought about the end of the Victorio Campaign.

Nevertheless, both Colonel Grierson and General Ord were confident that the Apaches had suffered at least 30 casualties and were in no condition to oppose 'any organized force', arguing that the large force gathering in New Mexico under Colonel Buell (see next chapter) would be able to catch and finish off the remaining Apaches.[133] The argument that Victorio had taken serious losses appears to have been optimistic. First, an Apache leader losing at least 30 warriors in the space of just over two weeks would rapidly have lost his influence. Second, on 25 August 1880, Brinkerhoff received the following information:

> American scouts from Carrizal yesterday report that Victorio travelled for several miles with his herds and people directly on the stage road from this place [Fort Bliss, Texas] to Chihuahua, while enroute to Candelaria Mountains. Mexican people reports the bands as strong, defiant and aggressive.[134]

This does not sound like a spent military force. Victorio may have been outmanoeuvred by Grierson, but the Apaches had not been badly physically damaged by the campaign. The most decisive long-term element of the Tenth Cavalry's success was in preventing the Apaches from reaching New Mexico to sell their loot for fresh supplies of rifles and ammunition. The campaign in the Trans-Pecos region had consumed a significant amount of ammunition yet, as we shall see in Chapter 14, it had not quite precipitated a critical shortage of ammunition for Victorio.

Victorio retreats to Mexico

Grierson's requests that he be allowed to pursue Victorio into Mexico were turned down,[135] though there were enough rumours to the effect that Grierson had crossed into Mexico to generate an urgent request from the Adjutant General to General Ord asking the latter to verify such information.[136] Grierson had to content himself with sending some scouts to shadow the Apaches south of the border. The scouts reported that Victorio had returned to the Candelaria Mountains by the middle of August 1880 to rest and recuperate, his warriors having been 'very severely punished during their short stay in Texas'.[137]

133 Ord to AG Chicago Ill. 27 Aug., 1880 in 'Victorio Papers', NA, M666, Roll 528.

134 Brinkerhoff to AAAG, SF, 27 Aug., 1880 in Letters Received, DoM 1868-98, RG 393, Entry A1-1 2601, Box 93.

135 'Grierson's Report, Sept.1880'; NA, RG393, Part 1, Entry 2546, pp.639-644; Matthews, 1993, p.41.

136 Whipple to Ord, 20 Aug., 1880, NA, RG393, Part 1, Entry 2539, Press Copies of Letters and Endorsements Sent, MDoM, Vol. 13, p.527; Mason, AG DoTx to AG Chicago 20 Aug., 1880, 'Victorio Files', NA, RG393, M1495, Roll 14.

137 'Grierson's Report, Sept.1880'; NA, RG393, Part 1, Entry 2546, pp.639-644; Ord to AG Chicago, 25 Aug., 1880 in 'Victorio Papers', NA, M666, Roll 528; Whipple to Sheridan, 26 Aug., 1880, NA, RG393, Part 1, Entry 2539, Press Copies of Letters and Endorsements Sent, MDoM, Vol. 13, p.540; see also Brinkerhoff to AAAG SF, 13 Aug., 1880, Telegrams Sent DoNM, Vol.3, Jan. – Nov. 1880 NA, RG393, Part 3, Entry 431, p.737; Whipple AAG to Sheridan, 19 Aug., 1880, NA, RG393, Part 1, Entry 2538, p.364; 'Town and County', the *Grant County Herald*, 28 Aug., 1880.

These scouts, two Lipan Apaches, two Pueblos, and Sergeant Tippett from the Seminole scouts, led by Charles Berger, were sent across the border by Grierson on 18 August.[138] Berger discovered that the Apaches had camped for two days approximately two to three miles across the border, and had hastily killed about 20 cattle. Berger reported that the main trail then traversed very rough ground to a spring in the Borracho Valley. He also noted that at that point a trail of about 20 horses split away from the main trail and made off westwards. He assumed this group to be warriors.

Information that this smaller trail passed round the northern flank of the Sierra Borracho was reported by other Pueblo scouts sent over the river from Fort Quitman by Captain Nolan. The Captain was less than impressed when they returned within two days stating that the Apaches were making for the Candelaria Mountains and citing the poor state of their horses for their quick return.[139]

Berger noted that the main group of Apaches had attempted to hide their trail leading from the spring in the Borracho valley by scattering. Berger, who knew that there was a good source of water five miles distant, made straight for the Ojo Del Borracho,[140] but was surprised to find that there was no sign of the Apaches having rendezvoused at this point. He camped for the night above the spring and, on the morning of 21 August, looked for, but could not see, any smoke indicating the near presence of an Apache camp. The trail was re-discovered at a rendezvous to the south west of Berger's camp, in a canyon with both good water and grass. The Apaches had stayed at this spot for two days and had killed their remaining cattle and cured the meat. Berger also found evidence that they were caring for a number of wounded and that some of their horses were exhausted. The trail from this camp was easy to follow, going in a direction slightly south of east for about 22 miles before arriving at the Alcapparra Mountains. Here, Berger concluded that the trail was going towards the Candelaria Mountains, and left it and made for Canta Recio. From that point, he was confident that he could pick up the trail, as Canta Recio was only 20 miles, as the crow flies, from the Candelaria Mountains.

This manoeuvre would allow Berger to avoid an arduous and potentially dangerous journey, as the trail deliberately crossed the most difficult terrain, in a very dry section of the country. Berger also wished to look for the smaller trail, which he estimated would pass to the north of the main trail. Finally, he estimated that he was six days behind the main group of Apaches, and needed to make up some time. Berger cut the second trail 14 miles to the north, before camping at the Passo del Amargosa. This trail was also moving in the direction of the Candelaria Mountains. Berger arrived at Canta Recio on 22 August, and entered the settlement ahead of the party, for fear that, if not forewarned of the presence of US army Indian scouts, Mexican soldiers or citizens would attack his companions.

At Canta Recio, the small garrison of soldiers under Francisco Mesa informed Berger that the Apaches had passed 25 miles to the south of them on the morning of 15 August.[141] Mesa also informed him that, in the late afternoon of that day, five Mexican scouts attached to Mesa's command had skirmished for about half an hour with five Apaches near Canta Recio, losing one

138 Berger to Beck, 23 Aug., 1880 in Unregistered Letters 1878-1881, HQ Records DoP 1878-1881, NA, RG393, M1381, Roll 2; Beck to CO Fort Quitman, 18 Aug., 1880 in Letters Sent 23 Aug., to 31 Dec., 1880, HQ Records DoP 1878-1881, NA, RG393, M1381, Roll 1, Letter No.146; 'Grierson's Report, Sept.1880'; NA, RG393, Part 1, Entry 2546, pp.639-644; See also Thrapp, 1967, p.207; Haley, 1952, p.335; Rister, 1928, p.215.

139 Nolan to AAG, DoP, 19 Aug., 1880 in Telegrams Rec'd by General Grierson in the Field 30 Jun.-14 Sept., 1880, HQ Records DoP 1878-1881, NA, RG393, M1381, Roll 4.

140 Berger estimated that this spot was 30 miles S.E. of Fort Quitman on the slope of the Borracho Mountains.

141 Berger to Beck, 23 Aug., 1880 in Unregistered Letters 1878-1881, HQ Records DoP 1878-1881, NA, RG393, M1381, Roll 2.

horse killed, before federal soldiers from Carrizal and San Jose arrived and drove the Apaches off. These troops had then followed the Apaches towards the Candelaria Mountains. Prior to this skirmish, the Apaches had ambushed three Mexican smugglers in the Passe de la Ventana. Two of the smugglers had been killed, with the third managing to escape.[142] At least one other attack was reported from northern Chihuahua: on 15 August, herders guarding horses belonging to the Mexican Army had been attacked. A vigorous fire-fight had ensued, but with no casualties. The Apaches had managed to make away with only one horse.[143]

Grierson later stated that his scouts had confirmed that the Apaches were in the Candelaria Mountains 'in a badly crippled and demoralized condition'.[144] An apparent casualty, was Victorio's sister, Lozen, who failed to reappear when the Apaches re-grouped in Old Mexico. As the Apaches did this at least twice between May and August 1880 the date of her disappearance is difficult to determine. A careful reading of Kaywaykla's account suggests that this separation took place as the Apaches retreated over the Rio Grande in August 1880.[145] This remarkable woman, had apparently rejected marriage for fighting alongside the warriors. She also had 'power'. Most successful Apache warriors and war leaders were credited with some form of 'power'. In Lozen's case she was credited with an ability to detect enemies.[146] At some point Lozen became separated from the band, staying with a Mescalero woman in labour, and escorting her back to the Mescalero reservation.[147] She did not rejoin her companions until after the climax of the Victorio Campaign at Tres Castillos in October 1880.

Yet if one reads Berger's report, while the Apaches were carrying wounded, it hardly reads as if they were in a crippled state. The information noted above, which was relayed to Brinkerhoff, regarding the strength and aggression displayed by the Apaches as they travelled to the Candelaria Mountains, also undermines this impression. Thus, when one reads that Berger accused Mexican troops of making no attempt, unless directly attacked, to block the Apaches as they made for the Candelaria Mountains,[148] one suspects that these scattered detachments were too weak to confront Apaches who were in no mood to give up the fight. Indeed, Grierson was contacted by Dr Mariano Samaniego, who had examined the trail left by the Apaches as they made towards the Candelaria Mountains. Samaniego estimated that there were at least 500 cattle and horses in this group, and stated that the *federales* had 'made some marches, but no advance against the main body of the Indians'.[149] Samaniego also reported that the Apaches were closely monitoring every move-

142 Report of Francisco Mesa, In Command of Detachment camped at Santa Recio, 22 Aug., 1880 translated by Charles Berger & Berger to Beck, 23 Aug., 1880 in Unregistered Letters 1878-1881, HQ Records DoP 1878-1881, NA, RG393, M1381, Roll 2; See also Hatch (citing telegram from Samaniego to Brinkerhoff) to AAG Fort Leavenworth, 17 Aug., 1880, Telegrams Sent DoNM, Vol.3, Jan. – Nov. 1880 NA, RG393, Part 3, Entry 431, p.749; Platt to AAG HQ MDoM 18 Aug., 1880 in 'Victorio Papers', NA, M666, Roll 528; Platt to AAG HQ MDoM, 18 Aug., 1880, 'Victorio Files', NA, RG393, M1495, Roll 14.

143 Hatch (citing telegram from Samaniego to Brinkerhoff) to AAG Fort Leavenworth, 18 Aug., 1880, Telegrams Sent DoNM, Vol.3, Jan. – Nov. 1880 NA, RG393, Part 3, Entry 431, pp.751-752.

144 Ord to AG Chicago Ill. 27 Aug., 1880 in 'Victorio Papers', NA, M666, Roll 528; 'Grierson's Report, Sept.1880'; NA, RG393, Part 1, Entry 2546, pp.639-644.

145 Ball, 1970, pp.76-77.

146 See Ball, 1970, pp.86-87.

147 Buchanan, 1986, p.32; Ball, 1962, p.40; Ball, 1970, pp119-120; Roberts, 1998, p.192.

148 Berger to Beck, 23 Aug., 1880 in Unregistered Letters 1878-1881, HQ Records DoP 1878-1881, NA, RG393, M1381, Roll 2; Ord to AG Chicago Ill. 27 Aug., 1880 in 'Victorio Papers', NA, M666, Roll 528; Victorio's Murdering Band', *The New York Times*, 28 Aug., 1880.

149 Grierson to AAG, DoTx, 22 Aug., 1880 in Telegrams Sent 23 Jun.-30 Nov., 1880, HQ Records DoP 1878-1881, NA, RG393, M1381, Roll 1, p.122, Letter No.427.

ment made by the Mexican troops.[150] The latter were split into small detachments to guard the settlements near the Candelaria Mountains.[151] Samaniego predicted that, if not pursued, Victorio would linger in the Candelaria Mountains before drifting on to the Laguna de Guzman.[152] It seemed likely Colonel Valle, with a small detachment of troops en route from El Paso del Norte to Chihuahua City, had had a narrow escape, as the main party of Apaches had crossed the road the Colonel was on only hours after his troops had passed.[153]

Grierson argued that the failure of the Mexican Army under Valle to blockade the Rio Grande, combined with the refusal of the Mexican Government to allow Grierson to cross the border, had allowed the Apaches an easy escape, perhaps not realising, or forgetting, that he had managed to lose track of Victorio in the Sierra Diablo. Nevertheless, Grierson accused many Mexican citizens of actively colluding with the Apaches to facilitate their flight. Grierson stated that:

> There seems to be a tacit understanding between Victorio and many Mexicans, that so long as he does not make war upon them in earnest, he can take whatever food and other supplies he may need for his warriors.[154]

While this accusation had a great deal of truth to it, the Colonel did not appreciate that this often reflected a less than stable political situation south of the border. Ordinary Mexican citizens in isolated settlements or ranches often depended on good relations with the Apaches to ensure their very survival.

Grierson also reported that the Mexican troops had withdrawn to Chihuahua City to counter a threatened internal insurrection.[155] However, far from undermining operations against the Apaches prior to their return to the Candelaria Mountains in mid-August, these troop movements had not been ordered until late August. This news was transmitted to Captain Brinkerhoff by Samaniego on 1 September 1880.[156] It is also quite clear that Valle intended to return to the frontier to resume operations against the Apaches once the internal difficulties had been resolved.[157] (See document file no. 100.)

Grierson was too harsh on the Mexican Army. He had already erroneously claimed that it had left the corresponding section of the border in the aftermath of the engagement at Tinaja de las Palmas, when it had temporarily withdrawn to El Paso del Norte for additional supplies. In fact, Valle had only withdrawn from the border in mid-August. Grierson was so annoyed at what he perceived to be Valle's actions that he went so far as to contact Captain Brinkerhoff, instructing

150 Ibid.

151 Hatch (citing telegram from Samaniego to Brinkerhoff) to AAG Fort Leavenworth, 18 Aug., 1880, Telegrams Sent DoNM, Vol.3, Jan. – Nov. 1880 NA, RG393, Part 3, Entry 431, pp.751-752.

152 Hatch (citing telegram from Samaniego to Brinkerhoff) to AAG Fort Leavenworth, 17 Aug., 1880, Telegrams Sent DoNM, Vol.3, Jan. – Nov. 1880 NA, RG393, Part 3, Entry 431, p.749.

153 Report of Francisco Mesa, In Command of Detachment camped at Santa Recio, 22 Aug., 1880 translated by Charles Berger & Berger to Beck, 23 Aug., 1880 in Unregistered Letters 1878-1881, HQ Records DoP 1878-1881, NA, RG393, M1381, Roll 2; Ord to AG Chicago Ill. 27 Aug., 1880 in 'Victorio Papers', NA, M666, Roll 528.

154 Rister, 1928, p.215.

155 Grierson to AAG, DoTx, 26 Aug., 1880 in Telegrams Sent 23 Jun.-30 Nov., 1880, HQ Records DoP 1878-1881, NA, RG393, M1381, Roll 1, pp.131-133, Letter No.444; 'Grierson's Report, Sept.1880'; NA, RG393, Part 1, Entry 2546, pp.639-644.

156 Brinkerhoff to AAAG 1 Sept., 1880 & Brinkerhoff to AAAG 2 Sept., 1880 in NA, RG393, Part 3, Entry 439, pp.808-809 & pp.803-804.

157 Brinkerhoff to AAAG 8 Sept., 1880, NA, RG393, Part 3, Entry 439, p.821; CO Ft Bliss to Hatch, 8 Sept., 1880, Telegrams Sent DoNM, Vol.3, Jan. – Nov. 1880 NA, RG393, Part 3, Entry 431, p.807; See also Pope to AAG, HQ MDoM, 10 Sept., 1880, 'Victorio Files', NA, RG393, M1495, Roll 14.

him to contact Valle to demand the return of the supplies that Grierson had sent over to the Mexicans when Valle and Grierson had met at Old Fort Quitman.[158] One can only hope that Captain Brinkerhoff had the diplomacy to ignore this request.

This situation was exacerbated by the US troops' inability to cross the border in hot pursuit of the Apaches. First, in February 1880, a clear instruction that US troops could pursue Apaches across the border had been suspended as a result of diplomatic pressure from Mexico. On 22 June 1880, the Mexican federal government refused permission for US troops to cross the border. (See Chapter 8.) The State Department had persevered in its efforts to persuade the Republic of Mexico to allow US troops to cross, but these efforts were in vain, and on 29 July 1880, the US Minister to Mexico was again informed, by the Mexican Minister for Foreign Affairs, that such permission would not be granted.[159] On 26 August 1880, Grierson was sent word by Ord that, 'There are no orders permitting troops to cross into Mexico when in pursuit of Indians.'[160]

The next stage of the Victorio Campaign would show that, in response to the continued resistance of Victorio's Apaches, actors within both the United States and Mexico would find an 'unofficial' diplomatic solution to cross-border relations. A hint of what this might entail was given when Charles Berger, returning from his scout into Mexico, encountered Roman Aranda. The latter informed Berger that he had 'papers and credentials from both the Governor of the State of Chihuahua, and the officer commanding the Mexican forces, empowering him to make a proposition to the District Commander to cross his troops into Mexico for the purpose of aiding in the contemplated movement against Victoria, now at Laguna Guzman'.[161]

Before we examine the diplomatic negotiations between the USA and Mexico concerning the war with Victorio, we must return to New Mexico. While Grierson was campaigning against the Apaches in western Texas, the troops in New Mexico had been re-fitted and reinforced.

---

158 Grierson to CO, Fort Bliss, 18 Aug., 1880 in Telegrams Sent 23 Jun.-30 Nov., 1880, HQ Records DoP 1878-1881, NA, RG393, M1381, Roll 1, pp.108-109, Letter No.403.

159 Secretary of State to the Secretary of War, 30 Aug., 1880 in Papers relating to the Frelinghuysen-Romero Agreement of Jul. 29, 1882, providing for reciprocal crossings of the international boundary by troops of the United States and Mexico in pursuit of hostile Indians, Feb. 1862-Jun. 1867; Letters Rec'd by the AGO (Main Series), 1881-1889, NA, M689, Roll 81.

160 Mason, AG, DoTx to Grierson, Eagle Springs via CO Fort Davis, 26 Aug., 1880 in Telegrams Rec'd by General Grierson in the Field 30 Jun.-14 Sept., 1880, HQ Records DoP 1878-1881, NA, RG393, M1381, Roll 4.

161 Nolan to AAAG, DoP, 16 Sept., 1880 in Letters Rec'd File 19 Mar., 1878, 14 Feb., 1881, HQ Records DoP 1878-1881, NA, RG393, M1381, Roll 2.

12

The Ninth Cavalry Regroups, June–August 1880

While Grierson and Valle were directing operations against Victorio, the US field commanders in Arizona and New Mexico were faced with several problems. First, the effect Victorio's continued resistance might have on other potentially hostile American Indians: in particular, the Navajos, on their reservations to the north of Victorio's territory; the remaining Mescalero Apaches, held on their reservation near Fort Stanton; and the Chiricahua Apaches on the San Carlos reservation. Second, was it too late to negotiate a settlement with Victorio? Third, Colonel Hatch had to try and rest, re-equip and reinforce the New Mexico garrison. Finally, once these troops had been rested, if Victorio remained at large, how should they be deployed against him?

Navajo and Mescalero Apaches

The persistent failure to defeat Victorio had encouraged other potentially militant American Indian warriors. For the Navajos, the Victorio war became a factor in an already problematic situation. Captain Bennett, CO Fort Wingate, had reported Navajo hostility, up to and including death threats against Galen Eastman, their reservation agent, as early as 16 April 1880. Bennett correctly identified Eastman's evangelical approach to his work as the source of the unrest. Frustrated by the Navajos' complete indifference to his strict Christian practices, Agent Eastman refused to issue government supplies to his charges until they adopted his beliefs. Bennett also noted that the trouble, at that point, was confined to a small group of Navajos, but that the Utes were also attempting to foment trouble on the reservation.[1] The previous year, Colonel Buell, commanding the Fifteenth US Infantry Regiment in the area, had reported that a lack of clarity concerning the southern boundary of the Navajo reservation had led to friction between them and settlers in the San Juan Valley. This concerned perceived incursions of Navajo herders with vast flocks of sheep. Buell argued that the situation would become increasingly tense unless the boundary was clearly marked and enforced.[2]

There had been several potentially explosive incidents. On 17 May 1880, the driver of the mail buckboard was stopped between San Mateo and Bacon Springs by a group of five Navajos, all reported to be drunk. One of the Navajos threatened and assaulted the driver, and cut the mail bags, before the driver made his escape on the buckboard. No mail was lost, and the other four

1 Bennett to AAAG DoNM, 16 Apr., 1880 in Letters Received by HQ_DoNM Sept. 1865-Aug. 1890, NA, RG393, M1088, Roll 40, Jan.-Jun. 1880; Bennett to AAAG, DoNM, 24 Apr., 1880 in Letters Received by HQ_DoNM Sept. 1865-Aug. 1890, NA, RG393, M1088, Roll 40, Jan.-Jun. 1880; Loud to Hatch, Mescalero Agency (Operator Mesilla to forward by first mail), 20 Apr., 1880, Telegrams Sent DoNM, Vol.3, Jan. – Nov. 1880 NA, RG393, Part 3, Entry 431, pp.322-323.

2 Buell to AAG, DoM, Fort Leavenworth, KS. 4 Nov., 1879, NA, RG393, Part 1, Entry 2546, pp.239-243.

Navajos made no effort to intervene on either side.[3] Also in May, Navajos killed three Anglo-Americans and wounded another in two separate instances. In the second case, agency workers had gone out to bury one of the men and had been threatened with the same fate by Navajos.[4]

During May 1880, fearing a Navajo revolt in response to a combination of Victorio's successes and agitation sponsored by emissaries from the Utes and Mormons, Colonel Buell was sent with a force of five companies of the Fifteenth Infantry to pre-empt any trouble on the Navajo reservation.[5] In a council with the Navajos, it was found that the unrest amongst them was mainly caused by their agent.[6] Dudley and Buell also reported that Navajo resistance had been somewhat encouraged by Victorio's successes.[7] There were rumours that Victorio had held a council with the Navajos and Zunis at Alamocito, and that some Navajo warriors had joined him.[8] Captain Bennett, Commanding Officer, Fort Wingate, had already recommended that the Agent should not be re-appointed,[9] and then found himself recommended for that post by Buell.[10] By mid-June, Bennett was able to report that the tension on the Navajo Reservation had been much reduced.[11]

This sparked yet another conflict between the War Department and the Indian Bureau, and the latter reinstated their employee. The Navajo immediately reacted against the evangelising agent and the army, now very concerned about Navajo warriors joining Victorio, simply removed Eastman for a second time. Captain Bennett, sent to replace Eastman, found the agency in a very poor physical and financial situation. In a further council with the Navajos, he found them to be very hostile towards Eastman. He also reported that this state of affairs had been exacerbated by news of troubles with the Utes to the north and the Apaches to the south.[12]

The situation on the reservation was reported to have deteriorated again by November 1880. This time, the problem centred around the sale of alcohol. Hatch telegraphed General Pope concerning what powers of arrest he might have over traders selling alcohol. Pope informed him that, if these men were caught on the reservation, there was no doubt as to his power. Such people should be arrested and turned over to the civil authorities. A more challenging problem arose when traders

---

3 Affidavit of George A. Taylor given to Lieut. T.F. Davis, Adjutant 15th Infantry, Fort Wingate, 18 May, 1880, NA, RG393, Part 1, Entry 2546, pp.469-470.

4 Bennett, Captain Ninth Cavalry, Monthly Report (July) from the Navajo and Moqui Indian Agencies to the Honorable CoIA, Washington D.C., 8 Aug., 1880, NA, RG393, Part 1, Entry 2546, pp.581-590.

5 Sheridan to Townsend, 26 May, 1880, NA, RG393, Part 1, Entry 2539, Press Copies of Letters and Endorsements Sent, MDoM, Vol. 13, pp.274-275; Platt to Colonel Hatch, Fort Craig, New Mexico, 7 Jun., 1880, NA, RG393, Part 3, Entry 440, p.19; Platt AAG, to AAAG, DoNM, SF, N.M. 9 Jun., 1880, NA, RG393, Part 3, Entry 440, p.23.

6 Buell to AAG Fort Leavenworth 16 Jun., 1880, Telegrams Sent DoNM, Vol.3, Jan. – Nov. 1880 NA, RG393, Part 3, Entry 431, pp.526-528.

7 Dudley to AAAG, DoNM, 4 Jun., 1880 & Buell to AAG, DoM, 8 Jun., 1880 in Letters Received by HQ DoNM Sept. 1865-Aug. 1890, NA, RG393, M1088, Roll 40, Jan.-Jun. 1880; Moore, p.230 & p.236.

8 Hatch to AAAG, SF 12? Jun., 1880; 'DoNM/GSFO/L&T', NA, RG393, Part 3, Entry 475, Vol. 7, p.367.

9 Loud to Hatch, Mescalero Agency (Operator Mesilla to forward by first mail), 20 Apr., 1880, Telegrams Sent DoNM, Vol.3, Jan. – Nov. 1880 NA, RG393, Part 3, Entry 431, pp.322-323.

10 Buell to AAAG, DoNM, 13 Jun., 1880 in Letters Received by HQ DoNM Sept. 1865-Aug. 1890, NA, RG393, M1088, Roll 40, Jan.-Jun. 1880.

11 Buell, Fort Wingate to AAAG, DoNM, 14 Jun., 1880 in Letters Received by HQ DoNM Sept. 1865-Aug. 1890, NA, RG393, M1088, Roll 40, Jan.-Jun. 1880.

12 Platt to AAAG DoNM 26 May, 1880, NA, RG393, Part 3, Entry 440, pp.39-40; See also Platt AAG to Colonel Hatch, Fort Craig, New Mexico, 7 Jun., 1880, NA, RG393, Part 3, Entry 440, p.19; Pope's Annual Report Year ending 22 Sept., 1880, NA, RG393, Part 1, Entry 2546, pp.611-612; Cozzens, p.331.

in alcohol chose to set up their businesses in close proximity to the reservation.[13] On 23 November 1880, Pope commented that those Navajos who remembered their defeat by the US army in the 1860s were being superseded by younger men. The Navajos could muster a considerable force of fighting men who might, if provoked further, decide to opt for war. In view of this situation, Pope recommended that it would be wise to send reinforcements to Fort Wingate.[14]

Where the Mescalero Apaches were concerned, instructions were given to the Commanding Officer, Fort Stanton, to maintain a close guard on the captive Mescaleros. He was to prevent their escape to Mexico, where the rest of the Mescaleros were assumed to have fled. It was also assumed that the Mescaleros who had left the reservation would have returned, had it not been for the 'influence of Victorio'.[15] It was suggested that messengers be sent to these Apaches to persuade them to return 'as the Troops are not allowed to cross the border for them'.[16] As noted earlier, this effort to contact at least some of the Apaches allied to Victorio failed to materialise when the Commanding Officer at Fort Stanton informed Santa Fé that he could not find any Mescalero willing to undertake this mission.[17] In September 1880, the Mescaleros changed their minds. Messengers were sent in search of the independent Mescalero Apaches on the 26 and 27 September, but had not returned by the end of October.[18]

The San Carlos Chiricahuas and Negotiations with Victorio

As we shall see, the reorganization of troops in New Mexico indicated that a major operation against Victorio was being prepared, with the strong probability that it would involve significant numbers of US troops entering the Republic of Mexico. Yet Hatch was still willing to enter into negotiations with Victorio. Two days after the Palomas River fight, on 26 May 1880, Hatch responded to a query from Department Headquarters concerning the possibility of persuading Victorio to capitulate. He responded that, providing that Victorio and his warriors were given an amnesty and their families were returned to Ojo Caliente, they would probably surrender. The main difficulty, in Hatch's opinion, was that the Warm Springs Apaches 'will be in the future suspicious and easily alarmed, the promises made the Hot Springs have been violated in nearly every instance by the Interior Department'.[19]

Equally, as noted in earlier chapters, Hatch vacillated between two polar opinions concerning Victorio. On the one hand, he sympathised with Victorio's plight; but at times he also advocated the complete destruction of the Apaches:

> I do not approve of asking him to come in, he should be driven to terms or killed. Probably the Indians who are asked to visit him will bring in his head if paid for it. I don't believe Victorio

13 Hatch to AAG, DoM, 20 Nov., 1880, & Pope to Sheridan 29 Nov., 1880 NA, RG393, Part 1, Entry 2546, pp659-661.

14 Letter written by Pope 23 Nov., 1880, NA, RG393, Part 1, Entry 2546, pp.662-666.

15 Loud to CO Fort Stanton, 28 Jun., 1880 in Letters Sent by '9MD/DNM/DoNM', NA, RG393, M1072, Roll 6, Jan. 1880-Aug. 1881, Letter No.317, pp.210-211.

16 Ibid.

17 Hatch to AAG, DoM, Fort Leavenworth, 22 Jul., 1880 in Letters Sent by '9MD/DNM/DoNM', NA, RG393, M1072, Roll 6, Jan. 1880-Aug. 1881, Letter No.369, p.239.

18 Conrad, CO Fort Stanton, to AAAG, DoNM 27 Oct., 1880 in Letters Received by HQ DoNM Sept. 1865-Aug. 1890, NA, RG393, M1088, Roll 41, Jul.-Dec. 1880.

19 Hatch to Department HQ, 26 May, 1880, 'DoNM/GSFO/L&T', NA, RG393, Part 3, Entry 475, Vol. 5, p.273.

> will ever live at San Carlos. If he surrenders it should be unconditional. Jeffords can undoubtedly manage Victorio if that cause is considered advisable.[20]

The Indians Hatch refers to were probably involved in efforts to contact Victorio from San Carlos, in July 1880. In June 1880, Carr had a meeting with Juh and Naiche where they complained that sickness had taken a significant toll of their people since their removal to San Carlos. At least a third, possibly closer to half, of Naiche's following had died since coming to San Carlos in 1876. This had not been an issue at their old reservation in the Chiricahua Mountains.[21] They were also not happy at being kept under closer scrutiny than other Apaches on the reservation. Juh reminded Carr that he had come in voluntarily, and Naiche pointed out that he had been living peacefully at San Carlos for four years. Tom Jeffords informed Carr that these factors had almost led the Chiricahua Apaches to leave the reservation in June. Jeffords had intervened and persuaded them to stay.[22] The mortality rate at San Carlos was one of the factors which persuaded Victorio to leave the reservation in 1877. Nevertheless, Carr thought that because Victorio's wife and children were at San Carlos, he might be persuaded to come into the reservation. Communication with Victorio could be opened in the same way as Juh had first been contacted in 1879. Emissaries from the Warm Springs Apaches living at San Carlos could be sent into Mexico. Carr, through Bennett, Chief of the San Carlos Indian Police, let the Chokonen and Chihenne Apaches know that he was open to negotiation about contacting Victorio.[23] Jeffords also advised that the only chance of bringing Victorio in peacefully was on the 'promise of a white man in whom he has confidence; and that there is only himself and one other man, now in New Mexico, [probably Andrew Kelley] who could or would fill that bill'.[24]

At the same time, Hatch contacted Willcox 'to see if arrangements can be made with Victorio to live at San Carlos with his family'.[25] Willcox ordered Carr to quietly liaise with Hatch in order to see if Victorio could be contacted and persuaded to surrender.[26] As part of this process, Tiffany, the new Indian agent at San Carlos, moved the Chiricahuas 'from an unhealthy location to a more salubrious one'.[27] While openly reluctant[28] to make the opening moves in any negotiations with

20 Hatch to Carr, Camp Thomas, 11 Jul., 1880, Telegrams Sent DoNM, Vol.3, Jan. – Nov. 1880 NA, RG393, Part 3, Entry 431, p.600; Carr quoting Hatch to AG DoAz, 13 Jul., 1880, Troops in SE Arizona, DoAz, NA, RG393, Part 1, Entry 232, Vol.7, 18 May-6 Sept., 1880, Letter No.396, pp.118-119; See also Carr to AAG DoAz, 30 Jun., 1880, Troops in SE Arizona, DoAz, NA, RG393, Part 1, Entry 232, Vol.7, 18 May-6 Sept., 1880, Letter No.273, pp.104-108; Carr to Hatch, 10 Jul., 1880, Troops in SE Arizona, DoAz, NA, RG393, Part 1, Entry 232, Vol.7, 18 May-6 Sept., 1880, Letter No.384, p.113.

21 Carr to AAG DoAz, 30 Jun., 1880, Troops in SE Arizona, DoAz, NA, RG393, Part 1, Entry 232, Vol.7, 18 May-6 Sept., 1880, Letter No.273, pp.104-108; Carr to AG DoAz, 5 Jul., 1880, Troops in SE Arizona, DoAz, NA, RG393, Part 1, Entry 232, Vol.7, 18 May-6 Sept., 1880, Letter No.374, p.108.

22 Carr to AAG DoAz, 30 Jun., 1880, Troops in SE Arizona, DoAz, NA, RG393, Part 1, Entry 232, Vol.7, 18 May-6 Sept., 1880, Letter No.273, pp.104-108.

23 Ibid, pp.104-108.

24 Ibid, pp.107-108.

25 Martin to Carr, 8 Jul., 1880, NA, RG393, Part 1, Entry 169, Vol. 10, p.312.

26 Carr to Hatch, 10 Jul., 1880, Troops in SE Arizona, DoAz, NA, RG393, Part 1, Entry 232, Vol.7, 18 May-6 Sept., 1880, Letter No.384, p.113; Carr to Genl Hatch Comd Dist of NM 10 Jul., 1880, NA, RG393, Part 3, Entry 439, p.578.

27 Willcox to AG, Presidio, San Francisco, 13 Jul., 1880, NA, RG393, Part 1, Entry 169, Vol. 10, p.318; Carr to AG DoAz, 10 Jul., 1880, Troops in SE Arizona, DoAz, NA, RG393, Part 1, Entry 232, Vol.7, 18 May-6 Sept., 1880, Letter No.385, pp.113-114.

28 Bell, Acting Secretary, Dept. of the Interior to The Secretary of War, 24 Aug., 1880, citing a letter dated 20 Jul., 1880 from Agent Tiffany concerning his meeting with Col. Carr in 'Victorio Files', NA, RG393, M1495, Roll 14. Part of this reluctance was on general principle, Carr's reluctance to negotiate with

Apaches, Carr was pragmatic enough to realise that the attempt to bring an end to hostilities was feasible, as there were Chihenne Apaches at San Carlos who could open negotiations with Victorio.[29] Carr also noted that Tom Jeffords was amenable the idea that he should participate in this cross-border venture.[30] However, while Willcox clearly agreed that an attempt to end hostilities by negotiation should be undertaken, he also suggested that Carr investigate other means 'for bringing in Victorio dead or alive and probable expense'.[31] Yet it was also clear that Willcox was aware of the circumstances behind Victorio's resistance:

> It is believed by many that Victorio was unjustly dealt with in the first instance by the abrupt removal of his people from Ojo Caliente N.M. to San Carlos and that such removal if not a breach of faith was a harsh and cruel measure from which the people of New Mexico have reaped the bitter consequence.[32]

General Pope shared this opinion, noting that while Victorio and his followers would probably have to be hunted down, it was believed that Victorio was willing to surrender if all the Warm Springs Apaches were given a reservation at Ojo Caliente. As far as Pope was concerned, the whole trouble with Victorio had been caused by the Department of the Interior's insistence that the Chihenne Apaches be deported to San Carlos.[33] (See document file no. 102.)

However, it was Tiffany who pointed out the key flaw in any effort to persuade Victorio to settle at San Carlos. Tiffany argued that it was unlikely that Victorio would now be able to settle at San Carlos, as he would be a 'marked man' as far as the 'San Carlos' Apaches were concerned, due to the casualties inflicted among them by Victorio's followers during the campaign. Indeed he pointed out that at Ash Creek in May 1880, a popular leader had been killed and his followers had vowed to shoot Victorio on sight.[34] (See document file no. 101.) Therefore, we not only have to appreciate that Victorio was fighting for a reservation at Ojo Caliente, but we also have to realize that the manner in which he was doing so completely ruled out any peace settlement which had Victorio returning to the San Carlos reservation. It also has to be acknowledged that Victorio's followers, had they returned to San Carlos, might have wished to settle scores for those Chihennes killed by San Carlos scouts on the Palomas River on 24 May 1880. Any return to San Carlos by Victorio was a recipe for future trouble between the two groups of Apaches.

In September 1880, the Warm Springs Apaches at San Carlos contacted Lieutenant Wright, then recruiting Apache scouts, and reiterated their desire to live at Ojo Caliente, for the same reasons as advanced before: the poor water, poor health and poor relations with other Apache groups at San Carlos. They also stated that they thought Victorio would return to Ojo Caliente and live in peace. Wright also revealed that he had not only sat down and talked to Loco and Jaralche,

---

Apaches can also be explained by the fact that he was worried that Victorio might move from Chihuahua into Arizona and had sent out scouts in an attempt to frustrate such a move. (Willcox to AG, Presidio, San Francisco, 13 Jul., 1880, NA, RG393, Part 1, Entry 169, Vol. 10, p.318.

29 Carr to Genl Hatch Comd Dist of NM 10 Jul., 1880, NA, RG393, Part 3, Entry 439, pp.578-579.

30 Carr to Genl Hatch Comd Dist of NM 10 Jul., 1880, NA, RG393, Part 3, Entry 439, p.579; Carr to Hatch, 10 Jul., 1880, Troops in SE Arizona, DoAz, NA, RG393, Part 1, Entry 232, Vol.7, 18 May-6 Sept., 1880, Letter No.384, p.113.

31 Willcox to Carr, 15 Jul., 1880, NA, RG393, Part 1, Entry 169, Vol. 10, p.32.

32 Martin to AG, Presidio, San Francisco, 11 Sept., 1880, NA, RG393, Part 1, Entry 169, Vol. 10, pp.418-419; Report of General O.B. Willcox, 11 Sept., 1880, in AR-WD 1880, NA, M997, Roll 35, 1880 Vol. I, p.206.

33 Pope to Whipple, AAG Chicago, 3 Jun., 1880, 'Victorio Files', NA, RG393, M1495, Roll 14.

34 Bell, Acting Secretary, Dept. of the Interior to The Secretary of War, 24 Aug., 1880, citing a letter dated 20 Jul., 1880 from Agent Tiffany concerning his meeting with Col. Carr in 'Victorio Files', NA, RG393, M1495, Roll 14.

but had also spoken with Victorio's wife. Unfortunately, Wright did not make it clear if she was with the two leaders. If it was a separate meeting, he gave no details as to what Victorio's wife had to say on the matter.[35]

The Ninth Cavalry Regroups

Hatch, or more accurately General Pope, now took the opportunity to reorganise the troops in southern New Mexico. At the beginning of June, General Pope informed his superiors that the Ninth Cavalry were effectively crippled, and would not be able to perform field duty for some time. Pope recommended that approximately 75 Apache scouts be stationed in New Mexico. In view of the vociferous press campaign against the troops in New Mexico, and in particular against their commander, Colonel Hatch, General Pope was quick to point out that much of the information coming from the press and other sources in New Mexico was inaccurate, and though he promised to investigate such reports, he predicted that most would be found to have little foundation.[36]

In June 1880, Pope visited New Mexico to see the current state of affairs for himself. While praising Hatch and his command's strenuous efforts, and crediting them with having cleared the area of Apaches, he also censured Hatch for deploying his troops too widely, thus leaving each detachment (Pope gently derided Hatch's term 'column') too weak to effectively counter the Apaches. He also pinpointed this as the source of the very bad feeling, indeed hostility, towards Hatch expressed by the local population.[37] (See document file no. 103.) Nevertheless, J.J. Coppinger, Inspector General for the District of New Mexico, filed a report underlining the point that many of the leading critics of Hatch and, to a lesser extent Morrow, were a deeply unreliable source of information, listing an admixture of alcoholism, cowardice, excessive opium consumption and thievery as reasons for this unreliability.[38] Coppinger added, 'There are here many southern men who seem to delight in insulting negro soldiers, their officers & their Regt.'[39] However, the damage had been done; and it should be remembered that Hatch had inflicted some of this damage upon himself.

Orders were issued to post commanders to collect a record of all scouts and expeditions from the previous campaign.[40] Pope ordered a radical reorganisation of the troops in the area. This was intended to restore discipline among the Ninth Cavalry and Fifteenth Infantry Regiments. He thought that discipline had been undermined, due to prolonged detached service.[41] What he was

35 Wright to AAAG, New Mexican Column (thro. CO Batt. 9th Cav.) 18 Sept., 1880 in Letters Received by HQ DoNM Sept. 1865-Aug. 1890, NA, RG393, M1088, Roll 41, Jul.-Dec. 1880.

36 Pope to Whipple, AAG Chicago, 3 Jun., 1880, 'Victorio Files', NA, RG393, M1495, Roll 14; Pope to Col. Whipple AAG Chicago, 16 Jun., 1880 in 'Victorio Papers', NA, M666, Roll 527.

37 Pope to Sheridan 1 Jul., 1880, NA, RG393, Part 1, Entry 2546, pp.521-527; See also Pope's Annual Report Year ending Sept. 22 1880, NA, RG393, Part 1, Entry 2546, p.613.

38 Coppinger to AAG, DoM, 6 Jul., 1880 in Letters Received, DoM 1868-98, RG 393, Entry A1-1 2601, Box 92.

39 Coppinger to AAG, DoM, 6 Jul., 1880 in Letters Received, DoM 1868-98, RG 393, Entry A1-1 2601, Box 92.

40 General Order No. 3, 18 Jun., 1880, Printed Special Orders 1869-1888, DoNM, NA, RG393, Part 3, Entry 446; See also Loud to Morrow, Fort Bayard, 21 Jun., 1880, Telegrams Sent DoNM, Vol.3, Jan. – Nov. 1880 NA, RG393, Part 3, Entry 431, p.543.

41 In his Annual Report for year ending 22 September, 1881, Pope made the same point that the Ninth Cavalry and Fifteenth Infantry needed to be sent to another district on account of their long and arduous service against Apaches had had a detrimental effect upon effectiveness and discipline. These two regiments needing 'to re-establish discipline and tactical knowledge, which have been considerably impaired by the service they have had to perform for a number of years past.' (HQ DoM, Annual Report for Year ending 22 Sept., 1881, NA, RG393, Part 1, Entry 2546, p.850).

referring to was the need to split company strength into smaller detachments. Pope wanted to ensure that a situation would be created where any return by Victorio to New Mexico could rapidly be crushed.[42] One of the first reorganisations was the disbanding of the three battalions of New Mexico Troops organised by Hatch in February 1880.[43] As we shall see, this reorganisation was intended to be offensive as well as defensive, international borders notwithstanding.

US army bureaucracy also made its presence felt. Just before the Hembrillo Canyon operation, District Headquarters, New Mexico received a missive from the Department of the Missouri complaining that the majority of company commanders from the Ninth Cavalry and Fifteenth Infantry had not complied with Circular Number Two. This circular was a 'statement of the amount of ammunition they have on hand manufactured prior to January 1 1877'.[44] On 1 June 1880, the US army's Adjutant General, Edward D. Townsend, ordered that all officers in the field fill out their monthly returns promptly, and that the returns for New Mexico for February–April were 'desired at the earliest possible date'.[45] Loud informed the Adjutant General that:

> District Returns are made from the Post Returns. There has been but little opportunity afforded Company Commanders during the Campaign now going on in the District to render to their Post Commanders promptly the proper Returns, showing Casualties in district. They have been continuously in the field and on the march.[46]

Hatch notified his officers on 7 June 1880 that a full record of the operations of March, April and May 1880 should be submitted to the Adjutant General.[47] It should be noted that the information which was published in the Annual Report for the Secretary for War for 1880 cannot be described as 'a full record' of events.

One of the first things Hatch himself had set in motion was the recruitment of a handful of experienced Mexican-American and Anglo-American scouts to monitor Victorio's movements in Mexico. As we have seen, individuals such as 'Hurricane' Bill and 'Cherokee' Jim were not necessarily reliable sources of information. (See Chapter 8.) On 24 June, District Headquarters contacted Lieutenant Davenport, Fort Craig, concerning information that there was a Mexican living in the area who knew the Warm Springs Apaches and who might be prevailed upon 'to go into Mexico to obtain information'.[48] On the same day, Morrow, at Fort Bayard, was also asked if he could find a couple of 'reliable persons' for scouting into Mexico to locate Victorio's band.[49] Morrow quickly found two men willing to undertake this difficult task and, on the following day, was instructed

42 Pope to Sheridan 1 Jul., 1880, NA, RG393, Part 1, Entry 2546, pp.521-527.

43 General Order No. 4, 26 Jun., 1880, Printed Special Orders 1869-1888, DoNM, NA, RG393, Part 3, Entry 446; See also Telegrams Sent (10 Jul., 1880) DoNM, Vol.3, Jan. – Nov. 1880 NA, RG393, Part 3, Entry 431, p.599.

44 Platt, AAG Fort Leavenworth to Co DoNM, 2 Apr., 1880 in Letters Received by HQ DoNM Sept. 1865-Aug. 1890, NA, RG393, M1088, Roll 40, Jan.-Jun. 1880.

45 Townsend to Comdg. General, DoM, 1 Jun., 1880 in Letters Received by HQ DoNM Sept. 1865-Aug. 1890, NA, RG393, M1088, Roll 40, Jan.-Jun. 1880.

46 Loud to the AG, U.S. Army, Washington D.C., 6 Jun., 1880 in Letters Sent by '9MD/DNM/DoNM', NA, RG393, M1072, Roll 6, Jan. 1880-Aug. 1881, Letter No.270, pp.175-176.

47 'DoNM/GSFO/L&T', NA, RG393, Part 3, Entry 475, Vol. 7, p.29.

48 Loud to Davenport, Fort Craig, 24 Jun., 1880, Telegrams Sent DoNM, Vol.3, Jan. – Nov. 1880 NA, RG393, Part 3, Entry 431, p.546.

49 Loud to Morrow, Fort Bayard, 24 Jun., 1880, Telegrams Sent DoNM, Vol.3, Jan. – Nov. 1880 NA, RG393, Part 3, Entry 431, p.547) Similar instructions were passed to the CO Fort Bliss. (Loud to CO Fort Bliss, 25 Jun., 1880, Telegrams Sent DoNM, Vol.3, Jan. – Nov. 1880 NA, RG393, Part 3, Entry 431, p.549.

to employ the pair and send them off into Mexico with all expediency.[50] Another scout had been sent out from Fort Stanton around the same time;[51] and a man named Valentine, who was believed to have been attached to Lieutenant Maney's Indian Scouts, was also sought for scouting duties. Instructions were sent that, as soon as Valentine was located, he was to report to Fort Cummings, no doubt to participate in this scouting activity.[52]

> You will use the men whom you were authorised to employ to watch Victoria's band, so that in case he crosses the Rio Grande to the east side below El Paso, the very earliest information of such movement can be telegraphed to Buell and to General Ord, at San Antonio.[53]

As to who these men were, the telegram is frustratingly silent, though it does confirm that Hatch's superiors approved his action in recruiting them. Some of this scouting was straight intelligence gathering concerning the number and movement of Victorio's following. A report was received on 28 August 1880, at Fort Cummings, stating that Victorio was in the Candelaria Mountains with a few wounded. It was estimated that he was accompanied by 100 to 120 men, 50 women and 500 animals.[54] It is significant that some of the people sought for scouting duties were known to be on familiar terms with the Chihenne Apaches, which suggests that negotiations were still considered an option.

Reinforcements were also dispatched to New Mexico. On 26 May 1880, Hatch was informed that three companies of the Fourth Cavalry and two companies of Infantry were to be sent to his district.[55] In mid-June, he also received word that the Thirteenth Infantry Regiment had been transferred from its station at New Orleans and was to be allocated to the District of New Mexico.[56] By 14 June, the reinforcements promised in May had begun to arrive in the area. L Company, Fourth Cavalry, was sent to Fort Cummings, while elements of the Sixteenth Infantry were sent into the San Mateo Mountains.[57] The other two companies of the Fourth Cavalry arrived at Fort Cummings, having taken almost a month to move from Kansas to New Mexico:

Table 12.1 Time Taken to Re-Deploy Companies A and H, Fourth Cavalry, from Kansas to New Mexico, June 1880.

1 June	Companies depart Caldwell, Kansas, and march to AT&SF Railroad at Wellington same day.
6 June	Arrive Belen, New Mexico.
14 June	Depart Belen New Mexico.
18 June	Arrive Fort Craig: distance marched 86 miles.
22 June	Depart Fort Craig for San Jose: distance marched 16 miles.
23 June	Depart San Jose for Canada Alamosa: distance marched 20 miles.
24 June	Depart Canada Alamosa for Cuchillo Negro: distance marched 15 miles.
25 June	Depart Cuchillo Negro for Las Palomas: distance marched 21 miles.
26 June	Depart Las Palomas for camp on Las Animas River: distance marched 15 miles.
27 June	Depart camp on Las Animas River for McEvers' Ranch: distance marched 15 miles
28 June	Departs McEvers' Ranch to camp in vicinity of Fort Cummings: distance marched 25 miles

Within two days, A Company, Fourth Cavalry, was scouting the road between Fort Cummings and Lloyd's Ranch, and I Company had been despatched to scout the land to the south of the Florida Mountains.[58] In the meantime, Colonel Carr was ordered to send two cavalry companies

58 Lt Budd, Co. I, 4th Cav. To AAAG, Dist of N.M., & Lt. Parker to AAAG, DoNM, 6 Jul., 1880 in Letters Received by HQ DoNM Sept. 1865-Aug. 1890, NA, RG393, M1088, Roll 41, Jul.-Dec. 1880.

Plate 12.1. Old Fort Cummings was used unofficially as a location to base small garrisons and scouting parties throughout the Victorio Campaign. However, it was officially reactivated in the summer of 1880 as the main base for a major offensive against the Apaches. Its strategic location cannot be overstated. The photo looks towards the eastern entrance of Cooke's Canyon. (Photo: Author)

Plate 12.2. The scattered stone outcrops seen in the brush below the hill at the centre of the photo are all that remains of the ruins of Old Fort Cummings. This photo gives a clear idea of the flat ground surrounding the fort, which was used by Buell to bivouac his troops as he concentrated his forces for the projected campaign against Victorio. (Photo: Author)

and an Apache scout company to scout the San Francisco River area.[59] The reinforcements and support from troops from Arizona allowed Hatch some leeway to reorganise his existing forces. Captain Dawson, with B Company, Ninth Cavalry, was immediately ordered to guard the mail route where it crossed the Mimbres River.[60] Detachments of Ninth Cavalry were also sent from Fort Cummings to Aleman and Las Palomas.[61] It was also clear that Fort Cummings, or more accurately the Fort Cummings reservation,[62] was intended to be the hub of any future operations against the Apaches. On 4 August 1880, Hatch recommended that Fort Cummings itself be re-occupied for 'operations against Indians in the future', being 'important in regards to the Mexican Frontier'.[63] Yet as early as 24 June, the commanding officer of troops stationed at Fort Cummings was asked to inform District Headquarters whether the water there could support nine companies of cavalry.[64] While this reorganization was completed, Major Morrow, at Fort Bayard, was ordered to keep some of his Apache scouts stationed close to the border, to give early warning of any move north on the part of the Apaches.[65]

The dreadful state of the Ninth Cavalry Regiment's horses had not improved by the end of June. Table 12.2 shows that the Ninth Cavalry recorded a dramatically reduced number of lost horses, yet the regiment still recorded a slight increase in unserviceable horses. By the end of June, not one company in the Ninth Cavalry Regiment was unable to mount 50 percent of its available manpower on serviceable horses. In fact, most companies were able to mount considerably less than half their men. (See Table 12.3.)

Table 12.2 Ninth Cavalry, Roster of Horses, January–June 1880.[66]

Ninth Cavalry	Serviceable Horses	Unserviceable Horses	Horses Lost in Action, Died, etc.
January 1880	438	103	36
February 1880	425	129	34
March 1880	441	140	10
April 1880	345	213	54
May 1880	244	277	62
June 1880	237	282	10

59 Martin to Carr, 5 Jun., 1880, & Comdg Dept to AG, Presidio, San Francisco, 10 Jun., 1880, NA, RG393, Part 1, Entry 169, Vol. 10, P.265 & p.271; Loud to Hatch, Fort Craig, 19 Jun., 1880, Telegrams Sent DoNM, Vol.3, Jan. – Nov. 1880 NA, RG393, Part 3, Entry 431, p.537; See also Carr to Hatch, 8 Jun., 1880, Troops in SE Arizona, DoAz, NA, RG393, Part 1, Entry 232, Vol.7, 18 May-6 Sept., 1880, pp.74-75.

60 Special Field Orders No. 37, para.5, 14 Jun., 1880, NA, RG393, Part 3, Entry 450.

61 Special Field Orders No. 38, para's.1-3, 19 Jun., 1880, NA, RG393, Part 3, Entry 450; Hatch to Morrow 7 Jun., 1880, 'DoNM/GSFO/L&T', NA, RG393, Part 3, Entry 475, Vol. 7, p.294.

62 i.e. the plot of land upon which the War Department had built Fort Cummings. Buell was authorised to establish a military camp on this ground even though the Fort itself was considered too 'dilapidated' to reoccupy. (Loud to Buell, 26 Jun., 1880 in Letters Sent by '9MD/DNM/DoNM', NA, RG393, M1072, Roll 6, Jan. 1880-Aug. 1881, Letter No.313 pp.207-208; Hatch to Buell, 7 Jul., 1880 in Letters Sent by '9MD/DNM/DoNM', NA, RG393, M1072, Roll 6, Jan. 1880-Aug. 1881, Letter No.333 p.220).

63 Hatch to AAG, DoM, Fort Leavenworth, 4 Aug., 1880 in Letters Sent by '9MD/DNM/DoNM', NA, RG393, M1072, Roll 6, Jan. 1880-Aug. 1881, Letter No.404, p.259; see also Hatch to AAG, DoM, 4 Aug., 1880 in Letters Received, DoM 1868-98, RG 393, Entry A1-1 2601, Box 92.

64 Loud to CO Fort Cummings, 24 Jun., 1880, Telegrams Sent DoNM, Vol.3, Jan. – Nov. 1880 NA, RG393, Part 3, Entry 431, p.547.

65 Loud to Morrow, Fort Bayard, 25 Jun., 1880, Telegrams Sent DoNM, Vol.3, Jan. – Nov. 1880 NA, RG393, Part 3, Entry 431, pp.551-552.

66 Derived from Returns From Regular Army Cavalry Regiments 1833-1916, 9th Cavalry 1873-1880, NA, M744, Roll 88

12.3 Serviceable, Unserviceable and Lost Horses to Available Men, Ninth Cavalry, June 1880.[67]

Company	Serviceable Horses	Unserviceable Horses	Available Men
A	18	17	44
B	24	20	52
C	19	19	50
D	16	23	49
E	0	36	54
F	12	20	45
G	30	17	65
H	18	29	53
I	23	22	55
K	9	45	61
L	21	17	63
M	33	17	64

The bi-monthly returns for the Ninth Cavalry (Table 12.4) reveal the same trend:

Table 12.4 Available Men to Serviceable Horses, Ninth Cavalry, March–June 1880.[68]

Co.	Available Men March–April 1880	Serviceable Horses March–April 1880	Available Men May–June 1880	Serviceable Horses May–June 1880
A	24	18	47	18
B	58	22	46	24
C	47	16	46	19
D	26	15	49	No Entry
E	46	29	50	1
F	27	7	44	12
G	66	40	63	30
H	57	No Entry	48	28
I	54	20	55	23
K	55	50	61	9
L	57	30	Missing from Archive	Missing from Archive
M	67	No Entry	62	33

Indeed, if we examine the period from January 1879 to December 1881 (see Figure 12.1), we can perhaps more clearly see the overall effect of the campaign against Victorio between January and June 1880 on the Ninth Cavalry's roster of horses:

67 Derived from Returns From Regular Army Cavalry Regiments 1833-1916, 9th Cavalry 1873-1880, NA, M744, Roll 88.
68 Derived Bi-Monthly Company Muster Rolls for Jan./Feb. & Mar./Apr. 1880, 9th Cavalry in NA, RG94

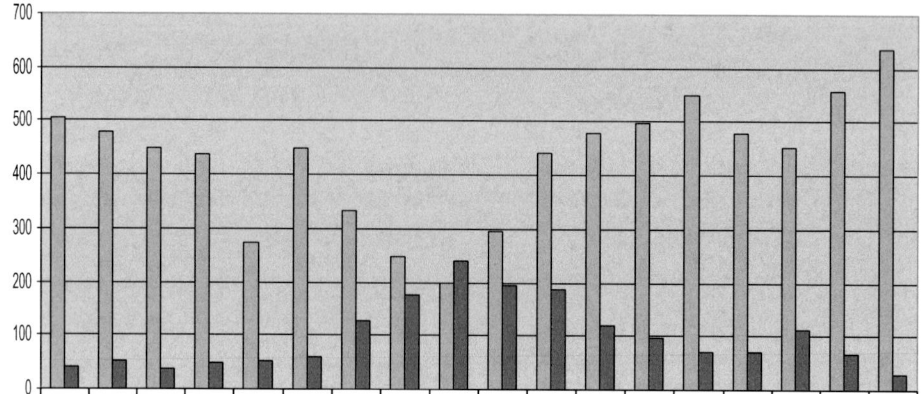

	Jan/Feb 1879	Mar/Apr 1879	May/Jun 1879	Jul/Aug 1879	Sep/Oct 1879	Nov/Dec 1879	Jan/Feb 1880	Mar/Apr 1880	May/Jun 1880	Jul/Aug 1880	Sep/Oct 1880	Nov/Dec 1880	Jan/Feb 1881	Mar/Apr 1881	May/Jun 1881	Jul/Aug 1881	Sep/Oct 1881	Nov/Dec 1881
Serviceable Horses	506	481	450	438	274	448	334	247	197	294	441	480	499	552	478	452	556	635
Unserviceable Hrses	40	52	37	48	51	59	127	176	241	193	189	121	96	71	72	112	69	30

Figure 12.1 Ninth Cavalry, Bi-Monthly Summary of Serviceable and Unserviceable Horses, 1879–81.[69]

However, the bi-monthly company rosters also reveal a key issue concerning our use of data from the monthly and bi-monthly regimental returns and other archival sources. Quite simply, the numbers do not tally: for example, the regimental return for June 1880 states that there were 237 serviceable and 282 unserviceable horses (see Table 12.2), whereas the bi-monthly roster for the end of June 1880 states that there were 197 serviceable and 241 unserviceable horses. (See Figure 12.1.)

What the reader must be aware of is that these returns, and indeed other sources from the archives, reveal trends but not absolutes. In this instance, both records indicate similar trends on the basis of similar, but different, sets of information. These records are dependent on the human foibles of their authors. Both sets of returns would have required the collation of detailed information on a blank form which must have taken some time for the person responsible to complete. We have already seen that the completion of these returns had been delayed by participation in this campaign. Therefore, the historian has no guarantee that the forms were completed on, or around, the date given on the form. The helpfulness of these records also depends on the varying levels of accuracy and handwriting legibility of the individuals who compiled them. Moreover, there would have been a political element to the filling out of these returns. For example, the general condition of the clothing, equipment and training of the men of each company of the Ninth Cavalry between January and August 1880 was recorded in the bi-monthly return. (See document file no. 104.) Here, the company commander had considerable leeway as to the picture he presented in this information. This meant that an officer who realised the importance of giving an accurate record of affairs could have submitted a very different return from a company commander desperate for promotion. Some company commanders recorded the exact state of their company. Others recorded the information in a way that makes the reader wonder whether their company had left its barracks. The only way for the historian to engage with such issues is to be aware of them, and to examine as many different sources as possible, if there are multiple data sources available. The reader needs to be warned that these figures indicate broad trends and the historian cannot vouch for them as absolute fact.

69 Derived 9th Cavalry Bi-Monthly Company Muster Rolls 1879-1881: NA, RG94.

With the above caveat in mind, it can be shown that there are jumps in horse fatalities during the Victorio War period; but can these be directly attributed to encounters with the Apaches? The Annual Report of the Secretary of War does not go into enough detail for us to be able to account for these casualties with any confidence as the result of the pursuit of the Apaches. However, where horses sold, died, lost or stolen are concerned, between 1876 and 1881 (see Figure 12.2), there are at least some indications that the Apaches were having an effect on the figures.

The numbers of horses killed or otherwise lost in 1878–80 are similar to those lost in 1876–77 (the Sioux War) and 1877–78 (the Nez Perce Campaign). It should be noted that, in 1879–80, the US army was not engaged in any sustained campaign against American Indians other than the Apaches.[70] On the other hand, these figures refer to *overall* US army losses and make no indication of the geographic location of the casualties. They also make no distinction between horses killed in action, by exhaustion, or by natural causes. Therefore, on their own, these figures should be treated with some caution.

However, by comparing the Ninth Cavalry's Regimental Return with those shown on the above table, it can be seen that the total number of US army horses that died, or were lost or stolen, for 1879–80 and 1880–81, or amounted to 1,181 and 569 respectively. In the same periods, the numbers of the Ninth Cavalry's horses that died, or were lost and stolen, totalled 395 and 120 respectively.[71] In other words, the Ninth Cavalry, one of ten US Cavalry Regiments, accounted for 34.4 percent of the US army's overall losses of horses in 1879–80 and 21 percent in 1880–81. This strongly suggests that the Apache tactic of targeting of the US army's horses had a major effect on the Ninth Cavalry's ability to remain 'fit for purpose'.

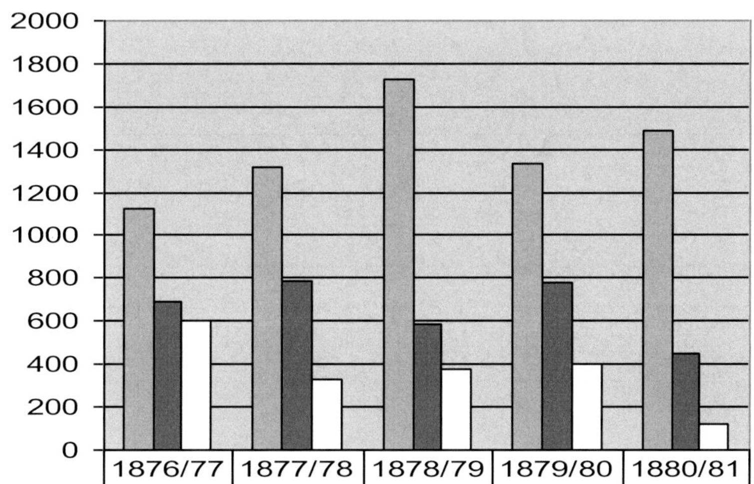

	1876/77	1877/78	1878/79	1879/80	1880/81
Sold	1121	1315	1725	1337	1487
Died	689	784	586	777	446
Lost/Stolen	599	326	377	404	123

Figure 12.2 Total US Army Horses Sold, Died, Lost or Stolen, 1876–81.[72]

70 The Ute Crisis of late 1879, while receiving far more attention than the Victorio Campaign, did not blow up into a major confrontation, though it did result in the commitment of a fairly large U.S. Army force to the area.

71 Derived from Returns From Regular Army Cavalry Regiments 1833-1916, 9th Cavalry 1873-1880, NA, M744, Rolls 88 & 89.

72 Derived AR-WD, 1877, p.290; 1878, p.348; 1879, p.307; 1880, p.421; 1881, p.324.

The number of mules sold, died, lost or stolen in the same period (see Figure 12.3), shows that during 1879–80 the US army suffered its highest loss in mules for the period 1876–81. This again suggests that the Apaches' strategy and tactics were having at least some effect.

Mules were an essential commodity for the pursuit of Apache guerrillas. They were more versatile than supply wagons, allowing detachments of cavalry to traverse very difficult terrain without losing contact with their supplies. The problem remained that, while increasing overall mobility, mules were just as susceptible to being irreparably 'broken down' or dying from exhaustion or gunshot wounds as the cavalry horses they accompanied.[73]

Figures 12.2 and 12.3 also show a high number of horses and mules being sold by the US army each year. There are two factors which are probably behind such a turnover of stock. First, the pursuit of Apaches was not only killing horses and mules but crippling them as well. Those animals that survived such service, but were judged no longer fit for active duty, could be sold on to other sources. Second, some of the animals bought by the US army were found, on delivery, to be unsuitable for field service and had to be sold.[74]

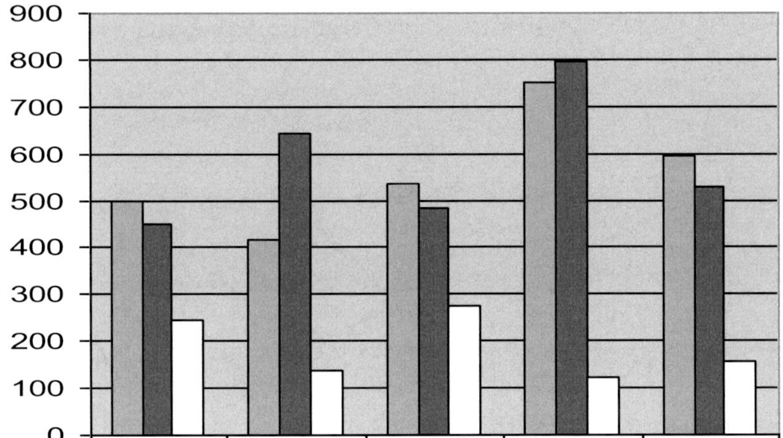

	1876/77	1877/78	1878/79	1879/80	1880/81
Sold	500	416	535	751	594
Died	449	644	482	797	529
Lost/Stolen	247	137	276	121	158

Figure 12.3 Total US Army Mules Sold, Died, Lost or Stolen, 1876–81.[75]

Where cost is concerned, there are some indications that the Apaches had some effect on the Army budget. The cost of horse purchases showed an overall downward trend between 1876 and 1881. However, the cost of horse purchases rose in 1879–80, and, while decreasing again in 1880–81, it did not drop below the lower cost recorded in 1878–79. (See Figure 12.4.)

73 Unfortunately, the Ninth Cavalry Returns do not give any figures on mules died, lost and stolen etc.

74 See Hatch to AAG, DoM, 3 Sept., 1879 in Letters Received, DoNM Oct. – Dec. 1879 NA, RG393, M1088, Roll 39.

75 Derived AR-WD, 1877, p.290; 1878, p.348; 1879, p.307; 1880, p.421; 1881, p.324

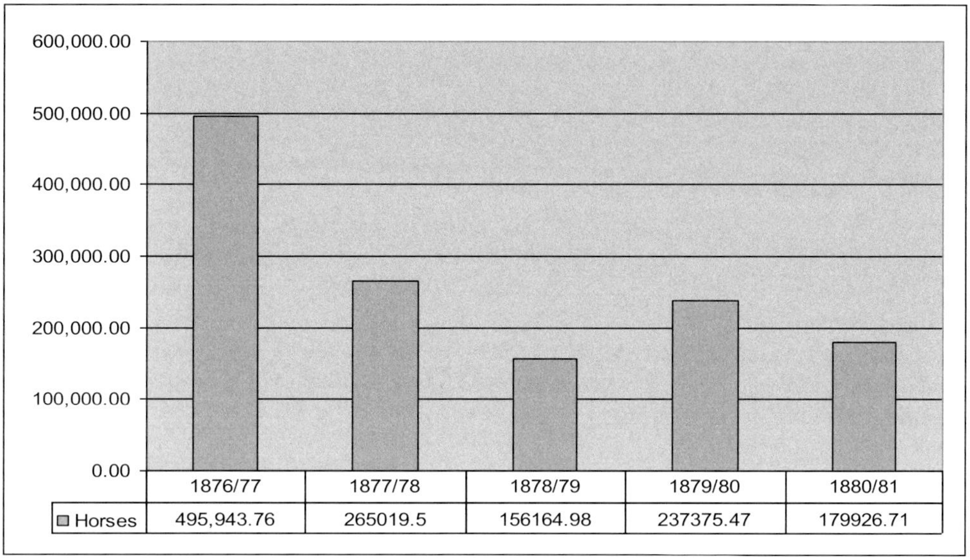

Figure 12.4 Total Cost ($) of US Army Horses (Cavalry and Artillery) Purchased, 1876–81.[76]

These rates also correspond with the numbers of horses being bought between 1876 and 1881. (See Figure 12.5.)

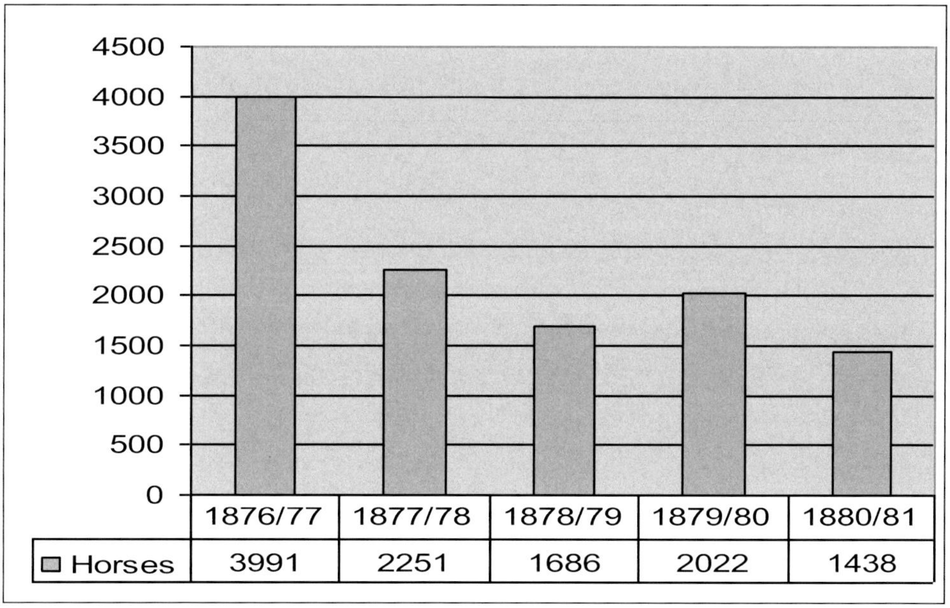

Figure 12.5 Total US Army Horses (Cavalry and Artillery) Purchased, 1876–81.[77]

76 Derived AR-WD, Report of the Quartermaster General 1877 to 1881.
77 Derived AR-WD, Report of the Quartermaster General 1877 to 1881.

While the average cost of horse purchases dropped from $124.26 in 1876–77, ($495, 943.76 (Figure 12.4) divided by 3991 horses (Figure 12.5)), to $92.62 in 1878–9 and then rose back to $125.12 in 1880–81, such fluctuations in price again suggest the Apaches had some effect on the increase in horse prices.

The cost and numbers comparison where mules are concerned shows, remembering that these are overall figures, a major peak in both numbers and cost which coincides with the year 1879–80 and suggests that the Apaches were a significant factor in this trend. (See Figures 12.6 and 12.7.)

As we have seen, the strongest indication that the Apaches had made a significant impact on the US army budget came in late May 1880, when General Sherman himself was forced to inform Hatch that there would be no money available to buy additional horses and mules until Congress approved the Army's appropriation in July.[78] (See Chapter 8.) The problem for the Ninth Cavalry was that the budget could not be stretched to purchase the numbers of horses and mules required to maintain continual pressure on the Apaches in the field.

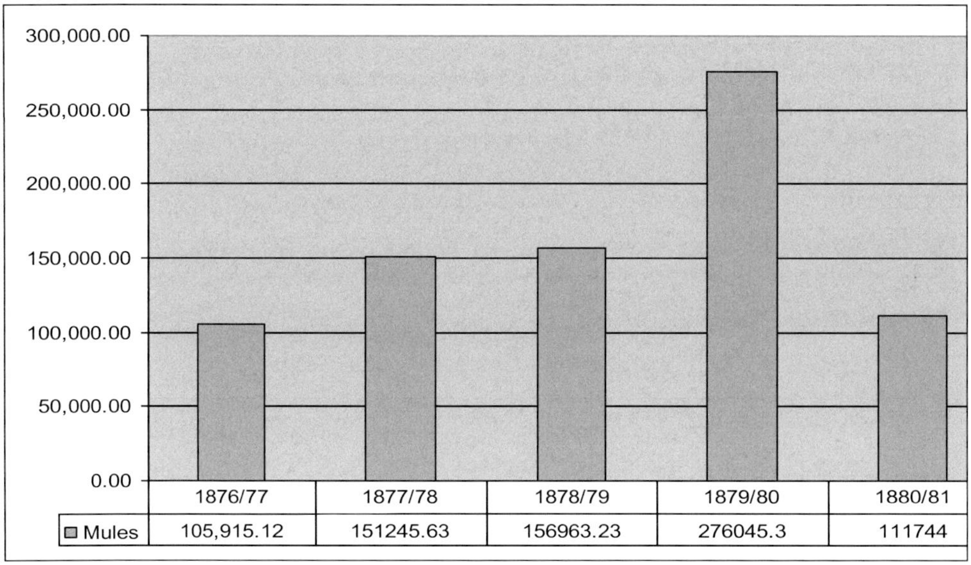

Figure 12.6 Total Cost ($) of US Army Mules Purchased, 1876–81.[79]

78 Sherman to Pope, 29 May, 1880, NA, RG393, Part 1, Entry 2539, Press Copies of Letters and Endorsements Sent, MDoM, Vol. 13, pp.290-291; Loud quoting Sherman's letter to Hatch, Fort Craig, 31 May, 1880, Telegrams Sent DoNM, Vol.3, Jan. – Nov. 1880 NA, RG393, Part 3, Entry 431, pp.452-453; Sherman to Sheridan, 28 May, 1880, 'Victorio Files', NA, RG393, M1495, Roll 14.

79 Derived AR-WD, Report of the Quartermaster General 1877 to 1881.

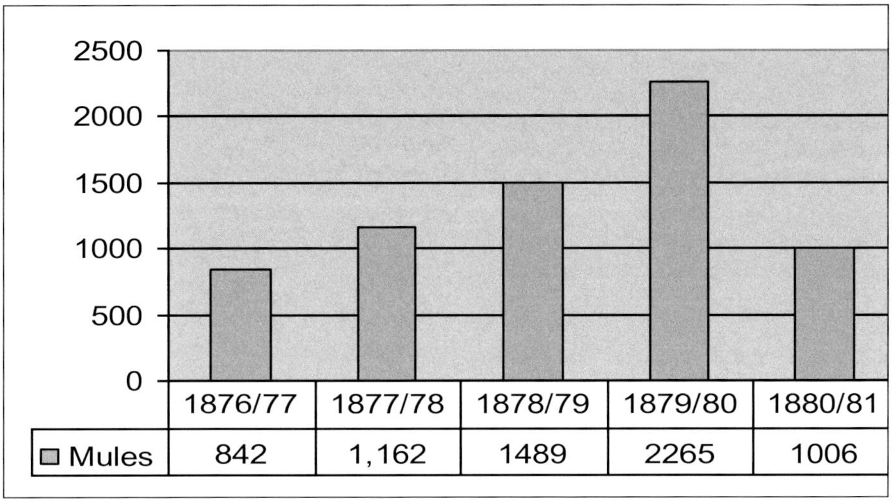

Figure 12.7 Total US Army Mules Purchased, 1876–81.[80]

The question is: did the Secretary of War take steps to inform Congress, through the President, that more money was required? The Annual Report of the Secretary of War for 1880 recommended that the army be raised from 24,000 to 25,000 enlisted men, to increase the efficiency of an overworked force.[81] However, this increase was more in reaction to a perceived overall lessening of the need to garrison the frontier, giving the US army the opportunity to turn its attention to becoming a 'European' army. It was not inspired by the need to combat Apaches, but by an ambition to 'tend to the more thorough drill and discipline of our small Army, by bringing together full regiments and fostering a proper *esprit de corps*'.[82] It would appear, from General Sherman's recommendation that Hatch seek extra horses and mules from other military districts and departments, that the Apache 'problem' was not seen as significant enough to warrant a change in the army's budget.[83] Thus, while the Apaches were clearly having an effect on the New Mexico troops, they were not causing enough problems for the US army as a whole. That the Apaches had caused so much chaos in New Mexico with approximately 150 warriors was a considerable achievement; there just were not enough of them to bring the fight for a reservation at Ojo Caliente to the attention of Congress.

On 26 June 1880, Hatch ordered a comprehensive garrisoning of south-western New Mexico. This encompassed the San Francisco Valley, to the west of the Mogollon Mountains, to the Sacramento Mountains in the east, using dismounted[84] elements of the Ninth Cavalry.[85] (See Table 12.5.)

Colonel Buell, commander of the Fifteenth Infantry Regiment, with B, D, K and I Companies of that regiment, were ordered from Fort Wingate to take post at Fort Cummings. Five companies

80 Derived AR-WD, Report of the Quartermaster General 1877 to 1881.
81 The AR-WD 1880, p.v.
82 The AR-WD 1880, p.vi.
83 See note 26 above.
84 Hatch had ordered Morrow to furnish him a list of all the serviceable horses in each company under his command. (Loud to Morrow, Fort Bayard, 26 Jun., 1880, Telegrams Sent DoNM, Vol.3, Jan. – Nov. 1880 NA, RG393, Part 3, Entry 431, p.553 & p.554).
85 NA, RG393, Part 3, Entry 450, Special Order 70, 26 Jun., 1880.

Colonel George Pearson Buell. Commander of the Fifteenth Infantry Regiment was brought in by General Pope to replace Colonel Hatch as field commander of the troops in the District of New Mexico. Hatch retained overall command of the District of New Mexico. Buell had a reputation with his superiors for picking unnecessary disputes and attempting to court-martial subordinate officers. One cannot help suspecting that Hatch was left in overall charge by Pope to minimise this aspect of Buell's behaviour. While a disruptive officer, Buell was also proved to be quite inept at internal US army politics. This leaves the suspicion that Buell, who without the benefit of any experience of the previous year's campaigning against Victorio, was placed in charge of direct operations against the Apaches in order that he be thoroughly censured if he failed. Nevertheless, as we shall see, Buell was not an incompetent field commander and even innovated in developing equipment designed for use in the field against the Apaches. (Carlisle Barracks)

from the Thirteenth US Infantry replaced these troops.[86] F Company, Fifteenth Infantry, was ordered from Fort Union, leaving a small detachment at that post, to join their commander at Fort Cummings.[87] The men with serviceable horses from B, C, D, F, K and L Companies, Ninth Cavalry, were ordered to report for duty under Colonel Buell at Fort Cummings, as was Lieutenant Maney's company of Indian scouts.[88] The battalion of the Fourth US Cavalry (A, H and L Companies) under Major H.E. Noyes, already at Fort Cummings, were also ordered to place themselves under Colonel Buell's direction when the latter arrived.[89] In the meantime, they were to scout south to the Florida Mountains and east to the Rio Grande.[90] By 4 July, Hatch was able to report that five companies of cavalry were at Fort Cummings and actively scouting the area.[91]

86 Loud to Buell, 25 Jun., 1880 in Letters Sent by '9MD/DNM/DoNM', NA, RG393, M1072, Roll 6, Jan. 1880-Aug. 1881, Letter No.307 pp.197-198; NA, RG393, Part 3, Entry 450, Special Order 70, par 2 & 3, 26 Jun., 1880; Special Order 73, par 2, 30 Jun., 1880; See also Fort Wingate Jul. 1880, Returns from U.S. Military Posts 1800-1916, NA, M617, Roll 1449.

87 NA, RG393, Part 3, Entry 450, Special Order 70, par 15, 26 Jun., 1880.

88 NA, RG393, Part 3, Entry 450, Special Order 70, par 5, 7, 9, 11, 13 & 32, 26 Jun., 1880. The arduous nature of commanding Apache scouts can perhaps be appreciated in comments made by Hatch in removing Maney from this command on the grounds of ill health. 'It is with pleasure the District Commander acknowledges the able and gallant manner in which Lieutenant Maney performed the arduous duties devolved upon him while in command of Indian Scouts.' (General Orders No.6, 29 Jun., 1880, Printed Special Orders 1869-1888, DoNM, NA, RG393, Part 3, Entry 446).

89 NA, RG393, Part 3, Entry 450, Special Order 71, par 2, Jun. 28 1880; See also Loud to Noyes, Fort Cummings, 28 Jun., 1880, Telegrams Sent DoNM, Vol.3, Jan. – Nov. 1880 NA, RG393, Part 3, Entry 431, p.560.

90 Loud to Noyes, Fort Cummings, 29 Jun., 1880, Telegrams Sent DoNM, Vol.3, Jan. – Nov. 1880 NA, RG393, Part 3, Entry 431, p.564.

91 Hatch to Asst. Adjt. Genl, Fort Leavenworth, Ks., 4 Jul., 1880, NA, RG393, Part 1, Entry 2546, pp.528-529 & p.560.

Table 12.5 Deployment of Dismounted Ninth Cavalry Detachments across South-Western New Mexico.[92]

Parent Post	Company	Locations	Number in Detachment
Fort Bayard	Dismounted men of B, C, H and M Companies, Ninth Cavalry	Parson William's Ranch	1 NCO, 9 Privates
		San Francisco/Mouth of Mineral Creek	1 NCO, 9 Privates
		Upper Plaza, San Francisco River	1 NCO, 9 Privates
		Hillsboro	1 Lt., 20 Privates
		Las Palomas	1 NCO, 9 Privates
		McEvers' Ranch	1 NCO, 9 Privates
		Cuchilla Negra	1 NCO, 9 Privates
Orders	To be rationed for 30 days, then receive rations from Fort Bayard. (Paragraph 4)		
Ojo Caliente	Dismounted men of K Company, Ninth Cavalry	Canada Alamosa	1 NCO, 9 Privates
Fort Craig		San Jose	1 NCO, 5 Privates
Orders	To be rationed for 30 days, then former to receive rations from Ojo Caliente, latter from Fort Craig. (Paragraph 6)		
Fort Bayard	Dismounted men of D Company, Ninth Cavalry	Slocum's Ranch	1 NCO, 9 Privates
		Santa Barbara	1 NCO, 9 Privates
Orders	To be rationed for 30 days, then receive rations from Fort Bayard. (Paragraph 8)		
Fort Bayard	Dismounted men of L Company, Ninth Cavalry	Lloyd's Ranch	1 NCO, 9 Privates
Orders	To be rationed for 30 days, then detachment at Lloyd's Ranch to receive rations from Fort Bayard. (Paragraph 10)		
Fort Bayard	Dismounted men of E Company, Ninth Cavalry	Old Fort Tularosa	1 NCO, 9 Privates
Ojo Caliente		Pattersons	1 NCO, 9 Privates
		Luera	1 NCO, 9 Privates
Orders	To be rationed for 30 days, then receive rations from Ojo Caliente. (Paragraph 23)		
Fort Craig	Dismounted men of F Company Ninth Cavalry	Point of Rocks	1 NCO, 9 Privates
Fort Bliss		San Augustine	1 NCO, 9 Privates
Orders	To be rationed for 30 days, then former receive rations from Fort Craig, latter from Fort Bliss. (Paragraph 12)		
Fort Craig	Dismounted men of I Company, Ninth Cavalry	Round Mountain (Toussaint)	1 NCO, 9 Privates
		Aleman (Martin's) Wells	1 NCO, 9 Privates
Orders	To be rationed for 30 days, then receive rations from Fort Craig (Paragraph 25)		
Fort Stanton	Dismounted men of A and G Companies, Ninth Cavalry	San Nicholas	1 NCO, 5 Privates
		Riconada	1 NCO, 10 Privates
		Dowling's Mills	1 NCO, 10 Privates
Orders	To be rationed for 30 days, then receive rations from Fort Stanton. (Paragraph 27)		

92 Special Order 70 26 Jun., 1880, NA, RG393, Part 3, Entry 450; Station of Troops by Companies – Station of Detachments of the Ninth Cavalry in the Field, NA, RG393, Part 1, Entry 183; See also Loud to CO, Company I, 9th Cav., Aleman, 29 Jun., 1880, Telegrams Sent DoNM, Vol.3, Jan. – Nov. 1880 NA, RG393, Part 3, Entry 431, p.564

Captain Hooker was ordered to hand over the Hotchkiss gun assigned to his disbanded third battalion to Colonel Noyes.[93] He was also ordered to hand over all his pack mules and equipment to Morrow, to equip the scout company at Fort Bayard with a full pack train.[94] Major Morrow was carefully instructed that this particular company was not to be enlisted as Indian scouts, but to be taken on as 'trailers and scouts'.[95] Finally, Lieutenant Colonel Nathan Augustus Monroe Dudley, Ninth Cavalry, was ordered to join and serve under Colonel Buell at Fort Cummings.[96]

Elsewhere, the mounted troopers of H and M Companies, Ninth Cavalry, a company of Indian scouts commanded by Lieutenant Goodwin, and D Company, Sixteenth Infantry, were to march from Fort Bayard and take up a position at Knight's Ranch under the command of Major Morrow.[97] The mounted troopers from E and I Companies, Ninth Cavalry, were ordered to take up a posting at Fort Wingate. Fort Craig was occupied by H Company, Sixteenth Infantry, leaving behind a small detachment at Fort Marcy. From their new station they were directed to provide adequate escorts for surveyors from the Atchison, Topeka and Santa Fé Railroad.[98] All surplus horses belonging to the headquarters of the Ninth Cavalry were to be handed over to 'First Lieutenant *G. Valois* R.Q.M. Ninth Cavalry, A.A.Q.M. in the field, Fort Craig, New Mexico to be held by him for further orders'.[99] Finally, the mounted element of A and G Companies, Ninth Cavalry, with G Company, Fifteenth Infantry, were ordered to 'remain in camp at the Mescalero Indian Agency until further orders'.[100] These men were tasked with guarding approximately 300 Mescaleros to prevent their aiding Victorio or other groups of independent Apaches.[101] Another reason given for the continued confinement of the Mescalero Apaches, in the summer of 1880, was the employment of Apache and Pueblo scouts, who at any time could pursue Apaches onto the reservation. If friendly Indians left this confinement, they might be mistakenly killed by such scouts.[102]

The Apache raids on the San Lorenzo and Santa Clara ranches in Chihuahua for horses (see Chapter 9) put troops along the border on the alert. It was assumed that now Victorio had fresh mounts, he would soon return to New Mexico.[103] Lieutenant Maney's company of Apache scouts

93 NA, RG393, Part 3, Entry 450, Special Order 74, par 5, Jul. 2 1880. Major Noyes was ordered to send a detail with two mules to Ojo Caliente to move the Hotchkiss Gun to Fort Cummings. This type of gun must therefore have been small enough for the gun and its ammunition to be packed on two mules.

94 Loud to Morrow, Fort Bayard, 26 Jun., 1880, Telegrams Sent DoNM, Vol.3, Jan. – Nov. 1880 NA, RG393, Part 3, Entry 431, p.555.

95 Loud to Morrow, Fort Bayard, 28 Jun., 1880, Telegrams Sent DoNM, Vol.3, Jan. – Nov. 1880 NA, RG393, Part 3, Entry 431, pp.558-559.

96 NA, RG393, Part 3, Entry 450, Special Order 71, par 2 & 3, 28 Jun., 1880.

97 NA, RG393, Part 3, Entry 450, Special Order 70, par 4, 26 Jun., 1880; See Station of Troops by Companies – Troops operating in the Field in Southern New Mexico – Knight's Ranch, Aug. 1880, NA, RG393, Part 1, Entry 183; 'Town and County', the *Grant County Herald*, 26 Jun., 1880

98 Hatch to AAG Fort Leavenworth, 3 Jul., 1880, Telegrams Sent DoNM, Vol.3, Jan. – Nov. 1880 NA, RG393, Part 3, Entry 431, p.583; NA, RG393, Part 3, Entry 450, Special Order 70, par 16 & 21, 26 Jun., 1880.

99 Special Field Orders, No.40 para.3, (Fort Craig) 30 Jun., 1880, NA, RG393, Part 3, Entry 450.

100 NA, RG393, Part 3, Entry 450, Special Order 70, par 28, 26 Jun., 1880; Hatch to AAG Fort Leavenworth, 3 Jul., 1880, Telegrams Sent DoNM, Vol.3, Jan. – Nov. 1880 NA, RG393, Part 3, Entry 431, p.583.

101 Letter dated South Fork, Jul. 3 1880, in The Walter Lowry Finley Collection.

102 Loud to CO Fort Stanton, 28 Jun., 1880 in Letters Sent by '9MD/DNM/DoNM', NA, RG393, M1072, Roll 6, Jan. 1880-Aug. 1881, Letter No.317, pp.210-211.

103 Hatch to Morrow, Fort Bayard, and Major Noyes, Fort Cummings, 30 Jun., 1880, Telegrams Sent DoNM, Vol.3, Jan. – Nov. 1880 NA, RG393, Part 3, Entry 431, pp.571-572; Hatch to Coppinger, 2 Jul., 1880, Telegrams Sent DoNM, Vol.3, Jan. – Nov. 1880 NA, RG393, Part 3, Entry 431, p.582.

were ordered to search the area to the south of Fort Cummings.[104] By 6 July, there was a small picket of US troops stationed in the Florida Mountains, with Apache scouts deployed further south.[105] A week later, Lieutenant Goodwin's scouts were also in the vicinity; but neither company of scouts found any signs of Apaches.[106] Luckily for the troops in New Mexico, Victorio was then moving towards western Texas to challenge Grierson's command. For the moment, the reorganization of the US troops in New Mexico continued with an alert, and anxious, eye to the situation in western Texas.[107]

By early July, Hatch had turned his attention from the purchase and deployment of pack mules, wagons and horse trappings to Fort Cummings and Knight's Ranch.[108] By mid-July, as the campaign in western Texas was beginning, he had stationed seven companies of cavalry and one Indian scout company at Fort Cummings and two companies of cavalry and an Indian scout company at Knight's Ranch. Five companies of infantry were making their way towards Fort Cummings, and a further company of infantry was en route to Knights Ranch. Hatch also requested that Knight's Ranch be connected to the telegraph line to aid the prosecution of military operations.[109] Finally, Colonel Buell notified Hatch that he was en route to Fort Cummings and expected to arrive at that point on 22 July, 1880.[110] A large shipment of ammunition[111] was ordered on 24 July, for delivery to Buell at Fort Cummings,[112] though Hatch noted that the hire of non-army transportation was proving to be a very unreliable method of transporting supplies.[113]

On travelling through southern New Mexico, making his way to Fort Cummings, Buell was clearly shocked at the disposition of small, and seemingly useless, detachments of both infantry and cavalry scattered across the region. While he was quite correct to suggest this was a poor state of military affairs in theory, he clearly had had no understanding of the previous year's campaigning against the Apaches. On his earlier-than-expected arrival at Fort Cummings, he sent a tactless letter to General Pope, dated 19 July 1880, which bypassed Hatch, and was not a good start. If

104 Loud to Morrow, Fort Bayard, 3 Jul., 1880, Telegrams Sent DoNM, Vol.3, Jan. – Nov. 1880 NA, RG393, Part 3, Entry 431, p586-587.

105 Hatch to AAG Fort Leavenworth, 6 Jul., 1880, Telegrams Sent DoNM, Vol.3, Jan. – Nov. 1880 NA, RG393, Part 3, Entry 431, p.594; Hatch to Carr, 11 Jul., 1880, Telegrams Sent DoNM, Vol.3, Jan. – Nov. 1880 NA, RG393, Part 3, Entry 431, p.601.

106 Hatch to AAG Fort Leavenworth, 14 Jul., 1880, Telegrams Sent DoNM, Vol.3, Jan. – Nov. 1880 NA, RG393, Part 3, Entry 431, p.609 see also p.611.

107 See Loud to Morrow, 14 Jul., 1880, Telegrams Sent DoNM, Vol.3, Jan. – Nov. 1880 NA, RG393, Part 3, Entry 431, pp.611-612.

108 See Hatch, 3 & 6 Jul., 1880, Telegrams Sent DoNM, Vol.3, Jan. – Nov. 1880 NA, RG393, Part 3, Entry 431, pp.584-585 & 591-593.

109 Loud to Lt. Allen, Officer in Charge of the Military Telegraph Line, New Mexico Division, SF, 30 Jul., 1880 in Letters Sent by '9MD/DNM/DoNM', NA, RG393, M1072, Roll 6, Jan. 1880-Aug. 1881, Letter No.387.

110 249 Hatch to AAG Fort Leavenworth, 14 Jul., 1880, Telegrams Sent DoNM, Vol.3, Jan. – Nov. 1880 NA, RG393, Part 3, Entry 431, p.612; Hatch to AAG Fort Leavenworth 22 Jul., 1880, Telegrams Sent DoNM, Vol.3, Jan. – Nov. 1880 NA, RG393, Part 3, Entry 431, p.640.

111 76,000 rounds of Carbine and 5,000 rounds of Rifle ammunition. 400 Rounds & 575 Primers for the Hotchkiss Mountain Gun. (Hatch to Fort Union Arsenal, 24 Jul., 1880, Telegrams Sent DoNM, Vol.3, Jan. – Nov. 1880 NA, RG393, Part 3, Entry 431, pp.648-649) Subsequently, Hatch increased the requisition for Rifle ammunition from 5,000 to 25,000. (Hatch to Fort Union Arsenal, 29 Jul., 1880, Telegrams Sent DoNM, Vol.3, Jan. – Nov. 1880 NA, RG393, Part 3, Entry 431, p.662).

112 Hatch to Fort Union Arsenal, 24 Jul., 1880, Telegrams Sent DoNM, Vol.3, Jan. – Nov. 1880 NA, RG393, Part 3, Entry 431, pp.648-649.

113 Hatch to AAG Fort Leavenworth, 28 Jul., 1880, Telegrams Sent DoNM, Vol.3, Jan. – Nov. 1880 NA, RG393, Part 3, Entry 431, pp.660-661; See also Hatch to Grierson, Eagle Springs, and to Col. Buell, Fort Cummings, 1 Aug., 1880, Telegrams Sent DoNM, Vol.3, Jan. – Nov. 1880 NA, RG393, Part 3, Entry 431, pp.685-686.

nothing else, the date meant that Buell had not bothered to contact the District Commander about his concerns, but had decided to report directly to General Pope: a clear breach of the military courtesy (at the very least) due to one's immediate superior.[114] To compound such political stupidity, Buell appears to have made no effort to investigate the practicalities and, more importantly, the impracticalities, of the prosecution of a war against Apache guerrillas. Conventional organisation and appearances were not going to win an Apache War.

In response to this issue, General Pope wrote very detailed instructions to Buell as to how he expected the latter to prosecute the anticipated campaign against Victorio. Pope concluded this letter as follows:

> I rely upon your energy and activity which are well known, and the only apprehension I have arrives from what is equally well known, viz: your strong propensity for controversy.
>
> You see I write you with entire frankness. I am greatly interested in your success, both on your own personal account, and on account of the public interests and I wish you to understand exactly what I think to be your weak point, which should watch with particular solicitude.[115]

Where Colonel Buell was on firmer ground was in his condemnation of the state of the telegraph service in southern New Mexico. Between his arrival in mid-July and 27 July, the line was down twice, including a break for four days. The Colonel reported a general lack of energy among operators, and was flabbergasted to find that the lines were not manned in shifts for twenty-four hours a day. He was also cut off in the middle of the transmission of an important telegram by an operator.[116] It may not have been practicable to routinely man the telegraph stations around the clock. Nevertheless, it would have made sense to so operate them during field operations against the Apaches. The immediate forwarding of scout reports and communications between headquarters was essential when campaigning against such mobile guerrillas.

By August 1880, Colonel Buell had a formidable force concentrated at Fort Cummings. Lieutenant Colonel N.A.M. Dudley was in charge of the mounted elements of six companies: B, C, D, F, K and L, Ninth Cavalry. Major H.E. Noyes commanded A, H and L Companies, Fourth Cavalry. Also present were B, D, F, I and K Companies, Fifteenth Infantry, and two assistant surgeons, J.J. Kane and W.R. Hall and two acting assistant surgeons, W.N. Handy and S.C. Benedict.[117] In mid-August, the Secretary of War authorised Buell to buy 40 pack mules.[118] However, Buell expressed concern that replacement horses for the dismounted men stationed at various points in southern

114 Buell to AAAG, DoNM, 19 Jul., 1880 in Letters Received, DoM 1868-98, RG 393, Entry A1-1 2601, Box 92. While the letter was addressed to the AAAG, District of New Mexico, its opening sentence instructed its recipient, Captain Loud, to forward the letter to both Col. Hatch and General Pope. If Loud failed to transmit this communication on to Pope he would be disobeying the orders of a superior officer and one who already had a reputation for resorting to court martialling junior officers, often on the flimsiest grounds. Loud had been cleared of an earlier charge brought against him by Buell and would have been very wary of provoking him. If Buell had genuine concerns he should have first voiced them to Hatch, and if not receiving satisfaction, have approached Pope.

115 Pope to Buell, 30 Aug., 1880 in Letters Received, DoM 1868-98, RG 393, Entry A1-1 2601, Box 93.

116 Buell to AAG, DoM, 27 Jul., 1880 & Buell to AAAG, DoNM, 4 Aug., 1880 in Letters Received, DoM 1868-98, RG 393, Entry A1-1 2601, Box 92.

117 Station of Troops by Companies – Troops operating in the Field in Southern New Mexico – Fort Cummings, Aug. 1880, NA, RG393, Part 1, Entry 183; See also Hatch to Valois, 28 Jul., 1880, Telegrams Sent DoNM, Vol.3, Jan. – Nov. 1880 NA, RG393, Part 3, Entry 431, p.657.

118 Meigs, Quartermaster General to Comdg Gen'l, Div. Mo., 12 Aug., 1880, NA, RG393, Part 1, Entry 2546, pp.577-578 & p.579. Forty pack mules passed through Silver City on the 28 Aug., 1880 on their way to Fort Cummings. ('Town and County', the *Grant County Herald*, 28 Aug., 1880).

New Mexico had not arrived.[119] Hatch, who had already been lobbying the Department of the Missouri for more horses,[120] informed Buell that the replacement horses would be provided 'as soon as they can be purchased in open market'.[121] He also told Buell that General Pope had ordered the dismounted men to be stationed at scattered points throughout south-western New Mexico and, for the moment, there was no urgent need to remount these detachments. General Pope recognised the political value of deploying these small detachments to provide some reassurance to the citizens of the Territory. Hatch pointedly reminded Buell that these detachments were not under Buell's command, and until further notice, they were to remain at their allocated stations.[122]

However, on 27 August 1880, the dismounted detachments of Ninth Cavalry at Las Palomas and Cuchillo Negro were ordered to join the detachment based at Hillsboro. Any men whose mounts had recovered were then ordered to join their mounted comrades at either Fort Cummings or Knight's Ranch. The dismounted detachments stationed on the San Francisco River were also instructed to send any men whose mounts had recovered to their proper companies at either Knight's Ranch or Fort Cummings.[123]

On 30 August 1880, a flurry of orders was issued directing various mule trains and supply wagons to report to either Knight's Ranch or Fort Cummings.[124] Those assigned to Fort Cummings would join the 251 mules, 28 wagons and associated equipment in various stages of repair already held at that post.[125] This equipment included a large water wagon.[126] In comparison to the resources available for Morrow's earlier pursuits of Victorio, an unprecedented amount of logistical capability was being concentrated at Old Fort Cummings and Knight's Ranch. An extension to the overall size of the military reservation at Fort Cummings was authorised on 4 September 1880, to accommodate the large number of troops stationed there.[127]

However, problems remained. Buell reported that:

> no horse equipments available. Col. Dudley now trying to borrow some from Fourth cav'y to equip his command so soon as Lt. Dimmick arrives with [replacement] horses the cav'y from here will be mounted and put in condition to take the field & act under my orders. I understand company K has much property at Ojo Caliente including horse equipments which should be sent in transportation all needed here.[128]

119 Hatch to AAG Fort Leavenworth, 3 Aug., 1880, Telegrams Sent DoNM, Vol.3, Jan. – Nov. 1880 NA, RG393, Part 3, Entry 431, p.692.
120 Hatch to AAG, DoM, 23 Jul., 1880 in Letters Sent by '9MD/DNM/DoNM', NA, RG393, M1072, Roll 6, Jan. 1880-Aug. 1881, Letter No.375, p.213; same letter in Letters Received, DoM 1868-98, RG 393, Entry A1-1 2601, Box 92.
121 Hatch to Buell. 4 Aug., 1880, Telegrams Sent DoNM, Vol.3, Jan. – Nov. 1880 NA, RG393, Part 3, Entry 431, pp.698-699.
122 Hatch to Buell, 4 Aug., 1880, Telegrams Sent DoNM, Vol.3, Jan. – Nov. 1880 NA, RG393, Part 3, Entry 431, pp.698-699.
123 NA, RG393, Part 3, Entry 450, Special Order 98, par 1 & 2, 27 Aug., 1880; See also Humphreys to AAAG 4 Sept., 1880, NA, RG393, Part 3, Entry 439, pp.800-801.
124 See in particular Various Telegrams Sent DoNM, Vol.3, Jan. – Nov. 1880 NA, RG393, Part 3, Entry 431, pp.772-774, pp.778-782 & p.785.
125 Buell to AAAG SF 28 Aug., 1880, NA, RG393, Part 3, Entry 439, pp.399-403.
126 NA, RG393, Part 3, Entry 450, Special Order 99, par 10, 30 Aug., 1880.
127 AG to Lieut General P.H. Sheridan, 4 Sept., 1880, NA, RG393, Part 1, Entry 2546, pp.593-594.
128 Buell to AAAG 20 ???? 1880, NA, RG393, Part 3, Entry 439, pp.106-107.

It should be noted that the Chief Quartermaster, District of New Mexico, had been instructed, on 20 July 1880, to 'take immediate steps' to ensure that Colonel Buell's command was properly supplied.[129] He ordered the dispatch of the items listed in Table 12.6 by the end of July.

Table 12.6 Supplies sent to Colonel Buell's Command.[130]

Carpenter's Equipment		Blacksmith's Tools		Wheelwright's Tools	
From Fort Union Depot:					
Three Months' Supply of Horse Medicine and Instruments					
100	Pack Saddle Blankets	150	Woollen Blankets	450	Rubber Blankets
40	Campaign Hats	20	Mess Pans	900	Rubber Ponchos
200	Common Tents	300	Shelter Tents	500 lbs each	Horse and Mule Shoes
From Headquarters, District of New Mexico, Santa Fé					
900	Forage Caps	600	Cavalry Blouses	600	Cavalry Trousers
400	Campaign Hats	300	Infantry Blouses	900	Drawers
900	Boots	1,800	Stockings		

By the beginning of September, this situation was steadily improving. On 2 September, Special Order 101, noting the arrival of replacement horses, ordered the detachments stationed at Canada Alamosa, San Jose, San Nicholas, Rinconada, Dowling's Mills, Slocum's Ranch, Santa Barbara and Lloyd's Ranch to report to Fort Cummings.[131] These redeployments imply that the US army had concluded that the Apaches were, in the main, based in Mexico. This negated the need for widespread detachments across south-western New Mexico, and allowed the concentration of all available cavalry near the Mexican border.

On 20 September, E Company, Ninth Cavalry, and two companies of the Thirteenth Infantry were redeployed from Fort Wingate to Fort Craig,[132] with E Company detachments based along or near the San Francisco Valley being ordered to march to Fort Craig by way of Ojo Caliente.[133] The Ninth Cavalry detachments based at Aleman and Round Mountain were also redeployed to Fort Craig.[134] These deployments were designed to provide some protection to the local economy should Victorio's Apaches evade Buell and attempt to return to their mountain strongholds in the United States.

Hatch also made renewed efforts to recruit additional Apache scouts from San Carlos. While Carr estimated that approximately 220 Apache scouts might be recruited, he reported that there were no reliable civilian 'leaders' available to direct these scouts, though he again voiced his belief that, even with such 'leaders', Apache scouts would not be much use unless backed by US army units.[135] He was also certain that sufficient numbers of rifles were not readily available to arm such a dramatic increase in the numbers of Apache scouts.

129 Loud to Chief Quartermaster, DoNM, 20 Jul., 1880 in Letters Sent by '9MD/DNM/DoNM', NA, RG393, M1072, Roll 6, Jan. 1880-Aug. 1881, Letter No.363, p.236.
130 Chief QM, DoNM, to Post QM, Fort Cummings, 28 Jul., 1880 in Letters Received, DoM 1868-98, RG 393, Entry A1-1 2601, Box 92
131 Special Order 101, NA, RG393, Part 3, Entry 450, paragraphs 2 & 3.
132 NA, RG393, Part 3, Entry 450, Special Order 111, 17 Sept., 1880, paragraphs 1, 2 & 3.
133 NA, RG393, Part 3, Entry 450, Special Order 112, 20 Sept., 1880, paragraph 4.
134 NA, RG393, Part 3, Entry 450, Special Order 114, 23 Sept., 1880, paragraph 6.
135 Carr to Hatch 10 Sept., 1880, NA, RG393, Part 3, Entry 439, pp.396-398; Carr to AG DoAz, 10 Sept., 1880, Troops in SE Arizona, DoAz, NA, RG393, Part 1, Entry 232, Vol.8, 6 Sept., 1880 – 12 Dec., 1880, Letter No.543, pp.7-8.

From San Carlos, Agent Tiffany[136] reported that between 100 and 150 San Carlos Apaches were willing to volunteer to go out after Victorio. Hatch thoroughly approved, and he estimated that the employment of the San Carlos scouts would end the war in six months.[137] He even offered to lead this group himself, if no other officer could be found, arguing that such units even helped to 'civilise' the Apaches by showing them disciplined army service.[138] General Pope agreed with the principle behind this proposal. He thought that the obvious hostility between the San Carlos Apaches and the Chihenne Apaches could be put to good use in hunting Victorio down. However, Pope was also concerned that such Apache volunteers should be accompanied by an experienced officer and detachments of US troops, in order that these warriors 'do not engage in hostilities with anybody except Victorio'.[139] However, Pope decided that he would wait to see if the next stage in the campaign met with any success before making a final decision as to whether these volunteers should be recruited.[140] Hatch's offer to feed and arm the volunteers would involve an expense of which he disapproved.[141]

By mid September, most of the mounted elements of the Ninth Cavalry, and a battalion of the Fourth Cavalry, were stationed near the Mexican border. Every effort had been made to ensure that they could operate with a full complement of wagon and mule transportation. Therefore, it was clear that the US army in New Mexico was gearing up for a major operation against the Apaches. Were such preparations geared towards detecting, and quickly defeating, Victorio's warriors the next time they crossed into New Mexico? Or was something bigger planned? Hatch's original orders to Colonel Buell, dated 26 June 1880, certainly suggest that no incursion into Mexico was planned:

> The Force now concentrating at old Fort Cummings will be under your Command. You are charged with the protection of the Mexican Frontier West of the Rio Grande River. It is probable the Hostiles who are driven into old Mexico will either return in force or in raiding parties to New Mexico. You will keep out Companies of Cavalry scouting the Country and guarding the main line of Travel West from the River.
>
> Should the Indians cross the border and pass your line, they must be followed with energy and persistency.
>
> (You are authorized to draw on Fort Bayard for Supplies so far as that Post can furnish them. It is however probable you must look to [Fort] Craig and the Terminus of the Rail Road for the great bulk of them.)[142]

---

136 Bell, Acting Secretary, Dept. of the Interior to The Secretary of War, 24 Aug., 1880, citing a letter dated 20 Jul., 1880 from Agent Tiffany concerning his meeting with Col. Carr in 'Victorio Files', NA, RG393, M1495, Roll 14; Tiffany to CoIA 13 Sept., 1880 (referring to Tiffany's original offer of the 20 Jul., 1880) in 'Victorio Papers', NA, M666, Roll 528; Tiffany's offer was eventually endorsed by the Acting Commissioner of Indian Affairs. E.M. Marble, Acting Commissioner to The Secretary of the Interior 14 Sept., 1880 in 'Victorio Papers', NA, M666, Roll 528.

137 Hatch to AAG DoM, 11 Sept., 1880 in 'Victorio Papers', NA, M666, Roll 528.

138 Hatch to AAG, DoM, Fort Leavenworth, 11 Sept., 1880 in Letters Sent by '9MD/DNM/DoNM', NA, RG393, M1072, Roll 6, Jan. 1880-Aug. 1881, Letter No.481, pp.310-312; Hatch to AAG DoM, 11 Sept., 1880 in 'Victorio Papers', NA, M666, Roll 528.

139 Pope to Whipple, AAG, Chicago, 29 Sept., 1880, 'Victorio Files', NA, RG393, M1495, Roll 14.

140 Pope to Whipple, AAG, Chicago, 29 Sept., 1880, 'Victorio Files', NA, RG393, M1495, Roll 14; Pope to Whipple AAG Chicago, 29 Sept., 1880 in 'Victorio Papers', NA, M666, Roll 528.

141 Hatch to AAG, DoM, Fort Leavenworth, 15 Sept., 1880 in Letters Sent by '9MD/DNM/DoNM', NA, RG393, M1072, Roll 6, Jan. 1880-Aug. 1881, Letter No.488, pp.315-316.

142 Loud to Buell, 26 Jun., 1880 in Letters Sent by '9MD/DNM/DoNM', NA, RG393, M1072, Roll 6, Jan. 1880-Aug. 1881, Letter No.313, pp.207-208.

The post surgeon for Fort Bayard also noted a number of troop movements from Fort Bayard to Knight's Ranch and Fort Cummings and stated that, 'All these movements of troops were occasioned in the deploying of troops, at different points, for the inauguration of a new campaign against Victorio's Indians, whose return from Mexico into the territory is expected soon to take place.'[143]

On 3 July 1880, General Pope had informed Hatch that, 'It would be a very serious misfortune to military character should Victoria recross the line into New Mexico, without immediate knowledge of the fact & prompt action with sufficient force.'[144] The following instructions concerning Buell's role, issued to Hatch on 14 July, suggested that something more than a secure border was being planned:

> Buell must have all the troops I specified as soon as possible. Give them to him with all information you have or can get about Indians, but leave him to act himself. He is responsible and must have freedom to act as he thinks best.[145]

The clearest statement of intent was delivered by General Pope on 1 July 1880:

> unless I get orders absolutely forbidding it, I shall, if these Indians of Victoria again enter the Territory, have them pursued into Mexico or elsewhere until they are caught. We have now or will have in a few days have a force on hand sufficient for the purpose and it would be foolish if not worse to fail to use it when the opportunity arises.[146]

Once it was realised that Victorio had not been crushed by Colonels Grierson and Valle in their campaigns of July and August, serious negotiations commenced between Colonel Buell and the Chihuahuan authorities to combine their efforts to catch and finish off the Apaches, and that this would involve a substantial force from the United States entering Chihuahua.

The main obstacle left to overcome was the difficult relations between the Republic of Mexico and the United States of America. The key to understanding this complex relationship is to realise that there were two levels of political action in both countries: the local and the federal. Actors at the local level were very aware of the nature of the problem and acted with the tacit approval of certain individuals within the more distant federal political structures. Individuals at the local level on both sides of the border were also more willing and able to cooperate with their opposite numbers. This was not a luxury necessarily open to both sets of superiors at the federal level.

The following chapter will examine these difficulties and argue that the proposed solution to the 'Victorio' problem was constructed through local 'unofficial' relations between local actors on both sides of the border, but in such a way that federal support for these measures could be officially denied.

143 Medical History, Fort Bayard NM May 1880, NA, RG94, Entry 257 Vol. 896, p.29.
144 Pope to Colonel Hatch, 3 Jul., 1880, NA, RG393, Entry 440, p.42.
145 Platt AAG to General Hatch, SF, 14 Jul., 1880, NA, RG393, Part 3, Entry 440, p.27.
146 Pope to Sheridan 1 Jul., 1880, NA, RG393, Part 1, Entry 2546, pp.521-527; See also Pope's Annual Report Year ending 22 Sept., 1880, NA, RG393, Part 1, Entry 2546, p.613.

13

Mexico and the United States Unite: 'Unofficial' and 'Official' Diplomacy Prevail, September–October 1880

The United States and Mexico: Official and Unofficial Relations

The central problem for the United States was trying to persuade the Mexican federal government that the US government had no ulterior motive for sending troops into Mexico. When, during June and July 1880, the US Department of State tried to apply diplomatic pressure by arguing that the Republic of Mexico was granting the Apaches asylum, it provoked an angry response from Mexico. Foreign Minister Miguel Ruelas rejected this rather undiplomatic accusation on the grounds that to grant such permission would be unconstitutional. He also condemned the US Indian reservation system for arming the Apaches, who then used these weapons indiscriminately on both sides of the border. Ruelas pointed out that the recent campaigns by General Trevino, and the current punitive expedition directed by Colonel Valle, clearly contradicted accusations that Mexico had granted asylum to the Apaches. Ruelas finally pointed out that the Mexican government had indicated its willingness to enter into negotiations concerning a reciprocal cross-border agreement between the two counties. That the US government had, so far, refused to countenance the idea of Mexican forces following Apaches into the United States was not the fault of the Republic of Mexico.[1]

We have already commented on the internal politics and lack of resources that the Mexicans faced when trying to confront the Apaches. However, the above situation reflects a long and difficult relationship between the two republics. Within living memory, the United States had thrown the Mexicans off a large portion of their sovereign territory, principally during the Mexican-American War of 1846–48 . Texan independence was a continuing source of annoyance. Though the United States had not officially involved itself, the driving force behind achieving Texan independence from Mexico had been Anglo-American immigrants. However, immediately after the end of the American Civil War, the US government had thrown considerable support behind the Mexican Republican President, Benito Juarez, to help him overthrow Emperor Maximilian.

Where the recent activities of Apaches were concerned, diplomatic relations between the United States and Mexico revolved around whether Mexico should grant passage to US troops *before* the United States recognised Diaz's regime, and whether it should wait till *after* recognition was granted to allow border crossings.[2] As late as 1 June 1877, in what came to be known as the 'Ord order'[3], the US government had unilaterally declared its right to pursue American Indians across

1 See Ruelas to Morgan, 23 Jul., 1880, Morgan to Ruelas, 24 Jul., 1880, 'Victorio Files', NA, RG393, M1495, Roll 14.

2 Dinges, 1987, pp.83-84.

3 So named as it was addressed to General Ord, Commander of the DoTx.

the border into Mexico, whether or not it had been given permission to do so by the Mexican government.[4] (See document file no. 105.)

It should also be noted that strict instructions were issued in this order concerning the conduct of US troops while on Mexican soil:

> The same courtesy and co-operation will be extended to Mexican troops, who may, when in pursuit of such raiders, cross into the United States, as we would be pleased to receive from them, when operating on their side of the river.[5]

It was also clearly stated that such courtesy would not be extended to Mexican 'revolutionists', and any such persons were to be disarmed and interned.[6] Finally, if there was a Mexican force present that was capable of apprehending any raiders being pursued by US forces, then the latter should not continue their pursuit into Mexico.[7]

While this order was attacked in the US Congress, it must also have been a very fresh and painful reminder to the Mexican government of the United States' assumption of supremacy over the western hemisphere under the auspices of the Monroe Doctrine of 1823. This 'doctrine' fostered the later expression of 'Manifest Destiny' as the rationale behind American expansion across the North American continent – an idea that was still very much in vogue in 1880. The problem for the Mexican federal government, in the light of the Monroe Doctrine and Manifest Destiny, was internal revolutionary activity, which centred around who would succeed Benito Juarez. Until Porfirio Diaz finally established his presidency of Mexico, the federal structures of government in the country could not control much of what transpired on the country's borders with the United States. Such border instability might provoke the US government to go further than it had done so far. In the interests of its citizens caught up in the turmoil, and with popular support, fuelled by notions of manifest destiny, it might annexe more of Mexico declaring itself more qualified to govern.

The Vice Consul's reports from El Paso del Norte and Chihuahua City for 1872–74 recount the rise and fall of various political factions within Chihuahua. It is clear from this correspondence that, during this period, most political actors in the State of Chihuahua had to focus all their efforts on their own political survival, which did not make for a coherent, let alone an effective, border security policy.[8] Even when Porfirio Diaz had established his regime, federal control of Mexico's border states was not assured in the face of the relative autonomy of the office of state governor. This office was prone to corruption and state-level revolution, and the federal authorities did not

4 Secretary of War, 1 Jun., 1877, to the General of the Army in Papers relating to the Frelinghuysen-Romero Agreement of 29 Jul., 1882, providing for reciprocal crossings of the international boundary by troops of the United States and Mexico in pursuit of hostile Indians, Feb. 1862-Jun. 1867 (hereafter referred to as 'Frelinghuysen-Romero Papers'); Letters Rec'd by the AGO (Main Series), 1881-1889, NA, M689, Roll 81; Hatfield, 1999, pp.23-24; see also Dinges, 1987, p.84; Wooster, 1988, p.95 & p.186; Sayles, 1976, p.296.

5 General of the Army, 9 Jun., 1877, to the Lieutenant General commanding MDoM; and by latter to Commanding General DoTx in 'Frelinghuysen-Romero Papers'; Letters Rec'd by the AGO (Main Series), 1881-1889, NA, M689, Roll 81.

6 General of the Army, 9 Jun., 1877, to the Lieutenant General commanding MDoM; and by latter to Commanding General DoTx in 'Frelinghuysen-Romero Papers'; Letters Rec'd by the AGO (Main Series), 1881-1889, NA, M689, Roll 81.

7 Secretary of War, 14 Jul., 1877 to the Commanding General DoTx in 'Frelinghuysen-Romero Papers'; Letters Rec'd by the AGO (Main Series), 1881-1889, NA, M689, Roll 81.

8 See Consular Despatches Cuidad Juarez (Paso del Norte), NA, Wash. D.C., M184, Roll 2 & Consular Despatches Chihuahua Mexico 1830-1906, NA, M289, Roll 1.

Porfirio Diaz.
President of the Republic of Mexico during the Victorio campaign. He was faced with the difficult task of negotiating with the nationalist and anti-American members of his government and the US government in negotiating cooperation between American and Mexican forces against the Apaches. He was unsuccessful in negotiating an agreement to allow both Mexican and American troops to cross each other's borders in pursuit of the Apaches in 1880. Nevertheless, Diaz probably turned a blind eye to unofficial cooperation between Mexican state troops and the US army in pursuit of Victorio in what became known as the Buell Expedition of September-October 1880. (National Archives)

have the resources or, on occasion, the inclination, to intervene if the incumbent governor was a supporter of the federal government.

Thus, the Diaz regime had to engage with the United States to convince the latter that the Mexican government could bring stability to the border. At the same time, such action could provoke resistance from regional political actors, even though the latter's sources of power could be quite ephemeral. The danger was that, if the federal government moved too quickly against such relative autonomy, these actors might garner more support and prove able to resist, or even possibly overthrow, central government. Nevertheless, despite the outrage felt at the Ord directive, the federal government of Mexico made a serious effort to calm its turbulent border regions.[9] Diaz had already despatched General Geronimo Trevino to calm the area. After the Ord directive was issued, General Trevino was given orders 'to repel with force the crossing of American troops into Mexican territory'.[10] There were a couple of incursions into Mexico by US troops where Mexican troops were encountered, but no shots were fired, Then, in June 1878, came what was potentially the most dangerous encounter between Mexican troops and a large US force – an encounter near Piedras Negras with US troops led by Colonel R.S. MacKenzie. However, both sides declined to enter into direct hostilities.[11]

Trevino's successes in pacifying the regions south of the border led to recognition of the Diaz regime in April 1878; but they failed to lead to the rescinding of the Ord directive, and led to Mexican nationalists blocking US-backed railroad construction proposals in the Mexican

9 Hatfield, 1999, 1999, pp.26-27.
10 Dinges, 1987, p.84.
11 Tabular Statement of Expeditions and Scouts against Indians & c., made in the DoTx during the Year ending 30 Sept., 1878, NA, RG393, Part 1, Entry 2551, Annual Reports of Departments 1879-1881, MDoM

Congress.[12] That same month, General Willcox informed his superiors that a telegram had been received informing him that the Mexican government had forbidden the troops of either country to cross the international border.[13] His superior, General McDowell noted that, up till that point, scouting parties from the military on both sides of the border could follow the trails of brigands and Indians into the other's territory and concluded that:

> Mexico cannot justly … nor can we … take exception to troops crossing the line in red hot pursuit, and there is no force on the opposite side to disarm the fugitives, who else can carry their depredations with utter impunity.[14]

However, as far as the Department of Arizona was concerned, the instructions from Mexico forbidding cross-border pursuits allowed some leeway in interpreting the term 'hot pursuit' in relation to Apache raiders. 'Orders cannot be given to pursue an enemy through Mexican Territory, but it is believed that in a close and hot pursuit, the command following would hardly have time to stop to examine as to exact boundary lines.'[15] By May 1879, General Trevino stated his aim to launch a campaign against Indians who were entering Mexico from the US. He also sought to coordinate his troops' efforts in conjunction with the US army 'to co-operate, as far as possible, with a view to securing a successful result of the campaign'.[16]

Unfortunately, while efforts were being made to convince the US government that the Mexican federal government was trying to assert control over its side of the border, other incidents suggested that the Diaz regime was making very slow progress. The San Elizario 'Salt War' of 1877–78, to the east of El Paso, caused some concern to the US authorities when it was discovered that Mexican US citizens were being aided by Mexican citizens in their fight to retain their salt rights. It was reported that the Mexican authorities in El Paso del Norte were less than cooperative in apprehending some Mexican murder suspects indicted in the United States, and very tardy in recovering the possessions of those US citizens killed during this dispute.[17]

Reports were received, during July and August 1878, that a large number of Mescalero Apaches were trading horses and mules stolen in the USA for guns and ammunition, in the town of Presidio del Norte. This prompted instructions from Sherman that raiding Indians be, if necessary, pursued into Mexico.[18]

The failure to resolve the general situation of lawlessness along the US-Mexican border prompted General Sherman to contact General Sheridan. The former suggested that martial law could be

---

12 Sayles, 1976, p.297; See also Dinges, 1987, p.84.

13 McDowell 8 Apr., 1878 in 'Frelinghuysen-Romero Papers'; Letters Rec'd by the AGO (Main Series), 1881-1889, NA, M689, Roll 81.

14 McDowell 8 Apr., 1878 in 'Frelinghuysen-Romero Papers'; Letters Rec'd by the AGO (Main Series), 1881-1889, NA, M689, Roll 81.

15 Martin AAG to CO DoAz, 22 Jun., 1879, NA, RG393, Part 1, Entry 169, Vol. 9, p.205.

16 Evarts U.S. Secretary of State (citing Ambassador Zamacona 10 Jun., 1879 and General Trevino10 May, 1879) to McCrary, U.S. Secretary of War, 2 Jul., 1879 in Letters Rec'd File 19 Mar., 1878-14 Feb., 1881, HQ Records DoP 1878-1881, NA, RG393, M1381, Roll 2.

17 See Schutz to the 2nd Assistant Secretary of State, 6 Mar., 1878 & 3 Dec., 1878 in Consular Despatches Cuidad Juarez (Paso del Norte), NARA, Wash.D.C., M184, Roll 2.

Schutz knew from January 1878 from a U.S. Citizen, Thomas Collins that a 'buggy' and horses belonging to two of the slain men, one Judge Howard & John Atkinson were in possession of Mexican citizens from Carrizal but these items were not returned until 12 January, 1879. (Schutz to 2nd Assistant Secretary of State, 12 Jan., 1879 & Schutz to 2nd Assistant Secretary of State, 18 Jul., 1880 in Consular Despatches Cuidad Juarez (Paso del Norte), NARA, Wash.D.C., M184, Roll 2).

18 Vincent, AAG, DoTx to CO, DoP, 27 Aug., 1878 in Letters Rec'd File 19 Mar., 1878-14 Feb., 1881, HQ Records DoP 1878-1881, NA, RG393, M1381, Roll 2.

declared in all the Texas counties bordering Mexico. Furthermore, a Mexican town could be temporarily seized, and a number of animals corresponding to the number stolen in Texas could be confiscated at random, to point out to the Mexican people the benefit of resolving the overall situation. Finally, Sherman suggested that the US break off diplomatic relations with Mexico until the border question was settled.[19] As far as Sheridan was concerned, the declaration of martial law might make sympathetic Mexican US citizens think twice about aiding and abetting Mexican citizens raiding in the United States The other proposals, he felt, would at the very least cause confusion, and might force the Mexican government into a situation of either declaring war on the United States or being deposed by its citizens. The breaking off of diplomatic relations would serve no purpose, and the idea failed to take account of the fact that the federal government of Mexico, while having difficulty in policing its own border, was not actually hostile to the United States.[20]

Having appeared rather sympathetic to the Mexican authorities, and having rejected Sherman's more 'radical', if not inflammatory, suggestions, Sheridan then proposed an even more provocative solution.

> I would suggest as the best way to settle this Rio Grande border trouble, that Congress pass an Act, providing that after a certain date from its passage, should any further raids from Mexico be made upon our soil by Indians or Mexicans, the President of the United States shall be authorized to occupy and hold the country from the Rio Grande to the Sierra Madre Mountains, and that such territory be retained until the Government of the United States is satisfied that its citizens will be no longer in danger of losing their lives and property. This declaration on the part of Congress will accomplish, in my opinion, the purpose desired, without further complications and without war. The fear of the occupation of this section by United States troops will be so great among its inhabitants that I believe it will effectually stop their marauding. If it does not, we can then get into position to stop it effectually ourselves.[21]

General Ord suggested a more conservative measure: the location in the border area of a mobile force with a pontoon train to pursue raiders into Mexico. The Mexican government should also be informed that any *ad hoc* attempt by Mexican citizens or the Mexican army to interfere would be considered as aiding the fugitives and, as such, would face attack by US forces. He also suggested that reprisals be aimed at those persons receiving stolen property. However, his primary recommendation was that those Indians haunting the borderlands be at first approached and offered land in the Indian Territory.[22]

Sherman rejected the idea of annexing the northern section of Mexico. In his opinion, this would not solve the problem and might lead to a situation where all of Mexico would eventually be annexed. This he felt could threaten the national character of the United States[23] 'Instead of our making them Anglo-Saxon, they may make us Mexicans. Therefore I am firm in my conviction that in no event, and under no circumstances should our national boundary move further south.'[24] Sherman then recommended that, as a first step, Mexico should be held accountable for border

19 Sherman to Sheridan 29 Jun., 1878 in 'Frelinghuysen-Romero Papers'; Letters Rec'd by the AGO (Main Series), 1881-1889, NA, M689, Roll 81.
20 Sheridan to Sherman, 2 Jul., 1878 in 'Frelinghuysen-Romero Papers'; Letters Rec'd by the AGO (Main Series), 1881-1889, NA, M689, Roll 81.
21 Ibid.
22 Ord to Sherman, 1 Jul., 1878 in 'Frelinghuysen-Romero Papers'; Letters Rec'd by the AGO (Main Series), 1881-1889, NA, M689, Roll 81.
23 Sherman to McCrary, 6 Jul., 1878 'Frelinghuysen-Romero Papers'; Letters Rec'd by the AGO (Main Series), 1881-1889, NA, M689, Roll 81.
24 Ibid.

security through naval action against its major ports. This could involve their blockade, occupation or destruction. Secondly, the US forces on the border should be strengthened, and all efforts made to catch and destroy raiders. Finally, Sherman proposed that the existing railroads in Texas be extended to the border. 'These would Stimulate Emigration and Trade, and Encourage a Class of men to settle who would defend their own property and lives, leaving the troops to deal with the larger parties.'[25]

This discussion of options does show the differing interpretations of the concept of manifest destiny at play: Sheridan was quite willing to risk a war with Mexico to solve the problem of a lawless border; Sherman, though quite willing to engage in limited hostilities with Mexico, was also aware of cultural 'threats' to the US's development of the North American continent. Whilst such concerns may appear ethnocentric, even ridiculous, in today's terms, these issues were taken very seriously at the time. The most effective measure proposed by Sherman was also cultural: his long-term solution was to thoroughly 'Americanise' the borderlands.

This discussion was academic. The Secretary of War had been informed that a conflict with Mexico, provoked by an act of the US forces, would not be countenanced by the President of the United States. For the moment, President Hayes was content that Ord should continue to act under the instructions issued on 1 June 1877.[26]

Unfortunately, any slight warming of relations between the two countries was interrupted when Victorio raided Chihuahua in January, and again in November, 1879. George W. McCrary, Secretary of War, had noted in his annual report for 1878 a significant reduction in cross-border incursions into Texas.[27] In Arizona, Colonel O.B. Willcox, who had recently taken over from Colonel Kautz, reported that the government of Mexico had forbidden their troops to pursue Apaches into the United States, and vice versa. However, Willcox noted a spirit of cooperation on the part of Mexican troops along the border that he could only ascribe to a change of policy on the part of the federal government of Mexico. Yet Willcox also recommended that, should this situation deteriorate, the order to remain on the US side of the border be suspended, in the short term, and that 'the common enemy be followed in the heat of pursuit across the border'.[28] By 1879, General Ord recommended that the Ord directive should be revoked, though the course of the Victorio war rapidly persuaded him to reverse this opinion.[29]

At first, the US diplomatic and military communities did not view Victorio's declaration of war as a threat to US-Mexican relations.[30] In reaction to Mexican complaints about raiding in Chihuahua in January 1879, the US authorities argued that US Apaches could not be held to account. First, they argued that many of these raids were more likely the work of Indians based in Mexico. Second, they pointed out that the US army regularly patrolled the border with its troops, whereas the Mexican army was nowhere to be seen along the Mexican side of the border.[31] This

25 Sherman to McCrary, 6 Jul., 1878 in 'Frelinghuysen-Romero Papers'; Letters Rec'd by the AGO (Main Series), 1881-1889, NA, M689, Roll 81.

26 McCrary to Sherman, 6 Aug., 1878 & Sherman to Sheridan, 9 Aug., 1878 in 'Frelinghuysen-Romero Papers'; Letters Rec'd by the AGO (Main Series), 1881-1889, NA, M689, Roll 81.

27 Report of the Secretary of War in AR-WD 1880, NA, M997, Roll 30, 1878 Vol. I-II, pp.v-vi.

28 Report of Col. O.B. Willcox in AR-WD 1880, NA, M997, Roll 30, 1878 Vol. I-II, pp. 193-194.

29 Annual Report, DoTx, 1 Oct., 1879, NA, RG393, Part 1, Entry 2551, Annual Reports of Departments 1879-1881, MDoM, p.6; Ramsey to General of the Army, 24 Feb., 1880, in 'Frelinghuysen-Romero Papers'; Letters Rec'd by the AGO (Main Series), 1881-1889, NA, M689, Roll 81; Dinges, 1987, p.86.

30 Sayles, 1976, p.298.

31 See correspondence attached to letter from F.W. Seward, Acting Secretary of State, to George W. McCrary, Secretary of War, 16 Aug., 1879, NA, RG393, Part 1, Entry 2546, pp.272-287; See also Foster to Ruelas, 18 Jul., 1879 & Foster to Evarts 23 Jul., 1879 in Letters Received by HQ DoNM Sept. 1865-Aug. 1890, NA, RG393, M1088, Roll 38 Jul.-Sept. 1879.

assertion was angrily rejected by the Mexican authorities, who argued that the Apache raiders could be shown to have been originally from US Indian reservations. They also pointed out that elements of the US government had recently praised the cooperation of US and Mexican forces along the border.[32] Indeed, it was privately acknowledged on the US side that, if there were incursions into Mexico, these were almost certainly coming from the Mescalero reservation.[33]

While the two countries bickered as to who was responsible for the Apache raids, on 1 October 1879, the US Consul in Mexico City made inquiries on behalf of the US government concerning the potential for the US and Mexican forces to co-ordinate their efforts against Victorio.[34] What is immediately apparent in this series of letters is a lack of any mention of cross-border operations. The United States merely expressed willingness to mount expeditions to pursue and punish Apaches. This received a warm welcome from Ruelas, but the thorny issue of just where these expeditions would operate was not mentioned.[35]

Over and above the understandable reluctance of the Mexican authorities to admit US troops into their territory, the former still harboured grave doubts concerning the direction of the USA's Indian policy. Mexico had never adopted a reservation policy towards Indians, and they viewed the US reservation system as merely providing the Apaches with secure bases from which they could raid Mexico with impunity.[36] Not only could Victorio gain arms and ammunition, he could also sell the plunder taken from raids in Mexico on US Indian reservations.[37] The Mexicans even went so far as to employ a spy on the San Carlos reservation in an attempt to keep track of Apaches and US troops.[38]

The spate of attacks in Mexico in November 1879, which, from a Mexican point of view, could have been interpreted as a result of Major Morrow's forcing Victorio into Mexican territory, prompted the Mexican federal army to take to the field. This must have had a positive effect, as the US Government rescinded the Ord order on 24 February 1880.[39] This decision was clearly influenced by the positive report concerning Mexican efforts to confront Apache raiders sent to the Secretary of State, William Evarts, by John Foster, Minister of the United States to Mexico, on 29 December 1879. (See document file no. 106.) Foster also noted that, in his opinion, this renewed interest in the border by the Diaz regime had been aroused by the United States' tough unilateral stance concerning pursuits across the border. Foster also warned that, while there had been positive

32 M. de Lamacona to William M Evarts, The Secretary of State, 16 Mar., 1880 in 'Victorio Papers', NA, M666, Roll 527; Ruelas to Foster, 19 Jul., 1879 notes Gen. Trevino in the field with two columns and noting the passage of at least two parties of 'barbarous' Indians crossing from the United States into Mexico on the 10 and 18 of Jun., 1879 in Letters Received by HQ DoNM Sept. 1865-Aug. 1890, NA, RG393, M1088, Roll 38 Jul.-Sept. 1879.

33 See collection of reports attached to report submitted by Ord to HQ MDoM, 9 Jul., 1879, NA, RG393, Part 1, Entry 2546, p.170-193; See also Pope to Whipple, 4 Sept., 1879, NA, RG393, Part 1, Entry 2546, pp.198-202; Hatch to the AAG, DoM, 14 Aug., 1879, NA, RG393, Part 1, Entry 2546, pp.202-205.

34 Dinges, 1987, p.84.

35 Wm. M Evarts, Secretary of State to George W. McCrary, Secretary of War, 10 Nov., 1879, NA, RG393, Part 1, Entry 2546, pp.244-249.

36 Hatfield, 1999, 1999, p.9, p.34, pp.41-42 & 56; Sayles, 1976, pp.304-305.

37 Hatfield, 1999, p.35.

38 Ibid, p.9.

39 Ramsey, Secretary of War, to The General of the Army, 24 Feb., 1880, NA, RG393, Part 1, Entry 2546, pp.343-345; Ramsey to General of the Army, 24 Feb., 1880, in 'Frelinghuysen-Romero Papers'; Letters Rec'd by the AGO (Main Series), 1881-1889, NA, M689, Roll 81; Hatfield, 1999, p.37-According to Hatfield it was revoked on the 1 Feb., 1880; Sayles, 1976, p.298, Wooster, 1998, p.95; Dinges, 1987, p.84; Loud to General Hatch, Fort Bayard, 9 Mar., 1880, Telegrams Sent DoNM, Vol.3, Jan. – Nov. 1880, NA, RG393, Part 3, Entry 431, p.205.

efforts on the border, the political situation in Mexico, with a looming presidential election, would not necessarily guarantee a continued state of stability on the question.[40]

When the Apaches retreated to Mexico in late May 1880, the US Consul in Mexico City renewed the US's request for permission to cross the border. As we saw at the beginning of this chapter, some of the efforts to gain such permission were made in a rather undiplomatic way, and permission was twice refused. Nevertheless, there came a point when President Diaz initiated negotiations for reciprocal border crossings in pursuit of Apaches. On the one hand, he was all too aware of the negative effect of allowing US troops into Mexico during an election campaign. On the other hand, a failure to deal with the Apaches could delay Mexico's economic and political development. In fact, military cooperation between the two countries was to lead to further economic and political stability and development on both sides of the border. The Atchison, Topeka and Santa Fé (AT&SF) Railroad, then nearing El Paso, had 'secured charters' from the Republic of Mexico and intended to construct a line from El Paso, via Chihuahua, Durango and Zacatecos, to Leon. Work had already commenced on a railroad from Mexico City to Leon.[41] In 1881 it was noted that the AT&SF intended to construct a railway line between El Paso and Guaymas.[42]

Filibusters and Counter-Revolutionaries

Another concern for the federal Mexican government was a resurgence in the potential for 'filibustering' activity in what could be defined as an independent application of that vague term 'manifest destiny'. In other words, groups of independent political entrepreneurs, often backed by US capital, but not necessarily by the US government, would try to take advantage of the instability of Mexico to carve out 'independent' fiefdoms. It is clear from consular dispatches sent in 1872 from El Paso del Norte (present day Cuidad Juarez), that, seeking to profit from revolutionary activity in Mexico at the time, 'interested parties' in Texas, and allegedly from both Chihuahua and Sonora,[43] were lobbying the US Consul for the creation of a US protectorate over these regions. Some of the more extreme elements were even arguing that the states of Chihuahua and Sonora, if not Mexico itself, should be annexed.[44] These sentiments were endorsed by some officials in the US State Department. The US Vice Consul at El Paso del Norte submitted a report stating that, in effect, Mexico, by 1872, was a 'lost cause' as an independent nation, having failed to thrive since throwing off Spanish rule:

40 John W. Foster to Wm. M. Evarts, 27 Dec., 1879, NA, RG393, Part 1, Entry 2546, pp.336-340.

41 Report of the General of the Army in AR-WD, NA, M997, Roll 35, 1880 Vol. I-II, pp.55-56

42 Report of Major O.M. Poe, Aide-de-Camp, General of the Army in AR-WD, NA, M997, Roll 38, 1881 Vol. I-II, p.2820. Poe had been commissioned by General Sherman to survey the progress of railway construction in Texas and southern New Mexico and this was carried out between 20 Dec., 1880 and 22 Feb., 1881.

43 See letter dated 29 October to the Consul from F. Maemanno? 'one of the most wealthy and popular merchants of the State of Chihuahua' in William M. Pierson U.S.V. Consul to the 2nd Assistant Secretary of State, Washington D.C., 4 Nov., 1872 in Consular Despatches Cuidad Juarez (Paso del Norte), NARA, Wash.D.C., M184, Roll 2.

The motivation for such sentiment appears to be the unstable political situation in Mexico which was the despair of any businessman who required stability to maximise their business opportunities and the 'forced loans' levied by the various political factions 'revolutionary' or otherwise.

44 William M. Pierson U.S.V. Consul to the 2nd Assistant Secretary of State, Washington D.C., 4 Nov., 1872 & Pierson to 2nd Assistant Secretary of State, Washington D.C., 17 Nov., 1872 with attached correspondence in Consular Despatches Cuidad Juarez (Paso del Norte), NARA, Wash.D.C., M184, Roll 2.

> Mexico in her present condition can hardly claim a greater right in the soil than was vested in the Montezummas when discovered by Cortez, namely possession, and occupancy, and such a title has ever been liable to be extinguished under international law by discovery, purchase, or conquest … Mexico is in a state of barbarism bearly[45] above the common average of the Indian tribes of North America and that she is entitled to no greater consideration than other tribes of big Indians bordering on the United States, and in the very nature of things in order to preserve the peace and dignity of the family of nations on the American Continent, must, in time, be protected by, and counted[46] within the limits of the union, and the sooner the rule is applied as laid down in the above cited cases[47] the more speedy will the public interest be served, and the great an popular current of the public mind be gratified.[48]

One major incentive for the United States to intervene in Mexico was the country's rich supply of precious metal and mineral resources, which had been exploited by the Spanish but abandoned by the Mexicans.[49]

Another consideration was that US merchants operating in Mexico were periodically subject to what was, in effect, official banditry. The nominated, but not yet appointed, US Consul in Chihuahua, Louis H. Scott, reported that one Henry Millar, a merchant in Chihuahua City, held to ransom by an armed faction in November 1876. Scott went so far as to enquire whether, if such an incident should occur in the future, for example, through kidnapping or imprisonment on refusal to pay a 'loan' to whatever political faction, he should 'ask the assistance of the Military in Texas or merely advise the [State] Department?'[50] Scott was convinced that such incidents would continue, and wanted assurance from the State Department that, when he was officially empowered to act as consul, he would have 'ample power to protect all the American Citizens in this state from outrage and robbery, to which [they] have become so familiar during the past year, and I desire also to feel assured that my Govt. will sustain me in what I undertake to do'.[51] His attitude did not prevent Mexican troops from violating the consulate, in November 1879, to remove money deposited there by US businessmen, which they took as a forced loan to pay for the revolution which, as we have seen, removed Governor Trias from office.[52]

In May 1877, the local garrison commander at El Paso del Norte, one Colonel Macharro, requiring money to pay his troops, levied it from 14 businessmen operating in that town, 10 of whom were US citizens. The consular agent protested this action, but noted that there was little that could be done as US troops at that time had been withdrawn from Fort Bliss. He further noted that, in effect, the Mexican side of the frontier was being run by political factions with very

45 As spelled in original document.

46 I am reasonably certain that this word is 'counted' but am not 100 per cent certain.

47 Johnson Vs. McIntosh & Fletcher Vs. Peek: In effect Peirson appears to be making an argument that certain unilateral federal actions within the United States, I suspect he is referring to post civil war reconstruction and the Kansas Missouri border wars can be applied outside the United States concerning Mexico.

48 William M. Pierson U.S.V. Consul to the 2nd Assistant Secretary of State, Washington D.C., 7 Nov., 1872; See similar sentiments expressed in Pierson to 2nd Assistant Secretary of State, 13 Jan., 1872 in Consular Despatches Cuidad Juarez (Paso del Norte), NARA, Wash.D.C., M184, Roll 2.

49 Pierson, U.S. Vice Consul to the 2nd Assistant Secretary of State, Washington D.C., 8 Nov., 1872 in Consular Despatches Cuidad Juarez (Paso del Norte), NARA, Wash.D.C., M184, Roll 2.

50 Scott to the Department of State. 23 Jan., 1877 in Consular Despatches Chihuahua Mexico 1830-1906, NA, M289, Roll 1.

51 Scott to the Second Assistant Secretary of State, Washington D.C., 21 Mar., 1877 in Consular Despatches Chihuahua Mexico 1830-1906, NA, M289, Roll 1.

52 Scott to Hunter, 2nd Assistant Secretary of State, Washington D.C., 14 Nov., 1879 in Consular Despatches Chihuahua Mexico 1830-1906, NA, M289, Roll 1.

little respect for anything short of direct military force.[53] In the event, when 'Colonel Macharro' attempted to widen the scope of this forced loan, he and his men were confronted by armed citizens and, after a lively gun battle, were forced to flee to the United States. The victorious citizens then proceeded to round up everybody who was supposed to have supported the previous petit-regime 'with the avowed purpose of shooting them'.[54] The anarchy threatened to continue when the new 'petit-regime' demanded the return of Macharro and threatened to invade the United States if this was refused.[55]

What is clear from the consular dispatches from El Paso del Norte and Chihuahua City is the state of official anarchy existing in Chihuahua, even after the establishment of the Diaz regime in Mexico. At least some Mexican authorities were inclined to blame 'speculators' and 'enemies' based in the United States for the inability of both countries to unite to exterminate the common enemy of both nations.[56] However, the United States discouraged such political entrepreneurship on its side of the border by actively opposing the activities of filibustering or revolutionary bands. In August 1877, troops from Fort Duncan arrested a group of 44 suspected would-be invaders and turned them over to the civil authorities in Texas. In March and April 1878, patrols from Fort Duncan were turned out to search for a group of filibusters under a man called Salinas. One of these patrols captured four of these men, all Mexicans, and again turned them over to the civil authorities.[57] Even as Buell was organising his forces in New Mexico and Grierson was finishing off his campaign in western Texas, General Ord had to reassure the Mexican Consul in San Antonio that, contrary to some newspaper reports, there was no 'Grand Army of Occupation organizing, partly in Texas, to invade Mexico'.[58]

The reference to 'enemies' as well as 'speculators' above refers to political opponents of the Diaz regime who wished to overthrow his government by force. Again, while not supported by the US government, such groups could use the relatively sparsely populated south-western USA as a springboard for their revolutionary activities. One Leonardo Marquez, presumably the person who held 'general' rank under the Emperor Maximilian in the 1860s, was first reported to be in the border area in early May 1880. Willcox informed the Mexican Consul (in Tucson?) that Marquez was camped near Algadones station with between 60 and 130 men. He also reported that a Mexican gunboat and 400 troops were heading towards the mouth of the river (Colorado?) to oppose Marquez.[59] Carr issued orders that one Sergeant Jerome Sawlor should 'proceed to Sonoita in the state of Sonora, Mexico with dispatches for General Marquez or the leader of the Revolutionists in Mexico'.[60] These dispatches politely informed Marquez that, should any of his forces cross the border, Carr would be obliged to disarm them, in view of the US Neutrality Laws. Carr also expressed the hope that recent depredations committed by Mexicans on Papago Indians

53 Schulz to 2nd Assistant Secretary of State, Washington D.C., 30 May, 1877 in Consular Despatches Cuidad Juarez (Paso del Norte), NARA, Wash.D.C., M184, Roll 2.

54 Schulz to 2nd Assistant Secretary of State, Washington D.C., 5 Jun., 1877 in Consular Despatches Cuidad Juarez (Paso del Norte), NARA, Wash.D.C., M184, Roll 2.

55 Schulz to 2nd Assistant Secretary of State, Washington D.C., 5 Jun., 1877 in Consular Despatches Cuidad Juarez (Paso del Norte), NARA, Wash.D.C., M184, Roll 2.

56 Document "F" From the "Periodico Official," Monterey, Saturday, 7 Sept., 1878 [Official organ of the Government of the State of Nuevo Leon, Mexico] in, NA, RG393, Part 1, Entry 2551, Annual Reports of Departments 1879-1881, MdoM.

57 Tabular Statement of Expeditions and Scouts against Indians & c., made in the DoTx during the Year ending 30 Sept., 1878, NA, RG393, Part 1, Entry 2551, Annual Reports of Departments 1879-1881, MdoM.

58 Ord to AG, Chicago, Ills., 9 Aug., 1880, NA, RG393, Part 1, Entry 2546, p.575 7 p.576.

59 Willcox to Mexican Consul, 7 May, 1880, NA, RG393, Part 1, Entry 169, Vol. 10, p.211.

60 Special Orders No. 21, HQ Troops in the Field in SE Arizona, Fort Lowell, A.T. 27 May, 1880, Special Orders Oct. 1879-Jan. 1881, DoAz, Vol. 2, NA, RG393, Part 1, Entry 239, p.3.

had not been carried out by any of Marquez's forces.[61] Carr did take the precaution of informing General Otero, the Mexican commander in Sonora, that he had been ordered to communicate thus with Marquez.[62] Meanwhile, Willcox contacted the Mexican Consul, on 13 June, to inform the latter that he could not arrest Mexican fugitives unless they had violated the neutrality laws or intended to wage war. If either of these charges could be proved, then every effort would be made to disarm and confine such men.[63] Two days later Carr was given permission to arrest Marquez, if he thought the latter intended to violate the neutrality laws.[64]

Marquez's activities were investigated by Deputy US Marshall J.W. Evans. He found that Marquez had been operating in Mexico before moving into the United States, but that there was no evidence that neutrality laws had been violated. Marquez had subsequently attempted to invade Sonora, again from the United States, with followers he had partially gathered from Tucson. This was a clear violation of US neutrality, and Evans reported that there was enough evidence to warrant Marquez's arrest.[65] Colonel Carr reported that, in late June 1880, he had been directed by his district headquarters to break up a small expedition that Marquez had organised in Arizona to take action against Mexico.[66] A group of approximately 40 revolutionaries were intercepted and scattered by a Sixth Cavalry company. This was probably a detachment commanded by Captain Rafferty, Sixth Cavalry, who was ordered to deal with Marquez on 21 June, 1880.[67] Three days later, Rafferty sent word that Marquez had disbanded his group.[68] When Marquez was subsequently spotted boarding a train for Yuma,[69] Willcox ordered the commanding officer, Fort Yuma, to keep an eye on him.[70] When Marquez departed north on a train for San Francisco, Willcox reported that, in his opinion, the attempted arrest by the Sixth Cavalry had, in the short term, neutralised Marquez's revolutionary activities.[71]

A small band of brigands posing as revolutionaries, under the command of one Brigido Reyes, was reported to have crossed the border into Mexico on 9 August 1880. Reyes had set out with approximately 22 men, but news of their departure did not reach the US military until two days after the event. This meant there was not enough time for Reyes to be intercepted by the Sixth

61 Carr to Marquez, 27 May, 1880, Troops in SE Arizona, DoAz, NA, RG393, Part 1, Entry 232, Vol.7, 18 May-6 Sept., 1880, Letter No.293, pp.50-51.

62 Carr to Otero, 27 May, 1880, Troops in SE Arizona, DoAz, NA, RG393, Part 1, Entry 232, Vol.7, 18 May-6 Sept., 1880, Letter No.296, p.53.

63 Willcox to Prieto, Mexican Consul, Tucson, 13 Jun., 1880, NA, RG393, Part 1, Entry 169, Vol. 10, p.276.

64 Martin to Carr, 15 Jun., 1880, NA, RG393, Part 1, Entry 169, Vol. 10, p.278 see also p.280, p.281 & p.288.

65 Willcox to AG, Presidio, San Francisco, 12 Jul., 1880, NA, RG393, Part 1, Entry 169, Vol. 10, p.317; See also "Border Troubles" Martin/Willcox to AG, MDoP, Presidio, San Francisco, 11 Sept., 1880, NA, RG393, Part 1, Entry 169, Vol. 10, p.422; Report of General O.B. Willcox, 11 Sept., 1880, in AR-WD 1880, NA, M997, Roll 35, 1880 Vol. I, p.209.

66 Tabular Statement of Scouts and Expeditions of Companies 6th Cavalry from 1 Jul., 1879-31 Jul., 1880, NA, RG393, Part 1, Entry 240.

67 Record of Events Jun. 1880 in Returns From Regular Army Cavalry Regiments 1833-1916, 6th Cavalry Regimental Returns 1875 to 1880, NA, M744, Roll 63; Bi-Monthly Company Muster Rolls for Company M, 6th Cavalry, May/Jun. 1880 in NA, RG94.

68 Willcox to AG, Presidio, San Francisco, 24 Jun., 1880, NA, RG393, Part 1, Entry 169, Vol. 10, p.291; Report of Col E.A. Carr, 29 Aug., 1880; Report of Col. E.A. Carr, 29 Aug., 1880, in AR-WD 1880, NA, M997, Roll 35, 1880 Vol. I, p.218; See also Carr to Rafferty, 16 Jun., 1880, Troops in SE Arizona, DoAz, NA, RG393, Part 1, Entry 232, Vol.7, 18 May-6 Sept., 1880, Letter No.354, pp.91-94.

69 And before anybody asks I don't know if it was the 3:10 ...

70 Willcox to AG, Presidio, San Francisco, 26 Jun., 1880, NA, RG393, Part 1, Entry 169, Vol. 10, p.293.

71 Willcox to AG, Presidio, San Francisco, 30 Jun., 1880, NA, RG393, Part 1, Entry 169, Vol. 10, p.297.

Captain William A. Rafferty, Sixth Cavalry. Throughout the campaign against Victorio, the Sixth Cavalry in Arizona provided periodic support to the troops in New Mexico by patrolling the border between the two territories and sending detachments to reinforce Hatch's forces. They also had to contend with American and Mexican brigandage across the Arizona-Mexico border and the activities of Mexican 'counter-revolutionaries' using Arizona as a base for invading northern Mexico. Captain Rafferty was involved in the attempts to detain two groups of such 'counter-revolutionaries' during the summer of 1880. (Carlisle Barracks)

Cavalrymen sent in pursuit.[72] Further activities by Reyes seem to have involved little more than political banditry in Magdalena, Sonora, where he was reported to have been raising forced loans, amounting to $10,000 for his 'revolution'.[73] Reyes was then reported to have been defeated and to have fled back into the United States. Rumours that a sheriff had arrested 20 of his men prompted Willcox to instruct Captain Rafferty to provide troops to support[74] the civil authorities if necessary.[75] Reyes was viewed by the US authorities as 'a mere brigand' and Headquarters, Department of Arizona, made strong representations that those now held in jail should not be viewed as 'political refugees',[76] noting the effect their activities had on US citizens engaged in the economic development of the Republic of Mexico, including mining and railway construction:

72 Martin to U.S. Marshall, Prescott, Arizona Territory, 14 Aug., 1880, NA, RG393, Part 1 Entry 169, Vol. 10, p.365; See also "Border Troubles" Martin/Willcox to AG, MDoP, Presidio, San Francisco, 11 Sept., 1880, NA, RG393, Part 1, Entry 169, Vol. 10, p.422; Report of Col E.A. Carr, 29 Aug., 1880; Report of General O.B. Willcox, 11 Sept., 1880, in AR-WD 1880, NA, M997, Roll 35, 1880 Vol. I, p.209.

73 Reports & Tabular Statements of Scouting Expeditions 1867-91, Capt Whitside, 6th Cavalry, to Kerr AAAG 16 Aug., 1880; NA, RG391 Entry 841; See also AR-WD 1880, NA, M997, Roll 35, 1880 Vol. I, p.223. Contributions to this loan were apparently encouraged by the summary execution of a local judge and a merchant. ('News from Sonora', the *Grant County Herald*, 28 Aug., 1880).

74 One is tempted to suggest that they were ordered to support their local sheriff ...

75 Willcox to AG, Presidio, San Francisco, 25 Aug., 1880, NA, RG393, Part 1, Entry 169, Vol. 10, pp.376-377; See also "Border Troubles" Martin/Willcox to AG, MDoP, Presidio, San Francisco, 11 Sept., 1880, NA, RG393, Part 1, Entry 169, Vol. 10, p.422; Record of Events Aug., 1880 in Returns From Regular Army Cavalry Regiments 1833-1916, 6th Cavalry Regimental Returns 1875 to 1880, NA, M744, Roll 63; Bi-Monthly Company Muster Rolls for Company M, 6th Cavalry, Jul./Aug. 1880 in NA, RG94.

76 See "Border Troubles" Martin/Willcox to AG, MDoP, Presidio, San Francisco, 11 Sept., 1880, NA, RG393, Part 1, Entry 169, Vol. 10, p.422; Report of General O.B. Willcox, 11 Sept., 1880, in AR-WD 1880, NA, M997, Roll 35, 1880 Vol. I, p.209.

> When these so-called filibusters swoop down on the peaceful inhabitants, our own citizens in Sonora suffer equally with the Mexicans, and for us to shield the robbers in their flight redhanded to our soil, is only to aid in the robbing of our own citizens.[77]

That the United States did act against such revolutionaries can be seen from the conviction of Brigido Altanaramo for 'setting on foot a military expedition and enterprise against a foreign power'. Altanaramo was given two years in the Detroit House of Corrections.[78]

Finally, it has to be acknowledged that, over and above the conflict with the Apaches, in 1880 there was a general level of organised brigandage, particularly horse thievery, operating across the Arizona, Chihuahua, New Mexico and Sonora lines. The posse comitatus laws prevented troops from aiding the civil authorities, 'which in that sparsely settled region, amount to nothing', in combatting such organised crime.[79] In other words, if they were being honest, the US authorities would admit they had not established strong political control of the international border areas in Arizona and New Mexico.

An 'Unofficial' Solution to an Official Problem

Over and above the specific issues raised by filibusters and revolutionaries, the question of Mexico's national sovereignty was a delicate issue, which raised significant obstacles to cross-border cooperation in dealing with the Apaches. One such obstacle was: what would the federal Mexican government be saying about its ability to rule if it allowed US forces to operate inside Mexico?

In 1880, this problem was resolved by the Chihuahuan state government arranging a local agreement which allowed the US army to cross the border. The fact was that, despite the fluctuations in their respective republics' relations, the civil and military authorities on both sides of the US-Mexican border were in regular communication with each other. These communications were often quite cordial, and are aptly illustrated by General Ord's communication to General Servado Canales asking him to convey his condolences to the President of the Republic of Mexico on the death of his wife. Canales' response was to express his thanks, and promise that he would immediately telegraph Ord's communication, via the Mexican Secretary of War, to President Diaz.[80] While the Diaz regime had started to reverse this situation, in 1880, some Mexican State Governors were still able to exercise a great deal of independence in their relations with their federal government. The opportunity for the Chihuahua state governor to exercise enough relative autonomy to contemplate taking an independent attitude to US troops crossing the border had arisen in the past. In 1862, in response to Confederate envoy James Reily's inquiry about Mexican permission for Union troops to pass through northern Mexico, Luis Terrazas, Governor of Chihuahua, had informed him that even if the federal government allowed the passage of troops

77 See "Border Troubles" Martin/Willcox to AG, MDoP, Presidio, San Francisco, 11 Sept., 1880, NA, RG393, Part 1, Entry 169, Vol. 10, p.422; Report of General O.B. Willcox, 11 Sept., 1880, in AR-WD 1880, NA, M997, Roll 35, 1880 Vol. I, p.209.

78 Report received dated 5 Aug., 1880 in Letters Rec'd 1880-1881, HQ Records of Fort Cummings, New Mexico, 1863-1873 & 1880-1884, NA, RG393, M1081, Roll 5.

79 See "Border Troubles" Martin/Willcox to AG, MDoP, Presidio, San Francisco, 11 Sept., 1880, NA, RG393, Part 1, Entry 169, Vol. 10, p.423; Report of General O.B. Willcox, 11 Sept., 1880, in AR-WD 1880, NA, M997, Roll 35, 1880 Vol. I, p.209.

80 Canales to Ord, 11 Apr., 1880, NA, RG393, Part 1, Entry 2546, pp.401-402: See also efforts made by Canales to apprehend men believed to have killed a Mr Bishop and attempted to rape his wife and servant on 16 May, 1880, over a supposed money debt owed by Bishop. (Ord to Sheridan, with enclosed correspondence, 20 May, 1880, NA, RG393, Part 1, Entry 2546, pp.454-458).

through Mexico to attack Texas, Terrazas would still not give them permission to pass through the state of Chihuahua.[81] It is thus clear that the Governor had been willing to defy the government of Mexico should it pass a bill allowing the entrance of foreign troops. The Governor had implied to Reily that he had the authority to grant permission for a cross-border incursion lasting less than one month, but he also informed Reily that he was not in favour of a previous governor's granting of permission for US troops to pursue Indians deep into Chihuahua. However, if Indian raiding persisted, then Terrazas undertook to 'take the steps necessary to act upon it before the Congress of the Union'.[82] Thus, in 1862, Terrazas had made it clear that, while he was in charge of the governing of Chihuahua, he was quite capable of making his own arrangements concerning a foreign power, even if that ran contrary to the wishes of the Federal government of Mexico. Prior to the Ord order, the Chihuahuan authorities had approached General Ord concerning Indians 'and invited our co-operation on their side of the river'.[83] It should be noted that, by 1880, in taking such a path, Terrazas was pushing at the boundaries of what would be tolerated by the Mexican federal government. Nevertheless, in the face of the problem posed by Victorio's Apaches, Terrazas clearly judged that this was a worthwhile risk. Indeed, while there was serious nationalist opposition to be overcome in the Mexican congress, President Diaz was finally granted the authority to officially allow US troops to cross the border on 16 October 1880.[84] (See document file no. 107.)

In August, 1879, the state government of Sonora had also been in contact the Department of Arizona concerning operations against brigands and Indians.[85] As part of these communications, Major A.K. Arnold, Fort Grant, sent a map of southern Arizona to Angel Elias, commanding troops based in Frontera, Sonora. This was in response to a wider request to help each other against the Apaches by communicating information concerning their movements. Arnold requested that, if the Mexican commander's orders allowed him, he should send a corresponding map of 'the northern and eastern States of Mexico'.[86] Elias stated that he would be happy to coordinate movements with US troops through the commanding officer, Fort Huachuca, or by courier contact with Camp Supply. He also hoped that any news from the United States would be sent as soon as possible:

> We shall do badly the Military authorities of both Republics and not appear Brotherly if we do not try the most effacious means in our power to punish severely the Indians and evil-doers that are hostile to both sides of the line.[87]

Elias thanked the US military for the map (suggesting that Mexican troops had been given tacit permission to cross the border) but regretted that, for the moment, the request by the US army for

81 Hall, 1956, p.235; The Union authorities were aware of Col. Reilly's activities see Carlton to Major David Fergusson, 13 Jan., 1863 & Fergusson to Carleton, 14 Feb., 1863 in Consular Despatches Chihuahua Mexico 1830-1906, NA, M289, Roll 1.

82 Hall, 1956, p.236.

83 Report of General Ord in AR-WD 1880, NA, M997, Roll 26, 1876 Vol. I-II, pp.487-488.

84 Jose Fernandez, Dept. of Foreign Affairs to Morgan, U.S. Minister to Mexico, 15 Oct., 1880 in 'Frelinghuysen-Romero Papers'; Letters Rec'd by the AGO (Main Series), 1881-1889, NA, M689, Roll 81; See also Sayles, 1976, pp.301-302; Hatfield pp.37-38; Dinges, 1987, p.94.

85 Angel Trias to HQ, Troops in the Field, Territory of Arizona, 25 Aug., 1879, NA, RG393, Part 1, Entry 235, p.30.

86 Arnold to Commander of Mexican Forces Stationed at Fronteras, 11 Aug., 1879, Troops in SE Arizona, DoAz, NA, RG393, Part 1, Entry 232, Vol.4, 3 Jul.-13 Dec., 1879, Letter No.47, pp.29-30; See also Arnold to CO Camp Huachuca, 13 Aug., 1879, Troops in SE Arizona, DoAz, NA, RG393, Part 1, Entry 232, Vol.4, 3 Jul.-13 Dec., 1879, Letter No.56, p.36.

87 Angel Trias to HQ, Troops in the Field, Territory of Arizona, 25 Aug., 1879, NA, RG393, Part 1, Entry 235, p.31.

equivalent maps could not be complied with: 'I have asked for them from the Colonel Comd'g and as soon as they are sent me, I shall take great pleasure in sending them in charge of Lieut Bailey.'[88]

Prior to the operation to abolish the Chiricahua reservation in 1876, General Schofield had recommended that the Mexican authorities be alerted, to give them an opportunity to block any attempt by Chiricahuas to flee into Sonora. He had also strongly implied that Governor Safford had already contacted the military authorities in Sonora concerning this matter.[89] It was thus understood that US commanders in the Department of Arizona were actively encouraged to cooperate with their opposite numbers in Sonora:

> Commanding General directs me to acknowledge receipt your telegram regarding out-break of Mescalero Indians. Have you informed the commanding officer at Fronteras? If not, please do so.[90]

However, the sort of opportunities that allowed Mexican army and state actors to exercise relative autonomy were far less likely to lead to interpretation, or even defiance, in the United States. Lew Wallace, Governor of New Mexico, had already aroused the ire of no less a person than General Sherman when he had attempted to use the US army as a resource in his efforts to pacify the Lincoln County War. General Pope was immediately informed that the Governor had the right neither to call upon troops to intervene[91] nor to 'declare Martial law, nor to do any act which incidentally changes the status or duties of Army Officers'.[92] Adjutant General Townsend wrote to Sheridan stating that Wallace's request to use US troops to enforce martial law in Lincoln and Dona Ana Counties should not be obeyed.[93] This was reinforced by a letter stating that the Governor had no powers to declare martial law. Only the President of the United States, as the Commander-in-Chief, could make such a declaration and order the army to act.[94] Finally, however, Special Field Order No. 1, District of New Mexico, 25 June 1878,[95] ordered the Commanding Officer, Fort Stanton, to report to the Governor at Lincoln and place his troops under the latter's command. Colonel Hatch had earlier that month issued orders that US troops could not be used as a *posse comitatus* and therefore could not be used to enforce civil law in Lincoln County. However, the state of anarchy had reached such a level that Hatch felt obliged to intervene to assist the Governor to restore order. Hatch's order was described as 'extremely unusual and doubtful of legality or policy' by General Sherman, and as 'objectionable' by US Secretary of War, G.W. McCrary.[96] These objections were thoroughly approved by Sheridan:

88 Ibid, p.32.
89 Schofield to AG U.S.A., 20 May, 1876 in Correspondence relating to the removal of the Chiricahua Apache Indians to the San Carlos Indian Agency, Arizona Territory, 1876-77: Letters Rec'd by the AGO (Main series). 1871-80. NA, M666, Roll 265.
90 F.A. Smith, AAAG to Major Arnold, Fort Grant, 10 Sept., 1879, NA, RG393, Part 1, Entry 235, p.7; See also NA, RG393, Part 1, Entry 169, Vol. 9, p.334.
91 AG Townsend to Comdg. General, DoM, 15 Mar., 1879 in Letters Received by HQ_DoNM Sept. 1865-Aug. 1890, NA, RG393, M1088, Roll 37 Apr.-Jun., 1879.
92 AG Townsend to Comdg. General, DoM, 21 Mar., 1879 in Letters Received by HQ_DoNM Sept. 1865-Aug. 1890, NA, RG393, M1088, Roll 37 Apr.-Jun., 1879.
93 Townsend to Comdg. General DoM 15 Mar., 1879, NA, RG393, Part 1, Entry 2546, pp.65-67.
94 Townsend to Comdg. General DoM 21 Mar., 1879, NA, RG393, Part 1, Entry 2546, pp.108-110.
95 (Loud to CO Fort Stanton, 25 Jun., 1878 in Letters Sent by '9MD/DNM/DoNM', NA, RG393, M1072, Roll 6, Letter No.299 p.212).
96 Comments made by Gen. Sherman & Secretary of War, G.W. McCrary transmitted by Gen. Sheridan through W.D. Whipple A.A.G. to Gen. Pope, Commanding DoM, 2 Apr. 1879, NA, RG393, Part 1, Entry 2546, pp.113-116.

Plate 13.1. Palace of the Governors, Santa Fé, New Mexico. (Photo: Author)

Plate 13.2. The House of Luis Terrazas, Chihuahua City, Mexico. (Photo: Author)

> the Governor seems imbued with the idea that he possesses the full powers of the President within the boundaries of New Mexico, particularly with regard to the land forces stationed therein.[97]

Wallace was quite capable of reaching beyond the legal limits of his powers, but it is also clear that the federal government of the United States was quite capable of quickly stopping such independent policy initiatives when it chose to. However, not all of Wallace's independent policy initiatives were blocked by the federal authorities. When he gave Mexican troops permission to cross the US border in pursuit of Apaches in January 1880, the US troops in New Mexico were given orders to facilitate such arrangements, much to the delight of the Governor of Chihuahua and the territorial press.[98] (See document file no. 29.)

Thus, when Victorio returned to Mexico in May–June 1880, local authorities on both sides of the border tried to solve the problem within the parameters set by their respective federal governments. The first attempted solution was one where Mexican and US forces cooperated with each other, but did not cross the border. Colonel Valle had permission to cross the border in hot pursuit of Apaches during his campaign in July–August 1880; yet he did not do so. This may be due to the loss of his supply train to the Apaches crippling his room for manoeuvre; but there may be more to it than meets the eye. Valle, despite directing Chihuahua state troops as part of his expedition, was an officer in the Federal Army of Mexico. As such, he had to pay far more attention to the implications of cross-border operations for the Mexican federal government. Had Valle crossed the border, the United States could quite reasonably have expected a reciprocal arrangement which, at that time, was not going to be granted by the Mexican federal government. In other words, Valle may have been given verbal instructions not to cross the border under any circumstances, in order to avoid political and diplomatic complications for the Diaz regime. Therefore, cooperation between the two forces took the form of sending information relative to the whereabouts and predicted movements of the Apaches. This arrangement failed to bring the Victorio war to an end.

As noted in the last chapter, a major cross-border operation was certainly one option being considered by General Pope. The failure of joint operations between Valle and Grierson to bring about Victorio's capitulation, or destruction, probably convinced Hatch and Pope that an incursion into Mexico was necessary in order to defeat the enemy. From Luis Terrazas' point of view, such an operation was relatively straightforward, as he could effectively ignore protests from Mexico City. According to Thrapp, on 22 or 23 August 1880, Luis Terrazas sounded out Colonel Valle concerning his cooperation in this venture; but the latter flatly refused. The reasons given for Valle's refusal were that his troops and horses were exhausted.[99] As noted above, Valle was answerable to the Mexican federal government. He may have become aware that Luis Terrazas was already entering into negotiations about activities in which he could not become involved. Captain Brinkerhoff reported that, on 16 or 17 August, Governor Terrazas had made the first moves to invite US troops into Chihuahua[100] to cooperate with his forces in bringing about the

97 Sheridan's endorsement of Pope's letter to the AAG, MDoM 28 Mar., 1879, NA, RG393, Part 1, Entry 2546, pp.111-112.

98 See Osborne to AAAG DoNM, 12 Jan., 1880 in NA, RG393, Part 3, Entry 439, pp.500-501 & Humphreys to AAAG SF 12 Jan., 1880, NA, RG393, Part 3, Entry 439, p502-505; Telegrams Sent DoNM, Vol.3, Jan. – Nov., 1880 NA, RG393, Part 3, Entry 431, pp.38-39; Terrazas to Gen Edward Hatch Comd DoNM 17 Jan., 1880 NA, RG393, Part 3, Entry 439, pp.429-430; Ashenfelter Editorial, the *Grant County Herald*, 17 Jan., 1880.

99 Thrapp, 1973, p.293.

100 We shall examine this correspondence in more detail in the following chapter.

destruction of Victorio.[101] In fact, Dr Samaniego had contacted Colonel Buell on 18 August to clarify the meaning of the word 'pursuit', and to confirm that this would refer to the pursuit of a clear trail left by the Apaches going into the State of Chihuahua. Samaniego also asked Buell to temporarily delay proceeding with his operations as, 'Col. Valle has gone to Chihuahua to have an understanding with the General [Federal] Government & with the Gov. of the State.'[102] On 21 August, Buell instructed Brinkerhoff to, 'Ask Dr Samaniego to get cooperation with his Gov't. and the two of us will see what we can do with Victorio in or out of Mexico.'[103] These discussions would have had serious implications for Valle's position, and his refusal would strongly suggest that his loyalty was primarily focused on the federal government, which would not officially condone such an action. Yet Valle's refusal did not give Luis Terrazas cause for pause, and he dispatched his nephew, Colonel Joaquin Terrazas, to raise the necessary state troops to take part in the operation.

However, one could not treat the US federal government in such a cavalier manner without risking career-threatening sanctions. One of the main obstacles to the launching of an operation against Victorio in Mexico was the ongoing State Department negotiations with Mexico's Department of Foreign Affairs to allow US troops to cross the border into Mexico. These negotiations ultimately bore fruit two years later; but the threat of Victorio's continuing resistance was immediate. Thus the actors involved had to attempt to defeat the Apaches as quickly as possible, but they had to accomplish this without causing serious damage to official negotiations between the two countries.

It is not at all clear who came up with the tactic of presenting a letter from Colonel Valle, dated 9 August 1880, which was *interpreted* as stating that authority had been granted to the US army to cross the border. (See document file no. 108.1.) It was clearly intended that, by the time the State Department translated this letter and realised that permission had not been granted, it would be too late to prevent the proposed field operation. (See document file no. 108.2.) The idea that Colonel Valle had written a letter confirming that US troops had been invited into the state of Chihuahua probably originated in the following letter from Dr Mariano Samaniego:

> Fort Bliss Aug. 16-80
>
> To Genl Buell
> Cummings
> Capt. Brinkerhoff, Comd'g Fort Bliss, Tx.
> Commissioned and amply authorized by the Governor of Chihuahua.
>
> I have the honor to communicate to you that the U.S. troops may cross into the Territory of Chihuahua in pursuit of Victorio and his band operating in combination with the Mexican forces. Col. Valle assuring you at the same time if it should be necessary the Authority of the principal politico's authority of this frontier.
> (sgd) Dr. Samaniego
>
> The Doctor states that if you come to El Paso, Tex., the highest local authority of the State will invite you formally to enter Chihuahua with your command:-
> (sgd) Brinkerhoff,
> Comd'g.[104]

101 Brinkerhoff to Buell, 16 & 17 Aug., 1880, Buell to Samaniego, 17 Aug., 1880, Samaniego to Buell, 18 Aug., 1880 in 'Victorio Papers', NA, M666, Roll 528.
102 Samaniego to Buell, 18 Aug., 1880 in 'Victorio Papers', NA, M666, Roll 528.
103 Buell to Brinkerhoff, 21 Aug., 1880 in 'Victorio Papers', NA, M666, Roll 528.
104 Samaniego to Buell, 16 Aug., 1880 in 'Victorio Papers', NA, M666, Roll 528.

It is immediately apparent that, while Valle's agreement is *implied* by Samaniego, there is no proof that Valle was actually aware of this letter. Subsequent events would lend some weight to the idea that Valle, a federal army officer, did not agree with this venture. What is also clear from this letter is that Samaniego stated that he was speaking on behalf of the Governor of Chihuahua. This communication was accepted at face value at District Headquarters:

> Headqrs Dist of New Mexico
> Santa Fé, N.M. August 18, 1880
>
> Respectfully forwarded to the Asst Adjt General Dept of the Missouri, recommending the co-operation as suggested. The proposal, it is presumed, means that no regard is to be given to the lines between the United States and Mexico when troops of either country are in pursuit of Indians. The Indians mentioned are Apaches (the Indian supposed to direct their movements is Victoria) who are simply a large band of assassins, a general enemy, and if they can be hunted down and destroyed by joint arrangements between the two countries, I certainly recommend it in this instance.
> (Sgd) Edward Hatch
> Colonel 9th Cavalry
> Commanding.[105]

This information was passed up through the US army chain of command until it reached the Chief Clerk to the Secretary of War on 31 August 1880[106] and was duly sent to the Department of State. The following day, the State Department very quickly informed the Secretary of War that, in their opinion, Colonel Valle's letter did not grant permission for US troops to cross the border. (See document file no. 108.2.) This translation or interpretation appears to have originated in the above letter from Colonel Hatch, though Hatch phrased his interpretation very carefully. It is plain that Colonel Valle had not extended such an invitation. Nevertheless, it is also clear that the District of New Mexico had received a clear invitation to cross the border from the State of Chihuahua which *implied* that Colonel Valle, a servant of the Mexican federal government, was party to this agreement.

At this point, the Department of War was *requested* to suspend, for the moment, any troop movements across the Mexican border, and to provide the State Department with Valle's original letter.[107] The Department of War complied with these requests to the extent that it was stated that the Adjutant General had been 'directed' to 'prohibit the crossing of the boundary by United States Troops until further orders'.[108] The original letter was delivered to the State Department on 6 September, and the latter's translation confirming its interpretation of Valle's letter was sent to the Department of War on 14 September 1880.[109] It then took six days for the Adjutant General's Office to inform the Division of the Missouri that, 'It would appear that the Department of State

105 Hatch's 18 Aug., 1880 endorsement to a translation of Valle's letter, to Capt Brinkerhoff, 9 Aug., 1880, 'Victorio Files', NA, RG393, M1495, Roll 14; See also 'Victorio Papers', NA, M666, Roll 528.

106 Chief Clerk for the Secretary of War (in his absence) to the Secretary of State, 31 Aug., 1880 in 'Victorio Papers', NA, M666, Roll 528.

107 John Hay, Dept. of State to Ramsey, Secretary of War 1 Sept., 1880 in 'Victorio Papers', NA, M666, Roll 528.

108 Chief Clerk for the Secretary of War (in his absence) to the Secretary of State, 1 Sept., 1880 in 'Victorio Papers', NA, M666, Roll 528.

109 Hunter , Acting Secretary, Dept of State to Ramsey, Secretary of War, 20 Sept., 1880, 'Victorio Files', NA, RG393, M1495, Roll 14; See also Hunter , Acting Secretary, Dept of State to Ramsey, Secretary of War, 25 Sept., 1880 in Letters Received by HQ DoNM Sept. 1865-Aug. 1890, NA, RG393, M1088,

finds certain differences in the meaning of Col. Valle's communication where the translation made by that Department is compared with that forwarded with the original.'[110] This rather vague missive was only transmitted to the Department of the Missouri on 22 September 1880. The State Department had to reiterate its point of view to the Department of War on 25 September 1880,[111] by which time Buell's forces had already crossed the border into Mexico.

The delays in transmitting the State Department's instructions (the State Department perhaps not realising how a 'request' could be creatively interpreted), and the ambiguous manner in which it was transmitted, suggest that a cross-border operation against Victorio had tacit support at the highest level in the Department of War. Indeed, the way in which this whole episode unfolded shows that the group of individuals who connived at this deception were very keenly aware of the 'political' implications of their actions. They had endorsed an invasion of a neighbouring country (albeit with the tacit support of key political figures within the State of Chihuahua), in such a way as to minimise the risk to their own positions once all was revealed. In other words, the whole incident could be portrayed as an 'unfortunate misinterpretation' of a letter – a misinterpretation which had been confirmed as such too late to prevent Buell's expedition from entering Mexico. There is, of course, the possibility that Hatch genuinely misinterpreted the letter, but the manner in which information from the State Department was delayed long enough for Buell to cross the border suggests otherwise.

The careful deception must have been formulated at a much higher level than the Headquarters of the District of New Mexico. Hatch, with his record of clumsy public relations with the territorial press, is not the most obvious candidate for this level of sophisticated politicking. However, although he had been less than politically astute in his dealings with New Mexican citizens and press, this does not mean that he was incapable of subtle political manoeuvring.[112] It is also quite clear that, while Colonel Buell was at the centre of organizing the field expedition into Mexico,[113] he was unaware of the use of Valle's letter. Buell based the justification for his incursion into Chihuahua on the letter from Samaniego noted earlier in this chapter, which had cited, but not given any proof of, Colonel Valle's acquiescence, and a later – legally rather ambiguous – invitation from Juan B. Olguin, the Political Officer for El Paso del Norte.[114]

However, this politicking was probably part of a damage limitation exercise in Washington in support of independent action already taken in New Mexico. Buell and Hatch were probably not politically sophisticated enough to outmanoeuvre the State Department. Buell, in particular, adopted an attitude which reflected the local New Mexico perspective: that the defeat of Victorio was paramount, though this did not account for the wider diplomatic perspective concerning relations between the two federal governments. While the key individuals in the Department of War had to engage in some quick thinking to stave off the political consequences of an invasion of

Roll 41, Jul.-Dec. 1880; Letters Received by HQ DoNM Sept. 1865-Aug. 1890, NA, RG393, M1088, Roll 41, Jul.-Dec. 1880.

110 Hunter , Acting Secretary, Dept of State to Ramsey, Secretary of War, 20 Sept., 1880, 'Victorio Files', NA, RG393, M1495, Roll 14; See also Hunter , Acting Secretary, Dept of State to Ramsey, Secretary of War, 25 Sept., 1880 in Letters Received by HQ DoNM Sept. 1865-Aug. 1890, NA, RG393, M1088, Roll 41, Jul.-Dec. 1880; Letters Received by HQ DoNM Sept. 1865-Aug. 1890, NA, RG393, M1088, Roll 41, Jul.-Dec. 1880.

111 Hunter , Acting Secretary, Dept of State to Ramsey, Secretary of War, 20 Sept., 1880, 'Victorio Files', NA, RG393, M1495, Roll 14; See also Hunter , Acting Secretary, Dept of State to Ramsey, Secretary of War, 25 Sept., 1880 in Letters Received by HQ DoNM Sept. 1865-Aug. 1890, NA, RG393, M1088, Roll 41, Jul.-Dec. 1880; Letters Received by HQ DoNM Sept. 1865-Aug. 1890, NA, RG393, M1088, Roll 41, Jul.-Dec. 1880.

112 This becomes apparent in his dealings with Buell's expenditure in the aftermath of his expedition.

113 See Chapter 14.

114 See Chapter 14.

Mexico, the fact that they did so reflects their tacit (and deniable) support for a quick end to the Victorio campaign.

These consequences materialised in early November, when enquiries from Mexico City concerning an alleged invasion of Chihuahua by US troops prompted some pointed questions from the State Department. Governor Terrazas, in responding to Buell's request that he reveal the correspondence that took place prior to, and during, the 'Buell Expedition', makes the cryptic statement that 'I agree with you – all of this trouble was caused by Col. Valle',[115] which only reinforces the suspicion that Valle had remained loyal to Mexico City and had reported back on the whole affair. This would be understandable, as it had been Valle whose letter had been misrepresented in the first place, and there is no reason to suppose that this officer was party to the apparent deception. The Department of War passed the questions it received down to Colonel Buell and, after some delaying tactics, the latter submitted his correspondence with various political actors[116] from the State of Chihuahua. However, Buell insisted that the anonymity of these men be preserved and not revealed to Mexico City.[117] Buell noted that, 'I understand the Jeffe Politico has been arrested already, and do not wish to cause him more trouble.'[118] This demand received the backing of the Secretary of War[119] and was acquiesced to by the State Department.[120] Buell made it quite clear in his response that he had been invited to enter Chihuahua and that his only motive, shared by the 'Jeffe Politico' and others in Chihuahua, was to destroy Victorio and his followers, who had been causing such havoc on both sides of the border.[121]

Of interesting significance is the failure of the US consular official, an employee of the US State Department based in El Paso del Norte, to mention anything about these negotiations at the same time as Dr Samaniego and Captain Brinkerhoff were acting as conduits between the Chihuahuan and New Mexico authorities. Both US consuls, in El Paso del Norte and Chihuahua, make no mention of the Buell expedition, which lends weight to the argument that the State Department was kept in the dark at all levels. However, we should remember that an early, and enthusiastic, supporter of cross-border cooperation against the Apaches was Louis H. Scott, US Consul in Chihuahua City and an employee of the US Department of State.[122] There is no proof that Scott was aware of the intended cross-border operation, but one suspects that, if he had known of the intended operation against Victorio, he would not have reported this to his superiors. The more one considers this situation, the more one suspects that, despite the on-going difficulties between the two countries, there were individuals on both sides of the border capable of acting independently, or of turning a blind eye to how the war against Victorio was prosecuted.

What remains unclear is the level of involvement of federal actors in the United States and Mexico. Was this a situation where state or territory actors decided to co-operate to deal with a specific crisis *in spite* of their federal colleagues, thus creating a situation where they could keep

115 Terrazas to Buell, 9 Mar., 1881 in 'Victorio Papers', NA, M666, Roll 528.

116 Namely Juan B, Olguin, Dr M. Samaniego, Col. Joaquin Terrazas and Roman Aranda.

117 Buell to AAG, DoM, 12 Feb., 1881 in 'Victorio Papers', NA, M666, Roll 528.

118 Buell to Samaniego, 11 Feb., 1881 in 'Victorio Papers', NA, M666, Roll 528.

119 Ramsey to The Secretary of State, 5 Mar., 1881in 'Victorio Papers', NA, M666, Roll 528.

120 Blaine, Secretary of State to Robert T. Lincoln, Secretary of War, 9 Mar., 1881 in 'Victorio Papers', NA, M666, Roll 528.

121 NA, RG393, Part 1, Entry 2546, pp.791-797.

122 Scott to Hunter, 2nd Assistant Secretary of State, 4 Dec., 1879, Letters Received by HQ DoNM Sept. 1865-Aug. 1890, M1088, Roll 37 (Oct.-Dec. 1879); See also Scott to Hunter, 2nd Assistant Secretary of State, Washington D.C. 28 Nov., 1879 in Consular Despatches Chihuahua Mexico 1830-1906, NA, M289, Roll 1; Scott to Hunter 28 Nov., 1879 in Evarts, Dept. of State to Alexander Ramsey, Secretary of War, 16 Dec., 1879, 'Victorio Files', NA, RG393, M1495, Roll 14 see same letter in 'Frelinghuysen-Romero Papers'; Letters Rec'd by the AGO (Main Series), 1881-1889, NA, M689, Roll 81.

the latter at arm's length until they could present them with a *fait accompli*? What appears more likely is that certain individuals reporting to, or members of, the federal government unofficially gave their state-level colleagues the leeway they needed to tackle the problem posed by Victorio's Apaches. For example, on 4 August 1880, General Pope instructed Hatch, 'In short you must do everything possible to strengthen Buell & then leave him to do what he thinks best. This is best on all accounts.'[123] This rather vague passage just reeks of a written reminder of earlier discussions, the details of which were never going to be committed to paper. It also suggests that, if any repercussions did occur, Buell would be the US army's preferred scapegoat.

There is another possible reason for why Buell's expedition was allowed to proceed. This was the intention of Rutherford B. Hayes, President of the United States, to pass through southern New Mexico during September or October of 1880, as part of a wider tour of the western United States. It was earlier noted that serious negotiations to cross the border were initiated on 16 August 1880. General Pope had been notified of the intention of President Hayes to visit the area on 9 August. He was ordered to inform Colonel Hatch, who was to record the details of any escort that was arranged, but to refrain from issuing any written orders until the visit was confirmed.[124] (See document file no. 109.1.) By 26 August, it was known that the trip had been finalised and that the President and General Sherman, with various officials, would be crossing Arizona and New Mexico, travelling as far as they could by rail. They would be travelling east via the Southern Pacific Railroad (S.P.R.R.), then travelling by coach through southern New Mexico, via Fort Cummings and Fort Craig, where they would join the AT&SF railroad. They expected to pass through this area between 1 and 15 October 1880.[125] This information was transmitted on 26 August 1880.

This news must have horrified Hatch, as it was clear that the President would be travelling through the centre of what was effectively a war zone. Hatch ordered Buell to carefully patrol the country between the terminus of the Southern Pacific and that of the AT&SF railway and to station detachments of troops at Soldier's Farewell and McEvers' Ranch. Troops from Fort Cummings were to patrol the Mimbres Mountains and Cooke's Canyon.[126] These orders were issued on 21 September 1880, just as the Buell Expedition started for Mexico. Instructions were also issued that, during the President's visit, every effort should be made to maintain the telegraph lines. To this end, the COs of Forts Bliss, Cummings and Bayard were to provide properly equipped repair teams to act at a minute's notice should they be required.[127] General Sheridan was quick to dismiss any concerns about the President's safety, on the grounds that there were approximately 700 troops in the area.[128] However, Sherman seems to have been less complacent, and General Pope was clearly instructed to 'insure absolute safety' for the President and his entourage.[129]

123 Pope to Hatch 1 Aug., 1880, NA, RG393, Part 3, Entry 439, p.45.

124 Sheridan to Pope, 9 Aug., 1880, NA, RG393, Part 1, Entry 2539, Press Copies of Letters and Endorsements Sent, MDoM, Vol. 13, pp.495-497; See also Sheridan to Crook 9 Aug., 1880, NA, RG393, Part 1, Entry 2539, Press Copies of Letters and Endorsements Sent, MDoM, Vol. 13, p.494.

125 Letter to Gen. Hatch 26 Aug., 1880, NA, RG393, Part 1, Entry 2539, Press Copies of Letters and Endorsements Sent, MDoM, Vol. 13, pp.544-546.

126 Loud to Buell, 21 Sept., 1880 in Letters Sent by '9MD/DNM/DoNM', NA, RG393, M1072, Roll 6, Jan. 1880-Aug. 1881, Letter No.502, p.324.

127 Allen to AAAG, DoNM, 30 Sept., 1880 in Letters Received by HQ DoNM Sept. 1865-Aug. 1890, NA, RG393, M1088, Roll 41, Jul.-Dec. 1880.

128 Sheridan to Sherman 11 Sept., 1880, NA, RG393, Part 1, Entry 2539, Press Copies of Letters and Endorsements Sent, MDoM, Vol. 13, pp.586-587.

129 Sheridan to Pope 11 Sept., 1880, NA, RG393, Part 1, Entry 2539, Press Copies of Letters and Endorsements Sent, MDoM, Vol. 13, p.584; See also Sherman to Sheridan, 10 Sept., 1880, NA, RG393, Part 1, Entry 2546, p.600.

Significantly, Sherman also instructed Sheridan that, 'The troops should not cease to undertake to capture or kill the Victoria band.'[130] Sherman pointed out that, if the dangers were so severe, the presidential party would not make the trip. In the meantime 'some good officer' should monitor the situation and make the necessary preparations for the visit.[131]

There were added complications, as evidenced by Captain Brinkerhoff's consternation when Governor Terrazas requested that a Chihuahuan commission have talks with the President on 3 October 1880. While he felt that such a meeting could clearly be of great benefit, he was wise enough to pass this request up the chain of command. (See document file no. 109.2.) One can only imagine the reaction of both the federal government of Mexico and the US Department of State to the diplomatic implications of such a meeting.

The instruction to ensure the absolute safety of the presidential party issued by the Commanding General of the United States Army does raise the possibility that a major operation by US troops in northern Mexico would have been seen as the perfect means to keep the Apaches well away from the most high profile of targets.[132] This sentiment can only have been reinforced when, less than a month before the President's party was due to pass through the area, Apache guerrillas struck, with deadly effect, only 20 miles east of Fort Cummings.[133] This was on the very route it was proposed that President Hayes would travel. This development, combined with the presence of General Sherman in the presidential party, provided all the incentive required for collusion throughout the US army command structure to facilitate Buell's expedition into Mexico.

Whether these contemporaneous arrangements extended to offering prior support for Buell's expedition from the President or any of his entourage is doubtful, though not outside the realms of possibility. What may have been forthcoming was an indication of subsequent support for the army from the executive, should there be any repercussions from their unauthorised cross-border cooperation. It is only fair to note that, during October 1880, the presidential party passed through Apacheria without incident.[134]

130 Sherman to Sheridan, 11 Sept., 1880, NA, RG393, Part 1, Entry 2546, p.596.

131 Sherman to Hatch, 14 Sept., 1880, NA, RG393, Part 1, Entry 2546, pp.606-607) The intended visit of the President to the territory was published in mid-September. ('The Coming Guests', the *Grant County Herald*, 11 Sept., 1880; 'Town and County', the *Grant County Herald*, 18 Sept., 1880).

132 The road between Forts Cumming and Craig is littered with terrain far worse than the myriad of grassy knolls which also frequent this particular route.

133 See next Chapter.

134 Special Field Order No. 41, para.3, 25 Oct., 1880, NA, RG393, Part 3, Entry 450.

14

Buell's Goodsight Mountain Expedition, 6-8 September 1880

Before we cover the progress of the Buell expedition into Mexico, it is worth noting an episode where either Colonel Hatch or Colonel Buell allegedly sent 'Captain' Jack Crawford, the 'Poet Scout', to make one last diplomatic effort to persuade Victorio to surrender, sometime in late August or early September 1880.[1] Recent discoveries in the National Archives also necessitated a detailed investigation of Colonel Buell's attempt to trap Victorio in the Goodsight Mountains in early September 1880.

'Captain' Jack Crawford's 'Adventures' in Mexico

According to Thrapp, it was Hatch who commissioned Crawford's mission;[2] but Crawford's own account (see document file no. 110) suggests that Hatch had ordered him to depart from Fort Craig to scout south from the Mescalero reservation, to garner intelligence of any Mescalero Apaches operating in the Sacramento Mountains. Once this mission was completed, he was to report to General Buell at Fort Cummings. According to Crawford, it was Buell who requested that 'a man' undertake a very dangerous mission to persuade Victorio to surrender to the US authorities. Of the four scouts[3] accompanying Crawford, not one was willing to risk falling victim to brigands or Apaches by undertaking this mission. Crawford alone was prepared to do it.[4]

Crawford's account states that Colonel Buell sent him with 'Navajo Charlie', an Apache familiar with Victorio, and with Casimero, 'a fearless little Mexican', in search of Victorio.[5] Thrapp suspects that 'Casimero' may have been one Zebina Nathaniel Streeter. Clearly one of the more colourful characters of the Apache Wars, Streeter was certainly closely associated with the Apaches, to the extent of being suspected of accompanying Juh on raids.[6] Thrapp states that he had a Mexican alias 'Cassimiro'.[7] He was certainly fluent in Spanish, having been an interpreter at Fort Craig, and was known to have lived at Canada Alamosa, where he had been on speaking terms with Victorio himself.[8] At the time, Streeter had a price on his head as a result of his Apache associations. He

1 See 'The Pursuit of Victorio' By Captain Jack Crawford Socorro County Historical Society, Publications in History, Volume 1, Feb., 1965.
2 Thrapp, 1974, p.291.
3 Named as Jim Blain, Lew Fountain, Bill Crawford and Jim Dickinson. ('The Pursuit of Victorio' By Captain Jack Crawford Socorro County Historical Society, Publications in History, Volume 1, Feb., 1965).
4 'The Pursuit of Victorio' By Captain Jack Crawford Socorro County Historical Society, Publications in History, Volume 1, Feb., 1965.
5 Ibid.
6 See Thrapp, 1988, pp.1378-1379 for a full biography; see also Thrapp, 1974, p.372, Note 60.
7 Thrapp, 1974, p.372, Note 6.
8 Thrapp, 1988, p.1378; see also Thrapp, 1974, p.372, Note 6.

Poet Scout Jack Crawford.
Jack Crawford, known as the 'Poet Scout' was one of a number of American citizens employed as scouts by Hatch and Buell and deployed into northern Mexico to keep track of Victorio's movements. While undoubtedly dangerous duty, not only risking attack by Apaches but also arrest by Mexican authorities, Crawford's account of his scout into northern Chihuahua is probably exaggerated, though he did bring back important intelligence that the Apaches appeared to be short of ammunition. (National Archives)

may have been using his alias to avoid official detection.[9] Indeed, he may have taken advantage of reports of his demise in 1879 to adopt this persona, for on 29 August 1879, the *Arizona Citizen* reported that Streeter had been killed in Janos in a 'duel' with a 'Spanish Officer'. The paper made explicit comment on Streeter's alleged raiding activity with the Apaches.[10]

Three days after crossing the border, Crawford and his companions reached Laguna de Santa Maria.[11] From there, they made their way eastwards to the Candelaria Mountains, following a trail left by Victorio. One very significant detail garnered by Crawford during his two-day journey to the Candelarias concerned the Apaches' lack of ammunition.[12] Crawford and his fellow envoys apparently got to within sight of Victorio's camp in the Candelaria Mountains when, with apparently no explanation, Navajo Charlie refused to go on. Crawford attempted to persuade, and then coerce, his Apache guide, but to no avail. He considered entering Victorio's encampment, but as he later explained, as Victorio's warriors could not speak English and he had no Apache, he was forced to withdraw.[13]

9 Thrapp, 1974, p.372, Note 6.
10 *Arizona Citizen*, 29 August, 1879 in Library of Congress 'Chronicling America' website <http://chroniclingamerica.loc.gov/> (accessed 13/09/2018).
11 The Laguna de Santa Maria was estimated as being thirty miles south of border (Price to Benjamin AAG Prescott 9 Jan., 1881 NA, RG393, Part 1, Entry 181 p.2). On modern maps the Laguna would appear to be approximately eighty kilometres south of Columbus or seventy-five kilometres from the international line. See NH 13-1 – El Paso (USGS) & H13-1-Cuidad Juarez (INEGI). This translates into a distance of approximately forty five miles.
12 'The Pursuit of Victorio' By Captain Jack Crawford Socorro County Historical Society, Publications in History, Volume 1, Feb., 1965; See also Thrapp, 1974, p.291.
13 'The Pursuit of Victorio' By Captain Jack Crawford Socorro County Historical Society, Publications in History, Volume 1, Feb., 1965; Thrapp, 1974, p.292.

This story beggars belief. Both sides could have conversed easily in Spanish, with the 'fearless' Casimero translating. Both Thrapp and Kaywaykla make it quite clear that Victorio himself could speak Spanish.[14] It is far more likely that, by the time they had closed to within a mile of Victorio's camp, Navajo Charlie had picked up a message the nuances of which suggested that a diplomatic overture would be unwelcome. The small party beat a hasty retreat.

Crawford, realising that he had at least located Victorio, returned to El Paso and informed General Buell about the location and condition of the Apaches. In response, Buell instructed Crawford to meet his command at Palomas Lake and guide them to the camp in the Candelaria Mountains.[15]

There is a major obstacle to giving credence to the thrust of Crawford's version of events. As we have already seen, Buell and his superiors had been quietly negotiating with the Mexican authorities to move Buell's forces into Mexico, with the intention of defeating Victorio in the field. If Crawford's peace mission really did take place, it would have undermined the detailed preparations for this expedition, and it would have been seen as a momentous breach of faith by Buell's Mexican allies. The Mexican authorities had no faith in the US's reservation system and, as far as they were concerned, if Victorio returned to any reservation, this would merely store up trouble for the future.

One strongly suspects that Captain Jack had been ordered on a dangerous scouting mission so that he could monitor Victorio's movements, rather than directly contact the Apache leader. This would fit with Buell's use of non-Apache scouts to spy below the Mexican border prior to his expedition. If one compares Crawford's report of a skirmish he and two companions had with a small party of Apaches in the San Mateo Mountains, January 1881 (document file no. 149)[16] with his account of his trip into Mexico, the latter comes across as contrived, playing to a wider audience, rather than offering a clear military report. It is clear that Hatch was willing to make some effort to contact Victorio during June and July of 1880. Crawford makes it quite clear that Hatch had ordered him to leave Fort Craig[17] and to scout south from the Mescalero reservation to garner intelligence of any Mescalero Apaches operating in the Sacramento Mountains. He was then to report to Colonel Buell at Fort Cummings. The one piece of information concerning Crawford's role from a US army source does not mention a diplomatic mission, but reports that Hatch had 'directed Crawford to at once go and scout the country desired by you'.[18] Once again, Hatch seems to have swung back to a policy of unconditional surrender where Victorio was concerned: 'No terms can be made with Victorio, and none should be.'[19]

Meanwhile, north of the border, during August and September 1880, Colonel Buell continued to assemble a large expedition based at Fort Cummings and Knight's Ranch.[20] While the US army's attention was focused on operations against Victorio in western Texas in July and August, the situation in New Mexico remained quiet. Early in September, Buell received word that Victorio was based 15 miles south of the Laguna de Santa Maria.[21] On 28 August, eight Apaches ran off

14 Thrapp, 1974, p.xii; Ball, 1970, p. 53.
15 'The Pursuit of Victorio' By Captain Jack Crawford Socorro County Historical Society, Publications in History, Volume 1, Feb., 1965.
16 See 'With My Face To My Foes': Nana's War 1880-1881, forthcoming 2019.
17 Corporal Bode confirms Crawford's presence at Fort Craig around this time. (Smith, 1994, p.147).
18 Hatch to Buell, 12 Aug., 1880, Telegrams Sent DoNM, Vol.3, Jan. – Nov. 1880 NA, RG393, Part 3, Entry 431, p.727.
19 Hatch to AAG DoM, 11 Sept., 1880 in 'Victorio Papers', NA, M666, Roll 528.
20 See Special Orders for late July and August 1880 cited earlier, NA, RG393 Part 3, Entry 450; Thrapp, 1974, p.292.
21 Buell to AAAG SF 4 Sept., 1880, NA, RG393, Part 3, Entry 439, p.793.

200 horses belonging to Dr Samaniego from within five miles of El Paso del Norte.[22] The raiders drove the horses to the east before turning south and eventually turning to the west, towards the Laguna de Guzman.[23] Of course, there were the usual false alarms: 12 Apaches were seen within five miles of El Paso on the evening of 1 September, prompting Captain Brinkerhoff to alert District Headquarters, only to have to rescind his warning the following day. It turned out to be a group of armed Mexican ranchmen instead of Apaches.[24] In mid-September, an attack on the Cosette Mine turned out to be no more than shots fired at a crow by one of the miners.[25]

Despite having had almost three months to recover from the effects of their campaigns against Victorio, between January and early June, the Ninth Cavalry Regiment was still chronically short of horses.

Table 14.1 Ninth Cavalry, Roster of Horses, June–August 1880.[26]

	Serviceable Horses	Unserviceable Horses	Horses Lost in Action, Died, etc.
June 1880	237	282	10
July 1880	271	242	9
August 1880	323	170	8

As a whole, the number of unserviceable horses had dropped considerably; but by the end of August, the regiment still had 170 unserviceable horses. If we examine each company in the regiment, the ratio of serviceable horses to available cavalrymen had generally improved; but Table 14.2, based on figures from the regimental monthly returns, shows that a significant number of men were left without mounts. Therefore, despite having had almost three months to recover, most companies in the regiment were struggling to find serviceable mounts for between one third and one half of the available men.

Table 14.2 Serviceable, Unserviceable and Lost Horses to Available Men, Ninth Cavalry, June–August 1880.[27]

Company	Month	Serviceable Horses	Unserviceable Horses	Lost Horses	Available Men
A	June	18	17	0	44
	July	14	22	0	47
	August	20	16	0	42
B	June	24	20	1	52
	July	26	17	1	55
	August	29	11	3	50

22 Olguin to Brinkerhoff, 29 Aug., 1880 in 'Victorio Papers', NA, M666, Roll 528; Grierson to AAG, DoTx, San Antonio, 2 Sept., 1880, 'Victorio Files', NA, RG393, M1495, Roll 14.

23 Brinkerhoff to Grierson, 29 Aug., 1880 in Telegrams Rec'd by General Grierson in the Field 30 Jun.-14 Sept., 1880, HQ Records DoP 1878-1881, NA, RG393, M1381, Roll 4.

24 Brinkerhoff to AAAG SF 1 & 2 Sept., 1880?, NA, RG393, Part 3, Entry 439, p.810.

25 The *Grant County Herald*, 18 Sept., 1880.

26 Derived from Returns From Regular Army Cavalry Regiments 1833-1916, 9th Cavalry 1873-1880, NA, M744, Roll 88

27 Derived from Returns From Regular Army Cavalry Regiments 1833-1916, 9th Cavalry 1873-1880, NA, M744, Roll 88

Company	Month	Serviceable Horses	Unserviceable Horses	Lost Horses	Available Men
C	June	19	19	0	50
	July	28	10	0	43
	August	29	9	0	44
D	June	16	23	0	49
	July	16	23	0	46
	August	26	5	0	51
E	June	0	36	1	54
	July	1	27	8	55
	August	16	12	0	51
F	June	12	20	0	45
	July	16	16	0	41
	August	14	12	3	42
G	June	30	17	3	65
	July	19	30	0	61
	August	39	8	0	57
H	June	18	29	1	53
	July	22	36	0	60
	August	25	31	2	49
I	June	23	22	0	55
	July	23	22	0	57
	August	23	22	0	57
K	June	9	45	1	61
	July	45	9	0	58
	August	30	24	0	55
L	June	21	17	1	63
	July	29	19	0	61
	August	25	14	0	57
M	June	33	17	2	64
	July	39	11	0	63
	August	33	6	0	66

The bi-monthly company returns reveal a similar picture, as shown in Table 14.3. Therefore, if Buell set his command in motion, the companies from the Ninth Cavalry would be would be much reduced in strength. Buell had complained that his overall command had fallen 'several hundred'[28] short of its paper establishment. It was not the lack of manpower which was to blame for this shortfall; it was the lack of serviceable horses.

28 Buell, HQ, Fort Stanton N.M., to AAG, DoM (via AAAG DoNM), 20 Nov., 1880 in Letters Received by HQ DoNM Sept. 1865-Aug. 1890, NA, RG393, M1088, Roll 42, File 658-1658, Jan.-Apr. 1881; An almost illegible portion of this report is contained in 'Victorio Papers', NA, M666, Roll 528.

Table 14.3 Available Men to Serviceable Horses, Ninth Cavalry, May–August 1880.[29]

Company	Available Men May–June 1880	Serviceable Horses May–June 1880	Available Men July–August 1880	Serviceable Horses July–August 1880
A	47	18	45	20
B	46	24	49	29
C	46	19	39	2? Entry indecipherable
D	49	No Entry	51	17
E	50	1	45	16
F	44	12	37	16
G	63	30	51	39
H	48	28	40	25
I	55	23	54	19
K	61	9	52	30
L	Missing from Archive	Missing from Archive	48	25
M	62	33	65	33

According to Buell, the Ninth Cavalry battalion which accompanied his expedition consisted of B, C, D, F, K, and L companies. If Buell had commenced his operation at the beginning of September, this battalion would have been able to field a maximum of either 153 or 146 mounted Ninth Cavalrymen.

14.4 Comparison of Monthly and Bi-monthly Returns of Cavalrymen Available for Field Service within Buell's Ninth Cavalry Battalion.[30]

Company	Monthly Regimental Return		Bi-monthly Company Return	
	Serviceable Horses	Available Men	Serviceable Horses	Available Men
B	29	50	29	49
C	29	44	2? Entry indecipherable (assume 29)	39
D	26	51	17	51
F	14	42	16	37
K	30	55	30	52
L	25	57	25	48
Totals	153	299	146	276

In other words, by the beginning of September, Buell's Ninth Cavalry battalion could, depending on which set of returns one examines, mount between 51 percent and 53 percent of the available men. Yet on 4 September 1880, in response to the news of renewed raiding by Apaches in Mexico, the War Department informed the State Department that the troops in New Mexico were, 'in

29 Derived Bi-Monthly Company Muster Rolls for May/Jun. &Jul./Aug. 1880, 9th Cavalry in NA, RG94
30 Derived from Returns From Regular Army Cavalry Regiments 1833-1916, 9th Cavalry 1873-1880, NA, M744, Roll 88; Bi-Monthly Company Muster Rolls for May/Jun. &Jul./Aug. 1880, 9th Cavalry in NA, RG94

good condition, well posted, and in sufficient force to deal with them if they cross to this side of the line'.[31] Three days prior to this announcement, Apache guerrillas had mauled a Ninth Cavalry detachment in the Sacramento Mountains.

Agua Chiquita Canyon, 1 September 1880

Sergeant James Robinson, G Company, Ninth Cavalry, with 10 soldiers,[32] was attacked in Agua Chiquita Canyon[33] in the Sacramento Mountains on 1 September 1880.[34] This detachment had been stationed at a point known as 'Little Water' since a local ranch belonging to 'Messrs Dewlin and Co. of Fort Stanton' had lost 53 cattle to Apaches in mid-August.[35] The Apaches had suddenly opened fire from the cover of the thick woods surrounding the ranch building at between 10:00 and 11:00 a.m. on 1 September, and Robinson estimated that there were between 25 and 30[36] heavily armed Apaches. The purpose of the attack was for the Apaches to pin the Ninth Cavalrymen in the building, whilst one of their number tried to drive off four mules belonging to the detachment's supply wagon. These had been turned out to graze. When the intent of the attack was divined, Robinson led his men in a charge which drove off the Apaches. While this prevented the Apaches from stealing the mules, all four mules were hit in the engagement and three died from their wounds during the night. Robinson also lost Privates Daniel Stanton and Robert Smith, who died of their wounds early the following morning.[37] (See document file no. 111.)

In the aftermath of the attack, Sergeant Robinson sent Private Alonzo Drake to carry news of the attack to the military detachment based at South Fork, on the one surviving mule which, though wounded, was fit enough to travel the 70 miles in 21 hours. During his journey, Drake was refused the loan of a saddle for the mule by a rancher called Martin, whose ranch was situated on the Rio Penasco.[38] Both Sergeant Robinson and Private Drake were later cited for gallantry by Colonel Hatch.[39]

31 Chief Clerk to the Secretary of War (in his absence) to the Secretary of State, 4 Sept., 1880 in 'Victorio Papers', NA, M666, Roll 528.

32 Nine privates from the Ninth Cavalry, plus a single infantryman from Company C, Fifteenth Infantry.

33 Baylor mentions a small spring named the 'Aqua Chiquita' in the Sacramento Mountains. (Baylor, 1996, p.341).

34 March? Major 9th Cavalry to AAAG Dist New Mexico undated, NA, RG393, Part 3, Entry 439, p.409; Schubert, 1995, R Smith & D Stanton entries; Billington, 1991, p.97;see also web article The Ninth Regiment of Cavalry by Lt G. Hutcheson.

35 Russell to the CoIA, 6 Sept., 1880 in 'Victorio Papers', NA, M666, Roll 528.

36 On receipt of this News, Col. Grierson suggested that this might be the same party that had evaded Lebo by abandoning their supplies in the Sierra Diablo and attacked Kennedy in the Guadalupe Mountains on the 3/4 Aug., 1880. (Beck to Kennedy, 11 Sept., 1880 in Letters Sent 23 Aug.-31 Dec., 1880, HQ Records DoP 1878-1881, NA, RG393, M1381, Roll 1, Letter No.156).

37 Cusack to Adjutant, 9th Cavalry, SF, 15 Sept., 1880 in Letters Received by HQ DoNM Sept. 1865-Aug. 1890, NA, RG393, M1088, Roll 41, Jul.-Dec. 1880; See also Buell to AAAG DoNM SF 14 Dec., 1880, NA, RG393, Part 3, Entry 439, p.53; Pope to AG of the Army, Washington D.C. 10 Sept., 1880, NA, RG393, Part 1, Entry 2539, Pope to AG of the Army, Wash. D.C. 10 Sept., 1880 in 'Victorio Papers', NA, M666, Roll 528; Press Copies of Letters and Endorsements Sent, MDoM, Vol. 13, pp.580-581; See also collection of telegrams from Hatch to Platt AAG 7 and 8 Sept., 1880, in 'Victorio Files' NA, RG393, M1495, Roll 14; Chronological List, p.51; Webb, 1976, p.90.

38 Cusack to Adjutant, 9th Cavalry, SF, 15 Sept., 1880 in Letters Received by HQ DoNM Sept. 1865-Aug. 1890, NA, RG393, M1088, Roll 41, Jul.-Dec. 1880; See also Billington, 1991, p.98.

On the 11 December, Buell telegraphed HQ in SF that four Mescalero Apaches being held at Ft Stanton were members of the party who ambushed Robinson's detachment. 'I hope the Dist. Comdr will succeed in getting them sent to Leavenworth prison' (NA, RG393, Part 3, Entry 439, p.53).

39 Hatch, General Order No. 9, 7 Oct., 1880, General Orders, Circulars and Court Martial Orders 1870-1881, NA, RG393, Part 1, Entry 183; See also General Orders No.9, 7 Oct., 1880, Printed Special

This attack heralded a flurry of attacks near the Mescalero agency. On 2 September, five Apaches accosted the agency herd and eventually took two horses, a revolver and a rifle, plus clothing and blankets, from the herders. The culprits were known to the herders as Mescaleros who had left the reservation in March and had been assumed to have joined Victorio. They were described by Russell as, 'among the worst Indians belonging to the Mescalero tribe'.[40] These Apaches appeared above the agency on the following day and offered to exchange their loot for their families, who were held at the agency. They threatened that if this was not done, they would open fire on the camp to force those Mescaleros held prisoner to scatter or be killed. Later that day, less than three miles from the agency, a boy was robbed of his horse and clothes. On 4 September, Russell reported two further attacks. In the first, close to the agency, two Americans were ambushed and one was killed. The second occurred 30 miles to the west, with four men reported as being killed.[41] It was later stated that Francisco Baca, Secundino Dominguez, Manuel Teal and Ramon Aguilar were killed near La Luz on 4 September 1880.[42] Russell stated that this activity had, not surprisingly, paralysed herding and hay-cutting duties on the reservation. He also stated that the decision to hold the Mescalero prisoners at the agency, with its military guard, had discouraged this raiding party from doing much wider damage in the area[43]. Hatch thought that these attacks demonstrated that some Apaches had penetrated Grierson's picket lines in western Texas.[44]

The *Army & Navy Journal* also records the narrow escape of a Tenth Cavalry enlisted man from a small party of seven Apache warriors in the vicinity of Eagle Springs. This man had belonged to a small party who had spotted some loose horses, and he had become separated from the rest of the party. Suddenly he encountered six dismounted Apaches and a seventh Apache mounted on a mule. The trooper lost his horse but managed to outrun his pursuers. The Apache camp was later found, hurriedly abandoned, but equipment lost by 'one of the men in the main fight with Victorio' and some clothing belonging to a stage driver killed 'some time since' was recovered. The Apaches were trailed to the Rio Grande near Ojo Caliente, Texas.[45]

The Mescalero prisoners of war were not released until 12 September 1880.[46] Earlier attempts to have the prisoners released were vigorously opposed by General Pope, despite the efforts of the Department of the Interior.[47] The US army still believed that most of the Mescalero warriors were off the reservation. Yet it was clear that District Headquarters still thought that many were, as yet, acting independently of Victorio's following. To dissuade them from joining the Chihenne chief,

---

Orders 1869-1888, DoNM, NA, RG393, Part 3, Entry 446.

40 Russell to the CoIA, 6 Sept., 1880 in 'Victorio Papers', NA, M666, Roll 528.

41 Russell to the CoIA, 6 Sept., 1880 in 'Victorio Papers', NA, M666, Roll 528; See also 'Town and County', the *Grant County Herald*, 18 Sept., 1880.

A miner named Gordon was killed at his mine. The Apaches attacked and were repulsed at Wilson's Ranch. John Walters ranch was attacked. Walters lost one horse killed and another stolen. Finally, Rafael Andres Romero was stopped by the Apaches who demanded his horses. Romero, speaking Apache, dissuaded them but was warned to vacate the area. ('Town and County', the *Grant County Herald*, 18 Sept., 1880; See also 'Outrages by Victorio's Indians', *The New York Times*, 10 Sept., 1880).

42 Delegation of Citizens of Dona Ana County, La Luz, to Hatch, 11 Sept., 1880 in Letters Received by HQ DoNM Sept. 1865-Aug. 1890, NA, RG393, M1088, Roll 41, Jul.-Dec. 1880.

43 Russell to the CoIA, 6 Sept., 1880 in 'Victorio Papers', NA, M666, Roll 528.

44 Brinkerhoff to Grierson, 18 Sept., 1880 in Register of Telegrams Rec'd 11 Oct., 1879-8 Oct., 1880, HQ Records DoP 1878-1881, NA, RG393, M1381, Roll 2, p219., Letter No.387.

45 'Indian Affairs', *Army & Navy Journal*, Vol. 18, 2 Oct., 1880, p.169.

46 Letter dated Fort Stanton, 12 Jul., 1880, in The Walter Lowry Finley Collection.

47 Pope to Whipple 19 Jul., 1880 in 'Victorio Papers', NA, M666, Roll 527; Schurz to the Secretary of War, 24 Jun., 1880 in Letters Received, DoM 1868-98, RG 393, Entry A1-1 2601, Box 91.

the Commanding Officer of Fort Stanton, Captain Conrad, was encouraged to offer an amnesty to these Mescaleros through the offices of the remaining Mescalero leaders.[48]

The attack in Agua Chiquita Canyon prompted demands that enough infantry be sent to the Mescalero agency to guard the Mescalero prisoners. This would free Captain Cusack's two Ninth Cavalry companies, allowing them to scour the surrounding mountain ranges for an estimated 20–50 Apaches held responsible for the attack.[49] Buell decided that he was not in a position to immediately redeploy troops in response to Apaches at large in the Sacramento Mountains; he was about to launch an offensive against Victorio in Chihuahua. He suggested that, while he did not 'presume to command' Cusack, the latter should call in some of his small detachments, thereby mustering an effective force with which to scout the Sacramento mountains.[50] However, by 23 September, even as Cusack's cavalry were preparing to scout the Sacramento and Guadalupe Mountains, Conrad noted that the recently released Mescaleros were very quiet and that no further raiding had been reported.[51]

Buell's Goodsight Mountains Expedition, 6–8 September, 1880 (see document file no. 112 & Map 14.1.)

On 6 September 1880, a stagecoach was ambushed 16 miles[52] to the west of Fort Cummings. The driver, Alexander Le Beau, and two passengers, E.S. Madden[53] and I. Roberts were killed.[54] Buell acknowledged that the Apaches involved had managed to slip across the border and had successfully evaded his scouting detachments.[55] It seems likely that they had bivouacked at the as-yet-undiscovered campsite in the Goodsight Mountains (see Chapter 1), which was close to the stage road running from La Mesilla to Fort Cummings.[56] Buell later claimed that his 'citizen scouts' had

48 Loud to CO Fort Stanton, 18 Aug., 1880 in Letters Sent by '9MD/DNM/DoNM', NA, RG393, M1072, Roll 6, Jan. 1880-Aug. 1881, Letter No.429, p.280.

49 March? Maj 9th Cavalry to AAAG undated, NA, RG393, Part 3, Entry 439, pp.409-410.

50 Buell to AAAG SF 18 Sept., 1880, NA, RG393, Part 3, Entry 439, pp.416-418.

51 Conrad to AAAG DoNM, 23 Sept., 1880 in Letters Received by HQ DoNM Sept. 1865-Aug. 1890, NA, RG393, M1088, Roll 41, Jul.-Dec. 1880.

52 Stout places the attack to early August but Thrapp states that the attack took place in early September. As they both cite a report by Col Hatch dated 10 September, the latter date is correct. (See Stout, p.159 & note 1, p.193; Thrapp, 1967, note 55, p.207; Thrapp, 1974, p.290) Another report states that the attack took place 38 miles from Fort Cummings. (NA, RG391, Entry 744, Miscellaneous Records 1880-1914 – Orders Letters 4th Cavalry – document titled 'Chronological List of Battles Engagements ETC. with Indians since April 30 1865').

53 This was the son of Captain D Madden Sixth Cavalry (Carr to AG, Presidio, San Francisco, 9 Sept., 1880, NA, RG393, Part 1, Entry 169, Vol. 10, p.399; Thrapp, 1967, p.207; Stout, p.159).

54 Buell to AAAG 7 Sept., 1880, NA, RG393, Part 3, Entry 439, p.820; See also collection of telegrams from Hatch to Platt AAG 7 and 8 Sept., 1880, in 'Victorio Files' NA, RG393, M1495, Roll 14; Hatch to AAG Fort Leavenworth, 8 Sept., 1880, Telegrams Sent DoNM, Vol.3, Jan. – Nov. 1880 NA, RG393, Part 3, Entry 431, pp.804-805; Kerr AAAG to Arnold, Fort Grant, 8 Sept., 1880, Troops in SE Arizona, DoAz, NA, RG393, Part 1, Entry 232, Vol.8, 6 Sept.-12 Dec., 1880, p.5.

55 Buell to AAAG 8 Sept., 1880, NA, RG393, Part 3, Entry 439, pp.817-819; Hatch to AAG Fort Leavenworth, 8 Sept., 1880, Telegrams Sent DoNM, Vol.3, Jan. – Nov. 1880 NA, RG393, Part 3, Entry 431, pp.804-805; Hatch to AAG Fort Leavenworth, 8 Sept., 1880, Telegrams Sent DoNM, Vol.3, Jan. – Nov. 1880 NA, RG393, Part 3, Entry 431, pp.804-805; See also collection of telegrams from Hatch to Platt AAG 7 and 8 Sept., 1880, in 'Victorio Files' NA, RG393, M1495, Roll 14.

56 Buell, HQ, Fort Stanton N.M., to AAG, DoM (via AAAG DoNM), 20 Nov., 1880 in Letters Received by HQ DoNM Sept. 1865-Aug. 1890, NA, RG393, M1088, Roll 42, File 658-1658, Jan.-Apr. 1881.

kept him well-informed of Victorio's movements in Mexico until 2 September, that is, just before this attack, when they lost track of Victorio for several days.[57]

The troops at Fort Cummings were quickly mobilised to pursue the raiders when alerted by a courier from Captain Hale, whose company of Sixteenth Infantrymen were escorting a railroad survey party and were camped approximately two miles west of the ambush. The infantrymen had discovered the remains of the stagecoach and two of its occupants at around 10:00 p.m.,[58] possibly alerted by the sound of gunfire. Between midnight and 12:30 a.m., two detachments of Fourth Cavalry left Fort Cummings in search of the Apaches. Captain Leopold Parker, with A Company, accompanied by 10 Apache scouts, was sent east to take up the trail from the site of the attack.[59] Major Noyes, with H Company, and also with 10 Apache scouts, was sent south to the Florida Mountains to intercept the Apaches should they be making for those mountains. Noyes was also ordered to look out for Lieutenants Maney and Goodwin and their Apache scout detachments and put them on the trail of the Apaches.[60]

Captain Parker's detachment reached Hales camp at about 3:00 a.m. and waited until daylight before proceeding to the ambush site. Here they found the body of the third occupant, and by 8:00 a.m. they had started on the trail of the Apache raiders. Parker's scouts had determined that 10 to 15 Apaches had come up from the south and, after ambushing and looting the stagecoach, had returned south[61].

However, Parker reported that his scouts appeared to be reluctant to pursue the trail, and several times overtook them and questioned them as to the number of Apaches they were pursuing.[62] Parker does not mention this in his report, but he may have been concerned that the scouts' questions and their reluctance to pursue the trail reflected a suspicion on their part that a stronger force of Apaches was present. However, the scouts reiterated their estimate.[63] The trail of the Apache raiders was periodically marked by scattered mail and fruit[64] taken from the stagecoach,[65] and, given subsequent events, one suspects that this was a deliberate ploy on the part of the Apaches to ensure that they were followed.

By around 11:00 a.m., Parker's command was starting to ascend a very gentle ridge between higher hills. He had stopped to consult with his scouts again when he received a volley from his left

57 Buell, HQ Fort Stanton N.M., to AAG, DoM (via AAAG DoNM), 20 Nov., 1880 in Letters Received by HQ DoNM Sept. 1865-Aug. 1890, NA, RG393, M1088, Roll 42, File 658-1658, Jan.-Apr. 1881.
One has to admit some scepticism concerning this claim as it conveniently coincides and thus attempts to excuse the failure to detect the one raid launched by Victorio into New Mexico between June and September, 1880.

58 Hale to AAG, New Mexico Column, 12 September, 1880 in Letters Received, Dept. of Missouri 1868-98, RG 393, Entry A1-1 2601, Box 94.

59 Parker to AAG, New Mexico Column, 9 September, 1880 in Letters Received, Dept. of Missouri 1868-98, RG 393, Entry A1-1 2601, Box 94.

60 Noyes to AAG, New Mexico Column, 13 September, 1880 in Letters Received, Dept. of Missouri 1868-98, RG 393, Entry A1-1 2601, Box 94; Buell, HQ Fort Stanton N.M., to AAG, DoM (via AAAG DoNM), 20 Nov., 1880 in Letters Received by HQ DoNM Sept. 1865-Aug. 1890, NA, RG393, M1088, Roll 42, File 658-1658, Jan.-Apr. 1881. For an overview of this mini-campaign see document files nos.112-115.

61 Parker to AAG, New Mexico Column, 9 September, 1880 in Letters Received, Dept. of Missouri 1868-98, RG 393, Entry A1-1 2601, Box 94.

62 Ibid.

63 Parker to AAG, New Mexico Column, 9 September, 1880 in Letters Received, Dept. of Missouri 1868-98, RG 393, Entry A1-1 2601, Box 94.

64 I have examined Dudley's report repeatedly and the only likely word I can decipher is 'fruit', so I can only conclude that the coach was carrying some fruit as part of its load.

65 Dudley to AAG, New Mexico Column, 9 September, 1880 in Letters Received, Dept. of Missouri 1868-98, RG 393, Entry A1-1 2601, Box 94.

and centre at a range of between 45-50 yards, immediately followed by a volley from his front and right from a large number of concealed Apache warriors.[66] One trooper, Private William Macfee, and two Apache scouts, were killed (which suggests that at least some of the Apache scouts had not hung back), and three other enlisted men – Farrier Peacock and Privates Aker[67] and Lorenz – were wounded in the opening moments of the ambush.[68] Lieutenant James Lockett, in his first action, was even closer to the Apaches. He had his horse wounded and received between three and four bullet holes through his coat, but was miraculously not hit by hostile fire.[69] One A Company horse was killed, and another was so badly wounded that it had to be shot. Lieutenant Budd also reported that a horse from his company had been killed in action on 7 September.[70] Parker himself noted one horse killed and several wounded, one of which later died. Two horses were also abandoned on the return journey to Fort Cummings.[71]

The Apaches had hidden themselves on a very gentle 'slope' in some dead ground below the crest of a very low ridge.[72] This innocuous looking terrain bisected Parker's line of advance and, as seen by the Fourth Cavalrymen, rose very gently from left to right, ending in a small hillock to Parker's right flank.[73] The slight rise and small hillock which created the dead ground concealing the Apache warriors blended into the ridge behind, by dint of being well-hidden by bushes and

66 Parker to AAG, New Mexico Column, 9 September, 1880 in Letters Received, Dept. of Missouri 1868-98, RG 393, Entry A1-1 2601, Box 94; Buell to AAAG 8 Sept., 1880, NA, RG393, Part 3, Entry 439, pp.817-819; Hatch to AAG Fort Leavenworth, 8 Sept., 1880, Telegrams Sent DoNM, Vol.3, Jan. – Nov. 1880 NA, RG393, Part 3, Entry 431, pp.804-805; See also collection of telegrams from Hatch to Platt AAG 7 and 8 Sept., 1880, in 'Victorio Files' NA, RG393, M1495, Roll 14; Carr to AG, Presidio, San Francisco, 9 Sept., 1880, NA, RG393, Part 1, Entry 169, Vol. 10, p.399; Pope to AG of the Army, Washington D.C. 10 Sept., 1880, NA, RG393, Part 1, Entry 2539, Pope to AG of the Army, Wash. D.C. 10 Sept., 1880 in 'Victorio Papers', NA, M666, Roll 528; Press Copies of Letters and Endorsements Sent, MDoM, Vol. 13, pp.579-580; Sheridan to Sherman 11 Sept., 1880, NA, RG393, Part 1, Entry 2539, Press Copies of Letters and Endorsements Sent, MDoM, Vol. 13, pp.586-587; 'Again', the *Grant County Herald*, 11 Sept., 1880; Thrapp, 1967, p.207; Thrapp, 1974, p.290; Stout, 1974, p.159; Carter, USACMH webpage; Smith, 1994, p.164.

67 The unfortunate William Aker received a bullet wound 'through fleshy part of thigh and scrotum.' (Bi-Monthly Company Muster Rolls for Co. A, 4th Cavalry, 31 Aug.-31 Oct., 1880 in NA, RG94).

68 Bi-Monthly Company Muster Rolls for Co. A, 4th Cavalry, 31 Aug.-31 Oct., 1880 in NA, RG94; See also Buell, HQ Fort Stanton N.M., to AAG, DoM (via AAAG DoNM), 20 Nov., 1880 in Letters Received by HQ DoNM Sept. 1865-Aug. 1890, NA, RG393, M1088, Roll 42, File 658-1658, Jan.-Apr. 1881; NA, RG391, Entry 734 Regimental Histories 1855-1926, 4th Cavalry; 4th Cavalry 1878-1883 Sept./Oct. 1880, Returns from Regular Army Cavalry Regiments 1833-1916, NA, RG393, NA, M744 Roll 43; See also Chronological List, p.51; NA, RG391, Entry 744, Miscellaneous Records 1880-1914 – Orders Letters 4th Cavalry – document titled 'Chronological List of Battles Engagements ETC. with Indians since April 30 1865'; Webb, 1976, p.90; Sheridan to Sherman 11 Sept., 1880, NA, RG393, Part 1, Entry 2539, Press Copies of Letters and Endorsements Sent, MDoM, Vol. 13, pp.586-587.

Out of an entire box file relating to the Fourth Cavalry in NA, RG391, Entry 734 Regimental Histories 1855-1926, there are four versions of the regiments record of engagements with Indians. Only one mentions this skirmish in 1880.

69 Parker to AAG, New Mexico Column, 9 September, 1880 in Letters Received, Dept. of Missouri 1868-98, RG 393, Entry A1-1 2601, Box 94.

70 4th Cavalry 1878-1883 Sept./Oct. 1880, Returns from Regular Army Cavalry Regiments 1833-1916, NA, RG393, NA, M744, Roll 43.

71 Parker to AAG, New Mexico Column, 9 September, 1880 in Letters Received, Dept. of Missouri 1868-98, RG 393, Entry A1-1 2601, Box 94.

72 Hale to AAG, New Mexico Column, 12 September, 1880 in Letters Received, Dept. of Missouri 1868-98, RG 393, Entry A1-1 2601, Box 94.

73 Personal observation of the terrain by the author 9 July, 2014.

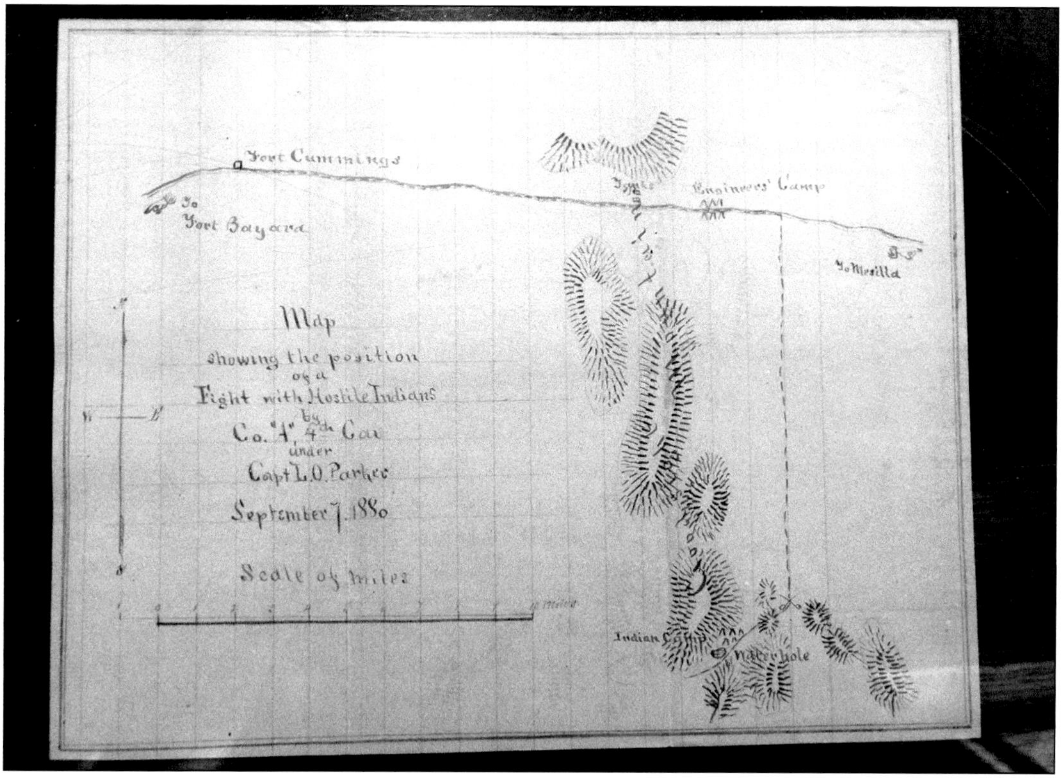

Plate 14.1. Photo of map accompanying Buell's Report.

soapweeds.[74] Buell reported that the Apaches had constructed small breastworks,[75] but there were no sign of these in 2014. What were present were several lines of natural rock formations which jutted out of the earth along the crest of the small hillock, and which provided perfect hard cover for the concealed Apache warriors.[76]

Confusion reigned, and the surviving Apache scouts retreated (or in Parker's words 'disappeared', along with their interpreter and mule packer) and took no further part in the battle. Parker rallied his company after a retreat of about 150 yards. After organising horse holders, he had about 30 soldiers available and deployed them in a skirmish line. Each man was ten yards apart, so the skirmish line was approximately 300 yards wide. The line advanced, and as they came within easy range, the Apaches opened up a heavy fire. Parker noted that the Apaches were still flanking him on both sides, which indicated a force considerably larger than the 10 to 15 Apaches whose trail they were following. Parker fell back and re-aligned his skirmish line to the right, in order to attack the slightly higher ground; but again he found the Apaches to be flanking him on both sides, and in no mood to vacate their positions. Moreover, he and one of his sergeants realised that some of the Apache warriors were using adjacent arroyos in an effort not only to surround his skirmish line

---

74 Personal observation of the terrain by the author 9 July, 2014., See also Hale to AAG, New Mexico Column, 12 September, 1880 in Letters Received, Dept. of Missouri 1868-98, RG 393, Entry A1-1 2601, Box 94.

75 : Buell, HQ Fort Stanton N.M., to AAG, DoM (via AAAG DoNM), 20 Nov., 1880 in Letters Received by HQ DoNM Sept. 1865-Aug. 1890, NA, RG393, M1088, Roll 42, File 658-1658, Jan.-Apr. 1881.

76 Personal observation of the terrain by the author 9 July, 2014.

but to threaten his horse-holders, who had been sent to the rear with the company's horses. Parker withdrew and regrouped again, making a final advance with his skirmish line. Finding that the Apaches were still willing to hold their positions to his front, and were simultaneously making efforts to move around the skirmish line, Parker withdrew his horses and men to a ridge a mile and a half distant.[77]

Despite the heavy fire, most of the serious casualties, human and equine, appear to have been sustained in the opening volleys from the Apaches.[78] Parker himself estimated that his lack of casualties sustained during the engagement was due to poor marksmanship by the Apaches. He also thought it had helped that, when not attempting to advance his skirmish line, he had ordered his men to lie down in the tall grass which grew at the bottom of the slope.[79] (See Map 14.2.)

Parker sent a courier to Captain Hale's detachment requesting his support.[80] It is not clear from the reports, but it would appear that this same courier brought the news which was telegraphed to Fort Cummings requesting their assistance.[81] Almost as soon as he had dispatched the courier, however, the captain had second thoughts, having spotted a number of mounted Apaches to the west moving northwards towards Hale's predicted line-of-march. Parker became concerned that he was facing a much larger force of Apache warriors than he had first anticipated, and that by calling for Hale's aid, he might have put the latter in considerable danger. His surviving Apache scouts had by this time re-appeared and were adamant that Parker was confronted by 'Victorio's whole outfit'.[82] Parker therefore withdrew about eight miles, until he joined Hale's detachment, and, shortly after that meeting, a courier from Buell and the first reinforcements from Fort Cummings joined them.[83]

In response to the message from Parker, which had been received at Fort Cummings at around 1:30 p.m., Lieutenant Colonel Dudley had set out with a battalion drawn from the Ninth Cavalry, and these troops had taken with them a mountain howitzer, a Gatling gun and a water wagon. This force left to join Parker at about 2:15 p.m. About half an hour later, Buell had mounted some of his infantry in wagons to take up the pursuit.[84] Buell had also sent a courier to Parker:

---

77 Parker to AAG, New Mexico Column, 9 September, 1880 in Letters Received, Dept. of Missouri 1868-98, RG 393, Entry A1-1 2601, Box 94; See also Buell, HQ Fort Stanton N.M., to AAG, DoM (via AAAG DoNM), 20 Nov., 1880 in Letters Received by HQ DoNM Sept. 1865-Aug. 1890, NA, RG393, M1088, Roll 42, File 658-1658, Jan.-Apr. 1881.

78 Buell to AAAG Santa Fe, 10 September, 1880 in Letters Received, Dept. of Missouri 1868-98, RG 393, Entry A1-1 2601, Box 94.

79 Parker to AAG, New Mexico Column, 9 September, 1880 in Letters Received, Dept. of Missouri 1868-98, RG 393, Entry A1-1 2601, Box 94.

80 Parker to AAG, New Mexico Column, 9 September, 1880 & Hale to AAG, New Mexico Column, 12 September, 1880 in Letters Received, Dept. of Missouri 1868-98, RG 393, Entry A1-1 2601, Box 94.

81 Parker to Buell, 1:35 p.m., 7 September, 1880. in Letters Received, Dept. of Missouri 1868-98, RG 393, Entry A1-1 2601, Box 94.

82 Ibid.

83 Parker to AAG, New Mexico Column, 9 September, 1880 & Hale to AAG, New Mexico Column, 12 September, 1880 in Letters Received, Dept. of Missouri 1868-98, RG 393, Entry A1-1 2601, Box 94; Buell, HQ Fort Stanton N.M., to AAG, DoM (via AAAG DoNM), 20 Nov., 1880 in Letters Received by HQ DoNM Sept. 1865-Aug. 1890, NA, RG393, M1088, Roll 42, File 658-1658, Jan.-Apr. 1881.

84 Buell, HQ Fort Stanton N.M., to AAG, DoM (via AAAG DoNM), 20 Nov., 1880 in Letters Received by HQ DoNM Sept. 1865-Aug. 1890, NA, RG393, M1088, Roll 42, File 658-1658, Jan.-Apr. 1881; See also Buell to AAAG 7 Sept., 1880, NA, RG393, Part 3, Entry 439, p.820; Hatch to AAG Fort Leavenworth, 8 Sept., 1880, Telegrams Sent DoNM, Vol.3, Jan. – Nov. 1880 NA, RG393, Part 3, Entry 431, pp.803-804; Collection of telegrams from Hatch to Platt AAG 7 and 8 Sept., 1880, in 'Victorio Files' NA, RG393, M1495, Roll 14; Hatch to AAG Fort Leavenworth, 7 & 8 Sept., 1880, Telegrams Sent DoNM, Vol.3, Jan. – Nov. 1880 NA, RG393, Part 3, Entry 431, pp.801-802 & pp.803-804.

Plate 14.2. Approaching the ambush site from Parker's perspective. One cannot see the cover used by the Apaches until one is almost within easy range. On the right horizon is the low rocky hill with the natural rock breastworks. (Photo: Author)

Plate 14.3. Opposite view, from behind the Apache position hidden on the low hill to the left down along a low hogback which provided excellent cover for the Apache warriors. (Photo: Author)

Plates 14.4 and 14.5. Two views of the natural breastworks utilised by the Apache warriors. (Photos: Author)

> Hold your enemy in check by retreating slowly if you can not cope with him in same ground.
> I come with whole command. Dudley far in advance with 9th Batt. Have sent courier to Noyes to come to you.[85]

Unfortunately, Parker had already retreated and joined Hale's command before this message reached him.

Lieutenant Colonel Dudley's battalion had managed to cover the 16 miles from Fort Cummings to, as far as he was concerned, an unexpected rendezvous with Parker's company, in about one and three-quarter hours. Given that this haste was prompted by the need to relieve Parker from a difficult predicament, a less than amused Dudley gathered up Parker's command and set out in pursuit of the Apaches.[86] On arriving at the site of the attack, Dudley sent out detachments to scour the ground for signs, and it was quickly noted that the Apaches had scattered. From the top of the ridge, which formed part of the southern face of the Goodsight escarpment,[87] Dudley could see a large dust cloud which he estimated was 15 miles away and only about five miles short of the Mexican border, which it was moving towards with all possible speed.[88] As we shall see below, at least some of these Apaches travelled south-east and moved through the West Potrillo Mountains and on to the East Potrillos before moving into Mexico. The scattered trails discovered around Dudley's immediate position re-converged at a camp a short distance away. This was located down a steep ravine leading out of the Goodsight Mountains, and which had a good water supply. It was estimated that the Apaches had been encamped there for two to three days. Realising they had not thrown off their enemies, the Apaches had had sufficient time to poison the waterhole at this camp with horses' entrails before they moved on towards Mexico. Dudley's cavalry camped two miles beyond this point on the evening of 7 September, having lost the trail in the darkness shortly after emerging from the Goodsight Mountains.[89]

Buell's infantry battalion followed the cavalry, at some point dismounting from their wagons and marching south through the night. This was in anticipation of helping Dudley, whom Buell hoped had surrounded the Apaches, to destroy the latter in the morning. They reached the camp recently abandoned by the fleeing Apaches, but could go no further and chose to bivouac at that point. This was estimated to have been 30 miles to the south-east of Fort Cummings.[90] Buell concluded that, without the presence of a mule train to carry food and water in casks, there was nothing to be

85 Buell to Parker, 7 September, 1880 in Letters Received, Dept. of Missouri 1868-98, RG 393, Entry A1-1 2601, Box 94.

86 Dudley to AAG, New Mexico Column, 9 September, 1880 in Letters Received, Dept. of Missouri 1868-98, RG 393, Entry A1-1 2601, Box 94.

87 The Goodsight Mountains seen from the east and north appear as a low range of hills. Yet from the west and south they present themselves as a much higher range of small mountains. Thus a traveller reaching the Goodsight Mountains from the south and west has a tough climb to reach the top of the range. However, the descent on the other side is an easy and short walk down to the level ground on the other side of the mountains. Thus the Goodsight Mountains define the edge of an escarpment where the level ground on each side of the range is significantly different in height to each other.

88 Dudley to AAG, New Mexico Column, 9 September, 1880 & Buell to AAAG Dist. of New Mexico, 10 September, 1880 in Letters Received, Dept. of Missouri 1868-98, RG 393, Entry A1-1 2601, Box 94.

89 Dudley to AAG, New Mexico Column, 9 September, 1880 in Letters Received, Dept. of Missouri 1868-98, RG 393, Entry A1-1 2601, Box 94; Buell, HQ Fort Stanton N.M., to AAG, DoM (via AAAG DoNM), 20 Nov., 1880 in Letters Received by HQ DoNM Sept. 1865-Aug. 1890, NA, RG393, M1088, Roll 42, File 658-1658, Jan.-Apr. 1881.

90 Buell to AAAG Dist. of New Mexico, 10 September, 1880 in Letters Received, Dept. of Missouri 1868-98, RG 393, Entry A1-1 2601, Box 94; See also Dudley to AAG, New Mexico Column, 9 September, 1880 in Letters Received, Dept. of Missouri 1868-98, RG 393, Entry A1-1 2601, Box 94.
Looking at the map on the following page thirty miles is a good estimate and it also places the camp very close to the place where Parker was first ambushed.

gained by following these Apaches into Mexico.[91] He also thought that this raid might have been a diversion to draw the troops away from another, more serious, incursion, and he moved his men back to Fort Cummings on the morning of 8 September.[92] On the march back to Fort Cummings, the force was joined by Major Noyes, whose detachment, finding no trace of Apaches and insufficient water in those mountains, had been contacted by a courier from Buell as they returned to the Little Floridas to water their horses.[93] Noyes was instructed by Buell's courier to march towards the engineer survey camp, and had already marched eastwards during the night when he spotted the dust cloud made by Dudley's cavalry as the latter turned for Fort Cummings.[94]

Buell thought that very little damage had been sustained by the Apaches: 'Do not think enemy recd more damage than loss of property by hasty flight.'[95] The three men killed were hurriedly buried. When a detachment of Ninth Cavalry scouting from Fort Cummings passed the graves on 29 November 1880, they found that coyotes had managed to dig up the bodies and had partially eaten them. The detachment reburied the remains of Private MacFee but 'did not have the time to inter the bodies of the two Yuma Indian Scouts'.[96]

Dudley subsequently lobbied Buell to court martial Parker for retreating several miles to the rear in the face of the enemy.[97] This demand was also reinforced by Dudley's outrage at discovering, on first encountering the Fourth Cavalry company, that Parker had withdrawn without recovering the bodies of the three slain men.[98] (See document file nos. 112.3 and 115.1.) Buell was also critical of Parker, and he thought that the Captain had made an error of judgement in advancing with only two flankers, one posted on either side of the front of his detachment. Buell also thought that Parker had clearly erred in retreating approximately eight miles after extricating himself from his immediate predicament. However, he was more inclined to blame Parker's Apache scouts, judging

91 Buell to AAAG 8 Sept., 1880, NA, RG393, Part 3, Entry 439, pp.817-819; Hatch to AAG Fort Leavenworth, 8 Sept., 1880, Telegrams Sent DoNM, Vol.3, Jan. – Nov. 1880 NA, RG393, Part 3, Entry 431, pp.804-805; Dudley to AAG, New Mexico Column, 9 September, 1880 in Letters Received, Dept. of Missouri 1868-98, RG 393, Entry A1-1 2601, Box 94; See also collection of telegrams from Hatch to Platt AAG 7 and 8 Sept., 1880, in 'Victorio Files' NA, RG393, M1495, Roll 14.

92 Buell, HQ Fort Stanton N.M., to AAG, DoM (via AAAG DoNM), 20 Nov., 1880 in Letters Received by HQ DoNM Sept. 1865-Aug. 1890, NA, RG393, M1088, Roll 42, File 658-1658, Jan.-Apr. 1881.

93 Noyes to AAG, New Mexico Column, 13 September, 1880 in Letters Received, Dept. of Missouri 1868-98, RG 393, Entry A1-1 2601, Box 94.

94 Noyes to AAG, New Mexico Column, 13 September, 1880 in Letters Received, Dept. of Missouri 1868-98, RG 393, Entry A1-1 2601, Box 94; Buell, HQ Fort Stanton N.M., to AAG, DoM (via AAAG DoNM), 20 Nov., 1880 in Letters Received by HQ DoNM Sept. 1865-Aug. 1890, NA, RG393, M1088, Roll 42, File 658-1658, Jan.-Apr. 1881.

95 Buell to AAAG 8 Sept., 1880, NA, RG393, Part 3, Entry 439, pp.817-819; Hatch to AAG Fort Leavenworth, 8 Sept., 1880, Telegrams Sent DoNM, Vol.3, Jan. – Nov. 1880 NA, RG393, Part 3, Entry 431, pp.804-805; See also collection of telegrams from Hatch to Platt AAG 7 and 8 Sept., 1880, in 'Victorio Files' NA, RG393, M1495, Roll 14.

96 Parker to AAAG, Troops in the Field, Fort Cummings, 30 Nov., 1880 in Reports of Scouts 2 Nov., 1880-1 Aug., 1882, HQ Records of Fort Cummings, New Mexico, 1863-1873 & 1880-1884, NA, RG393, M1081, Roll 8.

97 Dudley to AAAG SF 11 Nov., 1880, NA, RG393, Part 3, Entry 439, pp.609-613; See also Hatch to AAG Fort Leavenworth, 12 Nov., 1880, Telegrams Sent DoNM, Vol.4, Nov. 1880 – Jan. 1881, NA, RG393, Part 3, Entry 431, pp.35-36; Dudley to AAAG DoNM, 13 Nov., 1880, in Letters sent Vol. 7, 25 Oct., 1880-24 Jun., 1881,in HQ Records of Fort Cummings, New Mexico, 1863-1873 & 1880-1884, NA, RG393, M1081, Roll 1, Letter No. 137.

98 Dudley to AAG, New Mexico Column, 9 September, 1880 in Letters Received, Dept. of Missouri 1868-98, RG 393, Entry A1-1 2601, Box 94.

Plate 14.6. View from the southern edge of the Goodsight Mountains. It was from a similar perspective that Lieutenant Colonel Dudley spotted the dust cloud approximately 15 miles out on the plain, making for the Mexican Border. The West Potrillo Mountains can be seen marching across the distant left-centre horizon. (Photo: Author)

Plate 14.7. Similar perspective from the southern end of the Goodsight Mountains. The Florida Mountains are clearly visible on the right horizon, while the very edge of the West Potrillo Mountains can just be distinguished on the left horizon. (Photo: Author)

them to be worthless, as they had refused to take the point in Parker's advance and had fled during the ambush.[99]

Nevertheless, Buell concluded that, had Parker followed his instructions and retreated slowly, all the while holding the enemy at bay, the reinforcements from Fort Cumming would have been able to destroy the Apaches.[100] This conclusion is clearly flawed. The reinforcements from Fort Cummings followed Parker's trail. Victorio would have had clear warning of the approach of a superior force, and the Apaches would simply have scattered in the face of such opposition.

Buell acknowledged that the operation against the Apaches near Fort Cummings had disrupted his plans to coordinate his movements with those of both Terrazas and Carr, in order to attack Victorio in Mexico.[101] Nevertheless, a fresh trail leading into Mexico might give him the chance to launch an attack on Victorio. A few days after he had returned to Fort Cummings, Buell sent Captain Beyer, with approximately 80 Ninth Cavalrymen and 50 Apache scouts, into the East Potrillo Mountains. They were to establish the exact point at which the Apaches had crossed the border. Beyer located the crossing point, marched his command to Fort Bliss, and reported back to Buell by telegraph.[102] Buell now had a clear trail into Mexico, which would allow him to follow General Pope's instructions concerning crossing the border.[103]

Therefore, while Grierson had reported that Victorio had been damaged in Texas, these attacks in early September 1880, the number of warriors involved, and the ammunition they expended, suggest that Victorio still had a large following and good stocks of ammunition at that time. Nevertheless, the encounter with Parker may have expended a significant amount of ammunition.

For their own part, the Apaches appear to have been aware of the threat posed by Buell's force at Fort Cummings, and to have thoroughly scouted the borderlands between the Florida Mountains and El Paso. Two scouts, of either Anglo-American or Mexican origin, returned to Fort Bliss to report that Victorio was now based near the Laguna de Guzman. On their return, they had passed through the Potrillo Mountains and had found clear evidence that the Apaches were sending small parties to the highest points of this range, simply to keep a watch for hostile forces making their way south into Mexico.[104] (See document file no. 116.) The implication of this information was that if Victorio had scouts occupying the highest points of the Potrillo Mountains, any attempt to move large US forces south towards his position would be quickly spotted.

A remaining conundrum is the question of what Victorio was doing in the Goodsight Mountains in early September 1880? Why was the stagecoach attacked? And why did he ambush Parker?

That Victorio was present is strongly supported by the number of Apache warriors present at the battle. Moreover, Mescalero reports gathered by Buell in November 1880 at Fort Stanton include an interesting report by the widow of Mescalero Apache leader, Cab-al-es-so. He had been shot dead by Victorio in a leadership dispute, sometime during September, in the Potrillo Mountains.

---

99 Buell to AAAG Santa Fe, 10 September, 1880 in Letters Received, Dept. of Missouri 1868-98, RG 393, Entry A1-1 2601, Box 94; Buell, HQ Fort Stanton N.M., to AAG, DoM (via AAAG DoNM), 20 Nov., 1880 in Letters Received by HQ DoNM Sept. 1865-Aug. 1890, NA, RG393, M1088, Roll 42, File 658-1658, Jan.-Apr. 1881.

100 Buell to AAAG Santa Fe, 10 September, 1880 in Letters Received, Dept. of Missouri 1868-98, RG 393, Entry A1-1 2601, Box 94.

101 Buell, HQ Fort Stanton N.M., to AAG, DoM (via AAAG DoNM), 20 Nov., 1880 in Letters Received by HQ DoNM Sept. 1865-Aug. 1890, NA, RG393, M1088, Roll 42, File 658-1658, Jan.-Apr. 1881.

102 Buell to AAAG 12 Sept., 1880, NA, RG393, Part 3, Entry 439, p.404; Buell, HQ Fort Stanton N.M., to AAG, DoM (via AAAG DoNM), 20 Nov., 1880 in Letters Received by HQ DoNM Sept. 1865-Aug. 1890, NA, RG393, M1088, Roll 42, File 658-1658, Jan.-Apr. 1881.

103 Buell, HQ Fort Stanton N.M., to AAG, DoM (via AAAG DoNM), 20 Nov., 1880 in Letters Received by HQ DoNM Sept. 1865-Aug. 1890, NA, RG393, M1088, Roll 42, File 658-1658, Jan.-Apr. 1881

104 Brinkerhoff to AAAG SF 11 Sept., 1880, NA, RG393, Part 3, Entry 439, pp.405-408.

As the Goodsight Mountains are the next range of mountains to the north by north-west of the West Potrillo mountain range, and the former are sometimes described as an extension of the latter, this places Victorio in the immediate area. A number of possible explanations could be advanced for Victorio's presence in the Goodsight Mountains.

First, the stagecoach was attacked by an advance party of 10 to 15 Apaches as a target of opportunity. What may have caught the Apaches out was the unexpected presence of Major Hale's camp in the near vicinity. Thus, there was an unexpectedly quick response by the US army: first by Hale, then followed up by troops from Fort Cummings. This may have precluded a move north by a large group of Apache warriors to distract attention from a second group of dependents. Victorio had done this in the past, both successfully (New Mexico, January–February 1880) and unsuccessfully (Texas, July–August 1880). He may have gathered his following together in the Potrillo and Goodsight Mountains in preparation for such a manoeuvre, but have been forestalled by the quick response by the US army. Therefore, the large dust cloud seen by Dudley retreating into Mexico may have been Victorio's dependents, withdrawing across the border from the Potrillos, while the main group of warriors may have dispersed both into the Potrillos and down into Mexico in advance of the main party.

Second, we know that the Apaches were beginning to run relatively low on ammunition by September 1880. It has been assumed that Victorio's attempt to pass through Grierson's picket lines in Texas had caused this ammunition shortage, though Parker's fight on 7 September would appear to contradict this assumption. Nevertheless, Apache testimony and a couple of scout reports indicate that Victorio's following were short of ammunition from mid September 1880. So, knowing that they had good, yet dwindling, ammunition stocks, could the Apaches have been trying to lure Captain Hale's small detachment into an ambush, not necessarily to cause fatalities but to try to capture reserve ammunition from the company? Archaeological evidence from April 1880 shows that Victorio's following used large numbers of Springfield rifles and carbines whose 45:70 and 45:55 cartridges were interchangeable. Hale's infantrymen were probably armed with Springfield rifles, so they might have been considered a tempting target. Parker's troops, who were also probably armed with the Springfield carbines, may have offered the same opportunity.[105] Could this small party of Apaches have been used in an attempt to lure a US army detachment into a situation where a much larger group of Apaches could separate them from the reserve ammunition they had packed on mules and horses?

Third, could Victorio, who was aware of Buell's build-up of troops at Fort Cummings, have been merely testing out the preparedness of the troops in the immediate area? Finding the response faster than expected, the Apaches retreated, and stopped the initial pursuit in its tracks, before withdrawing into Mexico to take stock of the situation.

Finally, could Victorio have been trying to draw a significant number of US troops into a futile pursuit through the Potrillo Mountains, over the sand hill country in Northern Chihuahua, and into an ambush in the mountains to the north of the Lagunas de Guzman and Santa Maria? This had worked well for him in October 1879, when he had finally defeated Major Morrow's battalion and forced them to terminate their pursuit after following the same route. If this could be repeated, then Victorio might subsequently be able to get his following safely across an undefended border into secure winter quarters in the Black Range, San Mateo and Mogollon Mountains.

105 If I remember correctly at least some of the Fourth Cavalry were armed with a Hotchkiss carbine in 1882.

It should also be noted that both attacks in New Mexico gave General Pope an ideal opportunity to condemn the Mexican Government for, so far, refusing US troops permission to cross the border.[106]

> As long as we are prevented by the refusal of the Mexican government from sending a force into Mexico to hunt down this band of indians we are liable to these raids. I again ask that the Mexican government be requested to permit us a passage and break up this band in Mexico. The troops are well posted and in sufficient force to deal easily with Victorio's band; but whilst the Indians have a safe place ????? so near at hand they may at times be able to do such infamy as the above.[107]

The State Department, in response to Pope's statement, instructed the US Minister to Mexico, P.H. Morgan, to renew his efforts to get the Mexican government to grant permission for US troops to cross the line.[108] Morgan was instructed to 'press upon Mexico the necessity of allowing our troops to pursue across the border or assume the responsibility of harbouring and yet not disarming them'.[109] As late as 5 October, Hunter informed the Secretary of War that permission to cross the border could not be given until ratified by the Mexican Senate.[110]

106 Pope to AAG HQ MDoM, 9 Sept., 1880'Victorio Files' NA, RG393, M1495, Roll 14; Pope to AG of the Army, Wash. D.C. 10 Sept., 1880 in 'Victorio Papers', NA, M666, Roll 528.

107 Pope to AG of the Army, Washington D.C. 10 Sept., 1880, NA, RG393, Part 1, Entry 2539, Press Copies of Letters and Endorsements Sent, MDoM, Vol. 13, pp.581-582.

108 Hunter to Ramsey, Secretary of War, 15 Sept., 1880, 'Victorio Files' NA, RG393, M1495, Roll 14.

109 Hunter to Ramsey, 15 Sept., 1880 in 'Victorio Papers', NA, M666, Roll 528.

110 Hunter to Ramsey, Secretary of War, 5 Oct., 1880, 'Victorio Files' NA, RG393, M1495, Roll 14; Hunter to Ramsey, 15 Sept., 1880 in 'Victorio Papers', NA, M666, Roll 528; Hunter to Ramsey, 5 Oct., 1880 in Pope to Whipple AAG Chicago, 29 Sept., 1880 in 'Victorio Papers', NA, M666, Roll 528.

15

The Buell-Terrazas Campaign in Chihuahua, September–October 1880

Joaquin Terrazas Mobilises the Chihuahuan State Militia

South of the border, Luis Terrazas, Governor of Chihuahua, attempted to co-ordinate Mexican state and federal troops in a joint offensive against Victorio.

> He [Luis Terrazas] had secured a pledge of two hundred men from the political chief of Cuidad Guerrero, 111 miles by road west of Chihuahua City, and would immediately send rifles and ammunition for that number, money to hire mules, and supplies to pack them with. Orders had been issued to the political heads of Bravos and Galeana, 30 miles south-west of Casas Grandes, to raise what troops they could. Luis' directive stated that 'the government will pay four reales to the infantry and six to those who brought a horse and will pay rewards for Indian scalps, and the capture alive of women and children, according to the law, and 2,000 pesos for Victorio, dead or alive'. It added that 'all civilians enlisting for this campaign' would be under Joaquin's command.[1]

The Governor selected his cousin to head the State of Chihuahua's latest offensive against the Apaches. In response to this commission, Colonel Joaquin Terrazas embarked on a remarkable recruitment drive in the towns to the west and north of Chihuahua City.[2] He recruited a number of Tarahumara Indians as scouts and infantrymen. These men had the reputation of effortlessly keeping abreast of mounted men on the trail. Between 25 August and 29 September 1880, Terrazas passed through several towns collecting recruits or instructing them to follow in his path. He started at San Andres, then proceeded through Cuidad Guerrero, Namiquipa, Santa Clara, Ortega, San Lorenzo, and on to El Carmen. At the last location, he found a number of recruits, yet none of the guns promised by the central authorities. He also sent out messages asking volunteers from the Mexican border to link up with his forces at the Laguna de Patos. He continued on to San Buenaventura, Galeana and Corralitos, linking up with the expedition's second-in-command, Juan Mata Ortiz, who, like Terrazas, had considerable experience of fighting the Apaches.[3] Mata Ortiz had already gathered a group of over 100 volunteers, and had also sent out scouts to the north and west of Janos in search of the Apaches. By the time the force reached the Vado de Santa Maria, these scouts had returned without having seen any Apaches; but they had come across the tracks of 10 horses in the lakes region (presumably somewhere between the Laguna de Guzman[4] and the

1 Thrapp, 1974, p.294.
2 See Grierson to AAG, DoTx, San Antonio, 2 Sept., 1880, 'Victorio Files' NA, RG393, M1495, Roll 14; See Thrapp, 1974, pp.294-301 for a detailed account of Terrazas' recruitment drive and subsequent expedition against Victorio.
3 Thrapp, 1974, p.295.
4 Also known as Guzman Lake.

Laguna de Santa Maria). The tracks were moving to the east, towards the Candelaria Mountains.[5] The expedition carried on to the Laguna de Patos, where many of the militiamen promised for his force by settlements visited on his recruitment drive caught up with Colonel Terrazas on 29 September 1880.[6] Even as Terrazas waited for his militia to converge on the Laguna de Patos, his scouts fanned out northwards towards the Candelaria Mountains. Their orders were to carefully scout for Victorio's camp without alerting the Apaches. If there was a camp, Terrazas and his commanders would attempt a surprise attack. Once more, his scouts failed to find any Apaches, though they reported a trail moving eastwards out of the Candelaria Mountains.[7]

Terrazas' forces continued to grow, as the militia raised in the border region around El Paso del Norte joined him.[8] While the Colonel was encamped at the Laguna de Patos, he was also contacted by couriers from Buell.[9] By the time he left the Laguna de Patos, he commanded approximately 350 men.[10] With most of his forces gathered, he was now ready to set out after Victorio's band.

Luis Terrazas opens negotiation with Colonel Buell

As Joaquin Terrazas was gathering recruits, his cousin Luis Terrazas had already initiated a dialogue[11] (see document file no. 117) with Colonel Buell, principally through the offices of Dr Samaniego, though Juan B. Olguin and Roman Aranda were also used to help coordinate the campaign against Victorio. These men corresponded via Captain Brinkerhoff, at Fort Bliss, who provided the last link in the line of communication between Governor Terrazas and Colonel Buell. This correspondence opened on 16 August 1880, when Dr Samaniego informed Brinkerhoff that permission had been given for US troops to cross the border into Chihuahua in pursuit of Apaches.[12] This message was further reinforced by the Jefe Politico of the district of El Paso del Norte, Juan B. Olguin, when he requested that Brinkerhoff ask Buell to lend the citizens of Chihuahua as much military aid as possible to confront the Apaches.[13] As Buell had not yet received a direct communication from the Governor of Chihuahua, he asked for a letter to this effect, signed by Luis Terrazas.[14] In the meantime, Buell stated that, even if the Governor did not respond, if 'the people on your border want my assistance … they shall have it but, if a move is made I want it should be an effective one'.[15] Brinkerhoff was contacted by Samaniego[16] and told that the latter was expecting a letter from Luis Terrazas with further instructions. It was also stated in this letter that, 'I think [author's underline] the Jef. Politicos call is legal and sufficient to relieve you from all responsibility.'[17] Buell quickly contacted Olguin, on 31 August, estimating that he could put his forces in motion on 8 September. He also asked Olguin to furnish him two reliable guides.[18] The

5 Thrapp, 1974, pp. 295-297.
6 Ibid, p.298.
7 Ibid, p.297.
8 Ibid, p.298.
9 Thrapp, 1974, p.299; Crimmins, 1935, pp.138-139.
10 Thrapp, 1974, p.298.
11 This correspondence is repeated in full in Appendix Two of the previous chapter.
12 Brinkerhoff to Buell citing Samaniego to Brinkerhoff, 16 Aug., 1880 in 'Victorio Papers', NA, M666, Roll 528.
13 Olguin to Brinkerhoff, 29 Aug., 1880 in 'Victorio Papers', NA, M666, Roll 528.
14 Buell to Samaniego, 30 Aug., 1880 in 'Victorio Papers', NA, M666, Roll 528.
15 Buell to Jefe Politico, El Paso del Norte, 31 Aug., 1880 in 'Victorio Papers', NA, M666, Roll 528.
16 The letter does not mention him by name but it mentions the fact that the writer lost horses to the Apaches on the 28 Aug., 1880; this surely confirms the author as Samaniego.
17 Brinkerhoff to Buell, 31 Aug., 1880 in 'Victorio Papers', NA, M666, Roll 528.
18 Buell to Jefe Politico (through Brinkerhoff), 31 Aug., 1880 in 'Victorio Papers', NA, M666, Roll 528.

Plate 15.1. The well-preserved but abandoned hacienda at El Carmen, Chihuahua, Mexico. In September 1880, one would have expected to see this as the centre of activity as Colonel Terrazas gathered his forces to march against the Apaches. (Photo: Author)

Plate 15.2. The pass between Galeana and Casa Grandes. Terrazas probably used this route in September 1880. The photo gives the reader some idea of the vastness of the country that both the Mexicans and Apaches traversed in their many campaigns against each other. (Photo: Author)

following day, Buell informed Olguin that, unless the latter retracted his permission, the letter of 29 August, had, as far as Buell was concerned, sufficient legality for him to act.[19] However, on this point, it should be remembered that Samaniego had only expressed the opinion that he *thought* that the Jefe Politico's request was legal.

By 2 September, Buell and Samaniego were exchanging intended plans as to what US and Chihuahuan forces were available and where they should be deployed. Buell further asked for Mexican guides, and added a request for a map of the area. Finally, he also requested a meeting with Samaniego and/or Olguin at either Palomas Lake or Ascencion.[20] By 4 September, Buell sent his first communication to Joaquin Terrazas, informing him of the number of available US troops, and that his scouts placed Victorio approximately 15 miles from the Laguna de Santa Maria on the Santa Maria River. Buell proposed that he and Terrazas, in 'hearty cooperation', launch a joint attack on the Apaches.[21] In return, Joaquin Terrazas contacted Samaniego from the Hacienda de San Lorenzo, stating that he was more than willing to cooperate with Buell. He complimented Samaniego on the manner in which he had attempted to put the Governor's wishes into action without leaving Luis Terrazas open to being held to account for those actions. Colonel Terrazas also informed Samaniego of his intended plans, but added that, as he was still waiting for his men to gather, he proposed that Buell be asked to concentrate his forces at Boca Grande and Palomas Lake on 24 September 1880.[22] The stage was now set for these plans to be put into action, and on 9 September 1880, Luis Terrazas informed President Porfirio Diaz that he was about to send an expedition of several hundred men after Victorio.[23]

The US Army Organises an Expedition into Mexico

The planned operation to attack and destroy Victorio in Mexico was, from the US point of view, two pronged: from Arizona, Colonel Eugene A. Carr with six companies of the Sixth Cavalry was to sweep south to Casa Grandes and then eastwards towards Laguna de Guzman. The Sixth Cavalrymen would be fronted by three Apache scout companies,[24] who would operate in extended order, approximately 10 miles in advance of the US troops.[25] By 1 August 1880, Carr was informed that General Willcox 'desires you to cooperate with Col. Buell as far as possible'. The following day, Carr informed Buell that he did not possess a map of Northern Mexico.[26] By 3 August, a map had been found and was en route to Carr at Fort Bowie.[27] On 30 August, Carr had informed Willcox

19 Buell to Olguin, 1 Sept., 1880 in 'Victorio Papers', NA, M666, Roll 528.

20 Buell to Brinkerhoff, 2 Sept., 1880, Samaniego to Buell 2 Sept., 1880, Buell to Samaniego, 3 Sept., 1880 in 'Victorio Papers', NA, M666, Roll 528.

21 Buell to Col. Joaquin Terrazas (through Brinkerhoff, Samaniego and thence by courier), 4 Sept., 1880 in 'Victorio Papers', NA, M666, Roll 528.

22 Joaquin Terrazas to Samaniego, 11 Sept., 1880 in 'Victorio Papers', NA, M666, Roll 528.

23 Hatfield, 1999, p.38.

24 One of these scout companies, commanded by Lt Frederick Von Schrader, had been transported by rail to join Colonel Carr's expedition. This was the first time that U.S. troops had deployed by rail in Arizona. (Thrapp, 1988, p.1491).

25 Cruse, 1987, p.84; see also Thrapp, 1964, pp.218-219; 1974, p.299; Rasch, 1960, p.9; Carter, USACMH webpage.

26 Carr to Buell, 2 Aug., 1880, Troops in SE Arizona, DoAz, NA, RG393, Part 1, Entry 232, Vol.7, 18 May-6 Sept., 1880, pp.131-132.

27 Martin to Carr 3 Aug., 1880 NA, RG393, Part 1, Entry 169, Vol. 10 p.352.

that Victorio was, according to Buell, in the Candelaria Mountains. In Carr's opinion, this placed the Apaches out of easy reach of troops from Arizona.[28] This led Willcox to advise:

> that in assisting Buell you can do only what seems practicable and that appears to be to take what troops and transportation you can without stripping or distressing the southern posts and proceed as far only as may be necessary to cover Arizona: say the valley between the Sierra Madres and Chiricahuas [Mountains] and the San Francisco country and incidentally to hold for Buell any route or pass leading from Guzman. If this disposition of your force should lead to the discovery of the trail of the hostiles, you are at liberty to follow it. Finally, if you cannot well carry thirty (30) days rations take twenty (20).[29]

Following Wilcox's advice, Carr ordered the concentration of the units involved in the proposed expedition to commence around Fort Bowie, on 3 September 1880.[30] He intended to be ready to move on 9 September, but admitted that a few more days would allow him to concentrate more troops for his expedition.[31] Buell quickly responded that the forces in Arizona could have more than a few days to complete their mobilisation, as Buell was not quite ready to launch his expedition, due both to delays in recruiting Apache scouts for service with the New Mexican troops and to Colonel Terrazas' mobilisation of the Chihuahua state militia. Carr was told to wait until Buell instructed him to commence his field operations. Carr calculated that he would be leading 280 Sixth Cavalrymen and 55 Apache scouts into Mexico.[32] His only worry was a shortage of pack mules; but he proposed to move with wagons till he reached the Mexican border, before transferring supplies to the pack mules.[33]

Willcox and Carr appear to have been aware of the dubious legality of the operation. Willcox gave careful instructions not to move beyond certain boundaries; and Carr, alerted Willcox that if Victorio was to be found in the Candelaria Mountains, this would place Carr beyond such boundaries.

Further to the east in New Mexico, Buell had already concentrated a large force at Fort Cummings and Knight's Ranch. (See Chapter 12.) As the officer responsible for the overall direction of the US part of the campaign, Buell contacted Joaquin Terrazas, and a proposed plan of campaign was finalised by the beginning of September. The whole operation was aimed at coming upon Victorio from all sides. Carr was informed of the broad plan on 4 September 1880.[34] (See document file no. 118.) The US army's part in the campaign could be visualised as a horizontal line running west along the border from El Paso into Arizona. As those involved in the operation swung into action, Carr's segment in Arizona would act as a hinge on a door, pivoting on its junction with Buell's right flank and swinging around to the east.[35] (See Map 15.1.)

---

28 Martin to Carr (citing the latter's telegram of 30 Aug., 1880) 7 Sept., 1880, NA, RG393, Part 1, Entry 169, Vol. 10, pp.394-395.

29 Martin to Carr (citing the latter's telegram of 30 Aug., 1880) 7 Sept., 1880, NA, RG393, Part 1, Entry 169, Vol. 10, pp.394-395; Carr to Buell, 14 Sept., 1880, Troops in SE Arizona, DoAz, NA, RG393, Part 1, Entry 232, Vol.8, 6 Sept.-12 Dec., 1880, Letter No.553, p.13.

30 Special Orders No. 47, HQ, Troops in the Field in S.E. Arizona, Camp near Fort Bowie, A.T., 3 Sept., 1880, Special Orders Oct. 1879-Jan. 1881, DoAz, Vol. 2, NA, RG393, Part 1, Entry 239, pp.23-25.

31 Carr to Buell, 4 Sept., 1880, Troops in SE Arizona, DoAz, NA, RG393, Part 1, Entry 232, Vol.7, 18 May-6 Sept., 1880, Letter No.503, p.171.

32 Carr to AG DoAz, 6 Sept., 1880, Troops in SE Arizona, DoAz, NA, RG393, Part 1, Entry 232, Vol.8, 6 Sept.-12 Dec., 1880, Letter No.530, pp.2-3.

33 Ibid.

34 Carr to AG DoAz, 4 Sept., 1880, Troops in SE Arizona, DoAz, NA, RG393, Part 1, Entry 232, Vol.7, 18 May-6 Sept., 1880, Letter No.504, pp.171-172.

35 See Carr to Buell, 3 Sept., 1880, Troops in SE Arizona, DoAz, NA, RG393, Part 1, Entry 232, Vol.7, 18 May-6 Sept., 1880, p.160.

These plans were probably further refined on receipt of the news from Colonel Terrazas that he wished the US forces to be at Palomas Lake and the Boca Grande on 24 September 1880. Terrazas also outlined a detailed plan of campaign and sent this to Buell. This was written at San Lorenzo on 11 September, and probably took a few days to reach Buell. Terrazas confirmed that he understood Buell's intended plan of attack. He also informed Buell of the lay of the land between the Corralitos River and the Boca Grande Mountains, and indicated the likely camping places that Victorio might occupy. Finally, he sent proposals as to the sort of signals (fires at night; smoke during the day) the Chihuahua and US forces should use when operating within sight of each other. He even proposed a series of simple flag signals, should the two forces be close enough to see each other.[36] (See document files no's. 117 and 119.)

Joaquin Terrazas also informed Buell that he had received instructions from his cousin, on 31 August, that Chihuahuan State troops were not to cross the border into the United States. He informed Buell that he would cross the border if necessary but indicated that he would stay north of the border for as short a period as possible. 'I think with the good will manifested by the American Authorities, all will be right between the two Governments, if nothing is said about it.'[37] Thus, the permission for, and planning of, Buell's operation to trap Victorio was concluded with the authorities in Chihuahua on, or around, 15 September 1880.[38] This suggests that, before Buell entered Mexico, there was a three- to four-day gap in in the transmission of information between him and Joaquin Terrazas, whose plan of action had been written on September 11. This potential time lag would only improve once scouts from each command located each other and could communicate directly by mounted couriers. All that remained was for Buell to set his forces in motion.

In the meantime, Buell kept his superiors informed of his progress, though the latter were careful to downplay the point that the US army would be operating in northern Chihuahua. On 20 September, General Pope informed Sheridan that 'Buell, Carr and Terrassas, Governor of Chihuahua are making combined movement against Victorio which will probably culminate in Mexico.'[39] (See document file no. 120.) Buell clearly stated, on 18 September 1880, that he was 'now acting against Victorio in conjunction with Carr of Arizona & Terasas of Mexican forces'.[40] Two days later, probably to help justify the entry of US troops into Mexico, Pope reiterated the argument that the war would probably not have occurred had the Department of the Interior not been so insistent on the removal of the Warm Springs Apaches to San Carlos. He noted that one of the reasons for their resistance to this deportation was the hostility of other Apaches living on San Carlos towards the Warm Springs Apaches and that, when Victorio's followers had been settled at Ojo Caliente, there had been little trouble from them. Pope stated that the US army now faced a situation where Victorio and his followers had decided to fight to the finish and that their 'capture is not very probable, but the killing (cruel as it will be) can, I suppose, be done in time'.[41] (See document file no. 121.) It is interesting to note that in this 'official' document General Pope was careful

36 Joaquin Terrazas, San Lorenzo, 11 Sept., 1880 in 'Victorio Papers', NA, M666, Roll 528.

37 Ibid.

38 Buell, HQ Fort Stanton N.M., to AAG, DoM (via AAAG DoNM), 20 Nov., 1880 in Letters Received by HQ DoNM, Sept. 1865-Aug. 1890, NA, RG393, M1088, Roll 42, File 658-1658, Jan.-Apr. 1881.

39 Pope to Sheridan copied to General Ord, 20 Sept., 1880, NA, RG393, Part 1, Entry 2539, Press Copies of Letters and Endorsements Sent, MDoM, Vol. 13, p.621 & Sheridan to Ord, 20 Sept., 1880, NA, RG393, Part 1, Entry 2538, p.384; Pope to Sheridan, 20 Sept., 1880, 'Victorio Files' NA, RG393, M1495, Roll 14.

40 Buell to AAAG SF 18 Sept., 1880, NA, RG393, Part 3, Entry 439, p.417.

41 Pope's Annual Report Year ending 22 Sept., 1880, NA, RG393, Part 1, Entry 2546, p.613; Report of General John Pope, 22 Sept., 1880, in AR-WD 1880, NA, M997, Roll 35, 1880 Vol. I, pp.88-89.

to be quite ambiguous as to how US and Mexican forces were cooperating against the Apaches.[42] Yet on the same day, Pope stated that:

> To crush out these Indians finally it will be necessary to have authority to pursue and hunt them down wherever they go – whether within our limits or in Mexico – and I think arrangements now on foot will enable us to accomplish this object.[43]

The *New York Times* of 28 October 1880 quoted Buell's report, in which the latter stated that his expedition had been ordered by a telegram from General Pope dated 10 September 1880.[44]

Finally, the main concern for Buell was that Victorio might manage to elude US forces and take refuge in the Black Range.[45] If Buell, Carr and Terrazas were unable to contact each other quickly in the field, there was every opportunity that the Apaches would slip through the net. With this danger in mind, we shall turn first to Colonel Carr's part in the operation.

Colonel Carr's Expedition into Mexico

Of all the expeditions which set off into Mexico, that commanded by Colonel Carr made the most uneventful progress. Carr set off from Fort Bowie on 19 September 1880, intending to be in a position to blockade the Boca Grande passes on 24 September.[46] He commanded five companies of Sixth Cavalry (A, C, F, G, and M) and detachments from two more Companies (B and L), totalling 10 officers, including himself, and 243 other ranks divided into two battalions. He was also accompanied by A, C and D Companies, which were comprised of Indian scouts led by Lieutenants Cruse, Staunton and Mills, with 57 scouts, and a further 33 Sixth Cavalrymen who had been attached to these companies. The command was also accompanied by three guides, 27 mule packers, 20 Apaches classed as mule packers, and seven clerks.[47] (See document file no. 122.) Carr seems to have been most concerned as to how long he could keep his command in the field. Willcox moved swiftly to assure him that:

> arrangement will be made to supply your command in the field for any given period you may desire, if there is any chance by so doing for you to accomplish results. The peace of Arizona is endangered as long as Victorio remains on the warpath and it may take some time to bring him in, and the troops had better keep at it until he is brought in. Please designate as soon as practicable the point or points to which you want subsistence stores sent.[48]

---

42 Ibid.

43 Report of General John Pope, 22 Sept., 1880 in AR-WD, NA, M997, Roll 35, 1880 Vol. I-II, p.88.

44 'The Death of Victorio', *The New York Times*, 28 Oct., 1880.

45 Buell, HQ Fort Stanton N.M., to AAG, DoM (via AAAG DoNM), 20 Nov., 1880 in Letters Received by HQ DoNM Sept. 1865-Aug. 1890, NA, RG393, M1088, Roll 42, File 658-1658, Jan.-Apr. 1881.

46 Carr to AG DoAz, 17 Sept., 1880, Troops in SE Arizona, DoAz, NA, RG393, Part 1, Entry 232, Vol.8, 6 Sept.-12 Dec., 1880, p.17; Carr to Buell, 18 Sept., 1880, Troops in SE Arizona, DoAz, NA, RG393, Part 1, Entry 232, Vol.8, 6 Sept.-12 Dec., 1880, p.18.

47 Carr to AG DoAz, 19 Sept., 1880, Troops in SE Arizona, DoAz, NA, RG393, Part 1, Entry 232, Vol.8, 6 Sept.-12 Dec., 1880, Letter No.569, pp.19-20; Bi-Monthly Company Muster Rolls for Companies A, C, F, G, & M, 6th Cavalry, Sept./Oct., 1880 in NA, RG94; See also Special Orders No. 58, HQ, Troops in the Field in S.E. Arizona, Camp near Fort Bowie, A.T., 17 Sept., 1880, Special Orders Oct. 1879-Jan. 1881, DoAz, Vol. 2, NA, RG393, Part 1, Entry 239, pp.28-29.

48 Martin to Carr, 22 Sept., 1880, NA, RG393, Part 1, Entry 169, Vol. 10, p.415.

Colonel Eugene A. Carr.
Commander of the Sixth Cavalry is probably best remembered for his victory over the Cheyenne Dog Soldiers at Summit Springs in 1869. He commanded the Arizona troops who entered Mexico in support of Buell in September 1880. He was a vocal critic of what he saw as overreliance upon Apache scouts during the Victorio Campaign. He thought that the scouts should only be used to guide US troops to the enemy and then the fighting should be the responsibility of the accompanying soldiers. In August 1881, Carr led a mixed force of Sixth Cavalrymen and Apache scouts to arrest an Apache spiritual leader at Cibecue Creek. The Apache scouts mutinied and in the subsequent battle, the spiritual leader and seven Sixth Cavalrymen were among those killed. One wonders whether Carr's views concerning the proper deployment of Apache scouts led him to underestimate the capabilities of his Apache scouts and was partially to blame for provoking this violent incident. (National Archives)

One of Carr's actions was to reduce the amount of ammunition carried by the troops in his command. Instead of each man carrying 250 rounds, only 150 rounds of rifle or carbine ammunition were issued to each man.[49] Of the 150 rounds, each man was to carry 100 rounds on his person – or 60 rounds in the case of the Indian scouts – and the balance was to be carried by pack mules.[50]

Carr reported being delayed by heavy rains on the night of 20 September, and estimated that he would not be at the Corralitos River, let alone in the Boca Grande Mountains, by 24 September, as intended. Instead, he sent Lieutenant Mills, with his Apache scouts, ahead of his force, to make contact with Buell.[51] Carr's command reached Emory Springs, in the Hatchet Mountains, on 23 September 1880. Finding too little water and wood in that vicinity,[52] they marched on towards the Boca Grande Mountains.[53] By the evening of 24 September, Carr was camped on the Corralitos River, and he was issuing instructions to his command to pass through the Guzman Mountains to the Laguna de Guzman. Even as he issued these orders, both Blocksom's and Cruse's Apache

49 Para 3 Special order no.53.

50 Carr Special Orders No.54, 18 Sept., 1880, Special Orders Oct. 1879-Jan. 1881, DoAz, Vol. 2, NA, RG393, Part 1, Entry 239, p.30.

51 Carr to Buell, 21 Sept., 1880, Troops in SE Arizona, DoAz, NA, RG393, Part 1, Entry 232, Vol.8, 6 Sept.-12 Dec., 1880, Letter No.570, p.20; Mills to AAAG Troops in the Field in S.E. Arizona, Fort Lowell, 11 Oct., 1880 in Reports & Tabular Statements of Scouting Expeditions 1867-91, NA, RG391 Entry 841.

52 This implies that Carr was intending to establish a temporary base at Emory Springs but found this to be impracticable on arrival.

53 Carr Emory Springs, to AG DoAz, 2 Oct., 1880, Troops in SE Arizona, DoAz, NA, RG393, Part 1, Entry 232, Vol.8, 6 Sept.-12 Dec., 1880, Letter No.573, p.22-23.

scout companies were scouring these mountains for any sign of Victorio's people.[54] They were to try to spot Buell's command but, more importantly, should they encounter Victorio, they were to attempt to engage him until the main force under Carr arrived. Carr's main concern was that Victorio should not slip through between his command and Buell's.[55] Lieutenant Mills linked up with Buell's expedition on 24 September, but no firm contact was established between the New Mexico and Arizona troops.[56] In fact, the first Carr knew of this contact was around 9 October, when Lieutenant Mills arrived at Fort Bowie, having left Buell's command on 2 October 1880.[57] Lieutenant Mill's detachment (the last to come in) had followed Carr's expedition's trail as it moved north from the Corralitos River.[58] On his return, Lieutenant Mills stated that he had been informed that Captain Purington's company had passed through the site of the battle between Victorio and Morrow on 27 October 1879[59], and that they had found human remains which were believed to be those of Private Cochlovins, who had been reported missing in action, believed killed in that fight.[60] (See document file no. 123.)

Carr did not reach the Boca Grande range until 26 September 1880. He reported no contact with Buell, but did spot a large dust cloud far to the east, which he supposed belonged to one of Buell's columns.[61] Word eventually reached Carr from Buell, probably via couriers from Arizona, informing him that Buell expected him to move towards Lake Guzman.[62] While Carr stated that he was 'tempted' by such a move, he did not feel that he had authorisation to go that far.[63] He then picketed the Boca Grandes for almost six days with no further contact from Buell. From these picket lines, Carr sent out scouting parties east and south, as far as a rough line from Palomas Lake to the vicinity of Janos.[64] Seeing no signs of any human beings at all, let alone Apaches, Carr departed for Arizona on 1 October,[65] and had arrived back at Fort Bowie by 6 October 1880.[66] On his return to Arizona, he was asked to remain in the field by Department Headquarters. Carr noted that if he was to try to do so, he would require another 100 mules. He had not lost any mules during

54 Kerr, HQ Troops in the Field Camp on Corraletos or Jannos River, Mexico, 8:00 p.m. to Lieut Mills 24 Sept., 1880, NA, RG393, Part 1, Entry 240.

55 Orders presumably by Carr instructing Kerr to transmit orders to Blocksom, undated instructions written on telegraph form, NA, RG393, Part 1, Entry 240.

56 Mills to AAAG Troops in the Field in S.E. Arizona, Fort Lowell, 11 Oct., 1880 in Reports & Tabular Statements of Scouting Expeditions 1867-91, NA, RG391 Entry 841.

57 Ibid.

58 Mills to AAAG Troops in the Field in S.E. Arizona, Fort Lowell, 11 Oct., 1880 in Reports & Tabular Statements of Scouting Expeditions 1867-91, NA, RG391 Entry 841; Carr to AG, Whipple Barracks, 10 Oct., 1880, NA, RG393, Prt 1, Entry 169, Vol. 10, pp.456-457.

59 See Watt, 'I Will Not Surrender the Hair of a Horse's Tail: The Victorio Campaign 1879', p.276.

60 Mills to AAAG Troops in the Field in S.E. Arizona, Fort Lowell, 11 Oct., 1880 in Reports & Tabular Statements of Scouting Expeditions 1867-91, NA, RG391 Entry 841.

61 Carr to AG DoAz, 26 Sept., 1880, Troops in SE Arizona, DoAz, NA, RG393, Part 1, Entry 232, Vol.8, 6 Sept.-12 Dec., 1880, Letter No.572, pp.21-22; Return for Company G, 6th Cavalry, Sept./Oct., 1880 in NA, RG94.

62 Carr to AG DoAz, 25 Sept., 1880, Troops in SE Arizona, DoAz, NA, RG393, Part 1, Entry 232, Vol.8, 6 Sept.-12 Dec., 1880, Letter No.571, p.21.

63 Carr to AG DoAz, 26 Sept., 1880, Troops in SE Arizona, DoAz, NA, RG393, Part 1, Entry 232, Vol.8, 6 Sept.-12 Dec., 1880, Letter No.572, pp.21-22; See also Carr to Hatch, 7 Oct., 1880, Troops in SE Arizona, DoAz, NA, RG393, Part 1, Entry 232, Vol.8, 6 Sept.-12 Dec., 1880, Letter No.579, pp.25-26.

64 Carr to Buell, 17 Oct., 1880, Troops in SE Arizona, DoAz, NA, RG393, Part 1, Entry 232, Vol.8, 6 Sept.-12 Dec., 1880, p.30.

65 Carr Emory Springs, to AG DoAz, 2 Oct., 1880, Troops in SE Arizona, DoAz, NA, RG393, Part 1, Entry 232, Vol.8, 6 Sept.-12 Dec., 1880, Letter No.573, p.22-23; Carr to Buell, 17 Oct., 1880, Troops in SE Arizona, DoAz, NA, RG393, Part 1, Entry 232, Vol.8, 6 Sept.-12 Dec., 1880, p.30.

66 Returns for Companies A, C, F, G, & M, 6th Cavalry, Sept./Oct., 1880 in NA, RG94.

Lt Stephen Mills with Apache Scouts.
Lt. Stephen C.Mills, Twelfth Infantry, seen in a contemporary with his Apache scout company. His was the only force from Carr's expedition into Mexico which made direct contact with Buell's New Mexico force. On returning to Arizona, they reported that troops from New Mexico had discovered the remains of a Sixth Cavalryman, missing in action, believed killed, during the fight between Morrow's force and Victorio in Northern Mexico on the night of the 27-28 October, 1879. (See 'I Will Not Surrender the Hair of a Horse's Tail': The Victorio Campaign 1879, Chapter 11, p.276) (National Archives)

his incursion into Mexico, but many were in a very poor condition. Moreover, the team mules he had taken with him to Mexico had not performed well as pack mules.[67]

The Texas Rangers Move South of the Border

In response to Victorio's continued attacks on Mexican ranches, the local Chihuahuan Mexican militia commander, Roman Aranda, asked a small detachment of Texas Rangers to cross the border and help combat the Apaches.[68] Accordingly, Lieutenant Baylor, Sergeant Gillett and 12 Texas Rangers crossed the Rio Grande on 17 September 1880, 'to co-operate with him in exterminating the Apaches'.[69] Baylor anticipated that Victorio would move east from the Candelaria Mountains, in the face of the forces arrayed against him, and planned to block such a move with his detachment.[70]

---

67 Carr to AG DoAz, 5 Oct., 1880, Troops in SE Arizona, DoAz, NA, RG393, Part 1, Entry 232, Vol.8, 6 Sept.-12 Dec., 1880, Letter No.575, p.23-24.

68 Gillett, 1976, p.183.

69 Gillett, 1976, p.183; Brinkerhoff to AAAG 17 Sept., 1880, NA, RG393, Part 3, Entry 439, pp.825-826; Hatch to AAG Fort Leavenworth, 19 Sept., 1880, Telegrams Sent DoNM, Vol.3, Jan. – Nov. 1880 NA, RG393, Part 3, Entry 431, pp.839-840; Thrapp, 1974, p.299; Stout, p.171.

70 Brinkerhoff to Grierson, 16 Sept., 1880 in Register of Telegrams Rec'd 11 Oct., 1879-8 Oct., 1880, HQ Records DoP 1878-1881, NA, RG393, M1381, Roll 2, p.215, Letter No.379.

By 18 September 1880, it was reported that 75 men were picketing the eastern edge of the Candelaria Mountains.[71] The group that assembled at the Aranda Ranch numbered over 100, though not all would necessarily have been deployed to cover the Candelarias. As well as the Rangers, there were Mexican volunteers from both sides of the Rio Grande,[72] and scouts from Colonel Grierson's command were also believed to have joined this force.[73] (See document file no. 125.) It has always been assumed that the scouts from Grierson's command were Pueblo scouts, but it now appears that they were a small group of volunteers drawn from the Tenth Cavalry and led by Charles Berger. Berger and six 'soldiers' are reported to have left Fort Quitman on 27 September, 'with instructions to ascertain the present whereabouts of Victoria'.[74] Grierson clearly stated that some picked men from A and E Companies, Tenth Cavalry, accompanied Berger. He also noted that the six months' term of service of his Pueblo scouts had expired on 21 September, and that they 'could not be induced to re-enlist again for either love or money',[75] though he noted that some of these scouts were, in his opinion, 'worthless'.[76] In attempting to recruit more scouts, on 30 September, Lieutenant Nordstrom, Tenth Cavalry, found that the Pueblo Indians were very reluctant to re-enlist for their previous rate of pay. After several days of trying to recruit Pueblo scouts or Mexican citizens from the other side of the border, Nordstrom had to record complete failure to recruit any scouts. He attributed his failure to recruit more Pueblos to general indolence. His failure to recruit Mexican citizens he put down to rumours, spread by the Pueblo Indians, that if they served with the US army they would be kept on short rations and forced to 'drill among the Negroes'.[77]

On 19 September, the Texas Rangers discovered a rain-obscured trail to the south of the Rancheria Mountains[78] and spotted what they took to be signal fires to the east of the Aranda Ranch.[79] Gillett, five Rangers and 10 Mexican militiamen scouted towards these fires on 20 September. Before they could reach the area, they were ordered to occupy Rancheria Mountain and deny it to Victorio.[80] In the following days, Victorio was reported to be operating between Carrizal and the Candelaria Mountains. Although the Mexican militia and Texas Rangers moved into this

71 Brinkerhoff to Grierson, 18 Sept., 1880 in Register of Telegrams Rec'd 11 Oct., 1879-8 Oct., 1880, HQ Records DoP 1878-1881, NA, RG393, M1381, Roll 2, pp.218-219, Letter No.386.

72 Gillett, 1976, p.183.

73 Brinkerhoff to AAAG 17 Sept., 1880, NA, RG393, Part 3, Entry 439, pp.825-826; Hatch to AAG Fort Leavenworth, 19 Sept., 1880, Telegrams Sent DoNM, Vol.3, Jan. – Nov. 1880 NA, RG393, Part 3, Entry 431, pp.839-840.

74 Brinkerhoff to AAAG SF 27 Sept., 1880, NA, RG393, Part 3, Entry 439, p.120-121.

75 Grierson to AAG, DoTx, 31 Dec., 1880, in Letters Sent 23 Aug.-31 Dec., 1880, HQ Records DoP 1878-1881, NA, RG393, M1381, Roll 1, Letter No.168 (Note: This latter report contained as Letter No. 3 in Letters sent 1881); Nolan, Fort Quitman, 21 Sept., 1880 in Register of Letters Rec'd 23 Mar., 1878-30 Jan., 1881, HQ Records DoP 1878-1881, NA, RG393, M1381, Roll 2, p.54, Letter No.190; McLaughlan to Grierson, 21 Sept., 1880 in Register of Telegrams Rec'd 11 Oct., 1879-8 Oct., 1880, HQ Records DoP 1878-1881, NA, RG393, M1381, Roll 2, p.220, Letter No.389.

76 Grierson to AAG, DoTx, 23 Sept., 1880 in Telegrams Sent 23 Jun.-30 Nov., 1880, HQ Records DoP 1878-1881, NA, RG393, M1381, Roll 1, p.165, Letter No.495.

77 Nordstrom to Battalion adjutant 10 Oct., 1880 in Letters Rec'd File 19 Mar., 1878-14 Feb., 1881, HQ Records DoP 1878-1881, NA, RG393, M1381, Roll 2; See also Nolan to Smither, 6 Oct., 1880 in Register of Telegrams Rec'd 11 Oct., 1879-8 Oct., 1880, HQ Records DoP 1878-1881, NA, RG393, M1381, Roll 2, p.253, Letter No.457.

78 Thompson, Baylor's editor, states that this mountain constitutes a single elevation lying some ten miles to the north-east of the Candelaria Mountains.

79 Gillett, 1976, p.183.

80 Ibid, pp.183-184.

area, the Apaches managed to elude them.[81] Having failed to prevent Victorio moving eastwards, these troops made for Samaniego's ranch at San Jose.[82]

At San Jose, the Mexican militia and Texas rangers rendezvoused with Joaquin Terrazas' state troops, on 3 October 1880.[83] By that point, Colonel Terrazas was accompanied by approximately 200 cavalry and 100 infantry. Gillett described the cavalry and infantry as well-equipped with Remington pistols, carbines and muskets and ammunition,[84] and he clearly admired the minimal amount of baggage and food carried by the state troops. Nevertheless, Gillett noted that the infantrymen, Tarahumara Indians, had no difficulty in keeping up with the cavalry and were actually more effective than the mounted troops when operating in the mountains.[85] (See document file no. 126.2.) Reuben W. Creel, US Consul in Chihuahua City, writing in 1863, made very similar comments concerning the ability of the Chihuahua state troops to hold their own against the Apaches with relatively few resources.[86] (See document file no. 126.1.) Creel asserted that if well-armed and well led, the poor people who would make up the rank and file would 'do their duty'; but he noted that they were poorly led and equipped. He stated that the only officer of worth was 'decidedly brave and energetic' but was not formally trained, and was only fit to lead troops against Apaches or other guerrillas.[87] If Creel was referring to Joaquin Terrazas, the latter would seem exactly the man to track Victorio down.

By the time that Joaquin Terrazas rendezvoused with the Mexican militia raised by Aranda, and their Texas Ranger allies, his mobilisation and concentration was complete.

Colonel Buell's Expedition into Mexico (see document file no. 127.)

On 18 September 1880, Buell got his expedition under way. He contacted Samaniego, with a view to setting up an efficient system of couriers between his command, once it was in the field, and the telegraph office at Fort Cummings. He also advised Samaniego to organise a similar system between Terrazas' command and the telegraph office in El Paso. Buell required Terrazas to inform him of Victorio's current location, so that he could deploy his troops accordingly when Buell crossed the border.[88] However, this system of couriers was not implemented, thus losing the allies the opportunity to prevent delayed transmission times, and allowing the Apaches to slip by their opponents.[89] Where the use of the telegraph lines was concerned, a problem that had periodically plagued the US army surfaced again. Complaints by some officers that telegraph operators displayed 'a want of cordial cooperation' provoked a swift message to his men by the Acting Chief

81 Ibid, p.184.

82 This is probably the San Jose de Patos mentioned in Buell's report of the operation which almost certainly places its location to near the Laguna de Patos.

83 Gillett, 1976, p.184.

84 The term 'musket' may be a misnomer. This may refer to a breech loading rifle of longer barrel length rather than a muzzle-loading musket. The Winchester repeating arm came in carbine/rifle and musket variants. The latter was certainly a breech loading weapon with a longer barrel than the other two variants. (See Flayderman, pp.258-261; Finerty, 2001, p.238) Lt. Maus notes that in 1886, Terrazza's militiamen were armed with .44 calibre Remington rifles. (p.245).

85 Gillett, 1976, pp.184-185; see also Shipp, 2001, p.529; Smith, 1962, p.24.

86 Creery, U.S. Consul Chihuahua to the Secretary of State, Washington D.C, 30 Nov. 1863 in Consular Despatches Chihuahua Mexico 1830-1906, NA, M289, Roll 1.

87 Ibid.

88 Buell to Samaniego, 18 Sept., 1880 in 'Victorio Papers', NA, M666, Roll 528.

89 Note appended to Buell to Samaniego, 18 Sept., 1880 in 'Victorio Papers', NA, M666, Roll 528.

Signal Officer. 'Instruct your men to render commanding officers every possible assistance and under no circumstances to treat their demands in any other than with the greatest respect.'[90]

On the same day, Buell sent orders to some of his detachments. Captain Beyer was to move from El Paso[91] to the East Potrillo Mountains with his Ninth Cavalrymen, while Lieutenant Maney's Apache scouts were to station themselves on the western side of the Potrillo Mountains. They were all to move southwards into Mexico during the night of 23 September.[92] This first deployment was almost certainly in response to the news, brought to Captain Brinkerhoff on 11 September, that the Apaches were using the Potrillo Mountains to spy out the border. If there were any of Victorio's scouts present, these would hopefully be driven out just before Buell marched his main force to Palomas Lake. Of course, if Victorio was in the vicinity of the Laguna de Guzman, the Sierras Las Lilas and El Cartucho, to the west, and the Sierra San Blas and the Cerros Prietos, to the east, he would be ideally placed for stationing lookouts. The lookout stations to the east may have had their view of the Palomas Lake obscured by the Cerros La Rosina, but would have been able to spot Beyer and Maney's detachments at daylight on 24 September, as they moved into Mexico.[93] (See Map 15.2 for a summary of the Buell and Terrazas campaign against Victorio.)

Other detachments of US troops, stationed at Knight's Ranch and Fort Cummings, would also move south in several groups, and rendezvous south of the border at Palomas Lake by 24 September. Captain Theaker, with 70 Sixteenth Infantrymen, was to move south from Knight's Ranch, departing on 20 September.[94] Theaker was to join up with Buell's supply train and proceed to Palomas Lake.[95] Theaker was also accompanied by at least one company of Ninth Cavalry, which was commanded by Captain Purington and Lieutenant Rucker.[96] Theaker and Purington's detachments, while en-route to Palomas Lake, were encountered on the road by Captain Pollack, Acting Assistant Inspector General for the District of New Mexico, who was travelling to Knight's Ranch to inspect those very units. Pollack was completely unaware of the mounting of a major military operation into Mexico, and telegraphed Hatch asking for information about this operation on 21 September, after his encounter. He also used the occasion to observe that more pack mules were required if effective field service was to be rendered.[97]

Several detachments issued from Fort Cummings between 19 and 21 September: Buell's supply train, commanded by Captain Hartz, was set in motion on 19 September; and the following day, approximately 80 Fifteenth Infantrymen under Major Osborne left Fort Cummings. This command was accompanied by a water wagon which could carry in excess of 400 gallons, and had

90 Acting Chief Signal Officer to Lt Allen, SF, 16 Sept., 1880, NA, RG393, Part 1, Entry 2546, pp.608-609.

91 Brinkerhoff reports Beyer's detachment as consisting of Companies D and L Ninth Cavalry with a detachment of Indian scouts and having arrived at Fort Bliss on the 18 September, 1880. (Brinkerhoff to AAAG SF 19 Sept., 1880, NA, RG393, Part 3, Entry 439, p.413).

92 Buell, HQ Fort Stanton N.M., to AAG, DoM (via AAAG DoNM), 20 Nov., 1880 in Letters Received by HQ DoNM Sept. 1865-Aug. 1890, NA, RG393, M1088, Roll 42, File 658-1658, Jan.-Apr. 1881; See also Crimmins, 1935, p.136; Stout, 1974, p. 169.

93 See Cuidad Juarez H13-1 Map from the Instituto Nacional De Estadistica Geografia e Infromatica, Estados Unidos Mexicanos.

94 Buell, HQ Fort Stanton N.M., to AAG, DoM (via AAAG DoNM), 20 Nov., 1880 in Letters Received by HQ DoNM Sept. 1865-Aug. 1890, NA, RG393, M1088, Roll 42, File 658-1658, Jan.-Apr. 1881; See also Crimmins, 1935, p.135; Smith, 1994, p.158.

95 Buell, HQ Fort Stanton N.M., to AAG, DoM (via AAAG DoNM), 20 Nov., 1880 in Letters Received by HQ DoNM Sept. 1865-Aug. 1890, NA, RG393, M1088, Roll 42, File 658-1658, Jan.-Apr. 1881 See also Crimmins, 1935, p.138.

96 Pollack to Hatch 21 Sept., 1880, NA, RG393, Part 3, Entry 439, p.414.

97 Pollock to Hatch, 21 Sept., 1880 in NA, RG393 Part 3 Entry 439 p.415; Pollack to AAAG, DoNM, 23 Sept., 1880 in Letters Received by HQ DoNM Sept. 1865-Aug. 1890, NA, RG393, M1088, Roll 41, Jul.-Dec. 1880.

Plate 15.3. Fort Cummings. Little remains today of the large military fort around which Buell assembled his expedition. (Photo: Author)

Plate 15.4. This photo gives at least an impression of the perspective that troops leaving Fort Cummings for Mexico would have had. As one rounds the hill to the right of the photo, one is confronted by a long, deceptively 'flat' stretch of desert country, punctuated by: the Floridas, the Tres Hermanas, and on into northern Chihuahua. (Photo: Author)

been designed by Buell himself.[98] Finally, on 21 September, Buell departed Fort Cummings with two cavalry battalions. Lieutenant Colonel Dudley commanded the first battalion of approximately 100 Ninth Cavalrymen. The second battalion, consisting of 109 troops from the Fourth Cavalry, was led by Major Noyes.[99] The regimental returns suggest that this battalion consisted of A and H Companies, Fourth Cavalry.[100] The cavalry battalions were each equipped with a single Hotchkiss mountain howitzer.[101] To maintain communication between his commands, Buell provided each detachment with several civilian scouts. Sherman later upbraided him for employing such men, as this exceeded the army's strength as authorized by Congress.[102] Buell was making every effort to prevent Victorio from quietly slipping around his cordon and escaping into New Mexico, having had this possibility stressed to him by the Ninth Cavalry officers with the expedition, based on their previous experience. He thought that if he kept a number of civilian scouts active between his various detachments, such a manoeuvre by the Apaches might be detected quickly enough to prevent them evading his net.[103] In this context, it is worth noting that Colonel Hatch was not convinced that Buell knew how to manage his Apache scouts in such a way as to realise their maximum potential in the field.[104]

At District Headquarters, Hatch lost contact with Buell's command from 21 September until 2 October 1880,[105] when Roman Aranda arrived at Fort Bliss to report on progress up to that date.[106] Buell would then again 'disappear' for a few days, prompting Hatch to complain that he 'has not communicated with these Headquarters for weeks though ordered to do so'.[107]

The Ninth and Fourth Cavalry battalions failed to find water in the southern reaches of the Florida Mountains. Buell had to continue on through the night to Palomas Lake, reaching it well ahead of schedule at 6:00 a.m. on 23 September.[108] The original rendezvous was to have been at midnight on 23 September.[109] Major Osborne had already arrived with his infantrymen, and the rest of the force were concentrated at Palomas Lake early on 24 September. That night, contact with Lieutenant Mills's detachment of Apache scouts was established, but the actual location of Carr's

---

98 Buell, HQ Fort Stanton N.M., to AAG, DoM (via AAAG DoNM), 20 Nov., 1880 in Letters Received by HQ DoNM Sept. 1865-Aug. 1890, NA, RG393, M1088, Roll 42, File 658-1658, Jan.-Apr. 1881; See also Crimmins, 1935, pp.136-137; Thrapp, 1988, p.186.

99 Buell, HQ Fort Stanton N.M., to AAG, DoM (via AAAG DoNM), 20 Nov., 1880 in Letters Received by HQ DoNM Sept. 1865-Aug. 1890, NA, RG393, M1088, Roll 42, File 658-1658, Jan.-Apr. 1881; Note appended to Buell to Samaniego, 18 Sept., 1880 in 'Victorio Papers', NA, M666, Roll 528; See also Crimmins, 1935, p.137; F. Nolan, 1994, p.35.

100 4th Cavalry 1878-1883, Sept./Oct., 1880, Returns from Regular Army Cavalry Regiments 1833-1916 NA, RG393, NA, M744, Roll 43.

101 Crimmins, 1935, p.136.

102 Sherman, 10 Nov., 1880 in 'Victorio Papers', NA, M666, Roll 528.

103 Hatch to AAG, DoM, Fort Leavenworth, 15 Sept., 1880 in Letters Sent by '9MD/DNM/DoNM', NA, RG393, M1072, Roll 6, Jan. 1880-Aug. 1881, Letter No.488, pp315-316.

104 Hatch to AAG, DoM, Fort Leavenworth, 15 Sept., 1880 in Letters Sent by '9MD/DNM/DoNM', NA, RG393, M1072, Roll 6, Jan. 1880-Aug. 1881, Letter No.488, pp315-316.

105 Hatch to AAG Fort Leavenworth, 25, 27, 28, & 30 Sept., 1880, Telegrams Sent DoNM, Vol.3, Jan. – Nov. 1880 NA, RG393, Part 3, Entry 431, p.869, p.872, p.874 & p.879.

106 Hatch to AAG Fort Leavenworth, 2 Oct., 1880, Telegrams Sent DoNM, Vol.3, Jan. – Nov. 1880 NA, RG393, Part 3, Entry 431, p.889; Hatch to AAAG Fort Leavenworth, 2 Oct., 1880, 'Victorio Files' NA, RG393, M1495, Roll 14.

107 Hatch to AAG Fort Leavenworth, 6 Oct., 1880, Telegrams Sent DoNM, Vol.3, Jan. – Nov. 1880 NA, RG393, Part 3, Entry 431, p.905.

108 Buell, HQ Fort Stanton N.M., to AAG, DoM (via AAAG DoNM), 20 Nov., 1880 in Letters Received by HQ DoNM Sept. 1865-Aug. 1890, NA, RG393, M1088, Roll 42, File 658-1658, Jan.-Apr. 1881; See also Crimmins, 1935, p.137.

109 Pollack to Hatch 21 Sept., 1880, NA, RG393, Part 3, Entry 439, p.414.

force could not be ascertained.[110] Buell proceeded south to the Laguna de Guzman, being joined by Lieutenant Maney with his Indian scouts on 25 September.[111] Buell stated that the trail left by the Apaches in the aftermath of the skirmish on 7 September was followed from where it crossed the border to this point. It then turned to the south-east, making for the Candelaria Mountains.[112] In the hope that Carr would rendezvous with him, he halted by the Laguna de Guzman for part of the day. He then marched on to the Laguna de Santa Maria. Here he spent a whole day (26 September) waiting in vain for any sign of the Arizona troops.[113] Jack Crawford rejoined Buell just south of the border, at Palomas Lake, as earlier instructed. Buell sent Crawford with three men to move towards the Rio Grande to check for any signs that the Apaches had passed Beyer's left flank and made for New Mexico.[114]

Information was received at Santa Fé, through Fort Bliss, that Victorio had left the Laguna de Guzman area and had moved into the Candelaria Mountains on or around 18 September,[115] but this information does not seem to have reached Buell. Lieutenant Mills reported that it was a courier from Beyer's command who informed Buell that Victorio had gathered up his followers from around the Laguna de Guzman and made towards the Candelaria Mountains.[116] Buell estimated that Victorio had been surprised by such a major incursion of US forces, and had decided to withdraw to the Candelaria Mountains.[117]

The inference that Victorio had moved eastwards from the Laguna de Guzman can be drawn from the fact that the unfortunate Dr Samaniego's property was struck again on 18 September 1880. The raiders, 18 in number, were said to have captured 120 horses belonging to Dr Samaniego during a dawn attack on the San Jose stage station, on the road to Chihuahua City, 65 miles south

110 Buell, HQ Fort Stanton N.M., to AAG, DoM (via AAAG DoNM), 20 Nov., 1880 in Letters Received by HQ DoNM Sept. 1865-Aug. 1890, NA, RG393, M1088, Roll 42, File 658-1658, Jan.-Apr. 1881; See also Crimmins, 1935, pp.137-138; See also Mills to AAAG Troops in the Field in S.E. Arizona, Fort Lowell, 11 Oct., 1880 in Reports & Tabular Statements of Scouting Expeditions 1867-91, NA, RG391 Entry 841.

111 Buell, HQ Fort Stanton N.M., to AAG, DoM (via AAAG DoNM), 20 Nov., 1880 in Letters Received by HQ DoNM Sept. 1865-Aug. 1890, NA, RG393, M1088, Roll 42, File 658-1658, Jan.-Apr. 1881; Mills to AAAG Troops in the Field in S.E. Arizona, Fort Lowell, 11 Oct., 1880 in Reports & Tabular Statements of Scouting Expeditions 1867-91, NA, RG391 Entry 841.

112 Buell to AAAG, DoNM, 15 Oct., 1880 in NA, RG393, Part 3, Entry 439, pp.260-267; Hatch (passing on copy of Buell's Report) to AAG, Fort Leavenworth, 15 Oct., 1880, 'Victorio Files' NA, RG393, M1495, Roll 14; same letter contained in 'Victorio Papers', NA, M666, Roll 528; Buell, HQ Fort Stanton N.M., to AAG, DoM (via Office of AAAG, DoNM), 20 Nov., 1880 in Letters Received by HQ DoNM Sept. 1865-Aug. 1890, NA, RG393, M1088, Roll 42, File 658-1658, Jan.-Apr. 1881.

113 Buell, HQ Fort Stanton N.M., to AAG, DoM (via AAAG DoNM), 20 Nov., 1880 in Letters Received by HQ DoNM Sept. 1865-Aug. 1890, NA, RG393, M1088, Roll 42, File 658-1658, Jan.-Apr. 1881; See also Crimmins, 1935, p.138.

114 Buell, HQ Fort Stanton N.M., to AAG, DoM (via AAAG DoNM), 20 Nov., 1880 in Letters Received by HQ DoNM Sept. 1865-Aug. 1890, NA, RG393, M1088, Roll 42, File 658-1658, Jan.-Apr. 1881; 'The Pursuit of Victorio' By Captain Jack Crawford Socorro County Historical Society, Publications in History, Volume 1, Feb., 1965.

115 Hatch (citing Brinkerhoff, 20 Sept., 1880) to AAG Fort Leavenworth, 21 Sept., 1880, Telegrams Sent DoNM, Vol.3, Jan. – Nov. 1880 NA, RG393, Part 3, Entry 431, p.850; Information from Fort Bliss, 20 Sept. cited in Whipple? To Ord, 24 Sept., 1880, NA, RG393, Part 1, Entry 2539, Press Copies of Letters and Endorsements Sent, MDoM, Vol. 13, p.628; See also Crimmins, 1935, p.138; Stout, p.170.

116 Mills to AAAG Troops in the Field in S.E. Arizona, Fort Lowell, 11 Oct., 1880 in Reports & Tabular Statements of Scouting Expeditions 1867-91, NA, RG391 Entry 841; Buell, HQ Fort Stanton N.M., to AAG, DoM (via AAAG DoNM), 20 Nov., 1880 in Letters Received by HQ DoNM Sept. 1865-Aug. 1890, NA, RG393, M1088, Roll 42, File 658-1658, Jan.-Apr. 1881.

117 Buell, HQ Fort Stanton N.M., to AAG, DoM (via AAAG DoNM), 20 Nov., 1880 in Letters Received by HQ DoNM Sept. 1865-Aug. 1890, NA, RG393, M1088, Roll 42, File 658-1658, Jan.-Apr. 1881.

Plates 15.5 and 15.6. Two photos showing the terrain in northern Chihuahua to the south of Palomas Lake. The upper photo looks east towards the southern reaches of the Potrillo Mountains and Guzman Mountains. The lower photo looks north, and the Florida Mountains are just visible on the central horizon. This was the dry arid country that Buell's expedition had to cross when they entered Mexico. These photos were taken in September (2005) to convey the heat experienced and distances covered by US troops in search of Victorio. (Photos: Author)

of El Paso. The captured horses were driven off in the direction of the Candelaria Mountains. One Mexican 'boy' was killed at the stage station.[118] A force of Mexicans sent in pursuit recovered 65 horses and reported that the Apaches had gone in the direction of Laguna de Guzman.[119] It was later reported that, as the Apaches approached the Candelaria Mountains, they divided the herd, with one portion being driven off towards the Sierra del Fierro.[120]

At Palo Blanco, it was reported that a 'train' had been attacked and 11 animals had been stolen.[121] Torrential rain had hampered the pursuit, giving the Apaches a number of hours' start before they were pursued.[122] The splitting of the herd suggested that Victorio was not going to make a stand in the Candelaria Mountains, but was going to make for the Sierra del Fierro. This time, the Apaches, critically short of ammunition, could not deploy the tactic of drawing off their pursuers by using the majority of their warriors, while their dependents slipped away quietly. Victorio had only two options left other than to surrender: first, to completely evade his pursuers; or, if that failed, to stay so far ahead of the enemy that the latter's mounts would break down before his own horses collapsed. With the number of both Mexican and US forces converging on his position, Victorio must have known that his chances of giving all of these forces the slip would be small. Therefore, he raided for fresh horses, sending some to meet him in the Candelaria Mountains while the rest were driven on to the Sierra del Fierro to await his arrival. Thus he would be able to maintain a supply of fresh horses as he attempted to run those of his opponents into the ground.

From his bivouac at Laguna de Santa Maria, Buell also sent messages to forces in El Paso, and further east, to Colonel Grierson, warning them to watch out for any attempt by the Apaches to cross the Rio Grande.[123] He also asked Grierson to move across the border in support.[124] Much to Buell's chagrin,[125] Grierson refused, arguing that US troops had no authority to be operating

118 Brinkerhoff to AAAG SF 20 Sept., 1880, Telegrams Sent DoNM, Vol.3, Jan. – Nov. 1880 NA, RG393, Part 3, Entry 431, p.851; Information from Fort Bliss, 20 Sept. cited in Whipple? To Ord, 24 Sept., 1880, NA, RG393, Part 1, Entry 2539, Press Copies of Letters and Endorsements Sent, MDoM, Vol. 13, p.628; Brinkerhoff to AAAG, 20 Sept., 1880, NA, RG393, Part 3, Entry 439, pp.419-420; Hatch to AG Fort Leavenworth, 21 Sept., 1880, 'Victorio Files' NA, RG393, M1495, Roll 14; Thrapp, 1974, p.291; Stout, p.171; Gillett, 1976, p.183.

119 Rasch states that Lake Guzman is approximately 40 miles south of Columbus. (1960, p.9) On modern maps the Laguna would appear to be approximately sixty kilometres south of Columbus or fifty-five kilometres from the actual border. See NH 13-1 – El Paso (USGS) & H13-1-Cuidad Juarez (INEGI).

120 Brinkerhoff to Grierson, 22 Sept., 1880 & Nolan to AAAG, Fort Davis 22 Sept., 1880 in Letters Rec'd File 19 Mar., 1878-14 Feb., 1881, HQ Records DoP 1878-1881, NA, RG393, M1381, Roll 2; Brinkerhoff to Grierson. 22 & 25 Sept., 1880 in Register of Telegrams Rec'd 11 Oct., 1879-8 Oct., 1880, HQ Records DoP 1878-1881, NA, RG393, M1381, Roll 2, pp.221-222 & p.227, Letter No.392 & 399.

121 Baylor to Grierson, 30 Sept., 1880 Telegrams Rec'd, 18 May, 1880-4 Feb., 1881, HQ Records DoP 1878-1881, NA, RG393, M1381, Roll 4. The microfilm copy of this letter has not been properly flattened before copying and thus Baylor's report on the San Jose attack can be seen than a line is obscured but enough detail is left on the next page to suggest that the latter attack occurred about the same time.

122 Brinkerhoff to AAAG 31 Aug., 1880, NA, RG393, Part 3, Entry 439, pp.806-807; Brinkerhoff to AAAG SF, 23 Sept., 1880, Telegrams Sent DoNM, Vol.3, Jan. – Nov. 1880 NA, RG393, Part 3, Entry 431, p.866.

123 Buell, HQ Fort Stanton N.M., to AAG, DoM (via AAAG DoNM), 20 Nov., 1880 in Letters Received by HQ DoNM Sept. 1865-Aug. 1890, NA, RG393, M1088, Roll 42, File 658-1658, Jan.-Apr. 1881.

124 Buell (on road to Quitman, 4pm) to Grierson, 5 Oct., 1880 in Letters Rec'd File 19 Mar., 1878-14 Feb., 1881, HQ Records DoP 1878-1881, NA, RG393, M1381, Roll 2; Buell to Grierson, 5 Oct., 1880 in Register of Telegrams Rec'd 11 Oct., 1879-8 Oct., 1880, HQ Records DoP 1878-1881, NA, RG393, M1381, Roll 2, pp.248-249, Letter No.450.

125 Buell to AAAG, DoNM, 15 Oct., 1880 in NA, RG393, Part 3, Entry 439, pp.260-267; Hatch (passing on copy of Buell's Report) to AAG, Fort Leavenworth, 15 Oct., 1880, 'Victorio Files' NA, RG393, M1495, Roll 14; same letter contained in 'Victorio Papers', NA, M666, Roll 528; See also Buell, HQ

within the republic of Mexico.[126] In response, Buell requested command of Grierson's forces, but General Ord, while noting that that Grierson had been instructed to cooperate with Buell's forces, refused this request.[127]

Berger, with his small detachment of six Tenth Cavalrymen, arrived at Cantareccio[128] on 28 September.[129] They had already encountered three Apaches at the Tinaja de la Bandija, nine miles away. Berger had not charged them, being unsure whether these were Mexican volunteers or Apaches. At Cantareccio, he was informed that Roman Aranda, with 50 of his own men and the detachment of 13 Texas Rangers, were camped at Los Palos Blancos, near the Candelaria Mountains, waiting for the arrival of Colonel Terrazas. Berger concluded that the main part of Victorio's following had already crossed to either the Sierras Borracho, de Los Pinos or del Fierro and that Joaquin Terrazas was making for the Candelaria Mountains to pick up their trail.[130]. He reported that Terrazas and Buell had lost Victorio's trail on account of recent heavy rainfall between Laguna de Guzman and the Candelaria Mountains.[131] Berger determined to join Aranda and Baylor, and so these were probably the first US troops to make contact with Terrazas' forces. Indeed, Brinkerhoff reported that Terrazas' forces had still not made face-to-face contact with Buell's command by 29 September. Word had been received at Fort Bliss, from Baylor, that on 23 September, the tracks of approximately 50 Apaches had been discovered going across the El Paso to Chihuahua City road. The trail led towards the Sierra de Los Pinos.[132] Berger finally met Terrazas at a place called Los Blancos or Palos Blancos. Buell was expected, but had not arrived by the time that Terrazas left that point for San Jose with 400 men, on 30 September.

Fort Stanton N.M., to AAG, DoM (via AAAG DoNM), 20 Nov., 1880 in Letters Received by HQ DoNM Sept. 1865-Aug. 1890, NA, RG393, M1088, Roll 42, File 658-1658, Jan.-Apr. 1881; Dinges, 1987, p.93.

126 Grierson to Buell 4 Sept., 1880 in Telegrams Sent 23 Jun.-30 Nov., 1880, HQ Records DoP 1878-1881, NA, RG393, M1381, Roll 1, pp.148-149, Letter No.466; Grierson to AAG, DoTx, 3 Oct., 1880 in Telegrams Sent 23 Jun.-30 Nov., 1880, HQ Records DoP 1878-1881, NA, RG393, M1381, Roll 1, p.185, Letter No.540; Grierson to Buell, 6 Oct., 1880 in Telegrams Sent 23 Jun.-30 Nov., 1880, HQ Records DoP 1878-1881, NA, RG393, M1381, Roll 1, pp.196-198, Letter No.561; Grierson to AAG, DoTx, 31 Dec. in Letters Sent 23 Aug.-31 Dec., 1880, HQ Records DoP 1878-1881, NA, RG393, M1381, Roll 1, Letter No.168 (Note: This latter report contained as Letter No. 3 in Letters sent 1881.).

127 Vincent to Grierson, 8 Oct., 1880 in Register of Telegrams Rec'd 11 Oct., 1879-8 Oct., 1880, HQ Records DoP 1878-1881, NA, RG393, M1381, Roll 2, pp.260-261, Letter No.470; Vincent to Grierson, 8 Oct., 1880 in Telegrams Rec'd, 18 May, 1880-4 Feb., 1881, HQ Records DoP 1878-1881, NA, RG393, M1381, Roll 4; Hatch to Buell. 9 Oct., 1880, Telegrams Sent DoNM, Vol.3, Jan. – Nov. 1880 NA, RG393, Part 3, Entry 431, p.927.

128 Buell stated that Canta Recio was a Ranche owned by Roman Aranda. (Buell to Grierson, 4 Oct., 1880 in Register of Telegrams Rec'd 11 Oct., 1879-8 Oct., 1880, HQ Records DoP 1878-1881, NA, RG393, M1381, Roll 2, p.250, Letter No.453).

129 Brinkerhoff to AAAG 29 Sept., 1880, NA, RG393, Part 3, Entry 439, pp.122-123.

130 Brinkerhoff to AAAG 29 Sept., 1880, NA, RG393, Part 3, Entry 439, pp.122-123; Beck to CO, Eagle Springs, 2 Oct., 1880 in Letters Sent 23 Aug.-31 Dec., 1880, HQ Records DoP 1878-1881, NA, RG393, M1381, Roll 1, Letter No.168; Brinkerhoff to Beck, 29 Sept., 1880 Brinkerhoff to Grierson, 22 Sept., 1880 in Letters Rec'd File 19 Mar., 1878-14 Feb., 1881, HQ Records DoP 1878-1881, NA, RG393, M1381, Roll 2.

131 Berger to Nolan, 28 Sept., 1880 in Letters Rec'd File 19 Mar., 1878-14 Feb., 1881, HQ Records DoP 1878-1881, NA, RG393, M1381, Roll 2; Brinkerhoff to Grierson, 2 Oct., 1880 in Register of Telegrams Rec'd 11 Oct., 1879-8 Oct., 1880, HQ Records DoP 1878-1881, NA, RG393, M1381, Roll 2, pp.240-241, Letter No.435.

132 Brinkerhoff to Grierson, 26 Sept., 1880 in Register of Telegrams Rec'd 11 Oct., 1879-8 Oct., 1880, HQ Records DoP 1878-1881, NA, RG393, M1381, Roll 2, pp.229-230, Letter No.406.

From that point, Terrazas was going to advance towards the Sierra Borracho visiting all the springs and tanks to ensure that no Apaches had managed to get around behind him.[133] This implied that Terrazas was going to leave detachments of troops to picket these waterholes. Berger also stated that scouts sent out from Palo Blanco had discovered fresh camp sites, but no Apaches, and indications that Victorio was moving a large herd of horses and cattle.[134] This information reached Grierson, who immediately alerted Captains Nolan and Carpenter to double their vigilance in case Victorio should attempt to cross the Rio Grande into Texas.[135] By 7 October, Grierson had deployed two companies of cavalry at Old Fort Quitman and three cavalry companies near Ojo Caliente, Texas, and one company of cavalry had been ordered from Eagle Springs to Viejo Pass. This left one company of cavalry and one of infantry at Eagle Springs. A further company of cavalry was en route to Viejo Pass; and, finally, two companies of cavalry were based in the Guadalupe Mountains. Grierson's only worry was that Victorio would try to move even further down the Rio Grande to bypass his picket line, and he requested that Colonel Shafter, Commanding Officer, District of the Bravo, alert Lieutenant Bullis and his Seminole-Negro scouts.[136]

Returning to Buell's command, the Colonel's couriers had informed Colonel Terrazas that, 'we would get a fight with Victorio in the Candelaria Mountains'.[137] Late in the evening of 24 September, Buell had addressed a letter to Terrazas informing him that his command was camped on the Corralitos River, 20 miles to the north of the Laguna de Guzman. He added that his troops were preparing to set off for the Candelaria Mountains, moving in three detachments. The most northerly detachment was following a trail leading towards these mountains. Buell requested that Terrazas manoeuvre his forces to approach the south and east sides of the Candelarias by the morning of 26 September. If Terrazas was convinced that Victorio was still in the Candelarias, he was to block these sides of the mountains while Buell's forces would move in from the north and west. Buell also requested that Terrazas, 'Signal to me with flags wherever you are and two (2) small fires at night twenty (20) feet apart.'[138]

Buell initiated his movement towards the Candelarias by ordering Captain Beyer to carefully scout those mountains. Beyer was to follow the trail left by the Apaches, from the Lagunas de Guzman and Santa Maria towards the Candelarias.[139] His orders were not to attack the Apaches but to shadow them until Buell could bring the bulk of his forces into action.[140] This particular move, however, was frustrated by a nervous sentry accidentally firing his weapon and stampeding Beyer's mounts while his men were camped close to the Candelaria Mountains.[141]

---

133 Nolan to Carpenter 3 Oct., 1880 in Letters Rec'd File 19 Mar., 1878-14 Feb., 1881, HQ Records DoP 1878-1881, NA, RG393, M1381, Roll 2.

134 Nolan to Carpenter 3 Oct., 1880 in Letters Rec'd File 19 Mar., 1878-14 Feb., 1881, HQ Records DoP 1878-1881, NA, RG393, M1381, Roll 2.

135 Beck to CO, Eagle Springs, 2 Oct., 1880 in Letters Sent 23 Aug.-31 Dec., 1880, HQ Records DoP 1878-1881, NA, RG393, M1381, Roll 1, Letter No.168.

136 Beck to Shafter, 7 Oct., 1880 in Letters Sent 23 Aug.-31 Dec., 1880, HQ Records DoP 1878-1881, NA, RG393, M1381, Roll 1, Letter No.171; Smither to McLaughlen, Fort Davis, 7 Oct., 1880 in Letters Rec'd File 19 Mar., 1878-14 Feb., 1881, HQ Records DoP 1878-1881, NA, RG393, M1381, Roll 2.

137 Buell, HQ Fort Stanton N.M., to AAG, DoM (via AAAG DoNM), 20 Nov., 1880 in Letters Received by HQ DoNM Sept. 1865-Aug. 1890, NA, RG393, M1088, Roll 42, File 658-1658, Jan.-Apr. 1881; See also Crimmins, 1935, pp.138-139.

138 Buell to Terrazas, 10.30pm, 24 Sept., 1880 in 'Victorio Papers', NA, M666, Roll 528.

139 Buell, HQ Fort Stanton N.M., to AAG, DoM (via AAAG DoNM), 20 Nov., 1880 in Letters Received by HQ DoNM Sept. 1865-Aug. 1890, NA, RG393, M1088, Roll 42, File 658-1658, Jan.-Apr. 1881.

140 Mills to AAAG Troops in the Field in S.E. Arizona, Fort Lowell, 11 Oct., 1880 in Reports & Tabular Statements of Scouting Expeditions 1867-91, NA, RG391 Entry 841.

141 Brinkerhoff to AAAG SF 1 Oct., 1880, NA, RG393, Part 3, Entry 439, p.235; Hatch to AAG Fort Leavenworth, 1 Oct., 1880, Telegrams Sent DoNM, Vol.3, Jan. – Nov. 1880 NA, RG393, Part 3, Entry

Buell then moved the bulk of his forces eastwards towards the Candelaria Mountains from the Laguna de Santa Maria. Thus, all the cavalry and 30 infantry volunteers, commanded by Buell, marched directly towards the Candelarias on 28 September. This included Lieutenant Mills' Apache scout company, whom up until this point, the Lieutenant had declined to place under Buell's command, and had stationed on the eastern slopes of the Guzman Mountains to watch the country. Mills sent up smoke during the day and lit signal fires at night.[142] This was to both to attract the attention of Carr's command, and to discourage Apaches from moving in that direction. The balance of Buell's infantry and the supply train were sent on a long loop south up the Rio de Santa Maria, to San Jose de Patos (presumably near the Laguna de Patos), and on to El Lucero.[143]

During daylight on 29 September, Buell concealed his troops behind some small hills in the San Blas plains near the Candelaria Mountains and moved into those mountains during the night. The following day was spent in a fruitless search of the Candelarias,[144] with Buell implying that he was rather glad that Victorio had not chosen to make a stand in this rough terrain.[145] Buell himself estimated that a 'rearguard' of approximately 20 Apaches had departed on 26 September.[146] Lieutenant Mills reported that there was little water in the Candelaria Mountains, and that he had discovered only three tanks of water: one in the centre of the mountains, one on their west side, and one at their south-eastern tip. Victorio's trail was followed to the central tank, where the remains of his camp was discovered. The trail of the Apaches then left this camp moving in a north-easterly direction.[147] Captain Beyer had also managed to send some scouts into the mountains, and they reported that the Apaches were four days departed.[148] Buell was forced to march to El Lucero in search of water, reaching that point on 1 October. Beyer's company, having eventually recovered their stampeded horses, re-joined him at that point. The recovery of Beyer's animals was expedited by the assistance of the local Mexican population.[149] Mills stated that Buell had passed by the San Jasito (San Jose?)

431, pp.885-886; Mills to AAAG Troops in the Field in S.E. Arizona, Fort Lowell, 11 Oct., 1880 in Reports & Tabular Statements of Scouting Expeditions 1867-91, NA, RG391 Entry 841; Buell, HQ Fort Stanton N.M., to AAG, DoM (via AAAG DoNM), 20 Nov., 1880 in Letters Received by HQ DoNM Sept. 1865-Aug. 1890, NA, RG393, M1088, Roll 42, File 658-1658, Jan.-Apr. 1881; See also Crimmins, 1935, p.139; Stout, 1974, p.170.

142 Mills to AAAG Troops in the Field in S.E. Arizona, Fort Lowell, 11 Oct., 1880 in Reports & Tabular Statements of Scouting Expeditions 1867-91, NA, RG391 Entry 841.

143 Buell, HQ Fort Stanton N.M., to AAG, DoM (via AAAG DoNM), 20 Nov., 1880 in Letters Received by HQ DoNM Sept. 1865-Aug. 1890, NA, RG393, M1088, Roll 42, File 658-1658, Jan.-Apr. 1881; See also Crimmins, 1935, p.139.

144 Buell, HQ Fort Stanton N.M., to AAG, DoM (via AAAG DoNM), 20 Nov., 1880 in Letters Received by HQ DoNM Sept. 1865-Aug. 1890, NA, RG393, M1088, Roll 42, File 658-1658, Jan.-Apr. 1881; Brinkerhoff to AAAG SF 1 Oct., 1880, NA, RG393, Part 3, Entry 439, p.234; See also Crimmins, 1935, p.140.

145 Buell, HQ Fort Stanton N.M., to AAG, DoM (via AAAG DoNM), 20 Nov., 1880 in Letters Received by HQ DoNM Sept. 1865-Aug. 1890, NA, RG393, M1088, Roll 42, File 658-1658, Jan.-Apr. 1881.

146 'Indian Affairs', *Army & Navy Journal*, Vol. 18, 30 Oct., 1880, p.241.

147 Mills to AAAG Troops in the Field in S.E. Arizona, Fort Lowell, 11 Oct., 1880 in Reports & Tabular Statements of Scouting Expeditions 1867-91, NA, RG391 Entry 841.

148 Buell, HQ Fort Stanton N.M., to AAG, DoM (via AAAG DoNM), 20 Nov., 1880 in Letters Received by HQ DoNM Sept. 1865-Aug. 1890, NA, RG393, M1088, Roll 42, File 658-1658, Jan.-Apr. 1881; See also Crimmins, 1935, p.140; Thrapp, 1988, p.186.

149 Brinkerhoff to AAAG SF 1 Oct., 1880, NA, RG393, Part 3, Entry 439, pp.232-233, Brinkerhoff to AAAG SF 1 Oct., 1880, NA, RG393, Part 3, Entry 439, pp.234-235 & Unsigned and undated note in NA, RG393, Part 3, Entry 439, p.236; Hatch to AAG Fort Leavenworth, 1 Oct., 1880, Telegrams Sent DoNM, Vol.3, Jan. – Nov. 1880 NA, RG393, Part 3, Entry 431, pp.885-886; Bi-Monthly Company Muster Rolls for Company L, 9th Cavalry, Sept./Oct., 1880 in NA, RG94; Buell, HQ Fort Stanton N.M., to AAG, DoM (via AAAG DoNM), 20 Nov., 1880 in Letters Received by HQ DoNM Sept. 1865-Aug. 1890, NA, RG393, M1088, Roll 42, File 658-1658, Jan.-Apr. 1881.

Ranch, owned by Dr Samaniego, 12 miles to the south of the Candelaria Mountains. It was from this ranch that Victorio's warriors had earlier run off 120 horses.[150] Buell's supply train arrived on the following day.[151] Buell's main concern was that the Apaches would split into small groups after leaving the Candelarias and attempt to infiltrate back into the United States. However, his scouts confirmed that Victorio had not scattered, and that a clear trail led away from the Candelaria Mountains.[152] On 1 October, couriers from Terrazas also informed Buell that Victorio appeared to be making for the Sierra de Los Pinos.[153] Brinkerhoff received a report from Roman Aranda on 2 October, to the effect that Buell was pursuing Victorio towards the Sierra de Los Pinos, and that he and Terrazas had arranged to join their commands in those mountains.[154] Brinkerhoff also received a report, via stagecoach, that Buell and Terrazas had met face to face on 2 October, at Cantarrecio.[155] Terrazas estimated that he could get to the Sierra Borracho by 5 or 6 October.[156] The plan, at that point, was to force Victorio across the Rio Grande towards Grierson's forces.[157] Knowing that Terrazas was still to the south of him, Buell determined to move to Cantarrecio (or Santa Recia[158]), keeping himself between Victorio and the New Mexico border. To do this he marched his column up the Chihuahua to El Paso road and reached Cantareccio on 4 October. The following day, Buell sent couriers in search of Terrazas to inform him that he would station his forces to the north of the Sierra de Los Pinos while Terrazas was to approach these mountains from the south.[159] Their limited off-road transportation (i.e. mules) and unfamiliarity with the lie of the land to the east of El Lucero, also influenced his move to the north.[160] The clearest outline of the

150 Mills to AAAG Troops in the Field in S.E. Arizona, Fort Lowell, 11 Oct., 1880 in Reports & Tabular Statements of Scouting Expeditions 1867-91, NA, RG391 Entry 841.

151 Buell, HQ Fort Stanton N.M., to AAG, DoM (via AAAG DoNM), 20 Nov., 1880 in Letters Received by HQ DoNM Sept. 1865-Aug. 1890, NA, RG393, M1088, Roll 42, File 658-1658, Jan.-Apr. 1881.

152 Buell, HQ Fort Stanton N.M., to AAG, DoM (via AAAG DoNM), 20 Nov., 1880 in Letters Received by HQ DoNM Sept. 1865-Aug. 1890, NA, RG393, M1088, Roll 42, File 658-1658, Jan.-Apr. 1881; See also Crimmins, 1935, p.140.

153 Buell, Canta Recia to AAAG SF via Fort Bliss, 4 Oct., 1880, Telegrams Sent DoNM, Vol.3, Jan. – Nov. 1880 NA, RG393, Part 3, Entry 431, pp.908-909; Crimmins p.140; Stout, p.170; Rasch, 1960, p.9.

154 Brinkerhoff to AAAG SF 2 Oct., 1880, NA, RG393, Part 3, Entry 439, p.237; Hatch to AAG Fort Leavenworth, 2 Oct., 1880, Telegrams Sent DoNM, Vol.3, Jan. – Nov. 1880 NA, RG393, Part 3, Entry 431, p.889.

155 Brinkerhoff to Grierson, 5 Oct., 1880 in Letters Rec'd File 19 Mar., 1878-14 Feb., 1881, HQ Records DoP 1878-1881, NA, RG393, M1381, Roll 2; Brinkerhoff to Grierson, 5 Oct., 1880 in Register of Telegrams Rec'd 11 Oct., 1879-8 Oct., 1880, HQ Records DoP 1878-1881, NA, RG393, M1381, Roll 2, pp.247-248, Letter No.449; Hatch (citing Brinkerhoff telegram of 5 Oct., 1880) to AAG Fort Leavenworth, 6 Oct., 1880, Telegrams Sent DoNM, Vol.3, Jan. – Nov. 1880 NA, RG393, Part 3, Entry 431, p.905; Brinkerhoff to AAAG 5 Oct., 1880, NA, RG393, Part 3, Entry 439, p.242.

156 Buell, HQ Fort Stanton N.M., to AAG, DoM (via AAAG DoNM), 20 Nov., 1880 in Letters Received by HQ DoNM Sept. 1865-Aug. 1890, NA, RG393, M1088, Roll 42, File 658-1658, Jan.-Apr. 1881; See also Crimmins, 1935, p.140.

157 Terrazas to Buell, 6 Oct., 1880 in Letters Rec'd File 19 Mar., 1878-14 Feb., 1881, HQ Records DoP 1878-1881, NA, RG393, M1381, Roll 2; Buell, HQ Fort Stanton N.M., to AAG, DoM (via AAAG DoNM), 20 Nov., 1880 in Letters Received by HQ DoNM Sept. 1865-Aug. 1890, NA, RG393, M1088, Roll 42, File 658-1658, Jan.-Apr. 1881; See also Crimmins, 1935, p.141.

158 Buell, HQ Fort Stanton N.M., to AAG, DoM (via AAAG DoNM), 20 Nov., 1880 in Letters Received by HQ DoNM Sept. 1865-Aug. 1890, NA, RG393, M1088, Roll 42, File 658-1658, Jan.-Apr. 1881.

159 Buell to Terrazas, 5 Oct., 1880 in 'Victorio Papers', NA, M666, Roll 528; Buell, HQ Fort Stanton N.M., to AAG, DoM (via Office of AAAG, DoNM), 20 Nov., 1880 in Letters Received by HQ DoNM Sept. 1865-Aug. 1890, NA, RG393, M1088, Roll 42, File 658-1658, Jan.-Apr. 1881.

160 Buell, HQ Fort Stanton N.M., to AAG, DoM (via AAAG DoNM), 20 Nov., 1880 in Letters Received by HQ DoNM Sept. 1865-Aug. 1890, NA, RG393, M1088, Roll 42, File 658-1658, Jan.-Apr. 1881; See also Crimmins, 1935, p.140.

Buell expedition's course is given in the bi-monthly returns for D, I and K Companies, Fifteenth Infantry, taking as a starting point their departure from Fort Cummings on 20 September:

Table 15.1 Companies D, I and K, Fifteenth Infantry, during the Buell Expedition.[161]

Date	Campsite	Distance Travelled	Date	Campsite	Distance Travelled
20 Sept.	Kettle Springs	14 Miles	4 Oct.	Canta Recio	22 Miles
21 Sept.	Dry Camp	27 Miles	5 Oct.	San Ignacio	18 Miles
22 Sept.	Palomas Lake	18 Miles	6 Oct.	Along the Rio Grande	16 Miles
24 Sept.	Rio Janos	14 Miles	7 Oct.	4 Miles Below Quitman	12 Miles
25 Sept.	Lake Guzman	31 Miles	8 Oct.	Along the Rio Grande	14 Miles
26 Sept.	Santa Maria Lake	8 Miles	9 Oct.	Back up the Rio Grande	6 Miles
28 Sept.	Slocum's Ranch (Ojo Caliente)	11 Miles	10 Oct.	Opposite Quitman	15 Miles
1 Oct.	Carrisal	22½ Miles	11 Oct.	Rice's Station	17½ Miles
2 Oct.	El Lucero	18½ Miles	12 Oct.	Water Holes	22 Miles
3 Oct.	Water Holes	18 Miles	13 Oct.	San Elizario, TX	24 Miles

As far as the movements of the Chihuahuan state troops were concerned, Lieutenant Mills reported, on 2 October, that 100 Mexican volunteers belonging to Terrazas' command had passed by Samaniego's ranch marching to the north. More of Terrazas' troops were reported to be six miles to the south at San Jose. Mills noted that Terrazas himself had already moved towards the Sierra de Los Pinos.[162] Baylor observed that, if Victorio had occupied the Sierra De Los Pinos, the Apache leader would be difficult to defeat, as he invariably fortified his campsites. According to Baylor, the Sierra de Los Pinos offered a number of near impregnable grounds suitable for a camp.[163]

Not all the Apaches had departed eastwards. Lieutenant Stafford, left in command at Fort Cummings, reported an attempt to steal the cattle at that post on 1 October.[164] Hatch ordered out the available soldiers from Fort Craig to intercept these raiders.[165] Much to Hatch's annoyance,[166]

161 Bi-Monthly Company Muster Rolls for D, I & K Companies, 15th Infantry, Sept./Oct., 1880 in NA, RG94

It should be remembered that the above report lists the progress of Buell's supply train between 26 September and 2 October, while Buell had moved towards the Candelaria Mountains with his cavalry and some of his infantry.

162 Mills to AAAG Troops in the Field in S.E. Arizona, Fort Lowell, 11 Oct., 1880 in Reports & Tabular Statements of Scouting Expeditions 1867-91, NA, RG391 Entry 841.

163 Baylor to Buell, 6 Oct., 1880 in Letters Rec'd File 19 Mar., 1878-14 Feb., 1881, HQ Records DoP 1878-1881, NA, RG393, M1381, Roll 2.

164 Stafford to AAAG SF 1 Oct., 1880, NA, RG393, Part 3, Entry 439, p.232A; Stafford Ft Cummings to AAG, SF, NM, 1 Oct., 1880, NA, RG393, Part 3, Entry 440, p.91; Hatch to Carr 1 Oct., 1880, Telegrams Sent DoNM, Vol.3, Jan. – Nov. 1880 NA, RG393, Part 3, Entry 431, pp.880-881; Hatch to AAG Fort Leavenworth, 1 Oct., 1880, 'Victorio Files' NA, RG393, M1495, Roll 14.

165 Telegrams Sent DoNM, Vol.3, Jan. – Nov. 1880 NA, RG393, Part 3, Entry 431, pp.881-882; Hatch to AAG Fort Leavenworth, 1 Oct., 1880, 'Victorio Files' NA, RG393, M1495, Roll 14.

166 Hatch to AAG Fort Leavenworth, 7 Oct., 1880, Telegrams Sent DoNM, Vol.3, Jan. – Nov. 1880 NA, RG393, Part 3, Entry 431, pp.908-909.

'Buell is mistaken about no Indians in his rear. We are now scouting for small parties who have committed depredations.' (Hatch to AAG Fort Leavenworth, 7 Oct., 1880, Telegrams Sent DoNM, Vol.3, Jan. – Nov. 1880 NA, RG393, Part 3, Entry 431, pp.908-909).

Buell dismissed Stafford's report out of hand, on the grounds that Victorio's trail led eastwards out of the Candelaria Mountains leading towards the Sierra de Los Pinos , and thus 'he [Victorio] cannot beat this command into New Mexico either east or west'.[167] This betrayed a confidence born of an ignorance of Apache tactics. Buell seems to have assumed that the Apaches would operate in one group. Apache testimony from this period states that at least one group of warriors was absent, foraging for supplies, particularly ammunition. Such groups were adept at concealing their movements as a matter of routine. Nevertheless, Lieutenant Stafford was able to report that this party of Apaches passed on to El Colorado before doubling back to the Florida Mountains.[168] Stafford's was not the only report of Apache activity in New Mexico. Captain Brinkerhoff sent word to Grierson that two freight wagons en route to El Paso from Las Vegas had been attacked on 29 September, near San Augustin. Five Apaches wounded one of the freighters before departing to the south-east.[169]

Hatch concluded that the presence of so many troops in Chihuahua had caused the Apaches to fragment into smaller groups, thus making them far more difficult to track down. As far as he was concerned, all that had been achieved by the combined efforts of Buell and Carr was to send small scattered raiding parties into New Mexico. This must have been of great concern to Hatch, given the pending arrival of the President's entourage. He renewed his request for additional Apache scouts, and recommended that they be organised into companies of 25 scouts accompanied by a cavalry company with a pack train of 50 mules. He thought there should be a minimum of four such companies, but estimated that eight such companies would be required to finish off Victorio.[170]

Colonel Terrazas' Expedition

Up to 29 September, Joaquin Terrazas' offensive operations had been limited to opportunistic attempts to locate Victorio's camp and to act with those troops he had managed to gather. Having concentrated approximately 350 men at Laguna de Patos he then initiated a concerted operation to track down and destroy the Apaches. On 30 September, his command took stock of their equipment and gathered in limited food supplies from Carrizal. Terrazas also sent instructions to El Paso del Norte to arrange for more supplies to reach him on the march.[171]

The following day, Terrazas divided his command, sending one detachment to the north-east, under the leadership of Mata Ortiz, while he led the other eastwards towards the Sierra de Alcaparra. Mata Ortiz's command was to call at the waterhole at Cantarrecio to rendezvous with supplies from El Paso del Norte. He was then to swing to the south-east and search the rough country along the Rio Grande until he reached the Sierra Borracho.[172]

If Gillett has the correct date, the remaining Chihuahua state troops and the Texas Ranger detachment joined Terrazas' command somewhere between the Laguna de Patos and the Sierra

167 Buell to AAAG SF 4 Oct., 1880, NA, RG393, Part 3, Entry 439, p.240; Hatch (citing Buell telegram to Brinkerhoff, 4 Oct., 1880) to AAG Fort Leavenworth, 7 Oct., 1880, Telegrams Sent DoNM, Vol.3, Jan. – Nov. 1880 NA, RG393, Part 3, Entry 431, pp.908-909.

168 Stafford, Ft Cummings to AG, 8 Oct., 1880, NA, RG393, Part 3, Entry 440, p.90; see also Hatch to AAG Fort Leavenworth, 1 Oct., 1880, Telegrams Sent DoNM, Vol.3, Jan. – Nov. 1880 NA, RG393, Part 3, Entry 431, p.885.

169 Brinkerhoff to Grierson, 4 Oct., 1880 in Telegrams Rec'd, 18 May, 1880-4 Feb., 1881, HQ Records DoP 1878-1881, NA, RG393, M1381, Roll 4.

170 Hatch to AAG, DoM, Fort Leavenworth, 6 Oct., 1880 in Letters Sent by '9MD/DNM/DoNM', NA, RG393, M1072, Roll 6, Jan. 1880-Aug. 1881, Letter No.531, pp.340-341.

171 Thrapp, 1974, p.298.

172 Ibid, p.298.

Alcaparra on 3 October.[173] Terrazas scouted the Alcaparras and the surrounding country without encountering any sign of the Apaches. He then made his way north-east to rendezvous with Mata Ortiz in the Sierra Borracho.[174] Up until that point, his scouts had discovered nothing more than small trails leading eastwards. As the column passed over the plain between the Alcaparras and the Sierra Borracho, they reached Los Lagunas or Lagunita[175], where Victorio's band had obviously rested with a large number of horses and cattle.[176] At the end of October 1880, Charles Berger, leading a scout after Apache raiders (see Chapter 16) found the remains of a large camp in a mountain area just to the west of the Los Lagunas and estimated that Victorio had rested for up to eight days at that spot.[177] Terrazas' command discovered this camp as darkness fell. They found the remains of eight animals that the Apaches had butchered and partially eaten. Terrazas' men helped themselves to some of the meat.[178]

Assuming that Victorio had made for the Sierra Borracho, Terrazas was concerned about his supply train making for the same mountains. Without waiting for daybreak, he set his command marching through the night towards the Borrachos. In doing so, he lost contact with the Apache trail leading away from the Los Lagunas-Lagunita.[179] On 5 October, Terrazas joined Mata Ortiz in the Sierra Borracho but found no signs of the Apaches. They sent scouts on to the Sierra de Los Pinos,[180] and here they found signs that Victorio had camped on the top of these mountains for up to seven days.[181] Charles Berger again later reported that he had found a heavily fortified camp on top of the Sierra de los Pinos from which he estimated that the Apaches could have stood off a regiment of troops.[182] By 7 October, the command had been re-supplied by a wagon train from El Paso del Norte, with Terrazas allowing the Texas Ranger detachment to draw 10 days' rations from his commissary.[183]

The Mexicans moved southwards to the Sierra de Los Pinos where they met some of Buell's forces,[184] in the form of Lieutenant Maney, Henry K. Parker and 65 Apache scouts from the San Carlos reservation. They were accompanied by Lieutenant Schaeffer with 20 Ninth Cavalrymen.[185] Terrazas was now confident that he was between Victorio and the Rio Grande, and on 9 October 1880, he requested that the US army and Texas Rangers withdraw to the United States.[186]

---

173 Gillett, 1976, p.185.
174 In trying to map this area it would appear that the Sierra Borracho is either the Sierra La Amargosa or the Sierra San Jose Del Prisco.
175 Lagunita appears to refer to three lagunas in close proximity known today as the Laguna Las Flores, Laguna la Cincuenta y Cinco and the Laguna Garza.
176 Thrapp, 1974, p.298.
177 Berger's Report enclosed within Baldwin to Grierson, 10 Nov., 1880 in Letters Rec'd File 19 Mar., 1878-14 Feb., 1881, HQ Records DoP 1878-1881, NA, RG393, M1381, Roll 2.
178 Thrapp, 1974, pp.298-299.
179 Ibid, p.299.
180 Ibid.
181 Terrazas to Buell copied to Grierson by Nolan, 6 Oct., 1880 in Register of Telegrams Rec'd 11 Oct., 1879-8 Oct., 1880, HQ Records DoP 1878-1881, NA, RG393, M1381, Roll 2, pp.251-252, Letter No.455.
182 Berger's Report enclosed within Baldwin to Grierson, 10 Nov., 1880 in Letters Rec'd File 19 Mar., 1878-14 Feb., 1881, HQ Records DoP 1878-1881, NA, RG393, M1381, Roll 2.
183 Gillett, 1976, p.185; Thrapp, 1974, p.299.
184 Thrapp, 1974, p.299.
185 Buell to AAAG, DoNM, 15 Oct., 1880 in NA, RG393, Part 3, Entry 439, pp.260-267; Hatch (passing on copy of Buell's Report) to AAG, Fort Leavenworth, 15 Oct., 1880, 'Victorio Files' NA, RG393, M1495, Roll 14; same letter contained in 'Victorio Papers', NA, M666, Roll 528; Thrapp, 1974, p.299; Gillett, 1976, p.186.
186 Thrapp, 1974, pp.299-300; Gillett, 1976, p.186; Thrapp, 1988, p.186; Haley, 1981, p.331; Wellman, 1957, pp.174-175.

Buell's Expedition Returns to the United States

From Cantareccio, Buell had sent Lieutenant Maney's Indian scouts and Lieutenant Schaeffer with a Ninth Cavalry Company to contact Terrazas in the Sierra Borracho. Buell then took the balance of his forces north and east around the Sierra Borracho and into the Rio Grande valley.[187] As ever, Buell's prime concern was that Victorio might have scattered and was attempting to infiltrate northwards into New Mexico.[188] On 7 October, Buell's command camped to the south-east of Fort Quitman, on the Mexican side of the border. Buell sent out his scouts, supported by pack mules, to search further to the south-east down the Rio Grande.[189] On 9 October, Buell detached Lieutenant Colonel Dudley's Ninth Cavalrymen and sent them back to Fort Quitman to counter any attempt by the Apaches to move north into Texas. Buell retained the Fourth Cavalry battalion,[190] and he estimated that the forces now arrayed against Victorio would force the Apaches to move deeper into Mexico, though he conceded that Victorio might have escaped to the north-east. With this in mind, he ordered that the remaining cavalry and pack trains at Fort Cummings be sent to Fort Bliss should Dudley have to operate against Apaches in the Guadalupe and Sacramento Mountains. This measure would allow relatively fresh soldiers to take over the pursuit, as the troops involved in the recent Mexico expedition would require rest.[191] He noted in this report that, 'Terrazas and a part of my command move into the Pinos Mts tonight from the north & west I move with packs to the South & South East.'[192] This was probably on 8 October, as Brinkerhoff reported that Buell had moved towards the Sierras Borracho and de Los Pinos on the morning of 9 October 1880.[193] That night, Buell received information, and chose to interpret this as a request, from Joaquin Terrazas, that all US army units quit Mexico as, 'the farther advance of American troops into the territory of Mexico would be objectionable'.[194]

187 Buell, HQ Fort Stanton N.M., to AAG, DoM (via AAAG DoNM), 20 Nov., 1880 in Letters Received by HQ DoNM Sept. 1865-Aug. 1890, NA, RG393, M1088, Roll 42, File 658-1658, Jan.-Apr. 1881; Bi-Monthly Company Muster Rolls for Company L, 9th Cavalry, Sept./Oct., 1880 in NA, RG94; See also Crimmins, 1935, p.141; Thrapp, 1988, p.186; Rasch, 1960, p.9.

188 Buell to Terrazas or Baylor, 7 Oct., 1880 in 'Victorio Papers', NA, M666, Roll 528; Crimmins, 1935, pp.140-141.

189 Buell to Terrazas, 11.20am, 7 Oct., 1880 in 'Victorio Papers', NA, M666, Roll 528.

190 Hatch to AAG Fort Leavenworth, 10 Oct., 1880, Telegrams Sent DoNM, Vol.3, Jan. – Nov. 1880 NA, RG393, Part 3, Entry 431, pp.930-931; Buell, HQ Fort Stanton N.M., to AAG, DoM (via AAAG DoNM), 20 Nov., 1880 in Letters Received by HQ DoNM Sept. 1865-Aug. 1890, NA, RG393, M1088, Roll 42, File 658-1658, Jan.-Apr. 1881; See also Crimmins, 1935, p.141; Stout, pp.170-171; Rasch, 1960, p.9.

191 Buell to AAG Fort Leavenworth Camp in Mexico opposite Fort Quitman No date given NA, RG393, Part 3, Entry 439, pp.253-256; See also Stafford to AAG, SF, 6 Oct., 1880; Letters Rec'd at AAG, DoNM, 1872-1880, NA, RG393, Part 3, Entry 477.

192 Buell to AAG Fort Leavenworth Camp in Mexico opposite Fort Quitman No date given NA, RG393, Part 3, Entry 439, pp.255-256; Brinkerhoff Captain 15th Infantry to AAAG, SF, NM, 9 Oct., 1880, NA, RG393, Part 3, Entry 440, p.95.

193 Brinkerhoff to AAAG SF 9 Oct., 1880, NA, RG393, Part 3, Entry 439, p.258.

194 Buell to AAG Fort Leavenworth 15 Oct., 1880, NA, RG393, Part 3, Entry 439, p.264 & Buell to AAAG SF 19 Oct., 1880, NA, RG393, Part 3, Entry 439, p.272; Buell to AAAG, DoNM, 15 Oct., 1880 in NA, RG393, Part 3, Entry 439, pp.260-267; Hatch (passing on copy of Buell's Report) to AAG, Fort Leavenworth, 15 Oct., 1880, 'Victorio Files' NA, RG393, M1495, Roll 14; same letter contained in 'Victorio Papers', NA, M666, Roll 528; Sheridan to AG of the Army, Washington D.C, 22 Oct., 1880 in 'Victorio Papers', NA, M666, Roll 528; Thrapp, 1974, p299; Crimmins, 1935, p.141; Stout, 1974, p171; Rasch, 1960, p.9.

> Much as I regretted to give up the chase, I felt that I was in Mexico by the invitation of the Chihuahua or state authorities more than by any legal or proper right. I felt satisfied that Terrazas had received an intimation or order to forbid my advancing further towards Chihuahua, and that he had sent this message to me in a most gentlemanly manner. I therefore commenced the withdrawal of my advance the 10th day of October, and started back myself the 10th, en route to the American side of the Rio Grande.[195]

This at least shows that Buell was aware that he was acting without the sanction of the federal government of Mexico. Maney reported that Terrazas had, at that point, asked that US troops move *no further into Mexico*, and that Maney had agreed to wait two days for further instructions from Terrazas. However, Lieutenant Maney also informed Buell that Terrazas had assumed, rather than confirmed, that 1) Victorio had gone to the Sierra de Los Pinos and 2) that Victorio's trail had turned south, moving deeper into Chihuahua. Whether Terrazas had actually asked the US troops to leave Chihuahua is open to interpretation. However, the following day Buell received couriers from General Pope informing him that:

> Orders from War Department issued some time ago prohibits operations in Mexico by our troops. You will therefore recross the Rio Grande with your Command at the nearest convenient point & return to Cummings as soon as you can possibly do so without breaking faith with Gen'l Tarrasses & exposing him & his troops.[196]

These orders were not open to interpretation, and Buell reported that he had withdrawn all US forces from Mexico by 12 October.[197] This was effectively the end of Buell's expedition. Buell, as we saw earlier, was brought in to bring the Victorio campaign to a finish, and had failed to do so, Victorio being still alive and active in Chihuahua. For this reason, Buell lashed out at Carr for failing to cooperate with him in the field,[198] and General Willcox sent an angry communication to Carr outlining Buell's complaint and adding his own comments. He reminded Carr that his orders had been to remain in the field, and that Carr's rejection of logistical support such as additional pack mules constituted 'grave mistakes and are deeply regretted by the Dept. Comdr'.[199] Carr, never

---

195 Buell, HQ Fort Stanton N.M., to AAG, DoM (via AAAG DoNM), 20 Nov., 1880 in Letters Received by HQ DoNM Sept. 1865-Aug. 1890, NA, RG393, M1088, Roll 42, File 658-1658, Jan.-Apr. 1881; See also Crimmins, 1935, p.142.

196 Pope to Buell, (via CO Fort Quitman) 9 Oct., 1880 in 'Victorio Papers', NA, M666, Roll 528; A note added to this correspondence stated that this message was received by Col. Buell on the 10 October.
See also Buell, HQ Fort Stanton N.M., to AAG, DoM (via AAAG DoNM), 20 Nov., 1880 in Letters Received by HQ DoNM Sept. 1865-Aug. 1890, NA, RG393, M1088, Roll 42, File 658-1658, Jan.-Apr. 1881; Smither to Nolan, 10 Oct., 1880 citing Vincent, AAG, DoTx to Grierson 9 Oct., 1880 in Telegrams Sent 23 Jun.-30 Nov., 1880, HQ Records DoP 1878-1881, NA, RG393, M1381, Roll 1, p.221, Letter No.599; Dinges, 1987, p.93; Nolan to AAAG, DoP, 10 Oct., 1880 in Register of Telegrams Rec'd 11 Oct., 1879-8 Oct., 1880, HQ Records DoP 1878-1881, NA, RG393, M1381, Roll 2, p.266, Letter No.483.

197 Buell, HQ Fort Stanton N.M., to AAG, DoM (via AAAG DoNM), 20 Nov., 1880 in Letters Received by HQ DoNM Sept. 1865-Aug. 1890, NA, RG393, M1088, Roll 42, File 658-1658, Jan.-Apr. 1881; Nolan, Quitman citing information rec'd directly from Capt Baylor, to Beck, AAAG, 12 Oct., 1880 in Letters Rec'd File 19 Mar., 1878-14 Feb., 1881, HQ Records DoP 1878-1881, NA, RG393, M1381, Roll 2; Hatch to AAG Fort Leavenworth, 16 Oct., 1880, Telegrams Sent DoNM, Vol.3, Jan. – Nov. 1880 NA, RG393, Part 3, Entry 431, p.952; Hatch to AAG Fort Leavenworth, 19 Oct., 1880, Telegrams Sent DoNM, Vol.3, Jan. – Nov. 1880 NA, RG393, Part 3, Entry 431, p.960.

198 Carr quoting Buell Telegram of 11 Oct., 1880 to AG DoAz, 12 Oct., 1880, Troops in SE Arizona, DoAz, NA, RG393, Part 1, Entry 232, Vol.8, 6 Sept.-12 Dec., 1880, p.30.

199 AAAG to Carr, 9 Oct., 1880, NA, RG393, Part 1, Entry 169, Vol. 10, p.449.

one to take criticism lightly, hit back, accusing Buell of failing to send information about his movements and treating Carr 'shabbily'.[200] Carr also stated that he was surprised that Buell had expected him to join him, as that had never been his intention.[201] Indeed, the first mention of Carr joining Buell comes in a telegram dated 18 September, received by Carr on 25 September, where Buell sent instructions that Carr should move beyond the Boca Grande Mountains towards Guzman Lake.[202] As noted earlier, Carr felt that his orders from Headquarters, Department of Arizona, did not clear him to move beyond his positions in the Boca Grande Mountains. He also thought that Buell would have had more than enough men to deal with Victorio, had the New Mexico troops caught up with the Apaches.[203] Eventually, on 17 October, Carr, perhaps being unconsciously provocative, sent Buell a telegram expressing regret that Victorio had not been caught and concluding: 'wish you better luck next time. We must expect to make a great many fruitless expeditions to achieve a few successes.'[204] This was a statement of what was common knowledge among officers with long experience of campaigning against Apaches. Nevertheless, such 'sympathy' cannot have been received well by Buell, who had been brought in to deal with the 'Victorio problem' once and for all.

This seems to have been a clash born from the disappointment, and possibly humiliation, Buell felt from not inflicting a decisive defeat upon Victorio. If Victorio had moved west and managed to escape, then Carr's withdrawal could have been significant. Carr, as far as one can see, did picket the land to the west of Buell, as instructed by General Willcox. Where he may have been at fault was not picketing the area for as long as Willcox intended. However, Carr was confident that once Willcox had read his report, any desire by his superior to ascribe any blame to him would be dissipated.[205] For a couple of days, it looked as if this row might drift towards a court martial. Before the acrimony could reach such a pass, events at Tres Castillos would intervene and effectively smother any quest to apportion blame.

Buell also complained that the logistic support for his expedition had not been very effective. He had had to operate supported by a much-reduced pack train, since an order of100 additional pack mules from Texas and an order of an equivalent number of pack mule harnesses from San Francisco did not arrive until after his return from Mexico.[206]

Buell himself came under scrutiny for the unauthorised recruiting of citizens and Apache scouts. Hatch, who himself had authorized the recruitment of extra Apache scouts as mule packers, was rather quick off the mark in reporting to Department Headquarters that Buell had greatly exceeded the number of authorised Apache scouts, citizen scouts and mule packers.[207] As such Hatch pointed

200 Carr to AG, Whipple Barracks, 10 Oct., 1880, NA, RG393, Part 1, Entry 169, Vol. 10, pp.456-457.

201 Carr to Hatch, 7 Oct., 1880, Troops in SE Arizona, DoAz, NA, RG393, Part 1, Entry 232, Vol.8, 6 Sept.-12 Dec., 1880, Letter No.579, pp.25-26; See also Hatch to AAG, Fort Leavenworth, 9 Oct., 1880 in Letters Sent by '9MD/DNM/DoNM', NA, RG393, M1072, Roll 6, Jan. 1880-Aug. 1881, Letter No.532, pp.341-342.

202 Carr to AG DoAz, 25 Sept., 1880, Troops in SE Arizona, DoAz, NA, RG393, Part 1, Entry 232, Vol.8, 6 Sept.-12 Dec., 1880, Letter No.571, p.21.

203 See Carr to AG DoAz, 26 Sept., 1880, Troops in SE Arizona, DoAz, NA, RG393, Part 1, Entry 232, Vol.8, 6 Sept.-12 Dec., 1880, Letter No.572, pp.21-22; Carr to Hatch, 7 Oct., 1880, Troops in SE Arizona, DoAz, NA, RG393, Part 1, Entry 232, Vol.8, 6 Sept.-12 Dec., 1880, Letter No.579, pp.25-26; Carr to Buell, 17 Oct., 1880, Troops in SE Arizona, DoAz, NA, RG393, Part 1, Entry 232, Vol.8, 6 Sept.-12 Dec., 1880, p.30.

204 Carr to Buell, 17 Oct., 1880, Troops in SE Arizona, DoAz, NA, RG393, Part 1, Entry 232, Vol.8, 6 Sept.-12 Dec., 1880, p.30.

205 Carr to Willcox, 16 Oct., 1880, NA, RG393, Part 1, Entry 169, Vol. 10, pp.460-461.

206 Buell, HQ Fort Stanton N.M., to AAG, DoM (via AAAG DoNM), 20 Nov., 1880 in Letters Received by HQ DoNM Sept. 1865-Aug. 1890, NA, RG393, M1088, Roll 42, File 658-1658, Jan.-Apr. 1881.

207 Hatch to AAG, DoM, 15 Oct., 1880 in Letters Received by HQ DoNM Sept. 1865-Aug. 1890, NA, RG393, M1088, Roll 41, Jul.-Dec. 1880.

out that these men would have to be paid, and asked General Pope to confirm that these costs would be met.[208] It would appear that Buell had taken on up to 210 'employees' during his expedition, at an estimated cost of between $15,000 and $25,000. Hatch recommended that this be paid for under 'Incidental Expenses' ($15,000) and 'Transportation of the Army' ($10,000). The cost of fodder and water had not yet been ascertained but could be covered by a 'liberal' amount under 'Regular Suppliers'. Hatch also recommended that the additional Indian scouts should be paid, as they would not comprehend any reason given them for not being paid.[209]

Buell had most certainly exceeded his authority on the recruitment of US citizens as guides, couriers and mule packers; but he was probably not guilty of the hiring of unauthorised Apache scouts. What was ultimately at stake can be put no better than it was by General Sherman, when insisting that Buell had no right to hire Captain Fountain and six scouts as part of his force:

> The pressure on Officers to accept the services of volunteers on the Frontiers is very great and must be resisted, else every Officer in pursuit of Indians will accept the services of these bodies which profess to understand so much of the Indian character. No matter what may be the fact, we are restricted by the plain requirements of the law, to restrict the Army to the organization and numbers fixed by the statute.[210]

Hatch had a very clear motive for wanting to disguise his creative recruitment of Apaches in the first place; but he could not have asked for a more appropriate scapegoat than Colonel Buell. While Hatch had remained commander of the District of New Mexico, he had been effectively removed from directing field operations, and had been replaced by Buell. Moreover, Hatch had already had to deal with the contentious and vindictive nature Buell displayed in his treatment subordinate officers. Buell was an officer who would not hesitate to lay charges against other, usually more junior, officers. For example, on 13 November 1879, he charged Lieutenant Loud, Acting Assistant Adjutant General, with 'conduct unbecoming'. Hatch forwarded Buell's complaints concerning both Captain Charles Albert Woodruff and Lieutenant Loud with the clearest statement that, in his opinion, Buell was 'in the wrong'.[211] Buell's charges were completely dismissed by General Pope, who endorsed his decision with the statement that such charges should not be made lightly by a regimental commander.[212]

In a telegram (1 August 1880) to Hatch, General Pope gave the Colonel clear instructions concerning the spheres of control of both Colonel Buell and Major Morrow.[213] These two officers do not seem to have agreed with each other, and, reading between the lines, it seems that Buell had made a comment that he had been 'sent here to make a success of this campaign',[214] implying that those previously in charge had been found wanting. One suspects that Buell had also made these comments verbally to Morrow, the officer who probably had the best record[215] where maintaining

208 Ibid.

209 Hatch to AAG, DoM, 11 Dec. in Letters Sent by '9MD/DNM/DoNM', NA, RG393, M1072, Roll 6, Jan. 1880-Aug. 1881, Letter No.637 pp.403-404.

210 Drum, AG (enclosing Copy of Sherman's Letter) to Commanding General, DoM, 19 Nov., 1880 in Letters Received by HQ DoNM Sept. 1865-Aug. 1890, NA, RG393, M1088, Roll 41, Jul.-Dec. 1880.

211 Hatch to AAG, DoM, Fort Leavenworth, 22 Nov. 1879 in Letters Sent by '9MD/DNM/DoNM', NA, RG393, M1072, Roll 6, Jan.-Oct. 1879, Letter No.546, p.387.

212 Platt to Buell, 6 Dec. 1879 in Letters Received by HQ DoNM Sept. 1865-Aug. 1890, NA, RG393, M1088, Roll 39, Oct.-Dec. 1879.

213 Pope to Hatch 1 Aug., 1880, NA, RG393, Part 3, Entry 439, p.45.

214 Buell to AAAG SF 22 Jul., 1880, NA, RG393, Part 3, Entry 439, pp.555-557.

215 It has been noted that this success may have been born of Victorio's wish for Morrow to remain upon his trail and thereby cripple the ability of the U.S. Army to remain in the field.

contact with Victorio was concerned. Such statements, in telegrams to District Headquarters, cannot have made a good impression on Colonel Hatch. Buell accused Morrow of deliberately disobeying his orders, and there is some indication that Buell might have tried to have Morrow court martialled.[216] Hatch had to censure Buell on 28 July 1880 for attempting to circumvent his authority by writing directly to Department Headquarters.[217] On 31 July, Hatch responded to a telegram from Buell that District Headquarters was not competent to settle the controversy. He noted a number of 'irregularities' in Buell's practice which had been ignored in the wider interests of the service. He also indicated that telegrams from Buell which 'bordered on insubordination' had been 'borne' in the interests of maintaining a secure frontier.[218] Hatch and Pope seem to have reached an arrangement whereby Morrow was stationed out at Knight's Ranch while Buell was preparing his expedition at Fort Cummings;[219]. but the situation needed a more lasting resolution, and this was found when Morrow was sent to Europe to observe French military manoeuvres, by order of the Adjutant General.[220]

Buell was to cause further trouble for Colonel Hatch. Almost a year after his expedition, in September 1881, Buell was informed of the formation of a field camp under Major Guy V. Henry, near Fort Stanton, and learned too that Henry was 'independent of the orders of the post commander of Fort Stanton'.[221] Buell, still stationed at Fort Stanton, lobbied Hatch for overall command of this detachment, because Henry's command was supplied from that post. Hatch refused, and gave clear instructions that Henry's command was to remain independent.[222] Buell then appears to have vented his anger on Major Henry, accusing him of exceeding his authority in removing a company of the Fifteenth Infantry from Fort Stanton to his camp, and of personal disrespect, in removing an infantryman charged with looking after Buell's personal effects.[223] Henry replied that he had received clear instructions from the District Commander to act as he did, and that alternative arrangements had been made for the care of Buell's personal effects.[224] Henry also made it clear that he had not seen fit to complain about Buell's own lack of courtesy as the commanding officer at Fort Stanton.[225]

Buell was finally placed under arrest, on 1 November 1881,[226] for 'wilfully failing' to visit or report to Colonel Ranald MacKenzie when passing though Santa Fé. It was charged that it 'was necessary

---

216 Buell Fort Cummings, to AAAG SF, 21 Jul., 1880, NA, RG393, Part 3, Entry 439, p.554 & Buell to AAAG SF 22 Jul., 1880, NA, RG393, Part 3, Entry 439, pp.555-557.

217 Hatch to Buell, 28 Jul., 1880, Telegrams Sent DoNM, Vol.3, Jan. – Nov. 1880 NA, RG393, Part 3, Entry 431, p.658.

218 Hatch to AAG, DoM, Fort Leavenworth, 31 Jul., 1880 in Letters Sent by '9MD/DNM/DoNM', NA, RG393, M1072, Roll 6, Jan. 1880-Aug. 1881, Letter No.391, pp.251-252.

219 NA, RG393, Part 3, Entry 439, p.45.

220 Hatch to Morrow, 17 Aug., 1880, Telegrams Sent DoNM, Vol.3, Jan. – Nov. 1880 NA, RG393, Part 3, Entry 431, p.747; NA, RG393, Part 3, Entry 439, p.50; See also *Army & Navy Journal*, Vol. 18, 7 Aug., 1880, p.6.

221 Loud to CO Fort Stanton, 19 Sept. 1881 in Letters Sent by '9MD/DNM/DoNM', NA, RG393, M1072, Roll 7, 1881, Letter No.394, p.37.

222 Loud to CO Fort Stanton, 19 Sept. 1881 in Letters Received by HQ DoNM Sept. 1865-Aug. 1890, NA, RG393, M1088, Roll 43, May-Oct. 1881.

223 Buell to Henry, 10 Oct. 1881 in Letters Received by HQ DoNM Sept. 1865-Aug. 1890, NA, RG393, M1088, Roll 43, May-Oct. 1881.

224 Henry to Buell, 14 Oct. 1881 in Letters Received by HQ DoNM Sept. 1865-Aug. 1890, NA, RG393, M1088, Roll 43, May-Oct. 1881.

225 Henry to Buell, 14 Oct. 1881 in Letters Received by HQ DoNM Sept. 1865-Aug. 1890, NA, RG393, M1088, Roll 43, May-Oct. 1881.

226 Loud to Capt. Whittemore, 15th Infantry (with instructions to assume command of the HQ and Co's of that regiment) 1 Nov., 1881 in Letters Sent by '9MD/DNM/DoNM', NA, RG393, M1072, Roll 7, 1881, Letter No.447, p.70.

that Colonel Buell be checked in the insubordinate course which he has elected to commence'.[227] General Pope finally felt compelled to intervene and rebuke Buell in the most forthright manner concerning his behaviour, describing the Colonel's actions as 'obnoxious to all military propriety, or proper courtesy, as practiced among Officers of the Army and required by both military custom and the Regulations of the Army, as to be without excuse'.[228] (See document file no. 128.)

While these episodes show a thoroughly unpleasant side to Buell, which caused considerable annoyance to his superior officers, they also illustrate just what an ideal candidate he was, from Hatch's point of view, to lead the expedition into Mexico. Buell was quite happy to act unilaterally, without any reference to higher authority, whether it be recruiting scouts without authorisation or attempting to circumvent his superiors without permission if his actions were blocked. If there was going to be any political backlash from the incursion into Mexico, such a propensity for independent action made Buell an ideal scapegoat. Most importantly, if events did take such a course, Buell's downfall would be as much due to his failure to maintain his 'political capital' amongst his superiors as to events in Mexico. If Buell was targeted as the person to whom culpability would be attached, it was highly unlikely that any of his superiors would come to his rescue.

The Buell expedition had taken its toll of its men and animals. Lieutenant Colonel Dudley, on his return to Fort Cummings, reported that the men under his command were lacking in proper clothing, and that he had over 100 broken-down horses. He believed that if these animals were not adequately rested and sheltered, most would die. Those that survived would take months to make a full recovery.[229]

Table 15.2 Ninth Cavalry, Roster of Horses, September–October 1880.[230]

Ninth Cavalry	Serviceable Horses	Unserviceable Horses	Horses Lost in Action, Died, etc.
Sept. 1880	304	167	23
Oct. 1880	472	186	10

It is clear that Buell's expedition had increased the number of unserviceable horses. However, the Ninth Cavalry Regiment, as a whole, had increased the numbers of serviceable horses during the months of September and October. (See Table 15.2.) Those companies not involved in the Buell expedition (A, E, G, H, I and M Companies) all show an increasing number of serviceable horses, though the figures for I Company only start to improve at the end of October. (See Table 15.3.) This recovery in the figures can be explained through a combination of the purchase of new horses and the recovery of broken-down horses. However, the figures for those companies involved in the Buell expedition (B, C, D, F, K and L Companies) do not show consistent trends. We would expect to see an increase in the numbers of unserviceable horses and a decrease in serviceable horses; but

227 MacKenzie to AAG, DoM, 1 Nov., 1881 in Letters Sent by '9MD/DNM/DoNM', NA, RG393, M1072, Roll 7, 1881, Letter No.450, p.71; See also MacKenzie (noting Hatch's concerns as to Buell's conduct) to AAG, DoM, 15 Nov., 1881 in Letters Sent by '9MD/DNM/DoNM', NA, RG393, M1072, Roll 7, 1881, Letter No.466, pp.81-82.

228 Platt to Buell, 21 Dec. 1881 in Letters Received by HQ DoNM Sept. 1865-Aug. 1890, NA, RG393, M1088, Roll 44, Nov.-Dec. 1881.

229 Dudley to AAG DoNM 28 Letter No. 13, Oct., 1880, Letters sent Vol. 7 25 Oct., 1880-24 Jun., 1881 in HQ Records of Fort Cummings, New Mexico, 1863-1873 & 1880-1884, NA, RG393, M1081, Roll 1.

230 Derived from Returns From Regular Army Cavalry Regiments 1833-1916, 9th Cavalry 1873-1880, NA, M744, Roll 88

only B and D Companies appear to follow this expected trend. F Company recorded a reduction in unserviceable horses and an increase in serviceable horses. The remaining companies (C, K and L) show an expected increase in unserviceable horses, though in the case of L Company, this increase is tiny and recovers very quickly. Yet these companies also show an increase in their serviceable horses. This can probably be explained by the recovery of broken-down horses left behind at Fort Cummings or Knight's Ranch by Buell. The arrival of new horses in the absence of the expedition could also explain such an increase. The bi-monthly company returns for the Ninth Cavalry display the same trends. (See Table 15.4.)

Table 15.3 Serviceable, Unserviceable and Lost Horses to Available Men, Ninth Cavalry, September–October 1880.[231]

Company	Month	Serviceable Horses	Unserviceable Horses	Lost Horses	Available Men
A	August	20	16	0	42
	September	24	10	2	45
	October	45	7	0	55
B	August	29	11	3	50
	September	29	11	0	55
	October	14	16	0	57
C	August	29	9	0	44
	September	26	9	4	44
	October	34	21	4	56
D	August	26	5	0	51
	September	4	30	7	53
	October	14	37	0	61
E	August	16	12	0	51
	September	17	7	4	49
	October	41	7	0	53
F	August	14	12	3	42
	September	20	8	2	44
	October	40	5	1	57
G	August	39	8	0	57
	September	44	3	1	57
	October	62	4	0	51
H	August	25	31	2	49
	September	36	19	1	44
	October	45	25	1	48
I	August	23	22	0	57
	September	17	22	2	57
	October	20	19	0	53

231 Derived from Returns From Regular Army Cavalry Regiments 1833-1916, 9th Cavalry 1873-1880, NA, M744, Roll 88

Company	Month	Serviceable Horses	Unserviceable Horses	Lost Horses	Available Men
K	August	30	24	0	55
	September	30	24	0	54
	October	44	34	0	58
L	August	25	14	0	57
	September	20	18	1	56
	October	48	14	2	54
M	August	33	6	0	66
	September	33	6	0	64
	October	33	6	0	63

More importantly, given the previous experience of Ninth Cavalry pursuits of Victorio, we would expect to see an increase in the number of horses lost or broken down. Yet, there is nothing in Tables 15.2 to 15.4 which really stands out as being caused by hard field service in Chihuahua. The losses sustained by those Ninth Cavalry companies accompanying Buell do not appear to be particularly excessive. Some of these losses may be down to horses that had not recovered after the stampede near the Candelaria Mountains.

Table 15.4 Available Men to Serviceable Horses, Ninth Cavalry, July–October 1880.[232]

Company	Available Men July–Aug.	Serviceable Horses July–Aug.	Available Men Sept.–Oct.	Serviceable Horses Sept.–Oct.
A	45	20	52	40
B	49	29	55	44
C	39	2? Entry indecipherable	53	34
D	51	17	50	14
E	45	16	49	41
F	37	16	54	30
G	51	39	41	62
H	40	25	48	45
I	54	19	52	20
K	52	30	57	30
L	48	25	53	48
M	65	33	61	33

The most striking feature of this information is that, unlike previous pursuits of Apaches during the Victorio Campaign, the Ninth Cavalry had not sustained heavy horse and mule casualties. In fact, it had continued to recover its strength during Buell's incursion into Mexico. As noted above, this can certainly be partially explained by the commitment of only half the regiment's company strength to Buell's campaign. Yet even those companies that took part in the incursion into the Republic of Mexico do not appear to have been badly affected by their experience.

232 Derived Bi-Monthly Company Muster Rolls for Jan./Feb. & Mar./Apr. 1880, 9th Cavalry in NA, RG94

The relative lack of damage suffered by the Ninth Cavalry might be ascribed to their being better able to preserve their horses through experience; that is, as a result of their earlier campaigns against Victorio, they had learned to minimise their equine casualties.

However, these figures probably reflect a change in tactics and strategy by Victorio. The key difference is that the Buell expedition did not engage with, or even see, any Apaches. In the earlier period of the Victorio War, the Apache leader had deliberately ensured that the Ninth Cavalry had a fresh trail to follow in order to cripple or kill their horses. The relatively light casualties in broken-down and lost horses sustained during the Buell expedition can be attributed to the Apaches' shortage of ammunition. In other words, during the Buell expedition, Victorio made every effort to remain far ahead of his enemies and avoid all contact with US and Mexican troops. He did not try to distract his enemies by splitting his forces into two groups, because his did not have the ammunition stocks to sustain this strategy. Thus the trails left by the Apaches were not fresh enough to tempt Buell's troops into a horse-killing pursuit.

Perhaps Captain Byron Dawson, in his succinct summary of the expedition, gave the best picture of the frustration of the participants, when he stated that, 'nothing worthy of mention occurred during the trip'.[233] However, it must be noted that Buell's expedition, while hardly firing a shot, apart from nervous sentinels, and sustaining only average attrition rates among its horses,[234] was essential to the ultimate success of the Mexican operation. Victorio, low on ammunition, and faced by a large number of Apache scouts, simply couldn't afford an attempt to break through the US army's cordon. With the Chihuahuan militia mobilising to the south and west, he was faced with a semi-circular cordon running clockwise from Chihuahua City to the south, around to Grierson's border guards along the Rio Grande. He had to attempt to escape these large forces massing against him. The Buell expedition had forced the Apaches to keep moving eastward. Grierson's picket lines had also ruled out an attempt to escape from Mexico into Texas. We now have to turn our attention to the efforts made by Colonel Terrazas' expedition, once US troops had been asked to depart Mexico, to hunt down Victorio.

---

233 Bi-Monthly Company Muster Rolls for Company B, 9th Cavalry, Sept./Oct., 1880 in NA, RG94.

234 For example, Company A, Fourth Cavalry records that one horse died on the 29 September, 1880 and abandoned two horses on the 3 and 10 of October, 1880. Company H, Fourth Cavalry stated that five horses were abandoned on 4 October, (near Candelaria Mountains), 10 October, (near Guadalupe Mexico), 11 and 12 October, (near Fort Quitman) and the 15 October, (near Politas, Texas). (4th Cavalry 1878-1883, Sept./Oct., 1880, Returns from Regular Army Cavalry Regiments 1833-1916, NA, RG393, NA, M744, Roll 43).

16

Tres Castillos, October 1880

> Your dispatch just rec'd I present my heartiest congratulations for the extinction & destruction of Victorios band. It vindicates the army and will bring peace to our border. Hallelujah!
>
> JC Tiffany
>
> U.S. Indian Agent, 21 October, 1880.[1]

Victorio Attempts to Take Evasive Action

Despite Thrapp giving an excellent account of Colonel Joaquin Terrazas' expedition, the writer's analysis of Victorio's motivation during this campaign is open to challenge. All the signs found by both the US and the Mexican expeditions suggested that Victorio had retreated to the east. Thrapp interprets this move as a biblical exodus to an ultimate doom.[2] However, the reason Victorio had moved eastwards and, as we shall see, southwards, was that he was attempting to avoid both Buell's and Terrazas' forces.[3] It was certainly not to meet a predetermined doom or destiny. Rather, it was a manoeuvre born of grim necessity. Being so low in ammunition, and having responsibility for his accompanying dependants, he could ill afford an attempt to break through the loose cordon running from the south west round to the Rio Grande and to the north-east. Choosing a specific point in the cordon, and bringing local superiority of numbers to bear in creating a breach, could not be safely attempted. Indeed Victorio, after leading his enemies to the east, was trying to slip south and then west towards the sanctuary of the Sierra Madre. Kaywaykla states that, just before Tres Castillos, his grandmother told him that they were making for the Sierra Madre, or 'the land of Juh' as she termed these mountains.[4]

Kaywaykla was adamant that Victorio, Nana and other senior warriors were very worried about their lack of ammunition, and had sent a large detachment of their younger warriors on a long-range raiding trip in search of ammunition. Even with a full complement of warriors, the shortage of ammunition made the band vulnerable. Already exposed, if Victorio's people were to be caught by US or Mexican forces while some of his best warriors were absent seeking ammunition supplies, the result could be disastrous. While the Apaches were down, they were clearly not finished. A respite was required. This could not be gained by trying to break through the enemies, who were closing in from the north and the west. Victorio was also blocked from crossing the Rio Grande by Grierson's picket and patrol lines; though unbeknown to Victorio, the Tenth Cavalry, currently picketing the Rio Grande, were facing an outbreak of scurvy due to a lack of fresh vegetables. On 7 October, Acting Assistant Surgeon Henderson warned Captain Carpenter that if a large supply

1 Tiffany to Hatch 21 Oct., 1880, NA, RG393, Part 3, Entry 439, p.277.
2 Thrapp, 1974, pp.297-298.
3 Thrapp, 1974, pp.297-298; See also Ball, 1962, p.40.
4 Ball, 1970, p.93.

of vegetables was not procured very quickly, he would be forced to place a large number of men 'on Sick Report and send them into Fort Davis'.[5]

Victorio may also have faced a challenge to his leadership of those Mescalero Apaches who had allied themselves with him. On 14 November 1880, Captain Conrad, at Fort Stanton, reported a story that Victorio had shot Ca-bal-le-so[6] in the Potrillo Mountains 'about sixty days ago because he wanted to return here'.[7] (See document file no. 129.) This would place the Mescalero leader's death sometime around 16 September, and suggests that this might have been close to the attack on the stage coach in the Goodsight Mountains, on 6 September, and the subsequent clash with A Company, Fourth Cavalry, on the following day. The Apaches were reported as fleeing into Mexico via the Potrillo Mountains, and were not followed.[8] One suspects that the raid of 6–8 September was an abortive attempt to push deeper into New Mexico. This had been thwarted by the unexpected number of troops concentrated at Fort Cummings. If this was the case, then Ca-bal-es-so may have decided to leave Victorio, having lost faith in the latter's leadership. He had every right to take this option; but apparently Victorio challenged his right to lead the other Mescaleros away with him. The argument which flared up was settled when Victorio killed Ca-bal-le-so, as one paper put it, for 'insubordination'.[9]

Victorio must also have been aware that his authority, as a leader of his people, might have been somewhat undermined by their setbacks against Apache scouts in the latter part of May 1880, and the Tenth Cavalry in July–August 1880. Another military defeat would almost certainly cause him to lose the support of his Mescalero allies. The best overall solution, for the moment, would be to work his way around, rather than through, the opposition. To accomplish this, the Apaches, having managed to slip through the very loose cordon east of the Candelaria Mountains, would attempt to avoid all contact with their enemies. If their enemies did find a trail, then the Apaches had to maintain a sufficient lead to wear the enemies out before they caught up. The key factor in this tactic was for the Apaches to try to keep their horses in as good a condition as possible. Thus, as noted in the previous chapter, Victorio, once clear of his enemies, chose to camp for a number of days at a reliable water source (Los Lagunas-Lagunita) before moving on, as Terrazas and Buell moved east in search of his group. If one examines Map 16.1 the Apaches appear to have travelled, probably in separate groups, to the east and south, visiting a number of waterholes and lagunas (Lagunas Colorado, Salada, El Cuervo, Grande, and possibly El Uno; and Ojo del Carrizo and Tres Castillos). Visiting such water sources would allow Victorio to keep his own horses as fresh as possible, so that, should any of his enemies guess his whereabouts, or pick up his trail, the Apaches would be able to out-distance their pursuers. The raid on Samaniego's ranch, where half of the stolen horses were sent west towards the Candelaria Mountains, with the balance being sent east towards the Sierra El Fierro, corresponds to such a plan. Victorio was, at that point, moving his followers from the Lagunas de Guzman and de Santa Maria to the Candelaria Mountains. On their arrival at the Candelaria Mountains, they would find some fresh horses waiting for them.

5 Henderson to Carpenter, 7 Oct., 1880 & Carpenter to Beck, 7 Oct., 1880 in Letters Rec'd File 19 Mar.,1878-14 Feb., 1881, HQ Records DoP 1878-1881, NA, RG393, M1381, Roll 2.

6 Ca-bal-le-so was the Mescalero leader whom we last met just before the battle in Hembrillo Canyon when he had apparently left the Mescalero reservation to 'negotiate' with the independent Apaches. (Thrapp, 1974, pp.290-291; see also p.372 note 59).

7 Conrad, South Fork to Post Adjutant, Fort Stanton, 14 Nov., 1880 in Letters Received by HQ DoNM Sept. 1865-Aug. 1890, NA, RG393, M1088, Roll 41, Jul.-Dec., 1880; See also Buell to AAAG SF 3 Dec., 1880, NA, RG393, Part 3, Entry 439, p.4; Buell to AAAG, DoNM, 3 Dec., 1880, NA, RG393, Part 1, Entry 2546, p.698; *Evening Review, The*, Saturday 17 Jun., 1882.

8 See Chapter14.

9 *The Evening Review*, New Albuquerque, N.M. Saturday, 17 Jun., 1882 See also Thrapp, 1974, p.291; Haley, 1981, p.330.

As the Apaches continued eastwards in an effort to out-distance their enemies, they would find additional fresh horses awaiting them in the vicinity of the Sierra el Fierro.

Victorio was thus reasoning that the longer he could maintain a lead over US and Mexican forces, the more likely these enemies would be to drop out of the campaign, due to exhaustion and/or lack of supplies. If successful, Victorio might gain a respite in the Sierra Madre. Here the Apaches could rest, secure from their enemies, and could send out parties to seek fresh supplies of ammunition through a combination of trading and raiding. This tactic was in marked contrast to Victorio's earlier ones of overt aggression, to distract his enemies away from his families and/or plunder, and then wearing those enemies down in long pursuits, punctuated by periodic 'rearguard' actions, before he reformed his following, having exhausted his foes. Victorio's adoption of such a different tactic is, perhaps, one of the clearest indications of the Apaches' shortage of cartridges.

Victorio's change in tactics also suggests that Colonel Grierson had succeeded in damaging the Apaches' ability to wage war. Victorio's warriors had clearly expended a large proportion of their ammunition at Tinaja de Las Palmas and Rattlesnake Springs, with the expectation that they would be able to gain fresh supplies when they reached the Mescalero reservation. They had further depleted their stocks of ammunition during raids after their retreat into Chihuahua and, more particularly, in their abortive attempt to move into New Mexico on the 6-7 September. In attempting to capture further supplies of cartridges, they also had to gamble that they would gain more ammunition than they expended in each attack. For example, it should be remembered that when Sergeant Robinson's detachment was ambushed in Agua Chiquita Canyon, on 1 September, it was the mule train that had been targeted. The pack mules may have been carrying additional supplies of ammunition among their loads, and the failure to capture these mules would have been a great disappointment for the Apaches.

Colonel Terrazas takes the Offensive

While in the Sierra de Los Pinos, Terrazas had sent his scouts to the south-east, to investigate a small lake, the Laguna El Cuervo, at the northern end of a long chain of mountains which ran southwards, deeper into Mexico.[10] (See Map 16.1.) On the night of 8 October, a courier informed Terrazas that the scouts had learned that the Apaches had passed by the shores of the Laguna, apparently bound either for Cerro Lagrimas (Hill of Tears) or perhaps for the three hills known as Tres Castillos (Three Castles). The two destinations were situated, respectively, at approximately 27 miles and 45 miles to the south west.[11] On 11 October, Roman Aranda contacted Buell, informing him that Colonel Terrazas had broken camp at Ojo Del Cuerva [Cuerla?] the previous night, and was making for Ojo Del Carriso, 22 miles away, with an advance guard from his force. Aranda thought that no Apaches had attempted to cross the Rio Grande into Texas. If Victorio was at Ojo Del Carriso, Aranda estimated that Terrazas would strike him on 12 October.[12] In other words, when Colonel Terrazas asked the US army to proceed no further into Mexico, he remained unsure as to their exact location. In effect, Terrazas gambled that he would be able to catch and destroy Victorio without any assistance from U.S. forces.

Terrazas made final preparations for his 'search and destroy' mission. He pruned his forces by 90 men who, in his opinion, were not fit for further service. Brinkerhoff reported that Terrazas' command was 'on the brink of starvation & demoralisation that for these causes he [Terrazas] was

10 Thrapp, 1974, p.300.
11 Ibid.
12 Aranda to Buell, 11 Oct., 1880 in 'Victorio Papers', NA, M666, Roll 528.

Plates 16.1 and 16.2. Two photos taken on a 2005 trip to Tres Castillos. These were taken less than an hour before we sighted Tres Castillos, as we approached from the north-east. The mountains are either the Sierra La Lagrima or the Sierra Los Clanes. These photos should also give a clear idea of the arid terrain that Terrazas' troops crossed as they moved south in search of Victorio. (Photos: Author)

compelled to send 70 men back'.[13] (See document file no. 130.) Now down to approximately 260 men,[14] he left the Sierra de Los Pinos and moved south-eastwards to the Laguna El Cuervo to pick up the trail of the Apaches. However, the tracks turned out to be that of a small party of Apaches that made for the Cerro Lagrimas. They were not the trail left by a large party.[15] Terrazas was now unsure as to Victorio's approximate, let alone exact, location. Undeterred, he immediately set out to scout the mountain ranges to the south of the Laguna El Cuervo. First, there was the Sierra del Carrizo, then the Cerro Lagrimas, between which lay a waterhole called Ojo del Carrizo. Further south lay the Sierra Comenos, the Cerro Tosishue, and, finally, the Sierra de Puerto Frios, which lay almost 50 miles to the south of the Laguna El Cuervo.[16]

The entire column marched south to Ojo del Carrizo. Once again, they found no signs of the Apaches. The risk for Terrazas was that the Apaches had scattered into smaller groups to frustrate any pursuit and were now making their way westwards towards the Candelaria Mountains or the Lagunas de Guzman or Santa Maria. If this was the case, Terrazas did not have the logistical support to maintain such a pursuit.

On 12 October 1880, at Ojo Del Carrizo, Terrazas divided his force for a second time. Mata Ortiz was sent southwards, to investigate the Sierra Comenas and then to march on the Cerro Tosishue, 15 miles to the south of their present campsite. Terrazas, with his detachment, would scout westwards, on to the Llano de Los Castillos (Castillos Plains).[17] As Mata Ortiz moved southwards, Terrazas swung off to the west and the following morning:

> he cut tracks of three animals, at the edge of the Llanos de Los Castillos. They came down from the north, appearing very fresh. While his main force camped concealed in the chaparral, scouts worked onto the plains until little more than a league [approximately three miles] out, they came across the trail of the main body of hostiles. The sign showed that they had passed within a few days, seeming to make for Tres Castillos.[18]

Terrazas issued a flurry of orders: Mata Ortiz was to be contacted and recalled; a strong detachment was directed to scout further into the Llanos de Los Castillos. Presumably Terrazas rested the rest of his men, having spent the previous night scouting for tracks. Both the scouting detachment and Mata Ortiz's command rejoined him around dawn on 14 October. Mata Ortiz had found no sign of any Apaches, but Terrazas' scout force returned to report a myriad of tracks on the plains but no sightings of Apaches.[19] Issuing orders that Mata Ortiz should lead most of the column directly towards Tres Castillos, Terrazas, and a small detachment of 11 men, detoured to check a report of tracks leading from Tres Castillos towards Terrazas' former camp at Ojo del Carrizo. This report proved to be erroneous, and Terrazas and his small detachment turned westwards and made with all speed for Tres Castillos, which they reached at 2:00 p.m. on 14 October 1880.[20]

---

13 Brinkerhoff to AAAG SF 28 Oct., 1880, NA, RG393, Part 3, Entry 439, p.369

14 Brinkerhoff to AAAG SF 28 Oct., 1880, NA, RG393, Part 3, Entry 439, p.370. Baylor reported that Terrazas was down to two hundred men (Nolan, Quitman citing information rec'd directly from Capt Baylor, to Beck, AAAG, 12 Oct., 1880 in Letters Rec'd File 19 Mar.,1878-14 Feb., 1881, HQ Records DoP 1878-1881, NA, RG393, M1381, Roll 2)

15 Thrapp, 1974, p.300

16 Thrapp, 1974, p.296 & p300

17 Thrapp, 1974, p.300; Stout, p.176

18 Thrapp, 1974, pp.300-301

19 Thrapp, 1974, p.301

20 Thrapp, 1974, p.301

Tres Castillos, 14-15 October 1880

Despite his detour, Terrazas reached Tres Castillos well in advance of his main column. Tres Castillos consists of three jumbled rock outcroppings which rise to about 100 feet above the unusually flat plain which surrounds them. They run roughly north to south, and their length covers less than a mile. Their most important feature is the three quite substantial pools, which could normally be expected to be full during October, due to the summer rains.[21] The southern hill is the most rounded, but still consists of a rugged jumble of boulders and thick shrubs. Immediately to its north is a small but very steep fin of rock. One then traverses an open area, before encountering the main hill, which forms the other two points of Tres Castillos. At a distance, these look to be separate hills, but are joined by a saddle between the two. Again, these hills consist of a jumble of large boulders with thick bushes; but they are also much steeper than the southern hill.

Joaquin Terrazas climbed the northernmost of the three hills, and scanning the terrain, he spotted at least three distinct dust clouds drifting above the chaparral, approximately twelve miles to the south.[22] After some half an hour's study through his field glasses, he determined that the dust clouds were making for his location.[23] He left his 11 men to further scout and familiarise themselves with the lie of the land. They were then to withdraw northwards for between one and two miles and conceal themselves behind a small rock formation[24] until the Colonel could return with his entire force.[25]

Terrazas rejoined Mata Ortiz: 'about midway from their last camp to the Tres Castillos'.[26] Both commanders were veteran Apache campaigners and knew that seeing the approach of approximately 250 well-armed opponents would only serve to scatter the Apaches. However, in the open plain, there would be no way of concealing the approach of the troops in their usual formation. Terrazas and Mata Ortiz determined that their force should be formed into a long column formation no more than 20 men wide. They hoped that the Apaches might be encouraged to stand and fight, if apparently confronted by only 20 men. If the Chihuahua troops approached at speed, the bulk of the force would be hidden in the dust cloud raised by the front rank.

As the sun began to set, the Mexicans launched an attack on those Apaches who had arrived and camped at Tres Castillos. Terrazas estimated that two out of the three groups of Apaches whom he had spotted earlier that afternoon were camped at the base of the southernmost hill when the Mexicans attacked.[27] (See Map 16.2.)

Some of the Apache warriors accompanying these groups fanned out to meet the attack. Terrazas' Tarahumara Indian infantrymen responded by charging out of the column, firing as they went, killing at least one Apache warrior.[28] As the foot soldiers fanned out to confront the Apaches directly, the cavalry divided into two groups. Mata Ortiz took one group around the north end of Tres Castillos. He was no doubt joined by the 11 men left earlier by Terrazas. At the

---

21 Thrapp, 1974, p.301. We visited Tres Castillos in September 2005 and Thrapp's description of the terrain is very accurate. We spotted a lot of wildfowl, a couple of hawks and a Tarantula Wasp but did not, much to my disappointment, spot any eagles or rattlesnakes.
22 Thrapp, 1974, p.234 & 301
23 Thrapp, 1974, pp301-302
24 This small outcrop can be seen jutting out of the flat plain to the north and slightly west of the Tres Castillos.
25 Thrapp, 1974, p.302. It should be noted that some literature that has Col Terrazas and his men already in position waiting for Victorio at Tres Castillos and manages to trap them in a box canyon could not be further from the truth. (See for example Wellman, 1957, pp.175-176; Longstreet, p.96)
26 Thrapp, 1974, p.302
27 Ibid.
28 Ibid.

same time, Terrazas swung around to the south, until both groups of cavalry met on the other side of the hill formation. Both groups of cavalry dropped off men behind them as they went along, forming a cordon blocking any easy escape for the Apaches.[29] The Apaches, realising that they were surrounded and facing a much larger force than at first seemed to be the case, re-grouped as best they could on the southernmost hill of the three.[30] Buell later reported being told by Mescalero Apache survivors of the battle that the Apaches had managed to throw back a Mexican assault after they were surrounded.[31] Nevertheless, many of the Chihenne and Mescalero Apaches were taken completely by surprise, being killed or captured before they could reach cover.

The timing of Terrazas' attack was very fortuitous. One of the striking features of the terrain which surrounds Tres Castillos is that it is genuinely flat, unlike much of the ground between larger mountain ranges in the south-western USA and northern Chihuahua, where apparently flat ground, on closer inspection, is often very rough and lends itself to easy concealment. Terrazas' assault managed to coincide with the arrival of the Apaches. The latter had probably not had the time to send a lookout up to one of the two higher peaks which make up the middle and northern hills of Tres Castillos. A lookout stationed on the top of one of the hills might have been able to give the Apaches an earlier warning of the size of the force moving against them.

Moreover, had Terrazas launched his attack 10–15 minutes earlier, he would have caught the Apaches still on the move out on the plain. It is clear that most of the Apaches trapped had already dismounted, as Terrazas recovered 120 horses and 38 mules after the battle. He also claimed to have killed 78 Apaches and taken 68 women and children prisoner. If most of the Apaches had been mounted and on the move when Terrazas struck, they would simply have scattered back towards the thicker cover to the south. Here, Nana and his rearguard could have set up an ambush which, even with their limited supplies of ammunition, might have provided a sufficient check to Terrazas' pursuit long enough to allow most of the Apaches to escape.

On the other hand, had Terrazas arrived 10–15 minutes later, the Apaches might still have had time to mount up and scatter. Had Victorio followed standard Apache procedure, he would have stationed a lookout on the highest Tres Castillos hill. Even if the Apaches had not had time to scatter, they would have had time to occupy the higher middle and northern hills of Tres Castillos. As noted above, these two hills are as rugged as their lower neighbour, yet are steeper and joined by a narrow saddle which runs between them at a little less than half the elevation of the two peaks. The Apaches may have been short of ammunition, but the archaeological evidence from the Conline skirmish of 5 April 1880 reveals that the Apaches were still using archery as part of their arsenal. They were also steep enough to dislodge large boulders and send them down into their attackers. Even with such weapons, Victorio and his men could have mounted a far more effective defence from such positions. With Terrazas' men running low on food and morale, Apaches dug in on the northern peaks of Tres Castillos would have had a much better chance of holding out long enough to force Terrazas to withdraw through lack of supplies, or because of the arrival of additional Apache warriors. According to Kaywaykla, approximately 30 warriors arrived at Tres Castillos within twenty-four hours of the end of the battle, having successfully procured fresh stocks of ammunition. As it turned out, Terrazas had, with very good luck, timed his moment well in trapping a large number of Apaches on the southernmost hill of Tres Castillos.

At first glance, Tres Castillos appears to be a poor choice of campsite for Victorio, the hills there being surrounded by very flat and open plains. Yet we must consider the following: Victorio needed to keep his followers mounted to stay ahead of the pursuit. Tres Castillos was, at that time of year, an excellent source of water for a large group of Apaches and their horses and other stock. He

29 Ibid.
30 Ibid.
31 Buell to AAAG SF 3 Dec., 1880, NA, RG393, Part 3, Entry 439, p.4.

Plate 16.3. Looking south west, with the three peaks of the Tres Castillos clearly silhouetted against the mountains on the horizon. This is approximately the view Terrazas' troops would have had as they approached Tres Castillos. The terrain which surrounds these hills is unusually flat. (Photo: Author)

Plate 16.4. Looking north-east from just below the saddle between the central and northern hills of the Tres Castillos. The dark green patch is the dried up laguna, the northernmost of two such lagunas on the east side of the Tres Castillos. Mata Ortiz's cavalry crossed just above this laguna, moving from right to left. (See Diagram.) The photo again gives a clear idea of the very flat nature of the ground surrounding Tres Castillos. (Photo: Author)

may have had no option but to make for that point to refresh his mounts. The location had almost certainly been designated as the rendezvous point for those groups of Apaches foraging for fresh ammunition. What is also clear is that Victorio's change in strategy had almost worked. What appears to have happened is that Victorio had passed southwards, to the east of Tres Castillos, before turning and making for these hills. Unfortunately for the Apaches, Terrazas divined Victorio's probable destination and had taken a shortcut to the west to intercept the Apaches. Had Terrazas simply *followed* Victorio's trail, he would have been *at least* a day behind the Apaches, and the Chihuahuans were already running out of supplies. Terrazas would have been forced to suspend his campaign, and this would have given Victorio ample time to regroup either at the Lagunas de Guzman and/or de Santa Maria or even in the Sierra Madre. Victorio may have selected this point as being safe because he had calculated that, by the time he arrived there, his pursuers would not have been capable of catching him. It was another element of Terrazas' luck that, by correctly predicting Victorio's destination, he had been able to bring his force to Tres Castillos in just good enough condition to attack the Apaches.

Kaywaykla gives a graphic account of the Mexican attack. This differs from Terrazas' account only in the fact that one of the two groups of Apaches was in the process of arriving at the camp when the Mexicans attacked. Many of the Apaches were unaware of the attack until the Mexicans opened fire. Kaywaykla remembers the utter confusion as the Apaches scattered and tried to flee or take cover. He remained with his mother and they managed to find a temporary hiding place in a small crevice between two large rocks. Three Chihuahuan cavalrymen stopped right next to their refuge but failed to discover them. One remained behind to finish a cigarette before moving on.[32] (See document file no. 131.) This would suggest that Gouyen and Kaywaykla were almost caught by the first effort to trap the Apaches. As the Chihuahuan troops tightened their cordon, mother and son found themselves hiding outside it, but still dangerously close to the Mexican lines. Their only choice was to move quietly up the eastern side of the Tres Castillos hills, away from their enemies. Here, they encountered another woman and a girl, who refused to make the attempt to escape from Tres Castillos. If, again, the Apaches had followed standard procedure, another rendezvous point would have been chosen should they be attacked, either en route to, or at, Tres Castillos. Under the cover of darkness, both mother and son managed to crawl undetected through the Mexican picket lines, cross the plain and reach cover to the west of Tres Castillos. This took several hours and Kaywaykla reports sporadic shots coming from Tres Castillos throughout the night.[33] Kaywaykla also recalled a difficult climb at Tres Castillos to escape the Mexican cordon. This must have been up the saddle between the middle and northern hills. The rendezvous point would logically have been somewhere to the west and south of Tres Castillos, if the Apaches were returning towards the Lagunas de Guzman/Santa Maria, or the Sierra Madre, and hoping to link up with other Apache groups in that area. This may have made it necessary for the two fugitives either to scale the saddle, or to work their way around the northern end of Tres Castillos, before using the cover of darkness to pass over the plain undetected.

Opler also briefly mentions a Mescalero named Turquoise who was with Victorio at Tres Castillos:

> I outran even the bullets. I joined the Victorio bunch but was never even touched. I have been fired on at close range by infantry and never got a scratch. Victorio spoke to me many a time. When Victorio surrendered[34] I was right by his side. 'You're a man,' Victorio told me that day, 'but the end will be at sunrise.'[35]

---

32 Ball, 1970, pp.94-96: See also Kaywaykla, 1961, p.23 & p.38.
33 Ball, 1970, p.98; Kaywaykla, 1961, p.38.
34 One suspects that 'surrendered' may mean something more akin to 'trapped'.
35 Opler, 1969, p.82.

Plate 16.5 Closer view of the Tres Castillos. Those Apaches who failed to evade Terrazas' attack were trapped on the southernmost of the three hills, which is the lowest and most rounded of the three. (Photo: Author)

Plate 16.6. The southernmost hill of the Tres Castillos, viewed from the east. There is an abundance of jumbled rocks in which the trapped Apaches could take cover. (Photo: Author)

Two points are implied in this statement. First, that Victorio survived to the morning of 15 October; and second that he did not attempt to evade his enemies, which might mean that he was already wounded when he spoke to Turquoise. Nevertheless, Turquoise also made it clear that he himself managed to escape after the Apaches were surrounded by the Mexican state troops.

Having successfully surrounded the two groups of Apaches, Terrazas' men finished off or captured those Apaches they managed to catch in the open. Though, as noted, some Apaches managed to slip away during the night, the Mexicans were also largely successful in trapping the Apaches who had taken refuge on the southern hill. The third group of Apaches, the rearguard under the command of Nana, were still some distance from Tres Castillos and able to escape into the chaparral to the south.[36] The Mexicans also succeeded in capturing most of the horses and mules abandoned by the Apaches as the latter took cover on the southern hill of Tres Castillos.

Thrapp, in quoting Terrazas' report and memoirs, gives the impression that the Apaches were well-supplied with ammunition. Other sources suggest that this was not the case. Terrazas may be guilty of exaggerating the Apaches' ability to resist to enhance the magnitude of his own victory. It later emerged that he was less than confident in his troops' ability to confront Victorio, due to the effects of their own hunger.[37] Privately, Joaquin Terrazas acknowledged to Buell that he had been somewhat fortunate to catch Victorio at Tres Castillos.[38] This lends some weight to Brinkerhoff's suggestion that Terrazas' men were running low on both supplies and morale. Having emerged victorious, commanding troops weakened by hunger, Terrazas' triumphant language can be more readily understood.

Terrazas stated that, throughout the night, the Apaches: 'attempted to shoot their way from the peak, but were thrown back'[39], though we should judge this in the light of Kaywaykla's memory of desultory shots throughout the night. Nana's rearguard tried to set up a diversion by lighting a large fire to the south at about 10:00 p.m. This was answered by another fire lit high on the hill besieged by the Mexicans. Terrazas diverted some men to the south, and after a brief skirmish drove off some Apache warriors near the blaze.[40] Terrazas also reported that a 'death-song' was initiated among the trapped Apaches around midnight and continued till 2:00 a.m. The Apaches had also laboured throughout the night to raise up rock emplacements.[41]

At dawn, the Mexicans launched an all-out assault on the hill, and by 9:00 a.m.,[42] all the remaining Apaches had been killed or captured. Captain Brinkerhoff reported that

> the killing of Victorio & a portion of his band by the Mexican force under Terasas obviated the necessity of dispatch from me. The information comes from Lieut Ascarate of Terasas command who arrived at Carrisal on the 18th I have since been informed that the Lt reports that the Indians exhausted their ammunition in the fight & that the killing followed in the heat of the charge that every warrior who did not escape during the fight was killed.[43]

36 Thrapp, 1974, p.302.
37 Brinkerhoff to AAAG SF 28 Oct., 1880, NA, RG393, Part 3, Entry 439, p.370.
38 Joaquin Terrazas to Genl. G.P. Buell 12 Nov., 1880 (copy of document supplied by Dan D. Aranda, Las Cruces, New Mexico).
39 Thrapp, 1974, p.302; See also brief comment in David L. Hughes' 'An Early Chapter in the life of Apache Bill' pp.17-18.
40 Thrapp, 1974, pp.302-303; See also brief comment in David L. Hughes' 'An Early Chapter in the life of Apache Bill' pp.;17-18.
41 Thrapp, 1974, p.303.
42 Stout, 1974, p.176.
43 Brinkerhoff to AAAG SF 20 Oct., 1880, NA, RG393, Part 3, Entry 439, pp.273-274; See also Hatch to Willcox, 22 Oct., 1880, Telegrams Sent DoNM, Vol.3, Jan. – Nov. 1880 NA, RG393, Part 3, Entry 431, p.972.

Plate 16.7. A close-up of the cover on the hill where the Apaches were trapped. The southern laguna can be clearly seen. (Photo: Author)

Plate 16.8. Close-up of the cover on the southernmost hill of the Tres Castillos. The perspective is looking up the south-western slope. (Photo: Author)

The only other snippet of information concerning the final attack is a reference to one Juan Marcos, who was confronted by an Apache warrior as the former charged up the hill. Marcos won this personal combat but no further reliable[44] details can be drawn from this story.[45]

Terrazas claimed that some warriors and youths asked for and were given quarter. If this is the case, they were later reported as having been summarily executed.[46] This came from Kaywaykla's grandmother, who witnessed the aftermath as a captive. She, with four other female survivors, later managed to escape to the US after their being sold as slaves.[47]

Terrazas claimed that in the final assault his men faced Apache warriors who were dug in and made a fierce last stand, with the Mexicans having to finish their foes off at close quarters.[48] In his memoirs, Terrazas added a further detail:

> The warriors were killed, among the rocks, remaining only two of them in a cave, well armed and with plenty ammunition, who, with no thought of surrender, held out for more than two hours before they were killed, this despite the fact that their lives were offered to them by means of Indians already prisoners.[49]

Thrapp visited the site and he reports finding a 44-40 cartridge case at the entrance.[50] The cave is situated at the base of the southern hill, its mouth facing approximately north-west. It is quite small, but two men could have taken refuge there. It would have been difficult to approach, even from above, without giving the two Apaches a clear shot at their assailants. It is conceivable that one or two Apache warriors still had a good supply of ammunition, but, trapped by the attack, were unable to distribute their cartridges among other warriors.

The news of the defeat and death of Victorio arrived in the USA on 19 October 1880, in a letter from Dr Samaniego. Buell acknowledged this dispatch on the same day,[51] though the news of Victorio's death doesn't seem to have reached District of New Mexico Headquarters until 20 October.[52] A day earlier, Sheridan had briefed Sherman that the latest information concerning Victorio was that he and his followers were 'one hundred miles south of Quitman Mexican Troops in pursuit'. Sheridan had therefore concluded that the route chosen for the US President's trip through New Mexico would now 'be entirely safe'.[53] Colonel Grierson received the news while in

---

44 Rosson recounts this story as part of an account of the Victorio Campaign which is incomplete and the section on Tres Castillos does not match Thrapp's sources. However, I think it worth noting this particular detail as a possible lead in tracking down other versions of Tres Castillos as, so far, we have only Terrazas' and Kaywaykla's accounts to guide us. The short bibliography names a source called the 'Rural Citizen 1880' which might be a source worth tracking down.

45 Rosson, 1980, p.29.

46 Kaywaykla, 1963, p.21; Ball, 1980, p.83.

47 Ball, 1970, pp.169-170.

48 Terrazas cited in Thrapp, 1974, p.303; See also Buell to AAAG 22 Oct., 1880, NA, RG393, Part 3, Entry 439, pp.278-282.

49 Terrazas cited in Thrapp, 1974, p.303.

50 Thrapp, 1974, p.303.

51 Buell to Terrazas, 19 Oct., 1880 in 'Victorio Papers', NA, M666, Roll 528.

52 Hatch to Generals Sherman and Willcox, 20 Oct., 1880, Telegrams Sent DoNM, Vol.3, Jan. – Nov. 1880 NA, RG393, Part 3, Entry 431, p.961; Hatch to Pope, 21 Oct., 1880, Telegrams Sent DoNM, Vol.3, Jan. – Nov. 1880 NA, RG393, Part 3, Entry 431, pp.969-970) nor senior US army officers until the 22 of Oct. (Sheridan to the Adjutant of the Army, Washington D.C. 22 Oct., 1880, NA, RG393, Part 1, Entry 2539, Press Copies of Letters and Endorsements Sent, MDoM, Vol. 13, pp.725-727.

53 Sheridan to Sherman, 21 Oct., 1880, NA, RG393, Part 1, Entry 2539, Press Copies of Letters and Endorsements Sent, MDoM, Vol. 13, p.721.

Plate 16.9. View to the south-west from beneath the saddle between the northern and central hills of the Tres Castillos. After Gouyen and Kaywaykla had successfully passed through the Mexican lines, they were able to use the cover of darkness to cross the open land to the hills and mountains in the distance. (Photo: Author)

Plate 16.10. The small cave on the western side of Tres Castillos where two Apache warriors held out for several hours before eventually being killed. The cave would hold two men but is surprisingly small. (Photo: Author)

camp near Van Horn Wells on 22 October.[54] Lieutenant Leighton Finley, on patrol from Fresno Springs and Eagle Springs, noted, on arrival at the latter point on 24 October, that there was a rumour that Victorio had been killed by Mexican troops.[55] The *Army & Navy Journal* included an unconfirmed report that Victorio had been killed on 23 October,[56] but did not confirm his death until 30 October.[57] The news of Terrazas' success was splashed across the *Grant County Herald* on 23 October, leaving southern New Mexicans in no doubt that a great victory had been won.[58] (See document file no. 132.)

Samaniego stated that he had been informed by one of Terrazas' officers that 'Victorio with 50 grown Indians and 18 women & children dead. Moreover some 70 women & children were taken prisoners & 250 animals recovered.'[59] (See document file no. 133.) On 19 October, Henry Parker, Chief of Scouts, sent a telegram to his wife stating that, 'Terrasas killed Victorio and forty-nine Indians, sixteen women and children, captured sixty-eight women and children.'[60] These figures were also reported by Captain Brinkerhoff, though he warned that 'all these reports are doubtless upon the truth but may be exaggerated in some particulars.'[61] In fact, Terrazas (see document file no. 134) claimed that 62 warriors were killed out of a total of 78 slain Apaches, and that he took 68 prisoners. In return, he lost three killed, five seriously wounded and six slightly wounded.[62] It was reported that the Mexicans had captured 120 horses, 38 mules and 12 'Jacks'.[63] The Journal of the State of Chihuahua, dated 20 October 1880 (see document file no. 135), claimed that 62 men and 16 women and children had been killed, with a further 68 captured. They had also liberated two Mexican boys taken captive by the Apaches.[64] The two Mexican boys recaptured from the Apaches turned out to have been taken from the vicinity of Belen, New Mexico in April 1880.[65] Ten-year-old Felipe Padilla had survived the fight unscathed, but twelve-year-old Felix Carillo had been wounded in the leg.[66]

---

54 Grierson to AAG, DoTx, 31 Dec., 1880 in Letters Sent 23 Aug.-31 Dec., 1880, HQ Records DoP 1878-1881, NA, RG393, M1381, Roll 1, Letter No.168. Note: This report contained as Letter No. 3 in Letters sent 1881.

55 Leighton Finley Diary 6 Aug., 1880 entry Special Collections, University of Arizona Library, Tucson.

56 'Chief Victoria's War', *Army & Navy Journal*, Vol. 18, 23 Oct., 1880, p.227.

57 'Indian Affairs', *Army & Navy Journal*, Vol. 18, 30 Oct., 1880, p.241.

58 'Herald Extra-Special Dispatch to The Herald – S.P. Carpenter', the *Grant County Herald*, 23 Oct., 1880.

59 Buell to AAAG SF 19 Oct., 1880, NA, RG393, Part 3, Entry 439, p.271; See also Hatch to Pope, 21 Oct., 1880, Telegrams Sent DoNM, Vol.3, Jan. – Nov. 1880 NA, RG393, Part 3, Entry 431, p.969.

60 'Town and County', the *Grant County Herald*, 23 Oct., 1880.

61 Brinkerhoff to AAAG SF 20 Oct., 1880, NA, RG393, Part 3, Entry 439, pp.275-276.

62 Scott to Hunter, 2nd Assistant Secretary of State, Washington D.C., 22 Oct., 1880 in Consular Despatches Chihuahua Mexico 1830-1906, NA, M289, Roll 2; See also Thrapp, 1974, p.303; Haley, 1981, p.331.

Rasch adds that the Chihuahuans lost 3 killed and 12 wounded. He also states that 68 Apaches women and children were captured. (Rasch, 1960, p.9).

63 Scott to Hunter, 2nd Assistant Secretary of State, Washington D.C., 22 Oct., 1880 in Consular Despatches Chihuahua Mexico 1830-1906, NA, M289, Roll 2; Scott to Hunter, 22 Oct., 1880 attached to John Hay, Acting Secretary of State to Alexander Ramsey, Secretary of War, 10 Nov., 1880 in Letters Received by HQ DoNM Sept. 1865-Aug. 1890, NA, RG393, M1088, Roll 41, Jul.-Dec., 1880.

Sharp reported that the *Daily New Mexican* stated that Victorio, 60 men, 18 women and children were killed. They captured 70 men, women and children and recaptured 2 Mexican children. 280 horses and mules were also captured. (Sharp, 1957, p.12).

64 Copy of Journal of State Of Chihuahua in Brinkerhoff to AAAG SF 28 Oct., 1880, NA, RG393, Part 3, Entry 439, pp.374-385; Rasch, 1960, pp.9-10.

65 'Terrassas Talks' *Daily New Mexican* 30 Oct., 1880.

66 Loud to Mr Becker, Forage Agent, Belen N.M., 29 Oct., 1880, Telegrams Sent DoNM, Vol.3, Jan. – Nov. 1880 NA, RG393, Part 3, Entry 431, p.992.

The Mexican casualties indicate that the battle must have been a fairly one-sided affair, which confirms the belief that Victorio was short of ammunition.[67] Thrapp calls this more of a massacre than a battle.[68] If the Mexicans did clear the hill by assault, it would probably have been carried out by some of the militiamen pinning down the Apaches, while other Mexicans closed in on each position in turn and finished them off. Mescalero Apaches, returning to their reservation after the fight, reported that the trapped Apaches fought to their last bullet and surrendered on a given signal. By implication the surviving warriors were then killed.[69]

As noted earlier, the Apaches themselves reported that all of the adolescent males were summarily shot after the fighting was over, and these would have contributed to the figure of 68 warriors that Terrazas killed at Tres Castillos. During April 1880, at Cooney's mining camp, John Lambert stated that, from hiding, he had seen approximately 60 young men, 'in reality boys',[70] in Victorio's following, armed 'with the old fashioned store gun'.[71] Many of these adolescents were probably the same people whom Terrazas executed at Tres Castillos. Moreover, Kaywaykla estimated that, with several parties of warriors absent hunting or raiding, there were not as many as 68 warriors trapped and killed with Victorio.[72]

One ultimately undisputed fact was that Victorio was among the slain. Hatch noted that the two Mexican boys recaptured by Terrazas had reported that Victorio had definitely been killed in the engagement.[73] There are many versions of his death: The Apache version stated that, with three other warriors, he fought to his last bullet and then killed himself by driving his knife into his heart, his three companions sharing his fate.[74]

The Mexicans, however, recount a personal combat narrative. This took place between Mauricio Corredor, leader of the Tarahumara Indian infantry, and Victorio. The Apache leader was badly wounded in the exchange, and Corredor walked up and finished him off.[75] Corredor was feted as Victorio's killer and, over and above the 2,000 peso bounty on Victorio's head, he was presented

---

The return of the two boys was discussed at the highest levels by no less a trio as the Secretary's of the Interior, of State and of War concerning their return to the United States. (See Evarts to Ramsey, 8 Nov., 1880 in 'Victorio Papers', NA, M666, Roll 528); Owing to the 'severe wounds' received by one of the boys, necessitating his convalescence in Chihuahua City, they were not returned until fully recovered, the cost of their repatriation was borne by the United States (Luis Terrazas to Genl. Hatch 19 Nov., 1880 in Letters Received by HQ DoNM Sept. 1865-Aug. 1890, NA, RG393, M1088, Roll 41, Jul.-Dec., 1880; Hatch to AAG, DoM, Fort Leavenworth, 2 Dec., 1880 in Hatch to AAG Fort Leavenworth, 6 Dec., 1880 & Luis Terrazas to Hatch, 19 Nov., 1880 in 'Victorio Papers', NA, M666, Roll 528).

Hatch reminded the CO Fort Bliss that once the Mex. Authorities had handed back the two boys recaptured at Tres Castillos the latter was to make arrangements to reunite them with their families. (Hatch to CO Fort Bliss, 28 Dec., 1880, Telegrams Sent DoNM, Vol.4, Nov. 1880 – Jan. 1881, NA, RG393, Part 3, Entry 431, p.145).

67 'Chief Victoria's War', *Army & Navy Journal*, Vol. 18, 23 Oct., 1880, p.227.

68 Thrapp, 1967, p.209.

69 Buell to AAAG SF 3 Dec., 1880, NA, RG393, Part 3, Entry 439, p.5; Buell to AAAG, DoNM, 3 Dec., 1880, NA, RG393, Part 1, Entry 2546, pp.698-699; Buell, HQ Fort Stanton N.M., to AAG, DoM (via AAAG DoNM), 20 Nov., 1880 in Letters Received by HQ DoNM Sept. 1865-Aug. 1890, NA, RG393, M1088, Roll 42, File 658-1658, Jan.-Apr. 1881; Thrapp, 1974, p.305 & p.374 note 17.

70 Humphries, 1988, p.160.

71 Ibid. p.160.

72 Kaywaykla, 1961, p.22 & 1963, p.20.

73 Hatch to AAG, DoM, Fort Leavenworth, 8 Nov., 1880 in Letters Sent by '9MD/DNM/DoNM', NA, RG393, M1072, Roll 6, Jan. 1880-Aug. 1881, Letter No.574, p.366.

74 Kaywaykla, 1963, p.20; Ball, 1962, p.40 & 1970, p.102; 1980, p.50; Sonnichsen, 1973, p.210; Haley, 1981, p.331.

75 Stout, p.176; Thrapp, 1974, p.304; Keenan, 1997, p.239

with, 'a fancy nickled rifle by the grateful state of Chihuahua'.[76] Perez recounts an oral tradition that Corredor shot Victorio on the evening of 14 October, and during the night managed to creep close enough to see his body surrounded by grieving women.[77] It must be noted that those Apaches willing to discuss this question were scathing in their dismissal of Corredor as the killer of Victorio.[78]

Historian Martin L. Crimmins reports that Victorio was picked off by a Tarahumara sniper as he directed his warriors from the top of a hill.[79] Some accounts tell of the Apaches being trapped in a box canyon and wiped out.[80] Gillett, portrays him as riding a white horse on the morning of 15 October, rallying his trapped warriors, and being gunned down by the Mexicans.[81]

Lieutenant W.H. Beck, Tenth Cavalry, repeated a grisly story of Terrazas lining up 10 Apache prisoners at a time and asking them to give him Victorio's location. In a scene more reminiscent of a 'spaghetti' western, when each prisoner refused to reveal the location, they were immediately shot. Finally the 38th prisoner revealed his location, and Terrazas' orderly finished off the badly wounded Victorio.[82]

There are also traditions which argue that, while Victorio was slain, he was not killed at Tres Castillos. James A. McKenna records a skirmish between Victorio and some of his warriors and some prospectors, where Victorio was spotted by a couple of sharpshooters who shot his horse from under him, allegedly wounding the Apache leader. McKenna claims to have had information that Victorio had died of his wounds at Palomas Lake, and had been buried there, with another leader taking the chief's effects and subsequently being killed at Tres Castillos.[83] There are two reasons to doubt this version of events. First, an Apache leader would not have appropriated another, dead Apache's belongings, as their beliefs would have forbidden such an act.[84] Second, if Victorio had been killed by American prospectors, would the Apaches have allowed one of their most implacable foes (Terrazas) to have enjoyed a reputation for having perpetrated such a deed?[85] Cruse would have us believe that the battle did not take place at all. He argues that the Apaches had gone to the town of Santa Rosalia to trade. The Mexican inhabitants maintained a friendly visage while sending for Terrazas in secret. A fiesta was then staged and ended with the summary execution of Victorio.[86]

Of all the accounts of Victorio's death, the last three, particularly Cruse's, given Victorio's strict rules concerning minimal fraternising with Mexicans when trading, are the least convincing. Such accounts are probably more a symptom of the general chagrin that must have swept the US army

76 Thrapp, 1967, p.209; Lockwood, 1987, pp.232-233; Faulk, 1974, p.180; Sonnichsen, 1973, p.210; Smith, 1962, p.26 & 1965, p.138, note 35; Cocker, 1999, p.231; Rasch, 1960, p.10

77 Silver City Press, 30 Jun., 1998. Perez states that Mauricio Corredor's surname alluded to his ability as a runner, for which the Tarahumara Indians are famous. He adds that he came from Bocoyna and that his given Spanish surname was Gonzalez.

78 Ball, 1980, p.83.

79 Crimmins, 1935, p.142; See also Wellman, 1957, p.176; Longstreet, 1970, p.96; Rister, 1928, p.216.

80 Lockwood, 1987, p.232; Faulk, 1974, p.180; Yarbrough, 1969, p.69.

81 Gillett, 1926, p.47; 1976, p.188; Crimmins, 1935, p.142.

82 Thrapp, 1974, pp.304-305; Johnson, 1957, pp.9-10; Rasch, 1960, p.10.

83 McKenna, 1963, pp.190-193; See also Simmons, 1995, El Paso Times.

84 See Loring, 2001, p.196.

85 James A. McKenna's Black Range Tales is a highly entertaining collection of recollections of McKenna of his and others frontier experiences. Many of his stories feature Apaches and more particularly Victorio. However, where dates are mentioned concerning events they are usually wrong. For example he has Victorio alive in 1882 two years after he had been killed at Tres Castillos. (1963, p.188) As such McKenna should be treated with extreme caution as an accurate sources of events. It also has to be said that some of the stories have a ring of truth to them in their broad direction if not some of the detail.

86 Cruse, 1987, pp.85-86; Haley, 1981, p.331; Balmer, 1956, p.6.

that it had been Mexicans, and state militia at that, who had finally killed Victorio.[87] However, Thrapp is also quite correct that these stories, 'all reflect the imagination of the writer rather than the facts of that grisly day'.[88] The Mexicans might have known whom they were pursuing, but would not necessarily have known him by sight. Terrazas, in reporting his death stated:

> The indian Victorio is of the dead, according to the signs by which he is known ... according to those who tell me, those who knew him and the testimony of the captives, besides the wearing apparel and personal accoutrements which I have received, and which ... would only be carried by an Indian chief of some importance.[89]

However, recent research by Daniel D. Aranda has unearthed material which strongly suggests that the Mexicans quickly identified Victorio's body. A contemporary Chihuahua newspaper which clearly stated that Victorio was identified by the prominent facial scar and missing front teeth incurred at some point prior to the removal of the Chihennes to San Carlos in 1877.[90] This reinforces Allan Radbourne's argument that the photograph popularly supposed to be that of Victorio is not of that of the Apache leader.[91] We know that Victorio was shot in the face at close-range in the fight which ended the Pajarito brother's aspirations to lead the Chihenne Apaches in 1873.[92] It was possibly this wound which positively identified the Chihenne leader's body. This scarring was mentioned much later in the *The Arizona Silver Belt* which gives a more general description of Victorio at the time of his demise and also mentions another facial wound dating back to the mid-1860s: "At the time of his death, Victorio was about 55 years old, heavy-set, broad faced, square under jaw, prominent cheek bones, and bore a bullet mark in the cheek received at the hand of Barney Conly ... at Pinos Altos, N.M. in 1866."[93]

However, Terrazas' account may actually furnish us with a clue as to who killed Victorio. The most likely candidate for his killing may be an unfortunate un-named Mexican sergeant who was subsequently killed in an Apache ambush on 16 November 1880. On finding that he had been using Victorio's saddle and carried: 'a few trinkets from the body of the famed chief',[94] the Apaches had hacked the sergeant's body to pieces. One can only hope that they had not taken him alive.[95]

The only conclusion we can arrive at with any certainty, is that Victorio was killed at Tres Castillos, and that nobody knows exactly how he died. As far as his followers were concerned:

> The chief had died as he would have wished – in the defense of his people. He was the greatest of all Apache chiefs, yes, of all Indian chiefs. He had died as he had lived, free and unconquerable. We knew well the fate of Mangas Coloradas and of Cochise. They, too, would have preferred death in battle; they would have envied Victorio. So – we were not to mourn for him.

87 When the *Daily New Mexican* headlined Victorio's death, they gave Terrazas full credit for his victory. The article was also quick to argue that his triumph was in part due to the efforts of the US army in the movements prior to Tres Castillos. (*Daily New Mexican* cited in Sharp, 1957, p.12).

88 Thrapp, 1974, p.304.

89 Terrazas cited in Thrapp, 1974, p.304.

90 Aranda, unpublished article.

91 Radbourne, 2004, p.74

92 See Watt, 'I Will Not Surrender the Hair of a Horse's Tail: The Victorio Campaign 1879', p.93.

93 *The Arizona Silver Belt*, 29 Nov., 1890. Information courtesy of Daniel D. Aranda, email 13 September, 2018.

94 Thrapp, 1967, p.209.

95 Thrapp, 1967, p.209; 1974, pp.309-310; Stout, p.178; Rasch, 1960, p.10.

> He had been spared the ignominy of imprisonment and slavery, and for that he would have been thankful to Ussen.[96]

The winners of the battle were certainly Joaquin Terrazas and his militiamen. Feted by fellow Chihuahuans, Terrazas allegedly collected $17,250 scalp bounty and $10,200 from selling the captives into slavery.[97] Brinkerhoff had received information on 21 August, from Mexico, that the Governor of Chihuahua had made an offer of $2,000 for Victorio's scalp and $250 for each warrior's scalp.[98] This reward had apparently been recently raised to 3,000 dollars 'for the head of the Apache Chief Victoria'.[99] Obviously, Terrazas would have had to distribute some proportion of the profits among his troops. The militiamen were also allowed to retain any booty taken at Tres Castillos. A grateful populace contributed a further 17,000 pesos by voluntary subscription.[100] Terrazas and his men were honoured for their victory with a parade in Chihuahua City and generous speeches extolling their virtues as citizens of the State of Chihuahua.[101] This procession also involved the display of the Apache captives and Apache scalps suspended on poles.[102] (See document file no. 136.)

The Mexicans were not the only people in Chihuahua City celebrating the defeat of Victorio. US Consul Scott, in transmitting the news of Tres Castillos and the imminent arrival of the captives in Chihuahua City, added that some of the Apaches had escaped. He recommended the USA mete out the harshest punishment to them should they attempt to return to US reservations. If lenient measures were adopted, he argued, then the US risked losing the good will of the people of Chihuahua. He could not resist adding the following personal recommendation:

> I trust that the Department [of State] will recommend to the War Department and the Department of the Interior the immediate apprehension of the balance of this band as soon as they cross the border and either turn them over to the authorities of New Mexico or have the authorities of this State extradite and try them here.
>
> There is an opportunity now to teach these blood-thirsty Apaches a lesson that they will remember, and not one of this band should be permitted to escape the halter they so richly deserve.[103]

Buell also claimed, with some justification, that while his force had not contacted the Apaches, the presence of so many US troops in Mexico and picketing the Rio Grande had significantly contributed to Terrazas' victory.[104]

---

96 Kaywaykla cited in Ball, 1970, p.100; see also Roberts, p.189.

97 Thrapp, 1974, p.373 note 10; Smith, 1962, p.34; Alonso, p.99.
We should also perhaps be wary of the term 'slavery' in this case. It could involve conditions of cruel servitude, but it could also mean effective adoption into a Mexican household. (Alonso, p.44).

98 Brinkerhoff Ft Bliss to AAAG 21 Aug., 1880?, NA, RG393, Part 3, Entry 439, p.805; Rasch, 1960, p.10.

99 Brinkerhoff to AAAG SF 11 Sept., 1880, NA, RG393, Part 3, Entry 439, p.408; the *Grant County Herald*, 25 Sept., 1880.

100 Alonso, 1997, pp.99-100.

101 Alonso, 1997, p.100; Thrapp, 1974, pp.310-311; Rasch, 1960, p.10; Thompson, p.169.

102 'Greeting the Victors' *The Daily New Mexican*, 2 Dec., 1880; Thrapp, 1974, pp.310-311; See also Royal City News Webpage.

103 Scott to Hunter, 2nd Assistant Secretary of State, Washington D.C., 22 Oct., 1880 in Consular Despatches Chihuahua Mexico 1830-1906, NA, M289, Roll 2; Scott to Hunter, 2nd Asst. Sec. of State, 22 Oct., 1880 in 'Victorio Papers', NA, M666, Roll 528; Scott to Hunter, 22 Oct., 1880 attached to John Hay, Acting Secretary of State to Alexander Ramsey, Secretary of War, 10 Nov., 1880 in Letters Received by HQ DoNM Sept. 1865-Aug. 1890, NA, RG393, M1088, Roll 41, Jul.-Dec., 1880.

104 Buell, HQ Fort Stanton N.M., to AAG, DoM (via AAAG DoNM), 20 Nov., 1880 in Letters Received by HQ DoNM Sept. 1865-Aug. 1890, NA, RG393, M1088, Roll 42, File 658-1658, Jan.-Apr. 1881.

Tres Castillos: A Decisive Victory over the Apaches?

While the killing of Victorio and over 60 men and adolescent boys at Tres Castillos, accompanied by the loss of approximately 100 women and children to death, slavery or adoption, was a disaster for the Apaches, even this event was not necessarily as decisive as it would appear. The legend is that only 17 Apaches escaped from Tres Castillos, and that these were the sole survivors of the fight. However, there are good grounds for arguing that a large number of Apaches, following, or allied to, Victorio, were nowhere near, or escaped from, Tres Castillos. Under the leadership of Nana, and possibly of Mangus, son of Mangas Coloradas,[105] Chihenne Apache warriors would launch a series of retaliatory attacks on Mexicans and Anglo-Americans immediately after Victorio's death. In the longer term, throughout the winter of 1880 and the spring of 1881, the survivors of Victorio's band would continue their guerrilla war against the US and the Republic of Mexico. Thrapp states that in 1883, while General Crook confronted the Chiricahua Apaches in the Sierra Madre:

> Several other warriors rode into camp during the afternoon, including the important Ka-ya-ten-nae or 'Looking Glass,' as his name usually is translated, although there are other versions of what the Apache word meant. Although a young man, he had succeeded Victorio as war chief of the Warm Springs Indians, and took over his band of seventy nine, including fifty three fighting men.[106]

John G. Bourke reported at the time that Nana also had a personal following of 15 and, though he was still a man of power among the Chiricahuas, Looking-Glass appeared to be the leader.[107] Thrapp makes it quite clear that James Kaywaykla, 'always denied that Victorio had many warriors with him at the final battle. Most, he believed, were on other missions.'[108] He also cites a 'scout' called Riley who stated that a number of Apache warriors had killed at least 25 Mexicans in the aftermath of Tres Castillos, Terrazas' force having caught 'only the squaw camp with a few old men in it'.[109] Terrazas himself stated that he thought that there were at least 30 'Indians' still at large'.[110] Captain Brinkerhoff filed the following report on 20 October 1880:

> A portion of the band number unknown is reported to have captured about 300 horses at or near Horniga Mexico a ranch 50 miles south-east from Chihuahua on the 12th inst This detachment was probably not with Victorio at the time of his capture.[111]

On 28 October, Brinkerhoff added that:

> He [Terrazas] further states that the Indians who raided Hornigo ranche Oct 12th were not in the fight. 9 warriors of those with Victorio escaped early in the engagement. About 30 indians all of Victorio's band are still at large. The trails of the fugitives led in the direction of the Bosque Benito.[112]

105 While never reaching nor aspiring to the influence his father had exercised, the role Mangus played during the Victorio Campaign is virtually unknown. However, he did command a personal following and was respected as a leader. He was also known to the U.S. authorities and by 1881, along with Nana, was presumed by the US army to be a natural successor to Victorio.
106 Thrapp, 1972, pp.159-160.
107 Bourke, 2001ii, pp.384-385.
108 Thrapp, 1974, p.374, note 1.
109 Thrapp, 1974, p.308.
110 Terrazas telegram 25 Oct., 1880, cited in Haley, 1952, p.336.
111 Brinkerhoff to AAAG SF 20 Oct., 1880, NA, RG393, Part 3, Entry 439, pp.274-275.
112 Brinkerhoff to AAAG SF 28 Oct., 1880, NA, RG393, Part 3, Entry 439, pp.370-371.

Captain C.H. Conrad, Fifteenth Infantry, in charge at Fort Stanton, estimated that approximately 44 Mescalero Apaches had been killed at Tres Castillos, with a further 20 enslaved, accounting for between a third and half of the overall casualties inflicted by the Mexicans. This information was gained from Mescaleros recently returned to the reservation.[113] (See document file no. 137.)

Kaywaykla recalled a council held before Tres Castillos, where it was revealed that many warriors were absent foraging for food and ammunition. Nana wanted to send more warriors out to seek ammunition. After some debate, a warrior called Blanco was selected, and he rounded up a group of warriors and departed.[114] The absence of so many warriors left only 20 men, plus any warriors who had returned from earlier raiding expeditions. As they moved out from camp on the morning of 14 October, Kaywaykla implies that there were at least 400 people with Victorio.[115] He was a young boy at the time and could have easily miscalculated the numbers. Equally, this could mean that while Terrazas spotted evidence of three groups, there could have been other groups who completely escaped his scrutiny. The Apaches might well have split into a number of groups on the morning of 14 October, and might have agreed to a rendezvous several days later. Daklugie, son of Juh, echoed Kaywaykla's version of events, stating that most of Victorio's warriors were absent raiding in search of ammunition.[116] He also stated that Victorio had very few warriors with him, in the vanguard and 'a few more' with the rearguard.[117]

Yet these figures remain speculation. There are no reliable estimates of numbers of Warm Springs and Mescalero Apaches present in the vicinity of Tres Castillos who successfully evaded Terrazas' attack by avoiding the Colonel's scrutiny in the first place.

After Tres Castillos, it was Nana who gathered up the survivors with his rearguard warriors. He certainly had no thought of surrender, and within a day was thinking in terms of fighting back.[118] Nana had obviously kept a couple of scouts out monitoring Colonel Terrazas' movements. They had reported that a large party of militia, with most of the captured Apaches, had moved south, making for Chihuahua city. This was judged to be too strong to ambush. A smaller party, no doubt militiamen from the border region, had left Tres Castillos moving north towards their homes along the Rio Grande. The scouts had not managed to get close enough to determine how many prisoners were with the latter group, but Nana felt that he knew the country well enough to get ahead and attempt an ambush. A small patrol with a single Apache girl captive was ambushed and she managed to escape.[119]

Nana, in effect, mobilised as quickly as possible in order to take advantage of any opportunity to recover captives. Beyond the one rescue, this proved to be impossible. The Apaches re-grouped and, to avoid a potential ambush, Nana waited three days before returning to Tres Castillos to bury their slain.[120] It is difficult to determine numbers, but there may have been as many as 30 or 40 Warm Springs Apache warriors who had survived or avoided the disaster at Tres Castillos. Kaywaykla mentions that an additional party, who had detached themselves to hunt, caught them up some time after Tres Castillos. Led by Sanchez, they had separately returned to Tres Castillos

113 Conrad to Post Adjutant, Fort Stanton, 1 Dec., 1880 in Letters Received by HQ DoNM Sept. 1865-Aug. 1890, NA, RG393, M1088, Roll 41, Jul.-Dec., 1880; Conrad to Post Adjutant, Fort Stanton, N.M., 1 Dec., 1880, NA, RG393, Part 1, Entry 2546, pp.698-699;Conrad to Post Adjutant, Fort Stanton N.M. 1 Dec., 1880 in 'Victorio Papers', NA, M666, Roll 528; Thrapp, 1974, p.309.

114 Ball, 1970, p.90.

115 Ibid, p.91.

116 Ball, 1980, p.80 & p.83.

117 Ibid, p.83.

118 Ball, 1970, p.101.

119 Ibid, pp.101-102.

120 Ibid, p.102.

and tracked Terrazas down towards Chihuahua City. Finding no opportunity to effect a rescue of the captives, they had returned to seek out Nana.[121]

The decisive element of defeat for the Chihenne Apaches resided not in their immediate ability or otherwise to continue their resistance, but in the implications of Tres Castillos for their long-term survival. It was not just the loss of the slain and executed men and boys, but the loss of so many female Apaches into Mexican captivity. Not only would warrior losses be far harder to replace, but the skills of the women as the de facto experts in gathering and preparing foodstuffs and clothing had been lost. Daklugie implicitly acknowledged this fact, when he outlined his definition of genocide.[122]

The most immediate retaliation, in the immediate aftermath of Tres Castillos, was inflicted by Apache warriors in Texas.[123] The Tenth Cavalry had been informed that 30 Apaches were believed to have escaped from Tres Castillos and were roaming along the border.[124] On 28 October 1880, Apaches ambushed a 12-man patrol at Ojo Caliente, Texas, consisting of one sergeant, one corporal and ten privates from B and K Companies, Tenth Cavalry.[125] Almost the first thing Sergeant Perry and his men knew of their assailants was a shattering volley from close range, which killed Corporal W. Backus, and Privates C. Burns, J. Griffin, G. Mills and J. Stanley.[126] The official story was that the rest of the patrol made for cover and returned fire. Equally rapidly the Apaches seized four horses and two mules and disappeared.[127] However, the bi-monthly return for K Company, Tenth Cavalry, tells a very different story:

> Oct 26th – A detachment consisting of Corp'l Backus & 6 privates under charge of Sergt. Perry of Co "B", 10th Cav with 6 p'vts of the latter co, marched to Hot Springs, for picket duty. On the morning of the 28th at daybreak, this camp was surprised and attacked by about 30 Indians who came from the Mexican side of the river – Corp'l Backus and 2 pvts of Co "K" and 2 pvts of Co "B" were killed by the Indians – the rest of the men became demoralized and scattered to make their escape by running away – abandoning most of their clothing, arms, horses equipments & c. which were captured by the Indians and taken with them into Mexico.[128]

The Apaches had probably carefully scouted this detachment, possibly monitoring the its routine, on 27 October. They had camped behind a ridge three miles into Mexico, and had approached

121 Ibid, p.103.

122 Ball, 1980, p.79.

123 On 27 December, 1880, Lt. Beck reported that this attack was perpetrated by the thirty Apache warriors detached by Victorio to search for ammunition supplies. He also dates this attack to the 15 Oct., 1880. (Johnson, 1957, p.10).

124 Whipple to Pope, 27 Oct., 1880, NA, RG393, Part 1, Entry 2539, Press Copies of Letters and Endorsements Sent, MDoM, Vol. 13, pp.738-739.

125 Brinkerhoff to AAAG SF 29 Oct., 1880, NA, RG393, Part 3, Entry 439, pp.386-388; Brinkerhoff to AAAG SF 31 Oct., 1880, NA, RG393, Part 3, Entry 439, p.391; Ord to Pope, 1 Nov., 1880, NA, RG393, Part 1, Entry 2539, Press Copies of Letters and Endorsements Sent, MDoM, Vol. 13, p.752.
It was almost immediately assumed that the attack had been perpetrated by the thirty warriors reported by Col. Terrazas to have been absent from Tres Castillos. (Brinkerhoff to AAAG SF 29 Oct., 1880, NA, RG393, Part 3, Entry 439, pp.386-388).

126 Leckie, 1967, p.230, Stout, p.177, Schubert 1995 individual entries; Chronological List, p.51; Webb, 1976, p.90; Matthews, 1993, p.42.

127 Brinkerhoff to AAAG SF 31 Oct., 1880, NA, RG393, Part 3, Entry 439, pp.391-392; Leckie, 1967, p.230.

128 Bi-Monthly Company Muster Rolls for Company K, 10th Cavalry, Sept./Oct. 1880 in NA, RG94. It is worth noting that the largest number of fatalities inflicted by Victorio's Apaches upon the Ninth and Tenth Cavalry in a single engagement amounted to five men killed at Ojo Caliente NM, 4 September, 1879 and Ojo Caliente TX, 28 October 1880.

their target on foot.[129] At dawn on 28 October, they caught this detachment completely off guard, and those not immediately killed, fled. The first many of the detachment knew of their danger was when the Apaches 'rose up to fire a volley.'[130] Sergeant Perry escaped the attack, being outside the camp collecting his horse and preparing to go out on patrol.[131] Private Weoley Lively of K Company, recalled that Corporal Backus had:

> called to me to get up. He saw something in the bushes – the bushes were to my left, on the edge of the bank of the river and at the same time the Indians fired a volley from the bank of the river from behind the bushes and wounded four men in the tent. The balance of the men scattered and ran. I ran to where my horse was picketed and unfastened the lariat and mounted, when the horse was shot from under me. I then ran into the mountains and made my escape. I afterwards saw the Indians rounding up the herd.[132]

Private Thomas E. Murphy had better luck managing to mount his horse and escape. He recalled that the Apaches had surrounded the camp on three sides, and as Corporal Backus had put a bullet into his carbine and started to rise to make a challenge, the Apaches had opened fire. Those men sitting around the fire scattered.[133] Corporal Backus and one or two of the men spotted the Apaches just before the attack, but were not sure if they were Mexicans or Apaches until they opened fire.[134] The Apaches chose to strike at the point when Sergeant Perry went out to relieve the sentry.[135] This technique has clear echoes of Victorio's attack on Morrow's camp on 30 September 1879,[136] when the attack was timed to coincide with calling in all but one of the pickets for breakfast.

Private Cottman thought that most of the attackers were Mexican as, from his hiding place in the bushes, he heard them conversing in Spanish and that they 'looked different from any Indians I had ever seen,'[137] though he also recalled that his attackers wore shirts, hats and most of them wore their hair long.[138] The reference to the loss of most of their clothes strongly suggests that most of the survivors were rudely awakened and only had seconds to make a decision whether to choose 'fight' or 'flight'. Grierson later admitted that the Apaches had captured at least five horses and a corresponding amount of arms and equipment, though he tried to soften the blow by drawing attention to the quick response made to this attack by all of his detachments in the general area.[139]

---

129 Berger's Report enclosed within Baldwin to Grierson, 10 Nov., 1880 in Letters Rec'd File 19 Mar.,1878-14 Feb., 1881, HQ Records DoP 1878-1881, NA, RG393, M1381, Roll 2.

130 Baldwin to AAAG, DoP, 28 Oct., 1880 & Statement of Pvt. Thomas E. Murphy, Co.K, 10th U.S. Cavalry in Letters Rec'd File 19 Mar.,1878-14 Feb., 1881, HQ Records DoP 1878-1881, NA, RG393, M1381, Roll 2.

131 Baldwin to AAAG, DoP, 28 Oct., 1880 in Letters Rec'd File 19 Mar.,1878-14 Feb., 1881, HQ Records DoP 1878-1881, NA, RG393, M1381, Roll 2.

132 Statement of Pvt. Weoley Lively, Co. K, 10th U.S. Cavalry in Letters Rec'd File 19 Mar.,1878-14 Feb., 1881, HQ Records DoP 1878-1881, NA, RG393, M1381, Roll 2.

133 Statement of Pvt. Thomas E. Murphy, Co.K, 10th U.S. Cavalry in Letters Rec'd File 19 Mar.,1878-14 Feb., 1881, HQ Records DoP 1878-1881, NA, RG393, M1381, Roll 2.

134 Statement of Pvt's Thomas E. Murphy, Co. K &. Joseph Cottman, Co. B, 10th U.S. Cavalry in Letters Rec'd File 19 Mar.,1878-14 Feb., 1881, HQ Records DoP 1878-1881, NA, RG393, M1381, Roll 2.

135 Statement of Pvt. Joseph Cottman, Co. B, 10th U.S. Cavalry in Letters Rec'd File 19 Mar.,1878-14 Feb., 1881, HQ Records DoP 1878-1881, NA, RG393, M1381, Roll 2.

136 See Watt, 'I Will Not Surrender the Hair of a Horse's Tail: The Victorio Campaign 1879, p.221.

137 Statement of Pvt. Joseph Cottman, Co. B, 10th U.S. Cavalry in Letters Rec'd File 19 Mar.,1878-14 Feb., 1881, HQ Records DoP 1878-1881, NA, RG393, M1381, Roll 2.

138 Statement of Pvt. Joseph Cottman, Co. B, 10th U.S. Cavalry in Letters Rec'd File 19 Mar.,1878-14 Feb., 1881, HQ Records DoP 1878-1881, NA, RG393, M1381, Roll 2.

139 Grierson, Eagle Springs to AAG, San Antonio, Texas, 29 Oct., 1880 in Telegrams Sent 23 Jun.-30 Nov., 1880, HQ Records DoP 1878-1881, NA, RG393, M1381, Roll 1, p.225, Letter No.606; Grierson to

In fact, Captain Baldwin reported that 10 horses, four mules and 10 Carbines and revolvers, with their ammunition, had been lost and that he counted and buried four dead, with a further five men missing, though he was confident that three of these men were not actually dead.[140] Baldwin noted that, in fleeing, the men had abandoned their weapons.[141] Charles Berger re-examined the camp and verified that it had been Apaches who had ambushed the picket. He also criticised Lieutenant Ayers' choice of campsite for this particular detachment, and stated that the Lieutenant's choice of camp for his own picket station was even more open to attack.[142]

Captain Baldwin mounted a pursuit, but the Apaches had immediately crossed back into Mexico.[143] Baldwin did not pursue them into Chihuahua, because his instructions indicated that cross-border pursuit was strictly forbidden. The Apaches were believed to have returned to the Sierra Borracho.[144]

A final note on this attack concerns the epic night ride by Lieutenant Flipper which his own memoirs strongly imply was prior to the battle at Tinaja de Las Palmas.[145] However, there are a number of anomalies with this account which suggest that this event could not have occurred in July 1880. Flipper recalled that he rode to Eagle Springs to report an attack upon a picket of Tenth Cavalrymen where several had been killed. The first that was known of the attack was the arrival of two survivors "in their underclothing"[146] and Flipper and two soldiers were dispatched on an epic 98-mile ride to Eagle Springs to alert Colonel Grierson. Flipper's account then moves to an account of Tinaja De Las Palmas. It is difficult to see how Flipper could have ridden these distances to Eagle Springs and back to Old Fort Quitman and have time to return in time to rescue Grierson at Tinaja De Las Palmas. This is particularly anomalous given the poor physical shape he was in, by his own account, when he reported to Grierson at Eagle Springs.[147] However, his mention of a picket being ambushed, several killed and survivors arriving at his camp in their underclothes appears to be a very close match to the events on the 28 October, 1880. Flipper notes that the men were buried where they fell and that he was asked to lead the service "after which a volley was fired and the buglers sounded taps."[148] We know that the five men were buried at, or very near, to where they fell, as these graves have been formally memorialised at Ojo Calientes, Texas. So it would appear that Flipper's night-time courier duty was more likely undertaken on the night of the 29/30

AAG, DoTx, 31 Dec., 1880 in Letters Sent 23 Aug.-31 Dec., 1880, HQ Records DoP 1878-1881, NA, RG393, M1381, Roll 1, Letter No.168 (Note: This latter report contained as Letter No. 3 in Letters sent 1881).

140 Baldwin to AAAG, DoP, 28 Oct., 1880 in Letters Rec'd File 19 Mar.,1878-14 Feb., 1881, HQ Records DoP 1878-1881, NA, RG393, M1381, Roll 2; Capt Baldwin, Camp near Ojo Caliente, 28 Oct., 1880 in Register of Letters Rec'd Mar. 23, 1878-Jan. 30, 1881, HQ Records DoP 1878-1881, NA, RG393, M1381, Roll 2, p.46, Letter No.140.

141 Baldwin to Viele, Eagle Springs, Texas, 28 Oct., 1880 in Letters Rec'd File 19 Mar.,1878-14 Feb., 1881, HQ Records DoP 1878-1881, NA, RG393, M1381, Roll 2.

142 Berger's Report enclosed within Baldwin to Grierson, 10 Nov., 1880 in Letters Rec'd File 19 Mar.,1878-14 Feb., 1881, HQ Records DoP 1878-1881, NA, RG393, M1381, Roll 2.

143 Ord to AG Chicago, 30 Oct., 1880, 'Victorio Files' NA, RG393, M1495, Roll 14; Bi-Monthly Company Muster Rolls for Company D, 10th Cavalry, Sept./Oct. 1880 in NA, RG94 Matthews, p.41.

Wellman suggests that Capt. Baldwin lost four men killed in a fight with some of Victorio's warriors near Ojo Caliente, Texas, thereby preventing them returning to Victorio. As the war leader had arranged to meet this party at Tres Castillos he delayed his movement long enough to be caught by Col Terrazas. (1957, p.174) As we have seen on previous pages this interpretation of events is simply wrong. Indeed this story contradicts Wellman's account of how Victorio was trapped at Tres Castillos.

144 Brinkerhoff to AAAG SF 31 Oct., 1880, NA, RG393, Part 3, Entry 439, p.392.

145 Harris, 1997, p.32 & 34. See Chapter 10.

146 Ibid, p.32

147 Ibid, p.34

148 Ibid, p.34

Lt. Henry O. Flipper, Tenth Cavalry. He was the first African-American to graduate from West Point. He was credited with making a dangerous night ride from Old Fort Quitman to Eagle Springs to warn Colonel Grierson that Victorio had crossed the Rio Grande just prior to the fight at Tinaja de Las Palmas. A closer examination of his memoir strongly suggests that this incident actually occurred at the end of October after the attack upon the Tenth Cavalry detachment stationed at Ojo Caliente, Texas. (National Archives)

October to warn Grierson of the attack. This will have been just as potentially dangerous as, in the immediate aftermath of the attack Flipper could have had no idea of the subsequent activities of the Apaches who had perpetrated this attack.

It was at first supposed that the attackers were the 30 escaped Apaches reported by Terrazas,[149] but this estimate was quickly revised to suggest a group of 20 Mescaleros[150], who were thought to have been driven south when Buell was ordered to take four cavalry companies into the Sacramento Mountains on 22 September 1880.[151] This story seems unlikely, as Buell was moving his expedition into Mexico many miles to the west of the Sacramento Mountains on that date. Terrazas also reported his 30 Apaches as being too far away from Ojo Caliente, Texas. However, it was strenuously denied that this group could have left the Mescalero reservation. Since April, in the aftermath of Hembrillo Canyon, the Mescaleros detained on the reservation had remained under strong guard.[152] This is a clear example of the speculative 'it-must-have-been' approach used by the US army when attempting to calculate the numbers of Apache warriors at large, and who might be responsible for any attack. It also reinforces the argument that there were more Apache warriors at large who had not been trapped at Tres Castillos. Terrazas may well have been monitoring the movements of 30 Apache warriors, but quite how he managed to accomplish this after he had withdrawn his forces and celebrated his victory in Chihuahua City is not clear. Moreover, Terrazas' statement does not rule out another group of Apaches from Victorio's following, who had escaped his attention altogether. It also fails to acknowledge that Apache warriors, unencumbered by women and children, could travel long distances in a very short time. This could have been an attack by independent Mescaleros, who might have hidden in the Sacramento Mountains after the operation to disarm and dismount the Mescalero Apaches. However, this attack has all the hallmarks of a Chihenne/Chiricahua Apache-led attack. The *modus operandi* looks similar to techniques used by Victorio in his campaign against the US and Mexico. A glance at the Tenth Cavalry's casualty rate in 1880, compared with that of 1879, would suggest that, in the latter period,

149 Ord to AG Chicago 30 Oct., 1880 in 'Victorio Papers', NA, M666, Roll 528.
150 Pope to Whipple AAG Chicago, 29 Oct., 1880 in 'Victorio Papers', NA, M666, Roll 528.
151 'Indian Affairs' *Army & Navy Journal*, Vol. 18, 6 Nov., 1880, p.261.
152 NA, RG393, Part 1, Entry 2539, Press Copies of Letters and Endorsements Sent, MDoM, Vol. 13, pp.747-748.

the Mescalero Apaches chose to minimise direct conflict with the US army. In 1879, the Tenth Cavalry sustained two men wounded in action, whereas in 1880, between May and October, the Tenth Cavalry sustained 10 killed in action, and three wounded in action, plus two Pueblo scouts killed in action. The higher casualty rate coincides with a period when the Chihenne or Chiricahua Apaches, allied with Mescalero Apaches, were known to be operating in western Texas. While this information could be utilised to construct an argument that the Chihennes were more aggressive, or even courageous, than the Mescalero Apaches, this is not very convincing. A more plausible explanation is quite simple: the Chihennes had lost their reservation; the Mescaleros were still on their reservation. In other words, the Chihennes had far more to fight for than their Mescalero allies. For those Chihennes, including Victorio, who had chosen to fight, the San Carlos reservation was simply not an option. The attack at Ojo Caliente, Texas, was not something previously attempted by Mescalero Apaches during encounters with the Tenth Cavalry. The Ninth Cavalry's experience of campaigning against the Warm Springs Apaches, during 1879–80, was of a number of episodes where Chihenne Apaches were, in favourable circumstances, more than willing to stand and fight against large numbers of US troops. In September and October 1880, Victorio's followers had run short of ammunition. Victorio's death did not obviate this shortage, and his warriors' bold, point-blank assault, albeit in circumstances very much in their favour, netted 10 carbines and revolvers, plus a significant amount of ammunition. The Chihenne Apaches, so desperately short of munitions, simply had to take higher calculated risks in order to replenish their arms and ammunition, if they wished to continue their campaign for the return of their reservation in New Mexico. One suspects that Mescalero Apaches were probably present as allies of the Chihenne Apaches. In January 1881, Texas Rangers attacked a small camp of Mescalero Apaches, killing or scattering the Apaches in the 'Last Indian Fight in Texas'. The Rangers recovered some of the slain Tenth Cavalrymen's saddles from the abandoned campsite.[153]

Captain Baldwin may not have followed the Apaches into Mexico, but on 3 November 1880, Charles Berger, with 19 volunteers from B, I and K companies, Tenth Cavalry, led by Sergeant Diggs,[154] did track this party deep into Chihuahua. (See document file no. 138.) On the first day of the pursuit, Berger followed the trail to a hill 18 miles into Mexico, where the Apaches had stopped and thrown up breastworks, to monitor any immediate pursuit. Berger estimated that the party was made up of 20–25 warriors. The trail then led into the Sierra de Los Pinos where Berger's detachment camped, having covered some 30 miles. On the second day of his pursuit Berger found a strongly fortified camp at the top of the Sierra de Los Pinos, from which he judged the Apaches could have held off a regiment. Berger estimated that before these raiders had set off to attack the Tenth Cavalry, they had left their families at this strongpoint in the Sierra de Los Pinos.

153 Gillett, 1976, p.209; See also Dimmick to Hatch 3 Feb., 1881, NA, RG393, Part 3, Entry 439, p.115-116; NA, RG393, Part 1, Entry 204, Miscellaneous Records 1879-80, DoAz Record of events 14 Jan., 1881-4 Sept., 1882: Loud to AAG, DoAz, 3 Feb., 1881, NA, RG393, Part 1, Entry 181, pp.12-13 & p.14; McLaughlin, 5 Feb., 1881 in Register of Telegrams Rec'd 11 Oct., 1880 – 4 Feb., 1881, HQ Records DoP 1878-1881, NA, RG393, M1381, Roll 2, p.30, Letter No.75.

154 Grierson to AAG, DoTx, 31 Dec., 1880 in Letters Sent 23 Aug.-31Dec., 1880, HQ Records DoP 1878-1881, NA, RG393, M1381, Roll 1, Letter No.168 (Note: This report contained as Letter No. 3 in Letters sent 1881).

The men who travelled with Berger were: Co. B: Sgt. Charles Perry, Corp. Albert Tulsome, Trumpeter William Stanley, Blacksmith John Stewart and Privates Andrew Petry and James Riley; I Co. Sgt Robert Diggs, Farrier Lyam Parsons. Privates Jackson, Barlow, Charles Boyd, Andrew Drake, Hamson Rathis and Ben Polls; Co. K: Sgt. Lewis Conyus, Saddler John Thomas, Privates Scott Grand, E. Mussill. James Summers and Richard Budges. (Capt. Baldwin, 20 Nov., 1880 in in Letters Rec'd File 19 Mar., 1878-14 Feb., 1881, HQ Records DoP 1878-1881, NA, RG393, M1381, Roll 2).

The trail then travelled to the south, and turned briefly to the west after leaving the Sierra de Los Pinos, before turning south along the eastern side of the Sierra Borracho.[155] The Apaches had camped on a small mountain in the midst of this plain, 20 miles from the Sierra de Los Pinos. By that point, Berger estimated that they were following 30–35 ridden and 15–20 driven animals. The following morning, the trail was followed to the south west for another 10 miles, over very rough terrain, before they reached a place known as Los Tinajas, flanked by the Sierra el Fierro and the Sierra de Los Annons, or Arrons, Mountains. There was plenty of water, wood and game, and the detachment spent most of the day camped in this area. Berger reported that he had found the remains of a large camp of about 50 wickiups in the mountains to the west of Los Tinajas. He thought that this was the point where Victorio had camped for between eight and nine days after leaving the Laguna de Guzman with Terrazas 'after him'.[156] Having spent the nights of 5 and 6 November being assaulted by wind, rain, hail and even snow, and with his horses threatening to collapse, he still followed this trail for another three miles further south, before discovering the raiders' next camp. Following the trail over very rough terrain, another camp was discovered approximately 18 miles to the south. At this point, Berger judged that he was not gaining on the Apaches and turned for home. He followed his trail back to the Sierra de Los Pinos, rested his mounts for a day, and then made directly for Captain Baldwin's camp on the Rio Grande. On this leg of his journey, he confirmed that two groups of three and one group of four Apache ponies had left the group travelling south-east parallel to the Rio Grande. The detachment reached Captain Baldwin's camp late on 9 November 1880,[157] and Berger reached Fort Bliss on 13 November, from where Governor Terrazas was alerted to the passage of the Apaches through his territory. Berger was certain that none had returned to the United States.[158]

Lieutenant Nolan, commanding at Old Fort Quitman, predicted that these Apaches would move north of the border. To frustrate such an endeavour, he sent out several detachments of Tenth Cavalry to search along the Rio Grande for any signs that Apaches had crossed the border. Colonels Hatch, Buell and Terrazas were informed of these movements.[159]

After over a year's hard campaigning, Victorio had finally been killed. Although, as noted earlier, Nana and his following would continue the fight, one of the most accomplished leaders of the Apache Wars had come to the end of his struggle. If the following words were not uttered by Victorio, then they still reflect the thinking behind his resistance:

> Every struggle, whether won or lost, strengthens us for the next to come. It is not good for people to have an easy life. They become weak and inefficient when they cease to struggle. Some need a series of defeats before developing the strength and courage to win a victory.[160]

155 If one consults the overall map of the Victorio campaign (Map. 4.1, in Watt, 'I Will Not Surrender the Hair of a Horse's Tail: The Victorio Campaign 1879), the only clear link between modern maps and Berger's report are the Sierra del Pino and the Sierra El Fierro. Nevertheless, these two reference points give a broad indication of the path taken by the Apaches. One suspects that part of what is marked as the Sierra El Hueso on today's maps are the Sierra Borracho of Berger's report.

156 Berger's Report enclosed within Baldwin to Grierson, 10 Nov., 1880 in Letters Rec'd File 19 Mar.,1878-14 Feb., 1881, HQ Records DoP 1878-1881, NA, RG393, M1381, Roll 2.

157 Berger's Report enclosed within Baldwin to Grierson, 10 Nov., 1880 in Letters Rec'd File 19 Mar.,1878-14 Feb., 1881, HQ Records DoP 1878-1881, NA, RG393, M1381, Roll 2.

158 Berger's Report enclosed within Baldwin to Grierson, 10 Nov., 1880 in Letters Rec'd File 19 Mar.,1878-14 Feb., 1881, HQ Records DoP 1878-1881, NA, RG393, M1381, Roll 2; Brinkerhoff to AAAG SF NM 14 Nov., 1880, NA, RG393, Part 3, Entry 439, pp.616-619; Ist Lt. R.G. Smith to HQ, DoP, 19 Nov., 1880 in Letters Received by HQ DoNM Sept. 1865-Aug. 1890, NA, RG393, M1088, Roll 41, Jul.-Dec., 1880.

159 Brinkerhoff to AAAG SF 31 Oct., 1880, NA, RG393, Part 3, Entry 439, pp.393-394.

160 Victorio quoted in Miller, 1995, p.260.

It may seem strange to include this quote as a final comment on Victorio's death. Yet if these words can be ascribed to the Apache leader, it does reveal a lot about the attitudes and beliefs which motivated him. It is worth noting that by April 1881, even some of his enemies were referring to Victorio as having been a 'daring' leader, when describing his efforts to close the Black Range to Anglo-American intruders.[161] He had not taken the easy way out in his attempt to reach an accommodation with the Anglo-Americans in the early 1870s. Nor had he selected the path of least resistance when he eventually chose to resist Anglo-American efforts to move him and his people to San Carlos. There was, among some of the Apaches who chose to fight, an appreciation of the reality that they were unlikely to win. Yet, if we recall Opler's comments, no matter how great the odds, many Chiricahua warriors thought that, if they fought hard enough, there was always a chance of achieving victory. According to Ball, both Juh and Nana also adopted this attitude, in response to a growing realisation that they were not going to prevail.[162] Therefore, despite a heavy defeat on the Palomas River in May 1880, and setbacks at Tinaja de Las Palmas and Rattlesnake Springs in July–August 1880, Victorio seems to have retained the support of his followers and many of his allies. This has to be down to his outstanding status as a leader among his people but also shows their general commitment to the fight to win the return of their reservation at Ojo Caliente. Perhaps his role as a focal point for resistance to the Anglo-American reservation policy may help explain how the support of his followers lasted right up to, and beyond, his death at Tres Castillos.

161 The *Grant County Herald*, 2 Apr., 1881.
162 Ball, 1980, p.34.

17

Conclusion

> It is the old story, unjust treatment of the Indians by the Gov't., promises broken, treaties violated and the Indians moved from one reservation to another against their will, until finally they break out and go on the War path and the army is called in to kill them. It is hard to fight against and shoot men down when you know they are in the right and are really doing what our fathers did in the Revolution, fighting for their country.
>
> 2nd Lieutenant, Walter Finley Ninth Cavalry
> (Letter dated Fort Bayard, 11 November, 1879)[1]

There are a number of reasons why the Victorio Campaign has become a relatively obscure episode in the history of the Apache Wars that took place between 1860 and 1886. These factors could be linked by their political nature, being concerned with the distribution of resources both within and between different cultures. In other words, a broad definition of the politics related to this campaign would be recognised by any form of human society, no matter which of the myriad means by which societies practice politics it had chosen. Politics is about power, and how humans organise themselves into viable social groups. It is about conflict resolution, whether the conflict arises from within the social group or presents itself as an external threat. Such conflict arises from the attempt to distribute, and justify the distribution of, finite resources. For the Apaches, the small numbers of individuals involved, and the small range of roles (hunter/gatherer/raider/warrior) available, encouraged the development of a variant of direct democracy. In this, power was invested in successful practitioners and innovators in the roles central to their survival. Leaders had to succeed in holding together their social group through persuasion, mediation and, if all else failed, violence. Apache leaders also had to demonstrate their ability to deal with external threats in the same manner.

The Apaches' US and Mexican opponents acted according to the same principles, even if in a manner very different from that of these American Indians. Both countries explicitly recognised the concept of representative democracy, though the image and the reality of the practice could vary enormously. The size of US and Mexican societies precluded direct democracy; but these nations adopted different forms of representative democracy as the basic model to maintain social stability. The complex range of occupations in both societies necessitated the use of government institutions to provide leadership through persuasion, mediation and, if necessary, violence, in response to perceived internal and external threats to their social stability. Despite the complex organisation of government in the USA and Mexico, the basic goal of politics was the same as among the Apaches, just organised in a very different manner.

It is through a broad prism of 'politics' that we can examine various aspects of the Victorio Campaign. After all, as Clausewitz argued, to remove the 'political' from an act of war, renders that

1 The Walter Lowry Finley Collection.

act meaningless. A focus on politics will not cover all the factors relating to the campaign that we shall discuss; but it will provide a fresh insight into the motivation of many of the actors involved. The previous chapter recounted the death of Victorio, a central figure in the Apache resistance to the concentration policy devised for American Indians by the US Department of the Interior. Can his death be taken as an indication of his failure? The fact that his following showed no inclination to give up their campaign for the return of the reservation around Ojo Caliente, New Mexico, would suggest otherwise. If we examine the political goals of Victorio, Nana, Loco, Mangus and other Chihenne leaders, we might be able to evaluate the success or failure of their campaign for the return of Ojo Caliente by means of both war and peace.

Victorio and the Apache Resistance of 1876–1880 Re-evaluated

Although Victorio remained a rather elusive figure, there are indications that he and other Apache leaders had a clear notion of the above outline of politics. It was politics which influenced Victorio in his attempt to reach an accommodation with the USA in the early 1870s. It was also a political decision to turn from seeking accommodation to resistance. Victorio had been, in his eyes, given no other choice by the Department of the Interior. He clearly wanted to preserve an identity for his people, based around a reservation at Ojo Caliente. Whether he thought that a completely independent way of life could be maintained is unclear. We have seen occasions when disagreements occurred among the Apaches over the direction of both accommodation and resistance policies. The outcome of such disagreements could be lethal for the losing party. Yet we have also seen that, when the need arose, both Victorio and Juh could settle their alleged differences and fight shoulder-to-shoulder for a time; politics in Apache society being as varied and unpredictable as in our own society.

We can also ask ourselves whether the political decision to confront the USA and the Republic of Mexico was worth the consequences. While the US army did not 'win' the conflict between 1877 and 1881, one suspects that few Apaches would claim that *they* had won this fight. Both sides had failed to achieve their political goals; one side having failed to secure their reservation at Ojo Caliente; the other side having failed to force the Apaches onto a reservation where they did not wish to live. Yet it could be argued that the resistance mounted, and the sacrifices made, by Victorio, Nana and their followers between 1877 and 1881 was a key element of the resistance mounted by the Apaches between 1876 and 1886. It was this resistance which spared the Apaches from the ultimate logic of the Department of the Interior's policy of concentration.

In October 1881, there was a disturbance at the Mescalero reservation, following which two men fled into the hills. Their flight was triggered by a rumour that their tribe were about to be removed to San Carlos.[2] This caused a flurry of queries concerning whether a decision to effect the removal of the Mescaleros had already been taken. General Pope stated that if the Mescaleros were to be removed, then this operation should be turned over to the military. If not, he predicted that the men would de-camp en masse.[3] General Sheridan felt obliged to register a clear protest at any effort

---

2 Llewellyn, Indian Agent, Mescalero Agency to Col. G.V. Henry Camp La Luz, N.M. 18 Oct., 1881, NA, RG393, Part 1, Entry 2546, p.823.

3 Pope to AG, thro. HQ, MDoM, 29 Oct., 1881, NA, RG393, Part 1, Entry 2546, p.824 See also various correspondence concerning possible removal of the Mescalero Apaches, NA, RG393, Part 1, Entry 2546, pp.835-840; See also Letters Rec'd by the Office of the Adjutant General (Main Series), 1881-1889, NA, M689, Roll 44, Correspondence and reports mainly concerning efforts to capture hostile Apache Indians who were terrorising the border region of the District of New Mexico, Jul.-Dec. 1881.

to remove the Mescaleros, which certainly appears to have been rooted in recent experiences with the Chihenne Apaches:

> if such a removal is contemplated, I desire to register my protest against it. The reservation of these Indians has been the hot bed of sedition, theft and murder, and I think it best not to transfer these evils to any new place, which would be done by transferring these Indians, besides they would not stay at any other place, and we would have similar troubles to those created by the removal of Victorio's band over again.
>
> The best way to deal with these indians, and get security from them, is to let them stay where they are and turn the Agency over to the military.[4]

It is quite clear that in 1881–82 the complete removal of the Apaches from Arizona and New Mexico was being considered by the Department of the Interior. The stated reason was the continued trouble with the Apaches and the difficulty of dealing with them because of their close proximity to the Mexican border.[5] General Pope went as far as to inform Colonel MacKenzie, Commanding Officer, District of New Mexico, that he had learned 'unofficially' that the Mescaleros were to be removed to the 'Cimarron near Fort Union'.[6] Clearly the strong advice received from the likes of Pope and Sheridan prevailed; but it should also be noted that they themselves had earlier advocated the removal of the Mescaleros. What had happened to change their minds? In effect the resistance to concentration mounted by Chiricahua or Warm Springs and Mescalero Apaches had convinced Pope, Sheridan and most field officers that the concentration policy directed at the Apaches had failed.

It should be obvious that the warfare with the Apaches from 1877 to 1880 that led up to this intervention by the generals had largely been triggered by a political attempt to squeeze the Apaches onto a single reservation, in contravention of treaties signed by them with the US Government. In the case of Victorio, he and his people endured a great deal of provocation before a large element of the Warm Springs Apaches decided to fight to the finish, in an attempt to return to their reservation at Ojo Caliente. The question is, did Victorio's resistance achieve something, even in spite of his death? In one sense, the deportation of the Chiricahuas to Florida in 1886, and their subsequent treatment, could lead one to argue that the answer was an emphatic 'no'.

However, looking at the question from another angle, we can ask: without the implacable resistance to US concentration policy exhibited by Victorio and other Apaches between 1876 and 1886, would the Apache reservation system have looked the same? The long-term logic of the concentration policy seems to have been missed, probably because there was no further attempt to implement this policy. The concentration policy to put all the Apaches onto the San Carlos Reservation was not going to be the end of the process. The ultimate logic of the concentration policy was that the Apaches were destined for the Indian Territory. The consideration of this option in 1881–82 for the Mescalero Apaches does not necessarily mean that the option had not been considered, concerning the Apaches in general, by the US government. The reason that this policy was not carried further can be reduced to the fact that there was so much resistance generated by the first stage of the concentration policy, implemented in 1876 and 1877. It had become patently obvious what levels of resistance would be provoked if the next stage was implemented. To see the US army as the driving force behind US Indian policy, let alone as an autonomous and brutal machine for killing Indians, is grossly inaccurate. The army was at the forefront of resisting any further efforts at concentrating the Apaches upon one reservation; but the US army was but one element of the Federal Government of the United States. While the US army had to implement policies towards the American Indians, it was not formulating these policies. The Department of the Interior, through the Office of Indian Affairs, was the driving force behind Indian policy and, under the guise of assimilation, this policy was, effectively, intended to cram as many American Indians onto as little land as possible. Where the American Indians were concerned, the prime policy of the Department of the Interior was to clear as much land for the use of civilised Americans as possible. It was this basic policy, with the additional ingredients of political corruption and bureaucratic rationalisation, which caused the Apache Wars of 1876–86. Victorio's leadership was a key element of the resistance which succeeded in preventing the process of concentration proceeding to its logical conclusion.

Victorio himself remains a most elusive figure, due to his extreme caution concerning face-to-face dealings with Americans and Mexicans. Of those who encountered him, very few recorded their impressions. What we do know of him from these encounters, complemented by Apache recollections of him collected by Eve Ball, strongly suggests a great leader.

If one combines the military records of the campaign with knowledge of the general principles of Apache warfare, one can put forward a very strong case for Victorio's reputation as an unparalleled master of guerrilla warfare techniques.

During this campaign, he and his men quite simply ran the Ninth Cavalry Regiment into the ground, using strategies and tactics primarily designed to target the horses of his opponents in such a way as to simultaneously keep the pressure off his own logistics. This was so effective that by the end of May 1880, General Sherman was forced to inform Colonel Hatch that the US army could not spend the money required to purchase replacement horses and mules until the next appropriation of funds was approved by Congress at the beginning of July 1880. The Ninth Cavalry sustained approximately 34.4 percent of the overall losses of US army horses in the period July 1879 to June 1880. Not all these casualties can necessarily be laid at Victorio's door; but a high proportion must have been incurred due to the hard field service imposed by Victorio. When Victorio confronted Grierson's forces in western Texas in July–August 1880, an analysis of the probable intent of the Apaches shows this mini-campaign to have been a far closer run contest than was realized at the time, and one in which Grierson was quite lucky to have prevailed. When ammunition shortages prevented him from adopting one evasion strategy, Victorio changed his tactics and was profoundly unlucky to have been caught at Tres Castillos. He had come within an ace of outrunning and evading the large forces arrayed against him.

Nana's, and possibly Mangus's, continuation of the struggle after Victorio's death also shows that Victorio was a graduate of a social system which was adept at promoting its talented leadership candidates to the top. The Warm Springs Apaches did not collapse after Victorio's death, simply because there were other skilled and experienced leaders who were more than capable of continuing the struggle.

In acknowledging that the skill behind Apache guerrilla warfare techniques is the product of intelligent human beings, it must also be noted that the Apaches in general, and Victorio was no exception, were not infallible. Victorio was caught off guard several times during the campaign. At Cuchillo Negro in September 1879, he lost two warriors when the Apaches misjudged the size of the opposition and opted to fight instead of fleeing. Parker's Apache scouts inflicted a disastrous defeat in May 1880, but the decisive support for Parker's scouts did not materialise. In West Texas, Grierson managed to prevent Victorio's attempt to pass through to the Mescalero reservation in July and August 1880. This rebuff contributed to the ammunition shortages, and the risk-laden evasion tactics, forced on Victorio in September–October 1880, which ended in the disaster at Tres Castillos. As guerrilla warfare experts, the Apaches can be seen as masters of their art. But they were not perfect.

The key political point is that the tenacity of the Apaches' resistance certainly gave the US army pause for thought, and provoked them to a serious consideration of their stated goals. Thus, it can be argued that the Apache resistance had a measure of long-term success in staving off the full implications of the US concentration policy; and Victorio's short-term goal of a return of the Ojo Caliente reservation came very close to fruition.

There is very little evidence that justifies Victorio's alleged descent into an orgy of violence and cruelty. He may simply represent the more general nature of Apache guerrilla warfare, where all sides adopted an approach to war in which there were no accepted notions of non-combatants, illegitimate targets, neutrals, and similar exclusionary designations theoretically honoured by contemporary US and Mexican combatants. Another problem for the Apaches in this area is that they did not win. The old adage that 'the winners write history' is critical. The United States and Mexico were happy enough to adopt the very same 'total warfare' principles even as they condemned their use by the Apaches. Victorio may also, ironically, be a victim of his own personal success during his last period of resistance. Even given that many of the reports circulated at the time were exaggerated, it is clear that his last war killed a large number of people in the south west United States and northern Mexico. This number may never be fully quantified, but if one speaks to descendants of Mexican and American people in southern New Mexico today, one gets the distinct impression of a 'folk memory' of a dreadful period of conflict. This still survives in some of the older inhabitants of the state and those local historians who strive to keep the story alive. This has expanded in the telling over time, and is probably the root of Victorio's particularly fearsome reputation for cruelty. Victorio took few prisoners; but there is little evidence of an unusually savage war, which marks his resistance as different from other American-Apache conflicts.

Victorio was provoked into war by the policy of concentration, a failure to supervise reservation staff, and similar unjust practices. However, given the centrality of raiding and warfare to the Apache life-way, it would be unsafe to argue that, if the reservation policy had been implemented as promised, and honest personnel appointed to staff the reservations, there would have been no hostilities. Even when based at Ojo Caliente, the Warm Springs Apaches had been involved in raiding. Had the Chihenne Apaches been left on the reservation around Ojo Caliente, the chances are that Victorio and many of his followers would not have supported any subsequent conflict, and would almost certainly have acted directly against any militants themselves. In this case, the fighting would probably have been negligible and worthy only a footnote in the history of the Western Frontier.

The use of Apache scouts in General Crook's campaigns of the early 1870s, and from 1882 onwards, is well documented and acknowledged as the decisive factor in the defeat of independent Apaches during those years. The scouts' contribution to the Victorio campaign is equally decisive, but less well known. Their presence thwarted at least one ambush in the Guzman Mountains, in October 1879. Most of the skirmishes during the campaign in which the US army came off worst can be associated with a lack of Apache scouts. It is also clear that the independent Apaches made efforts to avoid Apache scouts if they knew of their presence. This is particularly evident from Nana's Raid in 1881. (See Volume III.) Where Nana encountered Apache scouts, he fought rearguard actions and attempted to evade his pursuers as quickly as possible. When he stood and fought, the odds may have been otherwise in his favour, but part of his calculations was that there were no Apache scouts present. Finally, on the Palomas River in May 1880, the Apache scouts inflicted by far the heaviest defeat that Victorio suffered on US soil.

Political Performance of the US Army between 1876 and 1881

When the concentration policy stirred up Apache resistance, the US army was expected to deal with such 'intransigence' through a mixture of force and negotiation. Where the Army failed to do this successfully, there has been a tendency to deal leniently with its version of events. In certain instances, casualties and skirmishes have been conveniently forgotten or glossed over. At a more general level, we have seen that officers involved in the campaign were amazed to find its absence from records and the inclusion of far less important expeditions and campaigns in the record. The

Victorio Campaign is unique in that all but one of the recipients of the Medal of Honor had to wait over a decade before having their bravery officially acknowledged. Racism aside, this may also reflect a 'feeling' in the upper reaches of the US army command that the less said about the Victorio Campaign the better. In fact, there seems to have been a deliberate attempt to play down the severity of the Apache Campaigns of 1879–81 as can be seen by the omission of this campaign from the official list of Indian campaigns sent to the US army pensions Office.

In 1879 Pope noted that:

> they [the Apaches] have not done much harm except in a small way, and that the troops are in the field most of the time to prevent this ... they continue to break out from time to time in small parties or individually, and rob and steal in a small but very irritating way.[7]

Sherman stated in his report for 1881 that:

> Whilst the troops have been kept very busy during the past year, no serious Indian or other war has occurred, but great progress has been made in collecting and locating Indians, hitherto hostile, on their proper reservations.[8]

Pope reiterated his original opinion at the end of the Victorio Campaign:

> The raids of the Apaches into Southern New Mexico for the last two years bear no resemblance to an Indian War or general outbreak. They rather resemble the operations of the cow-boys and other bands of robbers on the frontier, or to the parties of train-robbers in Missouri. There is no great difficulty in dealing with them when found. The difficulty is to find them.[9]

A senate resolution asking for the cost to the United States of Indian wars between 1872 and 1882 was passed on 24 January 1882.[10] The response, by Robert T. Lincoln, the then Secretary of War, lists a number of Indian wars and gives the distinct impression that war with the Apaches commenced in 1881, with a cost to the Quartermaster's Department of $43,850;[11] yet other elements of the report make it clear that Apache prisoners of war were being held from 1877–81.[12]

7 Gen. Pope's Report, 3 Oct., 1879 in Annual Reports of the War Department, NA, M997, Roll 33, 1879 Vol. I-II, p.83.

8 Annual Report of General Sherman, 3 Nov., 1881 cited in Personal File Eugene D. Dimmick, NA, RG94, Entry 297, Box 1496.

9 General Pope Annual Report 22 Sept., 1881 cited in Personal File Eugene D. Dimmick, NA, RG94, Entry 297, Box 1496; Headquarters Department of the Missouri, Annual Report for Year ending 22 Sept., 1881, NA, RG393, Part 1, Entry 2546, p.846.

10 Papers and a report of 4 Mar., 1882, from the Secretary of War relating to a statement of expenditures for Indian wars and for the observation and control of Indians from 1 Jul., 1871-20 Jun., 1882; Letters Rec'd by the Office of the Adjutant General (Main Series), 1881-1889, NA, M689, Roll 77.

11 See Statement A Cost of Indian wars since 1872 as shown by the records of the Quartermaster General in Papers and a report of 4 Mar., 1882, from the Secretary of War relating to a statement of expenditures for Indian wars and for the observation and control of Indians from 1 Jul., 1871-20 Jun., 1882; Letters Rec'd by the Office of the Adjutant General (Main Series), 1881-1889, NA, M689, Roll 77, p.3.

12 See Statement B Table showing expenditures incident to Indian wars entailed upon the Subsistence Department of the Army during the fiscal years 1872 to 1881, inclusive, over and above the cost of subsisting the Army during the same periods in Papers and a report of 4 Mar., 1882, from the Secretary of War relating to a statement of expenditures for Indian wars and for the observation and control of Indians from 1 Jul., 1871-20 Jun., 1882; Letters Rec'd by the Office of the Adjutant General (Main Series), 1881-1889, NA, M689, Roll 77, pp.3-4.

Later in the report, the conflict with the Apaches was stated to have occurred in 1879 and 1880–81, with the cost of the 1879 conflict to the Quartermaster's Department estimated at $43, 850.[13] The exact correspondence of two figures cannot be coincidental. All this achieves is to reinforce the impression that some effort was being made to 'downplay' the impact of the Victorio Campaign on the US army.

In 1908, the War Department issued the criteria for several campaign badges, including an Indian campaign badge. The Bannock War of 1878, operations against the Northern Cheyenne in 1878–79, and the Ute War of 1879–80 are included. There is no mention of operations against the Apaches in Arizona, New Mexico and Texas in 1879–81. The regulations state that a campaign medal will be awarded:

> in any serious action with hostile Indians in which there have been killed or wounded upon the side of the troops; decision to be made in each case of the latter class, upon individual application, whether the action concerned was such as to be properly considered serious within the meaning of the order.[14]

There was also a fairly widespread feeling among many field officers that Victorio was 'in the right'. They felt that the Office of Indian Affairs' policy and mismanagement had provoked the Victorio War.[15] It is fashionable to see the US Cavalry as a mindless 'Indian–killing' institution;[16] yet in this case, it can be argued that many officers felt that they had been handed a political problem that should never have happened. These officers were not alone. An article in the *New York Times* of 29 October 1880 gave an excellent review of the effects of Victorio's war and underlined the fact that had the Warm Springs Apaches been given the reservation they desired, such a war could have been avoided.[17]

However, the most interesting aspect of the Victorio campaign, where study of the US army is concerned, is the range of internal and external political obstacles, and how the field commanders, in some cases, overcame these barriers. One gets a strong impression that the US army performed far better than could be reasonably have been expected in spite of these political impediments.

'Buffalo Soldiers': The African-American Role in the Victorio Campaign

So far, use of the term 'buffalo soldier' has been kept to a minimum. Dobak and Phillips make the point that this label does not appear to have been widely used by the Ninth and Tenth Cavalrymen themselves.[18] Two out of the three instances when this term was used during the Victorio Campaign

13 See Statement C Expenditure on account of Indian wars from 1872 to 1881 in Papers and a report of 4 Mar., 1882, from the Secretary of War relating to a statement of expenditures for Indian wars and for the observation and control of Indians from 1 Jul., 1871-20 Jun., 1882; Letters Rec'd by the Office of the Adjutant General (Main Series), 1881-1889, NA, M689, Roll 77, p.5.

14 General Orders, No. 129. War Department, Washington, 13 Aug., 1908 cited in Personal File Michael Cooney, NA, RG94, Entry 297, Box 1067; See also General Orders, No. 170. War Department, Washington, 15 Aug., 1907 cited in Personal File George R. Burnett, NA, RG94, Entry 297, Box 941.

15 Public Affairs Office White Sands Missile Range Website: Hembrillo Battlefield; See also General Crook cited by Cocker, p.217.

16 To counter such a stereotypical view see comments by General Pope. (HQ DoM, Annual Report for Year ending 22 Sept., 1881, NA, RG393, Part 1, Entry 2546, pp.848-849).

17 'The End of Victorio', The New York Times, 29 Oct., 1880.

18 Dobak & Phillips, 2001, p.xvii & p.231.

stem from the territorial press, and in neither case was use of the term complimentary. For the purposes of this conclusion, however, it is a useful blanket term.

The most important point to note is that the Victorio Campaign is the buffalo soldiers' campaign. This is not to deny other US army units' involvement in the campaign; but bar the Palomas River battle in May 1880, and one or two other skirmishes, the buffalo soldiers were involved all of the major battles, and most of the skirmishes, in the Victorio Campaign.

The paradox, as outlined in the previous volume[19] is that buffalo soldier narratives tend to simultaneously highlight and obscure the role of the Apaches. However, if we examine the role of the Apaches and the African-American cavalrymen *as a whole*, during this the campaign, we gain a more robust view of both the Apaches and the Ninth and Tenth Cavalrymen. Where the buffalo soldiers are concerned, an overview of their performance in this campaign does tend to question the popular narrative, which tends to portray these troops as exemplary in all aspects of soldiering. This appears to have been born of a tendency to focus on particularly heroic episodes, and a generalisation derived from these soldiers' relatively low desertion and high re-enlistment rates. If we examine the Victorio campaign as a whole, the heroic instances remain; and comparative desertion rates were indeed low, though where the Ninth Cavalry was concerned the overall desertion rates increased noticeably between 1880 and 1881. Yet, in general, the Apaches experienced little difficulty when confronting the buffalo soldiers during this period.

There is a case to be made for saying that the Tenth Cavalry fared better against Victorio; but the area they were picketing was much smaller than that covered by the Ninth Cavalry. Most of the time, the Apaches, led by Victorio and Nana, out-manoeuvred and out-fought their buffalo soldier opponents. When we place the winning of the Regiment's Medals of Honor in the context of the overall campaign, these medals were usually won during episodes where the Apaches had taken the upper hand, or were even moving in for the kill. It should also be argued that the focus on admirably low desertion rates amongst the Ninth and Tenth Cavalry Regiments does not automatically indicate a higher discipline or fighting quality than amongst other US cavalry regiments.

So what conclusions can we draw concerning the overall performance of the buffalo soldiers? They were generally solid and reliable troops, whose experienced NCOs could usually be trusted to exercise independent command. Yet they were hamstrung by two factors: first, they were faced by an enemy whose principles of warfare were very difficult for US troops in general to effectively challenge without the help of Apache scouts; and second, as we have seen, they were further hampered in their ability to confront Apaches through both internal and external political factors. If we include this in our analysis of the campaign, then one does wonder at the buffalo soldiers' ability to stay in the field for as long as they did, particularly as Victorio often encouraged such pursuits for the damage he knew the buffalo soldiers would sustain. When we consider that Victorio effectively rendered the Ninth Cavalry unable to continue in the field by targeting the Regiment's horses and pack mules, we also have to acknowledge that the regiment was already short of horses, due to political factors beyond the comprehension of their Apache opponents. It should also be noted that this situation appears to have been a chronic complaint among the Cavalry Regiments in the south-west, be they black or white.

Nor is there any suggestion that white troops had a better record against the Apaches, though the territorial press of the time would generally have us believe otherwise. Captain Kramer and his Sixth Cavalry troops were easily dealt with by Victorio's warriors in Rocky Canon in May 1880. The Apaches also stopped Captain Parker's Fourth Cavalrymen with consummate ease near Fort Cummings in September 1880. Interestingly, both detachments were accompanied by Apache

19 See Robert N. Watt 'I Will Not Surrender the Hair of a Horse's Tail: The Victorio Campaign 1879.

scouts. Nevertheless, the key problem for the buffalo soldiers is that, despite their efforts, they did not inflict a defeat on either Victorio or Nana in the field.

One key aspect of the buffalo soldiers' involvement, however, must also be acknowledged. They were often active and willing participants in the forced removal of American Indians from their ancestral lands, and modern attempts to change this view should be seen as gross distortions of history. The buffalo soldiers are gaining increasing recognition for their role in the American West in 1866–91. They have yet to receive the measured recognition they deserve for their role as key participants in the Victorio Campaign; but this role pitted them against people defending what was rightfully theirs.

Mexican Involvement in the Victorio Campaign

North of the border, the Mexican population was often caught between the Apaches and their Anglo-American opponents. Knowing the widespread contempt in which they were held by many Anglo-Americans, some were probably very content to provide trading opportunities for the Apaches, in order to spite their common enemy. This did not, however, make them immune from attack by the Apaches, through the legacy of 'trade-hate' relations between the Apaches and the Mexicans.

The involvement of the Mexican state in combating the Apaches under Victorio meant it has been necessary for us to examine the complex political relationship between the federal government of Mexico and the United States. It has also allowed us to examine the relative political autonomy of the State of Chihuahua vis-à-vis the federal government of Mexico. While the latter was theoretically organised as a federal republic, the state of Chihuahua was politically more akin to a feudal state. This included a role in international affairs, where the State of Chihuahua felt able to reach 'unofficial' accords with actors employed by the US War Department *before* the federal government of Mexico ratified an agreement.

The military forces of the state of Chihuahua were far more effective than they are necessarily given credit for. They were certainly more effective than many civilian posses raised on the US side of the border. Alonso reveals a whole social structure that was geared towards actual service in, or contributions to, the maintenance of the state-level military units in Sonora and Chihuahua. It is quite clear that Mexico was riven with periodic political instability; yet despite such conflict, Mexican armed forces were, on an *ad hoc* basis, often far better organised and equipped than one would have expected in these circumstances.

The practice of collecting and handing in scalps for bounty, and the summary execution of prisoners, is now, and was then, seen in many quarters as distasteful in the extreme. Yet we must remember that these activities were not necessarily practiced in all circumstances. Both the Apaches and the Mexicans lived in, at least to outsiders, a bizarre relationship with each other, and were capable of perpetrating quite appalling acts against each other. Equally, both sides were willing to adopt captives, usually children, into their respective social groupings. In other words, both sides saw this complex relationship as a political solution that would allow the two communities to live in close proximity. To Victorio, such relations were fraught with danger, if one let one's guard down; but trading between Apaches and Mexican towns was an essential element to both communities. The fact remains: Mexicans on both sides of the border played a key role in the Victorio Campaign and, deserve recognition for this.

The Victorio Campaign: The Key Episode in the Apache Wars of 1876–86?

In late August 1881, the Apache Wars of popular historic perception flared up with a vengeance. In response to concerns about the activities of an Apache spiritual leader who was camped near Cibecue Creek in Arizona, Sixth Cavalrymen and Apache scouts under Colonel Carr attempted to affect his arrest. In the clash that followed, the Apache scouts mutinied and killed one officer and six troopers. The spiritual leader and a number of Apaches were also killed. The military build-up which followed this mutiny encouraged Juh, Naiche and many other Chiricahua warriors to leave with their families for Mexico.

The US army's actions at Cibecue and after are often portrayed as being heavy-handed and unnecessary. However, taken in the context of the sustained fighting against Victorio, and his successor Nana, over the previous two years, is the army's 'over-reaction' surprising? The latest round of fighting had only just died away. So, it seems justifiable to ask whether the rise of an Apache 'prophet', preaching a vision of white withdrawal from Apacheria, would have been taken so seriously if the event had not been preceded by two years of relentless guerrilla warfare. The rise of such a shaman merely reflected general dissatisfaction among the Apaches with their treatment by US federal authorities. It was these federal institutions, the Department of the Interior, which had decided to bring together a dangerous cocktail of Apache clans and tribes, who often saw each other as deadly enemies, on a single reservation. The US government had also failed to provide the promised resources by which those Apaches who had accepted the transition to reservation life could sustain themselves. Signs of increased unrest among the Apaches in general, and the potential effect on the Chiricahuas in particular, must have thoroughly alarmed the local US army command. Would their reaction have been the same if the Victorio Campaign had not occurred?

Victorio's resistance was a major, cumulative factor that fundamentally influenced the progress of events in August–September 1881 and beyond. One could go even further and argue that the Victorio Campaign had been the high-water mark of Chiricahua and Chihenne Apache resistance to the US and Mexico. It illustrated the utter chaos that could be inflicted by fewer than 200 Apache warriors. It was this experience that made it imperative that the US army deal with a similar coalition of Chiricahuas, which had gathered in the Sierra Madre by the summer of 1882.

The fact remains that while the campaigns of 1881–84 and 1885–86 are far better known and more frequently written about, it is only when they are viewed in conjunction with the Victorio Campaign that they can be seen to be the last acts in a much longer period of conflict dating back to 1876. The most intensive period of this warfare occurred during the attempt by Victorio and Nana to maintain their claim to their New Mexico homeland in 1879–81. The religious gathering at Cibecue was feared, by the US army, as the prelude to a repeat of the Victorio Campaign. This was to be avoided at all costs. In the short-term, the army failed, and the conflict did spread. In the long-term, however, the US army did avoid an escalation in warfare to the levels seen in the Victorio Campaign. Following the peace of 1883, after General Crook led his expedition into the Sierra Madres, there was no further raiding by the Chiricahua Apaches.[20] And in 1885, the General showed that he was well aware of just what a victory his Sierra Madre campaign represented:

> For more than two years there was not a single depredation committed by the Apaches, the first time within the memory of white men that so long an interval of peace had been enjoyed in Arizona and New Mexico. The destruction of Victorio and a portion of his band in Mexico, November 20, 1880 [15th October 1880], did not stop hostilities on the part of his survivors as

20 Crook to Assistant Adjutant General, HQ Division of the Pacific, Presidio of San Francisco, Cal. 9 Sept., 1885, NA, RG393, Part 1 Entry 187, Manuscript Reports, Dept of Arizona 1880-1885, p.14.

> was so confidently predicted at the time. The records at the Headquarters of my Department, incomplete as they possibly may be, show that in Arizona and New Mexico alone over fifty white people, men, women and children, were killed by these Indians between the time of Victorio's death and September 4, 1882, when I assumed command of the Department of Arizona, and this apart from their constant depredations and outrages in Mexico. I knew that there had not been a time within fifteen {15} years that the Chiricahuas had been at peace, but that during this whole time they had been constantly depredating either in Mexico or in this country. I fully realised that the property interests in Arizona and New Mexico had enormously increased since the campaign against Victorio and that we could not afford another war with these Indians, that would be so much more disastrous and marked by so much more of atrocity and destruction, owing to the increase in population and property interests and would also probably be of longer duration.[21]

The key achievement of General Crook's Sierra Madre campaign was to persuade this new gathering of Chiricahua warriors that their resistance was unsustainable. Led by Juh, Nana, Kaytennae, Chato, Chihuahua, Jolsanny and other seasoned leaders, these Apaches had the potential to repeat the chaos unleashed under the leadership of Victorio. Indeed at least two of Victorio's key lieutenants, Nana and Kaytennae, were highly influential leaders of this gathering. Crook delivered the political victory lacking in the Victorio Campaign and, most importantly, accomplished this *before* a repeat of that campaign could be unleashed.

Politics and the Victorio Campaign's Relative Obscurity

As Deverell argues, there are many facets to the overarching concept of the 'Old West' or the 'Wild West'. The element that binds these facets into a recognisable whole, to Deverell, is the exercise of political power by the state.[22]

The definition of politics advanced by Deverell is somewhat narrow compared with that concerning the use and distribution of resources within and between cultures used by Leftwich. Yet Deverell's position is an excellent launching pad for presenting the complex history of the Victorio campaign. It encompasses many patterns of conflict and cooperation, both within and between several cultures; but what links these together is their political nature.

The campaign itself marked failed attempts by both the Apaches and the US army to achieve their own immediate political goals: the former failed to hold onto an independent way of life in territory claimed by the United States; the latter failed to achieve the successful implementation of US Indian policy, on behalf of the Department of the Interior, by, as Clausewitz would put it, 'other means'.

There were a number of other complex political relationships between various groups and institutions who became embroiled in the Victorio Campaign. They included the relations within and between the federal and state levels of both the United States and the Republic of Mexico. And there were all the political constraints imposed on the US army by dint of its membership of a wider political system in which it was, and still is, regarded as a servant of Congress. This role, to be fair to its commanders, was broadly accepted by the army. Yet it is also plain that, within the broader confines of this bureaucratic arrangement, members of the structure of governance sometimes acted with relative autonomy, particularly when they believed that the overall structure

21 Crook to Assistant Adjutant General, HQ Division of the Pacific, Presidio of San Francisco, Cal. 9 Sept., 1885, NA, RG393, Part 1 Entry 187, Manuscript Reports, Dept of Arizona 1880-1885, pp.14-15.

22 See Deverell, 1996.

was undermining specific policy goals they supported. The two most obvious examples of this were, first, the recruitment of additional Apache scouts without official sanction; and second, the political manoeuvring which allowed Terrazas and Buell to cooperate with each other in Mexico, when they clearly had no *official* sanction from either federal government.

There is a subtle twist to this story which may explain the relative obscurity of the Victorio Campaign in the history of the Apache Wars. Most of the political factors covered in this work are not unique to this conflict on the western frontier. What is unique is the political failure of both sides to achieve their short-term political goals. The Victorio War is an excellent practical example of the Apache strategy and tactics deployed in an unrelenting period of guerrilla warfare between 1879 and 1881. It is also a very good example of how the US army fought, from their point of view, a limited war with an even more limited budget, yet still managed to generally perform better than could have been expected. In fact, this is a conflict between a large scale bureaucratic state organisation, with many components and levels, and a small-scale meritocracy. These are good examples of what Emile Durkheim termed mechanical and organic societies.[23] The key political driving force within each society concerns how individuals' beliefs in and expressions of, solidarity, or what we could term 'social loyalty', fundamentally influence their actions. Human beings within both types of society wish to express or experience a feeling of social solidarity. In a mechanical society, the loyalty of the individual is given to the society as a whole, based on a common identity. Apache society was small enough to be viewed as a 'segmented society', where solidarity was expressed by membership of the family within a political structure known as the tribe.

Organic society is far more complex, and the US army became an 'organ' operating within the much wider bureaucratic organisation of the United States. Yet the United States, as a society, was vast in comparison to that of the Apaches. Political and social solidarity would be clearly expressed to the United States through a loyalty to the US Constitution. Yet a more meaningful expression of loyalty would be towards the particular organ of society to which an individual belonged. Thus, US citizens who were, for example soldiers, Indian agents or diplomats would tend to have a closer solidarity with their immediate colleagues in the corresponding organ of state. They would often be shielded from any contact with those at the top of their organ of state. An Apache warrior who had decided to follow Victorio did so because of his personal knowledge of Victorio's record as a leader. Both systems of solidarity conferred a number of advantages and disadvantages when these cultures clashed.

The key advantage enjoyed by the Apaches was that their social organization enabled the swift and reliable coordination of, and execution of, plans. Apache warriors could react swiftly, flexibly and independently to changing circumstances, based on the personal ties between individual warriors. The disadvantage faced by the Apaches was the fragmented nature of their society, which prevented their banding together on a larger scale to confront the United States Their lack of numbers would ultimately finish their resistance to the United States. Once they adopted breech-loading rifles as their weapon of choice, they had to depend on a less-than-reliable network of small-scale traders and warfare to replenish their broken-down arms and provide additional ammunition.

This volume is littered with examples of the internal and external bureaucratic constraints and rivalries which acted against effective campaigning by the US army, despite the possession, by at least some of its field officers, of the knowledge of how to defeat the Apaches. The key advantage of such a large society was an attritional one; so that, even when the society neglected to channel sufficient resources into the promotion of its interests, the limited resources that it did have were still vast in comparison to the unreliable resources available to the Apaches. In truth, the damage caused by the Apaches, while locally quite devastating in physical, economic and psychological terms, was not

23 See Morrison, 2006, pp.160-168; Callinicos, 1999, pp.127-128; Nisbet, 1966, pp.84-85.

of sufficient magnitude to cause much concern for the US federal government. Nevertheless, it has to be noted that, in forcing the US army to temporarily run out of money, Victorio's strategy and tactics *almost* succeeded in registering their opposition to the concentration policy with sufficient effect within the US Congress, the very organ of US government that could have acted decisively to end such a policy. Whether Congress would have acted in such a manner is open to question, but there were certainly many US army officers from the most junior, for example Lieutenant Walter Finley, to the senior such as General George Crook who would have supported an end to concentration.

It is doubtful that Victorio understood the internal workings of US constitutional government, in modern parlances, his use of guerrilla warfare to lobby for a return of their Ojo Caliente reservation came very close to success.

Therefore, the Victorio campaign has probably been condemned to relative obscurity due to the fact that, in the short-term, none of the participants could have claimed to have achieved their political goals, and thus have claimed victory. In the long-term, the United States, which by 1886 had won the Apache Wars, could not point to any aspect of their war with Victorio or Nana which could be easily incorporated into a victory narrative. Even though the winners tend to write history, the campaign did not even make it into the US army pension records, and resulted in a surprised Thomas Cruse, who won a Medal of Honor fighting against the Apaches in 1882, discovering that he had not participated in an 'official' Indian campaign. As a result of the US army's wish to forget this piece of their history, the campaign has been generally relegated to a footnote in western frontier history; and the writings of John Clum have contributed to this effect. As a fervent proponent of the concentration policy, and an equally vociferous opponent of the US army, his argument that relative peace prevailed between 1876 and 1881 treated with the utmost suspicion. At best, the Victorio Campaign garners no more than a chapter in general histories of the Apache Wars. It is true that Thrapp and Stout both published histories of the campaigns in 1974, but new archaeological and archive research have dated both works. Victorio has far greater coverage in the Apache testimony gathered in the 1950s and 60s by Eve Ball, though for the military historian, this testimony presents a stimulating, but worthwhile, challenge in reconciling it with the voluminous US military records.

Finally, the history of the Victorio Campaign tells a gripping tale of a last-ditch resistance to US encroachment by some of the finest guerrilla fighters the world has seen. It also demonstrates the involvement of both African-American and Mexican actors from both sides of the border, who took key roles in this war, and whose contribution should not be forgotten. In hindsight, we can conclude that the Victorio Campaign was the last sustained attempt by the Apaches to preserve at least a semblance of their old way of life in territory claimed by the United States. Their failure to do so represented the long-term strategic victory of the US army, no matter how politically intangible this victory may have appeared to its commanders at the end of 1881. The US army and its Mexican equivalents found themselves dealing with intelligent, flexible and adaptive guerrillas whose principles of war made them very difficult to defeat. The attempt to concentrate the Apaches on one reservation, administered by (usually) thoroughly corrupt officials, provoked a sustained guerrilla war of a magnitude at least as great as the resistance offered by Cochise and others in the 1860s. It showed that the Apaches were more than capable of inflicting embarrassing defeats on their enemies. This war effectively paralysed economic activity in the area and pushed the US army in New Mexico close to a complete collapse.

On this basis alone, the Victorio Campaign should be remembered as one of the most important periods in the Apache Wars. In terms of our fascination with the Battle of the Little Bighorn, with discourses of heroism, and of 'going down fighting',[24] surely the Victorio Campaign deserves at

24 See Scott *et al*, 1998, pp.337-338.

least an acknowledgement as an epic last stand in its own right. The nature of Apache warfare may not lend itself to the romantic imagery of doomed Seventh Cavalrymen swamped by picturesque plains warriors; but realising what were the only options open to them, many Apaches chose that of the last stand. Such a choice was not necessarily the worst option. If one strove hard enough, and did not choose the path of least resistance, one might just win a better future. This was probably the thinking behind Victorio's resistance to what could be termed manifest destiny. Tacitus realised that opponents of the *Pax Romana* made excellent critics of the Roman administration of the Emperor Domitian, and could provide excellent metaphors to justify the reform of such regimes. Like Calgacus, who stood before his Caledonian warriors and declared of the Romans, 'where they make a desert,[25] they call it peace', Victorio might have said of the *Pax Americana*, 'where they take a desert, they call it democracy'. The most important historic and political lesson of the Victorio Campaign is that throughout its history, US imperial democracy, with the best of intentions, has made dreadful and avoidable mistakes when it has encountered resistance to its perceived 'manifest destiny'.

25 This is more often translated as 'desolation' but given the context of the Apache wars using 'desert' seems more analogous.

Appendix I

Materials Relating to Chapter 2

2.1 Instructions for the Transportation and Firing of the Hotchkiss Mountain Gun

It may come as some surprise that the Hotchkiss mountain gun was manned by cavalrymen and not artillerymen. However, it is clear that Ninth Cavalrymen had been trained to operate these guns. The following instructions from the manual would suggest that the Hotchkiss gun was quite simple in its operation and did not require specialist artillery training.

> HEADQUARTERS DISTRICT OF NEW MEXICO
> ACTING ASST. ADJUTANT GENERAL'S OFFICE,
> *Santa Fe, New Mexico, November21, 1879*
>
> The following instructions furnished these Headquarters from the Ordnance Depot at Cheyenne, Wyoming Territory, for the transportation and use of the Hotchkiss Mountain Gun, calibre 1.65, is hereby published for the information and government of all concerned, viz:-
>
> HARNESSING AND TRANSPORTATION
> The gun is drawn by one mule or horse, or, if need be, by two animals working in tandem
>
> The shafts are attached to the trail of the piece, and it is believed that in ordinary country a single animal in the shafts will be sufficient to draw the piece. If another animal is needed he should be attached in front of the other, and the team be driven in tandem.
>
> LOADING AND FIRING
> When the gun is not in use the breechblock is locked in. To load the piece, throw back the locking bar to the rear, and draw out the breech block to the right until the bore is clear. Insert the cartridge in the bore from the rear: if it sticks it may be pushed in a short distance by using the butt of the sponge staff and giving a steady pressure. The cartridge *must not* be pounded in. Push the breech block into its place to the left, (this will drive the cartridge home), and lock it in by throwing the locking bar forward. The piece is fired by a lanyard and friction primer in the usual manner.
>
> After firing, to reload, throw back the locking bar and draw out the breech block smartly to the right. If the ejector fails to throw out the empty shell push the breech block home and draw it out a second time. Sponge the piece carefully, insert a cartridge as before, set the breech block home, lock it and the piece is ready for firing.
>
> The sponge will work hard at first, and should be wet or oiled in serving the piece. The point blank range is about two hundred yards. For greater range a rear sight is provided.

The cartridges are all fixed and are ready for use. At the base of the cartridge there is a hole about one-eighth of an inch in diameter, situated in the center of the base. Through this hole, when clear of sawdust, an inner disc of copper is seen. The fulminate is between the outer base and this inner disc of copper and is ignited by the flame from the friction primer. This inner disc *should not be disturbed under any circumstance*, and the cartridge should be fired without any preparation whatsoever, as it is all fixed, ready for use, when packed in the ammunition boxes.

By command of Colonel HATCH
JOHN S. LOUD
First Lieut. And Adjutant 9th Cavalry,
Acting Assistant Adjutant General.

2.2 List of Stores at Fort Craig to be sent to Ojo Caliente, 7 January 1880[1]

1500 lbs	Bacon Issue	2025 lbs	Flour
150 lbs	Beans	150 lbs	Rice
100 lbs	Peas	300 lbs	Rio Coffee
1120 lbs	????? Sugar	21 ????	Conc. Vinegar
120 lbs	Candles	120 lbs	Laundry Soap
200lbs	Salt Issue	10 lbs	Black Pepper
150 lbs	Tobacco Plug	20 lbs	Breakfast Bacon
24 Cans	Green Corn	10 Cans	Lima Beans
10 Cans	Ham	6 Cans	Raspberry Jam
10 lbs	Lard	12 Cans	Lobsters
24 Cans	Oysters	20 lbs	Mackerel
10 Cans	Mushrooms	15 Cans	Peaches
24 Cans	Green Peas	24 Pint Bottles	Pickles
6 Cans	Plums	6 Cans	Pineapples
6 Cans	Damson Preserve	25 lbs	Table Salt
12 Boxes	Sardines	6 lbs	Corn Starch
6 Bottles	Worcester Sauce	10 lbs	Laundry Soda?
24 Cans	Tomatoes	50 lbs	???? Sugar
12 Cakes	Toilet Soap	30 lbs	Tobacco ???? Asstd
24 Cans	Yeast Powder	10 lbs	?????????????

Appendix II

Materials Relating to Chapter 4

4.1 Summary of Gatewood's Detachment of Apache scouts during March 1880

The number and continual manoeuvring of US army detachments and Apache raiding parties active during March 1880 makes it difficult to follow the movements of these groups. As Lieutenant Gatewood's scout detachment features regularly at different points in this chapter, it is useful to have a summary of these movements.

Date	Location	Activity
5 March	Camp Thomas, Arizona Territory	Ordered to proceed to the District of New Mexico.
21 March	Cienege Apache	Detachment encounters and pursues, to no avail, 10 Apache raiders.
22 March	From Camp French to Wheeler's Ranch	Detachment to verify rumour that Wheeler's Ranch has been attacked. If report false, they are to investigate possibility that the Apaches are east of the Rio Grande.
24 March	Caballo Mountains	Picketing the main pass through the Caballo Mountains.
25 to 28 March	Stationed near Las Palomas	On 28 March, Lieutenant Cruse, MacPherson and small detachment of scouts find remains of two wagons and two Sixth Cavalry deserters.

4.2 Company C, Sixth Cavalry, Tour of Duty, Southwest New Mexico, April–May 1880[1]

1 April	March to Knight's Ranch.
2 April	March to Cherry Creek.
3 April	Arrive Fort Bayard.
4 April	In camp at Fort Bayard.
5 April	March to Hudson's Hot Springs.
6 April	March to Old Fort Cummings.
7 April	March to McEvers' Ranch.
8 April	March to Santa Barbara.
9 April	In camp at Santa Barbara
10 April	March up Rio Grande to mouth of Rio Perchas.
11 April	March to Las Palomas.

12–14 April	In Camp at Las Palomas. Send detachment to Hillsboro for rations.
15 April	March to Arroyo Bonita.
16 April	Return to Santa Barbara.
17–18 April	In camp at Santa Barbara. Send detachment to Fort Cummings.
18–30 April	While based at Santa Barbara, detachments scout north to San Jose, west to McEver's Ranch and Rio Las Animas, and south west as far as Old Fort Cummings.
1 May	Leave Santa Barbara and pass through Fort Cummings, Hudson's Hot Springs, Silver City, Gila Crossing, Keller's Ranch, Deep Creek, Frisco River, Bush Valley, Blue River, Dry Creek, Duck Creek, Mangus Springs, Silver City, Cherry Creek, Knights Ranche…
24 May	… return to Fort Bowie.

Appendix III

Materials Relating to Chapter 10

10.1

Appendix 10.1

One version states that, having established his guard detachments throughout the region, the commander of the Tenth Cavalry was scouting the area when he spotted the Apaches, realised their destination, and reached it first.[1]

A second version is that, in reaction to the news that Victorio was almost certain to attempt a crossing of the Rio Grande, Grierson was in the process of moving himself closer to his Tenth Cavalry detachments. As he was approaching one of his garrisons at Eagle Springs, his own small detachment had a brief skirmish with a single Apache. The Apache was assumed to be part of the predicted advance into western Texas. Captain Nolan's Detachment of Tenth Cavalry, based at Fort Quitman, had also detected Victorio's crossing and had immediately dispatched couriers to Captain Gilmore at Eagle Springs. Lieutenant H.O. Flipper was one of these couriers. Lieutenant Flipper was the first African-American to graduate from West Point, in 1877, and had been posted to the Tenth Cavalry in 1878.[2] Flipper rode to Eagle Springs and informed Grierson of Victorio's movement. He then returned to Fort Quitman in enough time to participate in the looming battle.[3]

It should be noted that at least one version of this battle has 75 Tenth Cavalrymen being wiped out by Victorio's Apaches. Sowell, while mentioning no names, describes visiting a battlefield very similar to Tinaja de las Palmas, then proceeds to make up a story to fit the battle site.[4]

Appendix 10.2 Tenth Cavalry Deployments, July 1880[5]

Co.	Record of Event, July 1880
A	Arrive at Fort Quitman, 28 July. 30 July march to Eighteen Mile Waterhole to relieve Colonel Grierson; thence to Eagle Springs.[1]
B	Leave Chenati Mountains 25 July. March to Viejo Pass 27 July. Leave 29 July, with battalion under Captain Carpenter, for Eagle Springs. Arrive 30 July and join Grierson's command.[2]
C	Leave Fort Davis 25 July. Arrive Eagle Springs 29 July. Engage Apaches 30 July. Lose one man and five horses killed in action, one horse and one mule wounded in action.[3]
D	Captain Keyes, two officers and 53 enlisted men to Grierson Spring in June 1880 from Fort Concho.[4]
F	Captain Kennedy and 60 enlisted men to Black River, NM, in June 1880, from Fort Concho.[5] Leave Lost Chance Canon, Guadalupe Mountains. 1 July march to Guadalupe Canon. Leave on 3 July on Indian trail. Arrive at Camp Safford 26 July.
G	Arrive at Eagle Springs 24 July. Engage Apaches 30 July. One Officer and one enlisted man wounded in action and five horses killed or wounded in action.[6]
H	As Company B above.[7]
I	Arrive at Viejo Pass 27 July.
K	Leave Fort Davis 20 July, to march to El Muerto Stage Station, then to Fresco in Carrizo Mountains, then back to vicinity of El Muerto on 26 July. Small detachment leaves 25 July for Eagle Springs, returning to company 27 July. Leave camp on 31 July for Oak Springs, Carrizo Mountains.[8]
L	Camp Safford, engaged in scouting.
M	Captain Norvell, two officers and 63 enlisted men to North Concho River in June 1880 from Fort Concho.[9]

Notes

1 Bi-Monthly Company Muster Rolls for Company A, 10th Cavalry, Jul./Aug. 1880 in NA, RG94.
2 Bi-Monthly Company Muster Rolls for Company B, 10th Cavalry, Jul./Aug. 1880 in NA, RG94.
3 Bi-Monthly Company Muster Rolls for Company C, 10th Cavalry, Jul./Aug. 1880 in NA, RG94.
4 Return for Jun. 1880 in Returns From U.S. Military Posts 1800-1916, Fort Concho, Texas Jan. 1879-Jun. 1889, NA, M617, Roll 242.
5 Return for Jun. 1880 in Returns From U.S. Military Posts 1800-1916, Fort Concho, Texas Jan. 1879-Jun. 1889, NA, M617, Roll 242.
6 Bi-Monthly Company Muster Rolls for Company G, 10th Cavalry Jul./Aug. 1880 in NA, RG94.
7 Bi-Monthly Company Muster Rolls for Company H, 10th Cavalry Jul./Aug. 1880 in NA, RG94.
8 Bi-Monthly Company Muster Rolls for Company K, 10th Cavalry, Jul./Aug. 1880 in NA, RG94.
9 Return for Jun. 1880 in Returns From U.S. Military Posts 1800-1916, Fort Concho, Texas Jan. 1879-Jun. 1889, NA, M617, Roll 242.

5 Unless otherwise footnoted this table is derived from the Record of Events Jul. & Aug. 1880 in Returns From Regular Army Cavalry Regiments 1833-1916, 10th Cavalry Regimental Returns 1873 to 1880, NA, M744, Roll 96; See also Return for Jun. 1880 in Returns From U.S. Military Posts 1800-1916, Fort Concho, Texas Jan. 1879-Jun. 1889, NA, M617, Roll 242.

Bibliography

Primary Sources

National Archives Washington D.C. Microfilm Sources.

Letters Rec'd by the Office of the Adjutant General (Main series). 1871–80. RG94, M666, 593 rolls)

Roll (s)	File	Description
24	2465 AGO 1871	*Correspondence relating to the selection by Vincent Colyer of the Board of Indian Commissioners of sites for Apache Indian reservations at Tularosa Valley, and White Mountain, New Mexico Territory, and at Camp Grant and Camp Verde, Arizona Territory, 1871–72. Included is the order by General George Crook that the Apaches move onto the reservations by Feb 15, 1872, or be considered hostile.*
123	3383 AGO 1873	*Correspondence relating to the agreement with Cochise, chief of the Chiricahua Apache, negotiated by Gen. Oliver O. Howard and to Gen. George Crook's criticism of the agreement and his request to be allowed to subdue Cochise with force 1873–74*
265	2576 AGO 1876	*Correspondence relating to the removal of the Chiricahua Apache Indians to the San Carlos Indian Agency, Arizona Territory, 1876–77.*
326	1927 AGO 1877	*Correspondence relating to the arrest and removal of Geronimo's band of renegade Chiricahua Apache Indians from Ojo Caliente, New Mexico Territory, to the San Carlos Indian Agency, Arizona Territory, 1877*
366	5705 AGO 1877	*Correspondence relating to military operations against the Warm Springs Indians who fled from the San Carlos Indian Agency, Arizona Territory, 1877–79*
526–528	6058 AGO 1879	*Papers relating to military operations against Chief Victorio's band of Mescalero Apache in southern New Mexico, 1879–81, and one letter dated Mar. 13, 1886.*

Letters Rec'd by the Office of the Adjutant General (Main Series), 1881–1889. M689. 740 rolls. DP

Roll (s)	File	Description
44	4746 AGO 1881	*Correspondence and reports mainly concerning efforts to capture hostile Apache Indians who were terrorising the border region of the District of New Mexico, July–Dec. 1881.*

Returns From Regular Army Infantry Regiments June 1821-December 1916–1916 (Pamphlet Describing M665 from Record Groups 94 & 391)

Roll (s)	File	Description
166	N/A	*15th Infantry Jan. 1873–Dec. 1880*
167	N/A	*15th Infantry Jan. 1881–Dec. 1889*

Letters Rec'd by the Office of the Adjutant General (Main Series), 1881–1889. M689. 740 rolls. DP

Roll (s)	File	Description
77	364 AGO 1882	*Papers and a report of Mar. 4, 1882, from the Secretary of War relating to a statement of expenditures for Indian wars and for the observation and control of Indians from July 1, 1871-June 20, 1882*
81	663 AGO 1882	*Papers relating to the Frelinghuysen-Romero Agreement of July 29, 1882, providing for reciprocal crossings of the international boundary by troops of the United States and Mexico in pursuit of hostile Indians, Feb. 1882-June 1887*

Returns From Regular Army Cavalry Regiments 1833–1916 (Pamphlet Describing M744 from Record Groups 94 & 391)

Roll (s)	File	Description
43	N/A	*4th Cavalry 1887–1883*
63	N/A	*6th Cavalry 1875–1880*
64	N/A	*6th Cavalry 1881–1887*
88	N/A	*9th Cavalry 1873–1880*
89	N/A	*9th Cavalry 1881–1887*
96	N/A	*10th Cavalry 1873–1880*

Returns From U.S. Military Posts 1800–1916 (Pamphlet Accompanying M617 – from Record Groups 393)

Roll (s)	File	Description
87	N/A	*Bayard, Fort, N. Mex Aug. 1866–Dec. 1879*
88	N/A	*Bayard, Fort, N. Mex Jan. 1880–Dec. 1894*
117	N/A	*Bliss, Fort, Tex. Jan. 1872–Dec. 1885*
242	N/A	*Concho, Fort, Texas Jan 1879–June 1889*
262	N/A	*Craig, Fort, N. Mex Jan. 1871–June 1885*
298	N/A	*Davis, Fort, Texas Jan 1879–June 1891*
877	N/A	*Ojo Caliente, N. Mex May 1879–Mar. 1882*
1217	N/A	*Stanton, Fort, N. Mex Jan. 1868–Dec. 1877*
1218	N/A	*Stanton, Fort, N. Mex Jan. 1878–Dec. 1887*
1449	N/A	*Wingate, Fort, N. Mex Jan. 1872–Dec. 1882*

Microcopy M997: Annual Reports of the War Department

Roll	File	Description
26	N/A	*1876 Vol. I–II*
27	N/A	*1876 Vol. II–IV*
28	N/A	*1877 Vol. I–II*

29	N/A	*1877 Vol. III–IV*
30	N/A	*1878 Vol. I–II*
31	N/A	*1878 Vol. II*
32	N/A	*1878 Vol. III–IV*
33	N/A	*1879 Vol. I–II*
34	N/A	*1879 Vol. II–IV*
35	N/A	*1880 Vol. I–II*
36	N/A	*1880 Vol. II*
37	N/A	*1880 Vol. III–IV*
38	N/A	*1881 Vol. I–II*
39	N/A	*1881 Vol. II*
40	N/A	*1881 Vol. III–IV*

"Special Files" Created by the Military Division of the Missouri. Records of US Army Continental Commands, 1821–1920 M1495 (Record Group 393)

Roll (s)	File	Description
14		*Disturbances at El Paso, TX, Sept. 1877–May 1878*
		Victorio Campaign, Feb. 1879–Nov. 1880

Letters Sent by the 9th Military Department, the Department of New Mexico, and the District of New Mexico 1849–1890 M1072 (Record Group 393)

Roll (s)	File	Description
6		*Name and Subject Index to Volume 18 1878*
		Volume 18
		Name and Subject Index to Volume 19 Jan–Oct 1879
		Volume 19 1879
		Name and Subject Index to Volume 20
		Volume 20 1880
		Name and Subject Index to Volumes 20 and 21 1881
		Volume 20 Jan 1880–Aug 1881
7		*Name and Subject Index to Volumes 20 and 21 1881*
		Name and Subject Index to Volume 21 1882
		Name and Subject Index to Volumes 21 and 22 1883
		Volume 21 Aug. 1881–Aug.1883
		Name and Subject Index to Volumes 21 and 22 1883
		Volume 22 Sept. 1883–July 1887
		Volume 23 July 1887–Sept. 1890

Headquarters Records of Fort Cummings, New Mexico, 1863–1873 & 1880–1884 M1081
Rolls 1, 2, 3, 5 & 8

Letters Received by Headquarters District of New Mexico September 1865-August 1890 (Pamphlet Describing M1088 from Record Group 393)

Roll (s)	File	Description
37	658–1658	*Apr.–June 1879*
38	1664–2491	*July–Sept. 1879*
39	2506–3485	*Oct. –Dec. 1879*

40	806–1790	*Jan. –June 1880*
41	2103–4519	*July–Dec. 1880*
42	5–1544	*Jan. –Apr. 1881*
43	1568–4364	*May–Oct. 1881*
44	4368–5690	*Nov. –Dec.1881*

HQ Records of the District of the Pecos 1878–1881 Microcopy M1381
Rolls 1–5

Consular Despatches Chihuahua Mexico 1830–1906 M289
Rolls 1–2 Nov 30th 1830–May 13th 1901

Consular Despatches Cuidad Juarez (Paso del Norte) M184
Roll 2 Jan 16th 1871–Dec 31st 1884

National Archives Washington D.C. Non-Microfilm Sources
Record Group 94, Bi-Monthly Muster Rolls: Co A 4th Cavalry Regiment 1880
6th Cavalry Regiment 1880
9th Cavalry Regiment 1879–1881
10th Cavalry Regiment 1880
15th Infantry Regiment 1879–1881
Record Group 94, Entry 257, Medical History, Fort Bayard, New Mexico Vol. 896.
Record Group 94, Entry 297, Personal Record Files.

Martin B. Hughes	Box 483 AA1–10
John F. Guilfoyle	Box 481 AB1–18
Adam Kramer	Box 33 AC1–5
James H. French	Box 448 AD1-AD5
Matthias W. Day	Box 1 AE1-AE11
Henry Carroll	Box 476 AF1-AF12
John Conline	Box 279 AG1-AG16
Thomas Cruse	Box 1428 AI1–3
Eugene D. Dimmick	Box 1496 AJ1–17
Michael Cooney	Box 1067 AK1-AK5
George R. Burnett	Box 941 AL1-AL12
Patrick Cusack	Box 49 AN1-AN6
Samuel Woodward	Box 426 AO1-AO4
Augustus P. Blocksom	Box 463 AP1-AP11
Nicholas Nolan	Box 857 AQ1
Stephen C. Mills	Box 829 AR1-AR10
Leighton Finley	Box 600 AS1-AS2
Frank B. Taylor	Box 501 AT1-AT3
Henry H. Wright	Box 334 AU1-AU29
George W. Smith	Box 309 AV1-AV3
Louis H. Rucker	Box 180 AW1-AW4
Albert P. Morrow	Boxes 71 & 72 AX1-AX10
Tom Jeffords	Box 654 AY1

William H. Hugo Box 526 AZ1-AZ6

Record Group 94, Entry 561 Personal Papers of Medical Officers and Physicians ("Medical Officers Files":

Kennon, L.W.C. 1853–79 Box 1112

Record Group 391, Entry 734, Regimental Histories 4th Cavalry 1855–1926.

Record Group 391, Entry 744, Miscellaneous Records 1880–1914 Orders/Letters 4th Cavalry.

Record Group 391, Entry 841, Reports and Tabular Statements of Scouting Expeditions 1867–1891.

Record Group 391, Entry 909/911/919, Regimental Orders Issued 1876–1879.

Record Group 391, Entry 920, Letters, Telegrams and Endorsements Sent: and General and Special Orders and Circulars Issued by a Battalion July–September 1880.

Record Group 391, Entry 921, Letters & Telegrams sent by the Battalion on the Southern Pacific Railway at Separ NM Sept-Nov 1881.

Record Group 391, Entry 922, Letters & Telegrams Received by the Battalion on the Southern Pacific Railroad at Separ NM Sept-Nov 1881.

Record Group 391, Entry 923, Orders Issued by the Battalion on the Southern Pacific Railroad at Sepr NM Sept-Nov 1881.

Record Group 391, Entry 925, Endorsements Sent 1873–85, 10th U.S. Cavalry.

Record Group 391, Entry 933, Regimental History 1866–98, 10th U.S. Cavalry.

Record Group 393, Letters Received Dept. of the Missouri 1868–98 Entry A1–1 2601 Boxes 83–98

Record Group 393, Part 1, Entry 169, Letters Sent Vol. 9. Dept of Arizona 1879

Letters Sent Vol. 10. Dept of Arizona 1880

Letters Sent Vol. 11. Dept of Arizona 1881.

Record Group 393. Part 1, Entry 181, Letters Received, Dept of Arizona 1881.[1]

Record Group 393. Part 1, Entry 183, Dept of Arizona & District of New Mexico: General Orders, Circulars and Court Martial Orders 1870–1881.[2]

Record Group 393. Part 1, Entry 184, Dept of Arizona: Special Orders 1879–1881.

Record Group 393. Part 1, Entry 185, Dept of Arizona: General and Special Orders and other Orders Issued and Received.[3]

Record Group 393. Part 1, Entry 187, Dept of Arizona, Manuscript Reports 1880–85.

Record Group 393. Part 1, Entry 204, Dept of Arizona, Miscellaneous Records 1879–1880.

Record Group 393, Part 1, Entry 232, Dept of Arizona: Field Records – Troops in Southeastern Arizona 1878–1881.

Vol. 2. – September 1st 1878–May 27th 1879.

Vol. 3. – May 27th 1879–July 3 rd 1879.

Vol. 4. – July 3rd 1879–December 13th 1879.

Vol. 5. – December 13th 1879–May 7th 1880.

Vol. 6. – May 7th 1880–May 18th 1880.

Vol. 7. – May 16th 1880–September 6th 1880.

Vol. 8. – September 6th 1880–December 12th 1880.

1 I have photocopied all the material cited. I have numbered each photocopy in the order that I discovered them. In the text of this book they are cited as follows: (Sender to Recipient with date, RG393, Pt.1, Entry 181, page number (This number refers to the number that I have assigned to the telegram copy in my own files))

2 See Footnote 1.

3 See Footnote 1.

Record Group 393. Part 1, Entry 235, Dept of Arizona: Letters and Telegrams Rec'd 1878–1880.[4]
Record Group 393. Part 1, Entry 236, Dept of Arizona: Troops in South East Arizona Telegrams 1880.
Record Group 393. Part 1, Entry 238, Dept of Arizona: General Orders and Field Orders July 1879–January 1881.
Record Group 393. Part 1, Entry 239, Dept of Arizona: Special Orders Vols. I & II October 1879–January 1881.
Record Group 393. Part 1, Entry 240, Dept of Arizona: Miscellaneous Records 1878–1880.
Record Group 393. Part 1, Entry 244, Dept of Arizona: District of Apache – Telegrams Received 1881.
Record Group 393. Part 1, Entry 2538, Division of the Missouri: Letters Sent Vol. 6 1879–1881.
Record Group 393. Part 1, Entry 2539, Military Division of the Missouri: Press Copies of Letters and Endorsements Sent, Vols. 11–14 1879–1881.
Record Group 393. Part 1, Entry 2546, Military Division of the Missouri: Letters Received 1879–1881.[5]
Record Group 393. Part 1, Entry 2551, Military Division of the Missouri: Annual Reports of Departments 1879–1881.
Record Group 393, Part 3, Entry 431, District of New Mexico:
Telegrams Sent Vol. 2 – Jan. to Dec. 1879.
Vol. 3 – Jan. to Nov. 1880.
Vol. 4 – Nov. 1880 to Jan. 1881.
Vol. 5 – Feb. to Dec. 1881.
Record Group 393, Part 3, Entry 439, District of New Mexico: Telegrams Received 1870–1885 (Unarranged)[6]
Record Group 393, Part 3, Entry 440, District of New Mexico, Mail Copies of Telegrams Received 1880–1885 (Unarranged).[7]
Record Group 393, Part 3, Entry 446, District of New Mexico, Printed Special Orders 1869–1888.
Record Group 393, Part 3, Entry 450, District of New Mexico Printed Special Orders 1869–1888.[8]
Record Group 393, Part 3, Entry 451, District of New Mexico, Circular Letters Issued 1876–84.
Record Group 393, Part 3, Entry 453, District of New Mexico, Special Orders Rec'd from Sub-Commands.
Record Group 393, Part 3, Entry 472, District of New Mexico, Miscellaneous Records 1868–1889.
Record Group 393, Part 3, Entry 474, District of New Mexico, Press Copies of Letters and Telegrams Sent by Commander Hatch in the Field 1877 Ojo Caliente.
Record Group 393, Part 3, Entry 475 District of New Mexico General and Special Field Orders, Letters and Telegrams Volume 4–7.
Record Group 393, Part 3, Entry 477, District of New Mexico, Letters and Endorsements Sent 1877–1887.
Record Group 393, Part 3, Entry 479, District of New Mexico, Letters Received at AAG 1872–1880.

4 See Footnote 1.
5 See Footnote 1.
6 Note:- There are several problems with this material. Some of the telegrams are not clearly dated. They are not stored in order and some are illegible. I photocopied all the telegrams cited. I have numbered each telegram photocopy in the order that I discovered them. See also Footnote 1.
7 See Footnote 1.
8 Note that these also contain Special Field Orders issued by Headquarters in the Field.

Report of the Commissioner of Indian Affairs, Dept. of the Interior, Office of Indian Affairs. Washington November 1 1880.
John H. Ware V. the U.S. & Apache Indians, Depredation Claim No. 4584, 16E3/3/6/5 Box 375.

Government Documents

Chronological List of Actions, & c., with Indians, from January 1, 1866 to January 1891. *Adjutant General's Office.*
Record of Engagements with Hostile Indians within the Military Division of the Missouri from 1868 to 1882. Compiled from Official Records. Headquarters – Military Division of the Missouri, Chicago Illinois, August 1st 1882: *Lieutenant General P.H. Sheridan Commanding*
New Mexico State University Archives:
RG 98 Fort Bayard Interrement Record NMRA–902(8888).
Microfilm held in NMSU archives, Las Cruces, New Mexico
Lee Myers Papers: Boxes 6 & 7/25

Documents courtesy of William A. Dobak

Parker to CO Fort Wingate, 10 August, 1881, Department of Missouri, Letters Received, 6552 DMo 1881
Parker to A.A.A.General, District of New Mexico, Santa Fe N.M., 13 August 1881, Department of Missouri, Letters Received, 6552 DMo 1881
Carroll to Acting Assistant General, District of New Mexico, Santa Fe, N.M. 17 October 1881, Department of Missouri, Letters Received, 7266 DMo. 1881
Gardner to The Adjutant Batt. Ninthh Cavalry In the Field, Separ S.P.R.R., N.M. 28 October 1881, Department of Missouri, Letters Received, 7320 DMo. 1881
Gardner to The Adjutant Batt. Ninth Cavalry, Separ S.P.R.R., N.M. 31 October 1881, Department of Missouri, Letters Received, 7320 DMo. 1881
Carroll to A.A.A. General, Dist. Of New Mexico, Santa Fe N.M. 31 October 1881, Department of Missouri, Letters Received, 7330 DMo. 1881
Van C. Smith to Capt. Carroll Separ N.M. 23 October 1881, Department of Missouri, Letters Received, 7330 DMo. 1881
Following to do with a discussion concerning the relocation of Mescalero and San Carlos Reservations to Indian Territory Late 1881–1882
Bradley, CO Fort Wingate, to HQ District of New Mexico, 1 February 1882, Department of Missouri, Letters Received, 710 DMo. 1882
Mackenzie, to AAG Dept. Of Missouri, 5 February 1882, Department of Missouri, Letters Received, 710 DMo. 1882
Kirkwood, Secretary of the Interior to The Secretary of War 11 January 1882, Department of Missouri, Letters Received, 710 DMo. 1882
Randall, Capt. Twenty-Third Infantry CO Fort Reno, Indian Territory to Assistant Adjutant General, Department of the Missouri, 28 January 1882, Department of Missouri, Letters Received, 710 DMo. 1882
Guy V. Henry, Major Ninth Cavalry, Fort Sill to Assistant Adjutant General, Department of the Missouri, 27 January, 1882, Department of Missouri, Letters Received, 710 DMo. 1882

Documents courtesy of Berndt Kuhn

'Terrassas Talks' *Daily New Mexican* 30 October 1880
'Greeting the Victors' Victory Parade in Chihuahua City as reported in the *Daily New Mexican* 2 December 1880

Price to Act. Asst. Adjt. General, District of New Mexico, 25 July 1873 in Letters Received, District of New Mexico, RG393.

Documents courtesy of Daniel D. Aranda

David L. Hughes' 'An Early Chapter in the life of Apache Bill'

Parks, H.L. "Gavilan Canyon Fight – August 19, 1881" Letter dated 28 April 1956

Fountain to Bureau of Pensions, Dept. of the Interior, 12 September 1912

MacPherson Letters 1 January 1879 to 3 September 1880, University of Virginia at Charlottesville

Lt. M.B. Hughes to CO Ojo Caliente, 10 November 1877

Statement of Apache Indian Chiefs, Fort Wingate, 24 October 1877 in Letters Received, District of New Mexico 1877

Joaquin Terrazas to Genl. G.P. Buell 12 November 1880

Anon. 1, "Gavilan Canyon Fight – August 19 1881"

This document mainly quotes the Annual Report of the Secretary of War 1881, but includes some comments concerning US Army failures in Korea suggesting that this was written in the 1950s.

Anon. 2, "Fort Selden History: Month 1"

Misc. 1, "The Jim Santiago, Vidal Trujillo Gonzales Family" by Vidal T. Gonzales

Misc. 2, "Appendix A: Council of Mimbres Apaches held at Fort Tulerosa September 11 [12] 1872" RG 75 in National Archives also in Arizona Historical Society Microfilm MC 4

Source: Ed Sweeney via Dan Aranda

Misc. 3, "Spots of Interest in the Area"

This is a page-long article in three columns concerning the events surrounding the death and commemoration of Jim Cooney.

Misc. 4 "The Indian War in the Lava Beds"

Cuttings relating to the ambush of Eugene Van Patten's posse and other attacks perpetrated by Victorio's Apaches in October 1879.

Misc. 5 Declaration of Fransisco Montoya and supporting statement of Jose Abatos concerning and attack on Montoya's freight train in early May 1880.

Document sent by Karl Laumbach & Daniel D. Aranda

'The Pursuit of Victorio' By Captain Jack Crawford: Socorro County Historical Society, Publications in History, Volume 1, February 1965

Papers Held in the Gatewood Collection

Report of Captain C.B. McLellan, 6th U.S. Cavalry, 16 May 1880, On Operations in the District of New Mexico.

Report of Colonel E.A. Carr, 6th U.S. Cavalry, 29 August 1880, on Field Operations in South-Eastern Arizona.

From the Walter Lowry Finley Collection (AC 083-p), Angélico Chávez History Library, Museum of New Mexico, Palace of the Governors, Santa Fe, New Mexico, U.S.A.

Keith Humphries Collection, Geronimo Springs Museum, Truth or Consequences, New Mexico.

William M. Bates Interview Notes c. 1940

Fort Davis Museum Archive:

Robert Grierson's Diary, 10th July to 1st September 1880.

Special Collections, University of Arizona Library, Tucson
Leighton Finley Diary, 25th July to 15th November 1880.

Useful Biographical Sources
Browning, J.A. (1992), *The Western Reader's Guide: A Selected Bibliography of Nonfiction Magazines 1953–91* (Barbed Wire Press: Stillwater Oklahoma)
Browning, J.A. & McCravey, J.B. (2000), *A Complete Guide to Hunter's Frontier Times* (Eakin Press: Austin Texas)

Contemporary Newspapers
The *Grant County Herald & New Southwest* 1879–1881
Thirty-Four 1879–1880
Microfilms Courtesy of Ed Sweeney.
Crimmins, Colonel M. L. "The Mescalero Apaches" *El Paso Times* Sunday, May 31, 1931 & Sunday, June 7 1931
Las Vegas Daily Gazette, 30 December 1882.
'Nutt in a Nutshell' by 'Rambler',
http://chroniclingamerica.loc.gov/lccn/sn90051703/1882–12–30/ed–1/seq–4/#date1=01%2F01%2F1882&sort=date&date2=12%2F31%2F1882&searchType=advanced&language=&sequence=0&index=19&words=Kingston&proxdistance=5&state=New+Mexico&rows=20&ortext=&proxtext=&phrasetext=&andtext=kingston&dateFilterType=range&page=3
The New York Times
'Punishing Victorio's Band', 30 July 1880.
http://query.nytimes.com/mem/archive-free/pdf?res=9E05E1D81630EE3ABC4850DFB166838B699FDE
'Victorio's Murdering Band', 28 August 1880
http://query.nytimes.com/mem/archive-free/pdf?res=9A0DEFDB153BE033A2575BC2A96E9C94619FD7CF
'Outrages by Victorio's Indians', 10 September 1880
http://query.nytimes.com/mem/archive-free/pdf?res=9805E0D8143FEE3ABC4852DFBF66838B699FDE
'The Death of Victorio', 28 October 1880
http://query.nytimes.com/mem/archive-free/pdf?res=9B07E5DE173FE533A2575BC2A9669D94619FD7CF
'The End of Victorio', 29 October 1880
http://query.nytimes.com/mem/archive-free/pdf?res=9E02E7DA153BE033A2575AC2A9669D94619FD7CF
'The Murdering Apaches', 31 January 1881
http://query.nytimes.com/mem/archive-free/pdf?res=9806E4DA1F3AE533A25752C3A9679C94609FD7CF
'American Surveyors Murdered: Thirteen Men of the Mexico Central Force Found Dead' 7 July 1881
http://query.nytimes.com/mem/archive-free/pdf?res=9A02EFDC103CEE3ABC4F53DFB166838A699FDE

From the Walter Lowry Finley Collection (AC 083-p), Angélico Chávez History Library, Museum of New Mexico, Palace of the Governors, Santa Fe, New Mexico, U.S.A.

Weekly New Mexican, 27 September, 1879, p.2, c.2.

'The Fight on the Animas', *Weekly New Mexican*, 11 October 1879, p.1, c.3.

'The Indian War in the Southwest', *Weekly New Mexican*, 11 October 1879, p.2, c.1.

'Victorio the Indian Chief' *Weekly New Mexican*, 18 October 1879. p.1, c.4.

'Indian News' *The New Mexican*, 18 October 1879, p.2, c.5.

'The latest Indian News. Major Morrow follows Victoria into Mexico, and has a fight with him. The Savages are Dispersed with Heavy Loss.' *Weekly New Mexican*, 8 November 1879, p.2, c.3.

Secondary Sources.

Books

Adam, G.G.	2001	"Resolution Adopted at Meeting of Residents of Cochise County, Arizona, Regarding Outbreak of Indians From San Carlos Reservation" in Cozzens, *Eyewitnesses to the Indian Wars 1865–1890 Volume 1: The Struggle for Apacheria* (Stackpole Books: Mechanicsville) 414–424 First Published 1885
Aleshire, P.	1998	*Reaping the Whirlwind: The Apache Wars* (Facts on File: New York)
Alba, V.	1973	*A Concise History of Mexico* (Cassell: London)
Alonso, A.M.	1997	*Thread of Blood: Colonialism, Revolution, and Gender on Mexico's Northern Frontier* (The University of Arizona Press: Tuscon)
Altshuler, C.W.	1991	*Cavalry Yellow & Infantry Blue: Army Officers in Arizona between 1851 and 1886* (Arizona Historical Society: Tuscon)
Anderson, F.	2000	*Crucible of War: The Seven Years' War and the Fate of Empire in British North America. 1754–1766* (Faber & Faber: London)
Astor, G.	1998	*The Right to Fight: A History of African-Americans in the Military* (Presidio: Novato CA)
Ball, E.	1970	*In the Days of Victorio: Recollections of a Warm Springs Apache* (The University of Arizona Press: Tucson)
Ball, E.	1980	*Indeh: An Apache Odyssey* (University of Oklahoma Press: Norman)
Bancroft, H.H.	1889	*The Works of Hubert Howe Bancroft, Vol. XVI: History of the North Mexican States & Texas Vol. II 1801–1889* (The History Company: San Francisco)
Basso, K.	1996	*Wisdom Sits in Places: Landscape and Language Among the Western Apache* (University of New Mexico Press: Albuquerque)
Barnes, W.C.	1982	*Apaches & Longhorns: The Reminicinces of Will C. Barnes* (The University of Arizona Press: Tuscon) Copy of Edition Published in 1941
Barnes, W.C.	2001 (i)	"The Apaches' Last Stand in Arizona: The Battle of Big Dry Wash" in Cozzens, *Eyewitnesses to the Indian Wars 1865–1890 Volume 1: The Struggle for Apacheria* (Stackpole Books: Mechanicsville) 267–285 First Published 1931

Barnes, W.C.	2001 (ii)	"In the Apache Country" in Cozzens, *Eyewitnesses to the Indian Wars 1865–1890 Volume 1: The Struggle for Apacheria* (Stackpole Books: Mechanicsville) 615–624 First Published 1887
Barney, J.M.	1996	*Tales of Apache Warfare: True stories of Massacres, Fights and Raids in Arizona and New Mexico* (Trail to Yesterday Books: Tuscon) First published in 1933
Baylor, G.W. (Thompson, J.D. ed)	1996	*Into the Far Wild Country: True Tales of the Old Southwest* (Texas Western Press, The University of Texas at El Paso: El Paso)
Beck, W.A. & Haase, Y.D.	1969	*Historical Atlas of New Mexico* (University of Oklahoma Press: Norman)
Beck, W.A. & Haase, Y.D.	1989	*Historical Atlas of the American West* (University of Oklahoma Press: Norman) *Historical Atlas of the American West* (University of Oklahoma Press: Norman)
Benson, H.C.	2001	"The Geronimo Campaign" in Cozzens, *Eyewitnesses to the Indian Wars 1865–1890 Volume 1: The Struggle for Apacheria* (Stackpole Books: Mechanicsville) 552–556 First Published 1909
Betzinez, J.	1987	*I Fought with Geronimo* (University of Nebraska Press: London) First published by Stackpole 1959
Beyer, W.F. & Keydel	1971 (i)	"The Battle of Cuchillo Negra Mountains" cited in J.M. Carroll (ed), *The Black Military Experience in the American West* (Liveright: New York)
Beyer, W.F. & Keydel	1971 (ii)	"The Battle of Carrizo Canyon Mountains" cited in J.M. Carroll (ed), *The Black Military Experience in the American West* (Liveright: New York)
Beyer, W.F. & Keydel	1971 (iii)	"The Battle of Gavilan Canyon" cited in J.M. Carroll (ed), *The Black Military Experience in the American West* (Liveright: New York)
Beyer, W.F. & Keydel	1971(iv)	"The Battle of Membres Mountains" cited in J.M. Carroll (ed), *The Black Military Experience in the American West* (Liveright: New York)
Beyer, W.F. & Keydel	1971 (v)	"The Battle of Las Animas Canyon" cited in J.M. Carroll (ed), *The Black Military Experience in the American West* (Liveright: New York)
Beyer, W.F. & Keydel	1971 (vi)	"Tularosa" cited in J.M. Carroll (ed), *The Black Military Experience in the American West* (Liveright: New York)
Bigelow, J.	1986	*On the Bloody Trail of Geronimo* (Westernlore Press: Tuscon) First Published 1886–1887
Billington, M.L.	1991	*New Mexico's Buffalo Soldiers 1866–1900* (University Press of Colorado: Niwot)
Birtle, A.J.	2001	*U.S. Army Counterinsurgency and Contingency Operations Doctrine 1860–1941* (Center of Military History, United States Army: Washington D.C.)
Blevins, W.	1993	*The Wordsworth Dictionary of the American West* (Wordsworth Editions: Ware)
Bourke, J.G.	1980	*On the Border with Crook* (Time Life: New York) First published by Charles Scribners Sons 1891

Bourke, J.G. 1987 *An Apache Campaign in the Sierra Madre: An Account of the Expedition in Pursuit of the Hostile Chiricahua Apaches in the Spring of 1883* (University of Nebraska Press: London): First published by Charles Scribner's Sons 1886

Bourke, J.G. 2001 (i) "Crook's Campaign in '72" in Cozzens, *Eyewitnesses to the Indian Wars 1865–1890 Volume 1: The Struggle for Apacheria* (Stackpole Books: Mechanicsville) 141–143 First Published 1883

Bourke, J.G. 2001 (ii) "With Crook in the Sierra Madre" in Cozzens, *Eyewitnesses to the Indian Wars 1865–1890 Volume 1: The Struggle for Apacheria* (Stackpole Books: Mechanicsville) 346–385

Bowles, N. 1998 *Government and Politics of the United States 2nd Edition* (MacMillan Press: Basingstoke)

Boyer, R.M. & Gayton, N.D. 1992 *Apache Mothers and Daughters* (University of Oklahoma Press: Norman)

Brown, D. 1970 *Bury My Heart at Wounded Knee* (Vintage: London)

Bryan, H 1998 *True Tales of the American Southwest: Pioneer Recollections of Frontier Adventures* (Clear Light Publishers: Santa Fe)

Buchanan, K.M. 1986 *Apache Women Warriors* (South-western Studies No 81; University of Texas at El Paso: El Paso Texas)

Burton, A.T. 1999 *Black, Buckskin and Blue: African-American Scouts and Soldiers on the Western Frontier* (Eakin Press: Austin Texas)

Callinicos, A 1999 *Social Theory: A Historical Introduction* (Polity: Cambridge)

Carmony, N.B. 1996 *The Civil War in Apacheland: Sergeant George Hand's Diary-California, Arizona, West Texas, New Mexico 1861–1864* (High Lonesome Books: Silver City)

Carr C.C.C. 2001 "The Days of the Empire-Arizona 1866–1869" in Cozzens, *Eyewitnesses to the Indian Wars 1865–1890 Volume 1: The Struggle for Apacheria* (Stackpole Books: Mechanicsville) 18–35 First published 1889

Carroll, J.M. 1971 *The Black Military Experience in the American West* (Liveright: New York)

Cashin, H.V. 1993 *Under Fire with the Tenth U.S. Cavalry* (University Press of Colorado: Niwot) First Published by F. Tennyson Neelyin 1899

Chisman, C. 2001 "The Apache Campaign of 1885–1886" in Cozzens, *Eyewitnesses to the Indian Wars 1865–1890 Volume 1: The Struggle for Apacheria* (Stackpole Books: Mechanicsville) 540–545 First Published 1927

Chun, C.K.S. 2004 *US Army in the Plains Indian Wars 1865–91 (Battle Orders Number 5)* (Osprey Publishing: Oxford)

Clarke, P.H. 2001 "A Hot Trail" in Cozzens, *Eyewitnesses to the Indian Wars 1865–1890 Volume 1: The Struggle for Apacheria* (Stackpole Books: Mechanicsville) 630–641 First Published 1894

Clausewitz, C. 1968 *On War* (Penguin: London)

Clendenen, C.C. 1969 *Blood on the Border: The United States Army and the Mexican Irregulars* (Collier-Macmillan: London)

Clifford, F. & Nolan, F. (editor) 2011 *Deep Trails in the Old West: A Frontier Memory* (University of Oklahoma Press: Norman)

Cocker, M.	1999	*Rivers of Blood, Rivers of Gold: Europe's Conflict with Tribal Peoples* (Pimlico: London)
Coffer, W.E.	1982	*The Story of the Indians of Arizona and New Mexico* (Van Nostrand Reinhold Company: New York)
Coffman, E.M.	1986	*The Old Army: A Portrait of the American Army in Peacetime 1784–1898* (Oxford University Press: Oxford)
Cole, D.C.	1988	*The Chiricahua Apache 1846–1876: From War to Reservation* (University of New Mexico Press:Albuquerque)
Collins, C.	1994	*The Great Escape: The Apache Outbreak of 1881* (Westernlore Press: Tuscon Arizona)
Collins, C.	1999	*Apache Nightmare: The Battle at Cibecue Creek* (University of Oklahoma Press: Norman)
Cozzens, P.	2000	*General John Pope: A Life For The Nation* (University of Illinois Press: Urbana)
Cozzens, P.	2001	*Eyewitnesses to the Indian Wars 1865–1890 Volume 1: The Struggle for Apacheria* (Stackpole Books: Mechanicsville)
Cozzens, P.	2005	*Eyewitnesses to the Indian Wars 1865–1890 Volume V: The Army and the Indian* (Stackpole Books: Mechanicsville)
Cremony, J.C.	1983	*Life Among the Apaches* (University of Nebraska Press: London) First published by A. Roman and Company 1868
Crick, B	2005	*In Defence of Politics 5th Edition* (Continuum;London)
Crook, G.	2001 (i)	"Apache Affairs: An Interview with General Crook" in Cozzens, *Eyewitnesses to the Indian Wars 1865–1890 Volume 1: The Struggle for Apacheria* (Stackpole Books: Mechanicsville) 396–404 First Published 1883
Crook, G.	2001 (ii)	"Resume of Operations against Apache Indians, 1882 to 1886" in Cozzens, *Eyewitnesses to the Indian Wars 1865–1890 Volume 1: The Struggle for Apacheria* (Stackpole Books: Mechanicsville) 569–589 First Issued in 1886
Crook, G.	2001 (iii)	"The Apache Problem" in Cozzens, *Eyewitnesses to the Indian Wars 1865–1890 Volume 1: The Struggle for Apacheria* (Stackpole Books: Mechanicsville) 593–603 First Published 1886
Cruse, T.	1987	*Apache Days and After* (University of Nebraska Press: London) First published by The Caxton Printers Ltd 1941
Cruse, T.	2001	"From Hembrillo Canyon to Chevelon's Fork" in Cozzens, *Eyewitnesses to the Indian Wars 1865–1890 Volume 1: The Struggle for Apacheria* (Stackpole Books: Mechanicsville) 262–266 Letter written May 25th 1883
Dale, E.E.	1949	*The Indians of the Southwest: A Century of Development under the United States* (University of Oklahoma Press: Norman)
Daly, H.W.	2001	"The Geronimo Campaign" in Cozzens, *Eyewitnesses to the Indian Wars 1865–1890 Volume 1: The Struggle for Apacheria* (Stackpole Books: Mechanicsville) 447–487 First Published 1933
Davis, B.	1976	*The Truth About Geronimo* (University of Nebraska Press: London) First published by Yale University Press 1929

Davis, B.	2001	"The Difficulties of Indian Warfare" in Cozzens, *Eyewitnesses to the Indian Wars 1865–1890 Volume 1: The Struggle for Apacheria* (Stackpole Books: Mechanicsville) 488–494 First Published 1885
Debo, A.	1993	*Geronimo: The Man, His Time, His Place* (Pimlico: London)
Deverell, W.	1996	'Fighting Words: The Significance of the American West in the History of the United States', in C.A. Milner, *A New Significance: Re-Envisioning the History of the American West* (Oxford University Press: Oxford), pp.29–55
Discussion Forum II,	1968	'Discussions Part II', in R.B. Lee & I. DeVore, *Man the Hunter* (Chicago Aldine Publishing: Chicago)
Dixon, D.	1994	*Hero of Beecher Island: The Life and Military Career of George A. Forsyth* (University of Nebraska Press: London)
Dobak, W.A. & Phillips, T.D.	2001	*The Black Regulars 1866–1898* (The University of Oklahoma Press: Norman)
Downey, F. & Jacobson, J.N.	1973	*The Red-Bluecoats: The Indian Scouts* (Old Army Press: Fort Collins)
Driver, H.E.	1961	*Indians of North America* (The University of Chicago Press: London)
Dunlay, T.W.	1982	*Wolves for the Blue Soldiers* (University of Nebraska Press: London)
Dunn, J.P.	1958	*Massacres of the Mountains: A History of the Indian Wars of the Far West 1815–1875* (Archer House: New York)
Eaton, G.O.	2001	"A String for the Bow" in Cozzens, *Eyewitnesses to the Indian Wars 1865–1890 Volume 1: The Struggle for Apacheria* (Stackpole Books: Mechanicsville) 177–181 First published in 1938
Edge, R.J.	1971	"Braves of all Colors: The Story of Isaiah Dorman Killed at the Little Big Horn" cited in J.M. Carroll (ed), *The Black Military Experience in the American West* (Liveright: New York)
Elliott, C.P.	2001	"The Geronimo Campaign of 1885–1886" in Cozzens, *Eyewitnesses to the Indian Wars 1865–1890 Volume 1: The Struggle for Apacheria* (Stackpole Books: Mechanicsville) 427–446 First Published 1910
Evans, R.K.	2001	"The Indian Question in Arizona" in Cozzens, *Eyewitnesses to the Indian Wars 1865–1890 Volume 1: The Struggle for Apacheria* (Stackpole Books: Mechanicsville) 604–614 First Published 1886
Farrow, E.S.	2000	*Mountain Scouting: A handbook for Officers and Soldiers on the Frontiers: Foreword by Jerome A. Greene* (University of Oklahoma Press: Norman) First published by E.S. Farrow New York 1881
Faulk, O.B.	1969	*The Geronimo Campaign* (Oxford University Press: Oxford)
Faulk, O.B.	1974	*Crimson Desert: Indian Wars of the American Southwest* (Oxford University Press: New York)
Finerty, J.F.	2001	"On Campaign after Cibecue Creek" in Cozzens, *Eyewitnesses to the Indian Wars 1865–1890 Volume 1: The Struggle for Apacheria* (Stackpole Books: Mechanicsville) 236–261 First Published 1881
Fish, C. R.	1923	*American Diplomacy* (Henry Holt & Co.: New York)
Flanagan, M.	1999	*The Complete Idiot's Guide to the Old West* (Alpha Books: New York)
Flayderman, N.	1977	*Flayderman's Guide to Antique American Firearms … and their Values* (Follett Publishing Company: Chicago)
Forbes, J.D.	1994	*Apache, Navaho, and Spaniard 2nd Edition* (University of Oklahoma Press: Norman)

Foster, J.W. 1900 *A Century of American Diplomacy: Being a Brief Review of the Foreign Relations of the United States 1776–1876* (Houghton & Mifflin: Cambridge)

Fowler, A. 1996 *The Black Infantry in the West 1869–1891* (Greenwood Press: New York)

Fox *et al*, 1993 *Archaeology, History and Custer's Last Battle: The Little Big Horn Re-examined* (University of Oklahoma Press: London)

Frazer, R.W. 1965 *Forts of the West: Military Forts and Presidios and Posts commonly called Forts West of the Mississippi River to 1898* (University of Oklahoma Press: Norman)

Fuller, W.D. 2005 "Hunting with Apaches" in Cozzens, *Eyewitnesses to the Indian Wars 1865–1890 Volume V: The Army and the Indian* (Stackpole Books: Mechanicsville) 465–468 First published in 1872

Genung, C.B. 2001 "Indians and Indigo" in Cozzens, *Eyewitnesses to the Indian Wars 1865–1890 Volume 1: The Struggle for Apacheria* (Stackpole Books: Mechanicsville) 71–84 First published in 1911

Gibson, M. 1974 *The American Indian: From Colonial Times to the Present.* (Wayland Publishers: London)

Gillett, J.B. 1976 *Six Years with the Texas Rangers 1875 to 1881* (University of Nebraska Press: London) First published by Yale University Press 1925; Gillett copyright taken out in 1921

Glass, E. 1971 "Early Field Service" cited in J.M. Carroll (ed), *The Black Military Experience in the American West* (Liveright: New York)

Goodwin, G. 1998 *Western Apache Raiding and Warfare* (The University of Arizona Press: Tuscon)

Grant, A. 1994 *The American Political Process 5th Ed.* (Dartmouth: Aldershot)

Griggs, G. 1974 *History of the Old West* (Bronson Printing Co,: Las Cruces N.M.)

Griffen, W.B. 1988 *Apaches at War and Peace: The Janos Presidio, 1750–1858* (University of Oklahoma Press: Norman)

Haley, J.E. 1952 *Fort Concho and the Texas Frontier* (San Angelo Standard-Times: San Angelo, Texas)

Haley, J.L. 1981 *Apaches: A History and Culture Portrait* (University of Oklahoma Press: Norman)

Harris, T.D. (Ed.) 1997 Black Frontiersman: The Memoirs of Henry O. Flipper. (Texas Christian University Press: Fort Worth, Texas)

Hatfield, S.B. 1999 *Chasing Shadows: Apache and Yaquis Along the United States-Mexico Border, 1876–1911* (University of New Mexico Press: Albuquerque)

Hay, C. 1995 'Structure and Agency' in D. Marsh & G. Stoker, *Theory and Methods in Political Science* (MacMillan: Basingstoke)

Healy, D. 1978 "Imperialism" in De Conde (Ed), *Encyclopedia of American Foreign Policy: Studies of the Principal Movements and Ideas Volume II*, (Charles Scribners Sons: New York) pp.409–416

Heitman, F.B. 1903 *Historical Register and Dictionary of the United States Army 1789–1903* (Government Printing Office: Washington D.C.)

Hill, E.E. 1979 "John Q. Smith 1875–1877" in Kvasnicka, & Viola (Eds) *The Commissioners of Indian Affairs, 1824–1977* (University of Nebraska Press: London)

Hook, J.	1987	*The Apaches* (Osprey Publishing: London)
Hughes, F.G.	2001	"The Military and Cochise" in Cozzens, *Eyewitnesses to the Indian Wars 1865–1890 Volume 1: The Struggle for Apacheria* (Stackpole Books: Mechanicsville) 132–137 First Published in 1886
Humphries, K.	1988	*Apache Land From Those Who Lived It* (The Printing Corner: El Paso Texas)
Hyde, A.F. & Deverell, W.	1996	'Reintroducing a Re-envisioned West', in C.A. Milner, *A New Significance: Re-Envisioning the History of the American West* (Oxford University Press: Oxford), pp.300–305
Jennings, F.	1988	*Empire of Fortune: Crowns, Colonies, and Tribes in the Seven Years War in America* (WW Norton & Company: London)
Jett, W.B.	2001	"Engagement in Guadalupe Canyon" in Cozzens, *Eyewitnesses to the Indian Wars 1865–1890 Volume 1: The Struggle for Apacheria* (Stackpole Books: Mechanicsville) 495–496 First Published in 1937
Johnson, M.	1992	*The Native Tribes of North America: A Concise Encyclopedia* (Windrow & Greene: London)
Katcher, P.	1985	*US Cavalry on the Plains 1850–90* (Osprey Publishing: London)
Katz, W.L.	1996	*The Black West: A documentary and Pictorial History of the African American Role in the Westwards Expansion of the United States* (Simon & Schuster: London)
Kavanagh, T.W.	1996	*The Comanches: A History 1706–1875* (University of Nebraska Press: London)
Keenan, J.	1997	*Encyclopedia of American Indian Wars 1492–1890* (ABC-CLIO: Oxford)
Kemble, E.C.	2001	"Victorio and His Young Men" in Cozzens, *Eyewitnesses to the Indian Wars 1865–1890 Volume 1: The Struggle for Apacheria* (Stackpole Books: Mechanicsville) 203–210 First Published 1880
Kenner, C.L.	1999	*Buffalo Soldiers and Officers of the Ninth Cavalry 1867–1898* (The University of Oklahoma Press: Norman)
Knight, O.	1960	*Following the Indian Wars: The Story of the Newspaper Correspondents Among the Indian Campaigns* (University of Oklahoma Press: Norman)
Knight, O.	1978	*Life and Manners in the Frontier Army* (University of Oklahoma Press: Norman)
Kraft, L.	2000	*Gatewood & Geronimo* (University of New Mexico Press: Albuquerque)
Kühn, B.	2014	*Chronicles of War: Apache & Yavapai Resistance in the Southwestern United States and Northern Mexico, 1821–1937* (Arizona Historical Society: Tucson)
Latane, J.H. & Wainhouse, D.W.	1940	*A History of American Foreign Policy 2nd Edition* (Odyssey Press: New York)
Laughlin, W.S.	1968	'Hunting: An Integrating Biobehavior System and Its Evolutionary Importance', in R.B. Lee & I. DeVore, *Man the Hunter* (Chicago Aldine Publishing: Chicago)

Laumbach, K.W. 2001 *Hembrillo, An Apache Battlefield of the Victorio War: The Archaeology and History of the Hembrillo Battlefield* (Prepared for the White Sands Missile Range, New Mexico by Human Systems Research Inc)

Laumbach, K.W., Scott, D.D. & Wakeman, J. 2005 *Conline's Skirmish: An Episode of the Victorio War. Archaeological and Historical Documentation of an 1880s Skirmish Site on White Sands Missile Range.* (Prepared for The Directorate of Public Works, White Sands Missile Range, New Mexico by Human Systems Research Inc.)

Le Carré, J. 2006 *Smiley's People* – Sceptre Edition (Hodder & Stoughton: London)

Leckie, W.H. 1967 *The Buffalo Soldiers: A Narrative of the Negro Cavalry in the West* (University of Oklahoma Press: Norman)

Leckie, S.A. (Editor) 1989 *The Colonel's Lady on the Western Frontier: The correspondence of Alice Kirk Grierson.* (University of Nebraska Press: London)

Leckie, W.H. & Leckie, S.A. 1984 *Unlikely Warriors: General Benjamin Grierson and His Family* (University of Oklahoma Press: Norman)

Leckie, W.H. & Leckie, S.A. 2003 *The Buffalo Soldiers: A Narrative of the Black Cavalry in the West – Revised Edition* (University of Oklahoma Press: Norman)

Lee, R.B. 1968 'What Hunters Do for a Living or, How to Make Out on Scarce Resources', in R.B. Lee & I. DeVore, *Man the Hunter* (Chicago Aldine Publishing)

Lee, R.B. & DeVore, I. 1968 Problems in the Study of Hunters and Gatherers', in R.B. Lee & I. DeVore, *Man the Hunter* (Aldine Publishing: Chicago)

Leftwich, A 1983 *Redefining Politics; People Resources and Power* (Methuen: London)

Leftwich, A 1984 *What is Politics? The Activity and its Study* (Blackwell: Oxford)

Leftwich, A 2004 *What is Politics? The Activity and its Study* (Polity: Cambridge)

Lekson, S.H. 1987 *Nana's Raid: Apache Warfare in Southern New Mexico 1881* (Southwestern Studies No 81; University of Texas at El Paso: El Paso Texas)

Lewis, J.E. 1996 *The West* (Siena: Bristol)

Lloyd, F. 2001 "A Profile of the San Carlos Agency" in Cozzens, *Eyewitnesses to the Indian Wars 1865–1890 Volume 1: The Struggle for Apacheria* (Stackpole Books: Mechanicsville) 324–331 Letter written Feb 10th 1883

Lockwood, F.C. 1987 *The Apache Indians* (University of Nebraska Press: London) First published by MacMillan New York 1938

Longstreet, S. 1970 *War Cries on Horseback: The History of the Indian Wars* (Sphere: London)

Loring, L.Y. 2001 "Report on [the] Coyotero Apaches" in Cozzens, *Eyewitnesses to the Indian Wars 1865–1890 Volume 1: The Struggle for Apacheria* (Stackpole Books: Mechanicsville) 182–202 First Published 1875

Ludwig, L.L. & Stute, J.L. 1993 *The Battle at K-H Butte: Apache Outbreak – 1881: Arizona Territory* (Westernlore Press: Tuscon Arizona)

Lummis, C.F. 1893 *The Land of the Poco Tiempo*, (Charles Scribners Sons: New York)

Mails, T.E. 1974 *The People Called Apache* (BDD Illustrated Books: New York)

Maus, M.P.	2001	"Chasing Geronimo through the Sierra Madre" in Carmony, N.B. & Brown, D.E. (Eds) *Tough Times in Rough Places: Personal Narratives of Adventure, Death and Survival on the Western Frontier* (The University of Utah Press: Salt Lake City) 237–252 First Published 1896
McAnulla, S.	2002	'Structure and Agency' in D. Marsh & G. Stoker, *Theory and Methods in Political Science* 2nd Edition (Palgrave MacMillan: Basingstoke)
McChristian, D.C.	1995	*The US Army in the West, 1870–1880: Uniforms, Weapons, and Equipment* (University of Oklahoma Press: Norman)
McCracken, H.(Editor)	1960	*Frederic Remington's Own West: Written and Illustrated by Frederic Remington* (The Dial Press: New York)
McKenna, J.A.	1963	*Black Range Tales Chronicling Sixty Years of Life and Adventure in the Southwest* (Rio Grande Press: Chicago)
Merritt, W.	2001	"Incidents of Indian Campaigning in Arizona" in Cozzens, *Eyewitnesses to the Indian Wars 1865–1890 Volume 1: The Struggle for Apacheria* (Stackpole Books: Mechanicsville) 155–161 First published 1890
Miles, N.A.	2001	"On the Trail of Geronimo" in Cozzens, *Eyewitnesses to the Indian Wars 1865–1890 Volume 1: The Struggle for Apacheria* (Stackpole Books: Mechanicsville) 536–539 First Published in 1911
Miller, L.(Ed)	1995	*From the Heart: Voices of the American Indian* (Pimlico: London)
Moore, W.H.	1994	*Chiefs, Agents & Soldiers: Conflict on the Navajo Frontier 1868–1882* (University of New Mexico Press: Albuquerque)
Morrison, K.	2006	*Marx, Durkheim and Weber 2nd Edition* (SAGE:London))
Neifert, W.W.	2001	"Trailing Geronimo by Heliograph" in Cozzens, *Eyewitnesses to the Indian Wars 1865–1890 Volume 1: The Struggle for Apacheria* (Stackpole Books: Mechanicsville) 557–561 First Published 1935
Nickerson, A.H.	2001	"An Apache Raid, and a Long Distance Ride" in Cozzens, *Eyewitnesses to the Indian Wars 1865–1890 Volume 1: The Struggle for Apacheria* (Stackpole Books: Mechanicsville) 107–112 First Published in 1897
Nisbet, R.A.	1966	*The Sociological Tradition* (Heinemann: London)
O'Neal, W.	1991	*Fighting Men of the Indian Wars: A Biographical Encyclopedia of the Mountain Men, Soldiers, Cowboys and Pioneers Who Took Up Arms During America's Westward Expansion.* (Barbed Wire Press: Stillwater Oklahoma)
Ogle, R.H.	1970	*Federal Control of the Western Apaches 1848–1886* (University of New Mexico Press: Albuquerque)
Opler, M.E.	1969	*Apache Odyssey: A Journey between Two Worlds* (Holt, Rinehart and Wilson: London)
Opler, M.E.	1994	*Myths and Legends of the Chiricahua Apache Indians* (University of Nebraska Press: Lincoln) First published by the American Folk-Lore Society 1942
Opler, M.E.	1996	*An Apache Life-Way: The Economic, Social, & Religious Institutions of the Chiricahua Indians* (University of Nebraska Press: Lincoln) First published by the University of Chicago Press 1941

Panzeri, P. 1995 *The Little Big Horn 1876: Custer's Last Stand* (Campaign series No. 39; Osprey: London)

Parker, J. 1929 *The Old Army Memories 1872–1918* (Dorrance & Co: Philadelphia)

Parkman, F. 1908 *The Conspiracy of Pontiac and the Indian War after the Conquest of Canada Vol. II* (JM Dent & Sons: London)

Pegler, M. 1993 *US Cavalryman 1965–1890* (Warrior Series 4; Osprey: London)

Pettit, J.S. 2001 "Apache Campaign Notes–1886" in Cozzens, *Eyewitnesses to the Indian Wars 1865–1890 Volume 1: The Struggle for Apacheria* (Stackpole Books: Mechanicsville) 532–535 First Published 1886

Pletcher, D.M. 1978 "Manifest Destiny" in De Conde (Ed), *Encyclopedia of American Foreign Policy: Studies of the Principal Movements and Ideas Volume II*, (Charles Scribners Sons: New York) 526–534

Rakocy, W. & Jones, R.S. (Editors) 1977 *Mogollon Diary 1877–1977* (Rio Bravo Press)

Rakocy, W. 1983 *Ghosts of Kingston Hillsboro N. Mex. A Pictorial Documentary of the Great Black Range Country ca. 1880's* (Bravo Press: El Paso)

Randall, A.F. 2001 "In the Heart of the Sierra Madre" in Cozzens, *Eyewitnesses to the Indian Wars 1865–1890 Volume 1: The Struggle for Apacheria* (Stackpole Books: Mechanicsville) 394–395 First Published 1883

Rathbun, D.C. & Alexander, D.V. 2003 *New Mexico Frontier Military Place Names* (Yucca Tree Press: Las Cruces)

Reedstrom, E.L. 1990 *Apache Wars: An Illustrated Battle History* (Sterling Publishing Co.: New York)

Rickey, D. 1963 *Forty Miles a Day on Beans and Hay: The Enlisted Soldier Fighting the Indian Wars* (University of Oklahoma Press: Norman)

Rice, M.M. 2001 "Across Apache Land" in Cozzens, *Eyewitnesses to the Indian Wars 1865–1890 Volume 1: The Struggle for Apacheria* (Stackpole Books: Mechanicsville) 502–508 First Published 1895

Ridley, J. 1993 *Maximilian and Juarez* (Constable: London)

Rister, C.C. 1928 *The Southwestern Frontier* (Arthur Clark Company: Cleveland)

Roberts, D. 1998 *Once They Moved Like The Wind: Cochise, Geronimo and the Apache Wars* (Pimlico: London)

Robinson III, C.M. 2001 *General Crook and the Western Frontier* (The University of Oklahoma Press: Norman)

Robinson, S. 2000 *Apache Voices: Their Stories of Survival as Told to Eve Ball* (University of New Mexico Press: Albuquerque)

Rostow, E.V. 1993 *A Breakfast for Bonaparte: US National Security Interests from the Heights of Abraham to the Nuclear Age* (National Defense University Press: Washington D.C.)

Ruhlen, G. 1971 "Quitman: The Worst Post at Which I Served" cited in J.M. Carroll (ed), *The Black Military Experience in the American West* (Liveright: New York)

Russell, S. 1986 "The Social Construction of Artefacts: A Response to Pinch and Bijker" *Social Studies of Science* Vol. 16, SAGE, London, 331–46

Sanchez, R. 2000 *Cochise Remembers: A Story of Discovery and Reconciliation in New Mexico Genealogy and Family History* (R&R: San Diego)

Safford, A.P.K.	2002	"Something About Cochise" in Cozzens, *Eyewitnesses to the Indian Wars 1865–1890 Volume 1: The Struggle for Apacheria* (Stackpole Books: Mechanicsville) 124–131 First published 1872
Scott *et al*	1989	*Archaeological Perspectives on the Battle of the Little Bighorn* (University of Oklahoma Press: London)
Scott *et al*	1998	*They Died With Custer: Soldiers Bones from the Battle of the Little Bighorn* (University of Oklahoma Press: Norman)
Schubert, F.N.	1995	*On the Trail of the Buffalo Soldier: Biographies of African Americans in the U.S. Army 1866–1917* (Scholarly Resources: Wilmington, Delaware)
Schubert, F.N.	1997	*Black Valor: Buffalo Soldiers and the Medal of Honor, 1870–1898* (Scholarly Resources: Wilmington, Delaware)
Schubert, F.N.	2003	*Voices of the Buffalo Soldier: Records, Reports, and Recollections of Military Life and Service in the West* (University of New Mexico Press: Albuquerque)
Shaffer, D.R.	1999	*Developmental Psychology: Childhood & Adolescence 5th Edition* (Brooks Cole Publishing Co: London)
Shipp, W.E.	2001	"Captain Crawford's Last Expedition" in Cozzens, *Eyewitnesses to the Indian Wars 1865–1890 Volume 1: The Struggle for Apacheria* (Stackpole Books: Mechanicsville) 516–531 First Published in 1892
Sieber, A.	2001	"Military and Indians" in Cozzens, *Eyewitnesses to the Indian Wars 1865–1890 Volume 1: The Struggle for Apacheria* (Stackpole Books: Mechanicsville) 290–294 First Published 1882
Skogen, L.C.	1996	*Indian Depredation Claims 1796–1920* (University of Oklahoma Press: London)
Smith, S.L.	1990	*The View from Officer's Row: Army Perceptions of Western Indians* (University of Arizona Press: Tuscon)
Smith, T.T. (Editor)	1994	*A Dose of Frontier Soldiering: The Memoirs of Corporal E.A. Bode, Frontier Regular Infantry, 1877–1882* (University of Nebraska Press: Lincoln)
Sonnichsen, C.L.	1973	*The Mescalero Apaches 2nd Edition* (University of Oklahoma Press: London)
Spicer, E.R.	1962	*Cycles of Conquest: The Impact of Spain, Mexico, and the United States on the Indians of the Southwest, 1533–1960* (The University of Arizona Press: Tuscon)
Spude, R.L.	1992	"Native Americans and Gold Rushes. Two Views: 1860s Arizona and the Apache, 1900s Alaska and the Eskimo" in K. Tenfelde, in *Towards a Social History of Mining in the 19th and 20th Centuries: Papers Presented to the International Mining History Congress Bochum, Federal Republic of Germany, September, 3rd–7th 1989 (Verlag C.H. Beck: Munchen)*
Steffen, R.	1978	*The Horse Soldier 1776–1943 Volume II: The Frontier, the Mexican War, the Civil War, the Indian Wars 1851–1880* (University of Oklahoma Press; London)
Stockel, H.H.	1991	*Women of the Apache Nation: Voices of Truth* (University of Nevada Press: Reno & Las Vegas)

Stockel, H.H. 2004 *On the Bloody Road to Jesus: Christianity and the Chiricahua Apaches* (University of New Mexico Press: Albuquerque)

Stout, J.A. 1974 *Apache Lightning: The Last Great Battles of the Ojo Calientes* (University of Oxford Press: New York)

Sweeney, E.R. 1991 *Cochise: Chiricahua Apache Chief* (University of Oklahoma Press: Norman)

Sweeney, E.R. 1992 *Merejildo Grijalva: Apache Captive, Army Scout* (The University of Texas at El Paso: Southwestern Studies Series No 96, El Paso

Sweeney, E.R. (Editor) 1997 *Making Peace with Cochise: The 1872 Journal of Captain Joseph Alton Sladen* (University of Oklahoma Press: Norman)

Sweeney, E.R. 1998 *Mangas Coloradas: Chief of the Chiricahua Apaches* (University of Oklahoma Press: Norman)

Sweeney, E.R. 2010 *From Cochise to Geronimo: The Chiricahua Apaches 1874–1886* (University of Oklahoma Press: Norman)

Tate, M.L. 1999 *The Frontier Army in the Settlement of the West* (Oklahoma University Press: Norman)

Thompson, E.N. 1971 "The Negro Soldier and His Officers" cited in J.M. Carroll (ed), *The Black Military Experience in the American West* (Liveright: New York)

Thompson, C. 1985 *History of Marfa and Presidio County, Texas 1535–1946. Volume One, 1535–1900* (Nortex Press: Austin)

Thrapp. D.L. 1964 *Al Sieber Chief of Scouts* (University of Oklahoma Press: London)

Thrapp, D.L. 1967 *The Conquest of Apacheria* (University of Oklahoma Press: London)

Thrapp, D.L. 1972 *General Crook and the Sierra Madre Adventure* (University of Oklahoma Press: London)

Thrapp, D.L. 1973 *Juh: An Incredible Indian* (South-western Studies No 39 University of Texas at El Paso: El Paso Texas)

Thrapp, D.L. 1974 *Victorio and the Mimbres Apaches* (University of Oklahoma Press: London)

Thrapp, D.L (Editor). 1979 *Dateline Fort Bowie: Charles Fletcher Lummis Reports on an Apache War* (University of Oklahoma Press: Norman)

Thrapp, D.L. 1988 *Encyclopedia of Frontier Biography Vol I-III* (University of Nebraska Press in association with The Arthur H. Clark Company: London & Spokane)

Tripodi, C. 2011 *Edge of Empire: The British Political Officer and Tribal Administration on the North-West Frontier 1877–1947* (Routledge: Oxford)

Turney-High, H.H. 1991 *Primitive War: Its Practice and Concepts* (The University of South Carolina Press: Columbia)

Twitchell, R.E. 1963 *The Leading Facts of New Mexican History* (Horn & Wallace: Albuquerque)

Upham, F.K. 2001 "Incidents of Regular Army Life in Time of Peace" in Cozzens, *Eyewitnesses to the Indian Wars 1865–1890 Volume 1: The Struggle for Apacheria* (Stackpole Books: Mechanicsville) 85–93 First Published 1885

Utley, R.M. 1963 *The Last Days of the Sioux Nation* (Yale University Press: New Haven)

Utley, R.M.	1967	*Frontiersmen in Blue: The United States Army and the Indian, 1848–1865* (University of Nebraska Press: London)
Utley, R.M.	1973	*Frontier Regulars: The United States Army and the Indian, 1866–1891* (University of Nebraska Press: London)
Utley, R.M.	1977	*A Clash of Cultures: Fort Bowie and the Chiricahua Apaches* (National Park Service: Washington D.C.)
Utley, R.M.	1984 (i)	*The Indian Frontier of the American West 1846–1890* (University of New Mexico Press: Albuquerque)
Van Alstyne, R.W.	1978	"The Monroe Doctrine" in De Conde (Ed), *Encyclopedia of American Foreign Policy: Studies of the Principal Movements and Ideas Volume II*, (Charles Scribners Sons: New York) 584–596
Van Orden, J.	1991	*Geronimo's Surrender: The 1886 C.S. Fly Photographs* (Arizona Historical Society: Tuscon)
Wakeman, J. & Laumbach, K.	1999	'Victorio's Escape: GPS and Archaeology Recount the Tale of an Apache Battle' in K.L. Feder, *Lessons from the Past: An Introductory Reader in Archaeology* (Mayfield Publishing Company: London)
Watson, J.W.	2001	"Scouting in Arizona, 1890" in Cozzens, *Eyewitnesses to the Indian Wars 1865–1890 Volume 1: The Struggle for Apacheria* (Stackpole Books: Mechanicsville) 642–648 First Published 1897
Watson, J.W.	1976	*Chronological List of Engagements between the Regular Army of the United States and various tribes of Hostile Indians which occurred during the years1790–1898 inclusive* (AMS Press: New York)
Watt R.N.	2012	*Apache Tactics 1830–1886* (Osprey Publishing: Oxford)
Watt R.N.	2014	*Apache Warrior 1860–1886* (Osprey Publishing: Oxford)
Wellman, P. I.	(No date)	*Death in the Desert* (W. Foulsham & Co for the Fireside Press: London)
Wellman, P. I.	1957	*Death in the Desert* (Transworld Publishers:London)
Wharfield, Col. H.B.	1971	"The Tenth Cavalry in the Early Days" cited in J.M. Carroll (ed), *The Black Military Experience in the American West* (Liveright: New York)
Wheeler, K.	1978	*The Old West: The Scouts* (Time-Life Books: Alexandria Virginia)
White, J.M.	1979	*Everyday Life of the North American Indian* (Book Club Associates: London)
White, R.	1991	*"It's Your Misfortune and None of My Own": A New History of the American West* (University of Oklahoma Press: London)
Woodburn, J.	1968	'An Introduction to Hadza Ecology', in R.B. Lee & I. DeVore, *Man the Hunter* (Chicago Aldine Publishing: Chicago)
Wooster, R.	1988	*The Military and United States Indian Policy 1865–1903* (Yale University Press: London)
Worcester, D.E.	1979	*The Apaches: Eagles of the Southwest* (University of Oklahoma Press: Norman)
Wormser R.	1966	*The Yellowlegs: The Story of the United States Cavalry* (Doubleday: New York)
Wright, H.R.	2001	"In the Days of Geronimo" in Cozzens, *Eyewitnesses to the Indian Wars 1865–1890 Volume 1: The Struggle for Apacheria* (Stackpole Books: Mechanicsville) 497–501 First Published 1905

Wyatt, C.M. 2011 *Afghanistan and the Defence of Empire: Diplomacy and Strategy during The Great Game* (I.B.Taurus: London)

Journals

The *Army & Navy Journal* – Vols. 16–18 (August 1879 – July 1882)

Journal Articles

Aceves, J. "Who was Victorio? By Don Jesus Tarin as told to Jose Aceves" *Frontier Times* (September 1963), 24–25 & 71

Aranda, D.D. "An Episode From Victorio's War," *Real West* (February 1984), 14–19

Aranda, D.D. "Apache Depredations in Dona Ana County: An Incident in Victorio's War," *Southern New Mexico Historical Journal* Vol. 3, 1995, Issue 1, 2–8

Aranda, D.D. 'My Search for Victorio' [unpublished article]

Ayres, J. "A Soldier's Experience in New Mexico," *New Mexico Historical Review*, Vol. XXIV, No. 4 (October, 1949), 259–66

Ball, L.D. "Militia Posses: The Territorial Militia in Civil Law Enforcement in New Mexico Territory, 1877–1883," *New Mexico Historical Review*, Vol 55, No. 1 (January, 1980), 47–69

Ball, Eve. "The Fight for Ojo Caliente," *Frontier Times*, Vol. XXXVI, No. 2 (Spring, 1962), 22–23, 40

Balmer, J.W. "It was only 75 Years Ago" *The English Westerners Brand Book* Vol. 3, No. 1 (November 1956) 1–7

Baylor, G.W. "The Old Frontier; Events of Long Ago" *Frontier Times* Vol. 2, No.11, (August 1925), 12–13

Bernstein, J.H. "Secrets of Los Ladrones: Mysteries Shroud remote Rio Grande Valley Range," *New Mexico Magazine* Vol. 72, No 7 (July 1994), 72–79

Billington, M. "Black History and New Mexico Place Names," *Password* Vol. XXIX, No. 3 (Fall, 1984), 107–113

Bond, H.M. "The Negro in the Armed Forces of the United States Prior to World War I," *Journal of Negro Education*, Vol. 12, Issue 3, (Summer 1943), 268–287

Boucher, L.H. "Fort Cummings, Desert Sentinel,"*Real West*, Vol. XIII, No. 81 (April, 1970), 6, 44–47

Brumwell. S. "A Service Truly Critical: The British Army and Warfare with the North American Indians, 1755–1764" *War in History*, Vol. 5, No 2 (1998) 146–75

Clum, J.P. "Geronimo," *New Mexico Historical Review,* Vol. III, Nos. 1,2,3 (January, April, July 1928), 1–40, 121–44, 217–64.

Clum, J.P. "The Apaches," *New Mexico Historical Review,* Vol. IV, No. 2 (April, 1929i), 109–127

Clum, J.P. "The San Carlos Police," *New Mexico Historical Review*, Vol. IV, No. 3 (July, 1929ii), 203–219

Clum, J.P. "Apache Misrule," *New Mexico Historical Review,* Vol. V, Nos. 2 & 3 (April, July 1930i), 138–153, 221–239

Clum, J.P. "Victorio," *Arizona Historical Review*, Vol II, No. 4 (January, 1930ii), 74–90

Crimmins, Col. M.L.	"Colonel Buell's Expedition into Mexico in 1880," *New Mexico Historical Review*, Vol. X, No. 2 (April 1935), 133–142
Crimmins, Col. M.L.	"The Mescalero Apaches" *Frontier Times* Vol. 8, No.12, (September 1931), p.551
Cutter, D.C.	"The Legacy of the Treaty of Guadalupe Hidalgo," *New Mexico Historical Review*, Vol. 53, No. 4 (October, 1978), 305–315
Dinges, B.J.	"The Victorio Campaign of 1880: Cooperation and Conflict on the United States – Mexico Border," *New Mexico Historical Review*, Vol. 62 No. 1, (Jan 1987), 81–94
Dinges, B.J.	"Leighton Finley: A Forgotten Soldier of the Apache Wars" *The Journal of Arizona History*, Vol. 29, No.2, (Summer 1988), 163–184
Elliott, C.P.	"An Indian Reservation Under General George Crook," *Military Affairs*, Vol. 12, Issue 2 (Summer 1948), 91–102
Ellis, R.N. (Ed)	"The Apache Chronicle," *New Mexico Historical Review*, Vol. XLVII, No. 3 (July, 1972), 275–282
Gatewood, C.B.	"Campaigning Against Victorio in 1879," *The Great Divide*, (April, 1894), 102–104
Gibson, S.	'From the Archives: Sarah Gibson's Story' *Hillsboro Historical Society*, February 2016, Vol. 9, Number 1, 4–7 Richard E. Mitchem of Cedar City, Utah sent the story below to Sonja. We've seen several accounts of the 1879 Apache attack on McEver's Ranch, but this is the only first-hand description we've seen, told by one of the women who was living at the cienega, when the attack occurred. Mr. Mitchem received this manuscript from Judith Crawford of Deming, NM.
Gillett, J.B.	"Injun Fighting With The Texas Rangers" *Frontier Times* Vol. 3, No. 9, (June 1926)
Greever, W.S.	"Railway Development in the Southwest," *New Mexico Historical Review*, Vol. XXXII, No. 2 (April, 1957), 151–203
Hall, M.H.	"Colonel James Reily's Diplomatic Missions to Chihuahua and Sonora," *New Mexico Historical Review*, Vol. XXXI, No. 3 (July, 1956), 232–242
Harnin, W.	"Apache Siege at Alma" *True West* (June 1956) 8–10 & 30
Hart, R.L.	"Colonel Hatch and the Territorial Press during the Victorio War" *Southern New Mexico Historical Review* Vol. VI, No. 1, (January 1997) 44–49
Hastings, J.K.	"A Boy's-Eye View of the Old Southwest," *New Mexico Historical Review*, Vol. XXVI, No. 4 (October 1951), 287–301.
Hunter, J.M.	"The Fierce Apache Indians" *Frontier Times* Vol. 21, No. 7, (April 1944), p.299
Janda, Lance.	"Shutting the Gates of Mercy: The American Origins of Total War, 1860–1880" *The Journal of Military History*, Vol. 59, Issue 1 (Jan 1995), 7–26
Johnson, B.C.	"The Death of Victorio: Beck's Account" *The English Westerners Brand Book* Vol. 3, No. 9, (July 1957) 9–11
Jones, Calico.	"Nana: The Vengeful Ghost of the Apaches" *Western Digest* (November 1969), 52–61 & 74–81
Jones, Calico.	"Victorio's Vengeance Raid," *Real West*, Vol. XIII, No. 81 (April, 1970), 31–35,55,77
Jones, O.L.	"Lew Wallace: Hoosier Governor of Territorial New Mexico, 1878–81" *New Mexico Historical Review*, Vol. 60, (April, 1985), 129–158

Kayser, D. "The Southern Apache Agency" *El Palacio* Vol. 79, No. 2, (1973i), 16–23

Kayser, D. "Fort Tulerosa: 1872–1874" *El Palacio* Vol. 79, No. 2, (1973ii), 24–27

Kaywaykla, J., as told to Eve Ball. "I survived the Massacre of Tres Castillos," *True West*, Vol VIII, No. 6 (July-August, 1961), 22–23, 38.

Kaywaykla, J., as told to Eve Ball. "Nana's People," *True West*, Vol X No. 6 (July-August, 1963), 20–21, 66–67.

Leonard, T.C. "Red, White and the Army Blue: Empathy and Anger in the American West," *American Quarterly*, Vol. 26, Issue 2 (May 1974), 176–190

Matthews, J. "Squarely Fought: Fort Concho and the Campaign against Victorio, 1880," *West Texas Historical Association Year Book*, Vol. 69, (1993), 34–44

McChristian, D.D. "Grierson's Fight at Tinaja de las Palmas: An Episode in the Victoria (sic) Campaign," *Red River Valley Historical Review*, Vol. 7, (Winter 1982), pp.45–63

Meyer, D.L. "Early Mexican-American Responses to Negative Stereotyping," *New Mexico Historical Review*, Vol. LIII, No. 1 (January, 1978), 75–91

Miles, Bob. "Nine Against a Hundred" *Old West* (Fall 1971), p.20

Miles, N.A, "How U.S. Troops Caught Geronimo" *Frontier Times* Vol. 9 (February 1932), 193–196

Miller, H. "Nana's Raid of 1881," *Password,* Vol. XIX, No 2 (Summer 1974), 51–70

Miller, D.A. "The Role of the Army Inspector in the Southwest: Nelson H. Davis in New Mexico and Arizona, 1863–1873" *New Mexico Historical Review* Vol. 59, No. 2 (April 1984), 137–164

Myers, L. "Fort Webster on the Mimbres River," *New Mexico Historical Review*, Vol. XLI, No. 1 (January, 1966i), 47–57.

Myers, L. "The Enigma of Mangas Coloradas' Death," *New Mexico Historical Review*, Vol. XLI, No. 4 (October, 1966ii), 287–304

Myers, L. "Military Establishments in Southwestern New Mexico: Stepping Stones to Settlement," *New Mexico Historical Review*, Vol. XLIII, No. 1 (January, 1968), 5–48.

Nolan, F. "Van C. Smith:'A Very Companionable Gentleman'" *New Mexico Historical Review* Vol. 72, No. 2 (April 1997), 153–170

Nolan, F. "The Men of Fort Stanton," *Quarterly of the National Association for Outlaw and Lawman History*, Vol. 18 (Oct 1994), 37–45

Nolan, P.T. "Captain Jack Crawford: Veteran and Western Hero," *Real West*, Vol. XIII, No. 81 (April, 1970), 19–22 & 63

Norton, H.S. "Kaytennae and the End of the Apache Wars" *True West* (June 1988), p.14

O'Neal, B. "Captain Henry Carroll: Southwestern Indian Fighter" *Real West* (June 1982), p.55

Ogle, Ralph H. "The Apache and the Government – 1870's," *New Mexico Historical Review*, Vol. XXXIII, No. 2 (April, 1958), 81–102

Opler, M.E. "A Chiricahua Apache's Account of the Geronimo Campaign of 1886," *New Mexico Historical Review*, Vol. XIII, No. 4 (October, 1938), 360–386.

Opler, M.E. & Hoijer, H. "The Raid and War-Path Language of the Chiricahua Apache," *American Anthropologist* Vol. XLII, (Oct-Dec 1940), 617–34

Opler, M.E. & C.H. Opler. "Mescalero Apache History in the Southwest," *New Mexico Historical Review*, Vol. XXV, (January, 1950), 1–36

Porter, K.W. "Contacts in Warfare" *Journal of Negro History* Vol. 17, Issue 3, (July 1932), 298–306

Porter, K.W. "Notes Supplementary to 'Relations between Negroes and Indians" *Journal of Negro History* Vol. 18, Issue 3, (July 1933), 282–321

Porter, K.W. "Negroes and Indians on the Texas Frontier, 1831–1876," *Journal of Negro History* Vol. 41, Issue 3 (Jul., 1956i), 185–214

Porter, K.W. "Negroes and Indians on the Texas Frontier, 1831–1876," *Journal of Negro History* Vol. 41, Issue 4 (Oct., 1956ii), 285–310

Powers, N.B. "A Ride From Geronimo, The Apache," *New Mexico Historical Review*, Vol. XXXVI, No. 2 (April, 1961), 89–96

Radbourne, A. "Capturing The Apaches: The Photographs of A. Frank Randall." *Wild West*, (February, 2004), 74

Rasch, P.J. "The Death of Victorio" *The English Westerners Brand Book* Vol. 11, No. 3, (April 1960), 9–10

Reddick, L.D. "The Negro Policy of the United States Army, 1775–1945" *Journal of Negro History* Vol. 34, Issue 1, (Jan 1949), 9–29

Reeve, F.D. "The Federal Indian Policy in New Mexico, 1858–1880," *New Mexico Historical Review*, Vol. XII No 3 (July 1937), 218–269 & Vol. XIII Nos.1,2,3 (January April and July 1938) 14–62, 146–191, 261–313

Remington, F. "A Scout with the Buffalo Soldiers" *The Century Illustrated Monthly Magazine* New Series Vol. XV, (November 1888-April 1889), 899–912

Rolley, LaNelda "Buffalo Soldiers Ride Again: Belated Recognition extended to Black Regiments" *New Mexico Magazine* Vol. 72, No. 7, (July 1994), 26–31

Rosson, M. "The Pursuit of Victorio", *Real West* March 1980, p.26 repeated in *Real West* Special Issue 1981 p.14

Russell S. "The Social Construction of Artefacts; A Response to Pinch and Bijker" *Social Studies of Science*, (1986), 16, pp.331–346. (London: SAGE)

Sayles, S. "The Romero-Frelinghuysen Convention: A Milestone in Border Relations," *New Mexico Historical Review*, Vol. LI, No. 4 (October, 1976), 295–311

Schwatka, F. "Among the Apaches" *The Century Illustrated Monthly Magazine* New Series Vol. XII, (May 1887-October 1887), 41–52

Sharp, K. "Last Words on Victorio" *The English Westerners Brand Book* Vol. 3, No. 10, (August 1957), 11–12

Smith, R.A. "Apache Plunder Trails Southwards, 1831–1840," *New Mexico Historical Review*, Vol. XXXVII, No. 1 (January 1962), 20–42

Smith, R.A. "The Scalp Hunt in Chihuahua–1849," *New Mexico Historical Review*, Vol XL, No. 2 (April, 1965), 116–40

Sowell, A.J. "A Tragedy Of The Texas Frontier" *Frontier Times* Vol. 22, No. 10, (July 1945), 290–292

Steelhammer, C. "With the Apache Indians during the Revolt of 1879," *Military Affairs*, Vol. 18, No.2 (Summer 1954), 86–88

Tate, M.L. "John P. Clum and the Origins of an Apache Constabulary, 1874–1877" *American Indian Quarterly* Vol. 3, No.2 (Summer 1977), 99–120

Temple, F.M. "Federal Military Defense of the Trans-Pecos Region 1850–1880," *West Texas Historical Association Year Book*, Vol. 30, (1954), 40–60

Temple, F.M. "Colonel Grierson in the Southwest," *Panhandle Plains Historical Review*, Vol. 30, (1957), 27–54

Temple, F.M. "Colonel B. H. Grierson's Victorio Campaign," *West Texas Historical Association Year Book*, Vol. 35, (1959), 99–111

Temple, F.M. "Colonel B.H. Grierson's Administration of the District of the Pecos" *West Texas Historical Association Year Book* Vol. 37, (October 1962), 85–96

Utley, R.M. (1984ii) "The Buffalo Soldiers and Victorio" *New Mexico Magazine* 62: 3 (March 1984)

Wasson, J. "The Southwest in 1880," *New Mexico Historical Review*, Vol. V, No. 3 (July, 1930), 263–287

Watson. S "Military Learning and Adaptation Shaped by Social Context: The U.S. Army and Its "Indian Wars," 1790–1890" *The Journal of Military History*, Volume 82, No.2, (April 2018), 371–412

Watt, R.N. "Raiders of a Lost Art? Apache War and Society" *Small Wars & Insurgencies* Vol. 13, No. 3, (Autumn 2002), 1–28

Watt, R.N. "'Horses Worn to Mere Shadows': The Effects of Campaigning against Apaches upon the Ninth U.S. Cavalry Regiment in New Mexico Territory 1879–1881" *New Mexico Historical Review,* (Spring 2011), 197–222

Watt, R.N. "Apaches Without and Enemies Within: The U.S. Army in New Mexico 1879–1881" *War in History,* Vol. 18, Issue 2, (April 2011), 148–183

Watt, R.N. "Victorio's Military & Political Leadership of the Warm Springs Apaches" *War in History* Vol. 18, Issue 4, (November 2011), 457–494

Watt, R.N. "A Reevaluation of Colonel Benjamin H. Grierson's Trans-Pecos Campaign Against Victorio, July-August 1880." *Southwestern Historical Quarterly*, Vol. CXVIII, No.3, (January 2015), 240–261

Watt, R.N. "'An Exodus to Nowhere'?: Victorio's Tres Castillos Campaign, September-October 1880" *The Journal of Military History*, Volume 80, No.4, (October 2016), 1037–1072

White, R. "Race Relations in the American West," *American Quarterly*, Vol. 38, Issue 3 (1986), 396–416

Wilks, J. "A Negro Trooper Of The Ninth Cavalry" *Frontier Times* Vol. 4, No.7, (April 1927), p.11

Wilson, J.P. "How the Settlers Farmed: Hispanic Villages and Irrigation Systems in Early Sierra County, 1850–1900" *New Mexico Historical Review* Vol. 63, No. 4, (Oct 1988), 333–356

Woodward, A. "Side Lights on Fifty Years of Apache Warfare" *Arizoniana* Vol. 11, (Fall 1961), 3–14

Worcester, D.E. "The Beginnings of the Apache Menace of the Southwest," *New Mexico Historical Review*, Vol. XVI, No. 1 (January, 1941), 1–14

Worcester, D.E. "The Apaches in the History of the Southwest," *New Mexico Historical Review*, Vol. L, No. 1 (January, 1975), 25–44

Yarbrough, L. "Victorio, The Desert Fox" *Real West* (June 1969), 10–12, 65–66 & 69

Modern Newspaper Articles

Abarr (i), James. "Mining Memories," *Albuquerque Journal* October 18, 1998

Abarr (ii), James. "Desolate Outpost," *Albuquerque Journal* August 30, 1998

Associated Press, "1879 Battle Commemorated," *The Arizona Republic*, June 16, 1999

Digest, "Victorio's Name Cleared," *Albuquerque Journal*, July 4, 1995

El Paso Times 1 March 1942, "Apaches In Ambush Between Hillsboro, Lake Valley Killed 18 Frontiersmen, Buried In Single Grave On Spot Where They Fell"

Evening Review, The, Saturday 17 June 1882

Frentzel, Martin. "Trailing the Buffalo Soldiers," *Albuquerque Journal*, Dec 12, 1996

Jackson, David G. "Group Hikes Into History," *Albuquerque Journal*, November 16, 2000

The Los Angeles Times, "Leading the Charge: Danny Glover brings 'Buffalo Soldiers,' a Chronicle of the Famed Black Cavalry Corps to TNT," cited in the *Fort Worth Star-Telegram*, December 5, 1997

Lumpkin, John J. "Scientists Rewrite Cavalry, Apache Battle History," *Albuquerque Journal*, April 23, 1999

Neel, Ellis "Rewriting History: Buffalo Soldier Grit Backed by Evidence" Alamogordo Daily News cited in *The Denver Post* May 2, 1999.

Perez, L. "Memoir Recounts Death of Apache Chief Victorio" *Silver City Daily Press* Tuesday, June 30, 1998

Reed, Ollie Jr. "Colonel Lauded for Grave Work: Relocation Effort Leads to Prestigious Award," *The Albuquerque Tribune* cited in *The Denver Post*, June 20, 1999

Rene Romo Journal Southern Bureau, "Cavalrymen Honored Century After Battle," cited in *Albuquerque Journal*, September 14, 1996

Roberts, Chris. "Honoring Warriors," *Albuquerque Journal*, June 22, 1997.

Rocky Mountain News, "Apache Chief to be Honored: 19th Century Leader Victorio to be Inducted into Indian Hall of Fame in Oklahoma Ceremony" *Rocky Mountain News* August 18, 1991.

Saunders, Dusty. "A Wild Ride with 'Buffalo Soldiers' TNT Film Features Blacks' Encounters with Apaches and with White Military," *Rocky Mountain News*, December 7, 1997

Simmons, M. "New Mexico Scrapbook: Miners Flocked to Florida Mountains" *El Paso Times* 22nd January 1995

Sun-News. "Scientists Rewrite Cavalry, Apache Battle History" *Sun-News* Saturday, April 24, 1999

Whitney Herb. "He was a Guerrillla Fighter without Peer whose Nickname became a Battle Cry … Geronimo!," *The Arizona Republic* August 31, 1986

Internet Sites

Alma – New Mexico Ghost Town (*downloaded 24/03/2001*) http://www.ghosttowns.com/states/nm/alma.html

Ambush in Massacre Canyon: by G. Ballinger (*downloaded 17/03/99)* http://www.zianet.com/wblase/courier/ambush.htm

American Life Histories: Manuscripts from the Federal Writers' Project. 1936–1940 (*downloaded 03/03/2001* – See following entries)

Abran Miller
http://lcweb2.loc.gov/cgi-bin/query/D?wpa:41:./temp/~ammem_3Uyf::

Early Days Around Silver City

http://lcweb2.loc.gov/cgi-bin/query/D?wpa:15:./temp/~ammem_3Uyf::
Early Days In Silver City and Grant Co.
http://lcweb2.loc.gov/cgi-bin/query/D?wpa:1:./temp/~ammem_rPD9::
Incidents of the Early '80s
http://lcweb2.loc.gov/cgi-bin/query/D?wpa:4:./temp/~ammem_6794::
J.C. Brock
http://lcweb2.loc.gov/cgi-bin/query/D?wpa:14:./temp/~ammem_3Uyf::
J.F. Henderson
http://lcweb2.loc.gov/cgi-bin/query/D?wpa:39:./temp/~ammem_3Uyf::
J.H. (Jake) Byler
http://lcweb2.loc.gov/cgi-bin/query/D?wpa:44:./temp/~ammem_3Uyf::
Jose Apodaca
http://lcweb2.loc.gov/cgi-bin/query/D?wpa:17:./temp/~ammem_3Uyf::
Killing of Charlie Bachelor
http://lcweb2.loc.gov/cgi-bin/query/D?wpa:9:./temp/~ammem_3Uyf::
Louie Taren
http://lcweb2.loc.gov/cgi-bin/query/D?wpa:21:./temp/~ammem_3Uyf::
Mexican Boy Captured by Apache Indians
http://lcweb2.loc.gov/cgi-bin/query/D?wpa:3:./temp/~ammem_6794::
Mogollons of the Early Days
http://lcweb2.loc.gov/cgi-bin/query/D?wpa:1:./temp/~ammem_38gG::
Mr Eugene McCrohan
http://lcweb2.loc.gov/cgi-bin/query/D?wpa:1:./temp/~ammem_E2JH::
Mrs O.S. Warren
http://lcweb2.loc.gov/cgi-bin/query/D?wpa:18:./temp/~ammem_3Uyf::
Old Timers Dictionary
http://lcweb2.loc.gov/cgi-bin/query/D?wpa:23:./temp/~ammem_3Uyf::
The Alma Massacre
http://lcweb2.loc.gov/cgi-bin/query/D?wpa:2:./temp/~ammem_BRbY::
The Alms Massacre
http://lcweb2.loc.gov/cgi-bin/query/D?wpa:5:./temp/~ammem_6794::
Aragon – Fort Tularosa – New Mexico Ghost Town (*downloaded 12/12/2000*)
http://www.ghosttowns.com/states/nm/aragon-forttularosa.html
Benjamin H. Grierson by Chuck Barth, Tuscon Arizona (*downloaded 15/05/2001*)
http://www.cia-g.com/~rockets/NMGrierson.htm
The Buffalo Soldiers (1) (*downloaded 15/01/2000)*
http://www.zianet.com/wblase/courier/buffalo.htm
Buffalo Soldiers (2): Synopsis of TNT's Buffalo Soldiers: (*downloaded 13/09/99)*
http://turnerlearning.com/tntlearning/buffalo /entire.html
Buffalo Soldiers & Indian Wars (*downloaded 20/03/2001–05–17*)
http://www.buffalosoldier.net/index.htm
The Bulletin – Serving Las Cruces and the Mesilla Valley for Thirty Years. (*downloaded 15/01/2000)*
http://www.zianet.com/bulletin/1999/04_29_99/plaque.html
Articles:- *Plaque Commemorates 1880 Battle in San Andres* – M. Jaxson
Space Age Science Yields New View of Hembrillo Battle – J. Eckles
Cabinet Members Under Hayes (*downloaded 24/10/05*)
http://www.infoplease.com/ipa/A0101224.html
Cabinet Members Under Garfield (*downloaded 24/10/05*)
http://www.infoplease.com/ipa/A0101226.html

Cabinet Members Under Arthur (*downloaded 24/10/05*)
http://www.infoplease.com/ipa/A0101228.html
Chief Victorio (*downloaded 10/03/2001*)
http://www.kingsnake.com/hudspeth/victorio.htm
Chiz – New Mexico Ghost Town (*downloaded 12/12/2000*) http://www.ghosttowns.com/states/nm/chiz.html
Chloride, Sierra County NM (*downloaded 03/03/2001*)
http://village.globaldrum.com/sierra_newmexico/chloride.htm
Clairmont – New Mexico Ghost Town (*downloaded 24/03/2001*)
http://www.ghosttowns.com/states/nm/clairmont.html
Claridge, D. – Geronimo and Victorio – A Comparative Study (*downloaded 12/12 2000*)
http://www.zianet.com/snm/geronvic.htm
Cooney – New Mexico Ghost Town (*downloaded 12/12/2000*)
http://www.ghosttowns.com/states/nm/cooney.html
Cuchillo – New Mexico Ghost Town (*downloaded 12/12/2000*)
http://www.ghosttowns.com/states/nm/cuchillo.html
Electric Scotland.Com: Deaths which Occurred October 14th *(consulted 15/01/2000)*
http://www.electricscotland.com/history/today/1014.htm
Fort Davis Museum – Planning Outline for Rattlesnake Springs Exhibit *(downloaded 15/05/2001)*
http://turnerlearning.com/tntlearning/buffalo/davis.html
Fort Selden: New Mexico Territory–8 May 1865-April 1889 (*downloaded 15/01/2000)*
http://www.zianet.com/wblase/courier/fts.htm
General Sherman's Opinion – New Mexico History Index (*downloaded 13/12/2000*)
http://www.cia-g.com/~rockets/shermanopinion.htm
Glenwood New Mexico (Ref to approx location of the Cooney Fight of April 29th 1880) (*downloaded 06/08/99)*
http://www.zianet.com/snm/glenwood.htm

The Handbook of Texas Online:
Baylor, George Wythe (1832–1916): by T.W. Cutrer (*downloaded 13/09/99)*
http://www.tsha.utexas.edu/handbook/online/articles/view/BB/fbaar.html
Buffalo Soldiers: by M. Odintz (*downloaded 13/09/99*)
http://www.tsha.utexas.edu/handbook/online/articles/view/BB/qlbl.html
Byrne, James J: by T.W.Cutrer (*downloaded 11/07/2000*)
http://www.tsha.utexas.edu/handbook/online/articles/view/BB/fby5.html
Eagle Springs no named author (*downloaded 10/09/99)*
http://www.tsha.utexas.edu/handbook/online/articles/view/EE/rpel.html
Flipper, Henry Ossian (1856–1940): by B.J. Dinges (*downloaded 13/09/99)*
http://www.tsha.utexas.edu/handbook/online/articles/view/FF/ffl13.html
Gillett, James Buchanan (1856–1937): by M.F. Peirce (*downloaded 13/09/99)*
http://www.tsha.utexas.edu/handbook/online/articles/view/GG/fgi25.html
Grierson, Benjamin Henry (1826–1911): by B.J. Dinges (*downloaded 10/09/99)*
http://www.tsha.utexas.edu/handbook/online/articles/view/GG/fgr59.html
Rattlesnake Springs, Battle of.: by B.J. Dinges (*downloaded 10/09/99)*
http://www.tsha.utexas.edu/handbook/online/articles/view/RR/qfrpg.html
Tinaja De Las Palmas, Battle of: by D.C. McChristian (*downloaded 13/09/99)*
http://www.tsha.utexas.edu/handbook/online/articles/view/TT/qftl.html
Van Horn, Texas. by M.D. Kohout (*downloaded 11/06/2001*)
http://www.tsha.utexas.edu/handbook/online/articles/view/VV/hgv1.html

Hembrillo Battlefield (Public Affairs Office: White Sands Missile Range) (*downloaded 14/09/99)*
http://www.wsmr.army.mil/paopage/Pages/facts.htm
Hillsboro – New Mexico Ghost Town (*downloaded 12/12/2000*)
http://www.ghosttowns.com/states/nm/hillsboro.html
Hurst (1), J.W. – Kas-Tziden's Fury (Nana's Raid) (*Downloaded 12/12/2000–12–15*)
http://www.zianet.com/snm/nana.htm
Hurst (2), J.W. – Victorio and the Reservation System – A Prescription for Disaster
http://www.zianet.com/snm/victorio.htm
'Indian War Period Medals of Honour' (*downloaded 17/03/99)*
http://www.army.mil/cmh-pg/mohind.htm
Konstantin, P. – May 23rd to 31st in North American History (*downloaded 01/06/2001*)
http://members.tripod.com/~PHILICON/May4.html
Lake Valley – New Mexico Ghost Town
http://village.globaldrum.com/sierra_newmexico/lakevall.htm
Lake Valley – Sierra County NM (*downloaded 12/12/2000*)
http://www.ghosttowns.com/states/nm/lakevalley.html
Las Animas Canyon 1879–1997 by A. Apostolides (*downloaded 18/05/9)*
http://www.zianet.com/institute/LasAnim.htm
Library of Congress 'Chronicling America' website (http://chroniclingamerica.loc.gov/) First accessed July 2014.
This is a very useful site for searching old US Newspapers for articles on the Victorio Campaign. The simplest way to progress is to enter names or incidents into the search engine and take it from there … .
Map of New Mexico 1895 (*downloaded 06/08/99*)
http://fermi.jhvapl.edu/states/1895/nm_1895.jpg
Monticello or Placita – New Mexico Ghost Town. (*downloaded 12/12/2000*)
http://www.ghosttowns.com/states/nm/monticello.html
Ninth Cavalry Cemetery Dedication … site of the Battle of Las Animas in New Mexico: by K. Dusenberry, (*downloaded 14/09/99*)
http://www.coax.net/people/lwf/cem_ded.htm
The Ninth Regiment of Cavalry – Lt G. Hutcheson (Reprinted from Journal of the Military Service Institution, Vol. XVI, No 75, May 1895) *This article is also available from the US Army Center of Military History webpage* (*downloaded 14/09/99)*
http://www.coax.net/people/lwf/9thcav.htm
Perspectives: Between 1865 and 1890, 18 'buffalo soldiers' won the Medal of Honor in the American West. (*downloaded 15/05/2001*)
http://www.thehistorynet/MilitaryHistory/articles/1997/02973_text.htm
Outside View of New Mexico – New Mexico History Index (*downloaded 13/12/2000*)
http://www.cia-g.com/~rockets/dNMhist.view.htm
Royal City News – Victorio by C. Bennett. (*downloaded 14/08/2000*)
http://www.royalcity news.com/actio … p.section1.las&issue_name=curren[9]
Scientist Rewrite Cavalry/Apache Fight History (*downloaded 14/12/2000*)
http://www.webarchives.net/scientists_rewrite_cavalry.htm
Schubert, Frank N. "Remembering the Buffalo Soldier: Memorials to Black Soldiers of the Indian War Era" *(downloaded 12/11/2002)*

9 This webpage is one of the better summaries of the Victorio stories, though by no means complete or accurate. However, I had problems printing off the page and as such do not have a full web address available. I do have a copy of the article available for viewing.

http://www.captainbuffalo.com/memorials.html
USACMH – The US Army Center of Military History webpage.
Capt W.H. Carter – The Sixth Regiment of Cavalry
Lt J. Bigelow – The Tenth Regiment of Cavalry
Appendix 4 – Dates of Important Campaigns.
The U.S. Cavalry Versus The Indians 1832 through 1898 (*downloaded 15/05/2001*)
http://members.aol.com/aacsgtmike/indians.html
The United States Army Military History Institute Webpage
http://carlisle-www.army.mil/usamhi/DL/
Victorio Canyon – Diablo Mountains (*downloaded 10/03/2001*)
http://www.kingsnake.com/hudspeth/victorio_canyon.htm
Wakeman, J.(New Mexico State University) Laumbach, K. (Human Systems Research Inc.) (*downloaded 14/04/99)*
http://www.gpsworld.com/feature/1097victorio/bottom.htm
West Point Pioneer: Henry Ossian Flipper: by L.R. Jordan (*downloaded 09/03/99)*
http://www.aog.usma.edu/Pubs/Register/Flipper.htm
White Sands & Lake Lucero (*downloaded 26/02/2001*)
http://www.geocities.com/Athens/Parthenon/5883/whitesan.htm
24th U.S. Infantry at Fort Davis Texas (*downloaded 14/09/1999*)
http://www.coax.net/people/lwf/24th_fd.htm

Masters Thesis

Major Eric Leon Bradley, *Factors Influencing the Impacts on Security of Manning Military Posts on the United States-Mexico Border from 1865–1916*, A thesis presented to the Faculty of the U.S. Army Command and General Staff College in partial fulfilment of the requirements for the degree Master of Military Art and Science Military History, (Fort Leavenworth: Kansas, 2007) http://stinet.dtic.mil/cgi-bin/GetTRDoc?AD=ADA471719&Location=U2&doc=GetTRDoc.pdf (*Downloaded 12th June 2008*)

Maps

US Geological Survey Topographical 1:250,000 scale Maps
NI 12–6 – **St Johns**
NI 12–9 – **Clifton**
NI 12–12 – **Silver City**
NH 12–3 – **Douglas**
NI 13–4 – **Socorro**
NI 13–7 – **Tularosa**
NI 13–10 – **Las Cruces**
NH 13–1 – **El Paso**
NI 13–5 – **Ft Sumner**
NI 13–8 – **Roswell**
NI 13–11 – **Carlsbad**
NH 13–2 – **Van Horn**
NH 13–5 – **Marfa**
NH 13–8 – **Presidio**

Maps from the Instituto Nacional De Estadistica Geografia e Infromatica, (INEGI) Estados Unidos Mexicanos
H12–2 – **Nogales**
H12–5 – **Cananea**
H12–8 – **Hermosillo**
H12–3 – **Agua Prieta**
H12–6 – **Nacozari**
H12–9 – **Madera**
H13–1 – **Cuidad Juarez**
H13–4 – **Nuevo Casas Grandes**
H13–7 – **Buenaventura**
H 13–10 – **Chihuahua**
H13–5 – **San Antonio Del Bravo**
H13–8 – **Ojinaga**
H13–11 – **Cuidad Delicias**

David Rumsey Map Collection:
Historic Maps 77. Part of Central New Mexico. by Wheeler, G.M. from 1882
http://www.davidrumsey.com/detail?id=1–1–384–0091&name=77.+Part+of+Central+New+Mexico
AAA Arizona & New Mexico Road Map 1999

Index

Index of People

Index of Places

Index of Military Formations & Units

Index of Miscellaneous & General Terms